Kaplan Publishing are constantly finding
difference to your studies and our exciti
offer something different to students lo

This book comes with free MyKaplan or n
study anytime, anywhere. **This free online resource is ...**
separately and is included in the price of the book.

Having purchased this book, you have access to the following online study materials:

CONTENT	ACCA (including FBT, FMA, FFA)		FIA (excluding FBT, FMA, FFA)	
	Text	Kit	Text	Kit
Electronic version of the book	✓	✓	✓	✓
Knowledge checks with instant answers	✓		✓	
Material updates	✓	✓	✓	✓
Latest official ACCA exam questions*		✓		
Pocket Notes (digital copy)	✓		✓	
Study Planner	✓			
Progress Test including questions and answers	✓		✓	
Syllabus recap Videos		✓		✓
Revision Planner		✓		✓
Question Debrief and Walkthrough Videos		✓		
Mock Exam including questions and answers		✓		

* Excludes BT, MA, FA, FBT, FMA, FFA; for all other papers includes a selection of questions, as released by ACCA

How to access your online resources

Received this book as part of your Kaplan course?
If you have a MyKaplan account, your full online resources will be added automatically, in line with the information in your course confirmation email. If you've not used MyKaplan before, you'll be sent an activation email once your resources are ready.

Bought your book from Kaplan?
We'll automatically add your online resources to your MyKaplan account. If you've not used MyKaplan before, you'll be sent an activation email.

Bought your book from elsewhere?
Go to **www.mykaplan.co.uk/add-online-resources**
Enter the ISBN number found on the title page and back cover of this book.
Add the unique pass key number contained in the scratch panel below.
You may be required to enter additional information during this process to set up or confirm your account details.

This code can only be used once for the registration of this book online. This registration and your online content will expire when the examinations covered by this book have taken place. Please allow one hour from the time you submit your book details for us to process your request.

Please scratch the film to access your unique code.

Please be aware that this code is case-sensitive and you will need to include the dashes within the passcode, but not when entering the ISBN.

KAPLAN PUBLISHING

ACCA

Applied Skills

Audit and Assurance (AA)

EXAM KIT

KAPLAN
PUBLISHING

British Library Cataloguing-in-Publication Data

A catalogue record for this book is available from the British Library.

Published by:
Kaplan Publishing UK
Unit 2 The Business Centre
Molly Millar's Lane
Wokingham
Berkshire
RG41 2QZ

ISBN: 978-1-83996-691-0

Acknowledgements

This product contains copyright material and trademarks of the IFRS Foundation®. All rights reserved. Used under licence from the IFRS Foundation®. Reproduction and use rights are strictly limited. For more information about the IFRS Foundation and rights to use its material please visit www.ifrs.org.

CONTENTS

Features in this edition

In addition to providing a wide ranging bank of real past exam questions, we have also included in this edition:

- An analysis of all of the recently published new syllabus examinations.
- Subject specific information and advice on exam technique.
- Our recommended approach to make your revision for this particular subject as effective as possible.

  This includes step by step guidance on how best to use our Kaplan material (Study text, pocket notes and exam kit) at this stage in your studies.
- Enhanced tutorial answers packed with specific key answer tips, technical tutorial notes and exam technique tips from our experienced tutors.
- Complementary online resources including full tutor debriefs and question assistance to point you in the right direction when you get stuck.

You will find a wealth of other resources to help you with your studies on the following sites:

www.MyKaplan.co.uk

www.accaglobal.com/students/

Quality and accuracy are of the utmost importance to us so if you spot an error in any of our products, please send an email to mykaplanreporting@kaplan.com with full details.

Our Quality Co-ordinator will work with our technical team to verify the error and take action to ensure it is corrected in future editions.

INDEX TO QUESTIONS AND ANSWERS

INTRODUCTION

The majority of the questions within the kit are past ACCA exam questions, the more recent questions are labelled as such in the index. Where changes have been made to the syllabus, the old ACCA questions within this kit have been adapted to reflect the new style of exam and the new guidance. If changed in any way from the original version, this is indicated in the end column of the index below with the mark (A).

Note that

The specimen exam is included at the end of the kit.

KEY TO THE INDEX

EXAM KIT ENHANCEMENTS

We have added the following enhancements to the answers in this exam kit:

Key answer tips

All answers include key answer tips to help your understanding of each question.

Tutorial note

All answers include more tutorial notes to explain some of the technical points in more detail.

Top tutor tips

For selected questions, we walk through the answer giving guidance on how to approach the questions with helpful 'tips from a top tutor', together with technical tutor notes.

These answers are indicated with the 'footsteps' icon in the index.

ONLINE ENHANCEMENTS

Answer debrief

For selected questions, we recommend that they are to be completed in full exam conditions (i.e. properly timed in a closed book environment).

In addition to the examining team's technical answer, enhanced with key answer tips and tutorial notes in this exam kit, online you can find an answer debrief by a top tutor that:

- works through the question in full
- explains key elements of the answer
- ensures that the easy marks are obtained as quickly as possible.

These questions are indicated with the 'video' icon in the index.

Answer debriefs will be available on MyKaplan at:

www.mykaplan.co.uk

SECTION A-TYPE QUESTIONS

SECTION B-TYPE QUESTIONS

Planning and risk assessment

Internal controls

Substantive procedures, completion and reporting

Additional questions

ANALYSIS OF PAST EXAMS

The table below summarises the key topics that have been tested in the new syllabus published examinations to date.

	Specimen	M/J 21	S/D 21	M/J 22	S/D 22	M/J 23	S/D 23
Audit Framework							
Audit vs. assurance engagements							
Statutory audits							
Benefits/limitations of an audit							
Elements of assurance							
Corporate governance					✓	✓	
Audit committee							
Ethical threats	✓		✓				
Confidentiality and conflicts of interest							
Limited assurance engagements	✓						
Planning and risk assessment							
Acceptance		✓		✓			
Engagement letter					✓		
Quality management						✓	
Professional scepticism		✓					
Audit risk	✓	✓	✓	✓	✓	✓	✓
Analytical procedures	✓			✓	✓		
Materiality							
Understanding the entity							✓
Fraud & error			✓				✓
Laws & regulations							
Benefits of planning							
Audit strategy & plan	✓						
Interim & final	✓						
Audit documentation							

	Specimen	M/J 21	S/D 21	M/J 22	S/D 22	M/J 23	S/D 23
Internal control							
Components					✓		
Limitations of controls			✓				
Systems/tests of controls:							
– Revenue	✓		✓	✓		✓	
– Purchases	✓		✓			✓	
– Payroll		✓		✓	✓	✓	
– Non-current assets	✓		✓				
– Inventory			✓				
– Cash				✓			
Systems documentation	✓	✓					
IT controls	✓						✓
Internal Audit							
Scope/limitations	✓						
Contrast with external audit	✓						
Outsourcing internal audit							
IA assignments							
Audit Evidence							
ISA 500 Audit procedures							
Assertions	✓						
Audit sampling							
Sufficient appropriate evidence	✓						
Use of experts	✓						
Use of internal audit							
Service organisations							
Not-for-profit organisation							
Automated tools and techniques							
The audit of specific items:							
– Revenue/income				✓	✓		✓
– Purchases							
– Payroll		✓					✓

	Specimen	M/J 21	S/D 21	M/J 22	S/D 22	M/J 23	S/D 23
– Tangible non-current assets	✓		✓			✓	
– Research & development			✓				
– Trade receivables	✓	✓	✓	✓			✓
– Inventory		✓		✓			✓
– Bank					✓	✓	✓
– Trade payables/accruals					✓		
– Provisions	✓	✓	✓		✓	✓	✓
– Equity				✓			
– Directors' remuneration							
– Redundancy costs							
Completion & reporting							
Misstatements	✓						
Final review							
Subsequent events	✓					✓	
Going concern	✓						
Written representations							
Auditor's reports/opinions	✓	✓			✓		✓
Key audit matters			✓	✓			
Reporting to those charged with governance							

EXAM TECHNIQUE

GENERAL COMMENTS

- Read the questions and examination requirements **carefully**.
- **Divide the time** you spend on questions in proportion to the marks on offer:
  - there are 1.8 minutes available per mark in the computer based examinations so a 20 mark question should be completed in approximately 36 minutes
  - within that, try to allow time at the end of each question to review your answer and address any obvious issues

  Whatever happens, always keep your eye on the clock and **do not over run on any part of any question.**
- **Objective test case questions:**
  - Don't leave any questions unanswered. If in doubt, guess.
  - Try and identify the correct answer.
  - If you can't identify the correct answer, try and rule out the wrong answers.
- Spend the last **five minutes** of the examination:
  - reading through your answers, and
  - **making any additions or corrections.**
- If you **get completely stuck**, flag the question for review and **return to it later.**
- Stick to the question and **tailor your answer** to what you are asked.
  - Pay particular attention to the verbs in the question.
  - Apply your comments to the scenario.
- If you do not understand what a question is asking, **state your assumptions**.

  Even if you do not answer in precisely the way the examiner hoped, you may be given some credit, if your assumptions are reasonable.
- You should do everything you can to make things easy for the marker.

  The marker will find it easier to identify the points you have made if your **answers are understandable, well-spaced out and clearly referenced to the requirement being answered.**

OBJECTIVE TEST QUESTIONS

- Decide whether you want to attempt these at the start of the exam or at the end.
- No credit for working will be given in these questions, the answers will either be correct (2 marks) or incorrect (0 marks).
- Read the question carefully, as any alternative answer choices will be given based on common mistakes that could be made in attempting the question.
- If a question looks particularly difficult or time consuming, then miss it out first time through (make sure you flag it) and come back to it later.

CONSTRUCTED RESPONSE (LONG) QUESTIONS

- **Written elements**:

  Your answer should:

  - Have a clear structure
  - Be concise: get to the point!
- **Reports, memos and other documents**:

  Some questions ask you to present your answer in the form of a report, a memo, a letter or other document.

  Make sure that you use the correct format – there could be easy marks to gain here.

COMPUTER-BASED EXAMS – ADDITIONAL TIPS

- Do not attempt a CBE until you have **completed all study material** relating to it.
- On the ACCA website there is a CBE demonstration. It is **ESSENTIAL** that you attempt this before your real CBE. You will become familiar with how to move around the CBE screens and the way that questions are formatted, increasing your confidence and speed in the actual exam.
- Be sure you understand how to use the **software** before you start the exam. If in doubt, ask the assessment centre staff to explain it to you.
- Questions are **displayed on the screen** and answers are entered using keyboard and mouse.
- In addition to the traditional multiple choice question type, CBEs will also contain other types of questions, such as multiple response (select two or more), drop down list, drag and drop, hot spots and hot areas.
- You need to be sure you **know how to answer questions** of these types before you sit the exam, through practice.

SUBJECT SPECIFIC INFORMATION

THE EXAM

FORMAT OF THE EXAM

The exam will be in **TWO** sections

All questions are compulsory

		Number of marks
Section A:	3 objective test cases	
	5 questions worth 2 marks per case	30
Section B:	3 constructed response questions	
	2 × 20 mark questions (mainly scenario based)	40
	1 × 30 mark question (mainly scenario based)	30
		100

Time allowed: 3 hours.

In the AA exam the 'current' date will be 1 July 20X5. Year-end dates will then be flexed around this depending on the nature of the question. For example, a question set at the planning stage of the audit may have a year end of 30 June 20X5 or 31 July 20X5. A question set at the completion stage of the audit may have a year end of 31 January 20X5 or 31 March 20X5.

PASS MARK

The pass mark for all ACCA Qualification exams is 50%.

APPROACH TO THIS EXAM

Audit and Assurance is a computer based exam.

Any part of the syllabus can be tested in any section.

Section A

- The objective test case questions will be based around a short scenario and you will have to choose the correct answer(s) from the options given.
- You should begin by reading the OT questions that relate to the case, so that when you read through the information for the first time, you know what is required.
- Each OT question is worth two marks. Therefore you have 18 minutes (1.8 minutes per mark) to answer the five OT questions relating to each case.
- It is likely that all of the cases will take the same length of time to answer, although some of the OT questions within a case may be quicker than other OT questions within that same case.
- Work steadily. Rushing leads to careless mistakes and the OT questions are designed to include 'plausible distractors' i.e. answers which result from careless mistakes.

- If you don't know the answer, eliminate those options you know are incorrect and see if the answer becomes more obvious.
- After you have eliminated the options that you know to be wrong, if you are still unsure, guess.

Section B

- The constructed response questions will require a written response rather than being OT questions.
- Each question will contain some knowledge-based requirements. Knowledge of ISAs may be required in this section.
- The other requirements will require application of knowledge to the scenario provided. For these requirements it is important you relate your answers to the scenario rather than just regurgitate rote-learned knowledge.
- For the scenario based questions it is important to read the information carefully and only use this information to generate your answers. There are unlikely to be any marks awarded to students creating their own scenario and generating answers from that.
- **For each question**, read the requirements and then the detail of the question carefully.

  Always read the requirement first as this enables you to **focus on the detail of the question with the specific task in mind**.
- Take notice of the format required (e.g. letter, memo, notes) and identify the recipient of the answer . You need to do this to judge the level of sophistication required in your answer and whether the use of a formal reply or informal bullet points would be satisfactory.
- There are times when you are instructed to use tables to present your answer. This is the case when you are asked to link answers together. Pre-formatted tables will usually be set up in the workspace for you to use.
- Spot the easy marks to be gained in a question. Make sure that you do these parts first when you tackle the question.
- **Highlight questions for review if you are not sure and want to check your answers before you end your exam**.

The three questions in section B will usually focus on planning and audit risk assessment, internal controls and audit evidence.

Audit risks

Candidates need to explain audit risks by stating the specific area of the financial statements impacted (e.g. PPE, inventory, revenue, etc.) with an assertion (for example cut-off, valuation etc.), or, a reference to over/under/misstated, or a reference to inherent/ control/ detection risk. Credit is only awarded for misstated when it is clear that a balance could be either over or understated. Credit is not given for misstated if it is clear that a balance could only be overstated or could only be understated.

Control deficiencies and recommendations

Internal control deficiency questions typically require internal control deficiencies to be identified (½ mark each), explained (½ mark each) which must cover the implication of the deficiency to the company and a relevant recommendation to address the deficiency (1 mark). Candidates are required to explain the implication to the business to be awarded credit, for example that 'loss of revenue or loss of customer goodwill'. Recommendations must be described in sufficient detail.

Direct controls and tests of control

Questions typically require the direct control to be identified (½ mark each), explained as to why it is a direct control (½ mark each) and a test of control provided (1 mark). To explain why the control is a direct control, candidates must explain how the control will prevent or detect and correct a misstatement.

Audit evidence

Audit procedures must be clearly described. A well described substantive procedure will clearly detail the source of the evidence, clearly detail the purpose of the test, and state exactly 'how' the procedure should be performed.

All sections

- Don't skip parts of the syllabus. The AA exam has 18 different questions, each with multiple requirements, so the examination can cover a very broad selection of the syllabus each sitting.
- Practice plenty of questions to improve your ability to apply the techniques.
- Spend the last five minutes reading through your answers and making any additions or corrections.

Always keep your eye on the clock and do not over run on any part of any question!

DETAILED SYLLABUS

The detailed syllabus and study guide written by the ACCA can be found at:

https://www.accaglobal.com/gb/en/student/exam-support-resources/fundamentals-exams-study-resources/f8/syllabus-study-guide.html

KAPLAN'S RECOMMENDED REVISION APPROACH

QUESTION PRACTICE IS THE KEY TO SUCCESS

Success in professional examinations relies upon you acquiring a firm grasp of the required knowledge at the tuition phase. In order to be able to do the questions, knowledge is essential.

However, the difference between success and failure often hinges on your exam technique on the day and making the most of the revision phase of your studies.

The **Kaplan study text** is the starting point, designed to provide the underpinning knowledge to tackle all questions. However, in the revision phase, pouring over text books is not the answer.

Kaplan online tests help you consolidate your knowledge and understanding and are a useful tool to check whether you can remember key topic areas.

Kaplan pocket notes are designed to help you quickly revise a topic area, however you then need to practice questions. There is a need to progress to full exam standard questions as soon as possible, and to tie your exam technique and technical knowledge together.

The importance of question practice cannot be over-emphasised.

The recommended approach below is designed by expert tutors in the field, in conjunction with their knowledge of the examiner and their recent real exams.

The approach taken for the applied skills exams is to revise by topic area. However, with the professional stage exams, a multi-topic approach is required to answer the scenario based questions.

You need to practice as many questions as possible in the time you have left.

OUR AIM

Our aim is to get you to the stage where you can attempt exam standard questions confidently, to time, in a closed book environment, with no supplementary help (i.e. to simulate the real examination experience).

Practising your exam technique on real past examination questions, in timed conditions, is also vitally important for you to assess your progress and identify areas of weakness that may need more attention in the final run up to the examination.

In order to achieve this we recognise that initially you may feel the need to practice some questions with open book help and exceed the required time.

The approach below shows you which questions you should use to build up to coping with exam standard question practice, and references to the sources of information available should you need to revisit a topic area in more detail.

Remember that in the real examination, all you have to do is:

- attempt all questions required by the exam
- only spend the allotted time on each question, and
- get them at least 50% right!

Try and practice this approach on every question you attempt from now to the real exam.

EXAMINER COMMENTS

We have included the examiners comments to the specific new syllabus examination questions in this kit for you to see the main pitfalls that students fall into with regard to technical content.

However, too many times in the general section of the report, the examiner comments that students had failed due to:

- lack of knowledge or exam preparation
- candidates not adequately explaining audit risks
- candidates not clearly understanding/explaining the implication of control deficiencies
- audit procedures not clearly described
- substantive procedures being too generic and not related to the scenario given
- candidates re-writing the question requirement at the start of each question which is unnecessary and not an efficient use of time.

Good exam technique is vital.

ACCA SUPPORT

For additional support with your studies please also refer to the ACCA Global website.

THE KAPLAN AA REVISION PLAN

Stage 1: Assess areas of strengths and weaknesses

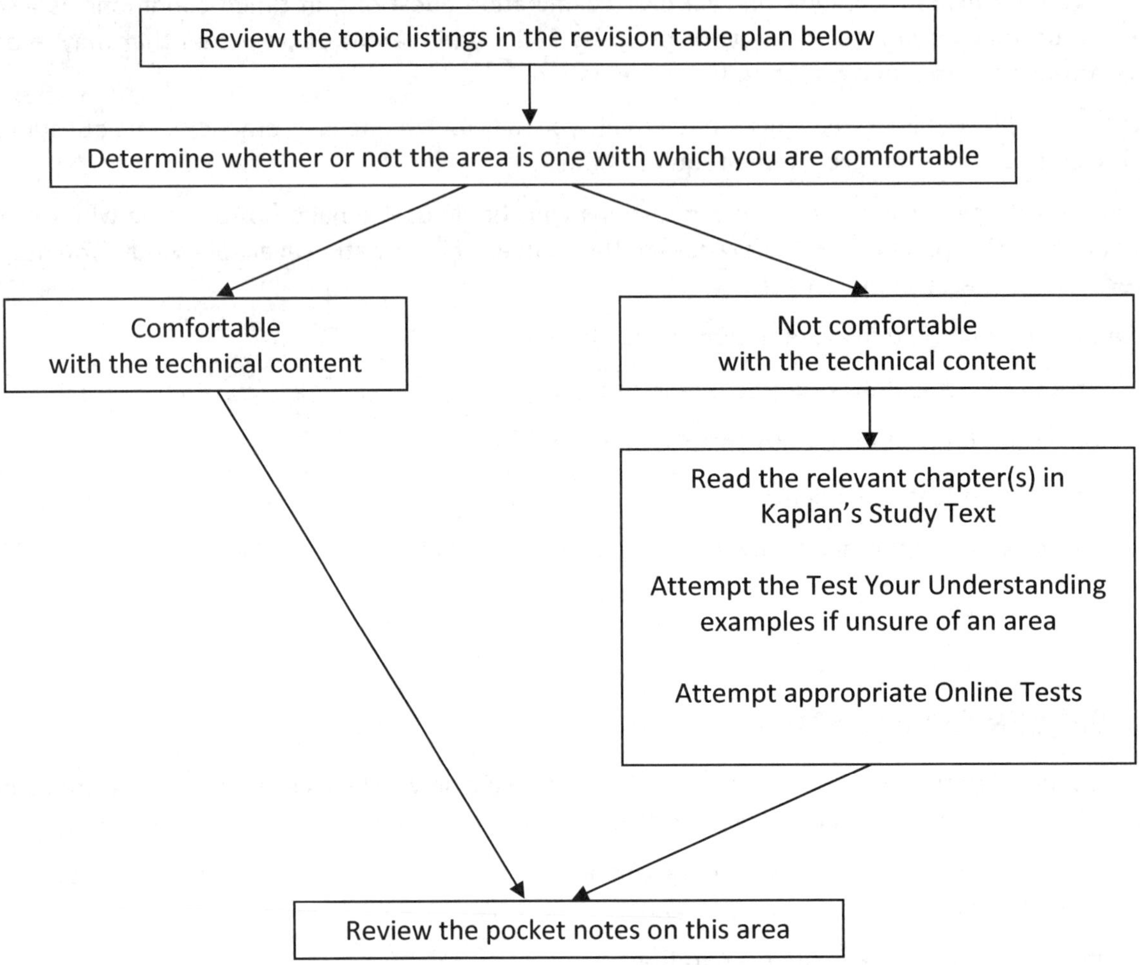

Stage 2: Practice questions

Follow the order of revision of topics as recommended in the revision table plan below and attempt the questions in the order suggested.

Try to avoid referring to text books and notes and the model answer until you have completed your attempt.

Try to answer the question in the allotted time.

Review your attempt with the model answer and assess how much of the answer you achieved in the allocated exam time.

Fill in the self-assessment box below and decide on your best course of action.

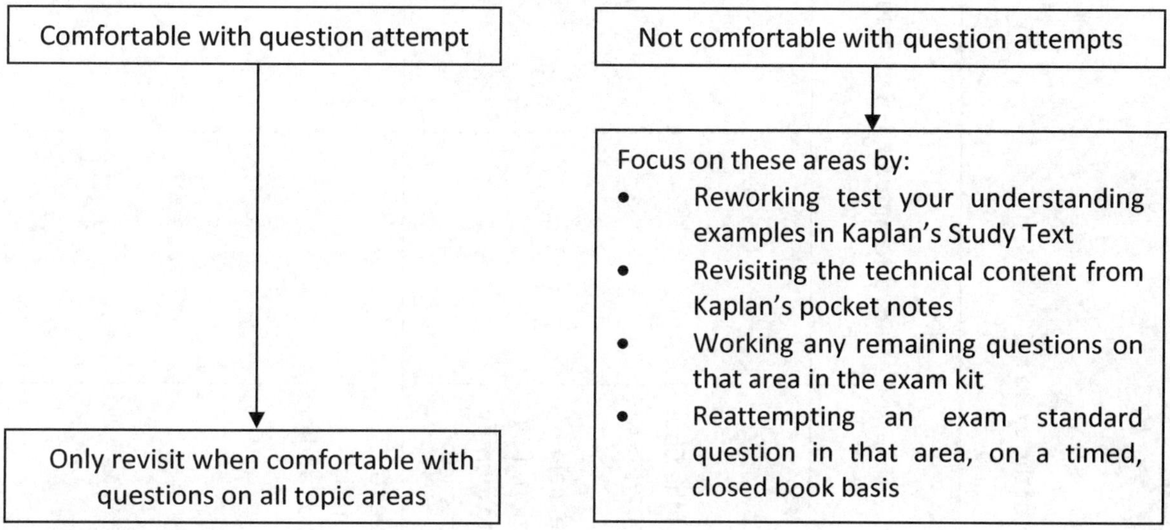

Note that:

The 'footsteps questions' give guidance on exam techniques and how you should have approached the question.

Stage 3: Final pre-exam revision

We recommend that you **attempt at least one mock examination** containing a set of previously unseen exam standard questions.

It is important that you get a feel for the breadth of coverage of a real exam without advanced knowledge of the topic areas covered – just as you will expect to see on the real exam day.

Ideally this mock should be sat in timed, closed book, real exam conditions and could be:

- a mock examination offered by your tuition provider, and/or
- the specimen exam in the back of this exam kit, and/or
- the last real examination.

KAPLAN'S DETAILED REVISION PLAN

In addition to the questions below, you should practise a selection of OT case questions from Section A of the exam kit.

Topics	Study Text (and Pocket Note) Chapter	Questions to attempt	Tutor guidance	Date attempted	Self-assessment
1 Audit framework and regulation	1, 2, 3, 4	Peach Hart Hurling Freesia Saxophone Enterprises Orange Financials OT cases 1 – 50	You must also be able to discuss the purpose of assurance and the levels of assurance offered by accountants. Make sure that you can define the elements of the Code of Ethics and that you practice applying the concepts to specific scenarios. You need to be able to identify and explain the main requirements of corporate governance regulations (e.g. UK Corporate Governance Code) and be able to identify when a company is not compliant with best practice.		
2 Planning and risk assessment	5 & 6	Lapis Magpie Esk Peach Corley Appliances Hart Scarlet Harlem Peony Darjeeling	Audit risk is a vital concept. You need to be able to: discuss what it is, including materiality; perform risk assessment for a client; and discuss its impact on audit strategy.		

Topics	Study Text (and Pocket Note) Chapter	Questions to attempt	Tutor guidance	Date attempted	Self-assessment
		Blackberry			
3 Internal controls	8, 9	Petra Daley Whittaker Pomeranian Castle Courier Swift Amberjack Freesia Camomile Raspberry Comet	You need to know how a simple financial control system (e.g. sales, purchases, payroll etc.) operates. You may be asked to identify deficiencies in control systems and provide recommendations. You may also be asked to explain the direct controls within a system and say how the auditor should test these controls.		
4 Audit evidence	7 & 10	Heron Pacific Spinach Danube Purrfect Sagittarii Encore Spadefish Hyacinth Jasmine Airsoft	It is vital that you are able to identify **specifically** what procedures are required (e.g. tests of control, analytical procedures) and what assertions are being tested (e.g. completeness, existence, accuracy) for a particular balance or issue given.		

Topics	Study Text (and Pocket Note) Chapter	Questions to attempt	Tutor guidance	Date attempted	Self-assessment
5 Review and reporting	11 & 12	Heron Spinach Encore Spadefish Hyacinth Jasmine Dashing Violet & Co OT cases 141 – 200	There are a wide range of issues that need to be considered at the completion stage of an audit. Typical examples include: subsequent events, going concern, written representations and evaluation of misstatements. It is important that you are able to assess a scenario and identify how it might impact upon the auditor's report and opinion. You also need to be able to discuss the content and purpose of the sections of an auditor's report. In addition, you should be able to identify matters which should be reported to those charged with governance.		

Section 1

OBJECTIVE TEST CASE QUESTIONS – SECTION A

AUDIT FRAMEWORK

The following scenario relates to questions 1 – 5

The board of directors of Sistar Co are concerned that they are not currently applying best practice in terms of corporate governance and are seeking to make improvements.

The company currently has three non-executive directors (NEDs) on the board, who are paid a fee which changes annually depending on company performance. The NEDs all sit on the audit, nomination and remuneration committees. There is currently no reference to the work of these committees in the annual report.

At present, Sistar Co does not have an internal audit function but the directors are establishing a team which will be responsible for a range of internal audit assignments.

The following is the current proposed structure for the internal audit (IA) department

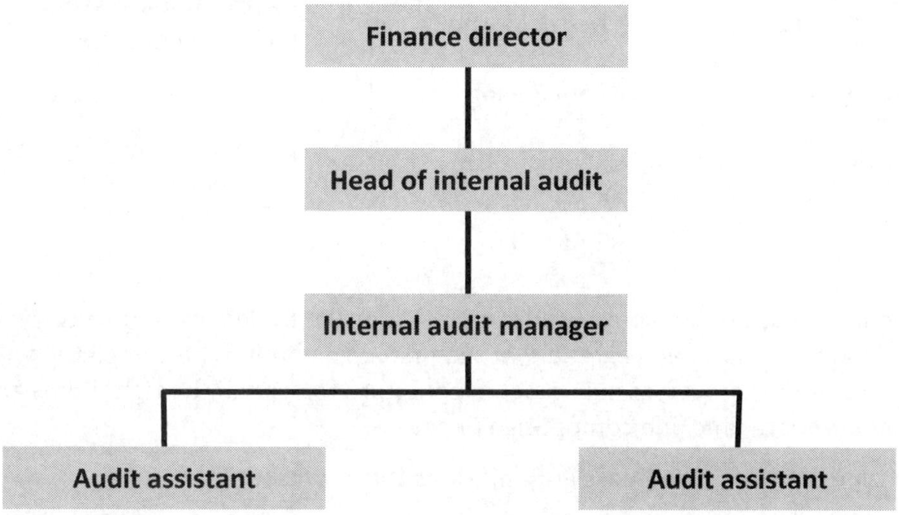

The only role still to be filled is the Head of internal audit. There are two potential candidates: Paul Belling a consultant who helped design and implement the company's current control system, and Maria Marquez who is currently an audit manager at Rossi & Bell, an audit firm which has never been used by Sistar Co.

Out of the other three members of the proposed IA department, two of them have moved from other departments in Sistar Co and one of the audit assistants has audit experience.

1 **Which of the following should be included in the annual report regarding the work of the audit committee?**

- o Responsibility for preparing the annual report and financial statements
- o Significant issues considered relating to the financial statements
- o A description of the principal risks the company faces
- o The process used to make appointments to the board **(2 marks)**

2 **Which of the following options correctly describes the deficiency relating to NEDs' remuneration and makes a valid recommendation for improvement?**

	Deficiency	**Recommendation**
o	Compromises NED independence	NEDs should be remunerated on the same basis as the executive team
o	Compromises the motivation of NEDs	NEDs' remuneration should be tied to profit targets
o	Compromises NED independence	NEDs' remuneration should be a set amount based on time committed
o	Compromises the motivation of NEDs	NEDs' remuneration should be linked to individual performance

(2 marks)

3 The board is in the final stages of establishing the IA department.

Select one option from each column which provides appropriate recommendations to improve the effectiveness and independence of the IA department.

Reports to
Finance director
Audit committee
Chief executive

Head of IA
Maria Marquez
Paul Belling

Remaining staff members
Appoint more senior staff with audit experience
No changes needed
All staff should be new to the company

(2 marks)

4 The board has started to compile a list of tasks for the IA department to carry out once it is up and running. It has been agreed that the first assignment to be completed will be for IA to review Sistar Co's processes over asset expenditure to verify if the right items are purchased at an appropriate time and competitive price.

What type of internal audit assignment does this represent?

- o A value for money audit
- o A management audit
- o A financial audit
- o An IT audit **(2 marks)**

5 When deciding on the role of the IA department in undertaking operational audits, which TWO of the following should the team NOT be involved in?

- o Observing procedures carried out by Sistar Co's staff
- o Reperforming procedures documented in procedures manuals
- o Designing and implementing internal control procedures to address deficiencies
- o Reporting findings directly to the board of directors
- o Authorising transactions and performing reconciliations **(2 marks)**

The following scenario relates to questions 6 – 10

You are an audit manager in Bark & Co and have been assigned to the audit of Foliage Co for the first time this year. Foliage Co is a listed company which specialises in manufacturing musical instruments. You will be taking over from Kim Baum, the audit manager who has been in charge of the audit for the last three years. Kim has just announced that he is leaving Bark & Co to join Foliage Co as the financial controller. Kim has recently completed the planning for the current year audit in preparation for the final audit which is due to commence next month.

Jane Leaf has been the audit engagement partner since Foliage Co became an audit client almost eight years ago. As she has completed seven years as the audit engagement partner, Jane has recently been rotated off the audit engagement. The new audit engagement partner, Chang Petiole, has suggested that in order to maintain a close relationship with Foliage Co, Jane Leaf should undertake the role of Engagement Quality Reviewer this year.

The total fees received by Bark & Co from Foliage Co in respect of all services provided in the last year amounted to 16% of the firm's total fee income. The current year's total fee income for audit, tax and other audit-related services is expected to be greater than last year.

---

6 What is the most appropriate response to the suggestion that Jane Leaf takes on the role of Engagement Quality Reviewer?

- o Jane Leaf could take the review role immediately
- o Jane Leaf could take the review role immediately but additional safeguards will be required
- o Jane Leaf should not serve as the Engagement Quality Reviewer for a period of at least five years
- o Bark & Co will need to consider resigning as auditor of Foliage Co **(2 marks)**

7 Which of the following is the LEAST appropriate response in relation to fee income received by Bark & Co from Foliage Co?

- o Bark & Co should assess whether audit and non-audit fees would represent more than 15% of gross practice income for two consecutive years
- o If the recurring fees are likely to exceed 15% of annual practice income this year Bark will need to resign as auditors of Foliage Co
- o If the recurring fees are likely to exceed 15% of annual practice income this year, additional consideration should be given as to whether the taxation and audit-related services should be undertaken by the firm
- o If the fees do exceed 15% this should be disclosed to those charged with governance at Foliage Co **(2 marks)**

8 What action should Kim Baum have taken when the possibility of employment with Foliage Co arose?

- o Kim should have notified Bark & Co of the potential employment so he could be removed from the audit team
- o Kim should have declined the offer of employment
- o Kim should not have applied for employment with an audit client while employed by Bark & Co
- o Kim should have asked for permission from Bark & Co before applying for a job with Foliage Co **(2 marks)**

9 Which ethical threat will be created when Kim Baum commences employment with the client and what action should be taken to manage the threat?

	Threat	Action
A	Intimidation	The manager should not be allowed to take the role of financial controller
B	Familiarity	The composition of the audit team must be reviewed and changed as appropriate
C	Confidentiality	The manager should not be allowed to take the role of financial controller
D	Self-review	The composition of the audit team must be reviewed and changed as appropriate

- o Option A
- o Option B
- o Option C
- o Option D **(2 marks)**

10 Select whether the following statements describe a rulebook approach or a conceptual framework approach to ethics.

Clearly defined laws for the auditor to follow	**Rule book approach**	**Conceptual framework approach**
Useful in a dynamic environment	**Rule book approach**	**Conceptual framework approach**
A set of guidelines with which the auditor uses judgement to apply to specific circumstances	**Rule book approach**	**Conceptual framework approach**
Easy to know what is allowed and not allowed	**Rule book approach**	**Conceptual framework approach**

(2 marks)

The following scenario relates to questions 11 – 15

You are an audit manager in Miranda & Co and you are planning the audit of Milberry Co which manufactures luxury handbags and other fashion accessories. Milberry Co has been an audit client of your firm for four years.

From a review of the correspondence file, you note that the audit engagement partner and the finance director have known each other socially for many years and in fact went on holiday together last summer with their families. As a result of this friendship, the partner has not yet spoken to the client about the fee for last year's audit, 20% of which is still outstanding.

The financial controller of Milberry Co was appointed two months ago. Prior to this appointment the financial controller was an audit senior at Miranda & Co and was a member of the audit team for Milberry Co.

Employees of Milberry Co are entitled to purchase handbags at a discount of 40% and during the planning meeting with the finance director, you and your audit team are offered the same level of staff discount.

The finance director has asked if your firm will prepare the company's tax return and provide tax advice to minimise the amount of tax payable.

11 Select which threat to objectivity is created by the information obtained from the review of the correspondence file.

The partner and the finance director have known each other socially for many years	**Advocacy**	**Familiarity**	**Self-interest**
40% of the fee for last year's audit is still outstanding	**Advocacy**	**Familiarity**	**Self-interest**

(2 marks)

12 Which is the MOST appropriate response to the outstanding fees from Milberry Co?

- O The auditor should resign from the client
- O The auditor should report the client to the ACCA
- O The auditor can continue working for the client but should ensure that the audit firm's credit control department are informed of the outstanding fees
- O The auditor's report for this year should not be issued until the fees have been paid

(2 marks)

13 Which of the following statements in respect of the relationship between the new financial controller and the audit firm are TRUE?

- o The audit approach should be revised to ensure procedures and items to be tested are not predictable
- o The audit team should comprise people who know the audit senior as this will make the audit run more smoothly and increase efficiency
- o The firm must resign as auditor as the threat to objectivity is too significant to safeguard
- o The audit senior should not be allowed to be the financial controller and should resign

(2 marks)

14 Which is the MOST appropriate response with respect to the discount offered by Milberry Co to the audit team?

- o The discount may be accepted as it is the same as that offered to the client's employees
- o The discount should be rejected as it is unlikely to be a trivial monetary amount
- o The discount should be rejected as gifts or hospitality are not acceptable per the ACCA Code of Ethics and Conduct
- o Audit manager approval must be obtained before the discount is accepted **(2 marks)**

15 Select the option which correctly identifies whether or not a self-review threat is likely to arise in relation to the tax services requested.

	Tax return	**Tax advice**
A	Yes	Yes
B	No	No
C	Yes	No
D	No	Yes

- o Option A
- o Option B
- o Option C
- o Option D

(2 marks)

The following scenario relates to questions 16 – 20

You are an audit manager in Tigger & Co, a large audit firm which specialises in the car manufacturing industry. Details of three companies operating in this industry are given below.

Winnie Co

Tigger & Co has audited Winnie Co for many years. The audit engagement partner for Winnie Co has been responsible for the audit for six years. The board of directors has asked if Tigger & Co will provide payroll and bookkeeping services, including providing advice on appropriate accounting policies. They have also suggested that the external audit fee should be renegotiated with at least 20% of the fee being based on the company's profit after tax as they feel that this will align the interests of Tigger & Co and Winnie Co.

Eeyore Co

Eeyore Co is a subsidiary of a major global car manufacturer. During the audit, the audit team discovered that Eeyore Co had developed and used a device which gave false readings during government tests which are required for all cars. The false readings enabled cars to meet government restrictions on carbon emissions which would otherwise have failed and therefore could not have been sold. The audit engagement partner has discussed the matter with senior management of Eeyore Co and advised them to report the matter to the industry regulator. Senior management has refused and reminded the engagement partner that the audit firm has a duty of confidentiality towards the company.

Piglet Co

Piglet Co has recently approached Tigger & Co to act as auditor due to the firm's expertise in the car manufacturing industry. Piglet Co is the main competitor of Winnie Co.

---

16 Which TWO of the following statements are TRUE in respect of the conflict of interest between Winnie Co and Piglet Co?

- o Tigger & Co must decline the audit engagement of Piglet Co
- o Winnie Co and Piglet Co may be concerned that commercially sensitive information may be disclosed by Tigger & Co to their competitor
- o Tigger & Co must ask permission of ACCA before accepting the audit of Piglet Co
- o Tigger & Co must obtain consent of both clients before continuing with the engagements **(2 marks)**

17 Which of the following is NOT an action that your firm should take to manage the conflict of interest between Winnie Co and Piglet Co?

- o Monitoring of safeguards by an engagement quality reviewer
- o Require every employee of Tigger & Co to sign a confidentiality agreement
- o Use separate engagement teams and engagement partners for each client
- o Operate secure data filing of all audit information **(2 marks)**

18 Which of the following statements is TRUE in respect of the audit of Winnie Co?

- o The audit engagement partner must be rotated
- o Providing the additional services for Winnie Co will create a confidentiality threat
- o Payroll and bookkeeping services cannot be provided to an external audit client
- o Providing advice on accounting policies is acceptable as long as the client is responsible for choosing the specific policies used **(2 marks)**

19 In relation to the proposal that 20% of the audit fee is based on the profit after tax of the company, which of the following statements is TRUE?

- o This will lead to fee-dependency which is a self-interest threat. The proposal should be rejected.
- o This is a contingent fee arrangement which creates an advocacy threat. The proposal should only be accepted if no more than 15% of the audit fee is based on profit before tax.
- o This is a contingent fee arrangement which creates a self-interest threat. The proposal should be rejected.
- o This will lead to fee-dependency which is a self-interest threat. The proposal should only be accepted if no more than 15% of the audit fee is based on profit before tax.

(2 marks)

20 Select whether the following statements are true or false in respect of the issue with Eeyore Co?

Senior management is correct that reporting the company will constitute a breach of confidentiality	**True**	**False**
Tigger & Co must report the breach of laws and regulations to the appropriate authority if the client refuses	**True**	**False**
Tigger & Co must report the breach of laws and regulations as it is a public interest matter	**True**	**False**
Tigger & Co must report the matter to the parent company and the audit firm responsible for the parent company audit	**True**	**False**

(2 marks)

The following scenario relates to questions 21 – 25

Cameron Co has recently become a listed company. Cameron Co is required to comply with corporate governance principles in order to maintain its listed status. The finance director, Lindsay Lewis has undertaken a review of compliance with corporate governance regulations.

Board composition

Cameron Co's board of directors comprises six members:

Name	**Role(s)**	**Length of service at Cameron Co**
Ola Osbourne	Chief executive and chair	5 years
Lindsay Lewis	Finance director	10 years
Hayden Huq	Sales director	5 years
Karie Khan	Human resources director	7 years
Jules Jardine	Non-executive director	10 years
Taylor Tahir	Independent non-executive director	3 years

Directors were last subject to re-election three years ago.

Ola Osbourne has been the chief executive of Cameron Co for five years and has recently been appointed as board chair. Ola Osbourne is considering appointing a close friend as a non-executive director.

Taylor Tahir is responsible for ensuring employee interests are represented in board discussions.

Directors' remuneration

Executive directors are paid a fixed salary which increases annually in line with inflation. There is no performance related pay or bonus awarded to the executive directors as the company does not want to provide incentive for financial results to be manipulated.

Audit committee

The company does not have an audit committee as the board of directors did not consider it necessary due to the experience of Lindsay Lewis. They are aware that an audit committee is now required and have proposed that one is established comprising the two non-executive directors, Lindsay Lewis and Ola Osbourne.

21 Select whether the following matters in respect of board composition represent a corporate governance strength or deficiency.

Ola Osbourne is the chair and chief executive	**Strength**	**Deficiency**
Taylor Tahir is the designated person to assist with workforce engagement	**Strength**	**Deficiency**
Ola Osbourne is considering appointing a close friend as a non-executive director	**Strength**	**Deficiency**

(2 marks)

22 Which of the following can be a member of the audit committee once established?

- o Ola Osbourne
- o Lindsay Lewis
- o Jules Jardine
- o Taylor Tahir

(2 marks)

23 Match the two issues given to the most appropriate response.

Issue	
1	The board is not balanced
2	Executive directors are paid a fixed salary which increases annually in line with inflation

Response	
A	An audit committee should be set up immediately
B	Establish specific criteria to assess candidates to ensure appointments are based on merit and relevant skills and experience
C	Introduce share options to align the remuneration of executive directors with the long-term success of the company
D	Appoint three more independent non-executive directors
E	Reduce the number of executive directors on the board

(2 marks)

24 Which of the following would NOT ensure Cameron Co is compliant with corporate governance principles?

- o Jules Jardine should replace Ola Osbourne as chair
- o All directors should be subject to re-election this year
- o A Nomination Committee should be established
- o Directors contracts should be reviewed to ensure notice periods are one year or less

(2 marks)

25 Select whether the following statements in relation to directors' remuneration are true or false.

Remuneration of directors should be set by the Nomination Committee	**True**	**False**
Workforce remuneration should be taken into consideration when setting the remuneration of executive directors	**True**	**False**
The company should be able to withhold bonuses and share awards from directors whose performance is not acceptable	**True**	**False**

(2 marks)

The following scenario relates to questions 26 – 30

Sycamore & Co is the auditor of Fir Co, a listed company operating in the computer software industry. The audit team comprises an engagement partner, a recently appointed audit manager, an audit senior and a number of audit assistants. The audit engagement partner has only been appointed this year due to the rotation of the previous partner who had been involved in the audit for seven years. Only the audit senior has experience of auditing a company in this specialised industry. The previous audit manager left the firm before the completion of the prior year audit and is now the finance director of Fir Co. The finance director and new audit manager are good friends.

The board of Fir Co has asked if Sycamore & Co can take on some additional work. The following additional non-audit services have been requested:

1 Routine maintenance of payroll records

2 Assistance with the selection of a new non-executive director

3 Tax services whereby Sycamore & Co would liaise with the tax authority on Fir Co's behalf.

Sycamore & Co has identified that the current year fees to be received from Fir Co for audit and other services will represent 16% of the firm's total fee income and totalled 15.5% in the prior year. The audit engagement partner has asked you to consider what can be done in relation to this self-interest threat.

26 In relation to the composition of the current audit team, select which of the fundamental principles is at risk and select an appropriate safeguard.

	Fundamental principle
1	Integrity
2	Professional competence and due care
3	Confidentiality
4	Objectivity

	Safeguard
A	Reinstate previous partner
B	Resign from the engagement
C	Assign a completely new audit team
D	Provide industry training for team members

(2 marks)

27 Select the type of threat which could arise as a result of the finance director's relationship with the audit manager and select an appropriate safeguard.

	Type of threat
1	Self-review
2	Familiarity
3	Advocacy

	Safeguard
A	The finance director must not have contact with the audit manager whilst the audit is ongoing
B	The firm should resign from the engagement
C	A different audit manager should be appointed

(2 marks)

28 Ignoring the potential effect on total fee levels, identify the threats to independence from providing the non-audit services.

Routine maintenance of payroll records	**Self-review**	**Self-interest**	**Advocacy**
Assistance with the selection of a new non-executive director	**Self-review**	**Self-interest**	**Advocacy**
Tax services whereby Sycamore & Co would liaise with the tax authority on Fir Co's behalf	**Self-review**	**Self-interest**	**Advocacy**

(2 marks)

29 Which of the following safeguards would NOT be relevant in mitigating the threat identified in relation to fees?

- o Disclosure to those charged with governance that fees from Fir Co represent more than 15% of Sycamore & Co's total fee income
- o A pre-issuance review to be conducted by an external accountant
- o The use of separate teams to provide the audit and non-audit services
- o Assign an engagement quality reviewer **(2 marks)**

30 During the audit of Fir Co, a suspicious cash transfer has been identified. The audit team has reported this to the relevant firm representative as a potential money-laundering transaction.

Which of the following statements is TRUE regarding the confidentiality of this information?

- o Details of the transaction can only be disclosed with the permission of Fir Co
- o If there is a legal requirement to report money laundering, this overrides the principle of confidentiality
- o Sycamore & Co is not permitted to disclose details of the suspicious transaction as the information has been obtained during the course of the audit
- o In order to maintain confidentiality, Sycamore & Co should report its concerns anonymously **(2 marks)**

The following scenario relates to questions 31 – 35

It is 1 July 20X5. You are an audit manager at Horti & Co and you are considering a number of ethical issues which have arisen on some of the firm's long-standing audit clients.

Tree Co

Horti & Co is planning its external audit of Tree Co. Yesterday, the audit engagement partner, Charlie Thrower, discovered that a significant fee for information security services, which were provided to Tree Co by Horti & Co, is overdue. Charlie hopes to be able to resolve the dispute amicably and has confirmed that he will discuss the matter with the finance director, Percy Marsh, at the weekend, as they are both attending a party to celebrate the engagement of Charlie's daughter and Percy's son.

Bush Co

Horti & Co is the external auditor of Bush Co and also provides other non-audit services to the company. While performing the audit for the year ended 31 March 20X5, the audit engagement partner was taken ill and took an indefinite leave of absence from the firm. The ethics partner has identified the following potential replacements and is keen that independence is maintained to the highest level:

Brian Smith	who is also the partner in charge of the tax services provided to Bush Co
Monty Nod	who was the audit engagement partner for the ten years ended 31 March 20X4
Cassie Dixon	who introduced Bush Co as a client when she joined the firm as an audit partner five years ago
Pete Russo	who is also the partner in charge of the payroll services provided to Bush Co

Plant Co

Plant Co is a large private company, with a financial year to 30 June, and has been an audit client of Horti & Co for several years. Alan Marshlow, a partner of Horti & Co, has acted as the engagement quality reviewer (EQR) on the last two audits to the year ended 30 June 20X4. At a recent meeting, he advised that he can no longer be EQR on the engagement as he is considering accepting appointment as a non-executive director and will sit on the audit committee of Plant Co.

The board of directors has also asked Horti & Co if they would be able to provide internal audit services to the company.

Weed Co

Weed Co, a listed company, is one of Horti & Co's largest clients. Last year the fee for audit and other services was $1.2m and this year it is expected to be $1.3m which represents 16.6% and 18.1% of Horti & Co's total income respectively.

31 Which of the following statements correctly explains the possible threats to Horti & Co's independence and recommends an appropriate safeguard in relation to the audit of Tree Co?

1 An intimidation threat exists due to the overdue fee and Tree Co should be advised that all fees must be paid prior to the auditor's report being signed

2 A self-review threat exists due to the nature of the non-audit work which has been performed and an engagement quality review should be carried out

3 A self-interest threat exists due to the relationship between Charlie and Percy and Charlie should be removed as audit partner

- 1, 2 and 3
- 1 and 2 only
- 2 only
- 3 only

(2 marks)

32 Taking into account the concern of the ethics partner, which of the partners identified as potential replacements should take over the audit of Bush Co for the year ended 31 March 20X5?

- Brian Smith
- Monty Nod
- Cassie Dixon
- Pete Russo

(2 marks)

33 Which of the following correctly identifies the threats to Horti & Co's independence and proposes an appropriate course of action for the firm if Alan Marshlow accepts appointment as a non-executive director of Plant Co?

	Threats	Course of action
o	Self-interest and familiarity	Can continue with appropriate safeguards
o	Self-interest and self-review	Must resign as auditor
o	Self-review and familiarity	Must resign as auditor
o	Familiarity only	Can continue with appropriate safeguards

(2 marks)

34 You are separately considering Plant Co's request to provide internal audit services and the remit of these services if they are accepted.

Which of the following would result in Horti & Co assuming a management responsibility in relation to the internal audit services?

1 Taking responsibility for designing and maintaining internal control systems

2 Determining which recommendations should take priority and be implemented

3 Determining the reliance which can be placed on the work of internal audit for the external audit

4 Setting the scope of the internal audit work to be carried out

- 1 and 3
- 2, 3 and 4
- 1, 2 and 4
- 3 and 4 only **(2 marks)**

35 **Which of the following actions should Horti & Co take to maintain its objectivity in relation to the level of fee income from Weed Co?**

1 The level of fee income should be communicated to those charged with governance

2 Separate teams should be used for the audit and non-audit work

3 Request payment of the current year's audit fee in advance of any work being performed

4 Request a pre-issuance review be conducted by an external accountant

- 1 and 4 only
- 3 and 4 only
- 2 and 3 only
- 1, 2, 3 and 4 **(2 marks)**

The following scenario relates to questions 36 – 40

You are an audit manager in CL & Co, an accountancy firm with six offices and 15 partners.

You are planning the audit of LV Fones Co, which has been an audit client for four years and specialises in manufacturing luxury mobile phones. During the planning stage of the audit you have obtained the following information.

The audit team of LV Fones Co are entitled to purchase mobile phone accessories at a discount of 10%. The finance director has commented that this is to encourage the audit team to be more favourable towards the company and to keep them on side. The audit engagement partner has assessed the potential value of the discount to be trivial and inconsequential to any individuals who wish to take advantage of this offer.

During the year, the financial controller of LV Fones Co was ill and unable to work. The company had no spare staff able to fulfil the role and a qualified audit senior of CL & Co was seconded to the client for three months. The fee income derived from LV Fones Co was boosted by this engagement and along with the audit and tax fee, now accounts for 25% of the firm's total fees.

From a review of the correspondence files you note that the audit engagement partner and the finance director have known each other socially for many years and in fact went on holiday together last summer with their families. As a result of this friendship the audit engagement partner has not yet spoken to the client about the fee for last year's audit, 20% of which is still outstanding.

36 Which of the following correctly identifies the threats to independence and proposes an appropriate course of action for the firm if any of the audit team takes advantage of the discount?

	Threats	Course of action
o	Self-interest	Decline the offer
o	Advocacy	The offer can be accepted
o	Familiarity	Consider whether the discount is given to employees
o	Intimidation	Continue with appropriate safeguards

(2 marks)

37 Which of the following actions should CL & Co take to maintain its objectivity in relation to the level of fee income from LV Fones Co?

1 Ensure partner compensation is not significantly influenced by client fees

2 Increase the client base

3 Perform a pre or post-issuance review of the engagement if fees exceed 30% of the firm's total income for five consecutive years

o 1 and 2 only

o 1, 2 and 3

o 2 and 3 only

o 1 and 3 only **(2 marks)**

38 Which of the following correctly identifies the threats to independence and proposes an appropriate course of action for the firm in respect of the audit senior's secondment to LV Fones Co?

	Threats	Course of action
o	Self-interest and self-review	The audit senior should not have been seconded to LV Fones Co
o	Self-interest only	The audit senior should be assigned to the audit team to increase efficiency of the audit
o	Self-review only	Perform an engagement quality review
o	Familiarity and self-review	The audit senior must not be assigned to the audit of LV Fones Co

(2 marks)

39 Which of the following actions should CL & Co take to maintain its objectivity in relation to the outstanding fees from LV Fones Co?

1 Ask the client to pay the outstanding amount

2 Have an independent review of the work performed

3 Do not issue the auditor's report for the current year until the fees are paid

- o 1 and 3 only
- o 2 and 3 only
- o 1, 2 and 3
- o 1 only

(2 marks)

40 Select one option from each column which identifies the type of ethical threat arising from the engagement partner's friendship with the finance director, and identifies an appropriate course of action the firm should take to manage the threat to an acceptable level.

Ethical threat
Intimidation
Familiarity
Self-interest

Course of action
Resign from the audit engagement
Structure the audit partner's responsibilities to reduce the potential impact to the engagement
Remove the audit partner from the audit

(2 marks)

The following scenario relates to questions 41 – 45

It is 1 July 20X5. You are an audit manager in NAB & Co, a large audit firm which specialises in the audit of retailers.

Mickey Co

Mickey Co, a food retailer, has approached NAB & Co to become its auditor. Mickey Co is looking for a new auditor as the previous firm resigned without prior notice three months ago without having started the audit for the year ended 31 December 20X4. Mickey Co has approached several other audit firms since the previous auditor resigned but all have declined to take the engagement. Mickey Co must file its financial statements by 30 September 20X5 in accordance with local legislation and therefore has stated that the audit must be completed before this date. NAB & Co currently audits Goofy Co, Mickey Co's main competitor.

Goofy Co

The audit engagement partner for Goofy Co has been in place for approximately six years and her son has just accepted a job offer from Goofy Co as a sales manager. This role would entitle him to shares in Goofy Co as part of his remuneration package.

Goofy Co has requested NAB & Co provides tax advice to minimise the company's tax liability. Management has suggested that the fee could be based on the level of tax saving achieved to ensure the payment for the service does not outweigh the benefit obtained. The fee is expected to be significant.

Goofy Co's management has decided to establish an audit committee. The company does not have any independent non-executive directors with recent and relevant financial experience and have requested our firm's assistance with this. Management has requested that the audit engagement partner assists by reviewing qualifications and advising on technical, financial competence of applicants.

41 Match the acceptance considerations with the MOST appropriate reason for why they should be considered by NAB & Co before accepting the audit of Mickey Co.

Acceptance consideration	
1	The previous audit firm resigned without notice and several firms have declined the engagement
2	The audit must be completed before 30 September 20X5
3	Mickey Co is a main competitor of Goofy Co, an existing audit client of NAB & Co

Reason	
A	There may be threats to objectivity and confidentiality that cannot be managed to an acceptable level
B	NAB & Co may not be competent to perform the audit
C	The fee may not be sufficient for the level of work that is required
D	The firm may not have enough resource to perform the audit at the time required
E	Management of Mickey Co may lack integrity

(2 marks)

42 What is the correct order of the steps that NAB & Co should take in respect of the conflict of interest arising?

1 Perform an engagement quality review

2 Obtain consent to act

3 Implement safeguards

4 Inform Mickey Co and Goofy Co

- 3, 1, 4, 2
- 4, 2, 3, 1
- 2, 4, 3, 1
- 4, 2, 1, 3 **(2 marks)**

43 Select one option from each column which identifies the SIGNIFICANT ethical threat arising from the audit engagement partner's son working for Goofy Co, and identifies an appropriate course of action the firm should take to manage the threat to an acceptable level.

Ethical threat
Intimidation
Familiarity
Self-interest

Course of action
Remove the audit engagement partner from the audit
Structure the audit partner's responsibilities to reduce the potential impact to the engagement
Inform Goofy Co that it should not employ the audit engagement partner's son

(2 marks)

44 Which of the following statements is TRUE in respect of Goofy Co's request for the tax advice fee to be based on the tax saving achieved?

- The fee basis is acceptable as it does not relate to the audit fee
- The fee basis is not acceptable as contingent fee arrangements are not acceptable for any accountancy work
- The fee basis is acceptable if both NAB & Co and Goofy Co agree to it
- The fee basis will not be acceptable as the fee is significant to the firm **(2 marks)**

45 Which of the following statements is TRUE in respect of the request for assistance with recruitment of independent non-executive directors for Goofy Co?

- No threat arises and no safeguards are required
- The audit engagement partner cannot provide assistance and another partner must provide assistance
- The audit firm cannot provide assistance and the request must be declined
- The audit engagement partner can provide the assistance but an engagement quality review must be performed **(2 marks)**

The following scenario relates to questions 46 – 50

You are an audit manager in Swift & Co responsible for the audit of Kingfisher Co, a retail company planning to list on a stock exchange within the next six months. The board of directors currently comprises the chair, chief executive, three executive directors and three non-executive directors. Details of the three non-executive directors is given below.

Teri Toucan

Teri was an employee of Kingfisher until retirement six years ago. On retirement, Teri became a non-executive director. Teri currently receives a pension from Kingfisher Co and a fixed salary for being a non-executive director. Teri does not own shares in Kingfisher Co.

Pat Parrot

Pat was an employee until ten years ago and was also a shareholder in Kingfisher Co as part of Pat's remuneration package included share options which had been exercised. Pat became a non-executive director three and a half years ago and on appointment, Pat left the company's pension scheme and sold all shares in Kingfisher Co.

Linda Lorikeet

Linda is an independent non-executive director of Kingfisher Co. Linda has been a member of the board for eight years and has extensive retail experience from previous employments.

Proposed changes

Kingfisher Co's management has been advised by the audit engagement partner about the need for compliance with corporate governance principles once the company is listed. The board of directors has identified two more potential independent non-executive directors to join Kingfisher Co. Once more directors are appointed, Kingfisher Co plans to establish an audit committee and a remuneration committee.

The two potential directors are:

Frances Finch

Frances is currently the finance director of a listed multi-national banking company and is a non-executive director and audit committee member for another company. Frances is agreeable to being a non-executive director for Kingfisher Co and to be paid a fixed fee which is not related to profits. Frances is being considered for the role of board chair as the current chair is due to retire in six months' time.

Mica Macaw

Mica, the sister of Kingfisher Co's chief executive, is currently a finance director of a small retail company, which does not compete with Kingfisher Co. Mica has expressed an interest in a role at Kingfisher Co provided a contract with a minimum three-year term is offered.

---

46 Which of the following recommendations is NOT required to be implemented by Kingfisher Co to bring the company in line with corporate governance best practice?

- o More independent non-executive directors must be appointed to ensure at least half of the board are independent
- o The board must appoint a workforce representative
- o Linda will need to be replaced as an independent non-executive director next year
- o The board chair must be appointed from within the company to ensure they have sufficient knowledge of the company **(2 marks)**

47 In respect of Frances Finch, which of the following statements is TRUE?

- o Frances could become board chair and sit on the audit committee as the person with recent and relevant financial expertise
- o Frances could sit on the remuneration committee but must not be committee chair
- o If Frances accepts the role of board chair, remuneration should be related to company performance to align the interests of the chair and the company
- o Frances cannot become board chair for Kingfisher Co whilst holding directorships at two other companies **(2 marks)**

48 In respect of Teri Toucan, which of the following will compromise independence?

- o Teri receives a pension from Kingfisher Co
- o Teri does not own shares in Kingfisher Co
- o Teri receives a fixed salary from Kingfisher Co
- o Teri was an employee of Kingfisher Co six years ago **(2 marks)**

49 Which of the follow are advantages of appointing Mica Macaw as a non-executive director of Kingfisher Co?

1 Mica has close links to Kingfisher Co's chief executive.

2 Mica's experience in retail will facilitate understanding of the issues faced by Kingfisher Co.

3 Mica's financial experience will be useful if appointed to the audit committee.

4 Mica wishes to commit to a three-year contract.

- o 1, 3 and 4 only
- o 2 and 3 only
- o 1, 2 and 4 only
- o 1, 2, 3 and 4 **(2 marks)**

50 Which TWO of the following correctly explains corporate governance guidelines in respect of succession and evaluation of directors?

- o A succession plan should be maintained for the board chair and chief executive
- o The annual report should explain the work of the nomination committee including the process for making appointments
- o Performance of the board chair, the board, the individual executive and non-executive directors and each committee must be evaluated annually
- o All members of the nomination committee must be independent non-executive directors **(2 marks)**

PLANNING AND RISK ASSESSMENT

The following scenario relates to questions 51 – 55

It is 1 July 20X5. You are planning the audit of Veryan Co for the year ending 31 July 20X5. Veryan Co is a new audit client which operates in the oil & gas exploration industry. Companies wishing to operate in this industry require a licence which is valid for 20 years. Licensing authorities take into account public health and safety, protection of the environment and protection of biological resources when granting licences. Veryan Co's activities are geographically spread across three continents in 35 locations.

Veryan Co has been in existence for 30 years and has grown its revenue at an average of 12% per annum. This is in line with the industry average. During your planning meeting with the finance director you were informed that the forecast profit before tax for this financial year is $9.5 million (20X4: $6 million) based on revenues of $124 million (20X4: $100 million).

You have completed the audit strategy and the risk assessment section identifies the following as areas of significant risk of material misstatement:

- Overstatement of receivables due to long outstanding debts
- Misstatement of intangible assets (licences) due to incorrect amortisation
- Overstatement of tangible non-current assets in one of the exploration areas due to damage caused by a recent hurricane
- Overstatement of inventory due to the inherent difficulty of establishing the quantity of oil and gas reserves

---

51 Which of the following is the LEAST significant audit risk to be considered when planning the audit of Veryan Co?

o Non-compliance with laws and regulations

o Understatement of trade payables

o Adequacy of provisions and contingent liabilities

o Foreign currency transactions **(2 marks)**

52 Which TWO of the following are appropriate responses to address the increased detection risk due to Veryan Co being a new audit client?

o Extended controls testing should be performed

o Obtain an understanding of Veryan Co

o Consideration should be given to relying on the work of an independent expert

o Reduce reliance on tests of controls

o Contact the previous auditor to request working papers **(2 marks)**

53 Which of the following is the LEAST appropriate materiality level to be used in the audit of Veryan Co?

- o $1.5 million
- o $1.0 million
- o $750,000
- o $475,000

(2 marks)

54 Select whether the following statements are consistent or not consistent with the movement in revenue.

Cut-off of revenue is an audit risk	**Consistent**	**Not consistent**
Completeness of revenue is an audit risk	**Consistent**	**Not consistent**
Occurrence of revenue is an audit risk	**Consistent**	**Not consistent**

(2 marks)

55 Match the audit risks given in the scenario with the MOST appropriate response the auditor of Veryan Co should take.

Audit risk
1 Receivables
2 Non-current assets
3 Intangible assets (licences)

Auditor's response
A Physically inspect a sample of exploration areas
B Contact a sample of customers to confirm the year-end balance
C Ask management to adjust the financial statements
D Inspect the licence agreement
E Review correspondence with customers
F Calculate the expected amortisation
G Review the results of management's impairment test

(2 marks)

The following scenario relates to questions 56 – 60

It is 1 July 20X5. You are an audit manager in Woodwind & Co and you are planning the audit of Flute Co, a new audit client for your firm which has a year ended of 30 June 20X5. Flute Co is a large mobile phone company which operates a network of stores in countries across Europe.

You have been provided with planning notes from the audit engagement partner following a planning meeting with the finance director.

During the year the company introduced a bonus based on sales for its sales team. The bonus target was based on increasing the number of customers signing up for 24-month phone line contracts. This strategy has been successful and revenue has increased by 15% compared with 20X4. In particular, there has been a significant increase in sales in May and June 20X5.

Technology companies which supply Flute Co with mobile phones release new versions with updated features every twelve months. When new phones are released, Flute & Co offers significant discounts on older versions.

You are to undertake a preliminary analytical review of the draft financial statements and have been provided with the following information:

	20X5 $	**20X4** $
Revenue	1,267,000	1,205,000
Cost of sales	1,013,000	965,000
Receivables	121,000	100,000
Payables	87,500	85,000
Inventory	160,000	125,000
Cash	123,000	140,000

Overvaluation of inventory and receivables are considered to be significant risks for this year's audit.

56 Which of the following statements is TRUE in relation to Flute Co being a new audit client of Woodwind & Co?

- Inherent risk is increased as the firm has no cumulative knowledge or experience of Flute Co
- The auditor may not be competent to perform the audit and should consider resigning
- The auditor should contact the previous auditor to ask if there are any professional matters of which they should be aware
- The auditor will need to increase the quality management procedures performed due to the increased risk **(2 marks)**

57 Which of the following is an appropriate explanation of the audit risk relating to the bonus for Flute Co's sales team?

- o There is an increased risk of a reduction in profit for the company as a result of irrecoverable debts
- o There is an increased risk of inappropriate cut-off of revenue
- o There is an increased risk of understatement of revenue
- o There is an increased risk of non-response from customers following direct confirmation audit testing **(2 marks)**

58 Using the financial information provided, calculate the following ratios for both years. Calculate your answers to the nearest round number and enter the answer into the relevant box.

	20X5	**20X4**
Receivables collection period		
Inventory holding period		

(2 marks)

59 Which of the following is NOT an appropriate audit response to the significant risks relating to inventory and receivables?

	Inventory	**Receivables**
o	Extend cut-off testing	Extend cut-off testing
o	Review controls over inventory levels	Review controls over the collection of debts
o	Discuss slow-moving inventory items with the finance director	Discuss long-outstanding receivables with the finance director
o	Perform post-year-end sales invoice testing	Perform post-year-end cash receipts testing

(2 marks)

60 Which TWO of the following statements BEST describe the purpose of using analytical procedures during the planning stage of Flute Co's audit?

- o To help form an overall conclusion on the financial statements
- o To obtain relevant and reliable audit evidence
- o To assist with identification of risks of material misstatement
- o To assist in identifying unusual transactions and events at Flute Co **(2 marks)**

The following scenario relates to questions 61 – 65

It is 1 July 20X5. You are an audit senior in Simone & Co. You are planning the audit of Epica Co for the year ending 31 July 20X5. The audit manager has held a planning meeting with the finance director and has provided you with notes of the meeting and financial statement extracts.

Epica Co has experienced difficult trading conditions this year which has resulted in sales prices being reduced. Despite this, revenue has continued to fall. In an attempt to improve profit, Epica Co has switched to a cheaper supplier which has resulted in lower quality goods being purchased and a corresponding increase in returns from customers.

During the year the directors performed a review of asset lives which has resulted in an increase in the useful life of the majority of tangible non-current assets. Accordingly, the depreciation charge has reduced from $1 million in 20X4 to $0.8 million in 20X5.

Financial statement extracts for year ending 31 July

	DRAFT 20X5	**ACTUAL 20X4**
	$m	$m
Revenue	12.5	15.0
Cost of sales	(7.0)	(8.0)
Gross profit	5.5	7.0
Operating expenses	(5.0)	(5.1)
Operating profit	0.5	1.9
Inventories	1.9	1.4
Receivables	3.1	2.0
Cash	0.8	1.9
Trade payables	1.6	1.2
Loan due for payment 31 January 20X6	1.0	1.0

61 Using the financial information provided, calculate the following ratios for both years. Calculate your answers to ONE decimal place and enter the answer into the relevant box.

	20X5	**20X4**
Gross profit margin		
Current ratio		

(2 marks)

62 In relation to the movement in the payables payment period, which of the following statements is most relevant to the auditor's consideration of audit risk?

- o The payables payment period has decreased which could indicate understatement of payables
- o The payables payment period has decreased which could indicate Epica Co is taking advantage of early payment discounts
- o The payables payment period has increased which could indicate Epica Co has cash flow problems
- o The payables payment period has increased which could indicate Epica Co is managing its working capital cycle by delaying payments to suppliers **(2 marks)**

63 Which THREE of the following describe audit risks that should be addressed during the audit of Epica Co?

- o Inventory may be overstated if sales prices have fallen below cost
- o Provisions for the return of goods may be understated
- o Epica Co has experienced difficult trading conditions causing revenue to fall
- o Sales prices have been reduced which will impact profitability
- o Lower quality goods have been purchased resulting in complaints from customers
- o Inventory may be misstated if returned goods have not been recorded back into inventory **(2 marks)**

64 Which TWO of the following describe appropriate auditor responses to the audit risk related to the increase in the useful life of tangible non-current assets of Epica Co?

- o Calculate whether the change in depreciation charge is material. If not material, no further action is necessary
- o Discuss with the directors the reason for the change in useful life
- o Compare the actual useful life of tangible non-current assets recently disposed of to the new depreciation policy to assess whether this reflects the actual useful economic life
- o Compare the fixtures and fittings depreciation rate this year to last year **(2 marks)**

65 Which of the following correctly describes the term performance materiality?

- o An amount which, through its omission or misstatement, would affect the economic decisions of the users taken on the basis of the financial statements
- o The maximum amount of misstatement the auditor is willing to accept and still conclude that the financial statements are fairly stated
- o An amount which reduces the probability that the aggregate of uncorrected and undetected misstatements exceeds materiality for the financial statements as a whole
- o An amount below which misstatements of balances and classes of transactions in the financial statements would be clearly trivial **(2 marks)**

The following scenario relates to questions 66 – 70

It is 1 July 20X5. You are an audit manager in Owl & Co responsible for the audit of Hawk Co. Hawk Co manufacture kites which it sells via its website directly to customers. You are currently planning the audit for the year ending 31 July 20X5.

Two issues have been brought to your attention during a planning meeting with the finance director.

Dismissal of financial controller

The financial controller of Hawk Co, who had been employed by the company for over 20 years, was dismissed in May 20X5. A claim for unfair dismissal has just been received. No replacement has been found for the financial controller as of yet and the tasks are being shared between the finance team until the role is filled.

Payables ledger supervisor

The payables ledger supervisor left in March 20X5 and a replacement has only been appointed in the last week. However, for this period no supplier statement reconciliations or trade payables account reconciliations were performed.

The finance director has also provided you with the most recent management accounts to enable you to perform preliminary analytical procedures and you have calculated the following ratios:

	20X5	**20X4**
Gross profit margin	17%	26%
Payables payment period	40 days	75 days
Receivables collection period	38 days	29 days

66 Which of the following are appropriate auditor responses to the increased audit risk created by the finance team being allocated the work of the financial controller?

1 The audit team should be fully briefed and be alert throughout the audit for additional errors

2 The auditor should appoint an expert to properly assess the risks of misstatement

3 The finance director should be requested to provide the audit team with assistance for matters that cannot be addressed by the remaining finance function

4 The auditor should consider resigning from the engagement as audit risk cannot be managed to an acceptable level

- o 1, 2 and 3
- o 2, 3 and 4
- o 1 and 3 only
- o 1 and 4

(2 marks)

67 Which THREE of the following statements are TRUE in relation to the lack of supplier statement reconciliations?

- o The auditor should perform the supplier statement reconciliations for Hawk Co
- o There is an increased risk of misstatement of trade payables
- o Misstatements in the purchase accrual balance may go undetected
- o The auditor will need to send requests for confirmation of balances to suppliers
- o Increased substantive testing will need to be performed over purchases and payables

(2 marks)

68 In respect of the unfair dismissal claim, which of the following audit procedures is NOT appropriate?

- o Review correspondence between the financial controller and the company
- o Review board meeting minutes
- o Review correspondence between the company and its lawyer
- o Discuss the claim with the financial controller

(2 marks)

69 Which audit risks can be identified from the preliminary analytical procedures performed?

	Gross profit margin	**Payables payment period**	**Receivables collection period**
A	Website sales may not be accurately recorded	Payables may not be accurately recorded	Extended credit terms may have been given to customers
B	Revenue may have been recognised too early	Suppliers may be withdrawing credit terms	Receivables may not be completely recorded
C	Revenue may not have occurred	Purchase invoices may have been recorded twice	Receivables may not exist
D	Website sales may not be completely recorded	Payables may not be completely recorded	Receivables may be overvalued

- o Option A
- o Option B
- o Option C
- o Option D

(2 marks)

70 Which of the following are reasons why analytical procedures will be performed during the planning of Hawk Co?

1 To help identify areas of potential risk

2 To help obtain an understanding of Hawk Co

3 To help detect material misstatements in the financial statement figures

- o 1 only
- o 1 and 2 only
- o 1, 2 and 3
- o 2 and 3 only **(2 marks)**

The following scenario relates to questions 71 – 75

It is 1 July 20X5. You are the audit manager responsible for the audit of Swandive Co, a company with a financial year ending 31 July 20X5. You are planning the audit and payroll has been identified as a significant audit risk this year.

You have designed the following procedures for inclusion in the audit plan.

1 For a sample of employees recalculate the gross and net pay and agree to the payroll records.

2 Perform a proof-in-total of wages and salaries and compare the expected total to actual wages and salaries in draft financial statements.

3 Select a sample of hourly paid employees and verify hours worked have been authorised by their line manager.

4 Review the payroll report for evidence of authorisation by the financial director before any payments are made to employees.

Payroll fraud

During the year, it was discovered that a payroll clerk had been setting up fictitious employees on the payroll system with the wages being paid into the clerk's own bank account. This clerk has subsequently left the company but you are concerned that additional frauds may have taken place in the wages department due to a lack of adequate and effective internal controls.

---

71 Which TWO of the procedures included in the audit plan describe substantive procedures to confirm the completeness and accuracy of Swandive Co's payroll expense?

- o 1 and 2
- o 2 and 3
- o 3 and 4
- o 1 and 4 **(2 marks)**

72 Select which section of the audit strategy of Swandive Co the following matters would appear. Audit strategy areas may be selected more than once or not at all.

Matter	
1	Risk of material misstatement including the risk of fraud
2	Use of professional scepticism
3	Selection of the audit team
4	Use of automated tools and audit techniques

Audit strategy section	
A	Characteristics of the engagement
B	Reporting objectives, timing of the audit and nature of communications
C	Significant factors, preliminary engagement activities, and knowledge gained on other engagements
D	Nature, timing and extent of resources

(2 marks)

73 With respect to the fraud at Swandive Co, which of the following statements is TRUE?

- o This fraud is an example of fraudulent financial reporting
- o The auditor will need to reduce control risk
- o Detection risk will need to increase as a result of the fraud
- o The audit team should discuss the susceptibility of Swandive Co to fraud **(2 marks)**

74 Which of the following additional controls is most effective at preventing fraud of this type occurring again?

- o An exception report should be generated when standing data is changed in the payroll system which is reviewed by the payroll manager
- o On a regular basis, department managers should be given a list of employees for their department from the payroll system to check
- o The people working in the payroll department should not be related
- o The finance director should compare the total payroll cost each month to prior month to identify significant differences **(2 marks)**

75 Which THREE of the following procedures would assist in the detection of further frauds of this type at Swandive Co?

- o Discuss with management whether they are aware of further frauds at Swandive Co
- o Report the fraud to the police to deter other employees from committing a similar fraud
- o Trace the amounts per the payroll records to the bank statements to identify any anomalies
- o Analyse the bank details of all employees to identify duplicate bank accounts
- o Review HR records for the names of employees and reconcile these to the names on the bank transfer lists **(2 marks)**

INTERNAL CONTROLS

The following scenario relates to questions 76 – 80

It is 1 July 20X5. You are an audit manager in Sandy & Co and you are responsible for the audit of Coastal Co for the year ending 30 September 20X5. The internal control systems in relation to purchases and payroll have recently been documented by the audit junior. Tests of controls have been performed to evaluate the effectiveness of the system. The audit junior has used narrative notes and an internal control questionnaire to document the system. You are reviewing the work performed by the audit junior before assessing the impact on the audit approach to be taken in respect of purchases and payroll.

The following features of the purchases and payroll systems have been noted in the audit junior's documentation:

1 Goods are counted and agreed to the supplier's delivery note before signing the delivery note to accept the goods.

2 The purchase invoice is matched to, and filed with, the related goods received note and purchase order by the purchase ledger team in the finance department.

3 Payroll standing data files are sent to department managers on a monthly basis for review.

4 Hours worked are entered onto a pre-printed payroll sheet by the wages clerk.

5 Before payroll payments are made, the finance director reviews the bank transfer list and signs to authorise the payments to be made.

76 Select whether the following advantages and disadvantages relate to narrative notes, internal control questionnaires or both.

	Narrative notes	Internal control questionnaires	Both
Advantages			
Can be prepared in advance			
Easy to understand			
Disadvantages			
May overstate the controls			
Some controls may be missed			

(2 marks)

77 Select whether the features of the purchases and payroll systems described are a strength or deficiency of the internal control system of Coastal Co.

1	**Strength**	**Deficiency**
2	**Strength**	**Deficiency**
3	**Strength**	**Deficiency**
4	**Strength**	**Deficiency**

(2 marks)

78 Which of the following control objectives is addressed by feature number 5?

- o To ensure payroll is classified correctly
- o To ensure only valid employees are paid
- o To ensure employees are paid for the correct hours
- o To ensure employee's salaries have been calculated correctly **(2 marks)**

79 You have reviewed the work of the audit junior and concluded that reliance can be placed on the internal controls. What impact will this have on the nature and extent of substantive audit procedures to be performed at the final audit?

- o Less importance can be placed on written representations from management
- o Greater use of tests of detail and less use of analytical procedures
- o Decreased sample sizes when performing substantive testing
- o Increased use of evidence from outside the entity **(2 marks)**

80 The payroll section of the audit plan of Coastal Co includes the following procedures. For each procedure select whether it is a test of control or a substantive procedure.

Recalculate the total of the bank transfer list	**Test of control**	**Substantive procedure**
Inspect the bank transfer list for evidence of the finance director's signature confirming the payment can be made	**Test of control**	**Substantive procedure**
For a sample of employees, agree the salary details in the standing data files to the calculation of the employee's monthly salary as per the payslip	**Test of control**	**Substantive procedure**
Review the procedures to ensure payroll files and documents are kept secure and confidential	**Test of control**	**Substantive procedure**

(2 marks)

The following scenario relates to questions 81 – 85

It is 1 July 20X5. You are an audit supervisor with Lzzy & Co, reviewing extracts from the sales and despatch systems documentation in preparation for the interim audit of Halestorm Co. The company's year end is 30 September 20X5.

Halestorm Co manufactures snacks such as potato chips which are supplied to large and small food retailers. Halestorm Co has experienced significant growth over recent years and in response to this growth, senior management has established an internal audit department to improve the control environment of the company. You are a member of the recently formed internal audit department.

Senior management of Halestorm Co has concerns about the effectiveness of the company's sales and despatch system and has instructed the internal audit department to perform a review of the system. Any deficiencies identified are to be reported to the finance director who will report the findings back to the board of directors at the next board meeting. Recommendations for improvements are also to be provided.

During the review the following deficiencies were identified:

(i) Availability of inventory is not checked until at the time of ordering

(ii) Telephone orders are initially noted on a piece of paper and then transferred to an order form after the call has ended

(iii) Order forms are not sequentially numbered

(iv) The online ordering system allows customers to place orders which exceed their credit limit.

81 Which of the following is NOT an objective of Halestorm Co's sales and despatch system?

- o To ensure that orders are only accepted if goods are available
- o To ensure that all orders are recorded completely and accurately
- o To ensure discounts received are accounted for completely and accurately
- o To ensure that all goods despatched are correctly invoiced **(2 marks)**

82 Match the control deficiencies to an appropriate explanation of the issue.

Deficiency
(i)
(ii)
(iii)
(iv)

Explanation	
A	Risk of incorrect orders being despatched
B	Risk of irrecoverable debts
C	Risk of orders not being fulfilled on a timely basis
D	Orders may go missing leading to unfulfilled orders

(2 marks)

83 Which TWO of the following are appropriate recommendations to address the credit limit system deficiency?

- o Credit limits should be reviewed by a responsible official on a regular basis and amended as appropriate
- o Sales order clerks should be allowed to use discretion to raise credit limits to avoid losing revenue
- o The online ordering system should be programmed to allow orders up to a maximum of 5% in excess of the credit limit
- o Orders which would cause a customer to exceed their credit limit should be sent to a responsible official for approval **(2 marks)**

84 Which of the following recommendations should be made to address deficiencies (ii) and (iii)?

1 Order clerks should have online access to view real-time inventory quantities at the time of ordering.

2 Order forms should be sequentially pre-numbered and a regular sequence check should be performed.

3 All orders should be entered directly into the ordering system as the customer is placing the order.

4 Customers should be instructed not to place orders by telephone.

- o 1 and 2
- o 2 and 3 only
- o 2, 3 and 4
- o 1, 3 and 4 **(2 marks)**

85 Which of the following statements is TRUE in respect of the review findings?

- o The findings will be communicated to the shareholders at the annual general meeting
- o The recommendations will need to be actioned before the external audit commences
- o The findings should be reported directly to the board of directors rather than the finance director
- o The findings should be discussed with the external auditor before being communicated to the finance director

(2 marks)

The following scenario relates to questions 86 – 90

It is 1 July 20X5. You are an audit supervisor with Marigold & Co, reviewing extracts from documentation describing Primrose Co's sales, inventory and purchasing systems in preparation for the interim audit. The company's year end is 30 September 20X5.

Primrose Co has recently upgraded its computer system to enable greater automation of transaction processing. The new system has integrated the sales, inventory and purchasing systems resulting in minimal manual entry.

Sales orders are entered into the system manually. The inventory system is automatically updated to reflect that inventory has been allocated to an order. The system will flag if there is insufficient inventory to fulfil the order. The inventory system is linked to the purchasing system so that when inventory falls to a minimum level a purchase order is automatically created and sent to the purchasing manager for authorisation. Once the manager clicks 'authorised' the order is automatically sent electronically to the approved supplier for that item. The system is backed up daily to ensure minimal loss of data in the event of a system failure.

Primrose Co's internal auditors were present during the implementation of the new system and performed tests during the process to ensure the information transferred into the new system was free from error. The internal audit plan of work has been updated to include regular tests of the system throughout the year to ensure it is working effectively.

Marigold & Co is planning to use automated tools and techniques during the audit for the first time this year as a result of the new system and is also planning to use the work of Primrose Co's internal audit department if possible.

86 Which of the following is NOT a test of control in respect of Primrose Co's system?

- o Trace a sample of purchase orders through to the approved supplier list to ensure the supplier used is approved
- o Trace a sales order through to the system and into the detailed sales listing to ensure it is recorded
- o Review a sample of purchases orders in the system to ensure they are authorised within the system
- o Inspect copies of the back-ups taken to ensure these are taken on a daily basis

(2 marks)

87 Select whether the following controls identified in Primrose Co's systems are general or information processing controls?

Daily backups of the system	**General**	**Information processing**
Authorisation of purchase orders	**General**	**Information processing**
Minimum order quantities	**General**	**Information processing**
Automatic updating of inventory once goods are sold	**General**	**Information processing**

(2 marks)

88 Which of the following procedures provides the MOST reliable evidence that the inventory system updates automatically once an order has been received?

- o Review the inventory level of an item, enter a sales order into the system and review the inventory level again after the order has been placed
- o Count a sample of items of inventory in the warehouse and agree the quantities to the quantities stated in the inventory system
- o Review the inventory report detailing quantities of items to identify unusually high or low quantities
- o Contact a sample of customers to enquire whether they have experienced delays in orders being processed due to insufficient inventory being held **(2 marks)**

89 Which can be tested by placing a dummy sales order for a large quantity of goods into the system? Select all that apply.

Control	
The inventory system is automatically updated to reflect that inventory has been allocated to a sales order	
The system will flag if there is insufficient inventory to fulfil the order	
When inventory falls to a minimum level a purchase order is automatically created and sent to the purchasing manager for authorisation	
The purchase order is automatically sent electronically to the approved supplier for that item	

(2 marks)

90 Which TWO of the following procedures should be performed by Marigold & Co to identify whether the work of Primrose Co's internal audit department can be relied upon?

- o Review the internal auditor's working papers to ensure sufficient appropriate evidence has been obtained
- o Engage an independent expert to assess the new system and validate the reliability of the internal audit department's work
- o Reperform a sample of procedures performed by the internal auditor to ensure the same conclusion is reached
- o Assess whether Primrose Co has an audit committee in place responsible for overseeing the internal audit function. If so, the external auditor can rely on the work performed by the internal auditor without the need for further work **(2 marks)**

The following scenario relates to questions 91 – 95

It is 1 July 20X5. Shroom Co is a manufacturer of vegetarian food including ready meals and plant-based sausages and burgers which it supplies to large grocery chains across the country. The company has grown significantly over the last five years with revenue increasing by 50%. Its year end is 31 July 20X5. You work in the internal audit department of Shroom Co which performs periodic reviews of internal controls, assesses the risk management processes of the company and performs fraud investigations when applicable. The following areas have been reviewed by the internal audit department over the last three years:

20X5	Non-current assets, revenue
20X4	Purchases, payroll
20X3	Inventory, cash

You are reviewing the internal controls over non-current assets and asset expenditure of the company which were last reviewed in 20X2.

You have been provided with the following information relating to the non-current assets cycle.

Shroom Co prepares a rolling five-year asset expenditure budget which is updated annually by the asset expenditure committee. The committee has three members. Each year the heads of department meet with the committee to discuss asset requirements for the budget period. All assets purchased must be included in the budget, except in exceptional circumstances for which there is a contingency fund set aside.

When asset expenditure is required, the relevant department head must send a requisition to the committee with quotations from at least two suppliers. The requisition is approved by the committee if the items requested are included in the budget and the quotation is acceptable. The approval is noted in the minutes of the meeting. A copy of the approved requisition form is sent to the purchasing department where a purchase order is completed and a copy of the approved requisition is kept with the order. Before the order is placed, the purchasing director must agree the order details to the approved requisition and sign the purchase order as evidence of the check.

On receipt, a goods received note (GRN) is completed. Each asset is checked to the authorised purchase order and checked for condition and evidence of these checks is noted on the GRN. Each asset is assigned a unique serial number which is recorded on the asset and written on the GRN. The GRN is forwarded to the finance team which maintains the non-current asset register. The asset is added to the register.

The non-current asset register contains a description of the asset, the serial number, the cost to be capitalised, the expected useful life, purchase date, department/location and estimated residual value. The non-current asset register is password protected and only a small number of people in the finance department know the password.

On a quarterly basis the management accounts detail the total asset expenditure incurred and the amount budgeted for the period with explanations of any variances greater than 5%.

Once a year the internal audit department agrees the physical assets to the asset register to ensure the register is complete.

91 Which TWO of the following control objectives are addressed by the work of the asset expenditure committee?

- o To ensure assets purchased are authorised
- o To ensure assets purchased are for a valid business use
- o To ensure the non-current asset register is complete
- o To ensure assets purchased represent value for money
- o To ensure all assets purchased are given a unique serial number **(2 marks)**

92 For each of the controls given below, select the type of control activity described.

The internal audit department agrees the physical assets to the asset register to ensure completeness	Physical or logical control	Verification	Reconciliation
Variances between actual and budgeted expenditure are analysed in the quarterly management accounts	Segregation of duties	Verification	Reconciliation
The non-current asset register is password protected	Physical or logical control	Segregation of duties	Authorisation

(2 marks)

93 Which THREE of the following documents together provide persuasive evidence that assets purchased during the year have been authorised?

1 Requisition

2 Order

3 Goods received note

4 Non-current asset register

5 Minutes of asset expenditure committee meetings

- o 1, 2 and 3
- o 2, 3 and 4
- o 3, 4 and 5
- o 1, 2 and 5 **(2 marks)**

94 Which of the following is NOT a test of control the external auditor of Shroom Co may perform in relation to non-current assets?

- Inspect a sample of assets purchased during the year for a serial number and trace this to the non-current asset register
- Review a sample of goods received notes for evidence of the check against purchase order and condition
- Compare actual asset expenditure with budgeted asset expenditure during the year and investigate any variances greater than 5%
- Review the internal audit working papers documenting the reconciliation of physical assets with the non-current asset register **(2 marks)**

95 The external auditor has this year expressed an interest in using some individuals from Shroom Co's internal audit department to provide direct assistance with external audit procedures.

For which of the following areas would it be appropriate for internal audit to provide direct assistance?

- Assessing controls over non-current assets
- Revenue recognition
- Valuation of inventory
- Performing cash counts **(2 marks)**

AUDIT EVIDENCE

The following scenario relates to questions 96 – 100

It is 1 July 20X5. Chester Co manufactures and sells pet toys to the wholesale market. It has prepared its financial statements to 31 March 20X5. You are an audit assistant with Durham & Co and you have been assigned the current liabilities balances in the audit work plan.

You have calculated the payables payment period to be 66 days in 20X5 (45 days in 20X4) and have asked the directors of Chester Co to provide an explanation for the increase in days.

Chester Co receives monthly statements from its main suppliers and performs regular supplier statement reconciliations. There were inconsistencies noted in respect of the following at 31 March 20X5.

Supplier	**Balance per supplier account**	**Balance per supplier statement**
	$	$
Oxford Co	151,480	296,120
Poole Co	(72,168)	84,235
Bath Co	82,348	92,340

Oxford Co

Chester Co has a credit agreement with Oxford Co under which it receives goods 14 days before the supplier raises the invoice. Chester Co received goods worth $144,640 on 18 March 20X5 for which the invoice was received shortly after the year end in accordance with the agreement. Chester Co entered the transaction into its accounting records at the date of invoice.

Poole Co

The difference on this balance has still to be investigated.

Bath Co

Chester Co's finance director has informed you that there was an error in closing the individual supplier accounts and they were closed three days early. Invoices received 29, 30 and 31 March 20X5 were posted to the 20X6 ledger. The directors of Chester Co have confirmed that following the discovery of this error, a manual journal adjustment was made.

96 Which of the following supplier balances would indicate a high risk in relation to the COMPLETENESS of the liability recorded at the year end?

- o A supplier with a high balance at the year end and with a low volume of transactions during the year
- o A supplier with a low balance at the year end and with a high volume of transactions during the year
- o A supplier with a low balance at the year end and with a low volume of transactions during the year
- o A supplier with a high balance at the year end and with a high volume of transactions during the year **(2 marks)**

97 Which of the following would correctly explain why the payables payment period has increased from 45 days in 20X4 to 66 days in 20X5?

- o Chester Co received a prompt payment discount from one of its suppliers for the first time in 20X5
- o Chester Co obtained a trade discount from one of its biggest suppliers which has reduced the amount owed to that supplier by 10% in the year
- o Chester Co purchased an unusually high level of goods in March 20X5 to satisfy a large order and had not paid for those goods by the year end
- o Chester Co took advantage of extended credit terms offered by a new supplier in respect of a large order which it had fully settled by the year end **(2 marks)**

98 Which of the following is an appropriate action in respect of the inconsistency in the balance with Oxford Co?

- o The auditor should take no further action as this is a timing difference which was resolved upon receipt and posting of the invoice
- o The auditor should request that the supplier's balance is amended at the reporting date to reflect the recent invoice
- o The auditor should contact the supplier and request a supplier statement as at the current date
- o The auditor should request that an accrual is created in respect of the goods received but not yet invoiced **(2 marks)**

99 Which of the following would be a valid explanation for the difference in respect of Poole Co?

1 An invoice for $156,403 has been paid twice

2 An invoice for $156,403 has been posted as a debit note

3 An invoice for $156,403 has been received and processed prior to receipt of the goods

- o 1 only
- o 1 and 2 only
- o 2 and 3 only
- o 1, 2 and 3 **(2 marks)**

100 Which of the following would NOT provide sufficient and appropriate audit evidence over the COMPLETENESS of the trade payables balance in respect of Bath Co?

- o Obtain the journal and confirm that all invoices recorded as received from Bath Co dated 29 – 31 March have been manually adjusted
- o Review the accruals listing to ensure goods received from Bath Co post year end for which an invoice has not been received have been recorded in the correct period
- o For post-year-end cash payments to Bath Co, confirm date of matching invoice and if pre year end, agree to liability
- o Review a sample of invoices received from Bath Co recorded post year end and match to GRN to determine if they should have been recorded at the year end **(2 marks)**

The following scenario relates to questions 101 – 105

It is 1 July 20X5. You are an audit senior in Jones & Co and are currently performing the final audit of Walker Co for the year ended 31 March 20X5. The company is a manufacturer and retailer of shoes and boots. The current audit senior is ill and you have been asked to complete the audit of payroll and revenue in their absence.

Payroll

You determine the following information from a review of the current year and prior year audit files:

- As at 31 March 20X4, Walker Co had 500 employees
- On 1 April 20X4, 10% of staff were made redundant, effective immediately, due to discontinuation of a product line
- On 1 June 20X4, all remaining staff received a 6% pay rise
- Over the course of the year, sales levels met performance targets which resulted in a fixed bonus of $1,500 being paid to each employee on 31 March 20X5

Revenue

The following audit procedures are included in the revenue section of the audit plan:

1 Review the treatment of a sample of post-year-end returns

2 Select a sample of goods despatch notes and agree to invoices in the detailed sales listing

3 Select a sample of invoices from the detailed sales listing and agree to goods despatch notes

4 Select a sample of invoices and recalculate the invoiced amount agreeing to price list

---

101 Which of the following statements explains the CUT-OFF assertion for wages and salaries?

- o Wages and salaries have been fairly allocated within the statement of profit or loss
- o Wages and salaries have been appropriately calculated taking into account all relevant taxation costs and adjustments
- o Wages and salaries which have been incurred during the period have been accounted for in respect of all personnel employed by Walker Co
- o Wages and salaries accounted for relate to the current year ended 31 March 20X5

(2 marks)

102 The following audit evidence has been gathered relating to the accuracy of wages and salaries for Walker Co:

1 Proof-in-total calculation performed by an audit team member

2 Written representation from the directors of Walker Co confirming the accuracy of wages and salaries

3 Verbal confirmation from the finance director of Walker Co confirming the accuracy of wages and salaries

4 Recalculation of the gross and net pay for a sample of employees by an internal audit team member of Walker Co

What is the order of reliability of the audit evidence starting with the MOST RELIABLE first?

- o 1, 2, 3, 4
- o 1, 4, 2, 3
- o 4, 1, 2, 3
- o 4, 1, 3, 2 **(2 marks)**

103 The prior year financial statements for Walker Co included $17 million for wages and salaries in the statement of profit or loss.

What would be the estimated current year wages and salaries expense, ignoring redundancy costs, based on the data gathered from the review of the audit files?

- o $16,740,000
- o $16,893,000
- o $16,815,000
- o $18,600,000 **(2 marks)**

104 **Select which TWO of the following are substantive ANALYTICAL PROCEDURES for wages and salaries.**

- o Trace and agree the total wages and salaries expense per the payroll system to the draft financial statements
- o Recalculate the gross and net pay for a sample of employees, agree to payroll records and investigate discrepancies
- o Compare the current year total payroll expense to the prior year and investigate any significant differences
- o Perform a proof-in-total calculation and compare expected expense to actual expense within the draft financial statements **(2 marks)**

105 **In respect of the revenue procedures included in the audit plan, select the assertion being tested.**

1	**Accuracy**	**Completeness**	**Occurrence**
2	**Accuracy**	**Completeness**	**Occurrence**
3	**Accuracy**	**Completeness**	**Occurrence**
4	**Accuracy**	**Completeness**	**Occurrence**

(2 marks)

The following scenario relates to questions 106 – 110

You are an audit senior of Viola & Co and are currently conducting the audit of Poppy Co for the year ended 31 March 20X5.

Materiality has been set at $50,000, and you are carrying out the detailed substantive testing on the year-end payables balance. The audit manager has emphasised that understatement of the trade payables balance is a significant audit risk.

Below is an extract from the list of supplier statements as at 31 March 20X5 held by the company and corresponding balance on the list of individual suppliers at the same date, along with some commentary on the noted differences:

Supplier	**Statement balance**	**List of individual suppliers**
	$000	$000
Carnation Co	70	50
Lily Co	175	105

Carnation Co

The difference in the balance is due to an invoice which is under dispute due to faulty goods which were returned on 29 March 20X5.

Lily Co

The difference in the balance is due to the supplier statement showing an invoice dated 28 March 20X5 for $70,000 which was not recorded in the financial statements until after the year end. The payables clerk has advised the audit team that the invoice was not received until 2 April 20X5.

106 The audit manager has asked you to review the full list of trade payables and select balances for which supplier statement reconciliations will be performed.

Which THREE of the following items should you select for testing?

- o Suppliers with material balances at the year end
- o Suppliers which have a high volume of business with Poppy Co
- o Major suppliers of Poppy Co with nil balances at the year end
- o Major suppliers of Poppy Co where the statement agrees to the balance on the list of individual suppliers **(2 marks)**

107 Which of the following audit procedures should be performed in relation to the balance with Lily Co to determine if the payables balance is understated?

- o Inspect the goods received note to determine when the goods were received
- o Inspect the purchase order to confirm it is dated before the year end
- o Review the post-year-end bank ledger account for evidence of payment of the invoice
- o Send a confirmation request to Lily Co to confirm the outstanding balance **(2 marks)**

108 Which of the following audit procedures should be carried out to confirm the balance owing to Carnation Co?

1 Review post-year-end credit notes for evidence of acceptance of return

2 Inspect pre-year-end goods returned note in respect of the items sent back to the supplier

3 Inspect post-year-end bank ledger account for evidence that the amount has been settled

- o 1, 2 and 3
- o 1 and 3 only
- o 1 and 2 only
- o 2 and 3 only **(2 marks)**

109 The audit manager has asked you to review the results of some statistical sampling testing, which resulted in 20% of the payables balance being tested.

The testing results indicate that there is a $45,000 error in the sample: $20,000 which is due to invoices not being recorded in the correct period as a result of weak controls and additionally there is a one-off error of $25,000 which was made by a temporary clerk.

What would be an appropriate course of action on the basis of these results?

- o The error is immaterial and therefore no further work is required
- o The effect of the control error should be projected across the whole population
- o Poppy Co should be asked to adjust the payables figure by $45,000
- o A different sample should be selected as these results are not reflective of the population **(2 marks)**

110 To help improve audit efficiency, Viola & Co is considering introducing the use of automated tools and techniques for some audits. You have been asked to consider how audit software and test data could be used during the audit of Poppy Co.

Select whether the following are examples of using test data or audit software for trade payables testing.

Selecting a sample of supplier balances for testing using monetary unit sampling	**Test data**	**Audit software**
Recalculating the ageing of trade payables to identify balances which may be in dispute	**Test data**	**Audit software**
Calculation of trade payables payment period to use in analytical procedures	**Test data**	**Audit software**
Inputting dummy purchase invoices into the client system to see if processed correctly	**Test data**	**Audit software**

(2 marks)

The following scenario relates to questions 111 – 115

It is 1 July 20X5. You are an audit supervisor in Seagull & Co and you are currently performing the audit of an existing client, Eagle Heating Co (Eagle), for the year ended 31 May 20X5. Eagle manufactures and sells heating and plumbing equipment to a number of home improvement stores across the country.

The following information has been obtained during discussions with the finance director.

Albatross Co

Albatross Co, one of Eagle's key customers has been experiencing financial difficulties. Eagle has agreed that Albatross Co can take a six-month payment break, after which payments will resume. The finance director does not believe that any allowance is required against this receivable. Your review of industry journals has identified several articles that suggest Albatross Co may soon cease trading.

Inventory

Eagle has experienced increased competition. In order to maintain its current levels of sales, it has decreased the selling price of its products significantly. Despite the reduction in selling price, inventory levels are significantly higher this year compared to the prior year. In addition to Eagle's inventory, there is inventory stored on behalf of a third party at the year end. Audit staff attended the year-end inventory count of Eagle which was held three days before the year end due to staff availability of Eagle. A reconciliation has been performed to determine the year-end inventory quantities.

Lawsuit

A customer has filed a claim against the company regarding a heating system that Eagle installed two months before the year end. The customer claims the installation was not done properly resulting in an explosion which caused damage to their home. The customer is claiming compensation of $50,000 which is material to the financial statements. The finance director believes that the claim is not probable to succeed so has not referred to it in the financial statements.

---

111 Which of the following substantive procedures will provide the MOST reliable evidence as to the recoverability of the outstanding balance from Albatross Co?

- o Obtain a direct confirmation letter from Albatross Co
- o Review the payment history of Albatross Co to assess the likelihood of payment
- o Review correspondence between Albatross Co and Eagle regarding when payment will be made
- o Review post-year-end cash receipts from Albatross Co **(2 marks)**

112 Which TWO of the following substantive procedures will provide evidence over the EXISTENCE of Eagle's trade receivables other than the balance owing from Albatross Co?

- o Calculate the receivables collection period and compare with prior year
- o Perform a receivables circularisation
- o Review post-year-end cash receipts from customers
- o Recalculate the allowance for irrecoverable receivables **(2 marks)**

113 Which TWO of the following factors may indicate overvaluation of inventory at Eagle?

- o Increased competition resulting in a decrease in selling price
- o Increased inventory levels
- o Increased inventory turnover ratio
- o Inventory consists of heating and plumbing equipment for home improvement stores
- o Inclusion of the third-party inventory within Eagle's inventory balance **(2 marks)**

114 Select whether the following are tests of control or substantive procedures in relation to Eagle's inventory balance.

Observe the client's staff to ensure co following the inventory count instructions	**Test of control**	**Substantive procedure**
Inspect the inventory for evidence of damage or obsolescence	**Test of control**	**Substantive procedure**
Reperform the reconciliation from the inventory count date to the year-end date for inventory to assess the accuracy of the inventory quantities	**Test of control**	**Substantive procedure**

(2 marks)

115 Which of the following are appropriate audit responses to the lawsuit?

1 Ask the finance director to include a provision in the financial statements

2 Inspect correspondence between the client and their legal advisers

3 Review board minutes to understand management's view about the claim

4 Contact the customer to understand the details of the claim

- o 2 and 3 only
- o 2, 3 and 4
- o 1, 3 and 4
- o 1 and 4 only **(2 marks)**

The following scenario relates to questions 116 – 120

It is 1 July 20X5. You are an audit senior in Staple and Co and you are preparing the audit procedures in respect of the audit of inventory for Gloss Co for the year ending 31 August 20X5. Gloss Co is a paint manufacturer and has been trading for over 50 years. It operates from one central site, which includes the production facility, warehouse and administration offices.

To avoid the disruption of a year-end inventory count, Gloss Co has this year introduced a continuous/perpetual inventory counting system. A timetable of inventory counts is maintained and regularly reviewed.

The following inventory counting processes have been implemented by Gloss Co:

1 The team prints the inventory quantities and descriptions from the system and these records are then compared to the inventory physically present.

2 Any discrepancies in relation to quantities are noted on the inventory sheets, including any items not listed on the sheets but present in the warehouse area.

3 Any damaged or old items are noted and they are removed from the inventory sheets.

4 During the counts there will continue to be inventory movements with goods arriving and leaving the warehouse.

5 Inventory belonging to third parties is removed from the warehouse before the count commences and kept in a separate location.

---

116 Which of the following statements are TRUE in respect of inventory counts?

1 The external auditor will perform the inventory count to ensure the inventory figure is accurate for the financial statements

2 The inventory count is used to ensure inventory is valued appropriately in the financial statements

3 All companies must cease production on days an inventory count is performed

4 The external auditor must attend the inventory count if inventory is a material balance

- o 1, 2 and 4 only
- o 2 and 3 only
- o 4 only
- o 1, 2, 3 and 4 **(2 marks)**

117 What is the primary reason for maintaining an inventory count timetable for the perpetual inventory counting system?

- o To ensure obsolete inventory is identified on a timely basis
- o To ensure the warehouse staff are not stealing inventory
- o To ensure all areas are counted during the year
- o To ensure damaged inventory is identified on a timely basis **(2 marks)**

118 Select whether the following statements are true or false in respect of Gloss Co's perpetual inventory system.

Staple & Co must attend at least one count to ensure adequate controls are applied	**True**	**False**
Cut-off testing will only need to be performed if a full count is carried out at the year end	**True**	**False**
All lines of inventory must be counted at least twice during the year	**True**	**False**
Staple & Co should visit the client's premises at least once a year and request a surprise inventory count	**True**	**False**

(2 marks)

119 Select whether the inventory count processes described represent strengths or deficiencies.

1	**Strength**	**Deficiency**
2	**Strength**	**Deficiency**
3	**Strength**	**Deficiency**
4	**Strength**	**Deficiency**
5	**Strength**	**Deficiency**

(2 marks)

120 During the inventory count you perform test counts agreeing inventory quantities on the count sheets to the physical inventory present in the warehouse and from the physical inventory to the count sheets.

Which assertions do these two procedures address?

	Count sheet to inventory	**Inventory to count sheet**
A	Existence	Completeness
B	Completeness	Existence
C	Accuracy, valuation and allocation	Existence
D	Rights and obligations	Accuracy, valuation and allocation

- o Option A
- o Option B
- o Option C
- o Option D

(2 marks)

The following scenario relates to questions 121 – 125

It is 1 July 20X5. You are an audit senior in Thor & Co and you have been assigned to the audit of Hemsworth Co for the year ended 31 May 20X5.

You are due to commence the audit of trade payables and the following procedures are listed in the audit plan:

Procedure		**Selection method**
1	For 20 invoices listed in the list of individual supplier balances, trace the amount recorded to the purchase invoice	Start at a random point and test every $100th
2	From the bank ledger account, select 10 payments made to suppliers in the first week of June 20X5 and trace to the related GRN. If the goods were received on or before 31 May 20X5 trace through to the list of individual supplier balances or accruals list	Highest value payments during the period specified
3	For 10 suppliers included in the list of individual suppliers, reperform supplier statement reconciliations	Any suppliers that have sent supplier statements at the year end

Sample sizes have been selected based on the results of the risk assessment performed at the planning stage.

121 Which THREE of the following should be considered when deciding whether to use sampling?

- o The time the auditor has available to perform the procedures
- o Appropriateness of the population
- o The size of the population
- o Completeness of the population
- o The ease with which the information is expected to be available **(2 marks)**

122 Identify whether the selection methods described represent sampling.

1	**Sampling**	**Not sampling**
2	**Sampling**	**Not sampling**
3	**Sampling**	**Not sampling**

(2 marks)

123 In respect of procedure 1, if the method stated to test every 100th item, which method would be described?

- o Monetary unit selection
- o Random selection
- o Systematic selection
- o Block selection **(2 marks)**

124 In relation to the procedures described, which of the following statements are TRUE?

1 Procedure 1 addresses the assertion of occurrence

2 Procedures 2 and 3 address the assertion of completeness

3 Procedure 2 uses the least reliable forms of evidence as compared with procedures 1 and 3

4 In respect of procedure 3, if supplier statements have not been retained by Hemsworth Co the auditor should contact the supplier directly

- o 1, 2, 3 and 4
- o 2 and 3 only
- o 1 only
- o 2, 3 and 4 **(2 marks)**

125 During the testing of Hemsworth Co's payables balance, several misstatements were found.

Which of the following is the most appropriate initial response your audit firm should take?

- o Report the matter to the client
- o Increase the amount of testing
- o Suggest the audit opinion is modified
- o Discuss the issue with the audit manager **(2 marks)**

The following scenario relates to questions 126 – 130

It is 1 July 20X5. You are an audit senior in Apollo & Co assigned to the audit of Delphic Co for the year ended 31 May 20X5. You are due to commence the audit of trade receivables. For the first time at this client, you have decided to use audit software to assist with the audit of the receivables balance.

Delphic Co is a wholesaler of furniture such as chairs, tables and cupboards. Delphic Co buys the furniture from six major manufacturers and sells them to over 600 different customers ranging from large retail chain stores to smaller owner-controlled businesses.

All financial information is stored on Delphic Co's computer systems, although previous audits have tended to adopt an 'audit around the computer' approach. Computer staff at Delphic Co are happy to help the auditor by providing access to the systems, although they cannot confirm completeness of systems documentation, and have warned that the systems have very old operating systems in place which limits file compatibility with more up-to-date programs. As the system is old, the auditor will be provided with copy files and not be allowed any direct access to Delphic Co's computer system.

126 Select whether the following explanations provide a valid explanation why audit risk increases when auditing 'around the computer'.

The actual computer files and programs are not tested therefore the auditor has no direct evidence that the programs are working as expected	**Valid**	**Not valid**
Where errors are found in reconciling inputs to outputs, it may be difficult or even impossible to determine why those errors occurred	**Valid**	**Not valid**

(2 marks)

127 Which of the following is NOT a limitation of using audit software at Delphic Co?

- o There may be substantial setup costs to use the software, especially where the computer systems of the client have not been fully documented
- o The computer audit department at Delphic Co cannot confirm that all system documentation is available, especially for the older systems currently in use
- o There are over 600 customers on the system making the use of audit software inappropriate at Delphic Co
- o The auditor will be provided with copy files and not be allowed any direct access to Delphic Co's computer system **(2 marks)**

128 Assuming that audit software can be developed for use on Delphic Co's systems, which of the following procedures could be carried out on the receivables balance?

1 Cast the receivables ledger to ensure it is arithmetically correct

2 Compare the balance on each receivable account with its credit limit to ensure this has not been exceeded

3 Stratify the receivables balances and select an appropriate sample for testing

4 Produce an aged receivables analysis to assist with the identification of irrecoverable receivables

- o 1 and 2 only
- o 1, 3 and 4 only
- o 2, 3 and 4 only
- o 1, 2, 3 and 4 **(2 marks)**

129 Which THREE of the following statements are TRUE in relation to audit software?

- o As the systems are old the audit software may slow Delphic Co's system down
- o The audit software will test the programmed controls of Delphic Co
- o The use of audit software may save time resulting in greater efficiency
- o Audit staff may need to be trained to use the audit software
- o The audit will be more expensive each year audit software is used **(2 marks)**

130 Delphic Co has informed you that they plan to implement a new computerised accounting system within the next year.

Which of the following would represent an appropriate audit response in respect of the new computerised accounting system?

1 The audit firm should delay the use of audit software to ensure it is designed to effectively work with the new system

2 The audit engagement partner should provide advice to Delphic Co on which system to implement

3 The external audit team must be present during the installation and testing of the new system

- o 2 and 3 only
- o 1 and 3 only
- o 1 only
- o 1, 2, and 3 **(2 marks)**

The following scenario relates to questions 131 – 135

It is 1 July 20X5. You are an audit manager who specialises in the audit of not-for-profit (NFP) organisations. You are currently assigned to two clients, Hightown and Stargazer which both have a year ended 31 March 20X5. Both audit teams include audit juniors who have only been involved with audits of companies and have not audited NFP organisations before. As the manager, you will be responsible for explaining the differences between the audits of NFPs and companies. The following information is to be communicated to the audit teams of each client.

Hightown

Hightown is a local government authority which receives an allocation of tax payer money from central government. Hightown has been notified by central government of a significant cut in its funding for the following financial year.

Stargazer

Stargazer is a local charity which operates several charity shops. People make donations of goods which the shop sells to customers. All sales are paid for in cash as transaction amounts are usually small and credit card charges incur too great a cost.

Stargazer employs one administrative assistant. All other staff and trustees are volunteers who commit between 1 and 5 hours per week to the charity. The administrative assistant is responsible for paying the bills, including their own wages, and recording the transactions in a spreadsheet. The administrative assistant is also responsible for preparing the financial statements and charity's tax return. Tax rules for charities are different to those for companies and individuals. Once prepared, they are sent to the trustees for approval. None of the trustees have any specific financial expertise.

131 Which TWO of the following statements is TRUE in relation to the audit of Hightown?

- o As Hightown is a local government authority the risk of manipulation of the financial statements is lower
- o Hightown requires an audit as it is funded by taxpayers
- o The auditor's report of Hightown will not be publicly available once issued
- o The audit of Hightown will take longer than the audit of a company
- o The audit team should include staff with experience of public sector audits **(2 marks)**

132 Which of the following statements is FALSE in respect of the notification regarding the cut in funding for Hightown?

- o Audit risk will increase due to the threat to the going concern status of the organisation
- o The auditor will need to review plans and forecasts to assess how the organisation will ensure it has sufficient funds to continue
- o The auditor's report for Hightown will not need to refer to going concern uncertainties as it is a local government authority
- o The auditor should review any plans Hightown has to reduce costs in the future to assess whether this could realistically be achieved and therefore indicate the organisation has sufficient funds to pay its liabilities when they fall due **(2 marks)**

133 Completeness of income has been identified as a significant audit risk for the audit of Stargazers. Select THREE procedures which will help identify if income is understated.

Compare income by shop and category to the prior year	
Inspect credit notes issued post year end	
Agree totals on till receipts to the detailed sales listing, bank statements and bank ledger account	
Obtain the detailed sales listing and cast to confirm accuracy	

(2 marks)

134 Which of the following risks require specific consideration for the audit of Stargazers?

1 Less segregation of duties

2 Uncertainty over future funding

3 Complexity of taxation rules

4 Competence of volunteer staff

- o 1 and 4 only
- o 1, 3 and 4 only
- o 1, 2 and 3 only
- o 1, 2, 3 and 4

(2 marks)

135 Select whether the following statements are ALWAYS true, NEVER true or MAY be true in respect of the audit of a charity such as Stargazers.

Management will have no financial qualifications therefore there is a greater risk of material misstatement	**Always true**	**May be true**	**Never true**
Internal control systems will not be as sophisticated as those for profit-making companies	**Always true**	**May be true**	**Never true**
There are fewer auditing standards applicable to audits of charities	**Always true**	**May be true**	**Never true**
Charities such as Stargazers will have different objectives to a profit-making company therefore the auditors' assessment of materiality will consider different factors	**Always true**	**May be true**	**Never true**

(2 marks)

The following scenario relates to questions 136 – 140

It is 1 July 20X5. You are an audit senior in Cork & Co and are currently performing the final audit of Bamboo Co for the year ended 31 May 20X5. The company is a manufacturer of environmentally-friendly packaging. You have performed the audit of equity (share capital and reserves). No misstatements have been identified during audit testing.

An extract from the draft financial statements is given below.

	Notes	**20X5**	**20X4**
		$m	$m
Ordinary share capital	1	100	50
Retained earnings		123	110
Revaluation surplus	2	100	90
		323	250

Notes:

1 A one for two bonus issue took place on 1 October 20X4. A one for three rights issue took place on 1 January 20X5.

2 Bamboo Co adopts a policy of revaluation of its properties. A revaluation of all of Bamboo Co's properties was performed by an independent expert on 20 May 20X5 resulting in a surplus of $10 million.

136 Which of the following provides the MOST reliable evidence in respect of the bonus issue of ordinary share capital?

- o Bank statements
- o Share register
- o Companies House information (or equivalent)
- o Notes of discussion with the finance director and chief executive **(2 marks)**

137 A dividend of $4 million was approved and paid in September 20X4 in respect of the year ended 31 May 20X4. A dividend of $6 million has been proposed in respect of the year ended 31 May 20X5. The proposed dividend is expected to be approved by shareholders in August 20X5. How should each of the dividends be reflected in the financial statements dated 31 May 20X5?

$4 million	Recognise in retained earnings	Disclose in the notes
$6 million	Recognise in retained earnings	Disclose in the notes

(2 marks)

138 In respect of the revaluation of property, select the assertion tested by the following procedures.

Inspect the independent expert's report	**Completeness**	**Cut-off**	**Valuation**
Match the physical properties to the independent expert's report and non-current asset register	**Existence**	**Completeness**	**Presentation**
Recalculate the depreciation on revalued properties	**Completeness**	**Existence**	**Valuation**

(2 marks)

139 Which TWO of the following statements are TRUE in relation to equity?

- o Equity is material by nature
- o The auditor must check that total equity is the same as total assets on the statement of financial position
- o The auditor will rely mainly on substantive analytical procedures when auditing equity
- o Movements in equity must be shown in the statement of changes in equity **(2 marks)**

140 Having completed the audit of equity, you are now auditing directors' emoluments.

Which of the following procedures should be performed to test COMPLETENESS of directors' emoluments?

1 Obtain a breakdown of payments made to each director, recalculate the total and agree to the financial statements

2 Trace amounts included on the breakdown of directors' emoluments to the bank statements and bank ledger account

3 Review board minutes for details of bonuses or additional payments to be made to directors

4 Inspect directors' service contracts for salaries and trace through to payroll reports for the year

- o 1, 2, 3 and 4
- o 1 and 4 only
- o 1, 2 and 3 only
- o 1, 3 and 4 only **(2 marks)**

REVIEW AND REPORTING

The following scenario relates to questions 141 – 145

It is 1 July 20X5. Viola Co is a manufacturer of shoes. You are an audit manager in Cello & Co and you are performing an overall review of the financial statements for the year ended 31 March 20X5 prior to the issue of the auditor's report. Profit before tax for the year was $131.4m (20X4: $120.9m).

Analytical procedures

As part of your overall review, you have performed analytical procedures over the draft financial statements and have noted that the trade receivables collection period is lower than it was during the interim audit performed in January 20X5. The credit controller of Viola Co left the company in February 20X5 and the directors have said that, as a result, the company is experiencing difficulties in debt collection.

Disclosures

During the year, Viola Co revalued its head office and as part of your review, you are considering the detail which is disclosed in the property, plant and equipment note in the draft financial statements.

Uncorrected misstatements

Your review also includes an assessment of uncorrected misstatements. These have been recorded by the audit team as follows:

		$000
1	Interest payable omitted in error	1,942
2	Additional allowance for receivables required	9,198
3	Error in sales invoice processing resulting in understatement of sales	8,541
4	Write off in respect of faulty goods	2,900

Faulty goods

The adjustment for faulty goods listed as an uncorrected misstatement above relates to an entire batch of shoes, which was produced on 12 March 20X5. The audit work concluded that the cost of this inventory exceeded its net realisable value by $2.9m. The directors dispute the audit team's figures and believe that the realisable value of the inventory still exceeds its cost.

141 Which of the following would form part of the auditor's overall review of the financial statements?

1 Establishing whether the preconditions for an audit are present

2 Assessing whether the information and explanations obtained during the audit are adequately reflected

3 Performing a detailed review of the audit working papers to ensure the work has been properly performed

4 Reviewing the adequacy of the disclosure of accounting policies

- o 1 and 2
- o 3 and 4
- o 1 and 3
- o 2 and 4 **(2 marks)**

142 Which of the following is a valid explanation for the INCONSISTENCY between the results of the analytical procedures on trade receivables and the directors' statement regarding debt collection problems?

- o A change in sales mix towards high value products
- o An increase in the proportion of cash sales since February 20X5
- o An increase in the rate of sales tax in March 20X5
- o Sales growth of 1% per month over the year **(2 marks)**

143 Which of the following details should be disclosed in respect of the revaluation of the head office if the auditor is to conclude that the disclosures are adequate?

1 Effective date of the revaluation

2 Name of the valuer

3 The amount of the revaluation increase

4 Carrying amount of the head office under the cost model

- o 1, 2 and 3 only
- o 1, 3 and 4 only
- o 2, 3 and 4 only
- o 1, 2, 3 and 4 **(2 marks)**

144 Which of the uncorrected misstatements numbered (1), (2) and (3) by the audit team MUST be adjusted for if the auditor is to issue an unmodified audit opinion?

- o Misstatements 2 and 3 only
- o Misstatements 1 and 3 only
- o Misstatements 1, 2 and 3
- o Misstatement 2 only **(2 marks)**

145 All adjustments required by the auditors have been made to the financial statements with the exception of adjustment (4) relating to the faulty goods.

Which of the following correctly describes the effect of this matter on the auditor's report?

- o Unmodified opinion with no further disclosure
- o Unmodified opinion with disclosure in an emphasis of matter paragraph
- o Qualified opinion due to material misstatement
- o Qualified opinion due to inability to obtain sufficient appropriate audit evidence

(2 marks)

The following scenario relates to questions 146 – 150

It is 1 July 20X5. You are an audit manager in Spring & Co responsible for the audit of Autumn Co. You are reviewing the audit file of Autumn Co for the year ended 31 March 20X5 which is nearing completion. You have noted several issues during your review:

- Several working papers which were prepared by the audit junior have not been signed as reviewed by the audit senior responsible for supervising the audit junior. You are aware that a review has been performed but this is not documented on the audit file.
- One audit working paper states that a sample of 30 purchase invoices should be tested but the results of the test show that only 15 invoices were tested. Several other areas document that samples sizes were reduced in order to save time.
- In the subsequent events review section of the file, the audit senior has documented that management have confirmed there are no subsequent events that affect the financial statements and that no further work is considered necessary as a result.

---

146 Which of the following statements are true in respect of the reduction in samples sizes?

1 The audit plan has not been followed

2 Sufficient appropriate evidence may not have been obtained

3 Material misstatements may go undetected

4 Those sections will need to be reviewed by a manager and the manager will form a conclusion on the balances

- o 1, 2 and 3 only
- o 2 and 4 only
- o 1, 3 and 4 only
- o 1, 2, 3 and 4

(2 marks)

147 Select whether the following statements are true or false in respect of the subsequent events review of Autumn Co.

Enquiry does not provide sufficient appropriate evidence on its own	**True**	**False**
The auditor has demonstrated a lack of professional scepticism	**True**	**False**
A written representation should have been obtained from management confirming that they have disclosed all subsequent events to the auditor	**True**	**False**
The auditor only needs to perform procedures if they are made aware of any subsequent events	**True**	**False**

(2 marks)

148 As a result of the quality issues encountered during the audit of Autumn Co, which of the following actions should now be taken?

1 The offending members of staff have demonstrated a lack of competence and due care therefore the firm should report them to the ACCA to be disciplined for failing to comply with ethical requirements

2 More frequent quality reviews may need to take place

3 Further training should be provided to staff

4 The firm's policies and procedures should be reviewed and updated if applicable

- 2 and 4 only
- 1 and 3 only
- 2, 3 and 4 only
- 1, 2, 3 and 4 **(2 marks)**

149 Engagement quality reviews are part of the audit firm's quality management system to ensure the audit is performed to a high standard. Which of the following statements is FALSE in respect of engagement quality reviews?

- An engagement quality review should be documented in the audit file
- An engagement quality review involves a discussion of the significant judgements arising during the audit
- An engagement quality review can be performed after the auditor's report has been signed
- Frequent communication between the engagement quality reviewer and audit team enhances the effectiveness of an engagement quality review **(2 marks)**

150 Select whether the following statements are true or false in respect of review of audit working papers.

The audit engagement partner will review all working papers on the audit file before issuing an opinion	**True**	**False**
If working papers have been reviewed there is no quality issue arising from the lack of documentation	**True**	**False**
All working papers should be signed by the person who prepared them	**True**	**False**
All team members' work should be reviewed by someone more senior than the preparer	**True**	**False**

(2 marks)

The following scenario relates to questions 151 – 155

It is 1 July 20X5. You are an audit manager in Elm & Co and you are finalising the audit of the financial statements of Oak Co for the year ended 31 March 20X5. The financial statements for the year ended 31 March 20X5 have been prepared on a going concern basis. The initial going concern assessment conducted by the management of Oak Co covers the six-month period to 30 September 20X5. You are reviewing the results of the final analytical procedures and other outstanding points on the audit file. The auditor's report is due to be signed in the next two weeks.

Results of analytical procedures

The following ratio analysis has been completed as part of the final analytical procedures:

	20X5 Final	**20X5 Planning**	**20X4 Final**
Gross profit margin	9%	11%	12%
Quick ratio	0.2	0.6	0.8
Payables payment period	45	40	37
Inventory holding period	50	40	42

Matters arising from discussion with the finance director

Discussions with the finance director have also revealed the following:

1 Oak Co lost a major customer, Beech Co, in March 20X5, but new business has been won post year end which has mitigated the impact of the loss of Beech Co.

2 Oak Co is due to repay a substantial loan on 30 September 20X5. Oak Co is currently negotiating revised terms with the bank but it is unlikely that negotiations will be concluded before the auditor's report is signed. This will be disclosed in the financial statements.

3 A number of personnel in the purchasing department left during the year and have not been replaced.

4 A major supplier to Oak Co has just gone out of business with a number of unfulfilled orders.

5 A new product which was due to account for 30% of revenue in 20X5 has not been successful.

6 A litigation claim was filed against Oak Co in April 20X5 with potential damages totalling 3% of this year's profit.

151 Which THREE of the issues identified could result in significant uncertainty over the going concern status of Oak Co?

- o 1
- o 2
- o 3
- o 4
- o 5
- o 6

(2 marks)

152 Select whether the following comments are consistent or inconsistent with the results of the final analytical procedures.

The company has increased the sales prices charged to customers while maintaining costs at a level comparable to 20X4	**Consistent**	**Inconsistent**
The company has become more reliant on its overdraft facility during the year	**Consistent**	**Inconsistent**
Due to cash restrictions, the company has encountered delays in paying suppliers	**Consistent**	**Inconsistent**
At the year-end inventory count, a lower level of slow-moving inventory was noted compared to prior year	**Consistent**	**Inconsistent**

(2 marks)

153 Which of the following procedures would provide the MOST reliable evidence in relation to the new business won post year end?

- o Review post-year-end sales orders from the new customer
- o Inspect email correspondence between the sales director of Oak Co and the new customer
- o Obtain a written representation confirming the level of business agreed with the new customer
- o Review board minutes discussing the contract with the new customer **(2 marks)**

154 Which of the following is an appropriate course of action for the auditor to take in respect of management's going concern assessment?

- o Request management extend the assessment to the date of the auditor's report
- o Design and carry out procedures to only assess going concern in the period from 31 March 20X5 to the date of the auditor's report
- o Request management extend the assessment to cover at least until 31 March 20X6
- o Accept the timeframe used by management as the going concern review is their responsibility **(2 marks)**

155 The audit engagement partner has concluded that the disclosure included in the financial statements in relation to the loan negotiations is adequate and commented that this disclosure is fundamental to the users' understanding of the financial statements.

Which of the following correctly identifies the implications for the auditor's opinion and report of Oak Co?

	Opinion	**Report**
o	Unmodified	No additional communication required
o	Unmodified	Material Uncertainty Related to Going Concern section
o	Modified	Emphasis of Matter paragraph
o	Modified	Key audit matters

(2 marks)

The following scenario relates to questions 156 – 160

It is 1 July 20X5. You are an audit manager in Blenkin & Co responsible for the audit of Sampson Co, a large listed retailer. The audit for the year ended 31 March 20X5 is nearing completion and the auditor's report is due to be signed next week.

You have been informed that the financial controller left Sampson Co on 28 February 20X5. As part of the subsequent events audit procedures, you reviewed post-year-end board meeting minutes and discovered that a legal case for unfair dismissal has been brought against Sampson Co by the financial controller. During a discussion with the Human Resources (HR) director of Sampson Co, you established that the company received notice of the proposed legal claim on 10 April 20X5.

The HR director told you that Sampson Co's lawyers believe the financial controller's claim is likely to be successful, but estimate that $150,000 is the maximum amount of compensation which would be paid. However, the directors do not intend to make any adjustment for a provision or to include any disclosures in the financial statements relating to the issue.

The draft financial statements currently show a profit before tax of $6.5 million and revenue of $66 million for the financial year ended 31 March 20X5.

---

156 Subsequent events procedures should be performed between the date of the financial statements and which date?

o The date the audit work for subsequent events is performed

o The date of approval of the financial statements

o The date of the auditor's report

o The date the financial statements are issued **(2 marks)**

157 Which of the following audit procedures should be performed to form a conclusion as to whether the financial statements require amendment in relation to the unfair dismissal claim?

1 Inspect relevant correspondence with Sampson Co's lawyers

2 Write to the financial controller to confirm the claim and level of damages

3 Review the post-year-end bank ledger account and bank statements for evidence the claim has been settled

4 Request management confirms their views in a written representation letter

- o 1, 2 and 3
- o 1, 2 and 4
- o 1, 3 and 4
- o 2, 3 and 4 **(2 marks)**

158 Select the type of opinion that is appropriate and the nature of any additional communications necessary if the unfair dismissal case is NOT adjusted for or disclosed within the financial statements.

Opinion
Unmodified
Qualified
Adverse
Disclaimer

Additional communications
No additional communication
Emphasis of Matter paragraph
Material Uncertainty Related to Going Concern section
Other matter paragraph

(2 marks)

159 You are drafting the auditor's report for Sampson Co and the audit engagement partner has reminded you that as Sampson Co is a listed company, the report will need to include a Key Audit Matters section.

According to ISA 701 *Communicating Key Audit Matters in the Independent Auditor's Report*, which of the following should be included in the Key Audit Matters section of the auditor's report?

- o Matters which required significant auditor attention
- o Matters which result in a modification to the audit opinion
- o All matters which were communicated to those charged with governance
- o All matters which were material to the financial statements **(2 marks)**

160 One month after the financial statements were issued the legal claim was finalised with the court awarding compensation of $500,000 to the ex-financial controller. The directors of Sampson Co have contacted Blenkin & Co to inform them of the outcome.

Which TWO of the following are appropriate actions for Blenkin & Co to take?

- o Discuss the matter with management and, where appropriate, those charged with governance
- o Obtain a written representation from management
- o Consider whether the firm should resign from the engagement
- o Enquire how management intends to address the matter in the financial statements where appropriate **(2 marks)**

The following scenario relates to questions 161 – 165

It is 1 July 20X5. You are an audit manager in Colorado & Co. You are responsible for the audit of Mississippi Co for the year ended 31 March 20X5. The audit is nearing completion and the auditor's report is due to be signed next week.

The draft financial statements recognise revenue of $18 million (20X4 – $17 million). The draft annual report of Mississippi Co contains a Chair's statement in which the chair has commented that revenue has increased by 20% this year. The report also includes an operating review, corporate social responsibility report, financial statements and notes to the financial statements.

The directors of Mississippi Co have indicated that they intend to distribute the annual report to prospective investors in order to obtain additional finance. The audit engagement partner has informed the directors that the auditor's report is only intended for reliance by the existing shareholders and that no liability will be assumed to any other party. The audit engagement partner has asked you to draft the auditor's report for Mississippi Co and requested that a paragraph referring to this restriction of liability is included.

---

161 Which of the following statements best describes the auditor's responsibilities in respect of other information?

- o The auditor provides limited assurance over the completeness and accuracy of the other information
- o The auditor must read the other information to ensure it is consistent with the financial statements and their knowledge of the entity obtained during the audit
- o The auditor must audit the other information and obtain sufficient appropriate evidence that the other information is true and fair
- o Other information only needs to be considered if it is made available at the start of the audit with the draft financial statements **(2 marks)**

162 Which of the following sections of Mississippi Co's annual report would NOT be considered 'Other Information'?

- o Chair's statement
- o Operating review
- o Corporate social responsibility report
- o Notes to the financial statements **(2 marks)**

163 How should the inconsistency between the Chair's statement and financial statements be referred to in the auditor's report of Mississippi Co?

- o Within the Other Information section
- o Within an Emphasis of Matter paragraph
- o Within an Other Matter paragraph
- o Within the Auditor's Opinion section **(2 marks)**

164 Select whether the following statements are true or false in relation to referring to the Chair's statement in the auditor's report of Mississippi Co.

Users may be misled if the other information contains incorrect information or information which contradicts the financial statements such as that in the Chair's statement	**True**	**False**
Users may believe the auditor has not audited the financial statements properly if the inconsistency is not highlighted	**True**	**False**
The auditor must expose management's incompetence	**True**	**False**
The inconsistency may undermine the credibility of your auditor's report if not highlighted	**True**	**False**

(2 marks)

165 In respect of the partner's request for restricting liability, how should this be addressed in the auditor's report?

- o Within the Auditor's Responsibility section
- o By including an Emphasis of Matter paragraph
- o By including an Other Matter paragraph
- o Within the Basis for Opinion section **(2 marks)**

The following scenario relates to questions 166 – 170

It is 1 July 20X5. You are an audit manager in Atlantic & Co responsible for the audit of Pacific Co. The audit of the financial statements for the year ended 31 March 20X5 is nearing completion and the auditor's report is due to be signed next week.

Included within receivables in the statement of financial position is a balance of $85,000 owed by Arctic Co, a key customer of Pacific Co. Arctic Co has just notified Pacific Co that it is unlikely to be able to pay the balance due to cash flow problems. The customer has asked for an extension of credit for a further three months as it expects its cash flow situation to improve in July and August. Pacific Co has agreed to this extension.

Due to the uncertainty over the recoverability of the debt, you believe that an allowance for receivables should have been made and you have discussed the issue with the finance director who has informed you that an adjustment for the balance will be made in the following year's financial statements if the debt is not paid during the extended credit period agreed with Arctic Co.

Revenue for the year is $2.6 million, profit before tax is $1.4 million and total assets are $7.5 million.

166 Which of the following statements is correct regarding the materiality of the irrecoverable debt?

- o The matter is material by nature
- o The matter is not material as the debt is less than 5% of revenue
- o The matter is not material as the debt is less than 10% of profit
- o The matter is likely to be material as it is over 1% of assets **(2 marks)**

167 Which THREE of the following procedures would allow the auditor to form a conclusion as to the level of adjustment required to the receivables balance?

- o Review correspondence with the customer indicating when payment will be made
- o Discuss with management why they feel an adjustment is not required in the current year
- o Perform a direct confirmation of the balance outstanding at the year end
- o Review post-year-end bank statements to identify if any payment has been received from the customer
- o Inspect the sales invoice and GDN relating to the receivable balance **(2 marks)**

168 Assuming the matter is considered material and Pacific's directors have refused to adjust the financial statements, what is the appropriate opinion to be issued?

- o Unmodified
- o Qualified
- o Adverse
- o Disclaimer **(2 marks)**

169 Select whether the following elements should be included in the auditor's report of Pacific Co.

Addressee	**Included**	**Not included**
Other Matter paragraph	**Included**	**Not included**
Other Information	**Included**	**Not included**
Emphasis of Matter paragraph	**Included**	**Not included**

(2 marks)

170 Which TWO of the following are reasons why the auditor would need to modify the auditor's opinion?

- o They conclude that there is a material inconsistency between the audited financial statements and the other information contained in the annual report
- o They wish to draw attention to a matter that is fundamental to the users' understanding of the financial statements
- o They conclude that the financial statements as a whole are not free from material misstatement
- o They have been unable to obtain sufficient appropriate evidence to conclude that the financial statements as a whole are free from material misstatement
- o They wish to restrict reliance on the auditor's report by third parties **(2 marks)**

The following scenario relates to questions 171 – 175

It is 1 July 20X5. You are an audit manager in Yellow Submarine & Co responsible for the audit of Magical Mystery Tour (MMT). The audit is nearing completion and the auditor's report is due to be signed next week.

MMT is a travel agency which has been trading for over five years. The company arranges holidays and hotel bookings in remote locations to individual customers and corporate clients. The company is financed partly through overdrafts and loans and also by several large shareholders. The overdraft facility is due for renewal later in July 20X5.

In January 20X5, a new competitor, Pure Shores Co, entered the market. Through competitive pricing, Pure Shores Co has gained considerable market share from MMT, including one of MMT's larger corporate clients which has moved its business to Pure Shores. In addition, a number of MMT's travel agents have left the company and joined Pure Shores. MMT has found it difficult to replace these employees due to the level of skills and knowledge of remote overseas locations required.

The directors have produced a cash flow forecast which shows a significantly worsening position over the coming 12 months. You have been informed that MMT's bankers will not make a decision on the renewal of the overdraft facility until after the auditor's report is issued. The directors have agreed to include brief disclosure of the uncertainty over going concern.

---

171 Which THREE of the following statements correctly describes the respective responsibilities of directors and auditors in relation to going concern?

- o The directors must assess whether the company can continue to trade for the foreseeable future
- o The auditors and the directors must make disclosure of going concern uncertainties in the financial statements
- o The auditor will evaluate management's assessment of going concern
- o The directors will usually prepare a cash flow forecast to assess whether the company is likely to be able to trade for the foreseeable future
- o The directors must assess a period of at least twelve months from the date the financial statements are issued **(2 marks)**

172 Which THREE of the following procedures should be performed to assess the uncertainty arising in relation to the overdraft renewal?

- o Calculate key ratios to identify possible financial problems
- o Inspect correspondence with the bank to identify any disputes which may indicate the overdraft facility will not be renewed
- o Review the level of profit made in previous periods to assess whether the company is likely to continue to trade
- o Enquire with management whether any alternative sources of finance have been considered if the bank does not renew the overdraft facility
- o Inspect board minutes for discussions of management as to how they plan to improve the financial position of MMT **(2 marks)**

173 What will be the impact on the auditor's report of MMT in the following circumstances?

Adequate disclosure of going concern uncertainties is made	**Unmodified opinion with no additional communication**	**Modified opinion**	**Unmodified opinion with Going Concern section**	**Unmodified opinion with Emphasis of Matter**
Adequate disclosure of going concern uncertainties is not made	**Unmodified opinion with no additional communication**	**Modified opinion**	**Unmodified opinion with Going Concern section**	**Unmodified opinion with Emphasis of Matter**

(2 marks)

174 In which of the following situations should a company NOT prepare financial statements using the break up basis?

- o The company has ceased to trade
- o A decision has been made to close the company
- o There are material uncertainties relating to going concern
- o The company has run out of cash and is unable to pay its debts **(2 marks)**

175 What will be the impact on the auditor's report of MMT if the auditor believes the basis of preparation of the financial statements is incorrect?

- o Unmodified opinion with no additional communication
- o Unmodified opinion with an Emphasis of Matter paragraph
- o Qualified opinion with Basis for Qualified Opinion
- o Adverse opinion with Basis for Adverse Opinion **(2 marks)**

The following scenario relates to questions 176 – 180

It is 1 July 20X5. You are an audit manager in Bond & Co responsible for the audit of Paddington Co for the year ended 31 March 20X5, which is nearing completion. You are now resolving the last few issues before deciding on the appropriate audit opinion.

During the audit the following issues have been identified:

1 Paddington Co's main competitor filed a lawsuit for $3 million alleging a breach of copyright. This case is ongoing and will not be resolved prior to the auditor's report being signed. Paddington Co's lawyers believe the claim is only possible to succeed. Paddington Co has sufficient cash to make the settlement if it loses the case. The lawsuit has not been mentioned in the financial statements or related disclosures.

2 A warranty provision of $25 million has not been recognised in respect of goods which require repair or replacement within the first twelve months if they do not perform as expected.

3 Depreciation in respect of property, plant and equipment has not been recognised in the financial statements. The auditor has estimated that a depreciation charge of $1 million should be recognised.

4 Intangible assets have been overstated by $12 million due to research costs being capitalised as development costs in the statement of financial position.

Paddington Co's profit before tax is $29 million.

---

176 Which of the issues identified during the audit is likely to lead to an adverse opinion on Paddington Co's financial statements?

- o Lawsuit
- o Warranty provision
- o Depreciation
- o Intangible assets **(2 marks)**

177 Which of the following statements is TRUE in respect of the lawsuit and its impact on the financial statements and auditor's report thereon?

- o A provision should be recognised in the financial statements of $3 million
- o A contingent liability should be disclosed in the notes to the financial statements
- o The matter is not material as it represents 10.3 % of profit before tax
- o The lawsuit does not need to be referred to in the financial statements as the case is not settled at the year-end date **(2 marks)**

178 The audit is now complete and the auditor's report is due to be issued next week. All adjustments requested have been corrected by management.

Which of the following correctly identifies the implications for the audit opinion and report of Paddington Co?

- o Unmodified opinion with no additional communication
- o Unmodified opinion with an Emphasis of Matter paragraph
- o Qualified opinion with Basis for Qualified Opinion
- o Disclaimer of opinion with Basis for Disclaimer of Opinion **(2 marks)**

179 Match the following auditor's report sections to the appropriate explanation of its purpose.

Element		**Purpose**	
1	Title	A	Provides a description of the professional standards applied during the audit to provide confidence to users that the report can be relied upon
2	Addressee	B	Identifies the intended user of the report
3	Basis for opinion	C	Identifies the person responsible for the audit opinion in case of any queries
4	Key audit matters	D	Clearly identifies the report as an Independent Auditor's Report
5	Name of engagement partner	E	Draws attention to any other significant matters of which the users should be aware which have been discussed with those charged with governance

(2 marks)

180 Which of the following correctly matches the opinion type with the wording for that opinion?

	Opinion	**Wording**
o	Unmodified	Except for
o	Disclaimer	Do not express an opinion
o	Adverse	True and fair view
o	Qualified	Do not give a true and fair view

(2 marks)

The following scenario relates to questions 181 – 185

It is 1 July 20X5. You are an audit manager in Grace & Co responsible for the audit of Humphries Co, a chain of food wholesalers. The audit of the financial statements for the year ended 31 March 20X5 is nearing completion and the auditor's report is due to be signed next week.

Revenue for the year is $78 million and profit before taxation is $7.5 million. The following events have occurred subsequent to the year end.

Receivable

Humphries Co has just become aware that one of its customers is experiencing significant going concern difficulties. There is a receivables balance in respect of this customer at the year end of $0.3 million. Humphries Co believe that as the company has been trading for many years, they will receive some, if not full, payment from the customer therefore no adjustment has been made for the balance in the financial statements.

Lawsuit

A key supplier of Humphries Co is suing them for breach of contract. The lawsuit was filed prior to the year end, and the sum claimed by them is $1 million. This has been disclosed as a contingent liability in the notes to the financial statements. Recent correspondence from the supplier indicates that they are willing to settle the case for $0.6 million. It is likely that Humphries Co will agree to this.

Warehouse

Following significant rain on 20 May 20X5, one of Humphries Co's three warehouses was flooded. All of the inventory stored there was damaged and has been disposed of. The insurance company has already been contacted but no response has been received as of yet. No amendments or disclosures have been made in the financial statements.

181 Calculate the materiality level of the receivable and settlement figure for the lawsuit by reference to profit before tax and state whether they are material. Answers to calculations should be rounded to the nearest whole number with no decimal places.

	Calculation		
Receivable		**Material**	**Not material**
Lawsuit		**Material**	**Not material**

(2 marks)

182 In respect of the receivable and lawsuit, select the type of event and the appropriate accounting treatment.

	Type of event		**Accounting treatment**	
Receivable	**Adjusting**	**Non-adjusting**	**Recognise**	**Disclose**
Lawsuit	**Adjusting**	**Non-adjusting**	**Recognise**	**Disclose**

(2 marks)

183 Which of the following is NOT an appropriate procedure to reach a conclusion on the outstanding receivable?

- o Contact the customer directly and enquire when they are likely to pay the outstanding balance
- o Review correspondence between the customer and Humphries Co to assess whether there is any likelihood of payment
- o Review the post-year-end period to see if any payments have been received from the customer
- o Discuss the outstanding debt with the credit control manager **(2 marks)**

184 Assuming that the receivable and warehouse issues are resolved but the lawsuit issue remains unresolved, which THREE of the following section titles MUST be included in the auditor's report?

Auditor Responsibilities for the Audit of the Financial Statements	**Included**	**Not included**
Basis for Opinion	**Included**	**Not included**
Basis for Qualified Opinion	**Included**	**Not included**
Key Audit Matters	**Included**	**Not included**
Opinion	**Included**	**Not included**
Qualified Opinion	**Included**	**Not included**

(2 marks)

185 Which of the following statements is TRUE in respect of the warehouse?

- o The value of the assets damaged during the flood should be written down to their realisable values
- o If the impact of the flood is material, the directors should include a disclosure note detailing the impact to the company
- o The insurance claim should be recognised as a contingent asset
- o As the flood occurred after the year end it will have no impact on the auditor's report **(2 marks)**

The following scenario relates to questions 186 – 190

It is 1 July 20X5. You are the manager responsible for the audit of Greenfields Co and you are performing the final review of the audit for the year ended 31 March 20X5. Greenfields Co specialises in manufacturing equipment which can help to reduce toxic emissions in the production of chemicals. The company has grown rapidly over the past eight years and this is due partly to the warranties that the company gives to its customers. It guarantees its products for five years and if problems arise in this period it undertakes to fix them, or provide a replacement product. The following issues have been left for your attention.

Receivable balance owing from Yellowmix Co

Greenfields Co has a material receivable balance owing from its customer, Yellowmix Co. During the year-end audit, your team reviewed the ageing of this balance and found that no payments had been received from Yellowmix Co for over six months, and Greenfields Co would not allow this balance to be circularised. Instead management has assured your team that they will provide a written representation confirming that the balance is recoverable.

Warranty provision

The warranty provision included within the statement of financial position is material. The audit team has performed testing over the calculations and assumptions which are consistent with prior years. The team has requested a written representation from management confirming the basis and amount of the provision are reasonable. Management has yet to provide this representation.

186 Select the appropriate words/phrases from the options to complete the sentences below. Options may be selected more than once.

A written representation ____________________ in respect of the receivable balance. This is because ____________________.

A written representation ____________________ in respect of the warranty provision. This is because ____________________.

- o Is appropriate
- o Is not appropriate
- o The matter is not material
- o The matter involves management judgement
- o Other procedures can be performed which provide more reliable evidence
- o An ISA specifically requires a written representation to be obtained for the item

(2 marks)

187 Assuming that the directors of Greenfields Co refuse to provide a written representation to the auditor, which of the following statements is TRUE?

- o The refusal to provide a written representation will only be a matter of concern if it relates to a material area of the financial statements
- o The refusal to provide a written representation may cast doubt over management integrity and as such the reliability of other evidence provided by the client may be called into question
- o The refusal to provide a written representation will result in the need for the auditor to report the directors to the industry regulator
- o The auditor will need to notify the shareholders of the issue in person

(2 marks)

188 Which TWO of the following audit reporting implications could result if Greenfields Co refuse to provide a written representation letter?

- o Unmodified opinion
- o Unmodified opinion with Emphasis of Matter paragraph
- o Qualified opinion due to material misstatement
- o Qualified opinion due to an inability to obtain sufficient appropriate evidence
- o Adverse opinion as the financial statements do not show a true and fair view
- o Disclaimer of opinion as the auditor does not have sufficient appropriate evidence to be able to express an audit opinion **(2 marks)**

189 Written representations are required by International Standards on Auditing in respect of subject-specific areas. Which of the following does NOT require a subject-specific written representation to be obtained?

- o Fraud and error
- o Laws and regulations
- o Analytical procedures
- o Subsequent events **(2 marks)**

190 Which TWO of the following MUST be included in every written representation according to ISA 580 *Written Representations*?

Plans or intentions of management that affect carrying values of assets	**Required**	**Not required**
Confirmation from management that they have provided the auditor with all information and access to records during the audit	**Required**	**Not required**
Confirmation from management that the financial statements are accurate/free from error	**Required**	**Not required**
Confirmation from management that all transactions have been reflected in the financial statements	**Required**	**Not required**

(2 marks)

The following scenario relates to questions 191 – 195

It is 1 July 20X5. You are an audit manager in Daffy & Co responsible for the audit of Minnie Co. The audit work for the year ended 31 March 20X5 is nearly complete and you are resolving the last few issues before deciding on the appropriate wording for the auditor's report and opinion. Profit before tax is $10 million.

The following matters have been left for your attention.

Property, plant and equipment

During the year, the property balance was revalued by an independent expert valuer at the request of Minnie Co's management.

Depreciation has been calculated on the total of land and buildings. In previous years it has only been charged on buildings. Total depreciation is $2.5 million and the element charged to land only is $0.4 million.

Computerised wages program

Minnie Co's computerised wages program is backed up daily, however for a period of two months the wages records and the back-ups have been corrupted, and therefore cannot be accessed. Wages and salaries for these two months are $1.1 million.

Lawsuit

Minnie Co's main competitor has filed a lawsuit for $5 million against them alleging a breach of copyright; this case is ongoing and will not be resolved prior to the auditor's report being signed. The matter is correctly disclosed as a contingent liability in the financial statements.

Draft extracts for the auditor's report

Extracts for the auditor's report have already been drafted as follows:

1 We conducted our audit in accordance with International Standards on Auditing applicable to this audit.

2 Our objectives are to obtain maximum assurance about whether the financial statements as a whole are free from material misstatements.

3 Misstatements can arise from deliberate manipulation by management or error.

191 Which TWO of the following statements are TRUE with respect to the work performed by the expert?

- Daffy & Co must consider the competence and objectivity of the expert
- Daffy & Co must assess the expert's work to ensure it is appropriate for audit purposes
- The following statement must be included in the auditor's report for Minnie Co:

  'In order to confirm property valuations, we relied on the work undertaken by an independent expert.'
- The auditor must document in the audit file how they have complied with ISA 620 *Using the Work of an Auditor's Expert*
- The audit fee will be higher due to the need for an expert **(2 marks)**

192 Which of the following statements is TRUE with respect to the depreciation on land and buildings?

- o The auditor does not need to ask management to adjust the financial statements as the misstatement is not material
- o A prior year adjustment will be required as the client's treatment was incorrect in the 20X4 financial statements
- o The auditor must ask management to increase property, plant and equipment by $0.4 million
- o The auditor must ask management to decrease property, plant and equipment by $0.4 million **(2 marks)**

193 In respect of the computerised wages issue only, select one option from each column which provides an appropriate conclusion.

Materiality
Not material
Material but not pervasive
Material and pervasive

Opinion
Adverse
Disclaimer
Qualified
Unmodified

Wording
Do not give a true and fair view
Give a true and fair view
'Except for'...give a true and fair view
Do not express an opinion

(2 marks)

194 In respect of the lawsuit only, which of the following correctly identifies the implications for the auditor's opinion and report?

- o Unmodified opinion with no additional communication
- o Unmodified opinion with an Emphasis of Matter paragraph
- o Qualified opinion with Basis for Qualified Opinion
- o Disclaimer of opinion with Basis for Disclaimer of Opinion **(2 marks)**

195 Which of the draft extracts for the auditor's report do not contain the correct wording as per ISA 700 *Forming an Opinion and Reporting on Financial Statements* and require amendment?

- o 1 only
- o 2 and 3 only
- o 3 only
- o 1, 2 and 3 **(2 marks)**

The following scenario relates to questions 196 – 200

It is 1 July 20X5. You are an audit manager in Shifu & Co responsible for the audit of Panda Co for the year ended 31 March 20X5. The draft financial statements show revenue of $55 million and profit before taxation of $5.6 million. Panda Co manufactures chemicals and has a factory and four offsite storage locations for finished goods. The final audit is almost complete and the financial statements and auditor's report are due to be signed next week.

The following two events have occurred subsequent to the year end. No amendments or disclosures have been made in the financial statements in respect of the two events.

Event 1 – Defective chemicals

Chemicals are manufactured up to one month before despatch to enable Panda Co to undertake extensive quality control checks prior to despatch. Testing on 3 April 20X5 found that a batch of chemicals produced in March 20X5 was defective. The cost of this batch was $850,000. In its current condition it can be sold at a scrap value of $100,000 with selling costs of $1,000. The costs of correcting the defect are too significant for Panda Co's management to consider this an alternative option.

Event 2 – Explosion

An explosion occurred at the smallest of the four offsite storage locations on 20 April 20X5. This resulted in some damage to inventory and property, plant and equipment. Panda Co's management have investigated the cause of the explosion and believe that they are unlikely to be able to claim on their insurance. Management of Panda Co has estimated that the value of damaged inventory and property, plant and equipment was $900,000 and it now has no scrap value.

196 Select the option which correctly identifies whether the events are adjusting or non-adjusting

	Event 1	Event 2
o	Adjusting	Adjusting
o	Adjusting	Non-adjusting
o	Non-adjusting	Adjusting
o	Non-adjusting	Non-adjusting

(2 marks)

197 At what figure should the defective inventory be valued in the financial statements?

- o $850,000
- o $100,000
- o $99,000
- o $849,000

(2 marks)

198 Which THREE of the following procedures should now be performed by the auditor of Panda Co?

- o Obtain written representation from management confirming all subsequent events have been communicated to the auditor
- o Inspect purchase invoices to confirm the cost of the defective inventory
- o Review the most recent quality control reports in to identify other instances of defective inventory included within inventory at 31 March 20X5
- o Obtain a schedule of assets damaged in the explosion to determine the amount of loss incurred
- o Review correspondence with the insurance company regarding the likelihood of a successful claim **(2 marks)**

199 Which of the following statements correctly identifies whether or not the events are material and whether the financial statements should be amended?

	Material	**Amendment**
o	Event 1 & Event 2	Event 1 only
o	Event 1 only	Event 1 only
o	Event 2 only	Event 2 only
o	Event 1 & Event 2	Event 1 & Event 2

(2 marks)

200 Assuming no amendments are made to the financial statements, which of the following will be included in the auditor's report for Panda Co?

- o Basis for qualified opinion
- o Adverse opinion
- o Emphasis of matter paragraph
- o Key audit matter paragraph **(2 marks)**

Section 2

PRACTICE QUESTIONS – SECTION B

PLANNING AND RISK ASSESSMENT

201 KNIGHT ELECTRONICS CO *Walk in the footsteps of a top tutor*

This scenario relates to four requirements.

It is 1 July 20X5. Your firm, Hercules & Co, has recently won the audit of a new client, Knight Electronics Co, for the year ending 30 September 20X5. Knight Electronics Co sells products enabling 'smart building' systems which allow customers to efficiently control their security, lighting and networking needs. The audit manager held a preliminary meeting with the finance director and has provided you with the following notes:

Planning meeting notes

Since its launch five years ago, Knight Electronics Co has experienced high levels of growth such that the founder and CEO, William Knight, is considering a stock exchange listing next year.

Knight Electronics Co has both corporate and domestic customers. On 1 October 20X4 Knight Electronics Co began to offer customers the option to purchase a three-year servicing agreement. This provides three annual services for products purchased. Customers pay for the servicing agreement in full at the start of the agreement.

Component parts are purchased from a number of suppliers. Prices of components have been steadily increasing over the past two years leading to a reduction in the gross profit margin. The forecast financial statements for the year ending 30 September 20X5 show inventory valued at cost.

In June 20X5, Knight Electronics Co decided to revalue its premises, which had previously been accounted for using the historic cost model. Properties with a carrying amount under the cost model of $3.8m were revalued to $8.4m based on a valuation performed by management. The finance director also carried out an extensive review of non-current asset lives and decided to extend the useful life of plant and equipment from five years to eight years.

In May 20X5, defective equipment used by Knight Electronics Co resulted in a small fire at its premises. The company has commenced legal action against the supplier of the equipment. Knight Electronics Co's lawyers have advised that the legal action is likely to be successful and, as a result, the finance director has included a receivable for the damages likely to be received from the supplier in the forecast financial statements.

During the year the company's credit controller was ill and was absent from work for four months. Due to staff shortages, no replacement credit controller was appointed. The receivables collection period has increased from 45 days to 75 days.

An instance of payroll fraud was also discovered during the year. A payroll clerk had set up a number of fictitious employees and the wages were then paid into the clerk's own bank account. Controls have now been implemented to prevent this from re-occurring and the clerk involved no longer works for the company. However, the audit manager is concerned that additional fraud may have taken place in the payroll department prior to the controls being implemented.

William Knight would like the audit to be completed by 31 October 20X5.

Requirements:

(a) **Briefly explain how each of the following sources of information will be used by Hercules & Co to gain an understanding of Knight Electronics Co at the planning stage of the audit: prior year audited financial statements, current year budgets and management accounts, prior year report to management, board meeting minutes and company website.**

Note: You do not need to refer to the scenario to answer this requirement. **(5 marks)**

(b) **Describe EIGHT audit risks and explain the auditor's response to each risk in planning the audit of Knight Electronics Co. (16 marks)**

(c) **Describe substantive procedures the auditor should perform to obtain sufficient and appropriate audit evidence in relation to Knight Electronics Co's revenue. (5 marks)**

ISA 240 *The Auditor's Responsibilities Relating to Fraud in an Audit of Financial Statements* provides guidance for auditors regarding fraud and error. Auditors must obtain sufficient appropriate audit evidence regarding the assessed risks of material misstatement due to fraud through designing and implementing appropriate responses.

(d) **Describe procedures which should be undertaken during the audit of Knight Electronics Co as a result of the payroll fraud. (4 marks)**

(Total: 30 marks)

202 LAPIS *Walk in the footsteps of a top tutor*

This scenario relates to two requirements.

It is 1 July 20X5. You are an audit supervisor with Indigo & Co and are planning the audit of your client, Lapis Co, for the year ending 30 September 20X5. Forecast profit before tax for the year is $68.9m and forecast revenue is $192.3m. The audit manager has attended a planning meeting with the finance director and has provided you with the following notes of the meeting:

Planning meeting notes

Lapis Co manufactures televisions at six factories located across Europe and purchases most of its raw materials from overseas suppliers. These raw materials are shipped directly to one of the company's factories and the goods are usually in transit for up to six weeks. Lapis Co has responsibility for goods in transit from the point of dispatch by the supplier.

The company's internal audit department undertakes controls testing across all factories, visiting each site at least once every year. The audit manager has discussed with the finance director that the external audit team may rely on the controls testing which is carried out by the internal audit department.

The company sells televisions to wholesale customers and directly to individual members of the public via the company's website. A significant wholesale customer has recently informed Lapis Co that it is experiencing financial difficulties, however the finance director indicated that an allowance for receivables is not required in the year-end financial statements.

Lapis Co offers customers a three-year warranty on any new televisions purchased. The finance director has confirmed that the warranty provision for the year ended 30 September 20X5 will remain at a similar level to the prior year. In December 20X4 Lapis Co changed one of its television speaker suppliers to a cheaper alternative. This has resulted in an increase in warranty claims for television speaker deficiencies.

In May 20X5, a payroll clerk was dismissed after it was discovered that they had carried out a number of fraudulent transactions. Controls have since been implemented to prevent this reoccurring.

The finance director has informed the audit manager that the intention I to disclose only the amount of remuneration payable to each director in the financial statements. Local legislation in the country in which Lapis Co is based requires disclosure of the names of the directors as well as the total amount of remuneration payable to each director.

One of Lapis Co's suppliers is offering the company an annual rebate on the condition that it purchases a minimum number of units by 30 September 20X5. The amount of the rebate will be claimed in November 20X5. It is likely from orders placed to date and forecast orders that Lapis Co will exceed the minimum volume required to claim this rebate, therefore, it is anticipated that the draft financial statements will include a receivable of $0.8m.

Lapis Co is developing a new smart television model. All $1.6m of costs incurred to date will be capitalised within intangible assets by the year end. The model is still under development and it is not anticipated that it will be available for commercial production until 20X6.

In order to finance the development of the new smart television model, Lapis Co secured a $2.5m interest-bearing bank loan in April 20X5. This is repayable in arrears over four years in quarterly instalments.

The directors of Lapis Co are intending to propose a final dividend once the financial statements are finalised.

Required:

(a) **In line with ISA 220 *Quality Management for an Audit of Financial Statements*, describe the auditor's responsibilities in relation to supervising and reviewing the work performed during the external audit of Lapis Co.**

Note: You do not need to refer to the scenario to answer this requirement. **(4 marks)**

(b) **Describe EIGHT audit risks and explain the auditor's response to each risk in planning the audit of Lapis Co.** **(16 marks)**

Audit risk	Auditor's response

(Total: 20 marks)

203 MAGPIE *Walk in the footsteps of a top tutor*

This scenario relates to three requirements.

It is 1 July 20X5. You are the audit supervisor at Crow & Co and are finalising the planning for your new client Magpie Co for the forthcoming audit for the year ending 31 July 20X5.

Magpie Co is a retailer of garden supplies which operates from 20 stores across the country and employs 400 staff. The audit manager has attended a meeting with the finance director and has provided you with the following notes of that meeting and financial statement extracts:

Notes of planning meeting

During the year the company spent $0.75m on refurbishing its stores to improve the customer experience. All of this expenditure has been recognised in the statement of financial position as property, plant and equipment. In addition, the company also installed a new sales system during the year which records all sales and receivables. The system enables daily sales from each store to be automatically reported to the centralised finance department at the end of each working day. As the system is from a market leading provider, it was not felt necessary to run the old and the new systems in parallel.

Customers are able to pay for their goods using either cash or credit card. At the end of the working day, the store manager generates a report from each cash register which confirms the cash takings. The cash is then counted and compared to the report. Since the new sales system was installed, head office now receives daily cash takings reports which have shown an increasing number of cash shortages at each store. These differences have not been investigated or reconciled on the basis that they have only been small amounts.

The company has a number of corporate customers who buy goods on 90-day credit terms and the level of receivables which are overdue for payment has increased from the prior year. However, the finance director does not intend to make any further allowance for receivables as overdue payments are becoming common in the industry.

The payables ledger clerk has carried out supplier statement reconciliations during the year and in a number of instances the supplier statements have shown a balance owing by the company which is higher than the balance on the list of individual supplier balances. These differences have been included as reconciling items on the supplier statement reconciliations by the payables ledger clerk, but no further work has been performed on these differences.

It has been discovered that the soil relating to a batch of plants with a cost price of $0.1m is contaminated, meaning that the plants may not be able to be sold. Tests are currently being carried out to determine whether the contamination can be remedied.

The report to management issued following the 20X4 audit indicated a significant number of deficiencies noted in the payroll cycle of the business.

Financial statement extracts for the year ending 31 July are as follows:

	Forecast 20X5	**Actual 20X4**
	$m	$m
Revenue	22	26
Cost of sales	(10.9)	(14.5)
Gross profit	11.1	11.5
Operating profit	0.4	1.2
Inventories	1.6	1.1
Receivables	9.0	7.2
Cash in hand	1.3	4.2
Trade payables	1.9	3.2

The audit assistant has already calculated some key ratios for Magpie Co which you have confirmed as accurate.

Ratio	**20X5**	**20X4**
Gross profit margin	50%	44%
Inventory holding period	54 days	28 days
Receivables collection period	149 days	101 days

Required:

ISA 210 *Agreeing the Terms of Audit Engagements* requires an auditor to issue an audit engagement letter.

(a) **Explain the PURPOSE of an audit engagement letter and list FOUR items which should be included in an audit engagement letter.** **(4 marks)**

(b) **Using the table below, calculate the following TWO ratios, for BOTH years, to assist you in planning the audit of Magpie Co.** **(2 marks)**

Note: Formulas are NOT required to be shown.

Ratio	**20X5**	**20X4**
Operating profit margin		
Payables payment period		

(c) **Using the information provided and the ratios calculated, describe SEVEN audit risks and explain the auditor's response to each risk, in planning the audit of Magpie Co.** **(14 marks)**

Audit risk	**Auditor's response**

(Total: 20 marks)

204 ESK *Walk in the footsteps of a top tutor*

This scenario relates to four requirements.

It is 1 July 20X5. You are an audit supervisor with Bannock & Co and are responsible for planning the audit of a new client, Esk Co, for the year ending 31 August 20X5. Your audit manager recently met with the finance director of Esk Co and has provided you with the following planning meeting notes and financial statement extracts.

Planning meeting notes

Esk Co is a manufacturer and wholesaler of plumbing supplies. It operates from two warehouses which are situated in the north and south of the country. Extracts from the forecast financial statements for the year ending 31 August 20X5 and the final financial statements for 20X4 are as follows:

	Forecast 20X5	**Final 20X4**
	$m	$m
Revenue	30.9	27.5
Cost of sales	(22.5)	(19.9)
Gross profit	**8.4**	**7.6**
Inventories	8.3	6.4
Receivables	7.2	4.9
Trade payables	2.4	3.5

In September 20X4, Esk Co purchased a patent for $2.6m which gives it the exclusive right to manufacture a waste disposal system for a four-year period. The purchase cost capitalised comprises the cost of the patent and other costs such as legal fees and administrative costs incurred in negotiating the contract. In order to finance this purchase, Esk Co obtained an interest-bearing bank loan of $2.5m during the year. The bank loan is payable in five equal annual instalments, with the first instalment due to be paid on 1 September 20X5.

The payables ledger clerk has recently discovered a batch of supplier invoices that had been mis-coded and therefore had not been recorded as trade payables. This error has now been corrected but investigations are still ongoing to determine how this happened and whether any other batches of invoices have been mis-coded.

There was a fire in the south warehouse in June 20X5 which resulted in damaged inventory. An inventory count immediately following the fire identified that inventory costing $1.1m required to be fully written off. The damaged inventory has not yet been replaced as there is sufficient inventory in the north warehouse to satisfy demand. The directors have raised a claim against Esk Co's insurance company to cover the full extent of the lost inventory. Although no confirmation has been received from the insurance company, the directors are confident that the full amount claimed of $1.1m will be received and have included this amount as other receivables within current assets.

Esk Co's sales staff receive bonuses if they meet sales targets each quarter. A higher level of sales bonus is available in the quarter to 31 August each year as a reward for efforts during the year as a whole. Esk Co offers its regular customers discounts of up to 10%, which are negotiated and documented by the sales director. This year, in order to easily monitor the amount of the customer discounts, they have been recorded separately as an expense in cost of sales. In previous years, revenue has been recorded net of the discount.

The manager in Esk Co's credit control department has been off work since December 20X4 due to ill health and has been replaced by an inexperienced temporary manager. As a result, Esk Co has not been monitoring the ageing of its receivables and only follows up on outstanding invoices when the system alerts credit control that a customer invoice has been outstanding for 90 days or more. The standard credit terms are 30 days.

During the year, Esk Co was informed by the tax authorities that it was under investigation for a breach of legislation relating to sales tax. Esk Co has appointed a tax consultant who has advised that there does appear to have been a breach of tax legislation and has estimated that a fine and penalty totalling $0.6m will be payable. The directors do not intend to record anything in the financial statements until final notification is provided by the tax authority, which is due to be received on 31 January 20X6.

Required:

ISA 210 *Agreeing the Terms of Audit Engagements* requires an auditor to establish whether the preconditions for an audit are present prior to accepting an audit engagement.

(a) **Describe the PRECONDITIONS for an audit that Bannock & Co should have established prior to accepting the audit of Esk Co. (4 marks)**

(b) **Using the table below, calculate the following FOUR ratios, for BOTH years, to assist you in planning the audit of Esk Co. (4 marks)**

Note: Formulas are NOT required to be shown.

Ratio	**20X5**	**20X4**
Gross profit margin		
Inventory holding period		
Receivables collection period		
Payables payment period		

(c) **Using the information provided and the ratios calculated, describe EIGHT audit risks and explain the auditor's response to each risk, in planning the audit of Esk Co. (16 marks)**

Audit risk	**Auditor's response**

(d) **Describe substantive procedures the auditor should perform to obtain sufficient and appropriate audit evidence in relation to Esk Co's trade receivables. (6 marks)**

(Total: 30 marks)

205 PEACH *Walk in the footsteps of a top tutor*

This scenario relates to five requirements.

It is 1 July 20X5. You are an audit supervisor with Apricot & Co and have been assigned to the audit of Peach Co, a soft drinks manufacturer which sells to wholesale customers. You are currently planning the audit for the year ending 31 August 20X5 and have received the following notes from the audit engagement partner. Materiality for the draft financial statements has been calculated as $153,000, which is 5% of profit before tax.

Planning meeting notes

A new accounting system was introduced via direct changeover in March 20X5. It had been successfully tested prior to its implementation and management had such confidence in the new system that they did not consider it necessary to undertake further testing after implementation.

Peach Co has been developing a new production process which will help to reduce sugar in its drinks by 50%. Development commenced on 1 November 20X4 and the total amount capitalised was $0.8m. On 1 May 20X5, the food safety authority approved the process and production of the new reduced-sugar soft drinks commenced.

Peach Co has inventories of high sugar drinks costing $227,000 which it can no longer sell in its home market due to lack of demand. The directors believe Peach Co can sell the remaining inventories to an international customer at a price that marginally exceeds cost but Peach Co will be responsible for all costs relating to the delivery and shipping of the drinks.

Peach Co replaced two items of machinery in its production line to accommodate a change in the type of bottles used. There were significant staff costs involved in preparing the site for the new machinery and in testing that the new machinery was operating correctly. These costs have been included within the wages and salaries expense for the period. Despite the old machinery being sold at a significant loss, during the year the directors of Peach Co decided to extend the useful lives of plant and machinery by an average of five years.

A member of the finance team was dismissed by Peach Co in May 20X5 after it was discovered that they had been fraudulently purchasing non-current assets for personal use. Peach Co started to investigate the fraud at the beginning of June 20X5 by reconciling all physical assets to the non-current asset register but will not have completed the reconciliation by the year-end date.

Peach Co entered into a contract on 1 May 20X5 with a new supplier of bottles. Peach Co has committed to a minimum order quantity of 150,000 bottles per month for a period of 12 months commencing 1 May 20X5. No costs have been accounted for to date as no amounts are payable for the first six months. Three equal instalments are then payable across the remainder of the contract term. Peach Co's previous supplier has launched a legal claim against Peach Co for breach of contract, stating that Peach Co did not have the right to exit the agreement early. Peach Co's lawyers have indicated that it is likely to lose the case and have estimated the amount payable to be in the region of $0.3m.

In order to fund the development of the new production process and the purchase of new machinery, Peach Co obtained an interest-bearing bank loan of $1.2m on 1 March 20X5 repayable over the next three years in arrears. In order to secure the bank loan, Peach Co agreed to maintain a minimum net profit margin and meet specific sales targets.

Required:

(a) Describe EIGHT audit risks and explain the auditor's response to each risk in planning the audit of Peach Co. (16 marks)

Audit risk	Auditor's response

(b) Describe Apricot & Co's responsibilities in relation to the prevention and detection of fraud and error. (4 marks)

Peach Co has been an audit client of Apricot & Co for the last 15 years. The audit staff of Apricot & Co and the client staff of Peach Co have always enjoyed a meal together at the start of the final audit. Alan Edward, the managing director of Peach Co has this year suggested that instead of a meal, all the audit staff and client staff go away for the weekend to a luxury hotel at Peach Co's expense.

Alan Edward has also suggested that the current year audit fee is renegotiated to be based on a percentage of Peach Co's net profit for the year.

This year, for the first time, Apricot & Co has been approached by Peach Co to help identify potential acquisition targets. Discussions are currently at an early stage and no work has been undertaken at present. The total fees in relation to the audit and other work would fall within acceptable levels in line with ACCA's Code of Ethics and Conduct.

Required:

(c) (i) Identify and explain TWO ethical threats which may affect the independence of Apricot & Co audit of Peach Co; and

(ii) For each threat, recommend an appropriate safeguard to reduce the threat to an acceptable level. (4 marks)

Ethical threat	Appropriate safeguard

(d) Describe substantive procedures the auditor should perform to obtain sufficient and appropriate audit evidence in relation to Peach Co's development expenditure. (6 marks)

(Total: 30 marks)

206 CORLEY APPLIANCES *Walk in the footsteps of a top tutor*

This scenario relates to three requirements.

It is 1 July 20X5. You are an audit supervisor with Woodward & Co and you are in the process of planning the audit of Corley Appliances Co, a company which sells domestic electrical appliances such as fridge freezers, TVs and washing machines. The company's year end is 31 August 20X5 and forecast revenue for the year is $12.2m, total assets are $6.8m and profit before tax is $2.8m. The audit manager held a meeting with the finance director and the notes from that meeting are provided below:

Notes from meeting with finance director

The company operates nationwide with 20 branches located across the country and sells goods to members of the public and to retailers.

The company has a returns policy which allows a customer to return goods within 28 days of purchase if they are not satisfied with the product. Historically, 5% of customers return goods within the return period. The company also provides a six-month warranty on its products which requires Corley Appliances Co to repair any defects, at its own cost, which arise within the warranty period. It is anticipated that the warranty provision in the draft financial statements will be lower than the prior year as the directors are confident the products sold by the company are built to a very high standard.

The company is based in Europe and its main supplier of appliances is based in Asia. Goods are shipped to the company's central warehouse by sea and are usually in transit for up to one month. Corley Appliances Co has responsibility for goods in transit from the point of despatch by the supplier. The central warehouse and all 20 branches will be carrying out a full year-end inventory count on 31 August 20X5 and it is expected that the value of inventory in Corley Appliances Co's financial statements will be $0.95m.

Over the last six months, the finance director has noticed that the company's receivables collection period is now an average of 55 days, whereas the company's target is 42 days. The credit controller is confident that all receivables will eventually pay as increases in receivables collection periods are starting to become common in the industry and has informed the finance director of this. The finance director believes it is unlikely that any increase in the allowance for credit losses/receivables will be necessary at the year end as compared to the prior year.

In June 20X5, a fraud was uncovered in the finance department. A payables ledger supervisor had diverted funds from the company's bank account using a fictitious supplier set up in the payables system. The employee was immediately dismissed, and the value of the fraud will be recognised as an expense in the statement of profit or loss. Since the dismissal of the supervisor, purchase invoices have not been recorded in the individual supplier accounts and it is unlikely that this backlog of invoices will be cleared by the year end.

During the year, the company purchased and installed a new automated despatch system for its central warehouse. The cost of the despatch system was $0.9m and has been recognised as an addition to property, plant and equipment. These capitalised costs include the purchase price of $0.6m, installation costs of $0.2m and staff training costs of $0.1m.

Due to the costs incurred in purchasing the new despatch system and the increase in the receivables collection period, the company's overdraft facility has increased significantly and at one point went over the agreed limit of $0.7m in early June 20X5. The bank has expressed concern about the way that the company is operating its bank overdraft and a decision will be made in November 20X5 as to whether the bank will continue to provide this overdraft facility, which the company is dependent on. The auditor's report is due to be signed in October 20X5.

Required:

ISA 210 *Agreeing the Terms of Audit Engagements* states that auditors should only accept, or continue an existing audit engagement, if the preconditions for an audit are present.

(a) Describe the PRECONDITIONS required for an audit. (3 marks)

(b) Describe SEVEN audit risks and explain the auditor's response to each risk in planning the audit of Corley Appliances Co. (14 marks)

Audit risk	Auditor's response

(c) Define the term 'professional scepticism' and explain TWO examples from the audit of Corley Appliances Co where the auditor should apply professional scepticism. (3 marks)

(Total: 20 marks)

207 HART *Walk in the footsteps of a top tutor*

This scenario relates to four requirements.

It is 1 July 20X5. You are an audit supervisor with Morph & Co responsible for planning the final audit of a new client, Hart Co, for the year ending 30 September 20X5. Hart Co specialises in the design and construction of customised playgrounds. The audit manager recently met with Hart Co's finance director and has provided you with the following notes.

Planning meeting notes

Hart Co has a forecast profit before tax of $12.2m (20X4: $9.8m) and total assets are expected to be $28.5m (20X4: $24.3m). The finance director has indicated that the directors are very pleased with the forecast performance for the year as the directors are paid a bonus based on a percentage of profit before tax.

Hart Co is undertaking the construction of playgrounds at 16 sites in various locations across the country. All playgrounds are constructed to specific customer specifications. Customers pay a 25% deposit on signing the contract, with the balance payable when control of the playground is transferred to the customer.

The balance of work-in-progress (WIP) at 30 June 20X5 is $7.6m in respect of the playgrounds under construction. A WIP count and valuation will be carried out at all sites on 30 September 20X5. Arrangements have been made for the audit team to attend only five of the WIP counts. Hart Co offers its customers a warranty at no extra cost, which guarantees that the playgrounds will function as expected for a period of three years. The warranty provision for the current year has been calculated as 2% of revenue. In the previous year the warranty was based on 6% of revenue. The finance director has made this change despite no significant difference in construction techniques or the level of claims in the year.

Hart Co has incurred expenditure of $1.8m relating to the research and development of a new type of environmentally-friendly building material. $0.6m of the expenditure to date has been written off to the statement of profit or loss. The remaining $1.2m has been capitalised as an intangible asset. No amortisation has been recognised to date as the material has not yet been brought into use.

In June 20X5, the company contracted to purchase new machinery costing $2.4m. It paid $1m on signing the contract to secure the machinery, which was due to be delivered in July 20X5. Due to a supplier problem, the delivery is delayed and is now scheduled to be delivered in October 20X5.

In order to finance the research and development costs and the machinery purchase, Hart Co made a rights issue to existing shareholders at a price of $0.75 for each $0.50 share.

Hart Co's payroll function is outsourced to an external service organisation, Chaz Co, which is responsible for all elements of payroll processing and maintenance of payroll records.

Hart Co's directors correctly disclosed their remuneration details in the forecast financial statements in line with IFRS Standards, however, local legislation in the country in which Hart Co is based, requires more extensive disclosure. The directors have stated that they consider this onerous and so do not intend to provide the additional information.

Required:

ISA 300 *Planning an Audit of Financial Statements* provides guidance to assist auditors in planning an audit.

(a) **Explain the benefits of audit planning.** **(4 marks)**

(b) **Describe EIGHT audit risks and explain the auditor's response to each risk in planning the audit of Hart Co.** **(16 marks)**

Audit risk	Auditor's response

(c) **Describe substantive procedures the auditor should perform to obtain sufficient and appropriate audit evidence in relation to Hart Co's directors' bonuses.** **(5 marks)**

At the end of the planning meeting, the finance director of Hart Co mentioned to the audit manager that one of the key reasons Morph & Co was appointed as auditor was because of its knowledge of the industry. There were some concerns however, as to how Morph & Co would keep information obtained during the audit confidential as it audits three other construction companies specialising in environmentally-friendly building materials, including Hart Co's main competitor.

(d) **Explain the safeguards which Morph & Co should implement to ensure that this conflict of interest is appropriately managed.** **(5 marks)**

(Total: 30 marks)

208 SCARLET *Walk in the footsteps of a top tutor*

This scenario relates to four requirements.

It is 1 July 20X5. You are an audit supervisor of Orange & Co planning the audit of a new client, Scarlet Co, for the year ended 31 May 20X5. Scarlet Co manufactures chemicals for use in domestic and commercial cleaning products.

The company's financial accountant was taken ill suddenly in May 20X5 and is unable to undertake the preparation of the year-end draft financial statements. As a result, the company recruited a temporary financial accountant in early June 20X5 who will prepare the draft financial statements.

The year-end financial statements need to be finalised quickly as the company is looking to raise finance through a bank loan to replace three machines in the production facility. The bank has asked for a copy of the audited year-end financial statements by the end of September 20X5 before they will agree to the loan and the directors are keen to report strong results in order to obtain this financing.

In the year, the company also purchased a specialised machine to develop a new range of chemicals for a major customer. Only trained staff are allowed to operate this machine and staff members had to undertake two days of training, followed by an assessment at the end of the training period. The training costs of $15,000 have been capitalised as part of the cost of the asset.

The company sources many of its raw materials to be used in the chemical manufacturing process from an international supplier and goods can be in transit for up to three weeks.

The agreement with the international supplier contains a clause which states that Scarlett Co is responsible for the goods as soon as they leave the suppliers warehouse.

You have carried out a preliminary analytical review which indicates that the receivables collection period has increased from 38 days to 52 days. The credit controller has confirmed that some customers are currently taking longer to pay than in previous years as they are awaiting payment from their customers.

On 29 May 20X5, the directors announced that one of its brands was being discontinued due to a fall in demand for the product. This resulted in four staff members being made redundant. The payroll department has calculated the levels of termination costs associated with the redundancy and they will be paid in the July 20X5 payroll run.

The directors each received a significant bonus in the year which has been included in the payroll charge for the year in the statement of profit or loss. Local legislation requires separate disclosure of directors' bonuses in the financial statements.

During the year the company sold a batch of chemicals to a customer for $120,000. At the beginning of May 20X5, the customer returned these chemicals because the chemical mix was not in line with the customer's specifications. A credit note is yet to be issued to the customer and the chemicals have been written down to their scrap value within inventory.

The company usually pays its suppliers by the end of each month. However, due to the financial accountant's illness, the payment run for May 20X5 was not performed until 1 June 20X5. The finance director has informed you that in order to show consistent results with the prior year, this payment run is shown as an unpresented item on the year-end bank reconciliation.

Required:

ISA 210 *Agreeing to the Terms of Audit Engagements* requires auditors to issue an engagement letter.

(a) **Explain the PURPOSE of an audit engagement letter and list FOUR items which should be included in an audit engagement letter. (4 marks)**

(b) **Explain WHY the following factors should have been considered by Orange & Co prior to accepting Scarlet Co as a new audit client. (5 marks)**

Pre-acceptance factors	Explanation
The outgoing auditor's response	
Management integrity	
Pre-conditions for an audit	
Independence and objectivity	
Resources available at the time of the audit	

(c) **Describe EIGHT audit risks and explain the auditor's response to each risk in planning the audit of Scarlet Co. (16 marks)**

Audit risk	Auditor's response

(d) **Describe substantive procedures the auditor should perform to obtain sufficient and appropriate audit evidence in respect of the redundancy costs. (5 marks)**

(Total: 30 marks)

209 HARLEM *Walk in the footsteps of a top tutor*

This scenario relates to five requirements.

It is 1 July 20X5. You are an audit supervisor of Brooklyn & Co and are planning the audit of Harlem Co for the year ending 30 September 20X5. The company has been a client of your firm for several years and manufactures car tyres, selling its products to wholesalers and retailers. The audit manager attended a planning meeting with the finance director and has provided you with the following notes of the meeting and financial statement extracts.

Planning meeting notes

Harlem Co sells approximately 40% of its tyres to wholesale customers. These customers purchase goods on a sale or return basis. Under the terms of the agreement, wholesale customers have 60 days during which any returns can be made without penalty. The finance director has historically assumed a return rate of 10%, however, but now feels that this is excessive and intends to change this to 5%.

The company purchased a patent on 30 September 20X4 for $800,000, which was capitalised in the prior year as an intangible asset. This patent gives Harlem Co the exclusive right to manufacture specialised wet weather tyres for four years. In preparation for the manufacture of the wet weather tyres, this year the company conducted a review of its plant and machinery. As part of this review, surplus items of plant and machinery were sold, resulting in a loss on disposal of $160,000.

In May 20X5, the financial controller of Harlem Co was dismissed after it was alleged that the financial controller had carried out a number of fraudulent transactions against the company. The financial controller has threatened to sue the company for unfair dismissal and disputes the allegations. The company has only recently started to investigate the extent of the fraud in order to quantify the required adjustment.

A problem occurred in June 20X5, during production of a significant batch of tyres, which affected their quality. The issue was identified prior to any goods being despatched and management is investigating whether the issues can be rectified and the tyres can subsequently be sold.

Harlem Co's finance director has informed you that in March 20X5 a significant customer was granted a payment break of six months, as it has been experiencing financial difficulties. Harlem Co maintains an allowance for credit losses/trade receivables and it is anticipated that this will remain at the same level as the prior year.

The report to management issued by Brooklyn & Co following last year's audit highlighted significant deficiencies relating to Harlem Co's purchases cycle.

The finance director has informed you that the company intends to restructure its debt finance after the year end and will be looking to consolidate its loans to reduce the overall cost of borrowing. As a result of the planned restructuring of debt, Harlem Co has not paid its shareholders a dividend this year, choosing instead to undertake a bonus issue of its $0.50 equity shares.

You have been asked by the audit manager to complete the preliminary analytical review and has provided you with the following information:

Financial statement extracts for year ending 30 September

	Forecast 20X5	**Actual 20X4**
	$000	$000
Revenue	23,200	21,900
Cost of sales	18,700	17,300
Gross profit	4,500	4,600
Finance costs	290	250
Profit before tax	450	850
Intangible asset	800	800
Inventories	2,100	1,600
Long and short-term borrowings	13,000	11,000
Total equity	10,000	9,500

The audit assistant has already calculated some key ratios for Harlem Co which you have confirmed as accurate. The audit assistant has ascertained that the trade receivables collection period has increased from 38 to 51 days.

Required:

(a) **Using the table below, calculate the following FOUR ratios, for BOTH years, to assist you in planning the audit of Harlem Co.** **(4 marks)**

Note: Formulas are NOT required to be shown.

Ratio	**20X5**	**20X4**
Gross profit margin		
Inventory holding period		
Gearing		
Interest cover		

(b) **Using the information provided and the ratios calculated, describe EIGHT audit risks and explain the auditor's response to each risk in planning the audit of Harlem Co.** **(16 marks)**

Audit risk	**Auditor's response**

(c) **In line with ISA 220 (Revised) *Quality Management for an Audit of Financial Statements*, describe the audit supervisor's responsibilities in relation to supervising and reviewing the audit assistants' work during the audit of Harlem Co.** **(4 marks)**

(d) **Describe substantive procedures the auditor should perform to obtain sufficient and appropriate audit evidence in relation to the VALUATION of trade receivables in the current year.** **(3 marks)**

(e) **Describe substantive procedures the auditor should perform to obtain sufficient and appropriate audit evidence in relation to the DISPOSAL of plant and machinery in the current year.** **(3 marks)**

(Total: 30 marks)

210 PEONY *Walk in the footsteps of a top tutor*

This scenario relates to two requirements.

It is 1 July 20X5. You are an audit supervisor of Daffodil & Co and are planning the audit of Peony Co for the year ending 30 September 20X5. The company is a food retailer with a large network of stores across the country and four warehouses. The company has been a client of your firm for several years and the forecast profit before tax is $28.9m. The audit manager has attended a planning meeting with the finance director and has provided you with the following notes of the meeting.

Planning meeting notes

Peony Co has an internal audit (IA) department which undertakes controls testing across the network of stores. Each store is visited at least once every 18 months. The audit manager has discussed with the finance director that the external audit team may rely on the controls testing which is undertaken by IA.

During the meeting, the finance director provided some forecast financial information. Revenue for the year is expected to increase by 3% as compared to 20X4; the gross profit margin is expected to increase from 56% to 60%; and the operating profit margin is predicted to decrease from 21% to 18%.

Peony Co values inventory in line with industry practice, which is to use selling price less average profit margin. The directors consider this to be a close approximation to cost. The company does not undertake a full year-end inventory count and instead undertakes monthly perpetual inventory counts, each of which covers one-twelfth of all lines in stores and the warehouses. As part of the interim audit which was completed in May, an audit junior attended a perpetual inventory count at one of the warehouses and noted that there were a large number of exceptions where the inventory records showed a higher quantity than the physical inventory which was present in the warehouse. When discussing these exceptions with the financial controller, the audit junior was informed that this had been a recurring issue.

During the year, IA performed a review of the non-current assets physically present in around one third of the company's stores. A number of assets which had not been fully depreciated were identified as obsolete by this review.

The company launched a significant TV advertising campaign in May 20X5 in order to increase revenue. The directors have indicated that at the year end a current asset of $0.7m will be recognised, as they believe that the advertisements will help to boost future sales in the next 12 months. The last advertisement will be shown on TV in early September 20X5.

Peony Co decided to outsource its payroll function to an external service organisation. This service organisation handles all elements of the payroll cycle and sends monthly reports to Peony Co which detail wages and salaries and statutory obligations. Peony Co maintained its own payroll records until 30 April 20X5, at which point the records were transferred to the service organisation.

Peony Co is planning to expand the company by opening three new stores during November 20X5 and in order to finance this, in June 20X5 the company obtained a $3m bank loan. This is repayable in arrears over five years in quarterly instalments. In preparation for the expansion, the company is looking to streamline operations in the warehouses and is planning to make approximately 60 employees redundant after the year end. No decision has been made as to when this will be announced, but it is likely to be in September 20X5.

Required:

(a) **Define and explain materiality and performance materiality.** **(4 marks)**

(b) **Describe EIGHT audit risks and explain the auditor's response to each risk in planning the audit of Peony Co.** **(16 marks)**

Audit risk	Auditor's response

(Total: 20 marks)

211 DARJEELING *Walk in the footsteps of a top tutor*

This scenario relates to five requirements.

It is 1 July 20X5. You are an audit supervisor of Earl & Co and are planning the audit of Darjeeling Co for the year ending 30 September 20X5. The company develops and manufactures specialist paint products and has been a client of your firm for several years. The audit manager has attended a planning meeting with the finance director and has provided you with the following notes of the meeting and financial statement extracts. You have been asked by the audit manager to undertake preliminary analytical procedures using the financial statement extracts.

Planning meeting notes

During the year Darjeeling Co has spent $0.9m, which is included within intangible assets, on the development of new product lines, some of which are in the early stages of their development cycle.

Additionally, as the company is looking to expand production, during the year it purchased and installed a new manufacturing line. All costs, incurred in the purchase and installation of that asset, have been included within property, plant and equipment. These capitalised costs include the purchase price of $2.2m, installation costs of $0.4m and a five-year servicing and maintenance plan costing $0.5m. In order to finance the development projects and the new manufacturing line, the company borrowed $4m from the bank which is to be repaid in instalments over eight years and has an interest rate of 5%. Developing new products and expanding production is important as the company intends to undertake a stock exchange listing in the next 12 months.

The company started a number of initiatives during the year in order to boost revenue. It offered extended credit terms to its customers on the condition that their sales order quantities were increased.

In addition, Darjeeling Co made an announcement in October 20X4 of its 'price promise': that it would match the prices of any competitor for similar products purchased. Customers who are able to prove that they could purchase the products cheaper elsewhere are asked to claim the difference from Darjeeling Co, within one month of the date of purchase of goods, via its website. The company intends to include a refund liability of $0.25m, which is based on the monthly level of claims to date, in the draft financial statements.

The finance director informed the audit manager that a problem arose in June 20X5 in relation to the mixing of materials within the production process for one particular product line. A number of these faulty paint products had already been sold and the issue was identified following a number of complaints from customers about the paint consistency being incorrect. As a precaution, further sales have been stopped and a product recall has been initiated for any of these specific paint products sold since June.

Management is investigating whether the paint consistency of the faulty products can be rectified and subsequently sold.

Financial statement extracts for year ending 30 September

	Forecast	**Actual**
	20X5	**20X4**
	$000	$000
Revenue	19,850	16,990
Cost of sales	(12,440)	(10,800)
Gross profit	7,410	6,190
Inventories	1,850	1,330
Trade receivables	2,750	1,780
Bank	(810)	560
Trade payables	1,970	1,190

Required:

(a) Explain why analytical procedures are used during THREE stages of an audit. **(3 marks)**

(b) Calculate THREE ratios, for BOTH years, which would assist you in planning the audit of Darjeeling Co. **(3 marks)**

(c) Using the information provided and the ratios calculated, describe EIGHT audit risks and explain the auditor's response to each risk in planning the audit of Darjeeling Co. **(16 marks)**

Audit risk	**Auditor's response**

(d) Describe substantive procedures the auditor should perform in relation to the faulty paint products held in inventory at the year end. **(3 marks)**

(e) Describe substantive procedures the auditor should perform to obtain sufficient and appropriate evidence in relation to Darjeeling Co's revenue. **(5 marks)**

(Total: 30 marks)

212 BLACKBERRY *Walk in the footsteps of a top tutor*

This scenario relates to two requirements.

It is 1 July 20X5. You are an audit senior of Loganberry & Co and are planning the audit of Blackberry Co for the year ending 30 September 20X5. The company is a manufacturer of portable music players and your audit manager has already had a planning meeting with the finance director. Forecast revenue is $68.6m and profit before tax is $4.2m.

Planning meeting notes

Inventory is valued at the lower of cost and net realisable value. Cost is made up of the purchase price of raw materials and costs of conversion, including labour, production and general overheads. Inventory is held in three warehouses across the country.

The company plans to conduct full inventory counts at the warehouses on 2, 3 and 4 October, and any necessary adjustments will be made to reflect post-year-end movements of inventory. The internal audit team will attend the counts.

During the year, Blackberry Co paid $1.1m to purchase a patent which allows the company the exclusive right for three years to customise their portable music players to gain a competitive advantage in their industry. The $1.1m has been expensed in the current year statement of profit or loss. In order to finance this purchase, Blackberry Co raised $1.2m through issuing shares at a premium.

In May 20X5, it was discovered that a significant teeming and lading fraud had been carried out by four members of the receivables ledger department who had colluded. They had stolen funds from wholesale customer receipts and then to cover this, they allocated later customer receipts against the older receivables. These employees were all reported to the police and subsequently dismissed. As a result of the vacancies in the receivables ledger department, Blackberry Co decided to outsource its receivables ledger processing to an external service organisation. This service organisation handles all elements of the receivables cycle, including sales invoicing and chasing of receivables balances and sends monthly reports to Blackberry Co detailing the sales and receivable amounts. Blackberry Co ran its own receivables ledger processing until 30 June 20X5, at which point the records were transferred to the service organisation.

In June 20X5, the financial accountant of Blackberry Co was dismissed, having been employed by the company for nine years. The financial accountant has threatened to sue the company for unfair dismissal. As a result of this dismissal, and until a replacement commences work in October, the financial accountant's responsibilities have been adequately allocated to other members of the finance department. However, for this period no supplier statement reconciliations or trade payables account reconciliations will be performed.

During the year, a receivable balance of $0.9m was written off by Blackberry Co as it was deemed irrecoverable as the customer had declared itself bankrupt. In June 20X5, the liquidators handling the bankruptcy of the company publicly announced that it was likely that most of its creditors would receive a pay-out of 40% of the balance owed. As a result, Blackberry Co plans to recognise $360,000 within the 20X5 financial statements in respect of the payout.

Required:

(a) **Describe Loganberry & Co's responsibilities in relation to the prevention and detection of fraud and error.** **(4 marks)**

(b) **Describe EIGHT audit risks and explain the auditor's response to each risk in planning the audit of Blackberry Co.** **(16 marks)**

Audit risk	Auditor's response

(c) **Describe substantive procedures the auditor should perform to obtain sufficient and appropriate audit evidence in relation to COMPLETENESS of Blackberry Co's trade payables.** **(4 marks)**

It is now 1 December 20X5 and the final audit has commenced. The audit manager assigned to the audit has been taken ill and you have been informed you will have to take on the role of audit manager as well as audit senior. There is no one available to review your work until the day before the auditor's report is due to be signed. Due to the reduction in resources assigned to the audit, the audit engagement partner has instructed you to reduce the number of procedures performed and reduce sample sizes to ensure the audit is completed by the deadline originally agreed with Blackberry Co.

(d) Describe THREE quality management deficiencies and provide a recommendation to address each deficiency to ensure compliance with quality management standards.

Note: The marks will be split equally between each part. **(6 marks)**

Quality management deficiency	Recommendation

(Total: 30 marks)

213 PRANCER CONSTRUCTION *Walk in the footsteps of a top tutor*

This scenario relates to three requirements.

It is 1 July 20X5. You are an audit supervisor of Cupid & Co, planning the final audit of a new client, Prancer Construction Co, for the year ending 30 September 20X5. The company specialises in property construction and providing ongoing annual maintenance services for properties previously constructed. Forecast profit before tax is $13.8m and total assets are expected to be $22.3m, both of which are higher than for the year ended 30 September 20X4.

You are required to produce the audit strategy document. The audit manager has met with Prancer Construction Co's finance director and has provided you with the following notes, a copy of the latest management accounts to June 20X5, and the prior year financial statements.

Meeting notes

The prior year financial statements recognise work-in-progress of $1.8m, which comprised property construction in progress as well as ongoing maintenance services for finished properties. The latest management accounts recognise $2.1m inventory of completed properties compared to a balance of $1.4m in September 20X4. A full year-end inventory count will be undertaken on 30 September at all of the 11 building sites where construction is in progress. There is not sufficient audit team resource to attend all inventory counts.

In line with industry practice, Prancer Construction Co offers its customers a five-year building warranty, which covers any construction defects. Customers are not required to pay any additional fees to obtain the warranty. The finance director anticipates this provision will be lower than last year as the company has improved its building practices and therefore the quality of the finished properties.

Customers who wish to purchase a property are required to place an order and pay a 5% non-refundable deposit prior to the completion of the building. When the building is complete, customers pay a further 92.5%, with the final 2.5% due to be paid six months later. The finance director has informed you that although an allowance for credit losses/receivables has historically been maintained, it is anticipated that this can be significantly reduced.

Information from management accounts

Prancer Construction Co's prior year financial statements and latest management accounts contain a material overdraft balance. The finance director has confirmed that there are minimum profit and net assets covenants attached to the overdraft.

A review of the management accounts shows the payables period was 56 days for June 20X5, compared to 87 days for September 20X4. The finance director anticipates that the September 20X5 payables days will be even lower than those in June 20X5.

Required:

(a) Describe the process Cupid & Co should have undertaken to assess whether the PRECONDITIONS for an audit were present when accepting the audit of Prancer Construction Co. (3 marks)

(b) Identify THREE main areas, other than audit risks, which should be included within the audit strategy document for Prancer Construction Co, and for each area provide an example relevant to the audit. (3 marks)

(c) Using all the information provided describe SEVEN audit risks, and explain the auditor's response to each risk, in planning the audit of Prancer Construction Co. (14 marks)

Audit risk	Auditor's response

(Total: 20 marks)

214 HURLING *Walk in the footsteps of a top tutor*

This scenario relates to four requirements.

It is 1 July 20X5. You are an audit supervisor of Caving & Co and you are planning the audit of Hurling Co, a listed company, for the year ending 30 September 20X5. The company manufactures computer components and forecast profit before tax is $33.6 million and total assets are $79.3 million.

Hurling Co distributes its products through wholesalers as well as via its own website. The website was upgraded during the year at a cost of $1.1 million. Additionally, the company has recently entered into a transaction to purchase a new warehouse which will cost $3.2 million.

Hurling Co's legal advisers are working to ensure that the legal process will be completed by the year end. The company issued $5 million of irredeemable preference shares to finance the warehouse purchase.

During the year the finance director has increased the useful economic lives of fixtures and fittings from three to four years as it was considered to be a more appropriate period. The finance director has informed the engagement partner that a revised credit period has been agreed with one of its wholesale customers, as they have been experiencing difficulties with repaying the balance of $1.2 million owing to Hurling Co.

In June 20X5, Hurling Co introduced a new bonus based on sales targets for its sales staff. This has resulted in a significant number of new wholesale customer accounts being opened by sales staff. The new customers have been given favourable credit terms as an introductory offer, provided goods are purchased within a two-month period. As a result, revenue has increased by 5% on the prior year.

The company has launched several new products this year and all but one of these new launches have been successful. Feedback on product Luge, launched four months ago, has been mixed, and the company has just received notice from one of their customers, Petanque Co, of intended legal action. They are alleging the product sold to them was faulty, resulting in a significant loss of information and an ongoing detrimental impact on profits. As a precaution, sales of the Luge product have been halted and a product recall has been initiated for any Luge products sold in the last four months.

The finance director is keen to announce the company's financial results to the stock market earlier than last year and in order to facilitate this, has asked if the audit could be completed in a shorter timescale. In addition, the company is intending to propose a final dividend once the financial statements are finalised.

Hurling Co's finance director has informed the audit engagement partner that one of the company's non-executive directors (NEDs) has just resigned, and has enquired if the partners at Caving & Co can help Hurling Co in recruiting a new NED.

Specifically, the finance director requested that the engagement quality reviewer, who was until last year the audit engagement partner on Hurling Co, assist the company in this recruitment. Caving & Co also provides taxation services for Hurling Co in the form of tax return preparation along with some tax planning advice. The finance director has recommended to the audit committee of Hurling Co that this year's audit fee should be based on the company's profit before tax. At today's date, 20% of last year's audit fee is still outstanding and was due to be paid three months ago.

Required:

(a) Define audit risk and the components of audit risk. **(4 marks)**

(b) Describe EIGHT audit risks, and explain the auditor's response to each risk, in planning the audit of Hurling Co. **(16 marks)**

Audit risk	Auditor's response

(c) (i) Identify and explain FIVE ethical threats which may affect the independence of Caving & Co's audit of Hurling Co, and

(ii) For each threat, recommend an appropriate safeguard to reduce the threat to an acceptable level.

Ethical threat	Appropriate safeguard

(10 marks)

(Total: 30 marks)

215 CENTIPEDE *Walk in the footsteps of a top tutor*

This scenario relates to four requirements.

It is 1 July 20X5. You are an audit supervisor of Ant & Co and are planning the final audit of Centipede Co, which is a listed company, for the year ended 30 June 20X5. The company purchases consumer packaged goods and sells these through its website and to wholesalers. This is a new client for your firm and your audit manager has already had a planning meeting with the finance director and has provided you with the following notes along with financial statement extracts.

Client background and notes from planning meeting

Rather than undertaking a full year-end inventory count, the company undertakes monthly perpetual inventory counts, covering one-twelfth of all lines monthly. As part of the interim audit which was completed earlier in the year, an audit assistant attended a perpetual inventory count in March and noted that there were a large number of exceptions where the inventory records were consistently higher than the physical inventory in the warehouse. When discussing these exceptions with the finance director, the assistant was informed that this had been a recurring issue all year. In addition, the audit assistant noted that there were some lines of inventory which, according to the records, were at least 90 days old.

Centipede Co has a head office where the audit team will be based to conduct the final audit fieldwork. However, there are four additional sites where some accounting records are maintained and these sites were not visited during the interim audit. The records for these sites are incorporated monthly through an interface to the general ledger. A fifth site was closed down in 20X4, however, the building was only sold in 20X5 at a loss of $825,000.

One of Centipede Co's wholesale customers is alleging that the company has consistently failed to deliver goods in a saleable condition and on time, hence it has commenced legal action against Centipede Co for a loss of profits claim. The directors have disclosed their remuneration details in the financial statements in line with International Financial Reporting Standards, which does not require a separate list of directors' names and payments. However, in the country in which Centipede Co is based, local legislation requires disclosure of the names of the directors and the amount of remuneration payable to each director.

Financial statement extracts for the year ended 30 June:

	Draft	**Final**
	20X5	***20X4***
	$000	$000
Revenue	25,230	21,180
Cost of sales	(15,840)	(14,015)
Gross profit	9,390	7,165
Operating expenses	(4,903)	(3,245)
Operating profit	4,487	3,920
Inventories	2,360	1,800
Trade receivables	1,590	1,250
Cash	–	480
Trade payables	3,500	2,800
Overdraft	580	–

Required:

(a) Describe the matters which Ant & Co should have considered prior to accepting the audit of Centipede Co. (5 marks)

(b) Using the table below, calculate the following FOUR ratios, for BOTH years, to assist you in planning the audit of Centipede Co. (4 marks)

Note: Formulas are NOT required to be shown.

Ratio	**20X5**	**20X4**
Gross profit margin		
Inventory holding period		
Payables payment period		
Current ratio		

(c) Using the information provided and the ratios calculated, describe EIGHT audit risks and explain the auditor's response to each risk, in planning the audit of Centipede Co. (16 marks)

Audit risk	**Auditor's response**

The finance director of Centipede Co informed Ant & Co that one of the reasons they were appointed as auditors was because of their knowledge of the industry. Ant & Co audits a number of other consumer packaged goods companies, including Centipede Co's main rival. The finance director has enquired how Ant & Co will keep information obtained during the audit confidential.

(d) Explain the safeguards which Ant & Co should implement to ensure that this conflict of interest is properly managed. (5 marks)

(Total: 30 marks)

216 AQUAMARINE *Walk in the footsteps of a top tutor*

This scenario relates to three requirements.

It is 1 July 20X5. You are an audit supervisor of Amethyst & Co and are currently planning the audit of your client, Aquamarine Co which manufactures elevators. Its year end is 31 July 20X5 and the forecast profit before tax is $15.2 million.

The company undertakes continuous production in its factory, therefore at the year end it is anticipated that work-in-progress (WIP) will be approximately $950,000. In order to improve the manufacturing process, Aquamarine Co placed an order in April for $720,000 of new plant and machinery; one third of this order was received in May with the remainder expected to be delivered by the supplier in late July or early August.

Included within intangible assets is a patent recognised at a cost of $1.3 million which was purchased at the beginning of the year. The patent gives Aquamarine Co the exclusive right to manufacture specialised elevator equipment for five years. In order to finance this purchase, Aquamarine Co borrowed $1.2 million from the bank which is repayable over five years.

In January 20X5 Aquamarine Co outsourced its payroll processing to an external service organisation, Coral Payrolls Co (Coral). Coral handles all elements of the payroll cycle and sends monthly reports to Aquamarine Co detailing the payroll costs. Aquamarine Co ran its own payroll until 31 December 20X4, at which point the records were transferred over to Coral.

The company has a policy of revaluing land and buildings and the finance director has announced that all land and buildings will be revalued at the year end.

During a review of the management accounts for the month of May 20X5, you have noticed that receivables have increased significantly on the previous year end and against May 20X4.

The finance director has informed you that the company is planning to make approximately 65 employees redundant after the year end. No decision has been made as to when this will be announced, but it is likely to be prior to the year end.

Required:

(a) Define audit risk and the components of audit risk. (5 marks)

(b) Describe SIX audit risks, and explain the auditor's response to each risk, in planning the audit of Aquamarine Co. (12 marks)

Audit risk	Auditor's response

(c) Explain the additional factors Amethyst & Co should consider during the audit in relation to Aquamarine Co's use of the payroll service organisation. (3 marks)

(Total: 20 marks)

217 VENUS *Walk in the footsteps of a top tutor*

This scenario relates to four requirements.

It is 1 July 20X5. You are an audit supervisor of Pluto & Co and are currently planning the audit of your client, Venus Magnets Co (Venus) which manufactures decorative magnets. Its year end is 30 September 20X5 and the forecast profit before tax is $9.6 million.

During the year, the directors reviewed the useful lives and depreciation rates of all classes of plant and machinery. This resulted in an overall increase in the asset lives and a reduction in the depreciation charge for the year.

Inventory is held in five warehouses and on 27 and 28 September a full inventory count will be held with adjustments for movements to the year end. This is due to a lack of available staff on 30 September. In June, there was a fire in one of the warehouses. Inventory of $0.9 million was damaged and this has been written down to its scrap value of $0.2 million.

An insurance claim has been submitted for the difference of $0.7 million. Venus is still waiting to hear from the insurance company with regards to this claim, but has included the insurance proceeds within the statement of profit or loss and the statement of financial position.

The finance director has informed the audit manager that the May and June bank reconciliations each contained unreconciled differences; however, it was considered that the overall differences involved were immaterial.

A directors' bonus scheme was introduced during the year which is based on achieving a target profit before tax. In order to finalise the bonus figures, the finance director of Venus would like the audit to commence earlier so that the final results are available earlier this year.

Required:

(a) **Identify and explain TWO factors which would indicate that an engagement letter for an existing audit client should be revised.** **(2 marks)**

(b) **List FOUR matters which should be included within an audit engagement letter.** **(2 marks)**

You have been asked by the audit engagement partner to gain an understanding about the new client as part of the planning process.

(c) **Identify FOUR sources of information relevant to gaining an understanding and describe how this information will be used by the auditor.** **(4 marks)**

(d) **Describe SIX audit risks, and explain the auditor's response to each risk, in planning the audit of Venus Magnets Co.** **(12 marks)**

Audit risk	Auditor's response

(Total: 20 marks)

218 SYCAMORE *Walk in the footsteps of a top tutor*

Answer debrief

This scenario relates to five requirements.

It is 1 July 20X5. You are the audit supervisor of Maple & Co and are currently planning the audit of an existing client, Sycamore Science Co (Sycamore), whose year end was 30 April 20X5. Sycamore is a pharmaceutical company, which manufactures and supplies a wide range of medical supplies. The draft financial statements show revenue of $35.6 million and profit before tax of $5.9 million.

During the year, a review of plant and equipment in the factory was undertaken and surplus plant was sold, resulting in a profit on disposal of $210,000.

Sycamore's previous finance director left the company in December 20X4 after it was discovered that following discovery that fraudulent expenses had been claimed from the company for a significant period of time. A new finance director was appointed in January 20X5 who was previously a financial controller of a bank, and the new appointee expressed surprise that Maple & Co had not uncovered the fraud during last year's audit.

During the year Sycamore has spent $1.8 million on developing several new products. These projects are at different stages of development and the draft financial statements show the full amount of $1.8 million within intangible assets. In order to fund this development, $2.0 million was borrowed from the bank and is due for repayment over a ten-year period. The bank has attached minimum profit targets as part of the loan covenants.

The new finance director has informed the audit partner that since the year end there has been an increased number of sales returns and that in the month of May over $0.5 million of goods sold in April were returned.

Sycamore decided to outsource its payroll function to an external service organisation. This service organisation handles all elements of the payroll cycle and sends monthly reports to Sycamore which detail wages and salaries and statutory obligations. Sycamore maintained its own payroll records until January 20X5, at which point the records were transferred to the service organisation.

Maple & Co attended the year-end inventory count at Sycamore's warehouse. The auditor present raised concerns that during the count there were movements of goods in and out the warehouse and this process did not seem well controlled.

Required:

(a) State Maples & Co's responsibilities in relation to the prevention and detection of fraud and error. (5 marks)

(b) Describe EIGHT audit risks, and explain the auditor's response to each risk, in planning the audit of Sycamore Science Co. (16 marks)

Audit risk	Auditor's response

(c) Explain the quality management procedures that Maple & Co should have in place during the engagement performance. (5 marks)

Sycamore's new finance director has read about review engagements and is interested in the possibility of Maple & Co undertaking these in the future. However, the finance director is unsure how these engagements differ from an external audit and how much assurance would be gained from this type of engagement.

(d) (i) Explain the purpose of review engagements and how these differ from external audits, and (2 marks)

(ii) Describe the level of assurance provided by external audits and review engagements. (2 marks)

(Total: 30 marks)

Calculate your allowed time, allocate the time to the separate parts..............

219 RECORDER COMMUNICATIONS *Walk in the footsteps of a top tutor*

This scenario relates to five requirements.

It is 1 July 20X5. Recorder Communications Co (Recorder) is a large mobile phone company which operates a network of stores in countries across Europe. The company's year end is 30 September 20X5. You are the audit senior of Piano & Co. Recorder is a new client and you are currently planning the audit with the audit manager. You have been provided with the following planning notes from the audit partner following a meeting with the finance director.

Recorder purchases goods from a supplier in South Asia and these goods are shipped to the company's central warehouse. The goods are usually in transit for two weeks and the company correctly records the goods when received. Recorder does not undertake a year-end inventory count, but carries out monthly continuous (perpetual) inventory counts and any errors identified are adjusted in the inventory system for that month. Manufacturers regularly bring out new models of mobile phones. When this happens, the old models have to be sold at a significant discount as customers usually want the latest model. Recorder has a number of older models in inventory.

During the year the company introduced a bonus based on sales for its sales persons. The bonus target was based on increasing the number of customers signing up for 24-month phone line contracts. This has been successful and revenue has increased by 15%, especially in the last few months of the year. The level of receivables is considerably higher than last year and there are concerns about the creditworthiness of some customers.

Recorder has a policy of revaluing its land and buildings and this year has updated the valuations of all land and buildings.

During the year the directors have each been paid a significant bonus, and they have included this within wages and salaries. Separate disclosure of the bonus is required by local legislation.

Required:

(a) Explain the benefits of audit planning. (5 marks)

(b) Describe SEVEN audit risks, and explain the auditor's response to each risk, in planning the audit of Recorder Communications Co. (14 marks)

Audit risk	Auditor's response

(c) Explain the audit procedures you should perform in order to place reliance on the continuous (perpetual) counts for year-end inventory. (3 marks)

(d) Describe substantive procedures you should perform to confirm the directors' bonus payments included in the financial statements. (4 marks)

(e) Explain the auditor's responsibility to consider laws and regulations in an audit of the financial statements. (4 marks)

(Total: 30 marks)

INTERNAL CONTROLS

220 SILVER CO *Walk in the footsteps of a top tutor*

This scenario relates to two requirements.

It is 1 July 20X5. You are an audit senior with Golden & Co and you are in the process of reviewing the inventory count arrangements for your audit client, Silver Co, in preparation for attendance at the full year-end inventory count on 30 September 20X5. The company manufactures household furniture such as tables, sofas and beds and has a factory and a large warehouse which are located on a single site.

Inventory count arrangements

The company manufactures goods 24 hours a day, seven days a week to meet customers' demands. Production will still be continuing during the inventory count as it is not possible for the company to stop producing goods. Movements of goods in and out of the factory and warehouse will also have to continue for operational reasons.

The count will be undertaken by 20 teams of two counters from the warehouse, and the warehouse supervisor will be overseeing the inventory count. Each team will be given a specific area of the warehouse to count using sequentially numbered inventory sheets which detail the items of inventory together with quantities held at the date of the count as per the inventory system. It has been left to the individuals within each team to decide how to allocate the responsibilities between them.

All goods present in the warehouse on 30 September 20X5 will be allocated into separate warehouse bays (designated areas of the warehouse) in preparation for counting. When a warehouse bay has been counted, it is crossed out on the warehouse map which is held in the office by the warehouse supervisor. The warehouse supervisor is confident that the 20 teams are familiar with the warehouse and the location of the inventory and concluded that that each bay only needs to be counted by one team. One area of the warehouse, which includes a large quantity of spare parts left over from production, will be segregated so that this inventory will not be counted, as the warehouse supervisor has stated that these items are unusable.

A numerical sequence check of the sheets will be carried out by the warehouse supervisor once the count is finished. The inventory sheets will then be passed to a warehouse assistant to update the inventory records to reflect the inventory physically present as per the inventory sheets.

Work in progress valuations have previously been carried out by an external inventory valuer. However, the warehouse supervisor has offered to undertake this valuation this year due to being having a detailed knowledge of the company's products. The directors have agreed to this on the basis that it will save costs.

Last week the company agreed to store 30 sofas belonging to a third party in its warehouse for the next four months as the third party's storage facilities became flooded. For convenience, these sofas have been stored alongside similar products which belong to Silver Co.

Requirements:

Auditors have a responsibility under ISA 265 *Communicating Deficiencies in Internal Control to Those Charged with Governance and Management* to communicate significant deficiencies in internal controls to those charged with governance.

(a) **Describe FOUR matters the auditor should consider in determining whether a deficiency in internal controls is significant.**

Note: You do not need to refer to the scenario to answer this requirement. **(4 marks)**

(b) **Identify and explain EIGHT deficiencies in Silver Co's inventory count arrangements and provide a control recommendation to address each of these deficiencies.**

(16 marks)

(Total: 20 marks)

Control deficiency	Control recommendation

221 PETRA *Walk in the footsteps of a top tutor*

This scenario relates to six requirements.

It is 1 July 20X5. Petra Co is a company listed on a stock exchange. It manufactures handbags which it supplies to retailers across the country. The company's year end is 30 September 20X5. You are an audit supervisor with Babylon & Co, preparing the draft audit programmes and reviewing the internal controls documentation in preparation for the forthcoming interim audit.

Payroll

Petra Co employs factory staff, who are paid based on the number of hours worked. They are paid in cash on a weekly basis due to commercial reasons. These staff each have a unique clock card which they use to enter and exit the factory at the beginning and end of their shift, and this process is supervised by security staff. The clock card system and the payroll system are linked.

The payroll system automatically calculates the gross and net pay along with relevant deductions and generates employee payslips. The payroll supervisor selects a sample of the payslips, reperforms the gross to net pay calculations and investigates any discrepancies. The sampled payslips are then signed as evidence of this review.

Factory staff receive an annual inflation-based pay increase every April. The revised hourly wage rates are communicated to the payroll department. The revised pay rates are entered into the system in April by a payroll clerk and each entry is checked by a senior clerk for input errors prior to processing that week's wages. The senior clerk signs a payroll listing of factory staff employees, which includes the revised hourly wage rates as evidence of undertaking this review.

Two members of the payroll department produce the cash pay packets. One member is responsible for preparing the pay packets by reference to the payslips generated by the system. The second member recounts the contents of the finished pay packets and confirms that this agrees to the payslips. Both members of staff are required to sign the weekly payroll listing on completion of this task.

Sales

Petra Co carries out credit checks for all new customers. Upon passing these checks, new customers are set up by an accounting clerk in the receivables ledger master file and a credit limit is set by the finance director. The credit limits are only reviewed if an increase is requested by the customer.

Petra Co generates revenue through visits by members of its sales department to customers' premises. When a customer places an order, sales staff check that the customer is within its credit limit and that the inventory is available and then complete a three-part pre-printed order form. One copy is left with the customer, the second is sent to the warehouse and the third to the finance department. The sales staff have monthly sales targets and are able to use their discretion in granting discounts up to a maximum of 8%. No review is undertaken of discounts granted.

Purchases

The company has a purchasing department based at its head office. All members of this department have full access to the supplier master file data and are able to make changes. When goods are received from a supplier they are processed by the warehouse team, who agree the delivery to the purchase order, checking the quantity and the quality of goods, and complete a sequentially numbered goods received note (GRN). The GRNs are matched to the purchase orders and are filed in the warehouse.

On receipt of the purchase invoice from the supplier, a payables ledger clerk, logs them into the payables ledger using document count controls to ensure that the correct number of invoices has been input.

Required:

(a) List FOUR control objectives of Petra Co's sales system. **(4 marks)**

(b) In respect of the PAYROLL system of Petra Co:

(i) Identify and explain THREE DIRECT CONTROLS on which the auditor may seek to place reliance, and

(ii) Describe a TEST OF CONTROL the auditor should perform to assess if each of these direct controls is operating effectively.

Note: The marks will be split equally between each part. **(6 marks)**

Direct control	Test of control

(c) Identify and explain FIVE DEFICIENCIES in Petra Co's SALES and PURCHASES systems and provide a recommendation to address each of these deficiencies.

Note: The marks will be split equally between each part. **(10 marks)**

Control deficiency	Control recommendation

(d) Describe substantive procedures the auditor should perform to obtain sufficient and appropriate audit evidence in relation to Petra Co's purchases and other expenses. **(4 marks)**

Petra Co has been a listed company for six years and the directors are aware of the need for compliance with corporate governance principles. The finance director has requested that the audit team undertakes a review of whether the company complies with the principles.

The board of Petra Co is appropriately comprised of executive and independent non-executive directors (NEDs). The Chair is planning to retire at the end of the financial year, and it is proposed by the nomination committee that the current marketing director is appointed into this role and that a new marketing director is recruited. Two directors are subject to re-election at each annual general meeting.

The NEDs are all members of the audit committee and are highly experienced in the industry in which Petra Co operates. Before joining Petra Co they were all previously involved in sales or purchasing roles. The level of executive directors' pay is set by the remuneration committee, comprised of independent NEDs. The remuneration for the NEDs is in the form of an annual bonus based on profit growth over the prior year.

(e) **Describe THREE corporate governance deficiencies faced by Petra Co and provide a recommendation to address each deficiency to ensure compliance with corporate governance principles.**

Note: The marks will be split equally between each part. **(6 marks)**

Deficiency	Recommendation

(Total: 30 marks)

222 DALEY *Walk in the footsteps of a top tutor*

This scenario relates to six requirements.

It is 1 July 20X5. Daley Co, a listed company, manufactures double glazed windows and doors. The company's year end is 30 September 20X5. You are an audit supervisor with Cooper & Co and you are in the process of reviewing the following extracts from the internal controls documentation in preparation for the forthcoming audit:

Payroll

The company employs 210 staff in its factory who are paid on a weekly basis by bank transfer. Factory staff have key cards and are required to swipe in and out at the beginning and end of their shift. This process is supervised. Hours worked by employees are recorded electronically using the key card system which is linked to the payroll system. Each week the hours worked are automatically transferred to the payroll system. As the process is automated, no checks over this transfer are performed.

The payroll is run on a weekly basis and the system automatically calculates the wages to be paid. On a sample basis, a payroll clerk checks gross to net pay calculations and compares these to the system-generated balances to ensure the accuracy of the payroll system. If any changes to the payroll data are required, the payroll clerk makes the amendment. An edit report of any amendments is produced weekly by the system but is not reviewed.

Non-current assets

Daley Co has a head office and ten factories, with a warehouse included at each factory. The company has an internal audit (IA) department which carries out a comparison between all of the assets recorded on the non-current asset register to those physically present in each of Daley Co's 21 sites. This year's programme of visits, which has been planned and carried out on the same basis as previous years, means that by 30 September 20X5, IA will only have completed this comparison at one factory and one warehouse.

During the year, the financial controller changed the company's capitalisation accounting policy. In accordance with the revised policy, only items of a capital (asset) nature exceeding $20,000 are accounted for as additions to non-current assets in the statement of financial position. Any non-current assets purchased below $20,000 are written off to the statement of profit or loss as an expense.

Bank and cash

On a weekly basis, a bank payments list is generated for supplier payments. The finance director reviews the total amount of the bank payments list and authorises it. The finance director then passes it to the financial controller who processes it for payment.

Daley Co incurs a lot of petty cash expenditure and the finance department maintains a petty cash float of $500 which is kept in the safe. It is used for making any sundry purchases by the company. When staff wish to purchase sundry items, the required sum of cash is given to the staff member who signs for it. The staff member is required to return any excess money to the finance department but there is currently no requirement for receipts to be provided.

The cashier reconciles the main current account on a monthly basis as this contains the highest levels of activity and reconciles the remaining three bank accounts every three months. The reconciliations are reviewed by the finance director who evidences this review.

Required:

ISA 315 (Revised 2019) *Identifying and Assessing the Risks of Material Misstatement* states that an entity's system of internal control consists of five components: control environment, the entity's risk assessment process, the entity's process to monitor the system of internal control, the information system and communication and control activities.

(a) **Using the table below, describe the five components of an entity's system of internal control.** **(5 marks)**

Note: You do not need to refer to the scenario to answer this requirement.

Component of internal control	Description
Control environment	
Entity's risk assessment process	
Entity's process to monitor the system of internal control	
Information system and communication	
Control activities	

(b) In respect of system of internal control of Daley Co:

(i) Identify and explain FIVE deficiencies

(ii) Recommend a control to address each of these deficiencies, and

(iii) Describe a TEST OF CONTROL the external auditors should perform to assess if each of these controls, if implemented, is operating effectively.

Note: The marks will be split equally between each part. **(15 marks)**

Control deficiency	Control recommendation	Test of control

(c) Describe substantive procedures the auditor should perform to obtain sufficient and appropriate audit evidence in relation to Daley Co's bank balances. (4 marks)

During the year, the Chair of Daley Co resigned due to other commitments and Fred Johnson, who is the chief executive of the company, took over this role. Fred has recently written to all shareholders to inform them that any questions or comments they may have could only be raised at the company's annual general meeting and that any other communication with the board is not possible.

The executive directors' remuneration is set by the remuneration committee. The non-executive directors' remuneration is set by the board and is based on pre-tax profit targets which are agreed by the board at the start of each financial year. As the board is of the view that the internal control environment is very effective, an audit committee has not been established.

(d) Describe THREE corporate governance deficiencies faced by Daley Co and provide a recommendation to address each deficiency to ensure compliance with corporate governance principles.

Note: The marks will be split equally between each part. **(6 marks)**

Deficiency	Recommendation

(Total: 30 marks)

223 WHITTAKER *Walk in the footsteps of a top tutor*

This scenario relates to four requirements.

It is 1 July 20X5. You are an audit supervisor with Walsh & Co. You are currently reviewing notes in relation to the internal controls in place at your client, Whittaker Co. Whittaker Co manufactures and sells luxury bed linen wholesale to the hotel trade and direct to the public from its factory store. It has a year ending 31 August 20X5.

Sales

Whittaker Co implemented a new sales system in May 20X5. The new system was fully tested prior to its implementation and will be run in parallel with the old system until the year end. Whittaker Co's internal audit (IA) department is responsible for comparing the output from the old and new systems, investigating any discrepancies and making recommendations for further action.

The company operates a fully automated credit check process for all its new hotel customers. The automated system generates a credit limit for each new customer which the sales director approves before the customer can place any orders. The sales director evidences approval of the credit limit in the system.

On a monthly basis, the receivables ledger clerk downloads the aged receivables report and reviews it for outstanding debts. In line with Whittaker Co's credit control policy, any debts which are greater than 30 days overdue are then passed to the credit control department which contacts the customers to resolve any issues and recover the debt.

Also, on a monthly basis, the accounts clerk reconciles the trade receivables account to the list of individual customer balances in order to verify the month-end receivables balance. Any reconciling items are documented, errors are corrected on a timely basis and then the reconciliations are reviewed and approved by the financial controller.

Payroll

Whittaker Co has a human resources (HR) department which is responsible for processing joiners and leavers, including preparing and sending authorised joiners forms to the payroll department so that new employees can be set up correctly on the payroll system. However, when additional staff are required at short notice, joiners' forms are not completed and instead, the production supervisor notifies the payroll department by email on the day they commence employment.

Staff are required to work overtime on a regular basis in order to meet production targets. Overtime is paid monthly in arrears, at the end of the month in which it is worked. All overtime reports are reviewed on a quarterly basis by the production supervisor after the overtime has been paid. Reviews of overtime reports are evidenced by signature of the production director.

The payroll system automatically calculates wages and deductions for all employees based on standing data. The standing data is reviewed regularly to ensure it is still accurate however no checks are performed on the monthly payroll calculations.

In May each year, all employees receive a bonus, the amount of which varies depending upon their performance. The payroll department receives written notification from the HR manager of the bonus, based only on the HR Manager's view of the employees' performance in the year. The bonuses for 20X5 were input into the payroll system by the payroll clerk. After May's payroll had been processed, a small number of employees notified the payroll department that the bonus they had been paid did not agree to their bonus confirmation letter. This was corrected in June 20X5.

Bank

Whittaker Co uses an internet banking system which requires a two-step verification process. A password is required to log on to the system. An additional passcode is then required to set up new payees or to withdraw funds. The login details including the password and the passcode are saved in a shared file which is accessible to all payables ledger staff in the accounts department.

The accounts clerk undertakes the bank reconciliations on a weekly basis. The reconciling items are documented and sent to the financial controller for review. The financial controller only investigates the reconciling items if the sum of these items is significant.

Required:

Auditors are required, under ISA 265 *Communicating Deficiencies in Internal Control to Those Charged with Governance and Management*, to communicate in writing to those charged with governance any significant deficiencies in internal control.

(a) **Describe FOUR matters the auditor may consider in determining whether a deficiency in internal control is significant.**

Note: You do not need to refer to the scenario to answer this requirement. **(4 marks)**

(b) **In respect of the SALES system of Whittaker Co:**

(i) **Identify and explain THREE DIRECT CONTROLS on which the auditor may seek to place reliance, and**

(ii) **Describe a TEST OF CONTROL the auditor should perform to assess if each of these direct controls is operating effectively.**

Note: The marks will be split equally between each part. **(6 marks)**

Direct control	Test of control

(c) **Identify and explain FIVE DEFICIENCIES in Whittaker Co's PAYROLL and BANK systems and provide a control recommendation to address each of these deficiencies.** Note: The marks will be split equally between each part. **(10 marks)**

Control deficiency	Control recommendation

(Total: 20 marks)

224 POMERANIAN *Walk in the footsteps of a top tutor*

This scenario relates to two requirements.

It is 1 July 20X5. Pomeranian Co is a manufacturer of fizzy drinks and operates across the country. The company's year end is 30 September 20X5. You are an audit supervisor with Poodle Co and you are reviewing extracts from the internal controls documentation in preparation for the forthcoming audit.

Sales

All new customers of Pomeranian Co are required to pass suitable credit checks. Upon passing the credit check, customers are set up in the customer master file and a credit limit is set by the sales director. The credit limits are only then changed when a customer requests an increase.

Customer orders are processed by Pomeranian Co's sales ordering department and goods are despatched from one of the company's warehouses. Sequentially numbered multi-part goods despatch notes (GDNs) are completed and a copy is filed in the warehouse when the goods are despatched. Copies of the GDNs are sent to the sales ordering department and the finance department on a weekly basis.

Pomeranian Co's credit controller is currently on maternity leave for six months and no one has taken over the credit controller's duties. As part of the month-end procedures, a clerk reconciles the trade receivables account to the list of individual customer balances and the reconciliations are only reviewed by the financial controller if there are any unreconciled differences.

Non-current assets

An annual asset expenditure budget is set for each department within Pomeranian Co and is referred to as part of the approval process. Board approval is required for any assets costing more than $0.5m. Asset expenditure below this level can be authorised by the relevant head of department.

Pomeranian Co has a head office and five factories, each of which includes a warehouse. The company has an internal audit (IA) department which is required, over a three-year cycle, to carry out a comparison between all the assets recorded on the non-current asset register to those physically present in each of the company's 11 sites. The programme of visits for the current year means that by the year end, IA will only have completed this comparison at one factory and one warehouse.

Purchases and inventory

Pomeranian Co maintains a perpetual inventory system in which finished goods and raw materials, stored in the warehouses, are counted monthly throughout the year rather than just being counted at the year end. Each of the five warehouse managers are responsible for supervising the inventory counts at their sites and ensuring that the counting teams are following the issued instructions.

The company calculates the cost of its inventory using standard costs, both for internal management reporting and for inclusion in the year-end financial statements. The basis of the standard costs was reviewed by the production department approximately two years ago. The company has a central purchasing department which is based at its head office. All members of this department have full access to the supplier master file data and a monthly exception report of any changes to master file data is automatically generated and then filed by a purchasing clerk.

Sequentially numbered goods received notes (GRNs) are produced by the company's warehouse department when goods are received, a copy of which is promptly sent to the purchasing and finance departments. On receipt of the purchase invoices, the finance clerk matches the invoices to the relevant purchase order and then passes the documents to the finance director for authorisation prior to input.

Required:

In order to obtain sufficient and appropriate audit evidence, an auditor cannot place complete reliance on an entity's system of internal control. In addition to performing tests of controls, auditors must always perform some substantive procedures due to the limitations of internal control.

(a) **Describe the LIMITATIONS of internal control.**

Note: You do not need to refer to the scenario to answer this requirement. **(4 marks)**

(b) **Identify and explain EIGHT deficiencies in Pomeranian Co's internal control system and provide a control recommendation to address each of these deficiencies.**

Note: The marks will be split equally between each part. **(16 marks)**

Control deficiency	Control recommendation

(Total: 20 marks)

225 CASTLE COURIER *Walk in the footsteps of a top tutor*

This scenario relates to five requirements.

It is 1 July 20X5. You are an audit supervisor of Apple & Co and are in the process of reviewing extracts of the systems documentation which has been completed on the payroll cycle of Castle Courier Co, as well as preparing the audit programmes for the forthcoming final audit for the year ending 30 September 20X5. Castle Courier Co is a package delivery company which operates from a large distribution centre.

Payroll

The company employs 200 staff of whom 120 of these staff are delivery drivers. All staff work a standard eight-hour shift each day and are paid monthly. All staff members are required to clock-in and out using a sequentially numbered key card which contains their unique employee number and name. Sequence checks on the key cards and the data recorded in the clocking-in system are carried out by the human resources (HR) supervisor on a regular basis. The clocking-in process is monitored by a camera on entry to the distribution centre and weekly checks are carried out by the HR department who review the video footage to ensure that no staff member clocks-in for someone else. Recordings are kept in date order in the HR department and logged on a spreadsheet together with the name of the person who has reviewed the footage.

The clocking-in system is directly linked to the payroll system and information regarding the hours worked by the staff is automatically transferred into the payroll system. The payroll system then automatically calculates gross pay, deductions and net pay. The payroll clerk confirms that the transfer of hours and calculations has been done correctly by recalculating a sample of employees' gross to net pay. A payroll supervisor then reviews this check which is evidenced by the supervisor's signature.

All staff are entitled to 22 days holiday a year. Employees are paid for any holiday which has not been taken at the end of the year. Department managers are required to approve all holiday requests by authorising employees' holiday forms, however this does not always occur.

The payroll system is password-protected, and the password is changed on a monthly basis by the payroll manager using a random password generator.

Once the payroll has been agreed by the payroll supervisor, the payroll clerk provides details of the net pay due to each employee to the financial controller who then prepares and authorises the bank transfer to be paid to the employees' bank accounts.

Each month, as part of the month-end procedures, the finance director undertakes a payroll account reconciliation and investigates any differences to ensure that the payroll figures have been posted into the accounting records correctly.

The company's HR department is responsible for processing starters and leavers using a joiner/leaver form to notify the payroll department of the change. On receipt of the joiner/leaver form a payroll clerk updates the payroll system. An edit report is generated which records the changes made but this report is not reviewed. Two staff members from the HR department have been absent for some time due to illness. As a result, the operations manager has processed six newly recruited temporary delivery drivers and instructed the payroll department to set up the new employees.

Delivery drivers are sometimes required to work overtime, particularly in busy periods. Where overtime is necessary, the operations manager has to authorise overtime in excess of five hours per week.

Some temporary delivery drivers receive their wages in cash. The delivery driver collects their pay packet from the finance department when it is ready. The member of staff in the finance department will ask for the delivery driver's name to check that there is a pay packet prepared and, if there is, they provide the delivery driver with their pay packet.

The company has to pay employment taxes to the tax authority by the end of each month. Each month the payroll supervisor calculates the total liability due to the tax authority and this is then passed to the financial controller who checks the calculations prior to the payment being made.

To encourage delivery drivers to make deliveries on time, the company pays a discretionary bonus to delivery drivers on a quarterly basis. The operations manager decides on the bonus to be paid and notifies the payroll clerk in writing every quarter as to who will receive a bonus and how much it will be.

As delivery drivers spend the majority of their day driving the company vehicles, they are required by law to take a 15-minute paid break in the morning and afternoon, as well as a one-hour lunch break. The company has no way of monitoring the length of these breaks as the delivery drivers are out on deliveries.

Required:

(a) **Describe the following methods for documenting internal control systems and for each explain a DISADVANTAGE of using this method.**

Note: The marks will be split equally between each part. **(4 marks)**

	Description	**Disadvantage**
Narrative notes		
Internal control questionnaires		

(b) **(i)** **Identify and explain FOUR DIRECT CONTROLS in Castle Courier Co's payroll system which the auditor may seek to place reliance on, and**

(ii) **Describe a TEST OF CONTROL the auditor should perform to assess if each of these direct controls is operating effectively.**

Note: The marks will be split equally between each part. **(8 marks)**

Direct control	**Test of control**

(c) **Identify and explain SIX DEFICIENCIES in Castle Courier Co's payroll system and provide a control recommendation to address each of these deficiencies.**

Note: The marks will be split equally between each part. **(12 marks)**

Control deficiency	**Control recommendation**

(d) **Describe substantive procedures the auditor should perform to obtain sufficient and appropriate audit evidence in relation to Castle Courier Co's payroll expense.** **(6 marks)**

(Total: 30 marks)

226 SWIFT *Walk in the footsteps of a top tutor*

This scenario relates to four requirements.

It is 1 July 20X5. Swift Co prints books which it sells online and supplies to retailers across the country. The company's year end is 30 September 20X5. You are an audit supervisor with Toucan & Co, preparing the draft audit programmes and reviewing the internal controls documentation in preparation for the interim audit.

Payroll

Swift Co employs factory staff who are required to work a standard shift of eight hours per day. No staff members are required to work overtime. All staff members are paid monthly by bank transfer. The company has a human resources (HR) department which is responsible for setting up all new joiners and a payroll department which processes wages and salaries.

When a new employee joins the company, HR completes a joiners' form which includes a unique employee number for each new employee. The joiners' form is then sent to the payroll department so that the new employee can be set up for payment. The unique employee number must be entered into the payroll system before the employee can be added to payroll. On a monthly basis, an exception report relating to changes to the payroll standing data is produced and reviewed by the payroll manager who evidences this review.

Employee hours worked and their hourly wage rates are preset into the system, which automatically calculates the gross and net pay along with relevant deductions and generates employee payslips. The payroll supervisor selects a sample of the payslips, reperforms the gross to net pay calculations and investigates any discrepancies. The sampled payslips are then signed as evidence of this review.

Purchases

The company has a purchasing department based at its head office. When raw materials are required, the production supervisors submit a requisition form to the purchasing department. A multi-part purchase order is generated and the purchasing manager authorises all orders up to $5,000. Orders over $5,000 are authorised by the purchasing director.

The warehouse team processes goods received from suppliers. They agree the goods received to the purchase order and check the quantity and the quality of the goods. On completion of those checks a goods received note (GRN) is produced. One copy of the GRN is then signed and filed in the warehouse. Another copy of the GRN is sent to the finance department.

A payables ledger clerk logs the purchase invoices in batches of 20 into the detailed purchase listing utilising control totals. A batch control sheet is completed for each set of 20 invoices and the clerk signs to evidence the checks undertaken.

Supplier statement reconciliations are performed on a monthly basis. All differences are fully investigated, and the financial controller reviews these reconciliations. Invoices are paid in accordance with the supplier's credit terms. The finance director authorises the bank transfer payment list for suppliers having first agreed the amounts to be paid to supporting documentation and having reviewed the list for duplicate payments.

Required:

Auditors are required to document a company's accounting and internal control systems as part of their audit process. Three methods available for documenting internal control systems are narrative notes, flowcharts and questionnaires.

(a) For each of the THREE methods identified in the table:

(i) Describe the method for documenting internal control systems, and

(ii) Explain an ADVANTAGE of using this method.

Note: The marks will be split equally between each part. **(6 marks)**

	Description	**Advantage**
Narrative notes		
Flowcharts		
Questionnaires		

(b) In respect of the internal control system of Swift Co:

(i) Identify and explain SEVEN DIRECT CONTROLS which the auditor may seek to place reliance on, and

(ii) Describe a TEST OF CONTROL the auditor should perform to assess if each of these direct controls is operating effectively.

Note: The marks will be split equally between each part. **(14 marks)**

Direct control	**Test of control**

(Total: 20 marks)

227 SNOWDON *Walk in the footsteps of a top tutor*

This scenario relates to four requirements.

It is 1 July 20X5. You are an audit supervisor with Rocky & Co, reviewing extracts from the internal controls documentation in preparation for the interim audit of Snowdon Co. The company's year end is 30 September 20X5. The company provides training services for individuals looking to become qualified engineers. Snowdon Co's customers are the employers that send their employees for training on a weekly basis. Snowdon Co runs classes in its 45 training centres across the country.

The company has a small internal audit (IA) department, which has experienced significant staff shortages and is currently under-resourced. This has resulted in a reduction in their programme of work for the year in many areas.

Non-current assets

Snowdon Co's training centres are either owned by the company or are held under a long-term lease. The company also has a head office and central warehouse for storage of training materials. Each training centre is set up as a separate department and is given an annual asset expenditure budget but some departments have already significantly exceeded their annual budgets.

When new equipment is acquired, the finance department classifies the expenditure between assets and expenses, noting the classification on the purchase order. The classification is made with reference to guidelines established by the finance director, who sample checks that the expenditure allocation has been correctly applied.

Part of the work which Snowdon Co's IA department is required to carry out is a comparison of the assets per the non-current asset register and those physically present in each of the centres. This year's programme of visits, which has been planned and carried out on the same basis as previous years, means that by the year end IA will only have visited the four largest centres and five of the other centres randomly selected.

Payroll

Snowdon Co has a human resources (HR) department, responsible for setting up all new joiners. Pre-printed joiners' forms, which require all necessary data, are completed by HR for new employees and once verified, a copy is sent to the payroll department so that the employee can be set up for payment. The joiner's form includes the staff member's assigned employee number and the system requires the new joiner's employee number to be entered before they can be added to payroll.

All members of the payroll department can amend employees' standing data in the payroll system as they have access to the password, which is changed by the payroll director on a quarterly basis.

On a monthly basis the employees are paid by bank transfer. The senior payroll manager reviews the list of bank payments and agrees this to the payroll records. If any discrepancies are noted, the senior payroll manager always makes the adjustment in the payroll records.

Sales and bank

After passing a credit card check, new customers are set up in the individual customer master file and a credit limit is set by the sales director. The credit limits then remain unchanged in the system unless a review is requested by the customer.

Each new customer is allocated a client services manager from Snowdon Co, who is responsible for managing the customer relationship and maximising sales. Standard credit terms for customers are 30 days and on a monthly basis sales invoices which are over 90 days outstanding are notified to the relevant client services manager to chase payment directly with the customer.

Every month, the cashier reconciles the bank statements to the bank ledger account. The reconciliations are reviewed by the financial controller, who also investigates all reconciling items and evidences that review by way of a signature.

Required:

Auditors are required, under ISA 265 *Communicating Deficiencies in Internal Control to Those Charged with Governance and Management*, to communicate in writing to those charged with governance any significant deficiencies in internal control.

(a) **Describe FOUR matters the auditor may consider in determining whether a deficiency in internal control is significant. (4 marks)**

(b) In respect of the internal control system of Snowdon Co:

(i) Identify and explain THREE DIRECT CONTROLS on which the auditor may seek to place reliance, and

(ii) Describe a TEST OF CONTROL the auditor should perform to assess if each of these direct controls is operating effectively.

Note: The marks will be split equally between each part. **(6 marks)**

Direct control	Test of control

(c) Identify and explain FIVE DEFICIENCIES in Snowdon Co's internal control system and provide a control recommendation to address each of these deficiencies.

Note: The marks will be split equally between each part. **(10 marks)**

Control deficiency	Control recommendation

(Total: 20 marks)

228 AMBERJACK *Walk in the footsteps of a top tutor*

This scenario relates to three requirements.

It is 1 July 20X5. You are an audit manager of Pinfish & Co and you are reviewing extracts of the documentation describing Amberjack Co's sales and despatch system following completion of the interim audit. Amberjack Co manufactures and distributes car tyres to a wide customer base both in its country and across the rest of the continent. Its year end was 30 April 20X5.

Amberjack Co has grown in size over the previous 18 months. All new customers undergo credit checks prior to being accepted and credit limits are subsequently set by the receivables ledger clerks who record the new customer details, assign a unique customer number and set credit limits in the master data file.

The company's credit controller is currently on secondment to the internal audit department for six months and no replacement has been appointed.

Customers wishing to order goods, telephone the company's sales order department and provide their unique account details. Sequentially numbered four-part sales orders are generated for all orders, after checking available inventory levels. One copy is retained by the sales ordering team to enable them to monitor progress of the sales orders, one copy is sent to the customer, one copy is sent to one of the company's warehouses for despatch and the final copy is sent to the finance department. Upon despatch, a three-part goods despatch note (GDN) is completed which is assigned the same sequential number as the order number; one copy is sent with the goods, one remains with the warehouse and one is sent to the finance department.

Due to the recent growth of the company, and as there are a large number of sales invoices, additional temporary staff members have been appointed to help the sales clerks to produce the sales invoices. The sales invoices are prepared using quantities from the GDNs and prices from the authorised sales prices list, which is updated every six months.

This year, in line with its main competitors, the company offered a 10% discount on all orders placed during one weekend in late November. Where a discount has been given, this has to be manually entered by the sales clerks onto the sequentially numbered invoice.

Customer statements are no longer being generated and sent out. The company only reconciles the trade receivables account at the end of April in order to verify the year-end balance.

Required:

(a) List FOUR limitations of internal control components. **(4 marks)**

(b) As the external auditor of Amberjack Co, write a report to management in respect of the sales and despatch system described which:

(i) Identifies and explains SEVEN deficiencies in the sales and despatch system and recommends a control to address each of these deficiencies, and

(ii) Includes a covering letter

Note: The marks will be split equally between each part. Two marks will be awarded within this requirement for the covering letter. **(16 marks)**

Control deficiency	Control recommendation

(Total: 20 marks)

229 FREESIA *Walk in the footsteps of a top tutor*

This scenario relates to seven requirements.

(a) Auditors are required to document a company's accounting and internal control systems as part of their audit process. Two methods available for documenting internal control systems are narrative notes and questionnaires.

Required:

For each of the two methods, NARRATIVE NOTES and QUESTIONNAIRES:

(i) Describe the method for documenting internal control systems; and

(ii) Explain an ADVANTAGE of using this method.

Note: The marks will be split equally between each part. **(4 marks)**

	Description	Advantage
Narrative notes		
Questionnaires		

It is 1 July 20X5. You are an audit supervisor with Zinnia & Co, preparing the draft audit programmes and reviewing extracts from the internal controls documentation in preparation for the interim audit. Freesia Co is a company listed on a stock exchange. It manufactures furniture which it supplies to a wide range of retailers across the region. The company has an internal audit (IA) department and the company's year end was 30 June 20X5.

Sales

Freesia Co generates revenue through visits by its sales staff to customers' premises. Sales ledger clerks, who work at head office, carry out credit checks on new customers prior to being accepted and then set their credit limits. Sales staff visit retail customers' sites personally and orders are completed using a four-part pre-printed order form. One copy is left with the customer, a second copy is returned to the sales ordering department, the third is sent to the warehouse and the fourth to the finance department at head office. Each sales order number is based on the sales person's own identification number in order to facilitate monitoring of sales staff performance.

Retail customers are given payment terms of 30 days and most customers choose to pay their invoices by bank transfer. Each day Lily Shah, a finance clerk, posts the bank transfer receipts from the bank statements to the bank ledger account and updates the list of individual customers. On a monthly basis, Lily performs the bank reconciliation.

Purchases and inventory

Receipts of raw materials and goods from suppliers are processed by the warehouse team at head office, who agree the delivery to the purchase order, check the quantity and quality of goods and complete a sequentially numbered goods received note (GRN). The GRNs are sent to the finance department daily. On receipt of the purchase invoice from the supplier, Camilla Brown, the purchase ledger clerk, matches it to the GRN and order and the three documents are sent for authorisation by the appropriate individual. Once authorised, the purchase invoices are logged into the suppliers' individual accounts by Camilla, who utilises document count controls to ensure the correct number of invoices has been input.

The company values its inventory using standard costs, both for internal management reporting and for inclusion in the year-end financial statements. The basis of the standard costs was reviewed approximately 18 months ago.

Payroll

Freesia Co employs a mixture of factory staff, who work a standard shift of eight hours a day, and administration and sales staff who are salaried. All staff are paid monthly by bank transfer. Occasionally, overtime is required of factory staff. Where this occurs, details of overtime worked per employee is collated and submitted to the payroll department by a production clerk. The payroll department pays this overtime in the month it occurs. At the end of each quarter, the company's payroll department sends overtime reports which detail the amount of overtime worked to the production director for their review.

Freesia Co's payroll package produces a list of payments per employee which links into the bank system to produce a list of automatic bank transfer payments. The finance director reviews the total to be paid on the list of automatic payments and compares this to the total payroll amount to be paid for the month per the payroll records. If any issues arise, then the automatic bank transfer can be manually changed by the finance director.

Required:

(b) In respect of the internal controls of Freesia Co:

(i) Identify and explain SIX deficiencies

(ii) Recommend a control to address each of these deficiencies, and

(iii) Describe a TEST OF CONTROL the external auditors should perform to assess if each of these controls, if implemented, is operating effectively to reduce the identified deficiency.

Note: The marks will be split equally between each part. **(18 marks)**

Control deficiency	Control recommendation	Test of control

Freesia Co deducts employment taxes from its employees' wages and salaries on a monthly basis and pays these to the local taxation authorities in the following month. At the year end, the financial statements will contain an accrual for employment tax payable.

Required:

(c) Describe the substantive procedures the auditor should perform to obtain sufficient and appropriate audit evidence in respect of Freesia Co's year-end accrual for employment tax payable. (4 marks)

The listing rules of the stock exchange require compliance with corporate governance principles and the directors of Freesia Co are confident that they are following best practice in relation to this. However, the chair recently received correspondence from a shareholder, who is concerned that the company is not fully compliant. The company's finance director has therefore requested a review of the company's compliance with corporate governance principles.

Freesia Co has been listed for over eight years and its board comprises four executive and four independent non-executive directors (NEDs), excluding the chair. An audit committee comprised of the NEDs and the finance director meets each quarter to review the company's internal controls.

The directors' remuneration is set by the finance director. NEDs are paid a fixed fee for their services and executive directors are paid an annual salary as well as a significant annual bonus based on Freesia Co's profits. The company's chair does not have an executive role and therefore has sole responsibility for liaising with the shareholders and answering any of their questions.

Required:

(d) Describe TWO corporate governance deficiencies faced by Freesia Co and provide a recommendation to address each deficiency to ensure compliance with corporate governance principles.

Note: The marks will be split equally between each part. **(4 marks)**

Deficiency	Recommendation

(Total: 30 marks)

230 CAMOMILE *Walk in the footsteps of a top tutor*

This scenario relates to three requirements.

(a) ISA 260 *Communication with Those Charged with Governance* provides guidance to auditors in relation to communicating with those charged with governance on matters arising from the audit of an entity's financial statements.

Required:

(i) **Explain why it is important for auditors to communicate throughout the audit with those charged with governance; and**

(ii) **Identify TWO examples of matters which the auditor may communicate to those charged with governance.**

Note: The marks will be split equally between each part. **(4 marks)**

Camomile Co operates six restaurant and bar venues which are open seven days a week. The company's year end is 31 July 20X5. It is 1 July 20X5. You are the audit supervisor reviewing the internal controls documentation in relation to the cash receipts and payments system in preparation for the interim audit, which will involve visiting a number of the venues as well as the head office. The company has a small internal audit (IA) department based at head office.

The purchasing department based at the company's head office is responsible for ordering food and beverages for all six venues. In addition, each venue has a petty cash float of $400, held in the safe, which is used for the purchase of sundry items. When making purchases of sundries, employees are required to obtain the funds from the restaurant manager, purchase the sundries and return any excess money and the receipt to the manager. At any time the petty cash sum held and receipts should equal the float of $400 but it has been noted by the company's IA department that on some occasions this has not been the case.

Each venue has five cash tills (cash registers) to take payments from customers. Three are located in the bar area and two in the restaurant area. Customers can pay using either cash or a credit card and for any transaction either the credit card vouchers or cash are placed in the till by the employee operating the till. To speed up the payment process, each venue has a specific log on code which can be used to access all five tills and is changed every two weeks.

At each venue at the end of the day, the tills are closed down by the restaurant manager who counts the total cash in all five tills and the sum of the credit card vouchers and these totals are reconciled with the aggregated daily readings of sales taken from each till. Any discrepancies are noted on the daily sales sheet. The daily sales sheet records the sales per the tills, the cash counted and the total credit card vouchers as well as any discrepancies. These sheets are scanned and emailed to the cashier at head office at the end of each week.

Approximately 30% of Camomile Co's customers pay in cash for their restaurant or bar bills. Cash is stored in the safe at each venue on a daily basis after the sales reconciliation has been undertaken. Each safe is accessed via a key which the restaurant manager has responsibility for. Each key is stored in a drawer of the manager's desk when not being used. Cash is transferred to the bank via daily collection by a security company.

The security company provides a receipt for the sums collected, and these receipts are immediately forwarded to head office. The credit card company remits the amounts due directly into Camomile Co's bank account within two days of the transaction.

At head office, on receipt of the daily sales sheets and security company receipts, the cashier agrees the cash transferred by the security company has been banked for all venues and also agrees the cash per the daily sales sheets to bank deposit slips and to the bank statements. The cashier updates the bank ledger account with the cash banked and details of the credit card vouchers from the daily sales sheets. On a monthly basis, the credit card company sends a statement of all credit card receipts from the six venues which is filed by the cashier.

Every two months, the cashier reconciles the bank statements to the bank ledger account. The reconciliations are reviewed by the financial controller who evidences the review by signature and these are filed in the accounts department. All purchases of food and beverages for the venues are paid by bank transfer. The finance director is given the total amount of the payments list to authorise at the relevant payment dates.

Required:

(b) Identify and explain EIGHT DEFICIENCIES in Camomile Co's cash receipts and payments system and provide a control recommendation to address each of these deficiencies.

Note: The marks will be split equally between each part. **(16 marks)**

Control deficiency	Control recommendation

(Total: 20 marks)

231 RASPBERRY *Walk in the footsteps of a top tutor*

Answer debrief

This scenario relates to five requirements.

It is 1 July 20X5. You are an audit manager of Grapefruit & Co, the auditor of Raspberry Co. The interim audit has been completed and you are reviewing the documentation describing Raspberry Co's payroll system. Raspberry Co operates an electric power station, which produces electricity 24 hours a day, seven days a week. The company's year end was 30 June 20X5.

Systems notes – payroll

Raspberry Co employs over 250 people and approximately 70% of the employees work in production at the power station. There are three shifts every day with employees working eight hours each. The production employees are paid weekly in cash. The remaining 30% of employees work at the head office in non-production roles and are paid monthly by bank transfer.

The company has a human resources (HR) department, responsible for setting up all new joiners. Pre-printed forms are completed by HR for all new employees and, once verified, a copy is sent to the payroll department for the employee to be set up for payment. This form includes the staff member's employee number and payroll cannot set up new joiners without this information.

To encourage staff to attend work on time for all shifts, Raspberry Co introduced a discretionary bonus, paid every three months, for production staff. The production supervisors determine the amounts to be paid and notify the payroll department. This quarterly bonus is entered into the system by a clerk and each entry is checked by a senior clerk for input errors prior to processing. The senior clerk signs the bonus listing as evidence of undertaking this review.

Production employees are issued with clock cards and are required to swipe their cards at the beginning and end of their shift. This process is supervised by security staff 24 hours a day. Each card identifies the employee number and links into the hours worked report produced by the payroll system, which automatically calculates the gross and net pay along with relevant deductions. These calculations are not checked.

In addition to tax deductions from pay, some employees' wages are reduced for such items as repayments of student loans owed to the central government. All employers have a statutory obligation to remit funds on a timely basis and to maintain accounting records which reconcile with annual loan statements sent by the government to employers. At Raspberry Co student loan deduction forms are completed by the relevant employee and payments are made directly to the government until the employee notifies HR that the loan has been repaid in full.

On a quarterly basis, exception reports relating to changes to the payroll standing data are produced and reviewed by the payroll director.

No overtime is worked by employees. Employees are entitled to take 28 holiday days annually. Holiday request forms are required to be completed and authorised by relevant line managers, however, this does not always occur.

On a monthly basis, for employees paid by bank transfer, the senior payroll manager reviews the list of bank payments and agrees this to the payroll records prior to authorising the payment. If any errors are noted, the payroll senior manager amends the records.

For production employees paid in cash, the necessary amount of cash is delivered weekly from the bank by a security company. Two members of the payroll department produce the pay packets, one is responsible for preparing them and the other checks the finished pay packets. Both members of staff are required to sign the weekly payroll listing on completion of this task. The pay packets are then delivered to the production supervisors, who distribute them to employees at the end of the employees' shift, as they know each member of their production team.

Monthly management accounts are produced which detail variances between budgeted amounts and actual. Revenue and key production costs are detailed, however, as there are no overtime costs, wages and salaries are not analysed.

Required:

(a) In respect of the payroll system of Raspberry Co:

(i) Identify and explain FIVE DIRECT CONTROLS which the auditor may seek to place reliance on; and

(ii) Describe a TEST OF CONTROL the auditor should perform to assess if each of these direct controls is operating effectively.

Note: The marks will be split equally between each part. **(10 marks)**

Direct control	Test of control

(b) **Identify and explain FIVE DEFICIENCIES in Raspberry Co's payroll system and provide a control recommendation to address each of these deficiencies.**

Note: The marks will be split equally between each part. **(10 marks)**

Control deficiency	Control recommendation

The finance director is interested in establishing an internal audit department (IAD). In the company the financial director previously worked for the IAD carried out inventory counts, however, as this is not relevant for Raspberry Co, has asked for guidance on what other assignments an IAD could be asked to perform.

Required:

(c) Compare and contrast the role of external and internal audit. **(5 marks)**

(d) Describe assignments the internal audit department of Raspberry Co could carry out. **(5 marks)**

(Total: 30 marks)

Calculate your allowed time, allocate the time to the separate parts..............

232 COMET PUBLISHING *Walk in the footsteps of a top tutor*

This scenario relates to six requirements.

It is 1 July 20X5. You are an audit supervisor of Halley & Co and you are reviewing the documentation describing Comet Publishing Co's purchases and payables system in preparation for the interim and final audit for the year ending 30 September 20X5. The company is a retailer of books and has ten stores and a central warehouse, which holds the majority of the company's inventory.

Your firm has audited Comet Publishing Co for a number of years and as such, audit documentation is available from the previous year's file, including internal control flowcharts and detailed purchases and payables system notes. As far as you are aware, Comet Publishing Co's system of internal control has not changed in the last year. The audit manager is keen for the team to utilise existing systems documentation in order to ensure audit efficiency. An extract from the existing systems notes is provided below.

Extract of purchases and payables system

Store managers are responsible for ordering books for their shop. It is not currently possible for store managers to request books from any of the other nine stores. Customers who wish to order books, which are not in stock at the branch visited, are told to contact the other stores directly or visit the company website. As the inventory levels fall in a store, the store manager raises a purchase requisition form, which is sent to the central warehouse. If there is insufficient inventory held, a supplier requisition form is completed and sent to the purchase order clerk, Oli Dancer, for processing. Oli sends any orders above $1,000 for authorisation from the purchasing director.

Receipts of goods from suppliers are processed by the warehouse team, who agree the delivery to the purchase order, checking quantity and quality of goods and complete a sequentially numbered goods received note (GRN). The GRNs are sent to the accounts department every two weeks for processing.

On receipt of the purchase invoice from the supplier, an accounts clerk matches it to the GRN. The invoice is then sent to the purchase ordering clerk, Oli, who processes it for payment. The finance director is given the total amount of the payments list, which is then authorised and bank payments are processed. Due to staff shortages in the accounts department, supplier statement reconciliations are no longer performed.

Required:

(a) **Explain the steps the auditor should take to confirm the accuracy of the purchases and payables flowcharts and systems notes currently held on file. (5 marks)**

(b) **In respect of the purchases and payables system of Comet Publishing Co:**

(i) **Identify and explain FIVE deficiencies**

(ii) **Recommend a control to address each of these deficiencies, and**

(iii) **Describe a TEST OF CONTROL the auditor should perform to assess if each of these controls, if implemented, is operating effectively to reduce the identified deficiency.**

Note: The marks will be split equally between each part. **(15 marks)**

Control deficiency	Control recommendation	Test of control

(c) **Describe substantive procedures the auditor should perform to obtain sufficient and appropriate evidence in relation to Comet Publishing Co's purchases and other expenses. (5 marks)**

Other information – conflict of interest

Halley & Co has recently accepted the audit engagement of a new client, Edmond Co, who is the main competitor of Comet Publishing Co. The finance director of Comet Publishing Co has enquired how Halley & Co will keep information obtained during the audit confidential.

(d) **Explain the safeguards which Halley & Co should implement to ensure that the identified conflict of interest is properly managed. (5 marks)**

(Total: 30 marks)

233 EQUESTRIAN *Walk in the footsteps of a top tutor*

This scenario relates to five requirements.

Equestrian Co manufactures smartphones and tablets. Its main customers are retailers who then sell to the general public. The company's manufacturing is spread across five sites and goods are stored in its nine warehouses located across the country.

It is 1 July 20X5. You are an audit supervisor in Baseball & Co, and in preparation for the forthcoming audit for the year ended 30 June 20X5, you are reviewing the following notes your audit manager has provided you with in relation to the company's internal controls.

Equestrian Co has a small internal audit (IA) department. During the year, IA started a programme of physically verifying the company's assets and comparing the results to the non-current asset register, as this type of reconciliation had not occurred for some time. To date only 15% of assets have had their existence confirmed as IA has experienced significant staff shortages.

During the year, Equestrian Co conducted an extensive reorganisation of its manufacturing process to improve efficiency. Due to the significant number of employee changes required, the human resources department (HR) has been very busy and to ease their workload during this period, the payroll department has assisted by setting up any new employees who have joined the company. In January 20X5, the wage rate paid to employees was increased by the HR director. The change in wage rate was communicated to the payroll department by email.

A new receivables system was introduced in May 20X5 and will continue to be run in parallel with the old system until IA has completed its checks between the two systems. New customers obtained by the sales team are required to undergo a full credit check. On the basis of this, a credit limit is proposed by sales staff and approved by the sales director via email. Credit limits are reviewed every six months by the sales managers and any amendments are made via a credit limit review form which must be authorised by the sales director.

Sales invoices are raised by the accounts department using the approved company price list, which is updated quarterly. Equestrian Co offers discounts to customers depending on the volume of orders, with an approved discount range of 2% to 10%. Discounts must be requested by a sales manager and authorised by the sales director to allow the accounts team to raise an invoice.

Monthly perpetual inventory counts are undertaken at each of the nine warehouses, as a full year-end inventory count is too disruptive for the company. High value items are stored in a secure area in each warehouse. Access is via a four-digit code, which for convenience is the same across all sites. Due to the company's reorganisation programme, some of the monthly inventory counts were not performed.

Bank reconciliations are undertaken monthly by an accounts clerk and details of all reconciling items are included. Where the sum of the reconciling items is significant, the reconciliation is sent to the financial controller for review.

In order to maximise cash balances, the finance director approves all purchase invoices for payment 75 days after receipt of the invoice. Payments are made by the cashier's office by bank transfer. Invoices are stamped as 'paid', and returned to the purchase ledger team who record the payment and file the invoices separately from invoices not yet paid.

Required:

(a) **Describe FOUR different types of control activities as given in ISA 315 (Revised 2019) *Identifying and Assessing the Risks of Material Misstatement* and, for each type, provide an example control a company may implement.** **(4 marks)**

(b) **In respect of the internal control systems of Equestrian Co:**

(i) **Identify and explain FIVE DIRECT CONTROLS which the auditor may seek to place reliance on; and**

(ii) **Describe a TEST OF CONTROL the auditor should perform to assess if each of these direct controls is operating effectively.**

Note: The marks will be split equally between each part. **(10 marks)**

Direct control	Test of control

(c) Identify and explain FIVE deficiencies in Equestrian Co's internal controls and provide a control recommendation to address each of these deficiencies.

Note: The marks will be split equally between each part. **(10 marks)**

Control deficiency	Control recommendation

The directors feel that the internal audit team needs to increase in size and specialist skills are required, but they are unsure whether to recruit more internal auditors, or to outsource the whole function.

(d) Explain the advantages and disadvantages for Equestrian Co of outsourcing the internal audit department. **(6 marks)**

(Total: 30 marks)

234 CATERPILLAR *Walk in the footsteps of a top tutor*

This scenario relates to three requirements.

Caterpillar Co is a clothing retailer which operates 45 stores throughout the country. The company's year end was 30 June 20X5. Caterpillar Co has an internal audit department which has undertaken a number of internal control reviews specifically focusing on cash controls at stores during the year. The reviews have taken place in the largest 20 stores as this is where most issues arise. It is 1 July 20X5. You are an audit supervisor of Woodlouse & Co and are reviewing the internal controls documentation in relation to the cash receipts system in preparation for the interim audit which will involve visiting a number of stores and the head office.

Each of Caterpillar Co's stores has on average three or four cash tills to take customer payments. All employees based at the store are able to use each till and individuals do not have their own log on codes, although employees tend to use the same till each day. Customers can pay using either cash or a credit card and for any transaction either the credit card payment slips or cash are placed in the till by the cashier. Where employees' friends or family members purchase clothes in store, the employee is able to serve them at the till point.

At the end of each day, the tills are closed down with daily readings of sales taken from each till. These are reconciled to the total of the cash in the tills and the credit card payment slips and any discrepancies are noted. Once this reconciliation has taken place, the cash is stored in the shop's safe until it is transferred to the bank via collection by a security company the same day. If the store is low on change for cash payments, a junior sales clerk is sent by a till operator to the bank with money from the till and asked to change it into smaller denominations.

The daily sales readings from the tills along with the cash data and credit card payment data are transferred daily to head office through an interface with the sales and cash receipts records. A clerk oversees that this transfer has occurred for all stores. On a daily basis, the clerk agrees the cash transferred by the security company has been banked in full by agreeing the cash deposit slips to the bank statements, and that the credit card receipts have been received from the credit card company. On a monthly basis, the same clerk reconciles the bank statements to the bank ledger account. The reconciliations are reviewed by the financial controller if there are any unreconciled amounts.

Required:

(a) **State FOUR control objectives of Caterpillar Co's cash receipts system.** **(4 marks)**

(b) **Identify and explain THREE DIRECT CONTROLS in Caterpillar Co's cash receipts system which the auditor may seek to place reliance on and describe a TEST OF CONTROL the auditor should perform to assess if each of these controls is operating effectively.**

Note: The marks will be split equally between each part. **(6 marks)**

Direct control	Test of control

(c) **Identify and explain FIVE DEFICIENCIES in Caterpillar Co's cash receipts system and provide a control recommendation to address each of these deficiencies.**

Note: The marks will be split equally between each part. **(10 marks)**

Control deficiency	Control recommendation

(Total: 20 marks)

235 BRONZE *Walk in the footsteps of a top tutor*

This scenario relates to seven requirements.

It is 1 July 20X5. You are an audit supervisor in Scarlet & Co and you are in the process of reviewing the systems testing completed on the payroll cycle of Bronze Industries Co (Bronze), as well as preparing the audit programmes for the final audit for the year ending 31 July 20X5.

Bronze operate several chemical processing factories across the country, it manufactures 24 hours a day, seven days a week and employees work a standard shift of eight hours and are paid for hours worked at an hourly rate. Factory employees are paid weekly, with approximately 80% being paid by bank transfer and 20% in cash; the different payment methods are due to employee preferences and Bronze has no plans to change these methods. The administration and sales teams are paid monthly by bank transfer.

Factory staff are each issued a sequentially numbered clock card which details their employee number and name. Employees swipe their cards at the beginning and end of the eight-hour shift and this process is not supervised. During the shift employees are entitled to a 30-minute paid break and employees do not need to clock out to access the dining area.

Clock card data links into the payroll system, which automatically calculates gross and net pay along with any statutory deductions. The payroll supervisor for each payment run checks on a sample basis some of these calculations to ensure the system is operating effectively.

Bronze has a human resources department which is responsible for setting up new permanent employees and leavers. Appointments of temporary staff are made by factory production supervisors. Occasionally overtime is required of factory staff, usually to fill gaps caused by staff holidays. Overtime reports which detail the amount of overtime worked are sent out quarterly by the payroll department to production supervisors for their review.

To encourage staff to attend work on time for all shifts Bronze pays a discretionary bonus every six months to factory staff; the production supervisors determine the amounts to be paid. This is communicated in writing by the production supervisors to the payroll department and the bonus is input by a clerk into the system.

For employees paid by bank transfer, the payroll manager reviews the list of the payments and agrees to the payroll records prior to authorising the bank payment. If any changes are required, the payroll manager amends the records. For employees paid in cash, the pay packets are prepared in the payroll department and a clerk distributes them to employees who knows most of these individuals and therefore does not require proof of identity.

Required:

(a) Explain why the auditor needs to obtain an understanding of the components of internal control relevant to the preparation of financial statements. (3 marks)

(b) In respect of the payroll system of Bronze Industries Co:

(i) Identify and explain FIVE internal control deficiencies

(ii) Recommend a control to address each of these deficiencies, and

(iii) Describe a test of control Scarlet & Co should perform to assess if each of these controls is operating effectively.

Note: The marks will be split equally between each part. **(15 marks)**

Control deficiency	Control recommendation	Test of control

(c) Describe substantive ANALYTICAL PROCEDURES you should perform to confirm Bronze Industries Co's payroll expense. (4 marks)

(d) Explain the factors to be considered in determining the suitability of using analytical procedures as a substantive procedure. (4 marks)

The directors of Bronze Industries Co are considering establishing an internal audit department next year, and the finance director has asked what impact, if any, establishing an internal audit department would have on future external audits performed by Scarlet & Co.

Required:

(e) Explain the potential impact on the work performed by Scarlet & Co during the interim and final audits, if Bronze Industries Co was to establish an internal audit department. (4 marks)

(Total: 30 marks)

236 TROMBONE *Walk in the footsteps of a top tutor*

This scenario relates to six requirements.

Trombone Co operates a chain of hotels across the country. Trombone Co employs in excess of 250 permanent employees and its year end is 31 August 20X5. It is 1 July 20X5. You are an audit supervisor of Viola & Co and you are currently reviewing the documentation of Trombone Co's payroll system, detailed below, in preparation for the interim audit.

Trombone Co's payroll system

Permanent employees work a standard number of hours per week as specified in their employment contract. However, when the hotels are busy, staff can be requested by management to work additional shifts as overtime. This can either be paid on a monthly basis or taken as days off.

Employees record any overtime worked and days taken off on weekly overtime sheets which are sent to the payroll department. The standard hours per employee are automatically set up in the system and the overtime sheets are entered by clerks into the payroll package, which automatically calculates the gross and net pay along with relevant deductions.

These calculations are not checked at all. Wages are increased by the rate of inflation each year and the clerks are responsible for updating the standing data in the payroll system.

Employees are paid on a monthly basis by bank transfer for their contracted weekly hours and for any overtime worked in the previous month. If employees choose to be paid for overtime, authorisation is required by department heads of any overtime in excess of 30% of standard hours. If employees choose instead to take days off, the payroll clerks should check back to the 'overtime worked' report; however, this report is not always checked.

The 'overtime worked' report, which details any overtime recorded by employees, is run by the payroll department weekly and emailed to department heads for authorisation. The payroll department asks department heads to only report if there are any errors recorded. Department heads are required to arrange for overtime sheets to be authorised by an alternative responsible official if they are away on annual leave; however, there are instances where this arrangement has not occurred.

The payroll package produces a list of payments per employee; this links into the bank system to produce a list of automatic payments. The finance director reviews the total list of bank transfers and compares this to the total amount to be paid per the payroll records; if any issues arise then the automatic bank transfer can be manually changed by the finance director.

Required:

(a) ISA 315 (Revised 2019) *Identifying and Assessing the Risks of Material Misstatement* describes the five components of an entity's internal control.

Identify and briefly explain the FIVE components of an entity's internal control. **(5 marks)**

(b) In respect of the payroll system of Trombone Co:

(i) Identify and explain FIVE deficiencies

(ii) Recommend a control to address each of these deficiencies, and

(iii) Describe a test of control Viola & Co should perform to assess if each of these controls is operating effectively.

Note: The marks will be split equally between each part. **(15 marks)**

Control deficiency	Control recommendation	Test of control

(c) Describe substantive procedures the auditor should perform at the final audit to obtain sufficient and appropriate evidence in relation to COMPLETENESS and ACCURACY of Trombone Co's payroll expense. (6 marks)

Trombone Co deducts employment taxes from its employees' wages on a monthly basis and pays these to the local taxation authorities in the following month. At the year end the financial statements will contain an accrual for income tax payable on employment income. You will be in charge of auditing this accrual.

Required:

(d) Describe the audit procedures required in respect of the year-end accrual for tax payable on employment income. (4 marks)

(Total: 30 marks)

237 LILY WINDOW GLASS *Walk in the footsteps of a top tutor*

This scenario relates to four requirements.

It is 1 July 20X5. You are an audit senior in Daffodil & Co and you are responsible for the audit of inventory for Lily Window Glass Co (Lily), including attending the year end inventory count.

Lily is a glass manufacturer, which operates from a large production facility, where it undertakes continuous production 24 hours a day, seven days a week. Also on this site are two warehouses, where the company's raw materials and finished goods are stored. Lily's year end is 31 July 20X5.

Lily is finalising the arrangements for the year-end inventory count, which is to be undertaken on 31 July 20X5. The finished windows are stored within 20 aisles of the first warehouse. The second warehouse is for large piles of raw materials, such as sand, used in the manufacture of glass. The following arrangements have been made for the inventory count.

The warehouse manager will supervise the count as due to being the individual who is most familiar with the inventory. There will be ten teams of counters and each team will contain two members of staff, one from the finance and one from the manufacturing department. None of the warehouse staff, other than the manager, will be involved in the count.

Each team will count an aisle of finished goods by counting up and then down each aisle. As this process is systematic, it is not felt that the team will need to flag areas once counted.

Once the team has finished counting an aisle, they will hand in their sheets and be given a set for another aisle of the warehouse. In addition to the above, to assist with the inventory counting, there will be two teams of counters from the internal audit department and they will perform inventory counts.

The count sheets are sequentially numbered, and the product codes and descriptions are printed on them but no quantities. If the counters identify any inventory which is not on their sheets, then they are to enter the item on a separate sheet, which is not numbered. Once all counting is complete, the sequence of the sheets is checked and any additional sheets are also handed in at this stage. All sheets are completed in ink.

Any damaged goods identified by the counters will be too heavy to move to a central location, hence they are to be left where they are but the counter is to make a note on the inventory sheets detailing the level of damage.

As Lily undertakes continuous production, there will continue to be movements of raw materials and finished goods in and out of the warehouse during the count. These will be kept to a minimum where possible.

The level of work-in-progress in the manufacturing plant is to be assessed by the warehouse manager. It is likely that this will be an immaterial balance. In addition, the raw materials quantities are to be approximated by measuring the height and width of the raw material piles. In the past this task has been undertaken by a specialist; however, the warehouse manager feels confident enough to perform this task.

Approximately 10% of the space in the finished goods warehouse has been rented out to third parties with similar operations. For completeness, the counters have been asked to count the inventory for all bays noting the third-party inventories on separate blank inventory sheets, and the finance department will make any necessary adjustments.

Required:

(a) **Identify and explain SEVEN DEFICIENCIES in Lily Window Glass Co's inventory count arrangements and provide a control recommendation to address each of these deficiencies**

Note: The marks will be split equally between each part. **(14 marks)**

Control deficiency	Control recommendation

(b) **Describe the procedures to be undertaken by the auditor DURING the inventory count of Lily Window Glass Co in order to gain sufficient appropriate audit evidence. (6 marks)**

Your manager wishes to utilise automated tools and techniques for the first time for controls and substantive testing in auditing Lily Window Glass Co's inventory.

Required:

(c) **For the audit of the inventory cycle and year-end inventory balance of Lily Window Glass Co, describe FOUR audit procedures that could be carried out using automated tools and techniques. (4 marks)**

(d) **Explain the potential advantages and disadvantages of using automated tools and techniques, including data analytics. (6 marks)**

(Total: 30 marks)

238 PEAR INTERNATIONAL *Walk in the footsteps of a top tutor*

This scenario relates to five requirements.

It is 1 July 20X5. You are an audit supervisor in Apple & Co and you are currently reviewing documentation of Pear International Co's internal control in preparation for the interim audit. Pear International Co (Pear) is a manufacturer of electrical equipment. It has factories across the country and its customer base includes retailers as well as individual consumers, to whom direct sales are made through its website. The company's year end is 30 September 20X5.

Pear's website allows individual consumers to order goods directly, and full payment is taken in advance. The website has some inbuilt validation checks to ensure details such as the customer's postcode and payment card details are in the correct format. Currently, the website is not integrated into the inventory system and inventory levels are not checked at the time orders are placed.

Pear's retail customers undergo credit checks prior to being accepted and credit limits are set accordingly by a sales manager. These customers place their orders through one of the sales team, who decides on sales discount levels. Sales invoices are raised by the accounts department using the GDNs. Monthly customer statements are sent to retail customers by the credit control team and the credit control team follow up on overdue debts as soon as they become overdue.

Goods are despatched via local couriers, however, they do not always record customer signatures as proof that the customer has received the goods. Over the past 12 months there have been customer complaints about the delay between sales orders and receipt of goods. Pear has investigated these and found that, in each case, the sales order had been entered into the sales system correctly but was not forwarded to the despatch department for processing.

Raw materials used in the manufacturing process are purchased from a number of suppliers. Factory supervisors check stock levels on a weekly basis and place a purchase requisition with the centralised procurement department. The requisitions must be authorised by the factory managers before the order is processed by the procurement department. Orders can only be placed with suppliers from the approved supplier list. The list is updated by the procurement team and a new supplier can only be added once the terms of the contract have been agreed and references obtained. As a result of staff changes in the payables ledger department, supplier statement reconciliations are no longer performed. Additionally, changes to supplier details in the supplier master file can be undertaken by payables ledger clerks as well as supervisors.

In the past six months Pear has changed part of its manufacturing process. A significant level of new equipment has been purchased, resulting in considerable levels of plant and equipment becoming surplus to requirements and disposed of during the year. Purchase requisitions for all new equipment have been authorised by production supervisors.

Required:

(a) In respect of the internal controls of Pear International Co:

(i) Identify and explain FIVE DIRECT CONTROLS which the auditor may seek to place reliance on, and

(ii) Describe a TEST OF CONTROL the auditor should perform to assess if each of these direct controls is operating effectively.

Note: The marks will be split equally between each part. **(10 marks)**

Direct control	Test of control

(b) Identify and explain FIVE DEFICIENCIES in Pear International Co's internal controls and provide a control recommendation to address each of these deficiencies.

Note: The marks will be split equally between each part. **(10 marks)**

Control deficiency	Control recommendation

(c) Describe substantive procedures the auditor should perform to obtain sufficient and appropriate audit evidence in respect of additions and disposals of plant and equipment. (6 marks)

The directors of Pear International Co are considering setting up an internal audit function but they are unsure whether it will be beneficial.

(d) Explain the factors to be taken into consideration when assessing the need for an internal audit function. (4 marks)

(Total: 30 marks)

SUBSTANTIVE PROCEDURES, COMPLETION AND REPORTING

239 LATTE CO *Walk in the footsteps of a top tutor*

This scenario relates to four requirements.

It is 1 July 20X5. You are an audit supervisor with Macchiato & Co currently working on the final audit of Latte Co, a supplier of catering equipment, for the year ended 31 March 20X5. Latte Co is a listed company with total assets of $22.7m and profit before tax of $3.2m. You are responsible for finalising the audit fieldwork in respect of the following:

Trade receivables

Latte Co's net trade receivables balance is $5.1m which comprises trade receivables of $5.5m and an allowance for receivables of $0.4m at 31 March 20X5 (20X4: receivables of $4.4m and an allowance of $0.6m). As a result of a lack of responses in prior years, the audit engagement partner has decided that a trade receivables circularisation will not be performed this year. Instead, the adut engagement partner has asked you to identify alternative substantive procedures to confirm the existence and valuation of trade receivables.

Provision for legal claim

A former employee of Latte Co has made a claim for $0.6m against the company in respect of an injury suffered while operating equipment which did not have the correct safety equipment installed. The directors have recognised a provision of $0.25m in the current year financial statements which is the maximum amount they are willing to pay to settle the claim.

Bank loan

Latte Co obtained a new three-year bank loan of $1m on 1 October 20X4 to finance the purchase of new equipment. The loan attracts an interest rate of 5%. Under the terms of the loan, 10 payments of $105,000, comprising capital and interest, are due to be made on a quarterly basis commencing 31 December 20X4. Latte Co did not make the quarterly payment due on 31 March 20X5 until 15 April 20X5.

Requirements

(a) **Describe substantive procedures the auditor should perform to obtain sufficient and appropriate evidence in relation to the EXISTENCE and VALUATION of Latte Co's trade receivables.** **(6 marks)**

(b) **Describe substantive procedures the auditor should perform to obtain sufficient and appropriate evidence in relation to Latte Co's provision for the legal claim.** **(4 marks)**

(c) **Describe substantive procedures the auditor should perform to obtain sufficient and appropriate evidence in relation to Latte Co's bank loan.** **(5 marks)**

It is now 12 August 20X5. During the audit of the legal claim against Latte Co, the audit team concluded that a provision of $0.6m should be recognised, rather than the $0.25m originally provided for. A significant increase in the provision was required, in order to comply with IAS 37 *Provisions, Contingent Liabilities and Contingent Assets*. The audit engagement partner has determined that the provision is now appropriately valued and that this issue should be communicated as a key audit matter (KAM) in accordance with ISA 701 *Communicating Key Audit Matters in the Independent Auditor's Report*.

(d) **(i)** **Describe the factors which the audit engagement partner would have considered in determining that this issue is a KAM; and**

(ii) **Describe the content of the KAM section of the auditor's report for Latte Co.** **(5 marks)**

(Total: 20 marks)

240 HERON *Walk in the footsteps of a top tutor*

This scenario relates to five requirements.

It is 1 July 20X5. You are an audit supervisor of Owl & Co, responsible for the final audit of Heron Co for the year ended 31 May 20X5 which is due to commence shortly. Heron Co is a manufacturer of colour dyes used in the textile industry. Its draft financial statements show total assets of $65.4m and profit before tax of $8.9m. The following matters have been brought to your attention:

Additions to plant and equipment

Heron Co incurred significant asset (capital) expenditure in the year as it purchased a new manufacturing line. All costs incurred in the purchase and installation of the manufacturing line have been recognised as plant and equipment within non-current assets. The amount capitalised of $3.6m includes the purchase price of $2.7m, delivery and installation costs of $0.3m, refundable purchase tax of $0.5m and $0.1m incurred in training staff on how to operate the new plant and equipment.

In addition to the $3.6m capitalised, Heron Co incurred costs of $0.2m testing the quality of the dye being produced by the new manufacturing line. The finance director has also capitalised this cost within plant and equipment. Heron Co started using the new manufacturing line in December 20X4 and it has a useful life of eight years.

Bank balances

The bank figure included in Heron Co's draft financial statements comprises four bank account balances: an overdraft of $2.4m which is the company's main current account and a total of $0.6m relating to three savings accounts. The finance director has informed the audit team that all four accounts have been reconciled as at the year end.

Provision for legal claim

Parrot Co, a customer of Heron Co, has made a claim for $0.8m against the company. Parrot Co is claiming that a customised yellow dye purchased from Heron Co in March 20X5 was substandard and that, as a result, Parrot Co had to scrap a large batch of clothes it was producing. The finance director has included a provision of $0.6m in the draft financial statements for the year ended 31 May 20X5 due to the belief that this is the likely sum to be paid to settle the claim. The yellow dye was not sold to any other customers and Heron Co does not hold any inventory of the dye at the year end.

Required:

(a) **Describe substantive procedures the auditor should perform to obtain sufficient and appropriate audit evidence in relation to the matters identified regarding Heron Co's ADDITIONS to plant and equipment.** **(5 marks)**

(b) **Describe substantive procedures the auditor should perform to obtain sufficient and appropriate audit evidence in relation to Heron Co's bank balances.** **(5 marks)**

(c) **Describe substantive procedures the auditor should perform to obtain sufficient and appropriate audit evidence in relation to Heron Co's provision for the legal claim.** **(5 marks)**

It is now 28 August 20X5 and the audit of Heron Co is almost complete. The auditor's report is due to be signed shortly. The following matter has been brought to your attention:

On 14 July 20X5, Sparrow Co, a customer of Heron Co with a receivables balance of $692,000 at 31 May 20X5, notified Heron Co that it was experiencing significant cash flow difficulties and would be unable to make any payments for the foreseeable future. The finance director of Heron Co believes that as Sparrow Co is a long-standing customer and has been trading for many years, the outstanding amount will be received in full in due course, and has therefore not adjusted the receivable balance in the financial statements for the year ended 31 May 20X5.

(d) (i) Explain whether the 20X5 financial statements of Heron Co require amendment in relation to the outstanding balance with Sparrow Co; and

(ii) Describe TWO audit procedures which should be performed in order to form a conclusion on any required amendment. (5 marks)

(Total: 20 marks)

241 PACIFIC *Walk in the footsteps of a top tutor*

This scenario relates to four requirements.

It is 1 July 20X5. Pacific Co operates a chain of 14 retail stores across the country, selling its own range of cosmetic products. You are the audit supervisor of Caribbean & Co and the final audit is due to commence shortly for the year ended 31 May 20X5. Draft financial statements show revenue of $45.2m and profit before tax of $4.1m. The following three matters have been brought to your attention:

Trade payables and accruals

As part of the year-end process, Pacific Co's payables ledger is closed at the end of the day on 31 May. Any invoices received after this date, relating to goods received before the year end, are recorded in the goods received not invoiced (GRNI) accrual.

This year, the payables ledger was kept open in error until 1 June 20X5. As a result, a significant payment run for suppliers made by bank transfer on 1 June 20X5 was recorded in the 20X5 payables ledger. The finance director has confirmed that the year-end trade payables balance was corrected using a journal.

Provision for legal claims

In March 20X5, a number of claims were received by the company from customers who suffered severe allergic reactions after using one of Pacific Co's products. They allege that the product ingredients listed on the label were incorrect. An internal investigation has suggested that one batch of the product had been incorrectly labelled. The finance director has recognised a provision in the draft financial statements of $0.5m.

Revenue

The company's revenue has increased by $3.9m during the year (20X4: total revenue $41.3m). The management accounts record information for revenue by key product line, of which there are eight, and also by store. In August 20X4, Pacific Co opened a new retail store, bringing the number of stores to 14. In addition, it launched a number of new products across most of the key product lines.

Required:

(a) Describe substantive procedures the auditor should perform to obtain sufficient and appropriate audit evidence in relation to the COMPLETENESS of Pacific Co's trade payables and accruals. (5 marks)

(b) Describe substantive procedures the auditor should perform to obtain sufficient and appropriate audit evidence in relation to Pacific Co's provision for the legal claims. (6 marks)

(c) Describe SUBSTANTIVE ANALYTICAL procedures the auditor should perform to obtain sufficient and appropriate audit evidence in relation to Pacific Co's revenue. (4 marks)

During the audit of Pacific Co's provision for the legal claims, the audit team gathered audit evidence showing that the provision should amount to $0.8m. The finance director has suggested that no adjustment is made in the 20X5 financial statements due to the belief that $0.5m is a reasonable estimate and that the difference of $0.3m is not material.

(d) Discuss the issue and describe the impact on the auditor's report, if any, should this issue remain unresolved. (5 marks)

(Total: 20 marks)

242 SPINACH *Walk in the footsteps of a top tutor*

This scenario relates to five requirements.

It is 1 July 20X5. You are an audit supervisor with Sweetcorn & Co and are responsible for the final audit of your existing client Spinach Co, which is due to commence in September 20X5. Spinach Co is a listed company which manufactures garden furniture. Its draft financial statements for the year ending 31 July 20X5 show revenue of $65.1m and profit before tax of $18.2m. The following matters have been brought to your attention:

Revenue

Spinach Co's revenue is generated through sales to individual customers via its website and also to wholesale customers such as garden centres and stores. Price increases in line with inflation were applied across all products in September 20X4. Spinach Co successfully launched three new product lines in February 20X5.

Wholesale customers place their orders on credit via Spinach Co's sales ordering department. Individual customers place their order online and immediately pay the full amount owing. The goods are normally despatched within seven days of the customer placing the order.

Inventory count

Spinach Co is forecasting a year-end inventory balance of $9.3m. The company undertakes continuous production and full year-end inventory counts will be carried out on 31 July 20X5. Spinach Co's raw materials and finished goods inventory are stored in its six warehouses which are located across the country. The company has one factory site and it is expected that there will be no significant work-in-progress held at the year end. Each inventory count will be supervised by a member of Spinach Co's internal audit department. There will be no movements of goods in and out of the warehouses during the counts. Sweetcorn & Co will only attend some of the counts.

The largest warehouse is located at the factory site and around 10% of this warehouse space is rented out to a third-party company, which stores its inventory of cleaning products there. The finance director has explained that the third-party inventory is located in one specific area of the warehouse.

Issue of share capital

The company is looking to expand its operations by securing an additional factory site in January 20X6. In order to raise sufficient capital to fund the factory purchase, Spinach Co issued ordinary shares at a premium in May 20X5, raising a sum of $4.3m.

Required:

(a) Describe substantive procedures the auditor should perform to obtain sufficient and appropriate audit evidence in relation to Spinach Co's revenue. (5 marks)

(b) Describe the audit procedures the auditor should perform as part of the audit of Spinach Co BEFORE and DURING the inventory count. (6 marks)

(c) Describe substantive procedures the auditor should perform to obtain sufficient and appropriate audit evidence in relation to Spinach Co's issue of share capital. (4 marks)

It is now 12 November 20X5. During the audit of Spinach Co's inventory, the audit team identified five product lines which were very slow moving and concluded that the net realisable value of these goods was below cost. A significant write down of inventory was required in order to comply with IAS® 2 *Inventories*. The audit engagement partner has determined that inventory is now appropriately valued and that this issue should be communicated as a key audit matter (KAM) in accordance with ISA 701 *Communicating Key Audit Matters in the Independent Auditor's Report.*

(d) (i) Describe the factors which the audit engagement partner would have considered in determining that this issue is a KAM, and

(ii) Describe the content of the KAM section of the auditor's report for Spinach Co. (5 marks)

(Total: 20 marks)

243 DANUBE *Walk in the footsteps of a top tutor*

This scenario relates to five requirements.

It is 1 July 20X5. Danube Co is listed on a stock exchange and sells consumer goods to wholesale customers. The company has a large head office and 18 warehouses. You are an audit supervisor of Mississippi & Co and the final audit for the year ended 31 March 20X5 is due to commence shortly. The draft financial statements show total assets of $198.5m and profit before tax of $56.1m. The following three matters have been brought to your attention.

Land and buildings

Danube Co historically recorded all property, plant and equipment (PPE) at cost less accumulated depreciation. However, during the year, management decided to change the accounting policy for land and buildings from the cost model to the revaluation model. The finance director hired an external independent valuer to undertake the valuation of all land and buildings, and this took place in July 20X4. Depreciation is calculated monthly on a pro-rata basis. Danube Co's year-end balance for PPE includes land and buildings of $79.2m (20X4: $64m).

Trade receivables circularisation

Danube Co's year-end trade receivables balance of $9.3m (20X4: $7.7m) has significantly increased compared to the prior year. Danube Co's list of individual customers is made up of a large number of customers with balances ranging from $15,000 to $50,000. A positive trade receivables circularisation has been undertaken by the audit team based on the year-end balances. The majority of responses from customers agreed to the balances as per Danube Co's list of individual customers at 31 March 20X5, however the following exceptions were noted.

Customer	Balance per Danube Co	Response from customer
Nile Co	$141,102	No response
Congo Co	$136,321	$122,189

Provision and receivable arising from the sale of defective goods

In December 20X4 Danube Co sold a number of hoverboards to a customer, Kalama Kids Co. It is alleged by Kalama Kids Co that these hoverboards are faulty, as there have been a few instances of the hoverboards overheating and catching fire. As a result, Kalama Kids Co is suing Danube Co for $3.9m. The court case is due to take place in August 20X5 and management believes that Kalama Kids Co's claim is likely to be successful. No hoverboards remain in Danube Co's inventory at the year end.

Danube Co purchased the hoverboards from a supplier, Thames Co. In February 20X5 Danube Co contacted Thames Co and requested that they reimburse Danube Co for damages which may become payable as a result of the sale of defective hoverboards. Danube Co is requesting a sum of $3.9m from Thames Co. The draft financial statements contain a provision of $3.9m in respect of the customer's claim and a receivable of $3.9m in respect of Danube Co's counter-claim against its supplier.

Required:

(a) Describe substantive procedures the auditor should perform to obtain sufficient and appropriate audit evidence in relation to Danube Co's land and buildings. (6 marks)

(b) Describe the procedures the auditor should perform in relation to the exceptions noted during the trade receivables circularisation in respect of Nile Co and Congo Co.

Note: The total marks will be split equally between each customer. **(4 marks)**

(c) Describe substantive procedures the auditor should perform to obtain sufficient and appropriate audit evidence in relation to the PROVISION and the RECEIVABLE arising from the sale of defective goods. (5 marks)

The audit engagement partner has determined that the issue relating to the provision and receivable arising from the sale of defective goods should be communicated as a key audit matter (KAM) in accordance with ISA 701 *Communicating Key Audit Matters in the Independent Auditor's Report.*

(d) (i) Describe the factors which the audit engagement partner would have considered in determining that this issue is a KAM, and

(ii) Describe the content of the KAM section of the auditor's report for Danube Co.

(5 marks)

(Total: 20 marks)

244 PURRFECT CO *Walk in the footsteps of a top tutor*

This scenario relates to four requirements.

It is 1 July 20X5. Purrfect Co manufactures and sells a variety of food for dogs and cats. Your firm, Kirano & Co, has audited the company for a number of years. You are about to commence the final audit for the year ended 31 March 20X5 and the draft financial statements show profit before tax of $23.1m and total assets of $99.2m.

Vego Dog – inventory valuation

Purrfect Co launched a new brand of vegan dog food, Vego Dog, in December 20X4 but sales have been lower than expected and the directors are considering a discounted sales price. Vego Dog products are valued using a standard costing method and the standard cost comprises raw materials, labour costs and production overheads. As at 31 March 20X5, Vego Dog products with a standard cost of $2.4m were included as finished goods in inventory.

Receivable – Ellah Co

One of Purrfect Co's major customers, Ellah Co, operates a chain of pet stores with 23 stores across the country. There have been reports in the press for several months that Ellah Co's sales and profits have been falling and, in March 20X5, Ellah Co announced that 11 of its stores were to close in May 20X5. As at 31 March 20X5, Purrfect Co's trade receivables included $2.6m outstanding from Ellah Co and no allowance has been included for this balance at the year end.

Contamination – legal claims

On 25 February 20X5, it was discovered that a batch of canned cat food had been contaminated with insecticide, which could be harmful to cats. This batch had been despatched in November 20X4 to 247 retail stores. By 31 March 20X5, Purrfect Co had received legal claims totalling $1.9m from consumers whose cats had eaten the contaminated food.

Required:

(a) **Describe substantive procedures the auditor should perform to obtain sufficient and appropriate audit evidence in relation to the matters identified regarding the inventory valuation of Vego Dog products.** **(6 marks)**

(b) **Describe substantive procedures the auditor should perform to obtain sufficient and appropriate audit evidence in relation to the receivable balance due from Ellah Co.** **(4 marks)**

(c) **Describe substantive procedures the auditor should perform to obtain sufficient and appropriate audit evidence in relation to the legal claims following the contamination.** **(5 marks)**

The final audit is now nearing completion. The audit team is satisfied that legal claims received to date have been appropriately reflected in the financial statements.

However, Purrfect Co's lawyer has advised you that it is possible that significant additional legal claims may be made by customers in future in respect of the contamination. The audit engagement partner has confirmed that this is a contingent liability that requires disclosure. The finance director has agreed to disclose some detail of the potential claims in the financial statements but the audit team is yet to confirm the adequacy of these disclosures.

(d) **Discuss the issue and describe the impact on the auditor's report of Purrfect Co of both adequate AND inadequate disclosure of the contingent liability.** **(5 marks)**

(Total: 20 marks)

245 SAGITTARII & CO *Walk in the footsteps of a top tutor*

This scenario relates to four requirements.

It is 1 July 20X5. You are an audit manager of Sagittarii & Co and you are in charge of two final audits which are due to commence shortly. Vega Vista Co and Canopus Co are both existing clients with a financial year ended 31 March 20X5. Vega Vista Co is a not-for-profit charitable organisation which raises funds for disadvantaged families and the draft financial statements show revenue of $0.8m. Canopus Co manufactures paint products in seven factories across the country and the draft financial statements show total equity and liabilities of $11.6m.

The following matters have been brought to your attention for each company.

Vega Vista Co

Income

Vega Vista Co generates income in a number of ways. The main source of income is via an annual food and music festival held in September every year. Tickets, which cost $35, are sold in the nine-month period prior to the event and can be purchased in advance online or on the day of the event for cash.

Approximately 15,000 people attended the September 20X4 event and more are anticipated for 20X5. At the event there are a number of stalls selling food and the charity receives a fixed percentage of these sundry sales. Also, during the festival, volunteers of the charity sign up individuals to make monthly donations, and these are paid by bank transfer to the charity. During the audit planning, the completeness and cut-off of income was flagged as a key audit risk.

Canopus Co

Restructuring provision

Canopus Co recently announced plans to fundamentally restructure its production processes due to a change in the focus of the company's operations. It has included a $2.1m restructuring provision in the draft financial statements. The restructure involves a refurbishment of the factories, the purchase of new plant and equipment and retraining of existing staff. These plans were finally agreed at a board meeting in March 20X5 and announced to shareholders and employees just before the year end.

Bank loans

In readiness for the operational changes, the directors of Canopus Co decided to restructure the company's bank loans. As a result, several long-term loans were repaid early and a new ten-year bank loan of $4.8m was taken out on 1 January 20X5. Repayments of $150,000 are due quarterly in arrears which includes interest.

Required:

(a) Describe substantive procedures the auditor should perform to obtain sufficient and appropriate audit evidence in relation to Vega Vista Co's income.

Note: You should assume that the charity adopts International Financial Reporting Standards.

(5 marks)

(b) Describe substantive procedures the auditor should perform to obtain sufficient and appropriate audit evidence in relation to Canopus Co's restructuring provision.

(5 marks)

(c) Describe substantive procedures the auditor should perform to obtain sufficient and appropriate audit evidence in relation to Canopus Co's bank loans. (5 marks)

During the audit of Canopus Co's restructuring provision, the audit team discovered that $270,000 of costs included did not meet the criteria for inclusion as per IAS 37 *Provisions, Contingent Liabilities and Contingent Assets*. The finance director has suggested that no adjustment is made in the 20X5 financial statements as the provision is a matter of judgement and the provision has been deemed reasonable by the board.

(d) Discuss the issue and describe the impact on the auditor's report, if any, should this issue remain unresolved. (5 marks)

(Total: 20 marks)

246 ENCORE *Walk in the footsteps of a top tutor*

This scenario relates to four requirements.

It is 1 July 20X5. You are an audit supervisor with Velo & Co and you are working on the final audit of Encore Co for the year ended 30 April 20X5. Encore Co is a waste management company, supplying its services to a variety of governmental and business organisations. Encore Co's draft profit before tax is $5.3m (20X4: $4.6m) and total assets are $40.1m (20X4: $33.9m). You have been provided with the following information regarding the draft financial statements.

Vehicle additions and disposals

On 1 February 20X5, Encore Co replaced 20 of its recycling vehicles. The old vehicles had a carrying amount of $1.8m, as recorded in the non-current asset register and were given in part-exchange against new vehicles costing $4.6m. Cash consideration of $3.9m was also paid.

Trade receivables

Encore Co's credit controller left the company in January 20X5 and has only recently been replaced. The trade receivables collection period increased from 49 days as at 31 December 20X4 to 66 days as at 30 April 20X5. Year-end trade receivables amounted to $9.1m (20X4: $7.1m) and an allowance for credit losses/receivables of $182,000 (20X4: $142,000) has been made.

Potential breach of transport regulations

In March 20X5, a former employee of Encore Co made a complaint to the transport authority, alleging that Encore Co has breached the regulations concerning maximum driving hours and compulsory rest breaks for drivers on a number of occasions. The transport authority has launched an investigation but the directors of Encore Co are not intending to disclose this issue or make any provision as they do not believe that the potential fine, which is $50,000 per breach, is material.

Required:

(a) Describe substantive procedures the auditor should perform to obtain sufficient and appropriate audit evidence in relation to Encore Co's vehicle additions and disposals. (6 marks)

(b) **Describe substantive procedures the auditor should perform to obtain sufficient and appropriate audit evidence in relation to the VALUATION of Encore Co's trade receivables.** **(5 marks)**

(c) **Describe substantive procedures the auditor should perform to obtain sufficient and appropriate audit evidence in relation to the potential breach of transport regulations by Encore Co.** **(4 marks)**

It is now 26 August 20X5 and the auditor's report for Encore Co is being finalised. On 12 August 20X5, the transport authority announced that it was taking legal action against Encore Co in respect of 17 breaches of the regulations. Encore Co's lawyers have advised that it is probable Encore Co will be found guilty of all of the breaches. Encore Co's directors have informed you that no provision will be made in respect of this matter, as the decision by the authority to take legal action was made after the year end, but they have agreed to disclose the issue in the notes to the financial statements.

(d) **Discuss the issue and describe the impact on the auditor's report, if any, should this issue remain unresolved.** **(5 marks)**

(Total: 20 marks)

247 SPADEFISH *Walk in the footsteps of a top tutor*

This scenario relates to four requirements.

It is 1 July 20X5 and you are an audit manager of Spadefish & Co and you are currently responsible for the audits of two existing clients:

Triggerfish Co manufactures hair products and its year ended on 31 May 20X5. You are finalising the audit programmes for the forthcoming audit.

Marlin Co is a distributor of electronic goods and its year ended on 30 April 20X5. The audit is almost complete and the auditor's report is due to be signed shortly.

The following matters have been brought to your attention for each company.

Triggerfish Co – Receivables

Triggerfish Co's draft year-end trade receivables are $3.85m (20X4: $2.45m) and revenue for the year is slightly increased on 20X4. Triggerfish Co has a large number of customers with balances ranging from $5,000 to $45,000. A positive receivables circularisation has been undertaken based on the year-end balances. The majority of responses from customers agreed to the balances as per Triggerfish Co's list of individual customers, however, the following exceptions were noted:

	Balance per Triggerfish	Response from customer
Albacore Co	$36,558	Nil response
Flounder Co	$24,115	$18,265
Menhaden Co	–$5,360 (Credit)	$3,450

Due to the increase in receivables, Triggerfish Co has recently recruited an additional credit controller to chase outstanding receivables. As a result of the additional focus on chasing outstanding receivables the finance director thinks it is not necessary to continue to maintain a significant allowance for credit losses/receivables and has reduced the closing allowance from $125,000 to $5,000.

Marlin Co – Going concern

During the year under audit Marlin Co has consistently paid a number of its suppliers significantly later than usual and only after several reminders. As a result, some of its suppliers have withdrawn credit terms meaning the company must pay cash on delivery. The company has also just received notification that its main supplier who provides the company with over 60% of its specialist electrical equipment has ceased to trade.

The overdraft has increased significantly over the year and the directors have informed you that the overdraft facility is due for renewal next month, and they are confident it will be renewed. The directors have decided that in order to conserve cash, no final dividend will be paid in 20X5.

Required:

(a) Describe the procedures the auditor should perform to resolve the exceptions noted for each customer during the positive receivables circularisation for Triggerfish Co. (8 marks)

(b) Describe substantive procedures the auditor should perform to obtain sufficient and appropriate audit evidence in relation to the allowance for credit losses/receivables in the current year. (4 marks)

(c) Identify and explain THREE potential indicators that Marlin Co is NOT a going concern. (3 marks)

(d) Describe the audit procedures the auditor should perform in assessing whether or not Marlin Co is a going concern. (5 marks)

(Total: 20 marks)

248 HYACINTH *Walk in the footsteps of a top tutor*

This scenario relates to five requirements.

It is 1 July 20X5. Hyacinth Co develops and manufactures computer components and its year end was 30 April 20X5. The company has a large factory, and two warehouses, one of which is off-site. You are an audit supervisor of Tulip & Co and the final audit is due to commence shortly. Draft financial statements show total assets of $23.2m and profit before tax of $6.4m. The following three matters have been brought to your attention:

Inventory valuation

Your firm attended the year-end inventory count for Hyacinth Co and confirmed that the controls and processes for recording work-in-progress (WIP) and finished goods were acceptable. WIP and finished goods are both material to the financial statements and the audit team was able to confirm both the quantity and stage of completion of WIP.

Before goods are despatched, they are inspected by the company's quality control department. Just prior to the inventory count, it was noted that a batch of product line 'Crocus', which had been produced to meet a customer's specific technical requirements, did not meet that customer's quality and technical standards. This inventory had a production cost of $450,000. Upon discussions with the production supervisor, the finance director believes that the inventory can still be sold to alternative customers at a discounted price of $90,000.

Research and development

Hyacinth Co includes expenditure incurred in developing new products within intangible assets once the recognition criteria under IAS 38 *Intangible Assets* have been met. Intangible assets are amortised on a straight-line basis over four years once production commences. The amortisation policy is based on past experience of the likely useful lives of the products. The opening balance of intangible assets is $1.9m.

In the current year, Hyacinth Co spent $0.8m developing three new products which are all at different stages of development.

Sales tax liability

Hyacinth Co is required by the relevant tax authority in the country in which it operates to charge sales tax at 15% on all products which it sells. This sales tax is payable to the tax authority. When purchasing raw materials and incurring expenses in the manufacturing process, the company pays 15% sales tax on any items purchased and this can be reclaimed from the tax authority.

The company is required to report the taxes charged and incurred by completing a tax return on a quarterly basis, and the net amount owing to the tax authority must be remitted within four weeks of the quarter end. The draft financial statements contain a $1.1m liability for sales tax for the quarter ended 30 April 20X5.

Required:

(a) Describe substantive procedures the auditor should perform to obtain sufficient and appropriate audit evidence in relation to the VALUATION of Hyacinth Co's inventory. (6 marks)

(b) Describe substantive procedures the auditor should perform to obtain sufficient and appropriate audit evidence in relation to Hyacinth Co's research and development expenditure. (4 marks)

(c) Describe substantive procedures the auditor should perform to obtain sufficient and appropriate audit evidence in relation to Hyacinth Co's year-end sales tax liability. (4 marks)

The audit is now almost complete and the auditor's report is due to be signed shortly. The following matter has been brought to your attention:

On 3 June 20X5, a flood occurred at the off-site warehouse. This resulted in some damage to inventory and property, plant and equipment. However, there have been no significant delays to customer deliveries or complaints from customers. Hyacinth Co's management has investigated the cause of the flooding and believes that the company is unlikely to be able to claim on its insurance. The finance director of Hyacinth Co has estimated that the value of damaged inventory and property, plant and equipment was $0.7m and that it now has no scrap value.

(d) (i) Explain whether the 20X5 financial statements of Hyacinth Co require amendment in relation to the flood, and

(ii) Describe audit procedures which should be performed in order to form a conclusion on any required amendment.

Note: The total marks will be split equally between each part. **(6 marks)**

(Total: 20 marks)

249 JASMINE *Walk in the footsteps of a top tutor*

This scenario relates to four requirements.

It is 1 July 20X5. Jasmine Co manufactures motor vehicle components and its year end was 30 April 20X5. You are an audit supervisor of Peppermint & Co and the final audit is due to commence shortly. Total assets are $43.2m and profit before tax is $7.2m. The following matters have been brought to your attention.

Trade receivables

Jasmine Co's list of individual customers comprises a large number of customers. In previous years, the audit team has undertaken a positive trade receivables circularisation to confirm year-end balances. However, the customer response rate has historically been low and so alternative audit procedures have been undertaken. A decision has been made that for the current year audit a circularisation will not be performed.

The year-end trade receivables balance is $3.9m (20X4: $2.8m) and the allowance for credit losses/trade receivables is $410,000 (20X4: $300,000).

Bank balances

The bank and cash figure included in Jasmine Co's draft financial statements is comprised of a number of bank account balances: an overdraft of $5.1m which is the company's main current account and $0.2m relating to several savings accounts. The finance director has informed the audit manager that all accounts have been reconciled as at the year end.

The overdraft of $5.1m has increased significantly since the prior year (20X4: $1.2m). The directors have informed you that the overdraft facility, which the company requires in order to operate on a daily basis, is due for renewal in August 20X5 and that they are confident it will be renewed.

Required:

(a) Describe substantive procedures the auditor should perform to obtain sufficient and appropriate audit evidence in relation to Jasmine Co's trade receivables. (5 marks)

(b) Describe substantive procedures the auditor should perform to obtain sufficient and appropriate audit evidence in relation to Jasmine Co's bank balances. (5 marks)

(c) Describe the audit procedures the auditor should perform in assessing whether or not Jasmine Co is a going concern. (5 marks)

During the final audit, the finance director has informed the audit team that Jasmine Co's bankers will not make a decision on the renewal of the overdraft facility until after the auditor's report is signed. The audit engagement partner is satisfied that the use of the going concern basis is appropriate.

The directors have agreed to include some brief going concern disclosures in the draft financial statements and the audit team still have to assess the adequacy of these disclosures.

(d) Discuss the issue and describe the impact on the auditor's report of Jasmine Co of adequate AND inadequate going concern disclosure. (5 marks)

(Total: 20 marks)

250 GOOSEBERRY *Walk in the footsteps of a top tutor*

This scenario relates to four requirements.

It is 1 July 20X5. You are an audit manager of Cranberry & Co and you are currently responsible for the audit of Gooseberry Co, a company which develops and manufactures health and beauty products and distributes these to wholesale customers. Its draft profit before tax is $6.4m and total assets are $37.2m for the financial year ended 30 April 20X5. The final audit is due to commence shortly and the following matters have been brought to your attention.

Research and development

Gooseberry Co spent $1.9m in the current year developing nine new health and beauty products, all of which are at different stages of development. Once they meet the recognition criteria under IAS® 38 Intangible Assets for development expenditure, Gooseberry Co includes the costs incurred within intangible assets. Once production commences, the intangible assets are amortised on a straight-line basis over three years.

Management believes that this amortisation policy is a reasonable approximation of the assets' useful lives, as in this industry there is constant demand for innovative new products.

Depreciation

Gooseberry Co has a large portfolio of property, plant and equipment (PPE). In June 20X5, the company carried out a full review of all its PPE and updated the useful lives, residual values, depreciation rates and methods for many categories of asset. The finance director felt the changes were necessary to better reflect the use of the assets. This resulted in the depreciation charge of some assets changing significantly for this year.

Bonus

The company's board is comprised of seven directors. They are each entitled to a bonus based on the draft year-end net assets, excluding intangible assets. Details of the bonus entitlement are included in the directors' service contracts.

The bonus, which related to the 20X5 year end, was paid to each director in May 20X5 and the costs were accrued and recognised within wages and salaries for the year ended 30 April 20X5. Separate disclosure of the bonus, by director, is required by local legislation.

Required:

(a) **Describe substantive procedures the auditor should perform to obtain sufficient and appropriate audit evidence in relation to Gooseberry Co's research and development expenditure. (5 marks)**

(b) **Describe substantive procedures the auditor should perform to obtain sufficient and appropriate audit evidence in relation to the matters identified regarding depreciation of property, plant and equipment. (5 marks)**

(c) **Describe substantive procedures the auditor should perform to obtain sufficient and appropriate audit evidence in relation to the directors' bonuses. (5 marks)**

During the audit, the team discovers that the intangible assets balance includes $440,000 related to one of the nine new health and beauty products development projects, which does not meet the criteria for capitalisation. As this project is ongoing, the finance director has suggested that no adjustment is made in the 20X5 financial statements. The finance director s confident that the project will meet the criteria for capitalisation in 20X6.

(d) Discuss the issue and describe the impact on the auditor's report, if any, should this issue remain unresolved. **(5 marks)**

(Total: 20 marks)

251 DASHING *Walk in the footsteps of a top tutor*

This scenario relates to six requirements.

It is 1 July 20X5. Dashing Co manufactures women's clothing and its year end was 30 April 20X5. You are an audit supervisor of Jaunty & Co and the final audit for Dashing Co is due to commence shortly.

The draft financial statements recognise profit before tax of $2.6m and total assets of $18m. You have been given responsibility for auditing receivables, which is a material balance, and as part of the audit approach, a positive receivables circularisation is to be undertaken.

At the planning meeting, the finance director of Dashing Co informed the audit engagement partner that the company was closing one of its smaller production sites and as a result, a number of employees would be made redundant. A redundancy provision of $110,000 is included in the draft financial statements.

Required:

(a) Describe the steps the auditor should perform in undertaking a positive receivables circularisation for Dashing Co. **(4 marks)**

(b) Describe substantive procedures, other than a receivables circularisation, the auditor should perform to obtain sufficient and appropriate audit evidence to verify EACH of the following assertions in relation to Dashing Co's receivables:

(i) Accuracy, valuation and allocation

(ii) Completeness, and

(iii) Rights and obligations.

Note: The total marks will be split equally between each part. **(6 marks)**

(c) Describe substantive procedures the auditor should perform to obtain sufficient and appropriate audit evidence in relation to the redundancy provision at the year end. **(5 marks)**

A few months have now passed and the audit team is performing the audit fieldwork including the audit procedures which you recommended over the redundancy provision. The team has calculated that the necessary provision should amount to $305,000. The finance director is not willing to adjust the draft financial statements.

(d) Discuss the issue and describe the impact on the auditor's report, if any, should this issue remain unresolved. **(5 marks)**

(Total: 20 marks)

252 AIRSOFT *Walk in the footsteps of a top tutor*

This scenario relates to five requirements.

It is 1 July 20X5. Airsoft Co is a listed company which manufactures stationery products. The company's profit before tax for the year ended 30 April 20X5 is $16.3 million and total assets as at that date are $66.8 million. You are an audit supervisor of Biathlon & Co and you are currently finalising the audit programmes for the final audit of your existing client Airsoft Co. You attended a meeting with your audit manager where the following matters were discussed:

Trade payables and accruals

Airsoft Co purchases its raw materials from a large number of suppliers. The company's policy is to close the payables account just after the year end and the financial controller is responsible for identifying goods which were received pre year end but for which no invoice has yet been received. An accrual is calculated for goods received but not yet invoiced (GRNI) and is included within trade payables and accruals.

The audit strategy has identified a risk over the completeness of trade payables and accruals. The audit team will utilise automated tools and techniques, in the form of audit software while auditing trade payables and accruals.

Bank overdraft and savings accounts

Airsoft Co's draft financial statements include a bank overdraft of $2.6 million, which relates to the company's main current account. In addition, Airsoft Co maintains a number of savings accounts. The savings account balances are classified as cash and cash equivalents and are included in current assets. All accounts have been reconciled at the year end.

Directors' remuneration

Airsoft Co's board comprises eight directors. Their overall remuneration consists of two elements: an annual salary, paid monthly and a significant annual discretionary bonus, which is paid in a separate payment run on 20 April. All remuneration paid to directors is included within wages and salaries. Local legislation requires disclosure of the overall total of directors' remuneration broken down by element and by director.

Required:

(a) Describe substantive procedures the auditor should perform to obtain sufficient and appropriate audit evidence in relation to the COMPLETENESS of Airsoft Co's trade payables and accruals. (4 marks)

Excluding procedures included in part (a):

(b) Describe audit software procedures which could be carried out during the audit of Airsoft Co's trade payables and accruals. (3 marks)

(c) Describe substantive procedures the auditor should perform to obtain sufficient and appropriate audit evidence in relation to Airsoft Co's year-end bank balances. (5 marks)

(d) Describe substantive procedures the auditor should perform to confirm the directors' remuneration included in the financial statements at the year end. (3 marks)

A member of your audit team has asked for information on ISA 701 *Communicating Key Audit Matters in the Independent Auditor's Report* having heard that this standard is applicable to listed clients such as Airsoft Co.

(e) Identify what a key audit matter (KAM) is and explain how the auditor determines and communicates KAM. (5 marks)

(Total: 20 marks)

253 INSECTS4U *Walk in the footsteps of a top tutor*

This scenario relates to four requirements.

It is 1 July 20X5. You are an audit manager of Snail & Co and you are in charge of two audits which are due to commence shortly. Insects4U Co is a registered charity which promotes insect conservation and has been an audit client for several years. Spider Spirals Co, also an existing audit client, manufactures stationery products and its draft total liabilities are $8.1 million. Both clients' financial year ended on 30 April 20X5. The following matters have been brought to your attention for each company.

Insects4U Co

Insects4U Co is a not-for-profit organisation which generates income in a number of ways. It receives monthly donations from its many subscribers and these are paid by bank transfer to the charity.

In addition, a large number of donations are sent through the post to the charity. Insects4U Co also sells tickets for their three charity events held annually. During the audit planning, completeness of income was flagged as a key risk.

Note: Assume that the charity adopts International Financial Reporting Standards.

Spider Spirals Co

Trade payables

The finance director of Spider Spirals Co has informed you that at the year end the individual supplier accounts were kept open for one week longer than normal as a large bank transfer and cheque payment run was made on 3 May 20X5. Some purchase invoices were received in this week and were recorded in the 20X5 accounts as well as the payment run made on 3 May.

Trade receivables

Spider Spirals Co has a large number of small customers; the normal credit terms offered to them is 30 days. However, the finance director has informed you that the average trade receivables days have increased quite significantly this year from 34 days to 55 days. This is partly due to difficult trading conditions and also because for six months of the year the role of credit controller was vacant. The company has historically maintained on average an allowance for credit losses/trade receivables of 1.5% of gross trade receivables.

Required:

(a) Describe substantive procedures the auditor should perform to obtain sufficient and appropriate audit evidence in relation to the COMPLETENESS of Insect4U Co's income. (4 marks)

(b) Describe substantive procedures the auditor should perform to obtain sufficient and appropriate audit evidence in relation to Spider Spiral Co's trade payables.
(6 marks)

(c) Describe substantive procedures the auditor should perform to obtain sufficient and appropriate audit evidence in relation to Spider Spiral Co's trade receivables.
(5 marks)

The finance director of Spider Spirals Co has informed you that there is no intention to make an adjustment for the trade payables payment run made on 3 May, as the total payment of $490,000 would only require a change to trade payables and the bank overdraft, both of which are current liabilities.

(d) Discuss the issue and describe the impact on the auditor's report, if any, should this issue remain unresolved. **(5 marks)**

(Total: 20 marks)

254 ELOUNDA *Walk in the footsteps of a top tutor*

This scenario relates to four requirements.

It is 1 July 20X5. Elounda Co manufactures chemical compounds using a continuous production process. Its year end was 30 April 20X5 and the draft profit before tax is $13.6 million. You are the audit supervisor and the final audit is due to commence shortly. The following matters have been brought to your attention.

Revaluation of property, plant and equipment (PPE)

At the beginning of the year, management undertook an extensive review of Elounda Co's non-current asset valuations and as a result decided to update the carrying amount of all PPE. The finance director, Peter Dullman, contacted a sibling, Martin, who is a valuer and requested that Martin's firm undertake the valuation, which took place in May 20X4.

Inventory valuation

Your firm attended the year-end inventory count for Elounda Co and ascertained that the process for recording work-in-progress (WIP) and finished goods was acceptable. Both WIP and finished goods are material to the financial statements and the quantity and stage of completion of all ongoing production was recorded accurately during the count.

During the inventory count, the count supervisor noted that a consignment of finished goods, compound E243, with a value of $720,000, was defective in that the chemical mix was incorrect. The finance director believes that compound E243 can still be sold at a discounted sum of $400,000.

Bank loan

Elounda Co secured a bank loan of two years ago. Repayments of $200,000 are due quarterly, with a lump sum of $800,000 due for repayment in October 20X5. The company met all loan payments in 20X4 on time, but was late in paying the January and April 20X5 repayments.

Required:

(a) Describe substantive procedures the auditor should perform to obtain sufficient and appropriate audit evidence in relation to the revaluation of Elounda Co's property, plant and equipment. **(5 marks)**

(b) **Describe substantive procedures the auditor should perform to obtain sufficient and appropriate audit evidence in relation to the VALUATION of Elounda Co's inventory.** **(6 marks)**

(c) **Describe substantive procedures the auditor should perform to obtain sufficient and appropriate audit evidence in relation to Elounda Co's bank loan.** **(4 marks)**

(d) **Describe the procedures which the auditor of Elounda Co should perform in assessing whether or not the company is a going concern.** **(5 marks)**

(Total: 20 marks)

255 ANDROMEDA *Walk in the footsteps of a top tutor*

This scenario relates to five requirements.

It is 1 July 20X5. Andromeda Industries Co (Andromeda) develops and manufactures a wide range of fast-moving consumer goods. Its year end is 31 July 20X5 and the forecast profit before tax is $8.3 million. You are an audit supervisor in Neptune & Co and the final audit is due to commence next month. The following information has been gathered during the planning process:

Inventory count

Andromeda's raw materials and finished goods inventory are stored in 12 warehouses across the country. Each of these warehouses is expected to contain material levels of inventory at the year end. It is expected that there will be no significant work-in-progress held at any of the sites. Each count will be supervised by a member of Andromeda's internal audit department and the counts will all take place on 31 July, when all movements of goods in and out of the warehouses will cease.

Rights issue

In order to fund ongoing research and development, Andromeda invited shareholders to participate in a 2 for 1 rights issue at a share price of $2.50 for each $1 share. The rights issue was taken up by the majority of the shareholders raising $10 million.

Research and development

Andromeda spends over $2 million annually on developing new product lines. This year it incurred expenditure on five projects, all of which are at different stages of development. Once they meet the recognition criteria under IAS 38 *Intangible Assets* for development expenditure, Andromeda includes the costs incurred within intangible assets. Once production commences, the intangible assets are amortised on a straight-line basis over five years.

Required:

(a) **Explain FOUR factors which influence the reliability of audit evidence.** **(4 marks)**

(b) **Describe the procedures to be undertaken by the auditor BEFORE and DURING the inventory count of Andromeda Industries Co in order to gain sufficient appropriate audit evidence.** **(5 marks)**

(c) **Describe substantive procedures the auditor should perform to obtain sufficient and appropriate audit evidence in relation to Andromeda Co's rights issue.** **(3 marks)**

(d) **Describe substantive procedures the auditor should perform to obtain sufficient and appropriate audit evidence in relation to Andromeda Co's research and development expenditure.** **(4 marks)**

The final audit is now nearing completion. During the audit, the team discovered that one of the five development projects, valued at $980,000 and included within intangible assets, does not meet the criteria for capitalisation. The finance director does not intend to change the accounting treatment adopted as the amount is considered to be immaterial.

(e) Discuss the issue and describe the impact on the auditor's report, if any, if the issue remains unresolved. (4 marks)

(Total: 20 marks)

256 HAWTHORN *Walk in the footsteps of a top tutor*

Answer debrief

This scenario relates to five requirements.

It is 1 July 20X5. Hawthorn Enterprises Co manufactures and distributes fashion clothing to retail stores. Its year end was 30 April 20X5. You are the audit manager and the final audit is due to commence shortly. The following three matters have been brought to your attention.

Supplier statement reconciliations

Hawthorn Enterprises Co receives monthly statements from its main suppliers and although these have been retained, none have been reconciled to the individual supplier accounts as at 30 April 20X5. The engagement partner has asked the audit senior to recommend the procedures to be performed on supplier statements.

Bank reconciliation

During last year's audit of Hawthorn Enterprises Co's bank and cash, significant cut off errors were discovered with a number of post-year-end cheques being processed prior to the year end to reduce payables. The finance director has assured the audit engagement partner that this error has not occurred again this year and that the bank reconciliation has been carefully prepared. The audit engagement partner has asked that the bank reconciliation is comprehensively audited.

Receivables

Hawthorn Enterprises Co's receivables balance has increased considerably during the year, and the year-end balance is $2.3 million compared to $1.4 million last year. The finance director has requested that a receivables circularisation is not carried out as a number of their customers complained last year about the inconvenience involved in responding. The engagement partner has agreed to this request, and tasked you with identifying alternative procedures to confirm the existence and valuation of receivables.

Required:

(a) (i) Identify and explain FOUR assertions relevant to classes of transactions and events for the year under audit; and

(ii) For each identified assertion, describe a substantive procedure relevant to the audit of REVENUE. (8 marks)

(b) Describe substantive procedures the auditor should perform to obtain sufficient and appropriate audit evidence in relation to the supplier statement reconciliations of Hawthorn Enterprises Co. (3 marks)

(c) Describe substantive procedures the auditor should perform to obtain sufficient and appropriate audit evidence in relation to the bank reconciliation of Hawthorn Enterprises Co. (4 marks)

(d) Describe substantive procedures the auditor should perform to obtain sufficient and appropriate audit evidence in relation to the EXISTENCE and VALUATION of Hawthorn Enterprises Co's receivables. (5 marks)

(Total: 20 marks)

Calculate your allowed time, allocate the time to the separate parts..............

257 PINEAPPLE BEACH HOTEL *Walk in the footsteps of a top tutor*

This scenario relates to five requirements.

It is 1 July 20X5. Pineapple Beach Hotel Co is a national hotel chain with 10 hotels around the country. Its year end was 30 April 20X5. You are the audit senior of Berry & Co and are currently preparing the audit programmes for the final audit of Pineapple Beach Hotel Co. You are reviewing the notes of last week's meeting between the audit manager and finance director where two material issues were discussed.

Revenue

Pineapple Beach Hotel Co's main source of revenue is generated from hotel bookings. Each hotel has its own leisure facilities which hotel guests can use for free. Memberships to the leisure centres are available to non-hotel guests on a monthly or annual contract with no joining fees. Each hotel also has a restaurant which offers meals to hotel guests and the general public. Business is seasonal due to the hotels being situated in beach resorts. Unlike many of their competitors, the hotels remain open all year round.

Depreciation

Pineapple Beach Hotel Co incurred significant asset expenditure during the year on updating the leisure facilities for the hotel. The finance director has proposed that the new leisure equipment should be depreciated over 10 years using the straight-line method.

Food poisoning claim

Pineapple Beach Hotel Co's directors received correspondence in March from a group of customers who attended a wedding at the hotel. They have alleged that they suffered severe food poisoning from food eaten at the hotel and are claiming substantial damages. The company's lawyers have received the claim and believe that the lawsuit against the company is unlikely to be successful.

Required:

(a) List and explain the purpose of FOUR items that should be included on every working paper prepared by the audit team. (4 marks)

(b) Describe substantive ANALYTICAL PROCEDURES the auditor should perform to should perform to confirm Pineapple Beach Hotel Co's revenue. (4 marks)

(c) Describe substantive procedures the auditor should perform to obtain sufficient and appropriate audit evidence in relation to Pineapple Beach Hotel Co's depreciation. (4 marks)

(d) Excluding written representation, describe substantive procedures the auditor should perform to obtain sufficient and appropriate audit evidence in relation to the food poisoning claim. (4 marks)

The date is now 1 September 20X5 and the audit is nearly complete. Suggested wording for the written representation letter has been given to the directors of Pineapple Beach Hotel, including a point confirming that the directors believe the food poisoning claim is appropriately accounted for and disclosed in the financial statements and all information in respect of the claim has been provided to the auditor. The directors have stated that they will not sign the written representation this year on the grounds that they believe the additional evidence that it provides is not required by the auditor.

(e) Discuss the issue and describe the impact on the auditor's report, if any, if the issue remains unresolved. (4 marks)

(Total: 20 marks)

ADDITIONAL QUESTIONS

THE FOLLOWING QUESTIONS ARE EXAM STANDARD BUT DO NOT REFLECT THE CURRENT EXAM FORMAT. THESE QUESTIONS PROVIDE VALUABLE PRACTICE FOR STUDENTS NEVERTHELESS.

258 SAXOPHONE ENTERPRISES *Walk in the footsteps of a top tutor*

Saxophone Enterprises Co (Saxophone) has been trading for 15 years selling insurance and has recently become a listed company. Saxophone is required to comply with corporate governance principles in order to maintain its listed status and the finance director has undertaken a review of whether or not the company complies.

Bill Bassoon is the chair of Saxophone and had been the chief executive until last year. Bill is unsure if Saxophone needs more non-executive directors as there are currently three non-executive directors out of the eight board members. Bill is considering appointing a close friend, who is a retired chief executive of a manufacturing company, as a non-executive director.

The finance director, Jessie Oboe, decides on the amount of remuneration each director is paid. Currently all remuneration is in the form of an annual bonus based on profits. Jessie is considering setting up an audit committee, but has not undertaken this task yet due to other work commitments. A new sales director was appointed nine months ago and has yet to undertaken the board training as this is normally provided by the chief executive and this role is currently vacant.

There are a large number of shareholders and therefore the directors believe that it is impractical and too costly to hold an annual general meeting of shareholders. Instead, the board has suggested sending out the financial statements and any voting resolutions by email; shareholders can then vote on the resolutions via email.

Required:

Describe FIVE corporate governance deficiencies faced by Saxophone Enterprises Co and provide a recommendation to address each deficiency to ensure compliance with corporate governance principles.

Note: The marks will be split equally between each part. **(10 marks)**

Deficiency	Recommendation

259 ORANGE FINANCIALS *Walk in the footsteps of a top tutor*

You are the audit manager of Currant & Co and you are planning the audit of Orange Financials Co (Orange), who specialise in the provision of loans and financial advice to individuals and companies. Currant & Co has audited Orange for many years.

The directors are planning to list Orange on a stock exchange within the next few months and have asked if the engagement partner can attend the meetings with potential investors. In addition, as the finance director of Orange is likely to be quite busy with the listing, the finance director has asked if Currant & Co can produce the financial statements for the current year.

During the year, the assistant finance director of Orange left and joined Currant & Co as a partner. It has been suggested that due to familiarity with Orange, the new partner should be appointed to provide an independent partner review for the audit.

Once Orange obtains its stock exchange listing it will require several assignments to be undertaken, for example, obtaining advice about corporate governance best practice. Currant & Co is very keen to be appointed to these engagements, however, Orange has implied that in order to gain this work Currant & Co needs to complete the external audit quickly and with minimal questions/issues.

The finance director has informed you that once the stock exchange listing has been completed, the engagement team would be invited to attend a weekend away at a luxury hotel with the Orange team, as a thank you for all their hard work. In addition, the finance director has offered a senior member of the engagement team a short-term loan at a significantly reduced interest rate.

Required:

(a) **(i)** **Identify and explain FIVE ethical threats which may affect the independence of Currant & Co's audit of Orange Financials Co, and**

(ii) **For each threat, recommend an appropriate safeguard to reduce the threat to an acceptable level.**

Note: The marks will be split equally between each part. **(10 marks)**

Ethical threat	Appropriate safeguard

(b) Orange's finance director has asked your firm to undertake a non-audit assurance engagement later in the year. The audit junior has not been involved in such an assignment before and has asked you to explain what an assurance engagement involves.

Required:

Explain the five elements of an assurance engagement. **(5 marks)**

(Total: 15 marks)

260 VIOLET & CO *Walk in the footsteps of a top tutor*

Answer debrief

You are the audit manager of Violet & Co and you are currently reviewing the audit files for two of your clients for which the audit fieldwork is complete. The audit senior has raised the following issues.

Daisy Co

Subsequent to the year end, the company's sales ledger has been corrupted by a computer virus. Daisy Co's finance director was able to produce the financial statements prior to this occurring; however, the audit team has been unable to access the sales ledger to undertake detailed testing of revenue or year-end receivables. All other accounting records are unaffected and there are no backups available for the list of individual customers. Daisy Co's revenue is $15.6m, its receivables are $3.4m and profit before tax is $2m.

Fuchsia Co

Fuchsia Co has experienced difficult trading conditions and as a result it has lost significant market share. The cash flow forecast has been reviewed during the audit fieldwork and it shows a significant net cash outflow. Management are confident that further funding can be obtained and so have prepared the financial statements using the going concern basis with no additional disclosures; the audit senior is highly sceptical about this.

The prior year financial statements showed a profit before tax of $1.2m; however, the current year loss before tax is $4.4m and the forecast net cash outflow for the next 12 months is $3.2m.

Required:

For each of the two issues:

(i) Discuss the issue, including an assessment of whether it is material.

(ii) Discuss whether a written representation is appropriate.

(iii) Recommend procedures the audit team should undertake at the completion stage to try to resolve the issue.

(iv) Describe the impact on the auditor's report if the issue remains unresolved.

Notes: 1 The total marks will be split equally between each issue.

2 Report extracts are NOT required.

(12 marks)

Calculate your allowed time, allocate the time to the separate parts..............

Section 3

ANSWERS TO OBJECTIVE TEST CASE QUESTIONS – SECTION A

AUDIT FRAMEWORK

1 OPTION 2

The annual report should describe the work of the audit committee including:

- Significant issues considered relating to the financial statements.
- How it has assessed the independence and effectiveness of the external audit process.
- Where there is no internal audit function, an explanation for the absence and how internal assurance is achieved.
- An explanation of how auditor independence and objectivity are safeguarded, if the external auditor provides non-audit services.

The other options would be included in the annual report but are not related to the work of the audit committee. Options 1 relates to the directors. Option 3 relates to the board. Option 4 relates to the nomination committee.

2 OPTION 3

NEDs' remuneration should not be tied to the performance of Sistar Co as this can compromise independence. NEDs' remuneration should be based on the time committed to carry out the role.

3

Reports to
Finance director
Audit committee
Chief executive

Head of IA
Maria Marquez
Paul Belling

Remaining staff members
Appoint more senior staff with audit experience
No changes needed
All staff should be new to the company

To ensure effectiveness of the internal audit function, it should report into the audit committee. Maria Marquez should be appointed Head Internal Auditor as she has audit experience and is independent of the company. Paul Belling helped design and implement the current control system which creates a self-review threat. Only one of the remaining internal audit staff members has audit experience therefore more staff should be appointed with audit experience.

4 OPTION 1

The assignment described represents a value for money audit as it is focused on assessing the economy, efficiency and effectiveness of Sistar Co's asset expenditure.

5 OPTIONS 3 AND 5

Authorisation of transactions and performing reconciliations are types of control procedures. Internal audit should not design and implement internal control procedures as this will create a self-review threat when they subsequently test the effectiveness of the controls implemented. Internal audit should report any deficiencies identified and provide recommendations for improvement. Management is responsible for implementing the recommendations.

6 OPTION 3

As Foliage Co is a listed company, Jane Leaf should not serve as the Engagement Quality Reviewer until a cooling-off period of five years has passed.

7 OPTION 2

Bark & Co should assess whether audit and non-audit fees would represent more than 15% of gross practice income for two consecutive years. If the recurring fees are likely to exceed 15% of annual practice income this year, additional consideration should be given as to whether the taxation and audit-related services should be undertaken by the firm. This is particularly important as the client is listed and many additional services are prohibited. In addition, if the fees do exceed 15% then this should be disclosed to those charged with governance at Foliage. Resigning as auditor would only be required if all other options do not reduce the threat to an acceptable level.

8 OPTION 1

The ACCA Code of Ethics and Conduct requires individuals to notify the firm of the possibility of employment with an audit client so they can be removed from the audit team.

9 OPTION B

There will be a familiarity threat because of Kim Baum's relationship with the audit team. The audit team may be too trusting of their ex-colleague. A self-review threat would be created if an employee of the client joined the audit firm and was assigned to the audit of their previous employer. A self-interest threat would have arisen during the recruitment process as the judgement of the audit manager may have been affected by the desire to be appointed financial controller.

10

Clearly defined laws for the auditor to follow	**Rule book approach**	**Conceptual framework approach**
Useful in a dynamic environment	**Rule book approach**	**Conceptual framework approach**
A set of guidelines with which the auditor uses judgement to apply to specific circumstances	**Rule book approach**	**Conceptual framework approach**
Easy to know what is allowed and not allowed	**Rule book approach**	**Conceptual framework approach**

The conceptual framework provides guidelines with the objective that the auditor chooses the most appropriate course of action in the circumstances. This allows flexibility to deal with all possible situations which is useful in a dynamic environment. The guidelines followed are professional guidance but are not law. Laws clearly outline what is acceptable and not acceptable in specific circumstances.

11

The partner and the finance director have known each other socially for many years	Advocacy	**Familiarity**	Self-interest
40% of the fee for last year's audit is still outstanding	Advocacy	Familiarity	**Self-interest**

The social relationship gives rise to a familiarity threat. Outstanding fees can create self-interest (and intimidation) threats.

12 OPTION 4

The audit firm should request that the fees are paid. The audit firm must not issue this year's auditor's report until the fees have been paid.

13 OPTION 1

The audit will need to be planned carefully to ensure that the work is not predictable, especially as the new financial controller is an ex-employee of the firm and will know the firm's procedures.

The composition of the audit team should be considered and anyone who has remained in close contact with the new financial controller should be removed from the team to avoid a familiarity threat.

It is unlikely that a significant familiarity threat would arise from an audit senior joining the audit client. The significance of the threat increases with the seniority of the person, e.g. an audit partner, therefore the audit firm would not need to resign. It is the audit firm's responsibility to manage any ethical threats and take appropriate action. They cannot stop someone from taking a job with another organisation.

14 OPTION 2

A discount of 40% is unlikely to be a trivial sum and therefore the most appropriate option is to reject the discount. The ACCA Code of Ethics and Conduct allows acceptance of goods and hospitality that are considered trivial and inconsequential. Approval would be sought from the audit engagement partner not the audit manager.

15 OPTION D

The ACCA Code of Ethics and Conduct states that preparation of tax returns does not generally create a self-review threat. This is because the audit firm would not be calculating the figures to include in the return. The procedure of preparing the tax return is mechanical in nature. Provision of tax advice could create a significant self-review threat as it may be discovered at a later date that the advice was not appropriate and the firm may be reluctant to admit this to the client.

16 OPTIONS 2 AND 4

The audit firm must obtain consent from both firms. If consent is not given, the firm must decide which client to keep. The firm does not have to choose its current audit client. It could decide to resign from the audit of Winnie Co and accept the audit of Piglet Co. There is no requirement for an audit firm to consult with ACCA and request permission when a conflict of interest such as the one described arises.

17 OPTION 2

The audit teams of each client would sign a confidentiality agreement but it would not be necessary to have all employees of the firm sign confidentiality agreements.

18 OPTION 4

Partner rotation is only a requirement for listed companies and only once the partner has been in place for seven years. Self-review is the main threat created when additional services such as payroll and bookkeeping are provided to an audit client. Confidentiality is not an issue as the information obtained relates to the same client and is not being provided to any other parties. Payroll and bookkeeping services can be provided to a non-listed audit client if they are routine and mechanical in nature. Advice on accounting policies is also acceptable as long as the client is responsible for making decisions on which accounting policies to use.

19 OPTION 3

A contingent fee arrangement, such as the one described, creates a self-interest threat. The auditor would have a financial interest in the client achieving a higher profit and may ignore misstatements which would reduce profit if adjusted. The proposal must be rejected as the ACCA Code of Ethics and Conduct does not allow contingent fee arrangements for assurance work.

20

Senior management is correct that reporting the company will constitute a breach of confidentiality	True	**False**
Tigger & Co must report the breach of laws and regulations to the appropriate authority if the client refuses	**True**	False
Tigger & Co must report the breach of laws and regulations as it is a public interest matter	**True**	False
Tigger & Co must report the matter to the parent company and the audit firm responsible for the parent company audit	**True**	False

In accordance with ISA 250 (Revised) *Consideration of Laws and Regulations in an Audit of Financial Statements*, the auditor has increased responsibility when non-compliance by a client is identified. The auditor must try and get the client to report the matter themselves in the first instance. If the client refuses and the breach is likely to be in the public interest, the auditor must report the matter to the appropriate authority.

As Eeyore Co is a global company and the issue relates to environmental pollution, it is highly likely to be considered a public interest matter. As Eeyore Co is a subsidiary, the matter must also be reported to the parent company and any other auditors involved such as the parent company auditor.

21

Ola Osbourne is the chair and chief executive	**Strength**	**Deficiency**
Taylor Tahir is the designated person to assist with workforce engagement	**Strength**	**Deficiency**
Ola Osbourne is considering appointing a close friend as a non-executive director	**Strength**	**Deficiency**

The chair and chief executive roles should be performed by different people to avoid too much power being held by one person. In addition, the chair should be independent on appointment and this is not the case with Ola Osbourne who has only recently been appointed chair after being chief executive for five years.

The board should understand the views of the company's other key stakeholders such as employees. The company should use a director appointed from the workforce, a workforce advisory panel or a designated non-executive director (NED). Taylor Tahir is a designated NED.

Directors, both executive and non-executive, should be appointed based on merit, relevant skills and experience.

22 OPTION 4

The audit committee must comprise independent NEDs, this means Lindsay Lewis (executive director), Ola Osbourne (executive director) and Jules Jardine (NED but not independent) cannot be members. In addition, the board chair cannot be a member of the audit committee which is another reason Ola Osbourne cannot sit on the audit committee. Therefore, only Taylor Tahir can be on the audit committee.

23 1D, 2C

At least half the board, excluding the chair should be independent NEDs. To balance the board of directors, three more non-executive directors need to be appointed. This will create a board of eight directors excluding the chair, four of which will be independent non-executive directors (3 new + Taylor Tahir). It is unlikely that a company would reduce the number of directors to achieve a balance.

Executive directors' remuneration should include performance related pay linked with the long-term sustainable success of the company, such as share options.

24 OPTION 1

The chair must be independent on appointment. Jules Jardine has been a member of the board for ten years. Independence is deemed to be compromised if a director has served on the board for more than nine years. Options 2, 3 and 4 are all provisions of the Corporate Governance Code.

25

Remuneration of directors should be set by the Nomination Committee	**True**	**False**
Workforce remuneration should be taken into consideration when setting the remuneration of executive directors	**True**	**False**
The company should be able to withhold bonuses and share awards from directors whose performance is not acceptable	**True**	**False**

Remuneration should be set by the remuneration committee to ensure a fair and transparent process. Remuneration of executive directors should be determined using formal and transparent procedures. Executive directors should receive performance related pay linked with sustainable long-term success of the company to incentivise the executive directors to grow the business and maximise shareholder wealth. This should be related to the long-term performance of the company rather than short term profits which could provide incentive to manipulate results. Non-executive directors should be paid a fixed salary which represents the time and commitment to the role, in order to improve independence.

Workforce remuneration and related policies should be considered when setting executive directors' remuneration.

Remuneration schemes should include provisions that enable the company to recover or withhold amounts or share awards to reduce the risk of directors being rewarded when the company is under-performing.

26 2D

The fundamental principle at risk is professional competence and due care as many of the audit team are new and do not have relevant experience in relation to the specialised industry in which Fir Co operates. It is not appropriate to reinstate the previous partner. As the previous partner has been rotated due to long association, a cooling-off period must be served before being involved with the client again. The audit firm should offer appropriate training for the audit team to ensure they have the necessary knowledge to carry out the work.

27 2C

As the previous audit manager is now finance director at the client, there is a familiarity threat due to the ongoing relationship between the old and new audit manager. The familiarity threat is not so severe that the firm would need to resign. It is not practical to prevent the audit manager speaking to the finance director during an audit as this will reduce the efficiency and effectiveness of the audit. A new audit manager should be appointed.

28

Routine maintenance of payroll records	**Self-review**	**Self-interest**	**Advocacy**
Assistance with the selection of a new non-executive director	**Self-review**	**Self-interest**	**Advocacy**
Tax services whereby Sycamore & Co would liaise with the tax authority on Fir Co's behalf	**Self-review**	**Self-interest**	**Advocacy**

As per the ACCA *Code of Ethics and Conduct*, the following threats would be created from carrying out the non-audit services requested by Fir Co:

Payroll – Self-review as the auditor will also be involved in auditing the figures included in the financial statements in relation to wages and salaries.

Recruitment – Self-interest as the auditor would be involved in selecting an officer of the company who has significant influence over the financial statements and audit.

Tax – Advocacy as the auditor may be perceived to be representing and promoting Fir Co's interest in liaising with the tax authority.

29 OPTION 3

Using separate teams will not address the self-interest threat from the fee levels as separating the teams will not alleviate the firm's potential financial dependence on Fir Co.

30 OPTION 2

As per ACCA *Code of Ethics and Conduct*, confidential information may be disclosed when such disclosure is required by law.

31 OPTION 4

In line with ACCA's *Code of Ethics and Conduct*, a self-interest threat would arise due to the personal relationship between the audit engagement partner and finance director.

A self-interest threat, not intimidation threat, would arise as a result of the overdue fee and due to the nature of the non-audit work, it is unlikely that a self-review threat would arise.

32 OPTION 3

Cassie Dixon has no ongoing relationship with Bush Co and would therefore be the most appropriate replacement as audit engagement partner to maintain independence. Appointing any of the other potential replacements would give rise to self-review or familiarity threats to independence.

33 OPTION 2

If Alan Marshlow accepts the position as a non-executive director for Plant Co, self-interest and self-review threats are created which are so significant that no safeguards can be implemented. As per ACCA's *Code of Ethics and Conduct*, no partner of the firm should serve as a director of an audit client and as such, Horti & Co would need to resign as auditor.

34 OPTION 3

Assuming a management responsibility is when the auditor is involved in leading or directing the company or making decisions which are the remit of management.

Designing and maintaining internal controls, determining which recommendations to implement and setting the scope of work are all decisions which should be taken by management.

35 OPTION 1

Weed Co is a listed company and the fees received by Horti & Co from the company have exceeded 15% of the firm's total fees for two years. Matters affecting independence must be disclosed to those charged with governance of a listed client and an appropriate safeguard should be implemented. In this case, it would be appropriate to have a pre-issuance review carried out prior to issuing the audit opinion for the current year.

36 OPTION 1

The offer of gifts from an audit client can create threats of self-interest and familiarity. The ACCA Code of Ethics and Conduct states that gifts must be declined if they are offered as an inducement to influence the auditor's behaviour, even if they are trivial and inconsequential. As the finance director has commented that the offer is intended to make the audit team more favourable toward the client, the offer is an inducement and must be declined.

37 OPTION 2

The ACCA Code of Ethics and Conduct states that when fees from a non-listed client represent 30% of the firm's total fees for five consecutive years, independence is threatened. The firm must take all three of the actions stated.

38 OPTION 4

The audit senior must not be assigned to the audit of LV Fones Co as a self-review threat will be created. The audit senior may be responsible for auditing areas for which they were responsible when on secondment and may not detect misstatements or may not wish to admit to misstatements if detected. A familiarity threat may also be created because the audit senior may have developed friendships with client staff whilst on secondment.

39 OPTION 3

All three actions should be taken by the audit firm if fees remain outstanding.

40

Ethical threat
Intimidation
Familiarity
Self-interest

Course of action
Resign from the audit engagement
Structure the audit partner's responsibilities to reduce the potential impact to the engagement
Remove the audit partner from the audit

Friendships between the auditor and client create a familiarity threat as the auditor may be too trusting of people they know well, and may therefore exercise less professional scepticism. The audit firm would only need to resign from the engagement if there was no alternative engagement partner that could be assigned to the audit of LV Fones Co. The audit engagement partner has the most influence over the audit and it would be impossible to structure the partner's responsibilities to reduce the potential impact whilst in charge of the engagement. The only way this can be achieved is to remove the partner from the audit and replace with a different partner.

41 1E, 2D, 3A

Difficulties retaining or obtaining an audit firm may indicate that management of Mickey Co lack integrity and audit firms are not willing to take on the engagement. As the audit is required to be completed within a tight deadline, the firm will need to go through the acceptance process, obtain an understanding of the client, plan and perform the audit and issue the auditor's report within three months. This will require sufficient resources to ensure the work can be completed to a high standard and the firm may not have sufficient resource to achieve this. As Mickey Co is a main competitor of Goofy Co, another audit client of the firm, a conflict of interest arises which creates a threat to objectivity and confidentiality.

42 OPTION 2

To manage the conflict of interest the firm must: 1. Inform Mickey Co and Goofy Co. 2. Obtain consent to act. 3. Implement safeguards. 4. Perform an engagement quality review.

43 OPTION 3

Ethical threat
Intimidation
Familiarity
Self-interest

Course of action
Remove the audit engagement partner from the audit
Structure the audit partner's responsibilities to reduce the potential impact to the engagement
Inform Goofy Co that it should not employ the audit engagement partner's son

It is unlikely that a sales manager would be in a position to influence the financial statements and therefore threats to familiarity or intimidation are unlikely to arise.

A significant self-interest threat is created by the son receiving shares as part of his remuneration. The ACCA Code of Ethics and Conduct states that a direct, or material indirect financial interest must not be held by the audit team or an immediate family member of the audit team. The partner will need to be removed from the audit.

44 OPTION 4

The ACCA Code of Ethics and Conduct states that contingent fee arrangements are not allowed for non-assurance services provided to audit clients if the fee will be material (significant) to the firm, therefore option 4 is the most appropriate answer.

45 OPTION 1

The ACCA Code of Ethics and Conduct states that reviewing qualifications and assessing competence of applicants does not generally create a threat to objectivity as the auditor is not making any management decisions that could cause a threat to objectivity. Goofy Co can provide this service if it will not result in the firm assuming management responsibilities.

46 OPTION 4

In accordance with the Corporate Governance Code, the board chair must be independent on appointment and must therefore be appointed externally.

At least half of the board, excluding the chair, must be independent non-executive directors. There should be workforce representation on the board. Independence is deemed to be compromised when a director has served for nine years. Linda can continue to be a member of the board if re-elected but will not be independent.

47 OPTION 2

The board chair must be independent on appointment. The board chair cannot sit on the audit committee but can be a member of the remuneration committee provided they are not the committee chair. Remuneration of non-executive directors must be a fixed salary. Restrictions on the number of directorships a person can take are only applicable to the largest 100 listed companies (e.g. FTSE 100).

48 OPTION 1

Independence is compromised if a non-executive director was employed by the company less than five years ago, has owned shares in the company within the last three years, or receives remuneration from the company other than a fixed salary for the role of non-executive director, such as a pension.

49 OPTION 2

The lack of independence due to the relationship with the chief executive, along with the request for a fixed three-year contract when all directors must stand for re-election annually, are both disadvantages to Mica taking a non-executive director position.

50 OPTIONS 2 AND 3

In accordance with the Corporate Governance Code, there should be a formal and rigorous annual evaluation of the performance of the board, its committees, the chair and the individual directors. The annual report should describe how the nomination committee has ensured appropriate appointments have been made including gender balance and diversity. A succession plan should be in place for the board and senior management, not just the chair and chief executive. The nomination committee must comprise a majority of independent non-executive directors but does not require all members to be INEDs.

PLANNING AND RISK ASSESSMENT

51 OPTION 2

Oil and gas companies are heavily regulated therefore the effect of non-compliance is likely to be a significant audit risk. Provisions and contingent liabilities may arise if there are issues such as oil spills or injury to employees in the workplace given the hazardous nature of the industry. As the company operates in three continents, foreign currency transactions are likely to be significant. Trade payables may be a risk for certain clients but in relation to the other risks stated, is unlikely to be a significant risk.

52 OPTIONS 2 AND 5

Detection risk is greater due to the lack of knowledge and experience of the client. In order to address this, the auditor must spend time obtaining an understanding of the client. The auditor can request copies of working papers from the previous auditor to help with this.

53 OPTION 1

Materiality ranges using traditional benchmarks:

Revenue (½% – 1%)	\$620,000 – \$1,240,000
Profit before tax (5% – 10%)	\$475,000 – \$950,000

As Veryan Co is a new audit client it is likely that materiality will be set at the lower end of the materiality scale to reflect the increased detection risk. Option 1 is 16% of profit and 1.2% of revenue and is therefore too high based on the traditional benchmark calculations. Options 2, 3 and 4 all sit within the ranges calculated above.

54

Cut-off of revenue is an audit risk	**Consistent** (shaded)	**Not consistent**
Completeness of revenue is an audit risk	**Consistent**	**Not consistent** (shaded)
Occurrence of revenue is an audit risk	**Consistent** (shaded)	**Not consistent**

Revenue has increased by 24% compared with 12% in previous years. Revenue may be overstated due to cut-off errors where sales relating to next year have been included in this year. Revenue may be overstated if sales have not occurred and are fictitious. Completeness would be a risk if revenue was lower than expected, however, as the profit margin has increased from 6% (6/100 × 100) to 7.7% (9.5/124 × 100) revenue appears to be overstated rather than understated.

55 1E, 2G, 3F

Receivables

To assess the recoverability of receivables, reviewing correspondence with customers may highlight any disputes which indicate that payment will not be made. Direct confirmation of a customer balance confirms existence of the debt but does not provide evidence that it will be paid.

Non-current assets

Damage caused by a hurricane is likely to lead to impairment of non-current assets. The client must perform an impairment review and consider whether an impairment charge is required, e.g. if carrying amount has fallen below recoverable amount. The auditor should review the results of management's impairment test to assess whether any impairment charge is adequate. Option A does not specify that the exploration site damaged by the hurricane would be physically inspected therefore this is not necessarily an appropriate procedure for the audit risk given.

Intangible assets (licences)

Amortisation of intangible assets can be checked by calculating the expected amortisation charge and comparing it with management's figure. Inspecting the licence agreement will only confirm the terms of the licence but will not state the amortisation charge that should be made each year.

56 OPTION 4

Increased audit risk arising from increased detection risk will result in increased quality management procedures such as the need for an engagement quality review. The auditor's lack of cumulative knowledge and experience of a client is a detection risk. Competence should have been considered **before** accepting. It is not professional to resign immediately after accepting an engagement. The audit firm should have contacted the outgoing auditor **before** accepting to enquire about any professional matters which would affect the acceptance decision.

57 OPTION 2

The risk of revenue cut-off errors increases with employees aiming to maximise their current year bonus. The increased risk of a reduction in profits as a result of irrecoverable debts is a business risk. Revenue is more likely to be overstated in order to achieve a higher bonus. The bonus would have no impact on the customer response level to direct confirmation requests.

58

	20X5	**20X4**
Receivables collection period	35 (121/1267) × 365	30 (100/1205) × 365
Inventory holding period	58 (160/1013) × 365	47 (125/965) × 365

Formulae:

Receivables collection period = receivables/revenue × 365

Inventory holding period = inventory/cost of sales × 365

59 OPTION 1

Cut-off testing would not provide relevant evidence to the potential valuation issues.

60 OPTIONS 3 AND 4

Option 1 refers to final analytical procedures performed at the completion stage of the audit. Option 2 refers to substantive analytical procedures performed during the fieldwork stage of the audit.

61

	20X5	20X4
Gross profit margin	44.0% (5.5/12.5 × 100)	46.7% (7/15 × 100)
Current ratio	2.2 (1.9 + 3.1 + 0.8)/(1.6 + 1.0)	4.4 (1.4 + 2.0 + 1.9)/1.2

Formulae:

Gross profit margin = gross profit/revenue × 100

Current ratio = current assets/current liabilities

As the loan is due for payment on 31 January 20X6, this is a current liability in 20X5 but not 20X4.

62 OPTION 3

	20X5	20X4
Payables payment period	83 (1.6/7 × 365)	55 (1.2/8 × 365)

Payables payment period = payables/cost of sales × 365

The payables payment period has increased by 28 days. This could indicate cash flow problems which the auditor will need to consider as part of its going concern assessment. If there are uncertainties over the company's ability to continue as a going concern, disclosure will be required in the notes to the financial statements and the auditor's report will need to reference the client's disclosure.

Options 1 and 2 are not correct as the payables payment period has increased not decreased. Option 4 would not need to be considered by the auditor as there is no indication of cash flow problems affecting going concern.

63 OPTIONS 1, 2 AND 6

Options 1, 2 and 6 are audit risks as they clearly describe how the financial statements may be materially misstated. Options 3, 4 and 5 are business risks as they describe issues the directors would be concerned about but which would not necessarily result in the financial statements being materially misstated.

64 OPTIONS 2 AND 3

Options 2 and 3 will allow the auditor to make an assessment of the appropriateness of the change. Option 4 is of no audit value as it is known the policy has changed during the year. In relation to option 1, the auditor will still need to assess the appropriateness of the change in useful life and discuss the matter with management if it is not appropriate. Whilst the change may not have a material impact this year, it may become material in subsequent years therefore the issue should be addressed as soon as it is identified.

65 OPTION 3

Option 1 describes materiality. Option 2 describes tolerable misstatement. Option 4 describes a clearly trivial threshold.

66 OPTION 3

There is no suggestion of any issue that would cause the auditor to consider resigning. The audit team should be fully briefed and advised to be vigilant. The finance director should also be advised that their assistance is likely to be requested by the audit team in the absence of a financial controller.

67 OPTIONS 2, 3 AND 5

Lack of supplier statement reconciliations can mean misstatements within payables and accruals go undetected. As controls are not effective in this area, increased substantive testing will need to be performed. The auditor should not perform the reconciliations as this is the responsibility of Hawk. There is no need to send requests for confirmations if the client has received a supplier statement. The issue relates to the client not reconciling the statement to its own ledgers.

68 OPTION 4

It would not be appropriate or professional for the auditor to discuss the claim with the financial controller, especially when legal proceedings are ongoing.

69 OPTION D

Gross profit margin

The ratio has decreased from 26% to 17% which indicates that website sales may not be completely recorded.

If sales had not occurred, the revenue balance would be overstated and the gross profit margin would increase.

If revenue had been recognised too early, the revenue balance would be overstated and the gross profit margin would increase.

Payables payment period

The ratio has decreased from 75 to 40 days which indicates understatement of payables i.e. payables may not be completely recorded.

Suppliers withdrawing credit terms is a business risk, not an audit risk.

If purchase invoices have been recorded twice, the payables balance would be overstated and the payables payment period would increase.

Receivables collection period

The ratio has increased from 29 to 38 days which indicates that receivables may be overvalued.

Extended credit terms may have been given to customers is not an audit risk.

If receivables are not completely recorded, the receivables balance would be understated and the receivables collection period would decrease.

70 OPTION 2

As the analytical procedures are being performed at the planning stage using the most recent management accounts of Hawk Co, the financial statement figures are not being tested. Analytical procedures at the planning stage are performed to help identify areas of potential risk and to obtain an understanding of the client. When the draft financial statement figures are available, **substantive** analytical procedures can be used to help detect material misstatements.

71 OPTION 1

Procedures 3 and 4 are tests of control not substantive procedures.

72 1C, 2C, 3D, 4A

Matter		Audit strategy section	
1	Risk of material misstatement including the risk of fraud	C	Significant factors, preliminary engagement activities, and knowledge gained on other engagements
2	Use of professional scepticism	C	Significant factors, preliminary engagement activities, and knowledge gained on other engagements
3	Selection of the audit team	D	Nature, timing and extent of resources
4	Use of automated tools and audit techniques	A	Characteristics of the engagement

73 OPTION 4

The fraud involves an employee stealing money from the company therefore is an example of misappropriation of assets. Detection risk will need to decrease as control risk is higher. For the employee to be able to commit this type of fraud, internal controls must not be working effectively therefore control risk is higher. The auditor can only assess control risk, they cannot influence it. Detection risk is the only component of audit risk the auditor can change. The risk of fraud must always be discussed with the audit team in accordance with ISA 240 *The Auditor's Responsibilities Relating to Fraud in an Audit of Financial Statements.*

74 OPTION 3

If employees working within the same department are related there is an increased risk of collusion which would circumvent any segregation of duties control. Therefore, to prevent frauds occurring in the payroll department, the people working together should not be related. Exception reports and review of employee lists by department managers would detect if fictitious employees had been set up on the payroll system. However, this would be after the fraud had occurred. Comparison of the monthly payroll cost with the prior month may detect fraud if the fraud is of sufficient scale to cause a significant variance but will not prevent fraud.

75 OPTIONS 1, 4 AND 5

A discussion with management would be useful to identify any other suspected frauds. Searching for duplicate bank account numbers would identify possible other frauds that are occurring. Reconciling the number of employees to the number of people being paid will identify fictitious employees on the payroll system.

Reporting the matter to the police is a management function and therefore not an audit procedure to detect further frauds.

As the employee had created fictitious employees to be paid in the payroll system, the details on the payroll records will match the payments in the bank statements therefore further fraud would not be detected.

INTERNAL CONTROLS

76

	Narrative notes	Internal control questionnaires	Both
Advantages			
Can be prepared in advance		✓	
Easy to understand			✓
Disadvantages			
May overstate the controls		✓	
Some controls may be missed			✓

Narrative notes are simple to record and easy to understand. However, controls may be difficult to pick out from the detail.

Internal control questionnaires are prepared in advance which can ensure that all typical controls are covered. However, the ICQ may not identify unusual controls. Management may overstate the controls by stating that they have the controls listed when in fact they don't. As the questionnaire is standardised it is easy to understand.

77

		Explanation
1	Deficiency	The goods received should be agreed to the authorised purchase order before signing the delivery note to ensure that only goods actually ordered are accepted. The supplier's delivery note will record what has been sent which may not be the same as the purchase order.
2	Strength	Matching the purchase invoice to the GRN ensures the goods being paid for have been received. Matching the GRN to the order ensures the goods received were ordered. Keeping the documents filed together provides a complete audit trail to support the transaction.
3	Strength	Monthly reviews of standing data by the department manager ensures that the correct details are held on a regular basis. Any employees who have left the company would be identified and could be removed from the payroll records before an invalid payment is made.
4	Strength	Pre-printed payroll sheets ensure that only genuine employees are paid. If any names are added to the sheets this will highlight a potential fraud or error which can be investigated before payment is made.

78 OPTION 2

By reviewing the payment list, the finance director will be able to identify any unusual names or duplicate names. This control will ensure only valid employees are paid. The bank transfer list will only show details of names and net pay therefore will not identify incorrect classification of costs, incorrect hours, or incorrect calculations unless a significant error was made.

79 OPTION 3

If reliance can be placed on the internal controls, reduced substantive testing can be performed. If the controls are working effectively it is likely that written representations from management will be more reliable rather than less reliable. Similarly, if controls are effective, the information used for analytical procedures is likely to be more reliable and therefore more reliance can be placed on analytical procedures as compared with tests of detail. Effective controls are unlikely to influence the amount of evidence obtained from a third party (although ineffective controls would influence the auditor to obtain more evidence from third parties as client generated evidence will be less reliable).

80

Recalculate the total of the bank transfer list	**Substantive procedure**
Inspect the bank transfer list for evidence of the finance director's signature confirming the payment can be made	**Test of control**
For a sample of employees, agree the salary details in the standing data files to the calculation of the employee's monthly salary as per the payslip	**Substantive procedure**
Review the procedures to ensure payroll files and documents are kept secure and confidential	**Test of control**

A substantive procedure is used to test the payroll figure in the financial statements.

A test of control is used to test the effectiveness of controls over payroll processing.

81 OPTION 3

Discounts received relate to the purchases system.

82 1C, 2A, 3D, 4B

Deficiency		**Explanation**	
(i)	Availability of inventory is not checked at the time of ordering	C	Risk of orders not being fulfilled on a timely basis
(ii)	Telephone orders are not recorded immediately	A	Risk of incorrect orders being despatched
(iii)	Order forms are not sequentially numbered	D	Orders may go missing leading to unfulfilled orders
(iv)	The online ordering system allows customers to exceed their credit limit	B	Risk of irrecoverable debts

83 OPTIONS 1 AND 4

The system should not allow credit limits to be exceeded by any amount. Changes to credit limits should only be performed by a responsible senior official.

84 OPTION 2

Orders should be sequentially pre-numbered and a regular sequence check performed to ensure the sequence is complete. Instructing customers not to place orders by telephone may result in sales being lost. A better system would be to enter the orders into the system immediately whilst the customer is placing the order. Option 1 is a recommendation for deficiency (i).

85 OPTION 3

To increase independence of the internal auditors, the findings should be communicated to those charged with governance. If the findings are reported directly to the finance director there is a risk that the finance director perceives any deficiencies as a criticism and may not report the findings to the board of directors.

An internal audit assignment is performed for the company. There is no requirement for findings to be communicated to the external auditor or the shareholders.

86 OPTION 2

Tracing a transaction through the system to ensure it is recorded in the detailed sales listing is a substantive procedure testing the assertion of completeness.

87

Daily backups of the system	**General**	**Information processing**
Authorisation of purchase orders	**General**	**Information processing**
Minimum order quantities	**General**	**Information processing**
Automatic updating of inventory once goods are sold	**General**	**Information processing**

Backups relates to the whole computer system therefore are a general control. Authorisation, minimum order quantities and automatic updating of inventory relate to the processing of information in the purchasing and inventory systems.

88 OPTION 1

Reviewing inventory levels immediately before and after a sales order has been processed enables the auditor to ensure the inventory level is updated automatically. Counting a sample of items to agree the quantities in the system does not prove the system updates automatically. The quantities may agree because that type of inventory may not have been sold recently and the quantities reflect the results of the last inventory count. Reviewing the inventory quantities in the system does not confirm the quantities held in the warehouse or that the system updates automatically. The auditor would not contact a customer to make an enquiry such as the one described.

89

Control	
The inventory system is automatically updated to reflect that inventory has been allocated to a sales order	✓
The system will flag if there is insufficient inventory to fulfil the order	✓
When inventory falls to a minimum level a purchase order is automatically created and sent to the purchasing manager for authorisation	✓
The purchase order is automatically sent electronically to the approved supplier for that item	✓

As all of the controls stated are computerised controls, a dummy order can be used to test them.

90 OPTIONS 1 AND 3

To rely on the internal auditor's work, Marigold & Co should review the internal auditor's working papers and reperform a sample of the tests again. An expert would not need to be used in this situation as the auditor can easily see if the internal auditor has performed the work properly by reperforming a sample of tests. The auditor cannot simply assume that the presence of an audit committee means the work of the internal auditor will be reliable, they must assess the work to ensure it is appropriate for audit purposes.

91 OPTIONS 2 AND 4

A control objective should describe a risk to be mitigated by an internal control. Options 1 and 5 describe the internal control but not the risk. Option 3 is a control objective relating to the recording of asset expenditure items but maintenance of the register is not the responsibility of the asset expenditure committee therefore is not a control objective addressed by its work.

92

The internal audit department agrees the physical assets to the asset register to ensure completeness	Physical or logical control	Verification	Reconciliation
Variances between actual and budgeted expenditure are analysed in the quarterly management accounts	Segregation of duties	Verification	Reconciliation
The non-current asset register is password protected	Physical or logical control	Segregation of duties	Authorisation

93 OPTION 4

The requisition is approved (authorised) by the asset expenditure committee. The purchase order is authorised by the purchasing director once checked against the approved requisition. Both of these documents contain signatures confirming authorisation/approval. The meeting minutes also contain evidence of the approval of the asset expenditure committee.

The GRN is not authorised although it should be matched to a copy of the authorised purchase order. This is not as persuasive as the signed requisition and order.

It will be assumed that if the controls have worked throughout the cycle, assets should not be able to be purchased and recorded in the non-current asset register unless they have been authorised. This is not as persuasive as the signed requisition and order.

94 OPTION 3

When an external auditor performs a comparison of actual to budget, this is a substantive analytical procedure. The other three procedures provide evidence that a control has operated effectively and are therefore tests of control.

95 OPTION 4

According to ISA 610 *Using the Work of Internal Auditors*, the external auditor must not assign work to the internal auditor which involves significant judgement, a high risk of material misstatement or with which the internal auditor has been involved. Cash counts will be the most appropriate as they do not involve significant judgement and there is nothing to indicate that the petty cash balance is material. The internal audit department is currently assessing internal controls over non-current assets therefore is work with which the internal auditor has recently been involved and may create a self-review threat. Revenue recognition is likely to involve significant judgement and possibly a high risk of material misstatement. Valuation of inventory for a manufacturer is likely to include significant work-in-progress which also involves significant judgement and a high risk of material misstatement.

AUDIT EVIDENCE

96 OPTION 2

A supplier with a low balance at the year end but with a high volume of transactions during the year may indicate that not all liabilities have been recorded at the year-end date.

97 OPTION 3

A purchase of a large volume of goods close to the year end would increase the payables payment period.

The prompt payment and trade discounts would both decrease the payables payment period, and the extended credit terms in this instance would have no impact as there is no closing balance with the new supplier.

98 OPTION 4

The difference of $144,640 with Oxford Co relates to goods which were received by Chester Co prior to the year end but were not recorded in the accounting records until after the year-end date. As Chester Co had a liability to pay for the goods at the date of receipt, an accrual should be created for the goods received not yet invoiced.

99 OPTION 1

The difference in respect of Poole Co may have arisen if the invoice had been paid twice in error as an additional $156,403 will have been debited to the supplier account.

100 OPTION 2

Reviewing the accruals listing would not help the auditor confirm the trade payables balance with Bath Co as accruals are recorded separately from trade payables.

101 OPTION 4

The cut-off assertion relates to transactions being recorded in the correct accounting period. In this case, payroll costs reflect payroll transactions for the period to 31 March 20X5. Options 1, 2 and 3 relate to the assertions of classification, accuracy and completeness.

102 OPTION 2

The most reliable evidence will be the work performed by the audit team member as auditor generated evidence is the most reliable. Verbal confirmation is the least reliable form of evidence as it can be disputed or retracted. Written confirmation is the next least reliable form of evidence as it is client generated.

103 OPTION 1

Prior year expense: $17,000,000

Employee numbers reduce from 500 to 450, a decrease of 10%.

Effect of redundancies: $17,000,000 × 90% = $15,300,000.

Effect of pay rise: ($15,300,000 × 2/12) + ($15,300,000 × 106/100 × 10/12) = $16,065,000

Effect of bonus: $16,065,000 + (450 × $1,500) = $16,740,000.

Alternatively, the calculation can be done as follows:

Prior year salaries adjusted for redundancies	= $17m × 0.9	= $15.3m
Adjust for wage rise for remaining staff	= $15.3m × 6% × 10/12	= $0.765m
Include bonus	= $1,500 × 450	= $0.675m
Total		= $16.74m

104 OPTIONS 3 AND 4

Analytical procedures evaluate trends and relationships between data. The auditor should investigate any unusual relationships which don't fit in with their expectation as it may indicate misstatement. A comparison to the prior year with an investigation of differences and a proof-in-total calculations are both examples of substantive analytical procedures. Recalculation is a simple arithmetical check. Agreeing the wages expense per the payroll system to the draft financial statements involves inspection.

105

1	Review the treatment of a sample of post-year-end returns	Accuracy	Completeness	**Occurrence**
2	Select a sample of goods despatch notes and agree to invoices in the detailed sales listing	Accuracy	**Completeness**	Occurrence
3	Select a sample of invoices from the detailed sales listing and agree to goods despatch notes	Accuracy	Completeness	**Occurrence**
4	Select a sample of invoices and recalculate the invoiced amount agreeing to price list	**Accuracy**	Completeness	Occurrence

The occurrence assertion means transactions have occurred and pertain to the entity, i.e. the sale is a genuine transaction of the business. Post-year-end returns would mean the transaction had not really occurred and should be removed from sales. Agreeing a sample of invoices to GDNs allows the auditor to confirm the sale is genuine. Selecting items from outside of the accounting records and tracing them into the records is a test for completeness. Recalculating invoices and confirming prices enables the auditor to test accuracy.

106 OPTIONS 1, 2 AND 3

Where completeness is the key assertion, the sample should be selected to verify where the balance may be understated and therefore should include suppliers with material balances, suppliers with a high volume of business with Poppy Co and major suppliers with no outstanding balance at the year end.

107 OPTION 1

In order to determine if the balance with Lily Co is understated, the auditor should determine if the goods should be included in payables at the year end by inspecting the goods received note. There is no need to send a confirmation request to Lily Co as a supplier statement has been obtained.

108 OPTION 3

To confirm the balance with Carnation Co, the auditor must determine if the liability exists for the disputed items at the year end by reviewing pre-year-end goods returned notes and post-year-end credit notes to verify that the goods have been returned and the order cancelled by the supplier.

109 OPTION 2

Although the control error is immaterial, the auditor must reach a conclusion on the population, based on the sample selected. In order to do so the effect of the error must be considered in relation to the whole population. It is not appropriate to project a one-off error across the population as by its nature it is not representative of the population.

110

Selecting a sample of supplier balances for testing using monetary unit sampling	**Test data**	**Audit software**
Recalculating the ageing of trade payables to identify balances which may be in dispute	**Test data**	**Audit software**
Calculation of trade payables payment period to use in analytical procedures	**Test data**	**Audit software**
Inputting dummy purchase invoices into the client system to see if processed correctly	**Test data**	**Audit software**

Test data involves inputting dummy transactions into the client's system to test how the transactions are processed. The other options are examples of audit software.

111 OPTION 4

Reviewing post-year-end receipts will confirm actual recoverability of the outstanding balance therefore provides the most reliable evidence.

A direct confirmation will confirm the amount outstanding but not the intention of the customer to pay this amount.

The payment history of Albatross Co does not ensure that current invoices will actually be paid.

Correspondence between Albatross Co and Eagle would be reliable, but not as reliable as the receipt of cash.

112 OPTIONS 2 AND 3

Options 1 and 4 relate to valuation.

113 OPTIONS 1 AND 2

A decrease in selling price may result in the cost of inventory being higher than net realisable value (NRV). Increased inventory levels for a company experiencing a reduction in sales may result in inventory not being sold and therefore NRV may be lower than cost. Inventory turnover would need to decrease to indicate valuation issues. There is nothing to indicate that the nature of the inventory would result in valuation issues. Eagle does not have the right to include third-party inventory in its financial statements. Inclusion would overstate inventory quantities but would not represent overvaluation.

114

Observe the client's staff to ensure they are following the inventory count instructions	**Test of control**	**Substantive procedure**
Inspect the inventory for evidence of damage or obsolescence	**Test of control**	**Substantive procedure**
Reperform the reconciliation from the inventory count date to the year-end date for inventory to assess the accuracy of the inventory quantities.	**Test of control**	**Substantive procedure**

Observing the count to ensure the count instructions are followed will provide the auditor with evidence that the controls over the inventory count are operating effectively. The other two tests are substantive in nature providing evidence over the accuracy, valuation and allocation assertion.

115 OPTION 1

The auditor needs to establish whether the claim is probable to succeed before they can ask the client to recognise a provision. If the claim is not probable to succeed it should not be recognised. If it is possible to succeed it should be disclosed as a contingent liability. This evidence should be obtained from the legal adviser as they are an independent expert. The auditor would review board minutes to ascertain the view of the board as a whole in respect of the claim. It would not be appropriate for the auditor to contact the customer making the claim against the client.

116 OPTION 3

The client performs the inventory count. The external auditor will perform a sample of test counts to ensure the count is accurate. The primary objective of the count is to ascertain accurate quantities. Some companies will produce items 24 hours a day. Provided the count is properly organised to ensure goods are not moved in and out of the counting area during the count the company does not need to cease production. ISA 501 *Audit Evidence – Specific Considerations for Selected Items* requires the auditor to attend the inventory count if inventory is a material balance.

117 OPTION 3

If the timetable is not monitored, some areas could be missed and all inventory may not be counted at least once a year.

118

Staple & Co must attend at least one count to ensure adequate controls are applied	**True**	**False**
Cut-off testing will only need to be performed if a full count is carried out at the year end	**True**	**False**
All lines of inventory must be counted at least twice during the year	**True**	**False**
Staple & Co should visit the client's premises at least once a year and request a surprise inventory count	**True**	**False**

119

1	**Strength**	**Deficiency**
2	**Strength**	**Deficiency**
3	**Strength**	**Deficiency**
4	**Strength**	**Deficiency**
5	**Strength**	**Deficiency**

Process 1 is a deficiency as counters may just agree with the quantity on the sheet and not actually count the goods.

Process 2 ensures discrepancies are highlighted for further investigation.

Process 3 will lead to understatement of inventory. Old or damaged items should be included until they are sold or scrapped.

Process 4 could result in cut-off errors as it will be difficult to identify goods already counted or not counted if movements are happening during the counting process.

Process 5 ensures inventory belonging to third parties is not recorded in Gloss Co's inventory records.

120 OPTION A

Agreeing the items listed on the count sheets to the physical inventory confirms existence. Agreeing the physical inventory quantities to the count sheet confirms completeness.

121 OPTIONS 2, 3 AND 4

When deciding whether to use sampling the population must be complete, accurate and appropriate for the purpose of the test. If the size of the population is small, sampling may not provide the most efficient method of obtaining evidence. Therefore, the size of the population would need to be considered. The time the auditor has available and the ease of obtaining evidence should not influence the audit procedures performed.

122

1	**Sampling**	**Not sampling**
2	**Sampling**	**Not sampling**
3	**Sampling**	**Not sampling**

Sampling involves selecting items for testing where all items have a chance of selection.

Procedure 1 describes monetary unit selection (MUS) which is a sampling method given in ISA 530 *Audit Sampling*.

Procedures 2 and 3 describe **selection** methods, not sampling methods. These procedures require items with specific characteristics to be tested, therefore all items will not have a chance of selection and as a result do not constitute sampling methods.

123 OPTION 3

Systematic sampling is where a sample is chosen with a constant interval. The starting point is chosen randomly.

124 OPTION 4

Procedure 1

This procedure will test the accuracy of the recorded amount.

The assertion of occurrence is not relevant to the audit of payables. Occurrence is relevant to purchases.

Tutorial note

To test occurrence of purchases, the GRN should be inspected and the invoice should be inspected for the name of the client in order to ensure the goods pertain to the Hemsworth Co.

Procedure 2

This procedure will test completeness of payables as it may identify invoices not included within payables or accruals at the year end.

The list of individual supplier balances, accruals listing, bank ledger account and GRNs are client generated evidence, therefore less reliable than third-party generated evidence.

Procedure 3

This procedure will test completeness of payables as well as rights and obligations and existence.

A payables circularisation would be performed if a supplier statement has not been retained or received.

Purchase invoices and supplier statements are third-party generated evidence, therefore more reliable than client generated evidence.

125 OPTION 2

The amount of testing should be increased before any further action is taken. The issue should then be discussed with the audit manager before discussing with the client. The audit opinion will only be modified if the errors are material and if they are not corrected by the client. This is the final action to be taken rather than the initial course of action.

126

The actual computer files and programs are not tested therefore the auditor has no direct evidence that the programs are working as expected	**Valid**	**Not valid**
Where errors are found in reconciling inputs to outputs, it may be difficult or even impossible to determine why those errors occurred	**Valid**	**Not valid**

As the system within the computer is not audited, the audit trail can be difficult to follow. This will mean direct evidence that the programs are working as expected cannot be obtained and it will be difficult to determine why the errors occurred.

127 OPTION 3

As there are 600 customers within the receivables listing, this makes the use of audit software much more beneficial to an auditor.

128 OPTION 4

All are procedures that could be performed using audit software.

129 OPTIONS 1, 3 AND 4

Audit software may slow Delphic Co's systems down. Test data is used to test the programmed controls. Audit software enables calculations and data sorting to be performed more quickly resulting in greater efficiency. Audit staff may need to be trained to use the software. Once the audit software has been designed there are no further costs (unless the client changes its systems). Therefore, the audit will only be more costly in the year of set up.

130 OPTION 3

If the partner advises Delphic Co which accounting system to choose, a self-review threat will be created. The external audit team does not need to be present during the implementation and testing. This may be impractical in terms of time and resource required. To save unnecessary time and expense, the audit firm should delay the use of audit software to ensure it is designed to effectively work with the new system.

131 OPTIONS 2 AND 5

The financial statements may still be manipulated to show a break-even position or to meet a specific target or objective imposed on the organisation. The auditor's report will be publicly available as taxpayers have a right to see the financial statements and associated auditor's report. The time required for the audit will depend on many factors such as complexity of the organisation and its transactions, the volume of transactions, etc., as is the case with company audits. An audit team should always be competent therefore the team should include people with public sector experience.

132 OPTION 3

An auditor's report for a local government authority will need to refer to going concern uncertainties in the same way as for a company.

133

Compare income by shop and category to the prior year	✓
Inspect credit notes issued post year end	
Agree totals on till receipts to the detailed sales listing, bank statements and bank ledger account	✓
Obtain the detailed sales listing and cast to confirm accuracy	✓

Inspection of credit notes issued post year end would identify possible overstatement of income rather than understatement.

134 OPTION 4

All risks given are relevant to Stargazers.

135

Management will have no financial qualifications therefore there is a greater risk of material misstatement	**Always true**	**May be true**	**Never true**
Internal control systems will not be as sophisticated as those for profit-making companies	**Always true**	**May be true**	**Never true**
There are fewer auditing standards applicable to audits of charities	**Always true**	**May be true**	**Never true**
Charities such as Stargazers will have different objectives to a profit-making company therefore the auditors' assessment of materiality will consider different factors	**Always true**	**May be true**	**Never true**

Some charities, particularly larger charities may have good internal control systems and predominantly qualified, paid staff responsible for the financial statements. Smaller charities may not have sufficient income to pay staff and may rely heavily on volunteers. Therefore options (1) and (2) MAY be true. Although ISAs are developed for audits of companies, they should still be followed in an audit of a charity or other NFP.

136 OPTION 3

Companies House (or equivalent) information provides independent evidence of the number of shares in issue. Option 1 is not relevant as a bonus issue does not generate cash. The bonus issue is debited against retained earnings in this case as there is no share premium account to utilise. Option 2 is client generated documentary evidence which is less reliable than third-party evidence. Option 4 is client generated verbal confirmation which is less reliable than documentary evidence or evidence from third parties.

137

$4 million	**Recognise in retained earnings**	Disclose in the notes
$6 million	Recognise in retained earnings	**Disclose in the notes**

Dividends paid during the year are debited to retained earnings and credited to bank. Dividends which are not approved by the year end cannot be recognised as no obligation has been created. Proposed dividends will be disclosed in the notes to the financial statements and recognised in the year they are approved.

138

Inspect the independent expert's report	**Completeness**	**Cut-off**	**Valuation**
Match the physical properties to the independent expert's report and non-current asset register	**Existence**	**Completeness**	**Presentation**
Recalculate the depreciation on revalued properties	**Completeness**	**Existence**	**Valuation**

The independent expert's report will show up-to-date values of the properties. This will only show the property values for those the client has requested and therefore does not confirm completeness. Cut-off is not a relevant assertion for non-current assets.

Matching the physical assets to the expert's report ensures that all properties have been revalued which is a requirement of IAS 16 *Property, Plant and Equipment* and matching into the non-current asset register confirms completeness of the assets in the financial statements.

Depreciation is used to reflect usage of an asset and affects the value of assets. Existence of assets is usually confirmed by physical inspection. Completeness relates to whether all assets have been recorded therefore not related to depreciation.

139 OPTIONS 1 AND 4

Total assets should equal total equity and liabilities on the statement of financial position.

The auditor will perform substantive tests of detail when auditing equity and reserves as they are material by nature and any movements will be one-off items which are not consistent year on year.

Movements in equity and reserves are shown in the statement of changes in equity.

140 OPTION 4

Procedure 2 tests the occurrence assertion as the procedure starts with the amount included in the financial statements and is agreed to supporting documentation. To test completeness, the procedure must start from outside of the accounting records and agreed into the accounting records.

REVIEW AND REPORTING

141 OPTION 4

As part of the overall review of the financial statements, the auditor should assess whether the information and explanations gathered during the audit and accounting policies are adequately reflected and disclosed.

Preconditions should be considered as part of the auditor's acceptance procedures and a detailed review of the audit working papers is conducted as part of the firm's quality management procedures.

142 OPTION 2

An increase in the proportion of cash sales since the interim audit would increase sales but not trade receivables resulting in a decreased trade receivables collection period.

143 OPTION 2

The effective date of the revaluation, the amount of the revaluation increase, and the carrying amount of the head office under the cost model are disclosures required by IAS® 16 *Property, Plant and Equipment*.

144 OPTION 1

Misstatements (2) and (3) are individually material and would require adjustment for an unmodified opinion to be issued. Misstatement (1) is immaterial and if Viola Co did not make this adjustment, an unmodified opinion could still be issued.

145 OPTION 1

Misstatement (4) is immaterial at 2.2% of profit before tax ($2.9m/$131.4m) and would not require further disclosure. As all other adjustments have been made, no material misstatement exists and an unmodified opinion can be issued.

146 OPTION 1

By not testing the sample sizes documented in the audit plan the audit plan has not been followed. Sample sizes will have been chosen based on the judgement of the auditor responsible for planning taking into consideration the requirement to obtain sufficient appropriate evidence. It is not acceptable to defer conclusions to the audit manager. If the sample sizes are considered acceptable at the lower quantities, the audit plan should be updated to reflect this. However, sample sizes should not be reduced simply to save time. If sufficient appropriate evidence is not obtained, material misstatements may go undetected and an inappropriate audit opinion could be issued.

147

Enquiry does not provide sufficient appropriate evidence on its own	**True**
The auditor has demonstrated a lack of professional scepticism	**True**
A written representation should have been obtained from management confirming that they have disclosed all subsequent events to the auditor	**True**
The auditor only needs to perform procedures if they are made aware of any subsequent events	**False**

Up to the date of the auditor's report the auditor must perform procedures to identify subsequent events and ensure they have been appropriately reflected in the financial statements. It is only after the auditor's report has been signed that they only need to take action if they become aware of any subsequent events. Enquiry alone is not sufficient. Choosing to rely only on enquiry of management demonstrates a lack of professional scepticism.

148 OPTION 3

The firm would not report staff to the ACCA. The matter will be dealt with internally through communication and training. Disciplinary measures may be taken by the firm if they consider it necessary to do so.

149 OPTION 3

Engagement quality reviews are performed on or before the date of the auditor's report.

150

The audit engagement partner will review all working papers on the audit file before issuing an opinion	**False**
If working papers have been reviewed there is no quality issue arising from the lack of documentation	**False**
All working papers should be signed by the person who prepared them	**True**
All team members' work should be reviewed by someone more senior than the preparer	**True**

151 OPTIONS 2, 4 AND 5

If the loan is not renegotiated the company may experience cash flow difficulties. The loss of a major supplier could have a serious impact on Oak Co if no alternative can be found. Poor results in a product line expected to account for 30% of revenue could also have a significant impact on the company going forward.

152

		Explanation
The company has increased the sales prices charged to customers while maintaining costs at a level comparable to 20X4	**Inconsistent**	The gross profit margin would improve if sales prices charged to customers had increased while costs were maintained. Gross margin has decreased which implies that the company is not making as much return as in the prior year. This would most likely be due to an increase in cost of sales or reduction in sales price. Therefore the comment regarding an increase in sales price contradicts the results of the analytical review.
The company has become more reliant on its overdraft facility during the year	**Consistent**	The deterioration in the quick ratio from 0.8 in 20X4 to 0.2 in 20X5 is consistent with increased reliance on an overdraft facility.
Due to cash restrictions, the company has encountered delays in paying suppliers	**Consistent**	The increase in the payables payment period is consistent with delays in paying suppliers.
At the year-end inventory count, a lower level of slow-moving inventory was noted compared to prior year	**Inconsistent**	A low level of slow-moving inventory would result in a decrease in the inventory holding period, however, the inventory holding period has increased significantly, implying that items are taking longer to sell. Given the comment regarding the observation made at the inventory count, this would warrant further investigation.

153 OPTION 1

The review of post-year-end sales orders provides the best evidence that the new customer is genuine and is ordering goods. This will allow the auditor to assess the level of sales being made to the new customer and to determine whether this does mitigate the loss of Beech Co. Email correspondence will give an indication of the nature of the relationship between the company and customer but this is not as persuasive as actual sales orders being received.

154 OPTION 3

If management assesses a period of less than twelve months from the date of the financial statements, the auditor must request them to extend the assessment to this date.

155 OPTION 2

The client has made adequate disclosure uncertainty related to going concern therefore the opinion will be unmodified. As per ISA 570 *Going Concern*, where there is a matter of fundamental importance to the users' understanding regarding an uncertainty related to going concern the auditor should include a Material Uncertainty Related to Going Concern section. The inclusion of this paragraph does not modify the opinion.

156 OPTION 3

As per ISA 560 *Subsequent Events*, the auditor has an active responsibility to carry out subsequent events procedures between the date of the financial statements and the date of the auditor's report.

157 OPTION 3

The auditor should not contact the financial controller who is no longer an officer of the company, and the party involved in the claim, to confirm the level of damages payable. All other procedures would be appropriate.

158

Opinion
Unmodified
Qualified
Adverse
Disclaimer

Additional communications
No additional communication
Emphasis of Matter paragraph
Material Uncertainty Related to Going Concern section
Other matter paragraph

The maximum damages of $150,000 is not material to the financial statements at 2.3% of profit before tax and 0.2% of revenue. Therefore, no modification to the audit opinion is required.

159 OPTION 1

As per paragraph 9 of ISA 701 *Communicating Key Audit Matters in the Independent Auditor's Report*, in determining key audit matters, the auditor shall determine from the matters communicated to those charged with governance, those which required significant auditor attention.

160 OPTIONS 1 AND 4

$500,000 represents 7.7% of profit before tax and 0.8% of revenue, therefore is material. Had this outcome been known before the financial statements were issued, they would have required adjustment. As per ISA 560 paragraph 15, in the circumstances described, the auditor should initially discuss the matter with management and understand how management intends to address the matter in the financial statements.

161 OPTION 2

The auditor must read the other information to ensure it is consistent with the financial statements and their knowledge of the entity obtained during the audit. They do not audit the other information. No assurance conclusion is expressed on the other information. Other information needs to be considered by the auditor if it is made available before the auditor's report is signed. The client may not have this information prepared at the start of the audit but may provide it to the auditor during the audit.

162 OPTION 4

Notes to the financial statements form part of the financial statements and are subject to audit.

163 OPTION 1

The auditor's report will include a section headed 'Other Information' which describes the auditor's responsibilities in respect of the other information, such as the Chair's statement. The inconsistency between the Chair's statement and the financial statements should be described in this section. The auditor's opinion does not cover the Chair's statement therefore will not need to be modified.

164

Users may be misled if the other information contains incorrect information or information which contradicts the financial statements such as that in the Chair's statement	**True**	**False**
Users may believe the auditor has not audited the financial statements properly if the inconsistency is not highlighted	**True**	**False**
The auditor must expose management's incompetence	**True**	**False**
The inconsistency may undermine the credibility of your auditor's report if not highlighted	**True**	**False**

Inconsistencies between the other information and the financial statements may undermine the credibility of the auditor's report as it may be perceived that the auditor has not identified the inconsistencies and therefore the audit was not performed properly. If the inconsistencies are not brought to the attention of the user they may be misled by the incorrect or inconsistent information.

165 OPTION 3

An Other Matter paragraph can be used to refer to matters concerning the auditor's responsibility. Any restriction of liability should be included in that paragraph.

166 OPTION 4

Materiality is calculated using the following benchmarks: ½ – 1% of revenue, 5 – 10% of profit before tax and 1 – 2% of total assets. The receivable is 3.3% revenue, 6.1% of profit before tax and 1.1% of assets. The irrecoverable debt is material by size. An irrecoverable debt is unlikely to be material by nature unless the effect of the adjustment was so significant it would change a profit to a loss.

167 OPTIONS 1, 2 AND 4

From the scenario the customer has agreed the balance is outstanding but is struggling to make any payments. Confirming an already confirmed balance will not provide evidence over the level of adjustment required. Inspecting the sales invoice and GDN does not provide evidence of when the balance will be received.

168 OPTION 2

The issue is only 6.1% of profit and 1.1% of assets and only affects receivables therefore is material but not pervasive. A qualified opinion is appropriate.

169

Addressee	**Included**	**Not included**
Other Matter paragraph	**Included**	**Not included**
Other Information	**Included**	**Not included**
Emphasis of Matter paragraph	**Included**	**Not included**

An Emphasis of Matter paragraph is only required if there is a matter disclosed adequately in the financial statements which the auditor considers to be fundamentally important and wishes to bring to the attention of the user. An Other Matter paragraph is only required if there is a matter not related to the financial statements that the auditor wishes to bring to the attention of the user such as further explanation of the auditor's responsibilities.

170 OPTIONS 3 AND 4

Option 1 would require the other information section of the report to provide a description of the inconsistency. Option 2 would require the inclusion of an Emphasis of Matter paragraph. Option 5 would be included in an Other Matter paragraph. These would not affect the audit opinion.

171 OPTIONS 1, 3 AND 4

The directors will assess whether the company can continue to trade for the foreseeable future. They will prepare forecasts to help with this assessment. The auditor will evaluate the directors' assessment to ensure that it is reasonable. The directors must make disclosure of going concern uncertainties in the financial statements. The auditor will highlight that disclosure in the auditor's report. The auditor does not make disclosure in the financial statements. The directors must consider a period of twelve months from the reporting date.

172 OPTIONS 2, 4 AND 5

Calculation of key ratios may identify indicators of going concern issues which need to be investigated further through audit procedures. However, the ratios do not provide evidence that the company is or is not a going concern. Ratios are calculated using historical information and the company may have already taken action to improve its financial position since that information was created. Reviewing the level of profit made in the past does not provide reliable evidence that the company will be able to trade in the future as the financial circumstances of the company may be different.

173

Adequate disclosure of going concern uncertainties is made	**Unmodified opinion with no additional communication**	**Modified opinion**	**Unmodified opinion with Going Concern section**	**Unmodified opinion with Emphasis of Matter**
Adequate disclosure of going concern uncertainties is not made	**Unmodified opinion with no additional communication**	**Modified opinion**	**Unmodified opinion with Going Concern section**	**Unmodified opinion with Emphasis of Matter**

The opinion will not be modified if the disclosures are adequate. The report will need to include a section referring to the Material Uncertainty Related to Going Concern. If the company does not make adequate disclosure the financial statements will be materially misstated which will require a modified opinion.

174 OPTION 3

The financial statements should be prepared on the break up basis if the company has ceased trading, intends to cease trading or has no realistic alternative but to cease trading. If a company cannot pay its debts when they fall due the company will have no alternative but to cease trading. If there are material uncertainties relating to going concern the financial statements will still be prepared on a going concern basis but disclosure of the uncertainties should be included in the notes.

175 OPTION 4

If the basis of preparation is incorrect the financial statements will be materially misstated to such an extent they do not give a true and fair view. This is material and pervasive which would require an adverse opinion. The basis for opinion will change to a basis for adverse opinion and will include an explanation as to why the adverse opinion has been given.

176 OPTION 2

Failure to recognise the warranty provision is likely to require an adverse opinion as the misstatement represents a substantial proportion of Paddington's profit. An adverse opinion is issued when the financial statements are pervasively misstated. This will mean they are unreliable as a whole.

Lawsuit	10% of profit	Material
Provision	86% of profit	Material and pervasive
Depreciation	3% of profit	Not material
Intangible assets	41% of profit	Material

177 OPTION 2

As the claim is only possible to succeed a contingent liability disclosure is required. A provision would only be required if the claim was probable to succeed. At 10.3% of PBT, the claim is material being greater than 5% of PBT.

178 OPTION 1

The matter is correctly treated in the financial statements therefore the opinion should be unmodified. Paddington Co has sufficient cash to make the settlement therefore there is no uncertainty facing the company and hence an emphasis of matter paragraph is not necessary.

179 1D, 2B, 3A, 4E, 5C

Element		Purpose
1	Title	Clearly identifies the report as an Independent Auditor's Report (D)
2	Addressee	Identifies the intended user of the report (B)
3	Basis for opinion	Provides a description of the professional standards applied during the audit to provide confidence to users that the report can be relied upon (A)
4	Key audit matters	Draws attention to any other significant matters of which the users should be aware which have been discussed with those charged with governance (E)
5	Name of engagement partner	To identify the person responsible for the audit opinion in case of any queries (C)

180 OPTION 2

A disclaimer of opinion states the auditor does not express an opinion.

An unmodified opinion means the financial statements give a true and fair view.

An adverse opinion means the financial statements do not give a true and fair view.

A qualified opinion states 'except for' the issue described, the financial statements give a true and fair view.

181

		Material	
	Calculation	Yes	No
Receivable	4% PBT (0.3/7.5 × 100)		✓
Lawsuit	8% PBT (0.6/7.5 × 100)	✓	

182

	Type of event		Accounting treatment	
Receivable	**Adjusting**	**Non-adjusting**	**Recognise**	**Disclose**
Lawsuit	**Adjusting**	**Non-adjusting**	**Recognise**	**Disclose**

The receivable and lawsuit are both issues that were in existence at the year end therefore are adjusting events. Adjusting events must be adjusted or recognised in the financial statements.

183 OPTION 1

It would not be appropriate to contact the customer directly to enquire about payment of the outstanding balance.

184

Auditor Responsibilities for the Audit of the Financial Statements	**Included**	**Not included**
Basis for Opinion	**Included**	**Not included**
Basis for Qualified Opinion	**Included**	**Not included**
Key Audit Matters	**Included**	**Not included**
Opinion	**Included**	**Not included**
Qualified Opinion	**Included**	**Not included**

As the adjustment is material, the opinion will need to be modified. The issue is material but not pervasive therefore a qualified opinion will be required. The section will be titled 'Qualified Opinion' and will be followed by a 'Basis for Qualified Opinion' section. Responsibilities of both auditors and management are included in every auditor's report. Key audit matters are only compulsory for listed companies. As the scenario does not specify that Humphries Co is a listed client, it cannot be assumed that a Key Audit Matters section must be included in the auditor's report.

185 OPTION 2

The condition causing the damage occurred after the year end therefore the event is non-adjusting. A non-adjusting event must be disclosed if it is material. If disclosure is required but not made the financial statements will be materially misstated which will impact the auditor's report. The amount claimed from the insurance company could only be recognised in the financial statements if the event was an adjusting event and if it was virtually certain the claim would be paid.

186 OPTIONS 2, 5, 1, 4

A written representation **is not appropriate** in respect of the receivable balance. This is because **other procedures can be performed which provide more reliable evidence**.

A written representation **is appropriate** in respect of the warranty provision. This is because **the matter involves management judgement**.

The client cannot confirm with confidence that the customer will pay their outstanding balance. Other procedures provide more reliable evidence such as after-date cash testing. Therefore, a written representation is not appropriate.

The warranty provision is decided by management based on their experience and judgement. As a result, there are limited other procedures that can be performed that would provide sufficient appropriate evidence. Therefore, a written representation is appropriate.

187 OPTION 2

The refusal to provide a written representation may cast doubt over the reliability of any other evidence provided by the client which means it will have a material effect. The shareholders will be made aware of the issue if the audit opinion is modified as the auditor will need to provide an explanation of the circumstances giving rise to the modification. The auditor will not need to specifically notify the shareholders of the issue in person. There is no requirement to notify an industry regulator in this situation.

188 OPTIONS 4 AND 6

Written representations are required by ISA 580. Therefore, without a written representation the auditor does not have sufficient appropriate evidence. If the auditor considers this to be material but not pervasive a qualified opinion will be issued. If it is deemed pervasive a disclaimer of opinion will be issued.

189 OPTION 3

ISA 580 *Written Representations* Appendix 1 identifies other auditing standards that require subject specific written representations. These include ISA 240 *The Auditor's Responsibilities Relating to Fraud in an Audit of Financial Statements*, ISA 250 *Consideration of Laws and Regulations in an Audit of Financial Statements* and ISA 560 *Subsequent Events.*

190

Plans or intentions of management that affect carrying values of assets	**Required**	**Not required**
Confirmation from management that they have provided the auditor with all information and access to records during the audit	**Required**	**Not required**
Confirmation from management that the financial statements are accurate/free from error	**Required**	**Not required**
Confirmation from management that all transactions have been reflected in the financial statements	**Required**	**Not required**

Plans or intentions of management will be specific to the entity therefore only included if relevant but not included in every written representation letter. Management cannot confirm the financial statements are accurate or free from error due to estimates and areas of management judgement affecting the financial statements.

191 OPTIONS 1 AND 2

The expert was arranged by Minnie Co (the audit client) therefore is a management's expert. The auditor must follow the requirements of ISA 500 *Audit Evidence* when relying on the work of a management's expert. This requires consideration of the competence and objectivity of the expert and making sure the work is appropriate for audit purposes. Management will have paid for the work therefore there is no impact on the audit fee. The auditor cannot reduce their responsibility for this area in the auditor's report, therefore a statement such as that given in Option 3 is not appropriate.

192 OPTION 3

Minnie Co has depreciated land which is not in accordance with IAS 16 *Property, Plant and Equipment.* The PPE balance in the financial statements will be understated and the depreciation charge overstated. The misstatement to depreciation and property, plant and equipment is 4% of profit before tax which is not material.

However, ISA 450 *Evaluation of Misstatements Identified During the Audit* requires the auditor to request management to correct all identified misstatements therefore Daffy & Co must request that management increases the value of PPE by $0.4 million. The prior year accounting treatment was correct as only buildings were depreciated, therefore there is no reason for a prior year adjustment to be made.

193

Materiality
Not material
Material but not pervasive
Material and pervasive

Opinion
Adverse
Disclaimer
Qualified
Unmodified

Wording
Do not give a true and fair view
Give a true and fair view
'Except for'...give a true and fair view
Do not express an opinion

The wages system issue means the auditor is unable to obtain sufficient and appropriate evidence in respect of wages. The amount that cannot be confirmed is $1.1 million which represents 11% of profit before tax which is material but not pervasive. A qualified opinion with the 'except for' wording is appropriate.

194 OPTION 2

The lawsuit is a material uncertainty. The matter has been correctly disclosed as a contingent liability, therefore the financial statements give a true and fair view and an unmodified opinion can be issued. An Emphasis of Matter paragraph will be required to draw the user's attention to the contingent liability disclosure made by Minnie Co.

195 OPTION 4

All three extracts require amendment. The correct wording for the extracts should be:

1 We conducted our audit in accordance with **International Standards on Auditing.**

2 Our objectives are to obtain **reasonable assurance** about whether the financial statements as a whole are free from material misstatements.

3 Misstatements can arise from **fraud or error**.

196 OPTION 2

The defective inventory is included in the financial statements as at 31 March 20X5. The quality control checks performed after the year end provide evidence of a condition in existence at the year end. This is an **adjusting event**.

The explosion occurred after the year and the damage caused was therefore not a condition in existence at the year end. This is a **non-adjusting event**.

197 OPTION 3

In accordance with IAS 2 *Inventories*, inventory must be valued at the lower of cost and net realisable value (NRV). NRV is the selling price less any costs that must be incurred to make the sale. Cost is $850,000. NRV is $100,000 – 1,000 = $99,000. Therefore, the defective inventory should be valued at $99,000.

198 OPTIONS 1, 4 AND 5

A written representation must be obtained in respect of subsequent events. A breakdown of the damaged items would be obtained to determine the value of assets damaged in the explosion. A review of correspondence with the insurance company will be required to determine the value of any possible reimbursement as this will affect the amount of loss incurred which will need to be disclosed. The auditor will have performed cost and net realisable value testing during the final audit. These procedures would not need to be repeated. Reviewing the most recent quality control reports would not identify defects in inventory held at 31 March 20X5 as they will relate to inventory due to be despatched in July as quality control checks are performed one month prior to despatch.

199 OPTION 4

Event 1: The write down of $751,000 (850k – 99k) is **material** as it represents 13.4% (751/5,600) of profit before tax and 1.4% (751/55,000) of revenue. The directors should **amend** the financial statements by writing down the inventory.

Event 2: The damaged assets of $900,000 are **material** as they represent 16.1% (900/5,600) of profit before tax and 1.6% (900/55,000) of revenue. The directors should **amend** the financial statements by including a disclosure note detailing the explosion and the value of the assets impacted.

200 OPTION 1

Both events are material and require amendment. The misstatements are not pervasive as they do not represent a substantial proportion of the financial statements. A qualified opinion is appropriate. The **basis for qualified opinion** will explain the reason for the qualified opinion and quantify the financial effects of the misstatements on the financial statements.

As the misstatements are not pervasive an adverse opinion is not appropriate. As Panda Co is not listed a key audit matter paragraph is not appropriate. An emphasis of matter paragraph is not appropriate as this is used to draw the user's attention to a matter correctly disclosed in the financial statements which is not the case here.

Section 4

ANSWERS TO PRACTICE QUESTIONS – SECTION B

PLANNING AND RISK ASSESSMENT

201 KNIGHT ELECTRONICS CO *Walk in the footsteps of a top tutor*

Key answer tips

Part (a) is a knowledge-based requirement for you to consider the relevance of different sources of information at the planning stage of the audit – in effect, how could the auditor use that information to inform planning. Try to make specific comments for each source of evidence.

Part (b) requires description of eight audit risks and the auditor's response to each risk. This lends itself to a 'tabular approach' when preparing your answer. For each risk described, match it with the auditor's response to manage or mitigate the risk.

Part (c) requires substantive audit procedures relating to the audit of revenue. This is a syllabus topic regularly examined. List each procedure separately so that is easier for the examiner to award marks as appropriate.

Part (d) is quite specific, relating to payroll fraud. Given the circumstances noted in the question, the procedures required should focus upon ascertaining the nature and extent of the fraud, management awareness and understanding of the fraud, and the possibility that other instances of fraud may have occurred. Also, the auditor should be alert to other possible indications of payroll fraud e.g. employees with identical names, unusual payments etc.

(a) Sources of information and their uses

Source	Use
Prior year audited financial statements	To gain insight into trends in performance, accounting policies and changes, company size and financial structure, and outcome of previous audits.
Current year budgets and management accounts	Provides relevant financial information for the year to date. It will also help the auditor at the planning stage to carry out preliminary analytical procedures and to identify risks.
Prior year report to management	To gain information on the system of internal control and any identified control deficiencies as, if these have not been addressed by management, the deficiencies may still be present and may impact upon the audit approach.
Board meeting minutes	To gain knowledge about the important issues affecting the business which were discussed by the directors and how these issues were addressed.
Company website	To gain information about the company's major products and services.

(b) Audit risks and responses

Audit risk	Auditor's response
Knight Electronics Co is a new client for Hercules & Co. As the team is not familiar with the accounting policies, transactions and balances of the company, there will be an increased detection risk on the audit.	Hercules & Co should ensure they have a suitably experienced team. Adequate time should be allocated for team members to obtain an understanding of the company and the risks of material misstatement, including a detailed team briefing to cover the key areas of risk.
There is also less assurance over opening balances as Hercules & Co did not perform the audit last year.	Increased audit procedures over opening balances will be required.
The company is considering a stock exchange listing and the CEO is likely to want to report a rising profit trend in the current year leading up to the listing. There is a possibility that the directors may try to manipulate the financial statements to achieve the desired result, resulting in possible profit, revenue and asset overstatement.	Hercules & Co should ensure that there is a suitably experienced audit team. The audit team should maintain professional scepticism and be alert to any manipulation throughout the audit. This is particularly the case in any areas which require the use of directors' judgement. A review of judgemental decisions and significant one-off journal entries should be performed.

Audit risk	**Auditor's response**
Prices of components have been increasing steadily leading to a reduction in gross profit margin but inventory is valued at cost. The net realisable value of components may have fallen below the cost incurred by the company, resulting in the inventory valuation being overstated.	The audit team should discuss with the finance director whether they are aware of this as an issue. They could also select a sample of inventory items and compare the cost shown on the purchase invoice with the sales price charged at and after the year end to confirm that NRV is above cost.
Property has been revalued from \$3.8m to \$8.4m based on a management revaluation. The accounting policy with respect to properties was changed during the year and property values have been substantially increased as a result. There is a risk that the revaluation has not been carried out on an appropriate basis but has been designed to inflate asset values in the light of the potential listing. This would result in an overstatement of property, plant and equipment.	The audit team should discuss with the directors the basis on which the revaluation has taken place. The audit team should review the methods used and the assumptions made. They should agree the values on the valuation records to the non-current asset register and confirm the revaluation has been recorded correctly.
The period over which plant and equipment is to be depreciated is to be extended from five to eight years. This will have the effect of reducing depreciation expense. Under IAS® 16 *Property, Plant and Equipment*, useful lives are to be reviewed annually, and if asset lives have genuinely increased, then the change to the depreciation charge is reasonable. However, there is a risk that this reduction has occurred in order to boost profits. If this is the case, then plant and equipment are overvalued and depreciation expense understated.	The audit team should discuss with the finance director the basis on which the decision was made. The auditor should review the condition of plant and equipment currently being used (**note**: since the company is only five years old, the plant will be a maximum of five years old) and whether profits or losses have been made when plant and equipment have been sold. If the depreciation rates in the past were too high, a profit on disposal would be likely. Also, the eight-year useful life should be compared to how often these assets are replaced, as this provides evidence of the useful life of assets.

Audit risk	Auditor's response
Knight Electronics Co has recognised a receivable in respect of damages it has claimed against a supplier as its lawyer has advised that the action is likely to be successful. IAS 37 *Provisions, Contingent Liabilities and Contingent Assets* states that contingent assets should only be recognised where it is virtually certain that they will be received. To be virtually certain, Knight Electronics Co would need to have it confirmed in writing by the supplier (or the supplier's lawyer) that the claim will be settled. If the receipt of damages by Knight Electronics Co is not virtually certain by the year end, then receivables and profits will be overstated.	The auditor should discuss with the directors the justification for treating the damages as virtually certain. The audit team should obtain written confirmation from the supplier's lawyer that the claim has been settled.
During the year, the company's credit controller was absent for four months, and they were not replaced. In addition, the receivables collection period has increased from 45 to 75 days.	Review and test the controls surrounding how the finance director identifies old or potentially irrecoverable receivables balances, especially during the period of absence of the credit controller, to ensure that they are operating effectively.
There is an increased risk with regards to the recoverability of receivables balances and an allowance may be required. If this is the case, receivables may be overvalued and the allowance understated.	Extended post year-end cash receipts testing and a review of the aged receivables to be performed to assess valuation. The need for an allowance should also be discussed with the finance director and the adequacy of any allowance for receivables assessed.
During the year, a payroll clerk carried out fraudulent transactions at the company and there is a concern that additional frauds may have taken place. There is a risk that the clerk may have undertaken a significant level of fraudulent transactions which have not yet been identified, leading to an increased control risk. Any additional payments would need to be written off to the statement of profit or loss. If these have not been uncovered, profit and payroll could be overstated.	Discuss with the finance director the details of the fraud perpetrated by the payroll clerk and what procedures have been adopted to date to identify any adjustments which are needed in the financial statements. In addition, discuss with the finance director what additional controls have been put in place to prevent any similar frauds. Additional substantive testing should be conducted over the affected areas of the accounting records, particularly payroll.

Audit risk	**Auditor's response**
	In addition, the team should maintain their professional scepticism and be alert to the risk of further fraud.
The client wants the audit to be completed one month after the year end. With a short timescale, and given that this is the first year Hercules & Co has audited this client, there is a risk that the client staff will be under pressure to complete the financial information ready for audit which may lead to increased errors. Further, there is an increased detection risk that the auditor will not gather sufficient audit evidence.	The auditor should assign more staff to the audit of Knight Electronics Co, as increased levels of substantive testing will be required due to the increased risk of error and detection risk. The composition of the audit team should be considered to ensure that staff have the necessary level of experience. The auditor should also consider the need for an interim audit.

(c) Revenue

- Compare the overall level of revenue against prior year and budget for the year and investigate any significant fluctuations.
- Perform a proof in total calculation for revenue, creating an expectation of the average price for the main 'smart building' products multiplied by the sales volumes for this year. This expectation should be compared to actual revenue and any significant fluctuations should be investigated.
- Obtain a schedule of sales for the year broken down into the main security, lighting and networking product categories and compare this to the prior year breakdown and for any unusual movements, discuss with management.
- Calculate the final gross profit margin for Knight Electronics Co and compare this to the prior year and investigate any significant fluctuations.
- Select a sample of sales invoices for customers and agree the sales prices back to the price list or customer master data information to ensure the accuracy of invoices.
- For a sample of invoices, recalculate invoice totals including discounts and sales tax.
- Select a sample of credit notes raised, trace through to the original invoice and ensure the invoice has been correctly removed from sales.
- For a sample of service agreements, recalculate the split of revenue recognised in the year and that recognised as deferred income (contract liability) and confirm that this has been recognised in line with the performance obligations in the contract.
- Select a sample of customer orders and agree these to the dispatch notes and sales invoices through to inclusion in the detailed sales listing and revenue general ledger accounts to ensure completeness of revenue.
- Select a sample of dispatch notes both pre and post year end and follow these through to sales invoices in the correct accounting period to ensure that cut-off has been correctly applied.

(d) Procedures due to payroll fraud

- Discuss with management and those charged with governance as to whether they are aware of any other payroll frauds or potential frauds.
- Review board minutes for evidence of management discussion of the materiality of the payroll fraud and to the existence of any additional instances of actual or suspected fraud.
- Discuss with the payroll manager the nature of the payroll fraud, how it occurred and the financial impact of amounts incorrectly paid into the payroll clerk's bank account.
- Review the supporting documentation to confirm the total of the fraudulent payments made and assess the materiality of this misstatement.
- Review and test the internal controls surrounding setting up of, and payments to, new joiners to assess whether further frauds may have occurred.
- Compare the list of employees from the payroll and agree to the list or contracts of employment in the human resources department.
- Review employee bank account details for indications of more than one employee with the same details.
- Consider whether other information obtained by the audit team indicates risks of additional material misstatements with regards to payroll fraud.
- Obtain a written representation from management acknowledging that they have disclosed to the auditors all knowledge of actual and suspected fraud.

ACCA marking guide

		Marks
(a)	Sources of information and their uses	
	1 mark per well-explained point	
	Restricted to	5
(b)	Audit risks and responses	
	New client	2
	Potential listing	2
	Revenue recognition	2
	Inventory valuation	2
	Property revaluation	2
	Change in useful lives	2
	Legal action	2
	Receivables	2
	Payroll fraud	2
	Reporting timetable	2
	Other	2
	Maximum 8 issues, 2 marks each	16
(c)	Revenue	
	1 mark per well-described procedure	
	Restricted to	5
(d)	Procedures due to payroll fraud	
	1 mark per well-described procedure	
	Restricted to	4
Total		**30**

Examiner's comments

This 30-mark question is based on Knight Electronics Co, which sells products enabling smart building systems. This question tests candidates' knowledge of understanding an entity, audit risks and responses, substantive procedures for revenue and procedures for a payroll fraud.

Requirement (a)

Knowledge requirements can sometimes have an opening statement referenced to an International Standard on Auditing (ISA), and this is useful for setting the scene and providing clarification on the aim of the question requirement. Also, when reviewing knowledge requirements, it is important to identify whether an understanding of the scenario is required to attempt the question. Where the knowledge requirement is not linked to the scenario a note is included confirming this. It is especially important that candidates understand exactly what the question is asking, and whether they need to apply their knowledge to a scenario, as candidates should be aiming to score full marks for knowledge requirements.

Some knowledge questions include a prepopulated table, and candidates are required to provide an explanation/description of the phrase/term included in the table. For a five-mark knowledge requirement such as this, candidates should aim to provide a well-explained point for each of the five terms included within the table. It is important to understand what the aim of the table is. In this case, five sources of information were available to the auditor to use in gaining an understanding of their new client Knight Electronics Co. Candidates were tasked with explaining HOW each piece of information could be used to achieve the aim of gaining an understanding of the new audit client.

When attempting this requirement candidates should consider each source of information, what they are and what information is available within them, then consider how this information could be used by the auditor. Without considering both elements of what the information is and how it can be used, it is difficult to achieve the available 1 mark per point. Considering how each of the sources of information differs will also ensure that there is not too much repetition of answer points.

Credit was awarded for prior year financial statements for gaining an understanding of the company's performance and position, and to undertake preliminary analytical review. Commonly awarded points in relation to budgets and management accounts included providing information for going concern, risk identification, or analytical review.

It was disappointing that many candidates confused the prior year report to management with the prior year audit report and so explained that they were looking for modifications to the opinion, no credit was awarded for this. For board minutes, credit was awarded for identification of key issues occurring during the year. To gain the 1 mark, this point needed to be expanded to also cover how those charged with governance had addressed these issues as this would be needed to assess whether audit risk has increased. The company's website could be used to review press releases and background on Knight Electronics Co's products and services. Candidates must take the time to carefully read and underline key words in the requirement to ensure their answer is relevant.

Requirement (b)

Marks are awarded for identification of audit risks (½ mark each), explanation of audit risks

(½ mark each) and an appropriate auditor's response to each risk (1 mark each). Good exam technique is critical with a scenario-based requirement such as this.

The scenario will typically contain more than the number of risks required, so it is important that candidates plan their time carefully and only attempt to list the required number of points.

The first step is to identify the factors which will give rise to an audit risk. This information can be found in the scenario. All of the information in the scenario should be read carefully, including the opening paragraph as this may include information relevant to the identification of audit risks. When undertaking this read through, it is good exam technique to use the highlight function as this provides a visual aid for quickly spotting audit risks. Having looked at the whole scenario and highlighted relevant points, candidates should pick their eight strongest points, re-read them from the scenario, and draft their answer as they go along.

Candidates often use the copy and paste function when drafting their answers for the identification of the risk. However, care should be taken to ensure that the risk is actually identified. Simply stating a fact from the scenario is not the same as identifying an audit risk. For example, stating that 'the company's credit controller was ill and absent from work for four months' is not in itself an audit risk, as if other members of the finance team are undertaking this work during the absence of the credit controller, then the audit risk is mitigated. However, in this case the scenario went on to state that the receivables collection period has increased from 45 to 75 days. Therefore, both facts together are required for the identify ½ mark, stating one without the other will not gain credit. Similarly, for the legal action raised against the company's supplier, it is the fact that a receivable for the likely damages has been included within the draft financial statements that creates the audit risk as this is a contingent asset.

Financial accounting knowledge is also important as audit risks will often focus on the accounting treatment used in the financial statements. In Knight Electronics Co, accounting issues which give rise to audit risks include those relating to revenue, inventory, revaluation of property, plant and equipment and contingent assets. Hence a strong knowledge of relevant accounting standards is required to fully understand the audit risk and therefore a relevant auditor response.

The risks least identified by candidates related to the audit timetable and potential stock exchange listing. Candidates should expect a range of topic areas within an audit risk scenario, some of which may be more challenging than others.

Having identified the risk factor, the next step is to explain the risk. To do this, candidates need to state the specific area of the financial statements impacted with an assertion (for example cut-off, valuation etc.), or, a reference to over/under/misstated, or, a reference to inherent/control/detection risk. 'Misstated' will only be awarded if it is clear the balance could be either over or understated.

For example, if the risk should have been described in terms of an understated balance, then no credit would be awarded if candidates referred to a misstated balance. Candidates cannot hedge their bets by providing both options.

The explanation of the risk must also clearly state the specific area of the financial statements impacted. For example, in respect of the issue relating to the change in useful lives, only noting 'non-current assets or assets could be overstated' would not be awarded credit. An appropriate explanation in this instance would be property, plant and equipment could be overstated.

Having identified and explained the risk, the next step is to provide the auditor's response.

Responses must be practical within the context of the scenario, and care should be taken to ensure the response is one an auditor would make and not a management response. In this session candidates often provided management responses for the audit risk relating to the increased receivables collection period, such as recruit a new credit controller. Candidates are advised to take a moment to read their responses and ensure that what they are recommending will help the auditor to form a conclusion on the identified audit risk.

In this session some candidates struggled to produce valid auditor responses for the risk relating to the audit timetable completion date of 31 October. Those candidates who attempted this risk suggested requesting the audit timetable be extended or that the audit engagement be declined. What was actually required was a focus on how sufficient and appropriate evidence could be obtained within the tight reporting deadline, such as undertaking an interim audit or increasing the size of the audit engagement team.

Additionally, some candidates gave general statements of the required accounting treatment. For example, for the inventory risk, it was common to see 'complete net realisable value (NRV) testing' rather than how the auditor would test whether the recent cost of the inventory was above or below NRV. This general statement approach indicates a lack of practise in tackling different risks and responses questions from previous exams. Candidates often suggest 'increased professional scepticism' for a whole range of audit risks, and whilst valid, on its own it is not a suitable auditor's response for 1 mark. This is because increasing scepticism does not, on its own, help the auditor to gain suitable audit evidence over the identified audit risk. For the payroll fraud risk, simply stating 'increase professional scepticism' will only gain ½ mark. To gain the full 1 mark, candidates need to focus on additional testing of payroll and the additional procedures adopted to identify the fraud and any necessary adjustments. Additionally, credit for increased professional scepticism, was only credited in relation to the payroll fraud and the potential stock exchange listing, it was not a valid response for any of the other audit risks.

Auditor responses do not have to be a detailed procedure, rather it is an approach the audit team will take. Care must be taken to ensure that the approach suggested actually addresses the risk identified and contains sufficient detail. A response of 'discuss with management' will not gain any credit as candidates need to be very clear exactly 'what' they are asking management about. For the receivables risk, responses which simply stated 'discuss with management the appropriateness of any allowances' were only awarded ½ mark as they also needed to first review the aged receivables report for long outstanding balances to gain the 1 mark available.

Where further documentary evidence is available to the auditor, candidates need to refer to this to gain the available 1 mark per response. Also, consideration should be given to the reliability of audit evidence gained. For example, evidence gained via confirmation from a third party will be more reliable than verbal assertions from management.

Future candidates are advised that audit risk is, and will continue to be, an important element in the syllabus and must be understood. Candidates must ensure that they include adequate question practice as part of their revision on this key topic.

The following published sample questions are all good scenario-based questions on audit risks and responses: Lapis Co March/June 2023, Magpie September/December 2022, Esk Co March/June 2022, Peach Co September/December 2021, Corley Appliances Co March/June 2021, Scarlet Co March/June 2020, Hart Co September/December 2020, Harlem Co September/December 2019, and Peony Co March/June 2019.

Part (c)

For substantive procedures requirements, one mark is available for each well-described procedure, therefore candidates should aim to produce five tests for this requirement. Candidates should plan their time accordingly.

When describing substantive procedures, one of the key things to consider is the level of detail provided. Many candidates fail to score well in this type of requirement because their procedures are vague or too brief. Tests must be sufficiently detailed noting clearly which source document should be used and what for. Candidates must ensure that they can distinguish between a substantive procedure and a test of control. Many candidates lose marks in this type of requirement by mixing up these procedures. Where substantive procedures are required for an account balance subject to an accounting standard then considering the rules of the standard can help in generating targeted substantive procedures.

Candidates who focused on casting the breakdown of sales and agreeing to financial statements, recalculating sales invoices, analytical review of total/monthly sales to prior year/budget, and 'cut-off testing' were able to gain credit.

Analytical procedures are very useful when auditing revenue and can be used to generate several valid tests. Comparisons can be made between total or monthly revenue and the prior year or budget; a breakdown of key product lines or customers can be compared to the prior year as well as a review of the gross margin for the current and prior year. In all cases, any significant fluctuations must be investigated, not just identified, and discussed with management. Without reviewing the fluctuations, only ½ mark is awarded. Another useful analytical review procedure is a proof in total where the prior year is adjusted for any known fluctuations in the year such as any new product lines, and then compared to the actual revenue in the year with significant fluctuations investigated.

Where the question requirement is for revenue, then no credit will be awarded for any receivables procedures. In this session it was common to see candidates stray into receivables tests such as reviewing after-date cash receipts and considering whether an allowance for receivables was necessary. Also, where detailed tests were provided, rather than testing to or from the listing of sales invoices, incorrect answers focused on the receivables ledger/detailed list of customer balances when agreeing to sales invoices and goods dispatched notes (GDNs). This was not valid and so would not have gained the available 1 mark. Additionally, when listing these types of detailed tests, the key point when the sale should be recognised is when the goods have been dispatched and so tests should begin or end with the GDN rather than the sales order.

When generating substantive procedures, it is important to ensure the tests have sufficient detail and are clear. For example, 'perform a cut-off test' without describing what the actual test is and what documents should be used will not gain any marks. It is important to stress that the source document is GDNs before and after the year end and that these need to be agreed to sales invoices to ensure they have been included in the correct accounting period. If sales invoices had been used as the source document rather than GDNs, then only ½ mark would have been awarded.

Care must also be taken not to produce tests of controls as these are not substantive procedures and would not gain any credit. Also, many candidates suggested reviewing disclosure of revenue, however this would not have gained any credit as revenue, along with most profit or loss account items, does not require disclosure notes.

Part (d)

When attempting a question such as this, it is important that candidates spend a few minutes considering the aim of the requirement. They should consider whether the procedures required are for the management of Knight Electronics Co or the auditor, Hercules & Co. Whether this is a knowledge requirement solely based on ISA 240 *The Auditors*

Responsibilities Relating to Fraud in and Audit of Financial Statements, or whether it is an application of knowledge from the ISA to the specific scenario.

The requirement is clear that what is needed are procedures to be undertaken during the audit, therefore only auditor procedures should be considered and not those of management. The requirement does not contain a note specifying that the scenario is not needed, and therefore an application of knowledge to the scenario is required.

The scenario contains details of an instance of payroll fraud where fictitious employees were set up by a payroll clerk who then made payments into their own bank account. In addition, the scenario states that controls have now been implemented to prevent this from reoccurring. The requirement is for four marks and so four well described procedures, which could be substantive or tests of control, would score full marks.

In considering the instance of fraud, the auditor would wish to understand how it occurred and its financial impact, what the new controls are which have been implemented, and how well they are now operating to prevent the risk of further payroll frauds.

Where attempted, candidates were able to gain some credit for discussing with management how the fraud occurred and discussing with management what new controls have been adopted. Some attempts at generating tests of control such as reviewing for duplicate payments to the same bank account and comparing the list of employees to contracts of employment gained credit. However, the tests of control were often too brief or vague and so only gained ½ mark. Obtaining a written representation was often suggested but with little detail as to what the auditor would be gaining representation for. To gain the available 1 mark, they needed to specify that management had notified all knowledge of actual and suspected fraud to the auditors.

Many candidates did not score well on this requirement. Incorrect answers focused on listing generic substantive procedures for auditing payroll expense, rather than the fraud, or they focused on the knowledge area of auditors' responsibilities relating to fraud, which did not gain any credit. Other incorrect answers focused on the controls management should adopt to prevent further frauds. This is the wrong focus as it does not consider what the auditors should do. Also, some candidates provided vague comments such as 'increase substantive testing' without any detail of what the increased testing would be. Candidates who suggested increasing professional scepticism did not gain any credit, as this is not an audit procedure, but an auditor response.

This requirement was challenging to many candidates as it was slightly unusual. However, those who considered the aim of the auditor in carrying out the procedures, and used the information available in the scenario, were able to score a sufficient number of points. Candidates should be prepared for unusual requirements and take a common-sense approach in tackling them.

202 LAPIS *Walk in the footsteps of a top tutor*

Key answer tips

Part (a) covers quality management responsibilities in respect of supervision and review of the audit team's work. Think about the role of the supervisor and the purpose of the review of working papers.

Part (b) asks for audit risks and responses. This requirement is examined every sitting. You must make sure the risk relates to either a risk of material misstatement or a detection risk. Read through the scenario to identify information which refers to something that will appear in the financial statements, e.g. intangible assets, receivables, provisions etc. Briefly explain the accounting treatment that should be applied. Think about common mistakes that the client could make either deliberately to manipulate the financial statements or unintentionally. State whether the item in the financial statements is at risk of under or overstatement. The response must be a response of the auditor, not the client and must directly relate to the risk you have given. The response may be a procedure or may be an approach that the auditor will take.

(a) Quality management

Overall, the audit engagement partner is required to take responsibility for overall supervision of the audit and reviews performed; however, this work is often performed by other senior members of the audit team.

Supervision

During the audit of Lapis Co, the auditor should keep track of the progress of the audit engagement, which includes monitoring progress against the audit plan, assessing whether the objective of work performed has been achieved and considering the ongoing adequacy of assigned resources.

The competence and capabilities of individual members of the engagement team should be considered, with on-the-job training and coaching provided to develop skills and competencies where necessary.

Supervision also includes creating an environment where engagement team members can raise any concerns without fear of repercussion.

In addition, part of the supervision process involves taking appropriate action to address any significant matters arising during the audit of Lapis Co and modifying the planned approach appropriately.

The supervising auditor is also responsible for identifying matters for consultation or consideration by more experienced engagement team members such as the audit manager or audit engagement partner.

Review

The auditor would be required to review the work completed by the team and consider whether this work has been performed in accordance with the audit firm's policies, International Standards on Auditing and other regulatory requirements.

The auditor should also consider whether all significant matters have been raised for audit engagement partner attention or for further consideration and, where appropriate consultations have taken place, whether appropriate conclusions have been documented.

The auditor should consider if there is a need to revise the nature, timing and extent of work performed. The auditor should also consider if the objectives of the engagement procedures have been achieved and if the work performed supports the conclusions reached and has been properly documented.

Overall, consideration should be given as to whether sufficient and appropriate evidence has been obtained to provide a basis for the auditor's opinion.

(b) Audit risks and auditor's response

Audit risk	**Auditor's response**
Goods in transit Lapis Co purchases its raw materials from overseas suppliers and has responsibility for goods at the point of dispatch, with materials in transit for up to six weeks. At the year end, there is a risk that cut-off may not be accurate and inventory, purchases and payables may be understated as the company may not correctly recognise the raw materials from the point of dispatch.	The audit team should undertake detailed cut-off testing of purchases of raw materials at the year end. The sample of shipping documentation immediately before and after the year end relating to goods from overseas suppliers should be increased to ensure that cut-off is complete and accurate.
Reliance on internal audit (IA) Indigo & Co may place reliance on the controls testing work undertaken by the internal audit (IA) department. If reliance is placed on work which is inadequate for the purposes of the audit, then the external audit team may form an incorrect conclusion on the strength of the internal controls at Lapis Co. This could result in Indigo & Co performing insufficient levels of substantive testing, thereby increasing detection risk.	The external audit team should meet with IA staff, read their reports and review their files relating to controls testing performed at the factories to ascertain the nature of the work undertaken. Before using the work of IA, the audit team will need to evaluate and perform audit procedures on the entirety of the work which they plan to use, in order to determine its adequacy for the purposes of the audit. In addition, the team will need to reperform some of the testing carried out by IA to assess its adequacy.
No allowance for receivables A significant wholesale customer has informed Lapis Co that it is experiencing financial difficulties. Lapis Co's finance director does not believe an allowance for receivables is required in the draft financial statements for the year ending 30 September 20X5.	Review and test the controls surrounding the way in which the finance director identifies old or potentially irrecoverable receivables balances and other credit control processes to ensure that they are operating effectively.

Audit risk	**Auditor's response**
There is a risk that trade receivables will be overvalued. This customer balance may not be recoverable and so trade receivables will be overstated and the allowance for receivables understated if an allowance is not recognised.	Review correspondence with this customer and discuss with the finance director the rationale for not maintaining an allowance for receivables, despite the financial difficulties experienced by this customer. Extend post-year-end cash receipts testing, in particular for this significant customer, in order to assess valuation and the need for an allowance for receivables.
Warranty provision The company changed one of its television speaker suppliers in December 20X4 to a cheaper alternative and this has led to an increase in warranty claims for television speaker deficiencies. If the overall number of customers claiming on the warranty has increased, then the warranty provision should possibly be higher. As the finance director is anticipating that the overall level of the provision will be similar to the prior year, there is a risk the provision and expenses are understated.	Discuss with management their procedures for estimating the warranty provision and specifically if they have identified the reason for the increase in claims and the effect of this on the estimate. Review the level of claims received during the year and post year end and compare this to the provision made at the year end to assess the adequacy of the provision.
Fraud In May 20X5, a payroll clerk was dismissed as they had carried out fraudulent transactions at Lapis Co. Controls have since been implemented to prevent this reoccurring. There is a risk that the clerk may have undertaken a significant number of fraudulent transactions which have not yet been identified. The loss as a result of the fraudulent transactions would need to be written off to the statement of profit or loss. If these have not been discovered, profit may be misstated. Control risk is also increased as the controls previously in place did not prevent the fraud.	Discuss with the finance director the details of the fraud perpetrated by the payroll clerk and what procedures have been adopted to date to identify any adjustments which are needed in the financial statements. In addition, discuss with the finance director what additional controls have been put in place to identify any similar frauds. Additional substantive testing should be conducted over the affected areas of the accounting records, particularly payroll, to establish if there have been any further fraudulent transactions. In addition, the team should maintain their professional scepticism and be alert to the risk of further fraud and errors.

Audit risk	**Auditor's response**
Directors' remuneration The directors only disclosed the amount of remuneration payable to each director, which does not comply with local legislation which also requires the names of the directors to be disclosed. The directors' remuneration disclosure will not be complete and accurate if the names and individual total payments are not disclosed and hence the financial statements will be misstated as a result of the non-compliance.	Discuss this matter with management and review the requirements of the local legislation to determine if the disclosure in the financial statements is included appropriately. If disclosure is inadequate, then request management to amend the directors' remuneration disclosures and review for compliance with local legislation.
Rebate receivable Lapis Co is planning to include a $0.8m receivable relating to a supplier rebate based on purchases for the year. The receivable should only be recognised if the company has purchased the required volume levels and the amount claimed is virtually certain to be received. If the annual volumes are overstated, then the value of the receivable recognised may be overstated and cost of sales may be understated.	Discuss with management the basis of the rebate calculation and agree the calculations back to supporting documentation, including the contract with the supplier. Review post-year-end correspondence with the supplier for evidence of the rebate being applied or post-year-end bank statements for evidence of receipt.
Development expenditure Lapis Co intends to capitalise all costs incurred of $1.6m in respect of the development of a new smart television model within intangible assets. IAS 38 *Intangible Assets* requires research costs to be expensed to profit or loss and only development costs which meet specific criteria to be capitalised as an intangible asset. All of this expenditure has been included as an intangible asset. If research costs have been incorrectly classified as development expenditure, there is a risk that intangible assets are overstated and expenses understated.	Obtain a breakdown of the expenditure capitalised and agree to supporting documentation as to whether the costs relate to the research or development stage. Discuss the accounting treatment with the finance director to assess whether the criteria for capitalisation under IAS 38 are being met.

Audit risk	Auditor's response
New loan A $2.5m interest bearing loan was obtained in April 20X5 and will be repaid in quarterly instalments over four years. If the loan is not allocated correctly between non-current and current liabilities, this would lead to a classification error with current and non-current liabilities being misstated. In addition, the company may fail to accrue for the interest, resulting in finance costs and accruals being understated.	Review the loan agreement to confirm the details and reperform the company's calculations to confirm that the loan has been correctly split between non-current and current liabilities. Recalculate the interest accrual and agree the amount to finance costs and the accruals schedule.
Dividend The directors are intending to propose a final dividend once the financial statements are finalised. In line with IAS 10 *Events after the Reporting Period*, the dividend is a non-adjusting event and should not be recognised as a liability in the 20X5 financial statements. The obligation only arises once the dividend is declared, and this occurs post year end. The dividends should, however, be disclosed in the notes to the financial statements assuming they are declared before the financial statements are authorised for issue. If the dividend is recognised, it will result in an overstatement of liabilities. Failing to disclose the proposed dividend will result in a lack of completeness of disclosure.	Discuss the issue with management and confirm that the dividend will not be recognised within liabilities in the 20X5 financial statements. The financial statements need to be reviewed to ensure that adequate disclosure of the proposed dividend is included in compliance with IAS 10.

ACCA marking guide

		Marks
(a)	**Quality management** 1 mark per well-explained point	
	Restricted to	**4**
(b)	**Audit risk and response** (only 8 risks required)	
	• Goods in transit	2
	• Reliance on IA	2
	• No allowance for receivables	2
	• Warranty provision	2
	• Fraud	2
	• Directors' remuneration	2
	• Rebate receivables	2
	• Development expenditure	2
	• New loan	2
	• Dividend	2
	• Other	2
	Max 8 issues, 2 marks each	**16**
Total		**20**

Examiner's comments

Requirement (a). Knowledge requirements such as this often have an opening statement, sometimes referenced to an International Standard on Auditing (ISA), and this is useful for setting the scene and providing clarification on the aim of the question requirement. It is especially important that candidates understand exactly what the question is asking, especially for knowledge questions, where candidates should be aiming to score full marks.

Question requirements such as this demonstrate the importance of having a detailed understanding of the ISAs, and in this case ISA 220 Quality Management. Additionally, this ISA has recently been revised and this amended standard was only examinable for the first time from September 2022 onwards. Therefore, candidates should have been prepared for a question on quality management.

For a four-mark knowledge requirement such as this, candidates should aim to provide four well-described points. For example, 'the auditor should consider whether sufficient and appropriate evidence has been obtained' would be awarded a ½ mark. In order to gain the additional ½ mark this should be expanded to include 'to provide a basis for the auditor's opinion'. Where credit was awarded, it was normally for 'monitoring the progress of the audit against the timetable,' 'considering the competence and capabilities of the engagement team members,' 'reviewing that all work has been adequately documented' and 'addressing significant matters which arose during the audit.' Credit was also awarded for 'considering whether the work performed is in line with ISAs'. However, it was disappointing that many candidates confused auditing and accounting standards, and so incorrectly focused on ensuring that accounting standards had been complied with, and no credit was awarded for this.

Care should be taken when reading the requirement to ensure that answer points focus on the right issues. For example, in this session many candidates incorrectly focused their answers on ethical and independence issues, auditors' responsibilities relating to fraud and the auditors' responsibilities to provide a true and fair opinion, all of which were not relevant and therefore scored no marks. Candidates must take the time to carefully read and underline key words in the requirement, in order to ensure their answer is relevant.

Requirement (b). Marks are awarded for identification of audit risks (½ mark each), explanation of audit risks (½ mark each) and an appropriate auditor's response to each risk (1 mark each). With a scenario-based requirement such as this, good exam technique is critical.

The scenario will typically contain more than the number of risks required, so it is important that candidates plan their time carefully and only attempt to list the required number of points.

The first step is to identify the factors which will give rise to an audit risk. This information can be found in the scenario. All of the information in the scenario should be read carefully, including the opening paragraph as this may include information relevant to the identification of audit risks. When undertaking this read through, it would be good exam technique to use the highlight function as this provides a visual aid for quickly spotting audit risks. Having looked at the whole scenario and highlighted relevant points candidates should pick their eight strongest points, re-read them from the scenario, drafting their answer as they go along.

Candidates often use the copy and paste function when drafting their answers for the identification of the risk. However, care should be taken to ensure that the risk is actually identified. Simply stating a fact from the scenario is not the same as identifying an audit risk. For example, stating that 'a significant customer is experiencing financial difficulties' is not in itself an audit risk. If adequate allowance is made for this receivable, then the audit risk is mitigated. However, in this case the scenario went on to state that no allowance for receivables was required. Therefore, both facts together are required for the identify ½ mark, and stating one without the other will not gain credit. Similarly, for the good in transit it's the fact that the company accepts responsibility from the point of dispatch that creates the audit risk. The warranty provision being unchanged only becomes an audit risk due to the fact that there has been an increase in customer claims due to the change in supplier.

Financial accounting knowledge is also important as audit risks will often focus on the accounting treatment used in the financial statements. In Lapis Co, accounting issues which give rise to audit risks include those relating to intangible assets. The risks least identified by candidates related to the receivable recognised for the rebate due to be received from a supplier and reliance on the work of internal audit (IA). Also, a number of facts from the scenario were incorrectly identified as audit risks, namely that there were overseas suppliers and that the company had six factories. Candidates should expect a range of topic areas within an audit risk scenario, some of which may be more challenging than others.

Having identified the risk factor the next step is to explain the risk. To do this, candidates need to state the specific area of the financial statements impacted with an assertion (for example cut off, valuation etc.), or, a reference to over/under/misstated, or, a reference to inherent/ control/ detection risk. 'Misstated' will only be awarded if it is clear the balance could be either over or understated. For example, if the risk should have been described in terms of an understated balance, then no credit would be awarded if candidates referred to a misstated balance. Candidates cannot hedge their bets by providing both options.

Some risk explanations were inappropriate. For example, candidates explained the issue of the proposed dividend as a manipulation of financial statements risk. Instead, this risk actually related to a possible overstatement of liabilities if the dividend had been accrued for, or incomplete disclosure if this non-adjusting event was not adequately disclosed. For the new loan risk some candidates incorrectly believed that needing a loan meant that a going concern risk arises, which is not the case and so no credit was awarded. Candidates must take the time to carefully read the scenario, noting any relevant information, to ensure that they correctly understand and describe the audit risks arising.

Having identified and explained the risk, the next step is to provide the auditor's response. Responses must be practical within the context of the scenario and care should be taken to ensure the response is one an auditor would make and not a management response. In this session, candidates in particular provided management responses for the audit risk relating to the goods in transit. Candidates are advised to take a moment to read their responses and ensure that what they are recommending will help the auditor to form a conclusion on the identified audit risk.

In this session, some candidates struggled to produce valid auditor responses for the risk relating to the reliance on work performed by IA. Many candidates focused on gaining comfort on the independence of IA or in general testing internal controls. What was actually required was a focus on evaluating and reperforming the work performed by IA. Additionally candidate responses for the new loan were vague. Rather than recalculating the split of the loan between current and non-current liabilities, candidates 'reviewed or confirmed the split.' This was not awarded credit as the response needs to be clearer as to how the split would be confirmed/reviewed.

Additionally, a significant minority of candidates gave general statements of the required accounting treatment. For example, for the intangible assets risk, it was common to see 'ensure that the development expenditure is capitalised in line with IAS 38 *Intangible Assets*' rather than how the auditor would address the capitalisation of all the development expenditure. This general statement approach indicates a lack of practice in tackling different risks and responses questions from previous exams.

Candidates often suggest 'increased professional scepticism' for a whole range of audit risks, and whilst often valid, it is not on its own a suitable auditor's response for 1 mark. This is because increasing scepticism does not, on its own, help the auditor to gain suitable audit evidence over the identified audit risk. For the payroll fraud risk, simply stating 'increase professional scepticism' will only gain ½ mark. To gain the full 1 mark, candidates need to focus on additional testing of payroll and the additional procedures adopted to identify the fraud and any necessary adjustments. Additionally, credit for increased professional scepticism was only awarded in relation to the payroll fraud. It was not a valid response for any of the other audit risks.

Auditor responses do not have to be a detailed procedure, rather it is an approach the audit team will take. Care must be taken however, to ensure that the approach suggested actually addresses the audit risk identified and contains sufficient detail. A response of 'discuss with management' will not gain any credit as candidates need to be very clear exactly 'what' they are 'asking management' about. For the intangible assets risk, responses which simply stated 'review the breakdown of development expenditure' were only awarded ½ mark as they also needed to agree the costs to invoices/supporting documentation to confirm whether the capitalisation criteria were met to gain the full 1 mark available.

Where further documentary evidence is available to the auditor, candidates need to refer to this to gain the available 1 mark per response. Also, consideration should be given to the reliability of audit evidence gained, for example evidence gained via confirmation from a third party will be more reliable than verbal assertions from management.

Future candidates are advised that audit risk is and will continue to be an important element in the syllabus and must be understood. Candidates must ensure that they include adequate question practice as part of their revision on this key topic.

203 MAGPIE *Walk in the footsteps of a top tutor*

Key answer tips

Part (a) requires knowledge of engagement letters. The engagement letter is the contract between the audit firm and client. The purpose of the engagement letter is the reason why we need to have a contract and the contents include the things that could cause issues or misunderstandings at a later date if not clarified and set out at the start of the engagement.

Part (b) requires calculation of two specified ratios. A formula sheet will not be provided in the exam so make sure you know how to calculate key ratios which the auditor will use when performing analytical procedures.

Part (c) asks for audit risks and responses. This requirement is examined every sitting. You must make sure the risk relates to either a risk of material misstatement or a detection risk. Read through the scenario to identify information which refers to something that will appear in the financial statements, e.g. non-current assets, receivables, etc. Briefly explain the accounting treatment that should be applied. Think about common mistakes that the client could make either deliberately to manipulate the financial statements or unintentionally. State whether the item in the financial statements is at risk of under or overstatement. The response must be a response of the auditor, not the client and must directly relate to the risk you have given. The response may be a procedure or may be an approach that the auditor will take.

(a) Engagement letter purpose and matters to be included

The audit engagement letter outlines the nature of the contract between the audit firm and the audit client. Its purpose is to minimise the risk of any misunderstanding of the terms of the engagement between the auditor and the client and it confirms acceptance of the engagement. The purpose of the engagement letter is to also set out the terms and conditions of the engagement and the responsibilities of the auditor and management.

Matters which should be included in the engagement letter include:

- The objective and scope of the audit
- The auditor's responsibilities
- Management's responsibilities
- Identification of the applicable financial reporting framework for the preparation of the financial statements
- Expected form and content of any reports to be issued by the auditor and a statement that there may be circumstances in which a report may differ from its expected form and content
- Elaboration of the scope of the audit with reference to legislation
- The form of any other communication of results of the audit engagement
- The requirement for the auditor to communicate key audit matters in accordance with ISA 701 *Communicating Key Audit Matters in the Independent Auditor's Report*
- The fact that some material misstatements may not be detected
- Arrangements regarding the planning and performance of the audit, including the composition of the audit team
- The expectation that management will provide written representations
- The expectation that management will provide access to all information relevant to or affecting the financial statements
- The basis on which fees are computed and any billing arrangements
- A request for management to acknowledge receipt of the audit engagement letter and to agree to the terms of the engagement
- Arrangements concerning the involvement of internal auditors and other staff of the entity
- Any obligations to provide audit working papers to other parties
- Any restriction on the auditor's liability

– Arrangements to make available draft financial statements and any other information.

(b) Ratios

Ratio	**20X5**	**20X4**
Operating profit margin	0.4m/22.0m × 100 = 1.8%	1.2m/26.0m × 100 = 4.6%
Payables payment period	1.9m/10.9m × 365 = 64 days	3.2/14.5m × 365 = 81 days

(c) Audit risks and auditor's response

Audit risk	**Auditor's response**
New audit client Magpie Co is a new client for Crow & Co. As the audit team are not familiar with the accounting policies, transactions and balances of Magpie Co, there will be an increased detection risk on the audit. There is also less assurance over opening balances as Crow & Co did not perform the audit last year	Crow & Co should ensure it has a suitably experienced team assigned to the audit. In addition, adequate time should be allocated for team members to obtain an understanding of Magpie Co and the risks of material misstatement including a detailed team briefing to cover the key areas of risk. Increased audit procedures should be performed over opening balances.
PPE expenditure During the year, the company has spent $0.75m on refurbishing its stores. This expenditure has been recognised as property, plant and equipment in the statement of financial position. There is a risk that some items of revenue expenditure may have been capitalised in contravention of IAS® 16 *Property, Plant and Equipment* (PPE) which would mean that PPE is overstated and expenses are understated.	Obtain a schedule of costs which have been capitalised as part of the refurbishment programme. Review supporting documentation such as invoices to establish that they are capital in nature.
New sales system During the year, a sales system was installed but it was not felt necessary to run the old and the new system in parallel. Opening balances from the old system may not have been transferred correctly. In addition, further errors could have arisen if there are issues with the operation of the new system. As a result, sales and receivables may be misstated.	The auditor should fully document and test the new accounting system. In addition, they should also perform substantive tests over the opening balances to ensure they have been correctly transferred from the old system. Discuss with the finance director whether any issues have arisen since the new sales system has been in operation which may give rise to a misstatement in the financial statements.

Audit risk	Auditor's response
Cash shortages Daily cash takings reports sent to head office show an increasing number of cash shortages at each store when comparing the contents of the cash registers to the reports. These differences have not been investigated or reconciled as they are only small amounts. This is a risk that these discrepancies are the result of fraud and several small cash shortages could become material when aggregated. In addition, an increase in control risk arises when internal controls detect a problem but it is being ignored.	Discuss with the directors whether these cash shortages may be indicative of fraud. The audit team must also apply professional scepticism throughout the audit recognising that fraud may have arisen as a result of the cash shortages. Extended substantive procedures over the cash sales cycle should also be carried out.
Receivables valuation There has been an increase in corporate customer accounts which are overdue for payment, but no increase has been made to the allowance for receivables in the financial statements. In addition, the receivables collection period has increased from 101 days to 149 days. There is a risk that some of the customers may not pay and that the receivables balances are not recoverable. This would result in receivables being overstated and the allowance for receivables being understated.	Discuss with the credit controller the likelihood of recovering the overdue balances and carry out extended post-year-end cash receipts testing to identify if the overdue balances have been properly cleared after the reporting date. Discuss with the finance director the need to increase the allowance for receivables in respect of other customers who may be unlikely to settle their debts.
Supplier statement reconciliations The payables ledger clerk has carried out supplier statement reconciliations and a number of supplier statements indicate a higher balance is owing by the company than is shown on the list of individual supplier balances. The differences have been included as reconciling items on the supplier statement reconciliations rather than being investigated. In addition, the payables payment period has decreased from 81 days to 64 days.	Review the supplier statement reconciliations and discuss with the payables ledger clerk why they have been included as reconciling items on the supplier statement reconciliation rather than investigated. Perform a review of after-date purchase invoices to determine if any relate to the current year. If any do relate to the current year, agree them to the accruals listing.

Audit risk	**Auditor's response**
There is a risk that cut-off is incorrect, resulting in trade payables, cost of sales and expenses being understated.	
Inventory valuation Inventory of $0.1m has been noted as being damaged due to containing contaminated soil. In addition, the inventory holding period has increased from 28 days to 54 days meaning the company is retaining inventory longer than the prior year. IAS 2 *Inventories* requires inventory to be valued at the lower of cost and net realisable value. If the contaminated soil cannot be remedied and the damaged inventory of $0.1m is not written down to its net realisable value (NVR), inventory will be overstated and cost of sales will be understated. In addition, if the inventory holding period suggests further inventory may need writing down to NRV, inventory will be overstated and cost of sales will be understated.	Discuss with the finance director whether the damaged inventory will be written down to its net realisable value and agree this write down to the final inventory valuation. Discuss with the directors why the inventory holding period has increased and whether further inventory may need to be written down to net realisable value. Perform review of post-year-end sales invoices to determine the price at which these items have been sold and compare to inventory valuation.
Prior year management report Last year's management report highlighted a number of significant deficiencies in the company's payroll cycle. If these deficiencies have not been addressed by management, the controls over the payroll may still contain deficiencies leading to an increased risk of misstatement. Wages and salaries expense and the year-end employment tax accrual may be misstated.	Discuss with the directors whether the recommendations made by the audit firm in respect of the payroll cycle have been implemented and carry out tests of controls to assess whether they are operating effectively. If the recommendations have not been implemented or there are no controls in place, adopt a fully substantive approach to address the completeness and accuracy of the wages and salaries expense and completeness of the year-end employment tax accrual.

Audit risk	Auditor's response
Profit margins The company's operating profit margin has reduced from 4.6% to 1.8% and gross profit margin has increased from 44% to 50%. There is a classification risk that costs may have been omitted from costs of sales or some direct costs have been included in overhead expenses incorrectly, meaning cost of sales is understated and operating costs overstated.	Review the nature of a sample of operating expenses during the year to identify if any direct costs have been incorrectly classified as overhead expenditure. Compare the classification of costs between cost of sales and operating expenses and compare with the prior year to ensure consistency and investigate any significant differences. Increase cut-off testing of purchases and accruals to verify that costs are included in the correct period.

ACCA marking guide

			Marks
(a)	**Engagement letter purpose and matters to be included** 1 mark per well-explained point		
		Restricted to	**4**
(b)	**Ratios**		
	• Operating profit margin		1
	• Payables payment period		1
			2
(c)	**Audit risk and response** (only 7 risks required)		
	• New client		2
	• PPE expenditure		2
	• New sales system		2
	• Cash shortages		2
	• Receivables valuation		2
	• Supplier statement reconciliations		2
	• Inventory valuation		2
	• Prior year management report		2
	• Operating profit and gross profit margins		2
		Max 7 issues, 2 marks each	**14**
Total			**20**

Examiner's comments

Part (a). One mark was available for each well-explained point regarding the purpose to a maximum of two marks and ½ marks for each of four items included in an engagement letter. This is a knowledge area that has been tested in previous diets. Candidates were able to confidently list four items which should be included and so scored the two available marks. In fact, many candidates listed more than four points, with the most common correct answers being scope, fees and auditor and management responsibilities. However, few candidates scored well in relation to the purpose of an engagement letter, as they simply ignored this part of the requirement or repeated items which would be included in the letter.

Where credit was awarded, it was normally for the engagement letter 'minimising the risk of misunderstandings of the engagement terms' and that 'it forms a written agreement or contract between the firm and client.' Candidates are reminded that they must take care in carefully reading the requirement and answering each sub-requirement carefully whilst avoiding overlap or repetition of points.

Part (b). Marks are awarded for the calculation of the relevant ratio for each year (½ mark each) and so four ratios should be calculated in just under four minutes. The marks are only awarded for the correct answer and the requirement clearly stated that formulas are not required to be shown. With only ½ marks available per ratio, credit is not awarded for the calculations. Therefore, if a candidate simply provides the calculation without the final answer, no credit will be given. It is clear from reviewing candidates' answers that some fail to bring a calculator into the exam, as they only list the calculations. Candidates are reminded that a calculator is required for ratio calculations as well as to assess materiality in audit report requirements. In this session candidates were able to confidently calculate both of the required ratios, relating to profitability and liquidity in this case. However, candidates must ensure that they are able to calculate all ratios within the syllabus, and not just the main profitability and liquidity ratios.

Part (c). Marks are awarded for identification of audit risks (½ mark each), explanation of audit risks (½ mark each) and an appropriate auditor's response to each risk (1 mark each). With a scenario-based requirement such as this good exam technique is critical. The scenario will typically contain more than the number of risks required, so it is important that candidates plan their time carefully and only attempt to list the required number of points. The first step is to identify the factors which will give rise to an audit risk. This information can be found in the scenario. All of the information in the scenario should be read carefully, including the opening paragraph as this may include information relevant to the identification of audit risks, such as whether this is a new client, as was the case in Magpie Co, and has in the past often been overlooked. When undertaking this read through it would be good exam technique to use the highlight function as this provides a visual aid for quickly spotting audit risks. Having looked at the whole scenario and highlighted relevant points candidates should pick their seven strongest points, re-read them from the scenario, drafting their answer as they go along. Candidates often use the copy and paste function when drafting their answers for the identification of the risk. However, care should be taken to ensure that the risk is actually identified. Financial accounting knowledge is also important as audit risks will often focus on the accounting treatment used in the financial statements. In Magpie Co, accounting issues which give rise to audit risks include those relating to property, plant and equipment and inventory valuation. The risk least identified by candidates related to the operating margins and gross margins changing. Candidates should expect a range of topic areas within an audit risk scenario, some of which may be more challenging than others. When tackling audit risk questions which also include ratios from an earlier requirement, the results of the calculations should be considered when identifying the risks. In this case, the significant movement of the inventory holding period along with the information in the scenario about the damaged inventory identifies a possible risk of overvaluation of inventory. Some candidates incorrectly used this information to generate two separate audit risks, both relating to overstated inventory with similar auditor responses. Candidates should note that if two pieces of information result in the same audit risk then credit is only available once as the information should be used in conjunction. Having identified the risk factor the next step is to explain the risk. To do this, candidates need to state the specific area of the financial statements impacted with an assertion (for example cut off, valuation, etc.) or a reference to over/under/misstated or a reference to inherent/ control/ detection risk. 'Misstated' will only be awarded if it is clear the balance could be either over or understated. For example, if the risk should have been described in terms of an understated balance, then no credit would be awarded if candidates referred to a misstated balance. For the damaged inventory risk some candidates explained that inventory could be under or overstated. In order to gain credit, they needed to be clear that the balance could be overstated. The explanation of the risk must also clearly state the specific area of the financial statements impacted. In addition, some risk explanations were inappropriate. For example, candidates explained the issue of the cash shortages on daily reports not being investigated as being a risk that cash is misstated. Instead, this risk should have been explained as leading to a control risk and increased fraud risk as cash shortages could be indicative of fraudulent behaviour. In addition, for the damaged inventory some candidates incorrectly assumed that the plants impacted by the contaminated soil were plant and equipment rather than inventory for a garden supplier, therefore their explanations incorrectly focused on the risk to property, plant and equipment, and no credit was awarded. Candidates must take the time to carefully read the scenario, noting any relevant information, to ensure that they correctly understand and describe the audit risks arising. Having identified and explained the risk, the next step is to provide the auditor's response. Responses must be practical within the context of the scenario and care should be taken to ensure the response is one an auditor would make and not a management response. In this session, candidates provided management responses for the audit risks relating to the cash shortages, new sales system and supplier statements not being reconciled. Candidates are advised to take a moment to read their responses. Suggesting that 'the company focus on training staff on the new sales system' will not help the auditor to form a conclusion on whether revenue or receivables are misstated due to the new system. In this diet some candidates struggled to produce valid auditor responses for the risks relating to the cash shortages, supplier statement reconciliations, changes in operating and gross margin and the management report deficiencies in the payroll cycle. In some instances, candidates' answers were vague and too brief, indicating a lack of practice in tackling different risks and responses questions from previous exams. Auditor responses do not have to be a detailed procedure, rather it is an approach the audit team will take. Care must be taken, however, to ensure that the approach suggested actually addresses the risk identified and contains sufficient detail. A response of 'discuss with management' will not gain any credit as candidates need to be very clear exactly what they are asking management about. For the refurbishment of the stores risk, responses which simply stated 'review the breakdown of capitalised expenditure' were only awarded ½ marks as they also needed to agree the costs to invoices/supporting documentation to confirm the nature of the expenditure to gain the full 1 mark available. Where further documentary evidence is available to the auditor, candidates need to refer to this to gain the available 1 mark per response. Also, consideration should be given to the reliability of audit evidence gained; for example, evidence gained via confirmation from a third party will be more reliable than verbal assertions from management. Candidates often suggest 'increased professional scepticism' for a whole range of audit risks, and whilst valid, it is not on its own a suitable auditor's response for 1 mark. This is because increasing scepticism does not, on its own, help the auditor to gain suitable audit evidence over the identified audit risk. For the cash shortages not being investigated risk, simply stating 'increase professional scepticism' will only gain ½ marks. To gain the full 1 mark, candidates need to focus on additional testing of the cash shortages and whether they relate to a fraud. Future candidates are advised that audit risk is and will continue to be an important element in the syllabus and must be understood. Candidates must ensure that they include adequate question practice as part of their revision on this key topic.

204 ESK *Walk in the footsteps of a top tutor*

Key answer tips

Part (a) asks for preconditions of an audit. This is knowledge from the study text that you either know or don't know. A common-sense approach will not help you here. If you don't have the knowledge, move on and try to compensate by scoring well on other requirements.

Part (b) asks for specific ratios to be calculated from the information provided. The question specifically states that formulas are not required, therefore, do not waste time typing these out as no marks will be awarded.

Part (c) asks for audit risks and responses. This requirement is examined every sitting. You must make sure the risk relates to either a risk of material misstatement or a detection risk. Read through the scenario to identify information which refers to something that will appear in the financial statements, e.g. intangible assets, bank loan, etc. Briefly explain the accounting treatment that should be applied. Think about common mistakes that the client could make either deliberately to manipulate the financial statements or unintentionally. State whether the item in the financial statements is at risk of under or overstatement. The response must be a response of the auditor, not the client and must directly relate to the risk you have given. The response may be a procedure or may be an approach that the auditor will take.

Part (d) asks for substantive procedures in respect of trade receivables. You must describe procedures that will help you address the relevant assertions such as valuation, existence, etc. Substantive procedures are used to detect misstatements in the financial statements. Tests of controls will not score marks. Remember that substantive procedures include analytical procedures, such as calculation of the receivables collection period, as well as tests of detail.

(a) Preconditions for an audit

In order to establish whether the preconditions for an audit are present, Bannock & Co must:

- Determine whether the financial reporting framework (for example IFRS®) to be applied by Esk Co in the preparation of its financial statements is acceptable. In considering this, the auditor should have assessed the nature of the entity, the nature and purpose of the financial statements and whether law or regulation prescribes the applicable reporting framework, and
- Obtain the agreement of the management of Esk Co that they acknowledge and understand their responsibility:
  - for the preparation of the financial statements in accordance with the applicable financial reporting framework, including where relevant their fair presentation.
  - for the design and implementation of internal controls which management considers necessary to enable Esk Co to prepare financial statements which are free from material misstatement, whether due to fraud or error, and

- to provide Bannock & Co with access to all information which is relevant to the preparation of the financial statements such as records, documentation and other matters. Access to information includes any additional information which Bannock & Co may request from management for the purpose of the audit and an agreement to provide unrestricted access to Esk Co's staff in order that Bannock & Co can obtain relevant evidence.

(b) Gross profit margin, inventory holding period, receivables collection period and payables payment period ratios

Ratio	20X5	20X4
Gross profit margin	8.4m/30.9m × 100 = 27.2%	7.6m/27.5m × 100 = 27.6%
Inventory holding period	8.3m/22.5m × 365 = 135 days	6.4m/19.9m × 365 = 117 days
Receivables collection period	7.2m/30.9m × 365 = 85 days	4.9m/27.5m × 365 = 65 days
Payables payment period	2.4m/22.5m × 365 = 39 days	3.5/19.9m × 365 = 64 days

(c) Audit risks and auditor's response

Audit risk	Auditor's response
New audit client Esk Co is a new client for Bannock & Co. As the audit team are not familiar with the accounting policies, transactions and balances of Esk Co, there will be an increased detection risk on the audit. There is also less assurance over opening balances as Bannock & Co did not perform the audit last year.	Bannock & Co should ensure it has a suitably experienced team assigned to the audit. In addition, adequate time should be allocated for team members to obtain an understanding of Esk Co and the risks of material misstatement including a detailed team briefing to cover the key areas of risk. Increased audit procedures should be performed over opening balances.
Patent cost Esk Co purchased a patent in the year and has capitalised all costs associated with the purchase. There is a risk that the costs, such as the administrative cost incurred in negotiating the contract, have been capitalised which is not in accordance with IAS 38 *Intangible Assets*. There is also a risk that amortisation has not been calculated and accounted for correctly. There is a risk that intangible assets and profit for the year are both overstated.	The audit team should obtain a breakdown of the total amount capitalised and review the costs to ensure they are all allowable under IAS 38. They should agree the purchase price of the patent to the contract and other costs to invoice and bank statements to confirm that the correct amount has been capitalised as an intangible asset. They should review the terms of the patent to agree its useful life of four years, recalculate the amortisation expense for the period and agree the carrying amount at the end of the period is correct.

Audit risk	Auditor's response
New bank loan Esk Co has borrowed $2.5m from the bank under a five-year loan. If the loan is not allocated correctly between non-current and current liabilities, this would lead to a classification error with liabilities being misstated. There is a risk that the finance cost associated with the loan has been omitted from the statement of profit or loss leading to understated finance costs and accruals.	The audit team should recalculate the split between current and non-current liabilities to ensure the classification is correct in accordance with relevant accounting standards and local legislation. Details of any security offered against the loan should be agreed to the loan agreement. The finance costs should be recalculated based on the loan amount and interest rates applied and agreed to the accruals schedule.
Miscoded invoices A batch of invoices was miscoded and was not recorded as trade payables. Investigations are still ongoing to identify whether there are any other batches of miscoded invoices. The payables payment period has decreased from 64 days to 39 days. There is a risk that there are other batches of miscoded invoices. If these are not identified and corrected by the year end, purchases and trade payables will be understated.	The audit team should discuss the matter relating to the miscoded invoices with management to understand how the issue arose, where the miscoded invoices had been originally posted to and whether all invoices have now been correctly posted. Detailed testing of the trade payables balance, including a review of supplier statement reconciliations, should be carried out to ensure that all liabilities are recorded.
Inventory damaged by fire Inventory of $1.1m was damaged as a result of the fire and has not been replaced. The inventory balance has increased by $1.9m in the year and the inventory holding period has increased from 117 days to 135 days. The increase in inventory and the holding period is inconsistent with the loss of inventory as a result of the fire. There is a risk that the damaged inventory has not been fully written off and remains within closing inventory or that there is other slow-moving inventory which has not been identified. Inventory may be overstated and cost of sales understated as a result.	The audit team should discuss with management the process for identifying damaged inventory items following the fire and review the outcome of the inventory count to agree that the items identified have been written off correctly. They should also attend the year-end inventory count to identify whether any of the damaged items are still held within inventory at year end and confirm how management intends to value this damaged inventory in the year-end financial statements.

Audit risk	Auditor's response
Insurance claim Esk Co has included a current asset of \$1.1m in respect of an insurance claim relating to the fire. To comply with IAS 37 *Provisions, Contingent Liabilities and Contingent Assets*, the amount claimed should not be recognised until the receipt of the claim is virtually certain. As the insurance company has not responded to the claim, recognising the amount claimed overstates profit and other receivables.	Discuss with management whether any notification of payment has been received from the insurance company and review the related correspondence. If virtually certain, the treatment adopted is correct. If payment has been received, agree to post-year-end bank ledger account. If receipt is not virtually certain, the auditor should request that management remove it from profit and receivables. If the receipt is probable, the auditor should request management include a contingent asset disclosure note.
Staff bonuses An additional bonus is payable to sales staff in the quarter to 31 August 20X5 which gives an incentive to achieve sales targets in that period. This increases the incentive for staff to create fictitious sales or to record sales in the incorrect period in order to achieve the additional bonus. There is an increased risk that revenue and receivables are overstated due to fictitious sales.	The audit team should remain alert to the risk of fictitious sales and sales being recorded in the wrong period. They should extend cut-off testing around the year end and review the level of returns or orders cancelled post year end.
Discounts Trade discounts offered to regular customers have been separately accounted for as an expense. Trade discounts should be offset against revenue. There has been an increase in revenue but the gross profit margin has fallen slightly from 28% to 27%, consistent with the fact that there are additional expenses recorded. There is a risk that revenue and cost of sales are overstated as a result of the accounting treatment adopted.	The audit team should discuss with management the rationale for including discounts in cost of sales, how discounts are calculated and accounted for. For a sample of sales, they should recalculate the discount and review a breakdown of revenue and cost of sales to agree that discounts have been accounted for correctly. The audit team should request that discounts are reclassified to revenue in accordance with IFRS 15 *Revenue From Contracts with Customers*.

Audit risk	**Auditor's response**
Credit control Esk Co's credit control manager has been off work since December 20X4 and has been replaced by an inexperienced manager. The receivables collection period has increased from 65 days in 20X4 to 85 days in 20X5, indicating that they are not collecting debts as efficiently in the current year. There is a risk that amounts will not be collected from credit customers and that receivables are overstated as a result.	Bannock & Co should discuss with the directors the credit control procedures in place and the process for identifying and following up on aged and irrecoverable debts. Extend post-year-end cash receipts testing and a review of the aged list of individual customer balances to be performed to assess valuation. Also consider the adequacy of any allowance for receivables.
Tax investigation Esk Co is under a tax investigation relating to sales tax and it is likely that the company will be required to pay a penalty and fine of $0·6m. Therefore, a provision should be recognised as there is a probable outflow of resources as a result of a past event. Esk Co has not recognised a provision nor has any disclosure been made. There is a risk that provisions are understated and that disclosures are inadequate.	The audit team should obtain a copy of the letter from the tax authorities and discuss the matter with the directors. They should obtain and review documentation from the tax consultant to assess the likelihood and amount of any penalties and fines to be paid.

(d) Substantive procedures – trade receivables

- Obtain a breakdown of the list of individual customer balances, cast and agree the total to the trial balance/trade receivables account.
- Obtain the prior year aged list of individual customer balances and for significant customers compare to the current year and prior year balances. Discuss with management any missing receivables or significantly lower balances.
- Select a sample of trade receivables from the listing and prepare a receivables circularisation.
- Review the after-date cash receipts and follow through to pre-year-end receivable balances.
- Inspect the aged receivables report to identify any slow-moving balances, discuss these with the credit control manager to assess whether an allowance or write down is necessary.
- For any old or slow-moving balances review customer correspondence to assess whether there are any invoices in dispute.
- Review board minutes/discuss with management to assess whether there are any significant concerns re recoverability of receivables.
- Select a sample of goods despatch notes from before the year end, agree to sales invoices and to inclusion in the year-end list of individual customer balances.

- Review the list of individual customer balances for any credit balances and discuss with management whether these should be reclassified as payables.
- Review customer correspondence to identify any balances which are in dispute or unlikely to be paid and discuss with management.
- Recalculate the allowance for trade receivables and compare any potential irrecoverable balances to assess if the allowance is adequate.

ACCA marking guide		
		Marks
(a)	**Preconditions for an audit**	
	• Determine whether financial reporting framework is acceptable	1
	• Responsibility for the preparation of the financial statements	1
	• Responsibility for the design and implementation of internal controls	1
	• Responsibility to provide audit firm with access to all relevant information	1
	Restricted to	**4**
(b)	**Ratios**	
	• Gross profit margin	1
	• Inventory holding period	1
	• Receivables collection period	1
	• Payables payment period	1
		4
(c)	**Audit risk and response** (only 8 risks required)	
	• New client	2
	• Patent cost	2
	• New bank loan	2
	• Miscoded invoices	2
	• Inventory damaged following fire	2
	• Insurance claim	2
	• Staff bonuses	2
	• Discounts	2
	• Credit control	2
	• Tax investigation	2
	Max 8 issues, 2 marks each	**16**
(d)	**Substantive procedures – trade receivables**	
	• Obtain a breakdown of the receivables listing, cast and agree the total to the trial balance/trade receivables account	1
	• Obtain the prior year aged receivables listing and for significant customers compare to the current year and prior year balances.	1
	• Circularise a sample of receivables	1
	• Review the after-date cash receipts	1
	• Inspect the aged receivables report to identify any slow-moving balances	1
	• Review customer correspondence to assess whether there are any invoices in dispute	1
	• Review board minutes/discuss with management to assess whether there are any significant concerns re recoverability	1
	• Select a sample of goods despatch notes from before the year end, agree to sales invoices and inclusion in the list of individual customer balances	1
	• Review the list of individual customer balances for credit balances	1
	• Review customer correspondence to identify any balances which are in dispute	1
	• Recalculate the allowance for trade receivables and assess adequacy by comparing with potentially irrecoverable balances	1
	Restricted to	**6**
Total		**30**

Examiner's comments

Requirement (a). This is a relatively straightforward knowledge requirement which has been tested in previous exam sessions. Knowledge requirements such as this often have an opening statement, sometimes referenced to an International Standard on Auditing (ISA), and this is useful for setting the scene and providing clarification on the aim of the question requirement. It is especially important that candidates understand exactly what the question is asking, especially for knowledge questions, where candidates should be aiming to score full marks. Question requirements such as this demonstrate the importance of having a detailed understanding of the ISAs, and in this case ISA 210 *Agreeing the Terms of Audit Engagements*. For a four-mark knowledge requirement such as this, candidates should aim to provide four well-described points. For example, 'management should confirm their preparation of financial statements' would be awarded ½ marks. In order to gain the additional ½ mark this should be expanded to include 'in accordance with the applicable framework'. Care should be taken when reading the requirement to ensure that answer points focus on the right issues. For example, in this session some candidates incorrectly focused their answers on pre-acceptance procedures such as ensuring adequate staff were available, obtaining professional clearance from the previous auditors, independence issues and preparing engagement letters, all of which were not relevant. Candidates must take the time to carefully read and underline key words in the requirement, in order to ensure their answer is relevant.

Requirement (b). Marks are awarded for the calculation of the relevant ratio for each year (½ mark each) and so eight ratios should be calculated in just over seven minutes. The marks are only awarded for the correct answer and the requirement clearly states that formulas are not required to be shown. With only ½ mark available per ratio, credit is not awarded for the calculations. Therefore, if a candidate simply provides the calculation without the final answer, no credit will be gained. It is clear from reviewing candidates' answers that some fail to bring a calculator into the exam, as they only list the calculations. Candidates are reminded that a calculator could be required for ratio calculations as well as to assess materiality in audit report requirements. In this session candidates were able to confidently calculate all of the required ratios and these all related to profitability and liquidity. However, candidates must ensure that they are able to calculate all ratios within the syllabus, and not just the main liquidity and profitability ratios.

Requirement (c). Marks are awarded for identification of audit risks (½ mark each), explanation of audit risks (½ mark each) and an appropriate auditor's response to each risk (1 mark each). With a scenario-based requirement such as this, good exam technique is critical. The scenario will typically contain more than the number of risks required, so it is important that candidates plan their time carefully and only attempt to list the required number of points. The first step is to identify the factors which will give rise to an audit risk. This information can be found in the scenario. All of the information in the scenario should be read carefully, including the opening paragraph as this may include information relevant to the identification of audit risks, such as whether this is a new client, as was the case in Esk Co, and is often overlooked. When undertaking this read through it would be good exam technique to use the highlight function as this provides a visual aid for quickly spotting audit risks. Having looked at the whole scenario and highlighted relevant points, candidates should pick their eight strongest points, re-reading them from the scenario, drafting their answer as they go along. Candidates often use the copy and paste function when drafting their answers for the identification of the risk. However, care should be taken to ensure that the risk is actually identified. For example, this session some candidates stated 'Esk Co purchased a patent for $2.6m' this in itself is not the audit risk, as it is the fact that 'administrative costs have been included within the intangible asset'. Financial accounting knowledge is also important as audit risks will often focus on the accounting treatment used in the financial statements. In Esk Co, accounting issues which give rise to audit risks include those relating to intangible assets, bank loans, inventory valuation, contingent assets and a provision. The risk least identified by candidates related to Esk being a new client. Candidates should expect a range of topic areas within an audit risk scenario, some of which may be more challenging than others. When tackling audit risk questions which include ratios, the results of the calculations should be considered when identifying the risks. Where the movement in the ratio year on year is minimal, as in the case of the gross profit margin which decreased from 27.6% to 27.2%, then it is unlikely this movement will lead to a significant audit risk. However, in the case of the significant movement of the receivables collection period along with the information in the scenario about the lack of an experienced credit controller, this identifies a possible risk of overvaluation of trade receivables. Some candidates incorrectly used this information to generate two audit risks, both relating to overstated receivables with similar auditor responses. Candidates should note that if two pieces of information result in the same audit risk then credit is only available once as the information should be used in conjunction. Having identified the risk factor, the next step is to explain the risk. To do this, candidates need to state the specific area of the financial statements impacted with an assertion (for example cut off, valuation etc.) or a reference to over/under/misstated or a reference to inherent/ control/ detection risk. 'Misstated' will only be awarded if it is clear the balance could be either over or understated. For example, if the risk should have been described in terms of an understated balance, then no credit would be awarded if candidates referred to a misstated balance. Candidates cannot play it safe by providing both options. For the new bank loan, some candidates explained that the split of the loan between current and non-current liabilities may not be correct. However, without stating the assertion, that the loan may be misclassified, credit would not be awarded. The explanation of the risk must also clearly state the specific area of the financial statements impacted. For example, in respect of the issue relating to the capitalisation of admin costs within the patent, only noting 'non-current assets or assets could be overstated' would not be awarded credit. An appropriate explanation in this instance would be 'intangible assets could be overstated'. In addition, some risk explanations were inappropriate. For example, candidates explained the issue of the sales staff being paid a bonus based on the last quarter's sales as being a risk over the calculation of the bonus. Instead, this risk should have been explained as leading to a cut-off risk with revenue being overstated in order for sales staff to maximise their bonus. Candidates must take the time to carefully read the scenario, noting any relevant information, to ensure that they correctly understand and describe the audit risks arising. Having identified and explained the risk, the next step is to provide the auditor's response. Responses must be practical within the context of the scenario and care should be taken to ensure the response is one an auditor would make and not a management response. In this session candidates provided management responses for the audit risks relating to the miscoded invoices, damaged inventory and lack of an experienced credit controller. Suggesting that 'the company appoint an experienced credit controller' will not help the auditor to form a conclusion on whether trade receivables are overvalued, this is a management response rather than an auditor's response. Candidates are advised to take a moment to read their responses with this in mind. Auditor responses do not have to be a detailed procedure, rather it is an approach the audit team will take. Care must be taken however, to ensure that the approach suggested actually addresses the risk identified and contains sufficient detail. A response of 'discuss with management' will not gain any credit as candidates need to be very clear exactly 'what' they are 'asking management' about. For the new bank loan risk, responses which simply stated 'recalculate the split of the loan in the financial statements' were only awarded ½ mark as they also needed to agree the loan to a loan agreement to gain the full 1 mark available. Where further documentary evidence is available to the auditor, candidates need to refer to this to gain the available 1 mark per response. Also, consideration should be given to the reliability of audit evidence gained; for example, evidence gained via confirmation from a third party will be more reliable than verbal assertions from management. Candidates should also consider the practicality of obtaining the evidence, suggesting 'the audit team should write to the insurance company to ask if the claim of $1.1m will be paid' is not valid, as the insurance company is still processing the claim so they will not provide an answer on this to the auditor. Additionally, for the insurance claim many candidates suggested 'contacting Esk Co's lawyer to understand the likelihood of the insurance claim being successful'. Contacting the company's lawyers is only valid in the case where Esk Co is suing or being sued by someone. Candidates often suggest 'increased professional scepticism' for a whole range of audit risks, and whilst valid, it is not on its own a suitable auditor's response for 1 mark. This is because increasing scepticism does not, on its own, help the auditor to gain suitable audit evidence over the identified audit risk. Future candidates are advised that audit risk is and will continue to be an important element in the syllabus and must be understood. Candidates must ensure that they include adequate question practice as part of their revision on this key topic.

Requirement (d). For substantive procedures requirements, one mark is available for each well-described procedure, therefore candidates should aim to produce six tests for this requirement. Candidates should plan their time accordingly. Also, candidates should note that it is not necessary to write out the question requirement at the beginning of their answer, it does not gain any credit and therefore wastes time. When describing substantive procedures, one of the key things to consider is the level of detail provided. Many candidates fail to score well in this type of requirement because their procedures are vague or too brief. Tests must be sufficiently detailed, noting clearly which source document should be used and for what purpose. For example, in this session some candidates included, 'review after-date cash receipts' and would have only gained ½ mark. In order to gain the 1 mark available this test would need to be expanded to 'follow these receipts through to the pre-year-end receivables balance'. Candidates must ensure that they can distinguish between a substantive procedure and a test of control. Many candidates lose marks in this type of requirement by mixing up these procedures. Where substantive procedures are required for an account balance subject to an accounting standard then considering the rules of the standard can help in generating targeted substantive procedures. In many substantive procedure questions analytical procedures can be an important source of evidence, but for one off types of expenditure then analytical review is unlikely to be useful. For trade receivables, valid analytical procedures such as 'comparing the trade receivables to the prior year with significant differences being discussed with management' would gain the full one mark. Candidates who 'compare the balance to the prior year and identify any significant differences' only gained ½ marks as the process of comparing current to prior year only identifies the differences. To gain the other ½ mark these significant differences need to be investigated or discussed further with management. Candidates who focused on 'casting the receivables listing and agreeing to financial statements', 'preparing a receivables circularisation', 'reviewing after-date cash receipts', 'reviewing the aged receivables reports for slow-moving balances and discussing with management the need for an allowance', 'reviewing customer correspondence for balances in dispute' and 'undertaking analytical review procedures' were able to gain credit. When generating substantive procedures for trade receivables or trade payables, it is imperative that the focus of the tests is on the statement of financial position balance rather than on revenue or purchases. In this session, some candidates incorrectly provided revenue procedures such as 'recalculate the total on the sales invoices' and 'agree goods despatch notes to the sales invoice and detailed sales listing,' and these did not gain credit. Take the time to read the question requirements carefully and spend time thinking about what is needed prior to producing an answer.

205 PEACH *Walk in the footsteps of a top tutor*

Key answer tips

Part (a) asks for audit risks and responses. This requirement is examined every sitting. You must make sure the risk relates to either a risk of material misstatement or a detection risk. Read through the scenario to identify information which refers to something that will appear in the financial statements, e.g. development costs, property, plant and equipment. Briefly explain the accounting treatment that should be applied. Think about common mistakes that the client could make either deliberately to manipulate the financial statements or unintentionally. State whether the item in the financial statements is at risk of under or overstatement. The response must be a response of the auditor, not the client and must directly relate to the risk you have given. The response may be a procedure or may be an approach that the auditor will take.

Part (b) asks for the auditor's responsibility in relation to prevention and detection of fraud and error. A good answer needs to refer to the requirements of the relevant auditing standard, ISA 240. If you can't remember the main points of the ISA, take a common-sense approach and think about a logical answer to score at least some marks.

Part (c) asks for ethical threats and safeguards from the scenario. To earn a full mark for each threat you must explain how the auditor's objectivity could be impaired i.e. how their behaviour could be affected by the situation which would result in them being biased towards the client.

Part (d) asks for substantive procedures in respect of the development expenditure. You must describe procedures that will help you evaluate whether the development costs have been correctly accounted for in accordance with the relevant accounting standard therefore think about the criteria set out in the standard and design procedures that will provide evidence that the criteria have been met.

(a) Risks and responses

Audit risk	**Auditor's response**
New accounting system A new accounting system was introduced in March 20X5 and post implementation testing has not been conducted. There is a risk of opening balances on the new system being misstated and loss of ongoing data if they have not been transferred from the old system correctly. If the new system is not operating effectively there is a risk of misstatement of the accounting records.	The audit team should undertake detailed testing to confirm that all balances have been completely and accurately transferred to the new accounting system. They should perform walkthroughs to document the new system and test the controls in place. They should discuss with management any issues which have occurred since the new system was implemented.

Audit risk	**Auditor's response**
Development costs Peach Co has been developing a new production process and $0.8m was capitalised in the year as development expenditure. IAS 38 *Intangible Assets* requires research expenditure to be recognised as an expense as incurred and development expenditure capitalised only if strict criteria are satisfied. There is a risk that research expenditure has been incorrectly classified as development expenditure resulting in overstated intangible assets and understated research expenses. The capitalised expenditure should be amortised over the life of the process, commencing when the new process is first brought into use in May 20X5. There is a risk that amortisation has not been correctly calculated for the period resulting in misstated amortisation.	The audit team should discuss with management the accounting policy applied, particularly in respect of identifying the research and development stages. A detailed review of the costs capitalised and supporting documentation should be carried out to determine the nature of the expenditure. Any development expenditure should then be agreed as meeting the relevant criteria for capitalisation as set out in IAS 38. The auditor should discuss the assessment of the useful life of the product with management and assess its reasonableness. They should also reperform amortisation calculations to confirm the amounts are accurate.
Inventory valuation Peach Co holds inventory of $227,000 that it can no longer sell in its home market. It believes it can be sold to an international customer, but there are significant additional costs that Peach Co will incur. There is a risk that the net realisable value (NRV) of the inventory is less than cost and therefore that the inventory is overstated and cost of sales understated.	The audit team should discuss with the directors their belief that the inventory can be sold and should review any agreement with the international customer to determine the likelihood of the sale and the selling price for the inventory. They should also obtain supporting documentation in respect of the delivery and shipping costs in order to establish NRV and discuss with management if a write-down is required.
Staff costs Peach Co has included in wages and salaries, significant staff costs involved in the preparation of the site for the new machinery and in testing the new machinery. IAS 16 *Property, Plant and Equipment* states that costs, directly attributable to bringing the asset to the condition necessary for its intended use, are capitalised as part of the cost of the asset. These directly attributable costs include costs of site preparation and costs of testing.	The audit team should discuss with management the accounting treatment applied and request that the relevant staff costs are included in the cost of PPE. The audit team should undertake a review of the staff costs expensed and the process for allocating staff costs to work undertaken to confirm the amounts that should be capitalised as part of the cost of machinery. If an adjusting journal is made by management this should be reviewed for accuracy.

Audit risk	Auditor's response
It appears that an incorrect accounting treatment has been applied in respect of the staff costs resulting in understated property, plant and equipment (PPE) and overstated wages and salaries expense.	
PPE useful lives The directors extended the useful lives of plant and machinery by an average of five years despite the fact that machinery had been disposed of at a significant loss. Under IAS 16 asset lives should be reviewed annually, and if the asset lives have genuinely increased, then the resulting decrease in depreciation may be reasonable. However, the fact that old items of machinery were sold at a substantial loss in the period does not support the decision to increase useful life. As such, it appears that plant and machinery is overstated and depreciation expense understated.	The audit team should discuss with the directors the rationale for any extensions of asset lives and reduction of depreciation rates. The revised useful life of a sample of assets should be compared to how often these assets are replaced and any gain or loss on disposal, as this provides evidence of the useful life of assets.
Fraudulent purchases A member of Peach Co's finance team fraudulently purchased assets for personal use. The reconciliation of physical assets to the non-current asset register will be ongoing at the year end, hence there is a risk that non-current assets are overstated as they may include the personal assets purchased. Control risk is also increased if the fraud has gone undetected for a period of time.	The audit team should discuss the fraud with management to understand how the fraud was detected and corrected. They must understand the internal controls in place to prevent other frauds occurring. Additional procedures should be performed, particularly in respect of non-current assets additions. When testing non-current assets, they should obtain a list of all non-current assets capitalised in the year and agree the new assets to an authorised purchase order. They should select an increased sample of assets from the non-current asset register to confirm the existence of the assets and that they are used in the business.

<table>
<tr><th>Audit risk</th><th>Auditor's response</th></tr>
<tr><td>New supplier costs

The directors have not accounted for any costs under the new contract for bottles as no amounts are due to be paid until after the year end.

There is a risk that the costs incurred to date have not been recognised and therefore costs and liabilities are understated and profit is overstated.</td><td>The audit team should review the terms of the contract to understand the amounts payable and terms of payment. They should review the goods received not invoiced accrual listing to ensure that amounts payable to the supplier for bottles received have been accrued despite not being invoiced.</td></tr>
<tr><td>Legal claim

A previous supplier has launched a legal claim against Peach Co. The claim has not been settled but Peach Co's lawyers believe that they are likely to have to pay an estimated $0.3m.

As it appears probable that Peach Co will have to pay the supplier, a provision is required to comply with IAS 37 Provisions, Contingent Liabilities and Contingent Assets.

There is a risk that provisions and expenses are understated if the company has not recognised a liability in respect of this legal claim.</td><td>The audit team should review correspondence with Peach Co's lawyer to understand the likelihood of the supplier winning the case and the amount of the payments to be made to them.</td></tr>
<tr><td>New bank loan

Peach Co obtained a new interest-bearing bank loan in the year repayable over three years.

There is a risk that the loan has not been correctly allocated between current and non-current liabilities which would give rise to a classification error and liabilities being misstated.

In addition, the finance costs are paid in arrears and may not have been correctly accrued at the year end resulting in understated accruals and finance costs.</td><td>The audit team should undertake a review of the loan agreement to confirm the details and reperform the company's calculations to confirm that the loan has been correctly classified between current and non-current liabilities.

The finance costs should be recalculated and agreed to the accruals schedule.</td></tr>
</table>

Audit risk	**Auditor's response**
Loan covenants Peach Co has strict covenants in place regarding the loan. A breach of covenants could result in fines and penalties or mean the loan would be instantly repayable. There is an increased risk that the existence of covenants gives an incentive to manipulate key balances by overstating revenue and profit to ensure covenants are met.	The audit team should review the loan covenants in detail to understand what Peach Co is required to comply with. They should calculate the covenants to understand whether any breaches have occurred and discuss the impact of any breaches with management. The team should maintain their professional scepticism to remain alert to the risk over revenue recognition and judgements which affect profit.

(b) Auditor's responsibilities in relation to the prevention and detection of fraud and error

- Apricot & Co must conduct an audit in accordance with ISA 240 *The Auditor's Responsibilities Relating to Fraud in an Audit* of Financial Statements and are responsible for obtaining reasonable assurance that the financial statements taken as a whole are free from material misstatement, whether caused by fraud or error.
- Apricot & Co is required to identify and assess the risks of material misstatement of the financial statements due to fraud.
- The auditor needs to obtain sufficient appropriate audit evidence regarding the assessed risks of material misstatement due to fraud, through designing and implementing appropriate responses.
- Apricot & Co must respond appropriately to fraud or suspected fraud identified during the audit, for example, the fraud regarding the purchase of assets for personal use identified by Peach Co.
- When obtaining reasonable assurance, Apricot & Co is responsible for maintaining professional scepticism throughout the audit, considering the potential for management override of controls and recognising the fact that audit procedures which are effective in detecting error may not be effective in detecting fraud.
- To ensure that the whole engagement team is aware of the risks and responsibilities for fraud and error, ISAs require that a discussion is held within the team.
- Apricot & Co must report any actual or suspected fraud to appropriate parties.

(c) Ethical threats and appropriate safeguards

Ethical threat	**Appropriate safeguard**
The managing director of Peach Co has this year suggested that instead of a meal, all the audit staff and client staff go away for the weekend to a luxury hotel at Peach Co's expense. This represents a self-interest and familiarity threat. The acceptance of goods and services, unless trivial and inconsequential in value, is not permitted as it may make the audit staff less likely to challenge Peach Co's assumptions and explanations.	As it is unlikely that the weekend away has an insignificant value, this offer should be politely declined. The normal meal at the start of the audit is likely to be acceptable, particularly if the audit team pay for themselves.
Peach Co has suggested that the audit fee is renegotiated to be based on a percentage of Peach Co's net profit. This is a contingent fee and leads to a self-interest threat. If the audit fee is based on profit the audit team may feel incentivised to allow incorrect accounting treatments in order to maximise profits.	Apricot & Co should not agree to the proposed basis for the fees and should communicate with those charged with governance to explain that the audit fee needs to reflect the level of work and the experience of the team required to obtain reasonable assurance.
Apricot & Co has been approached by Peach Co to assist with the identification of acquisition targets. The provision of this type of corporate finance work creates a potential advocacy threat as Apricot & Co may be seen to be promoting Peach Co as an investor. In addition, there may be a self-review threat if the potential acquisition is subsequently reflected in the financial statements and the audit team may be less likely to challenge the figures included.	Apricot & Co may be able to accept this type of work depending on the precise nature and provided that adequate safeguards can be put in place. Care must also be taken not to make management decisions. Safeguards would include using professionals who are not involved in the audit to perform the service (e.g. corporate finance) and having an appropriate reviewer who was not involved in providing the service review the audit work or service performed.

(d) Development expenditure

- Obtain a schedule of capitalised costs within intangible assets, cast it and agree the closing balance to the general ledger, trial balance and financial statements.
- Select a sample of capitalised costs and agree to invoices, payroll records or other source documentation in order to confirm that the amount is correct and that the cost relates to the project.
- Discuss with the directors the decision to capitalise the costs from 1 November 20X4 onwards and assess whether this is based on the project meeting all of the conditions for capitalisation in IAS 38.
- Review a breakdown of the nature of the costs capitalised to identify if any research costs have been incorrectly included. If so, request that management remove these and include within profit or loss.
- Select a sample of costs recorded as research expenses and development costs and agree to supporting documentation confirming the date of the expenditure to ensure that costs were allocated correctly.
- Review market research reports to confirm that there is a market for the new process and that the selling price is high enough to generate a profit.
- Review feasibility reports as at 1 November 20X4 and discuss with directors their view that the process was technically feasible at that date.
- Review the budgets in relation to the development project and the cash flow forecast in order to assess whether Peach Co had access to adequate cash resources to complete the project as at the date of capitalisation. Agree the budgets to supporting documentation.
- Discuss with the finance director the rationale for the useful life being applied, consider its reasonableness and agree to supporting documentation.
- Recalculate the amortisation charge and confirm that it covers the period for May to August 20X5.
- Review the disclosures for intangible assets in the draft financial statements in order to confirm that they are in accordance with IAS 38.

ACCA marking guide

		Marks
(a)	**Audit risk and response** (only 8 risks required)	
	• New accounting system	2
	• Development costs	2
	• Inventory valuation	2
	• Staff costs	2
	• PPE useful lives	2
	• Fraudulent purchases	2
	• New supplier costs	2
	• Legal claim	2
	• New bank loan	2
	• Loan covenants	2
	Max 8 issues, 2 marks each	**16**
(b)	**Fraud responsibilities**	
	• ISA 240 responsibilities	2
	• Respond appropriately	2
	Restricted to	**4**

(c)	**Ethical threats and appropriate safeguards** (only 2 threats required)	
	• Luxury weekend provided by client	2
	• Audit fee based on profit	2
	• Corporate finance service	2
	Maximum 2 threats, 2 marks each	**4**
(d)	**Substantive procedures for development expenditure**	
	• Obtain schedule of capitalised costs, cast and agree to general ledger, trial balance and financial statements	1
	• Agree a sample of costs from schedule to invoice, payroll records and other source documentation to confirm accuracy	1
	• Discuss the capitalisation policy with management and assess whether IAS 38 criteria are met	1
	• Review the breakdown to identify research costs incorrectly capitalised	1
	• Agree a sample of costs from schedule to supporting documentation to confirm the date and ensure correct allocation	1
	• Review market research reports to confirm there is a market and will generate a profit	1
	• Review feasibility reports to confirm technical feasibility	1
	• Review budgets in relation to the development project and cash flow forecast to assess whether Peach Co has adequate resources to complete the project	1
	• Discuss with the finance director the rationale for the useful life being applied, and consider its reasonableness	1
	• Recalculate the amortisation charge and confirm that it covers the period for May to August 20X5	1
	• Review the disclosures for intangible assets in the draft financial statements to confirm that they are in accordance with IAS 38.	1
	Restricted to	**6**
Total		**30**

Examiner's comments

Requirement (a). Marks are awarded for identification of audit risks (½ mark each), explanation of audit risks (½ mark each) and an appropriate auditor's response to each risk (1 mark each). With a scenario-based requirement such as this good exam technique is critical. The scenario will typically contain more than the number of risks required, so it is important that candidates plan their time carefully and only attempt to list the required number of points.

The first step is to identify the factors which will give rise to an audit risk. This information can be found in the scenario. All of the information in the scenario should be read carefully, including the opening paragraph as this may include information relevant to the identification of audit risks, such as whether this is a new client, which is often overlooked. When undertaking this read through, a useful technique which could be adopted would be to use the highlight function as this provides a visual aid for quickly spotting audit risks. Having looked at the whole scenario and highlighted relevant points, candidates should pick the points they are best able to develop, re-read them from the scenario, drafting their answer as they work through the issues taking care to address the number of risks stated in the requirement. In Peach Co the question requires eight risks to be identified and explained. Candidates should expect a range of topic areas within an audit risk scenario, some of which may be more challenging than others. In Peach Co for example many candidates failed to fully understand the risk relating to the costs omitted for the contract with the new bottle supplier.

Financial accounting knowledge is also important as audit risks will often focus on the accounting treatment used in the financial statements. In Peach Co, accounting issues which give rise to audit risks include those relating to intangible assets, property plant and equipment, inventory valuation and a legal provision.

Having identified the risk factor the next step is to explain the risk. To do this, candidates need to state the specific area of the financial statements impacted with an assertion (for example cut off, valuation etc.), or a reference to over/under/misstated, or a reference to inherent/control/ detection risk. 'Misstated' will only be awarded if it is clear the balance could be either over or understated. For example, if the risk should have been described in terms of an understated balance, then no credit would be awarded if candidates referred to a misstated balance. Candidates cannot hedge their bets by providing both options.

The explanation of the risk must also clearly state the specific area of the financial statements impacted. For example, in respect of the issue relating to development expenditure capitalised as part of intangible assets, only noting 'assets could be overstated' would not be awarded credit. An appropriate explanation in this instance would be 'intangible assets could be overstated'.

Care must also be taken to explain the risk based on the information within the scenario. For example, some candidates explained the issue of loan covenants relating to minimum profit and sales targets as being a going concern risk. However, there were no indications from the information provided that Peach Co was experiencing going concern difficulties or that this would be the consequence of any breach. In this case, the risk related to overstatement of profit and/or sales revenue in order to meet the covenants. Candidates must take the time to carefully read the scenario, noting any relevant information, to ensure that they correctly understand and describe the audit risks arising.

Having identified and explained the risk, the next step is to provide the auditor's response. Responses must be practical within the context of the scenario and care should be taken to ensure the response is an auditor's response and not a management response. Auditor responses do not have to be a detailed procedure, rather it is an approach the audit team will take. Care must be taken however to ensure that the approach suggested actually addresses the risk identified and contains sufficient detail. A response of 'discuss with management' will not gain any credit as candidates need to be very clear exactly 'what' they are asking management about. For the new bank loan risk, an appropriate response would be 'carry out a review of the loan agreement to confirm the details and reperform the company's calculations to confirm that the loan has been correctly classified between current and non-current liabilities'. This clearly addresses the issue identified.

Where further documentary evidence is available to the auditor, candidates need to ensure that they refer to this. Also, consideration should be given to the reliability of audit evidence gained; for example, evidence gained via confirmation from a third party will be more reliable than verbal assertions from management. In Peach Co, the scenario specifically refers to information based on an assessment by their legal advisers. Therefore, an appropriate response would have been to 'review correspondence from Peach Co's lawyer to understand the likelihood of the claim being successful and likely sum to be paid.' This response would be more relevant and reliable than a discussion with management as to the likely outcome.

Future candidates are advised that audit risk is and will continue to be an important element in the syllabus and must be understood. Candidates must ensure that they include adequate question practice as part of their revision on this key topic.

Requirement (b). Knowledge requirements such as this often have an opening statement, sometimes referenced to an ISA, and this is useful for setting the scene and providing clarification on the aim of the question requirement. It is particularly important that candidates understand exactly what the question is asking, especially for knowledge questions, where candidates should be aiming to score full marks.

Question requirements such as this demonstrate the importance of having a detailed understanding of the ISAs, and in this case ISA 240 *The Auditor's Responsibilities Relating to Fraud in an Audit of Financial Statements*. For a four-mark knowledge requirement such as this, candidates should aim to provide four well-described points. Care should be taken when reading the requirement to ensure that answer points focus on the right issues. For example, in this session some candidates incorrectly focused their answers on management's responsibilities. This is despite the requirement only relating to the responsibilities of auditors. Candidates must take the time to carefully read and underline key words in the requirement to ensure their answer is relevant.

Requirement (c). For questions which examine ethical threats and safeguards, candidates are generally asked to identify and explain a specified number of ethical threats from a given scenario and give a relevant safeguard to address the threats identified. Candidates are awarded ½ mark for identifying the ethical threat and ½ mark for explaining the implication of the threat. Candidates are awarded 1 mark for each well explained safeguard.

In order to be awarded ½ mark for identifying the threat candidates are required to identify the issue from the scenario and correctly state which type of ethical threat it relates to, for example self-review threat. Both aspects of this response are required. For example, in Peach Co candidates needed to identify that the audit team had been invited to a luxury hotel at Peach Co's expense and also to state that this gives rise to a self-interest or familiarity threat.

The next step is to explain the implication of the threat clearly. Candidates often fail to do this and miss out on the ½ mark available. The explanation needs to clearly explain why this is an ethical issue. For example, just stating that 'this will impact on the auditor's independence' would not be awarded credit. Candidates must explain HOW independence will be impacted, for example 'accepting goods/service which have significant value may result in the audit team feeling unable to challenge management's explanations.'

The final step is to then suggest a safeguard and it is important that this is phrased as an action; often candidates provide objectives rather than actions. For example, for the threat relating to audit fees being based on the level of Peach Co's net profit, an appropriate response in order to gain the 1 mark available would be, 'the audit firm should inform Peach Co that they cannot agree to the proposed fee basis', or 'Apricot & Co should inform management that the audit fee will be based on the level of work undertaken.'

Additionally, safeguards must be practical. Constantly recommending that 'the audit firm should resign' is unlikely to be a sensible safeguard. While resignation would remove the ethical threat, it would also result in the loss of the audit. Resignation should be viewed as the last resort when considering safeguards. Alternative options where available should be considered first.

Requirement (d). For substantive procedures requirements, one mark is available for each well-described procedure, therefore candidates should aim to produce six tests for this requirement. Candidates should plan their time accordingly. Also, candidates should note that it is not necessary to reproduce the question requirement at the beginning of their answer, it does not gain any credit and is a waste of time.

When describing substantive procedures one of the key things to consider is the level of detail provided. Many candidates fail to score well in this type of requirement because their procedures are vague or too brief. Tests must be sufficiently detailed noting clearly which source document should be used and what for. For example, in this session some candidates included 'review market research reports' without specifying why this was being done or for what purpose, and so would have only gained ½ mark. In order to gain the 1 mark available this test would need to be expanded to include 'to confirm the directors view that a market exists for this project'.

Candidates must ensure that they can distinguish between a substantive procedure and a test of control. Many candidates lose marks in this type of requirement by mixing up these procedures. For example, in this session some candidates provided test of controls such as 'ensure that the expenditure is authorised by the board of directors.' The purpose of this procedure is to ensure that the controls over the expenditure are operating effectively, therefore this is not a substantive procedure.

In many substantive procedure questions analytical procedures can be an important source of evidence. However, for one off types of expenditure such as development expenditure, analytical review is unlikely to be useful. The scenario clearly identified that development expenditure commenced on 1 November 20X4 and there was no information in the question to suggest that there was a balance in the prior year.

Candidates who focused on 'casting the development expenditure and agreeing to financial statements', 'agreeing costs to invoices/payroll records', 'recalculating the amortisation charge and confirming that it covers May to August 20X5' and 'reviewing the disclosure is in accordance with accounting standards' were able to gain credit.

Where substantive procedures are required for an account balance subject to an accounting standard then considering the rules of the standard can help in generating targeted substantive procedures. IAS 38 *Intangible Assets* prescribes a series of criteria which must be met in order for costs to be classified as development expenditure. Therefore, tests based on these such as 'reviewing cash flow forecasts to assess if Peach Co has enough resources to complete the project' would have been awarded credit.

Future candidates should take the time to read the question requirements carefully and spend time thinking about what is needed prior to producing an answer.

206 CORLEY APPLIANCES CO *Walk in the footsteps of a top tutor*

Key answer tips

Part (a) asks for the preconditions of an audit. This is knowledge you either know or don't know. If you don't know it move on and try to compensate by scoring well on other requirements.

Part (b) asks for audit risks and responses. This requirement is examined every sitting. You must make sure the risk relates to either a risk of material misstatement or a detection risk. Read through the scenario to identify information which refers to something that will appear in the financial statements, e.g. warranty, receivables. Briefly explain the accounting treatment that should be applied. Think about common mistakes that the client could make either deliberately to manipulate the financial statements or unintentionally. State whether the item in the financial statements is at risk of under or overstatement. The response must be a response of the auditor, not the client and must directly relate to the risk you have given. The response may be a procedure or may be an approach that the auditor will take.

Part (c) is a tricky requirement relating to a key characteristic of the auditor – professional scepticism. Professional scepticism requires an open and questioning mind, being alert to the possibility of misstatement and is important for the auditor to be able to detect material misstatement caused by fraud as fraud is likely to be concealed. Fraud is easier to hide in areas of the financial statements which require judgement, so to answer this question, think about the areas of the financial statements where management will need to use its judgement to determine the accounting treatment.

(a) Preconditions required for an audit

Auditors should only accept a new audit engagement or continue an existing audit engagement if the preconditions for an audit are present.

ISA 210 *Agreeing the Terms of Audit Engagements* requires the auditor to:

- Determine whether the financial reporting framework to be applied in the preparation of the financial statements is acceptable (for example IFRS Accounting Standards).

  In considering this, the auditor should have assessed the nature of the entity, the nature and purpose of the financial statements and whether law or regulation prescribes the applicable reporting framework.

- Obtain the agreement of management that it acknowledges and understands its responsibilities for the following:
  - preparing the financial statements in accordance with the applicable financial reporting framework;
  - internal control necessary for the preparation of the financial statements to be free from material misstatement whether due to fraud or error; and
  - providing the auditor with access to information relevant for the audit and access to staff within the entity to obtain audit evidence.

(b) Risks and responses

Audit risk	Auditor's response
Refund liability The company has a returns policy allowing a customer to return goods within 28 days of purchase if they are dissatisfied with the product. IFRS 15 *Revenue from Contracts with Customers* requires that revenue should only be recognised to the extent that goods will not be returned. The company should recognise a refund liability for goods which are expected to be returned. If the company has not correctly accounted for the refund liability, revenue will be overstated and the refund liability understated.	Enquire with the finance director how the returns policy has been applied at the year end and whether the provisions in IFRS 15 have been reflected. Review the assumptions underpinning the refund liability for reasonableness and whether they meet the historic 5% value of returns. Compare the level of post-year-end returns to the refund liability and discuss any significant differences with management.
Reduced warranty provision The company provides a six-month warranty on its products which require defects to be repaired at Corley Appliances Co's own cost. The directors have reduced this provision during the year on the grounds they feel the products they sell are built to a high standard. The company does not manufacture the goods (they only sell them) and therefore this is not a reasonable reason for reduction, hence if the company has reduced the warranty provision excessively at the year end, liabilities and expenses may be understated.	Review the calculation of the warranty provision and assess its reasonableness in light of the value of claims received in the period. Review the assumptions underpinning the warranty provision for reasonableness. Review the level of claims made under warranty post year end to assess the reasonableness of the reduced provision.

Audit risk	**Auditor's response**
Goods in transit/cut-off The company purchases their goods from its main supplier in Asia and has responsibility for goods at the point of despatch, the goods are in transit for up to one month. At the year end, there is a risk that the cut-off of purchases may not be accurate as they may not correctly recognise the goods from the point of despatch. There is also a risk that inventory and trade payables are understated at the year end.	Discuss with management the point at which inventory is recorded and review the contract with the supplier to verify the requirements in place. Review the controls the company has in place to ensure that inventory is recorded from the point of despatch. The audit team should undertake detailed cut-off testing of purchases of goods at the year end and the sample of shipping documentation immediately before and after the year end relating to goods from its main supplier in Asia should be increased to ensure that cut-off is complete and accurate.
Detection risk/inventory count The company's central warehouse and all 20 branches will be carrying out an inventory count at the year-end date of 31 August. It is unlikely that the auditor will be able to attend all sites which increases detection risk. It may not be possible to gain sufficient appropriate audit evidence over the inventory counting controls and completeness and existence of inventory for those sites which are not visited.	The audit team should assess which of the inventory counts they will attend. This should include the count for the central warehouse and a sample of branches which contain the most material balances of inventory and those which have historically had exceptions reported during the inventory count. For those not visited, the auditor will need to review the level of exceptions noted during the count and discuss any issues which arose during the count with management.
Allowance for credit losses Over the last six months, the receivables collection period has increased from 42 days to 55 days and the allowance for credit losses/receivables will be at the same level as the prior year. Some receivables may not be recoverable and if an additional allowance is not included in the financial statements, receivables will be overstated and the allowance for credit losses/receivables understated.	Review and test the controls surrounding the way in which the finance director assesses the recoverability of receivables balances and other credit control processes to ensure that they are operating effectively. Perform extended post-year-end cash receipts testing and a review of the aged list of individual customer balances in order to assess valuation and the need for an increased allowance for irrecoverable receivables. Discuss with the finance director whether an additional allowance will be required against balances older than the company's credit terms.

Audit risk	Auditor's response
Payables fraud The payables ledger supervisor was dismissed in June 20X5 due to a fraud. The value of this fraud has been recognised as an expense in the draft statement of profit or loss. If additional frauds committed by the payables ledger supervisor are not discovered, this could result in expenses being understated and payables being overstated. Control risk is also increased if the fraud has gone undetected for a period of time.	Discuss with the finance director the details of the fraud perpetrated by the payables ledger supervisor and what procedures have been adopted to date to identify any further adjustments which are needed in the financial statements. In addition, discuss with the finance director what additional controls have been put in place to prevent any similar frauds. The audit team should undertake additional substantive procedures over the payables balance, particularly the fictitious supplier set up in the payables system to ensure this has been removed. In addition, the team should maintain professional scepticism and be alert to the risk of further fraud.
Incomplete purchases & payables Since the dismissal of the payables ledger supervisor, purchase invoices have yet to be recorded in the individual supplier accounts. There is a risk that the purchases and trade payables balance at the year end will be understated if these invoices are not recorded or accrued before the system is closed down for the year.	Review the unprocessed invoices file at the year end to identify any invoices which relate to the supply of pre-year-end goods and ensure they have been properly accrued for in the year-end financial statements and recognised as a liability. Discuss with the finance director the approach to be adopted to resolve the issue of unprocessed purchase invoices.
Capitalised training costs The company purchased and installed a new despatch system. The costs which have been capitalised include staff training costs ($0.1m). As per IAS 16 *Property, Plant and Equipment*, the cost of an asset includes its purchase price and directly attributable costs only. IAS 16 does not allow staff training costs to be capitalised as part of the cost of a non-current asset, as these costs are not directly related to the cost of bringing the asset to its working condition. The training costs should be charged to profit or loss. Therefore property, plant and equipment (PPE) and profits are overstated.	Discuss the accounting treatment with the finance director and request that the training costs are written off to profit or loss to ensure treatment is in accordance with IAS 16. If adjusted, review the journal entry for accuracy.

Audit risk	Auditor's response
Renewal of overdraft facility The company breached the terms of its overdraft facility in June 20X5 and the bank will only confirm the decision whether, or not, to continue to support the business in November 20X5, which is after the auditor's report will be signed. The company is dependent on the overdraft facility. If the bank refuses to continue to support the company, there may be doubts as to the company's ability to continue as a going concern. The uncertainties may not be adequately disclosed in the financial statements.	Discuss with the finance director the availability of alternative financing if the bank is unwilling to continue to support the company and review the adequacy of any going concern disclosures in the financial statements. The audit team should undertake detailed going concern testing, in particular, reviewing the impact of a non-renewal of the overdraft facility.

(c) Professional scepticism and examples where professional scepticism should be applied

Professional scepticism is defined in ISA 200 *Overall Objectives of the Independent Auditor and the Conduct of an Audit in Accordance with International Standards on Auditing* as an attitude which includes a questioning mind, being alert to conditions which may indicate possible misstatement due to fraud or error, and a critical assessment of audit evidence.

Examples where the auditor should apply professional scepticism for Corley Appliances Co are as follows:

Revenue recognition

ISA 240 *The Auditor's Responsibilities Relating to Fraud in an Audit of Financial Statements* contains a rebuttable presumption that fraud in relation to revenue is high risk and hence the auditor must apply professional scepticism to Corley Appliances Co's revenue recognition policies, especially in relation to the company's returns policy which due to the judgement involved may be used as a way to manipulate revenue.

Warranty provision

Accounting for warranty provisions will include an element of estimation based on previous experiences of the costs incurred by the company to repair defective goods. The auditor should maintain professional scepticism keeping in mind that warranty provisions may include management bias to either deliberately over or understate the provision. Management has reduced the warranty provision in the year on the grounds they feel the goods they sell are built to a high standard. As the company is not involved in the manufacturing of the goods they sell, it may be unreasonable to reduce the warranty provision on this basis.

Fraud

As a fraud has been committed during the year, the auditor must maintain professional scepticism recognising the fact that internal controls may be weak, hence allowing for employee manipulation of such internal control deficiencies. The auditor must also consider the possibility that other frauds may have taken place during the year through management override of the entity's internal controls.

Bank overdraft

The company is reliant on its bank overdraft due to the significant levels of expenditure which it has incurred during the year on the new despatch system. Management may want to deliberately overstate profit and understate liabilities so that the bank renews the overdraft facility.

Receivables valuation

The receivables collection period has been increasing over the past six months, but the finance director does not envisage that an increase in the allowance for credit losses/receivables is required. The auditor must apply professional scepticism in considering whether management's assessment of recoverability is reasonable, as any increase in the allowance will reduce profits.

ACCA marking guide

		Marks
(a)	**Preconditions required for an audit**	
	1 mark per well-explained point	
	Restricted to	**3**
(b)	**Audit risk and response** (only 7 risks required)	
	Refund liability	2
	Reduced warranty provision	2
	Goods in transit	2
	Inventory count attendance	2
	Allowance for credit losses/receivables	2
	Fraud	2
	Incomplete purchases and payables	2
	Training costs capitalised	2
	Renewal of overdraft facility	2
	Max 7 issues, 2 marks each	**14**
(c)	**Professional scepticism and examples where professional scepticism should be applied**	
	Professional scepticism definition	1
	Examples	2
	Maximum	**3**
Total		**20**

Examiner's comments

Part (a). Knowledge requirements such as this often have an opening statement, sometimes referenced to an ISA, and this is useful for setting the scene and providing clarification on the aim of the question requirement. It is particularly important that candidates understand exactly what the question is asking, especially for knowledge questions, where candidates should be aiming to score full marks. Question requirements such as this demonstrate the importance of having a detailed understanding of the ISAs, and in this case ISA 210 *Agreeing the Terms of Audit Engagements*. For a three-mark knowledge requirement such as this, candidates should aim to provide three well-explained points. Care should be taken when reading the requirement to ensure that answer points focus on the right issues. For example, in this session some candidates incorrectly focused their answers on pre-acceptance procedures such as ensuring adequate staff were available, obtaining professional clearance from the previous auditors, independence issues and preparing engagement letters all of which were not relevant. Instead candidates should have made reference to the preconditions as set out in ISA 210.

Part (b). With this type of requirement good exam technique is critical. Marks are awarded for identification of audit risks (½ mark each), explanation of audit risks (½ mark each) and an appropriate auditor's response to each risk (1 mark each). The scenario will typically contain more than the number of risks required, so it is important that candidates plan their time carefully and only attempt to list the required number of points.

The first step is to identify the factors which will give rise to an audit risk. This information can be found in the scenario. All of the information in the scenario should be read carefully, including the opening paragraph as this may include information relevant to the identification of audit risks, such as whether this is a new client, which is often overlooked. When undertaking this read through it would be good exam technique to use the highlight function as this provides a visual aid for quickly spotting audit risks. Having looked at the whole scenario and highlighted relevant points candidates should pick the points they are best able to develop, based on the number stated in the requirement (in this case seven), re-read them from the scenario, drafting their answer as they work through the points. Financial accounting knowledge is also important as audit risks will often focus on the accounting treatment used in the financial statements. In Corley Appliances Co accounting issues which give rise to audit risks include risks relating to revenue recognition, goods in transit and a warranty provision. In identifying the audit risk, it is important candidates use the specific information in the scenario rather than making general statements. For example, in Corley Appliances Co stating that 'the company has a warranty provision' would not have been sufficient to gain credit. In this instance the key issue relates to the fact that the warranty provision is expected to be lower than the prior year.

Having identified the risk factor the next step is to explain the risk. To do this, candidates need to state the specific area of the financial statements impacted with an assertion (for example cut off, valuation etc.), or, a reference to over/under/misstated, or, a reference to inherent/control/detection risk. 'Misstated' will only be awarded if it is clear the balance could be either over or understated. For example, if the risk should have been described in terms of an understated balance, then no credit would be awarded if candidates referred to a misstated balance. Candidates cannot hedge their bets by providing both options. The explanation of the risk must also clearly state the specific area of the financial statements impacted. For example, in respect of the issue relating to training costs being capitalised as part of property, plant and equipment (PPE), only noting 'assets could be overstated' would not be awarded credit. An appropriate explanation in this instance would be 'PPE could be overstated'. In addition, a number of candidates explained the issue of goods in transit as inventory being overstated, however the company has responsibility for goods in transit from the point of despatch by the supplier and therefore the risk was that inventory could be understated. Candidates must take the time to carefully read the scenario, noting any dates and other relevant information, to ensure that they correctly understand and describe the audit risks arising. In order to correctly explain the risk, candidates must take the time to carefully read the information provided to ensure that they describe risks from the auditor's perspective. Where this is not done candidates often describe business risks which do not gain credit. For example, for the goods in transit issue some candidates explained the risk as 'leading to damaged or lost goods.' This is a business risk focus rather than audit risk and does not gain credit. To gain credit the focus should be on the potential impact on the inventory balance in the financial statements.

Having identified and explained the risk, the third step is to provide the auditor's response. An auditor's response does not have to be a detailed procedure, rather it is an approach the audit team will take. Care must be taken however, to ensure that the approach suggested actually addresses the risk identified and contains sufficient detail. A response of 'discuss with management' will not gain credit as candidates need to be very clear as to exactly 'what' they are 'asking management' about. In addition, where further documentary evidence is available to the auditor, candidates need to refer to this to gain the available 1 mark per response. For example, 'reviewing the aged reports and discussing the appropriateness of the allowance' would be an appropriate response to the receivable's valuation risk. A common error is for candidates to confuse the auditor's response and management's response. For example, in response to the risk of the fraud committed by the payables ledger supervisor, many candidates focused on how the company could avoid future frauds. This is not an auditor's response and therefore would not be awarded credit. From the audit perspective, the risk is that there may be other undetected frauds resulting in overstated profit. The auditor's response would need to address this risk.

Candidates should also consider whether their response is practical within the context of the scenario. Suggesting that the auditor ask the bank if they will continue to provide the overdraft facility would not be feasible, as the bank would not respond to this request.

Future candidates are advised that audit risk is and will continue to be an important element in the syllabus and must be understood. Candidates must ensure that they include adequate question practice as part of their revision on this key topic.

Part (c). This question tests candidates' understanding of professional scepticism. One mark is available for each well explained point so candidates should aim for three points. A brief definition/explanation of professional scepticism is required and there would be one mark available for this. Correct answers included 'having a questioning mind' or 'being alert to possible areas of misstatement in the financial statements' and both of these would gain the available one mark. Candidates need to be careful not to use circular language in their explanation, for example 'professional scepticism means being sceptical' would not gain any credit.

Having defined professional scepticism, candidates need to explain two examples from the scenario where scepticism is applied. As the requirement is 'explain' it would not be sufficient for one mark to simply list the area impacted. For example, stating that 'the warranty provision would be considered when applying scepticism' would only gain ½ mark as a full explanation needs to consider why or how the auditor should approach the area with scepticism. In this case that the provision may be subject to management bias would be an appropriate response. It is important that candidates only identify examples from the scenario of Corley Appliances Co as indicated in the requirement, as opposed to general financial statement transactions and balances where scepticism is required. This requirement also highlights the range of topics which the exam can cover.

207 HART *Walk in the footsteps of a top tutor*

Key answer tips

Part (a) is a straightforward knowledge question. Notice that the question asks for the benefits of planning. Answers which just state what activities are performed at the planning stage will not score marks. As planning is the most important stage of the process, students should be aware of the reasons why it is important to plan the audit.

Part (b) asks for audit risks and responses. This requirement is examined every sitting. You must make sure the risk relates to either a risk of material misstatement or a detection risk. Read through the scenario to identify information which refers to something that will appear in the financial statements, e.g. WIP, warranty, plant & machinery and briefly explain the accounting treatment that should be applied. Think about common mistakes that the client could make either deliberately to manipulate the financial statements or unintentionally. State whether the item in the financial statements is at risk of under or overstatement. The response must be a response of the auditor, not the client and must directly relate to the risk you have given. The response may be a procedure or may be an approach that the auditor will take.

Part (c) requires substantive procedures in respect of directors' bonuses. A substantive procedure is used to detect material misstatement in the balance. Think about how you will prove that the figure included in the financial statements is complete and accurate as well as disclosed appropriately.

Part (d) requires knowledge from the text book on how to manage conflicts of interest.

(a) Audit planning is addressed by ISA 300 *Planning an Audit of Financial Statements*. It states that adequate planning benefits the audit of financial statements in several ways:

- Helping the auditor to devote appropriate attention to important areas of the audit.
- Helping the auditor to identify and resolve potential problems on a timely basis.
- Helping the auditor to properly organise and manage the audit engagement so that it is performed in an effective and efficient manner.
- Assisting in the selection of engagement team members with appropriate levels of capabilities and competence to respond to anticipated risks and the proper assignment of work to them.
- Facilitating the direction and supervision of engagement team members and the review of their work.
- Assisting, where applicable, in coordination of work done by experts.

(b) Risks and responses

Audit risk	Auditor's response
New audit client Hart Co is a new client for Morph & Co. As the audit team is not familiar with the accounting policies, transactions and balances of Hart Co, there will be an increased detection risk on the audit. There is also less assurance over opening balances as Morph & Co did not perform the audit last year.	Morph & Co should ensure it has a suitably experienced team assigned to the audit and that adequate time is allowed for team members to obtain an understanding of the company and the risks of material misstatement, including a detailed team briefing to cover the key areas of risk. Increased audit procedures should be performed over opening balances.
Directors' bonus The directors are paid a bonus based on a percentage of profit before tax for the year. There is a risk that the directors will try to overstate the profit, and therefore their bonuses by increasing the revenue and income recorded and decreasing expenses. This is a particular risk relating to judgemental areas such as provisions and estimates.	The audit team should be aware of the increased risks of manipulation and should assign more experienced audit members to significant estimates and judgemental areas. Also, adequate time should be allocated for team members to obtain an understanding of the company and the significant risks of overstatement of profit, including attendance at an audit team briefing. The team needs to maintain professional scepticism and be alert to the increased risk of manipulation. Increased testing should be performed relating to adjusting journal entries.
Revenue recognition Customers pay a 25% deposit on signing the contract to purchase the playgrounds. The deposits should not be recognised as revenue immediately and instead should be recognised as deferred income (contract liabilities) within current liabilities until the performance obligations, as per the contracts, have been satisfied. This is likely to be at a point in time, when control of the playground is passed to the customer. There is a risk that revenue is overstated and current liabilities understated if the deposits have been recorded within revenue.	The audit team should obtain a copy of the contracts with customers and review them to understand the performance obligations. They should discuss with management the criteria for determining whether performance obligations have been satisfied and the treatment of deposits received to ensure it is appropriate and consistent with relevant standards. During the final audit, the audit team should undertake increased testing over the cut-off of revenue and the completeness of deferred income (contract liabilities).

Audit risk	**Auditor's response**
WIP The audit team will only attend the WIP counts at five of the 16 sites. WIP is a material balance and the valuation of WIP is a judgemental area. As the audit team is not attending all sites, detection risk is increased as the team will be unable to directly obtain evidence relating to WIP.	The auditor should assess which inventory counts the team will attend, most likely to be those with the most material WIP balances or which are assessed as having the greatest risk of misstatement. For those inventory counts not attended, the audit team will need to obtain and review documentation relating to the controls surrounding the counts and will need to review reports from any experts used to value the WIP, and any exceptions noted during the count and discuss with management any issues which arise during the count.
Warranty provision Hart Co offers its customers a warranty at no extra cost, which guarantees the playgrounds will function as expected for three years. The provision is calculated as 2% of revenue in the current year against 6% in the prior year, despite there being no changes in the construction techniques or the level of claims. Under IAS 37 *Provisions, Contingent Liabilities and Contingent Assets* this should be recognised as a warranty provision. Calculating warranty provisions requires judgement as it is an uncertain amount. There is a risk that the warranty provision could be understated, leading to understated expenses and liabilities.	The audit team should discuss with management the basis of the provision calculation and compare this to industry averages and the level of post-year-end claims, if any, made by customers. In particular, they should discuss the rationale behind reducing the level of provision this year. The audit team should also compare the prior year provision with the actual level of claims in the year, to assess the reasonableness of the judgements made by management.

Audit risk	**Auditor's response**
R&D Hart Co has recognised $0.6m of research expenditure in profit or loss with the remaining $1.2m having been capitalised as development expenditure. IAS 38 *Intangible Assets* has strict criteria as to which costs can be capitalised as development expenditure. There is a risk that the requirements of the standard have not been applied correctly. If research costs have been incorrectly classified as development expenditure, there is a risk that intangible assets could be overstated and research expenses understated.	The audit team should obtain a breakdown of the research expenditure recognised in profit or loss and of the development costs capitalised and review supporting documentation to determine whether they have been correctly classified. Any development expenditure should then be agreed as meeting the relevant criteria for capitalisation as set out in IAS 38. The team should also discuss the accounting treatment with the finance director and ensure it is in accordance with IAS 38.
PPE Hart Co placed an order for $2.4m of machinery, paying $1 m in advance. The machinery was due to be received in July 20X5 but will now be delivered post year end. Only assets which physically exist at the year end should be capitalised as property, plant and equipment (PPE). The $1 m deposit paid in advance should be recognised as a prepayment. If the deposit of $1m paid in advance has been capitalised within PPE then prepayments are understated and PPE will be overstated.	Review the non-current asset register to determine if the $1m paid in advance has been capitalised. Discuss the correct accounting treatment with management to confirm that the amount paid in advance is recognised as a prepayment and if incorrectly recognised review the correcting journal entry.
Rights issue Hart Co made a rights issue in the year. This is a non-standard transaction and there is increased risk that the issue has not been recorded correctly. The rights issue has been made at a premium and therefore requires to be split into its share capital and share premium elements. There is a risk that the split between share capital and share premium has not been accounted for correctly and that these balances are misstated. There is also a risk that the rights issue has not been disclosed in accordance with accounting standards and local company legislation.	The audit team should obtain legal documentation in support of the rights issue to agree the number of shares issued and the rights price. They should recalculate the split of share capital and share premium and agree this to the journal entry to record the rights issue. The audit team should also agree that disclosures are adequate and consistent with standards and legislation.

Audit risk	Auditor's response
Payroll Hart Co's payroll function is outsourced to an external service organisation. A detection risk arises as to whether sufficient and appropriate evidence is available at Hart Co to confirm the completeness and accuracy of controls over the payroll cycle and liabilities at the year end. Consideration should be given to the level of controls in place at the service organisation and whether the data is reliable. If any errors occurred these could result in the wages and salaries expense and any accruals being misstated.	Discuss with management any changes to the extent of records maintained at Hart Co since the prior year audit and any monitoring of controls which has been undertaken by management over payroll. Consideration should be given to contacting the auditor of the service organisation, Chaz Co, to confirm the level of controls in place. A type 1 or type 2 report could be requested. Consider the extent to which sufficient appropriate audit evidence can be obtained from records held at Hart Co in respect of the wages and salaries expense and liabilities.
Directors' remuneration Directors' remuneration disclosures have been made in line with IFRS Standards but not local legislation. Where the local legislation is more comprehensive than IFRS Standards it is likely that the company must comply with local legislation. The directors' remuneration disclosure will not be complete if the additional information is not disclosed.	Discuss this matter with management and review the requirements of local legislation to determine if the disclosure in the financial statements is included appropriately.

(c) Substantive procedures for directors' bonuses

- Obtain a schedule of the directors' bonus and cast the schedule to ensure its accuracy. Agree the amount to that disclosed in the financial statements.
- Review the schedule of current liabilities and confirm the bonus accrual is included as a year-end liability.
- Agree the individual bonus payments to the post-year-end payroll records.
- Recalculate the bonus payments and agree the criteria to supporting documentation and the percentage rates to be paid to the directors' service contracts.
- Confirm the amount of each bonus paid by agreeing to the post-year-end bank ledger account and bank statements.
- Compare the profit before tax used in the bonus calculation to the final profit before tax figure to confirm whether any adjustment is required to the bonus paid and discuss any differences with management.

- Agree the amounts paid to each director to board minutes and contracts to ensure the amounts included in the current year financial statements are fully accrued and disclosed.
- Review the board minutes to identify whether any additional payments relating to this year have been agreed for any directors.
- Obtain a written representation from management confirming the completeness of directors' remuneration including the bonus.
- Review the disclosures made regarding the bonus paid to directors and assess whether these are in compliance with local legislation.

(d) Safeguards

- Both Hart Co and its competitor should be notified that Morph & Co would be acting as auditors for each company and consent should be obtained from management of each company.
- Morph & Co should consider advising one or both clients to seek additional independent advice.
- Morph & Co must ensure it appoints separate engagement teams, with different engagement partners and team members to each client; once an employee has worked on one audit, such as Hart Co, then they should be prevented from being on the audit of the competitor for a period of time.
- Adequate procedures should be in place within the firm to prevent access to information, for example, strict physical separation of both teams, confidential and secure data filing.
- Morph & Co must set out clear guidelines for members of each engagement team on issues of security and confidentiality. These guidelines could be included within the audit engagement letters sent to each client.
- Morph & Co should consider the use of confidentiality agreements signed by all members of the engagement teams of Hart Co and the competitor.
- Work performed should be reviewed by an appropriate reviewer who is not involved in the audit to assess whether key judgements and conclusions are appropriate.
- Regular monitoring of the application of the above safeguards should be undertaken by a senior individual in Morph & Co not involved in either audit.

ACCA marking guide

		Marks
(a)	**Benefits of audit planning**	
	Appropriate attention to important areas	1
	Identify/resolve potential problems/risks	1
	Effective/efficient performance	1
	Assists in selection of audit team/assignment of work	1
	Facilitates direction/supervision/review	1
	Assists in coordination of work performed by experts	1
	Restricted to	**4**

(b)	**Audit risk and response** (only 8 risks required)	
	New client	2
	Directors' bonus	2
	Payment of deposit	2
	Audit team not attending all WIP counts	2
	Warranty provision decrease	2
	Treatment of R&D costs	2
	Payment for PPE in advance	2
	Rights issue	2
	Outsourced payroll function	2
	Directors' remuneration disclosure	2
	Max 8 issues, 2 marks each	**16**
(c)	**Substantive procedures for directors' bonuses**	
	1 mark per well-described procedure	
	Restricted to	**5**
(d)	**Safeguards**	
	1 mark per well-explained point	
	Restricted to	**5**
Total		**30**

Examiner's comments

Part (a) is a relatively straightforward knowledge requirement which has been tested in previous exam sessions. It demonstrates the importance of having a detailed understanding of the ISAs, and in this case, ISA 300 *Planning an Audit of Financial Statements* in particular. For a four-mark knowledge requirement such as this, candidates should aim to provide four well-explained points. It should be noted that the opening statement before the requirement specifically refers to ISA 300 which should provide the context for the response. Care should be taken when reading the requirement to ensure that answer points focus on the right issues. For example, in this session some candidates incorrectly focused their answers on determining the audit approach, gaining an understanding of the client or considering the audit timetable which were not relevant.

Part (b). With this type of requirement good exam technique is critical. Marks are awarded for identification of audit risks (½ mark each), explanation of audit risks (½ mark each) and an appropriate auditor's response to each risk (1 mark each). The scenario will typically contain more than the number of risks required, so it is important that candidates plan their time carefully and only attempt to list the required number of points. The first step is to identify the factors which will give rise to an audit risk. This information can be found in the scenario. All of the information in the scenario should be read carefully, including the opening paragraph as this may include information relevant to the identification of audit risks and is often overlooked. For example, in this question the opening paragraph of the scenario refers to the fact that Hart Co is a new client which therefore results in an increased detection risk. Financial accounting knowledge is also important as audit risks will often focus on the accounting treatment used in the financial statements. In Hart Co accounting issues which give rise to audit risks include risks relating to revenue recognition, a warranty and a share issue. Having identified the risk factor the next step is to explain the risk. To do this, candidates need to state the specific area of the financial statements impacted with an assertion (for example cut off, valuation etc.), or, a reference to over/under/misstated, or, a reference to inherent/ control/ detection risk. 'Misstated' will only be awarded if it is clear the balance could be either over or understated. For example, if the risk should have been described in terms of an understated balance, then no credit would be awarded if candidates referred to a misstated balance. Candidates cannot hedge their bets by providing both options.

The explanation of the risk must also clearly state the specific area of the financial statements impacted. For example, in respect of the issue relating to the research and development costs capitalised as an intangible asset, only noting 'assets could be overstated' would not be awarded credit. An appropriate explanation in this instance would be 'intangible assets could be overstated' as only by clearly identifying the specific area impacted by the risk can the auditor devise an appropriate response. In order to correctly explain the risk, candidates must take the time to carefully read the information provided to ensure that they describe risks actually highlighted in the scenario, rather than theoretical risks. For example, in Hart Co the revenue recognition risk relates to the correct treatment of the deposit, however, many candidates thought the risk was that the 75% outstanding balance may not be paid resulting in overstated receivables. There is no indication that recoverability of the balance is a potential issue in the scenario and therefore is not relevant. In addition, a number of candidates explained the issue of the auditors not attending all the WIP counts in terms of inventory being misstated, rather than as a detection risk. Candidates must take the time to carefully read the scenario, noting any dates and other relevant information, to ensure that they correctly understand and describe the audit risks arising. Having identified and explained the risk, the third step is to provide the auditor's response. An auditor's response does not have to be a detailed procedure, rather it is an approach the audit team will take. Care must be taken however, to ensure that the approach suggested actually addresses the risk identified. Selecting a suitably experienced audit team or ensuring adequate time is allocated to obtain an understanding of the client would be an appropriate response to the risk arising from a new audit client. A common error is for candidates to confuse the auditor's response and management's response. For example, in response to the risk of the directors' bonus, many candidates focused on whether the bonus should be based on profit and instead suggested it should be based on long-term performance. This is not an auditor's response and therefore would not be awarded credit. From the audit perspective, the risk is that of manipulation of profits by directors in order to achieve the targets required for the bonus to be paid. Candidates should also consider whether their response is practical within the context of the scenario. Suggesting that the auditor attend all 16 of Hart Co's inventory WIP counts at the year end would not be feasible or necessary. Future candidates are advised that audit risk is and will continue to be an important element in the syllabus and must be understood. Candidates must ensure that they include adequate question practice as part of their revision on this key topic.

Part (c). For substantive procedures requirements, one mark is available for each well described procedure. Candidates should plan their time accordingly. When describing substantive procedures one of the key things to consider is the level of detail provided. Many candidates fail to score well in this type of requirement because their procedures are vague or too brief. For example, in this session many candidates included, 'review board minutes' without specifying that this was being done to agree the amounts paid to the directors or 'obtain written representations' without specifying that this was for confirmation of completeness of the bonuses. Candidates must also take time to read any information provided and ensure that they tailor their procedures to the scenario rather than simply listing a series of rote-learned tests. In this session many candidates included irrelevant tests such as 'compare the bonus to prior year', 'review for authorisation of the bonus' or focused on auditing the profit before tax figure rather than the bonus itself. This demonstrates a lack of understanding of the scenario and the purpose of the substantive procedures. Candidates who focused on 'recalculating the bonus', 'agreeing bonus payments to post-year-end bank statements/bank ledger account', 'agreeing the bonus to payroll records' and 'reviewing the disclosure for compliance with legislation' were able to gain credit. Take the time to read the question requirements carefully and spend time thinking about what is needed prior to producing an answer.

Part (d). This question tests candidates understanding of ACCA's Code of Ethics and Conduct. One mark is available for each well explained point so candidates should aim for five points. Again, as for part (a) this requirement is relatively straightforward and an area where candidates should perform well. Key points include informing the competitors and obtaining consent, appointing separate engagement teams for each client, confidentiality agreements and attempts at putting in place physical barriers between each engagement team. This requirement also highlights the range of topics which the exam can cover. Questions on ethics may cover independence, confidentiality and conflict of interest and candidates must be equally prepared for any of these aspects.

208 SCARLET *Walk in the footsteps of a top tutor*

Key answer tips

Part (a) asks for an explanation of the purpose and a list of contents of an audit engagement letter. All section B questions are likely to include a knowledge requirement and students must prepare for these requirements. Often, these questions require knowledge of an auditing standard and therefore they can be difficult to answer unless you have revised the specific audit guidance. Also pay attention to the verbs in the question. To explain the purpose of the engagement letter you must say why it is important for a firm to have an engagement letter with a client. When listing the contents, no explanation is required.

Part (b) asks for an explanation as to why the factors given should be considered prior to acceptance. By presenting the question in this way, the examiner is making it clear that marks will only be available for explanations, not identification as the points have already been identified for you. This demonstrates the need to fully understand matters affecting the audit. It will be difficult to pass the exam by memorising the text book.

Part (c) asks for audit risks and responses. This requirement is examined every sitting. You must make sure the risk relates to either a risk of material misstatement or a detection risk. Read through the scenario to identify information which refers to something that will appear in the financial statements, e.g. plant and equipment, receivables, intangible assets, loans and briefly explain the accounting treatment that should be applied. Think about common mistakes that the client could make either deliberately to manipulate the financial statements or unintentionally. State whether the item in the financial statements is at risk of under or overstatement. The response must be a response of the auditor, not the client and must directly relate to the risk you have given. The response may be a procedure or may be an approach that the auditor will take.

Part (d) requires substantive procedures in respect of redundancy costs. A substantive procedure is used to detect material misstatement in the balance. Think about how you will prove that the figure included in the financial statements is complete and accurate as well as disclosed appropriately.

(a) Engagement letters

Purpose of an engagement letter

The letter of engagement outlines the responsibilities of both the audit firm and the audit client. Its purpose is to:

- Minimise the risk of any misunderstanding between the auditor and the client
- Confirm acceptance of the engagement; and
- Forms the basis of the contract by outlining the terms and conditions of the engagement.

Items to be included in an engagement letter

- The objective and scope of the audit
- The responsibilities of the auditor
- Responsibilities of management
- Identification of the financial reporting framework used in the preparation of the financial statements
- Expected form and content of any reports to be issued
- Elaboration of the scope of the audit with reference to legislation
- The form of any other communication of the results of the audit
- The fact that some material misstatements may not be discovered
- Arrangements concerning the planning and performance of the audit, including the composition of the audit team
- The expectation that management will provide written representations
- The basis on which the audit firm will calculate its fees
- A request for management to agree to the terms of the audit engagement and acknowledge receipt of the letter of engagement
- Arrangements concerning the involvement of internal audit and other staff employed at the company
- Any obligations to provide audit working papers to third parties
- Any restrictions on the auditor's liability; and
- Arrangements to make available draft financial statements and any other information.

(b) Factors to consider prior to accepting Scarlet Co as a new audit client

The outgoing auditor's response

Prior to accepting an audit engagement, the auditor is required to contact the previous auditors, after obtaining permission from Scarlet Co, to ask for all information relevant to the decision as to whether or not the firm should accept appointment.

The auditor should consider the outgoing auditor's response to assess whether there are any ethical or professional reasons why the firm should not accept appointment.

Management integrity

If Orange & Co's audit engagement partner has reason to believe that Scarlet Co's management lack integrity, there is a greater risk of fraud and intimidation. Orange & Co need to consider management integrity because if there are serious concerns regarding this, Orange & Co must not accept the audit engagement.

Pre-conditions for an audit

Orange & Co can only accept an audit engagement if the preconditions are present. The preconditions confirm that management will use an acceptable financial reporting framework under which they will prepare the financial statements and confirms that management acknowledges and understands its responsibilities for:

- Preparing the financial statements in accordance with the applicable financial reporting framework
- Internal control necessary for the preparation of the financial statements to be free from material misstatement; and
- Providing the auditor with access to information relevant for the audit and access to staff within the entity to obtain audit evidence.

If the preconditions are not present, Orange & Co cannot accept the audit engagement.

Independence and objectivity

The auditor must consider whether there are any threats to independence and objectivity which cannot be reduced to an acceptably low level by the use of appropriate safeguards, such as if any of Orange & Co's staff have shares in Scarlet Co or are related to staff employed at Scarlet Co. If such threats are present and cannot be sufficiently mitigated, Orange & Co must not accept the audit engagement.

Resources available at the time of the audit

Orange & Co must have adequate resources with the relevant experience available at the time the audit of Scarlet Co is likely to be carried out. All audit staff deployed to the audit of Scarlet Co must be capable of carrying out the audit in accordance with International Standards on Auditing (ISAs). If adequate resources will not be available, Orange & Co must not accept the audit engagement.

(c) Audit risks and auditor's responses

Audit risk	**Auditor's response**
New audit client Scarlet Co is a new audit client of the firm. The audit engagement team will be unfamiliar with the accounting policies, transactions and balances of the client, hence there will be increased detection risk on the audit. In addition, there is less assurance over opening balances as Orange & Co did not perform last year's audit.	Orange & Co should ensure that it has a suitably experienced team deployed on the audit. In addition, sufficient time must be set aside so that the team members can familiarise themselves with the new client, document its systems and controls and understand the risks of material misstatement. Increased audit procedures should be performed on the opening balances to confirm their reasonableness.

Audit risk	Auditor's response
Temporary accountant The company's financial accountant was taken ill suddenly in May 20X5 and a temporary accountant has been drafted in to help prepare the financial statements. There is an increased risk of errors in the financial statements as the temporary financial accountant may not be familiar with the company's activities and so errors/omissions may go unnoticed.	Discuss with management the technical competency and experience of the temporary financial accountant. In addition, the audit engagement team should ensure that increased substantive procedures are undertaken on the material areas of the financial statements to reduce audit risk, particularly those requiring judgement.
Risk of manipulation The year-end financial statements have to be prepared by the end of September 20X5 in order to secure bank finance and management wish to report strong results. This increases the risk that the directors may manipulate the financial statements, by overstating profits and assets and understating liabilities.	The audit engagement team should maintain professional scepticism throughout the course of the audit. Detailed cut-off testing on areas such as revenue, inventory and payables should be performed to ensure that cut-off has been correctly applied and substantive procedures performed on estimates and judgements to ensure accuracy.
Machinery A specialised machine was acquired and staff members had to be trained in the machine's use at a cost of $15,000 which has been capitalised as part of the cost of the machine. IAS 16 *Property, Plant and Equipment* prohibits training costs from being capitalised and therefore profits and property, plant and equipment will be overstated, and expenses understated if the training costs are not written off to the statement of profit or loss.	Discuss the accounting treatment with the directors and request that an adjustment is made to ensure appropriate treatment of the training costs. Obtain a breakdown of the remaining capitalised costs and agree to supporting documentation to ensure that they meet the recognition criteria in IAS 16.
Inventory cut-off The delivery time of three weeks from the company's international supplier is likely to result in goods in transit at the year end. The company has advised that the contract with the supplier means that Scarlet Co will be responsible for goods from despatch and therefore inventory should be recorded when the products are sent by the supplier. There is a risk that inventory is not recorded on despatch and therefore inventory and liabilities are understated at the year end.	Discuss with management the point at which inventory is recorded and review the contract with the supplier to verify the requirements in place. Review the controls the company has in place to ensure that inventory is recorded from the point of despatch. Extend cut-off testing by reviewing pre and post-year-end GRNs and supplier despatch notes to verify that inventory is recorded at the correct point.

Audit risk	**Auditor's response**
Receivables valuation Preliminary analytical procedures indicate that the receivables collection period has increased from 38 days to 52 days due to customers taking longer to pay. There is a risk that some receivables may not be recoverable and an allowance for credit losses/receivables is required, hence receivables may be overstated and the allowance understated.	Extend post-year-end cash receipts testing and perform a review of the aged receivables listing to assess the valuation of receivables. Discuss with management the adequacy of any allowance for credit losses/receivables.
Redundancy provision On 29 May 20X5, the directors announced that a brand was being discontinued resulting in four members of staff being made redundant. The costs of redundancy are being included in the July 20X5 payroll run. As there is a present obligation for which the costs can be reliably measured, and which will result in an outflow of funds, IAS 37 *Provisions, Contingent Assets and Contingent Liabilities* would require this provision to be recognised in the financial statements. If a provision is not recognised profit would be overstated and liabilities and payables would be understated.	Obtain the calculation of the redundancy payments and agree that a provision has been included as a liability in the year-end financial statements. Agree the redundancy payments have been paid post year end.
Directors' bonus The directors have each been paid a significant bonus at the year end and separate disclosure of this is required in the financial statements by local legislation. The directors' remuneration disclosure will be incomplete and inaccurate if the bonus paid is included in the payroll charge for the year and not separately disclosed in accordance with the local legislation.	Discuss this matter with management and review the disclosure in the financial statements to ensure it complies with local legislation.
Return of faulty goods A customer has returned $120,000 of faulty goods to the company prior to the year end but a credit note is yet to be issued. As this sale occurred pre year end, there is a risk that revenue and receivables are overstated if the credit note is not correctly recorded prior to the year end.	Inspect a copy of the credit note and confirm an adjustment to revenue and receivables has been recorded pre year end.

Audit risk	Auditor's response
Payment run The company's suppliers have been paid on 1 June 20X5 and the payment has been included as an unpresented item in the year-end bank reconciliation. This is possible evidence of window dressing which results in understated payables and bank balances.	Request that the bank reconciliation is amended to remove the supplier payments at the year end as these should be accounted for in the 31 May 20X6 financial statements. Review the journal entry correcting the payables and bank balances at the year end.

(d) Substantive procedures for the redundancy costs

- Review the board minutes for evidence of the decision to discontinue the brand of chemicals prior to the year end.
- Review supporting documentation to confirm that the decision to discontinue the brand was notified to the four members of staff prior to the year end.
- Obtain details of the redundancy calculated by employee, cast the schedule and agree to the trial balance/financial statements.
- Recalculate the redundancy provision to confirm completeness and agree components of the cost to supporting documentation such as employee contracts.
- Agree the redundancy payments made in July 20X5 to the bank ledger account/payroll records and compare these to the provision in the financial statements.
- Obtain a written representation from management confirming the completeness of the costs.
- Review the disclosures included in the financial statements to verify they are in compliance with requirements of IAS 37 *Provisions, Contingent Assets and Contingent Liabilities*.

ACCA marking guide

			Marks
(a)	**Purpose and contents of engagement letter**		
	• Purpose		2
	• Four examples of items to be included (½ mark each)		2
		Maximum	**4**
(b)	**Factors to consider prior to acceptance**		
	• Outgoing auditor's response		1
	• Management integrity		1
	• Pre-conditions		1
	• Independence and objectivity		1
	• Resources		1
		Maximum	**5**

(c)	**Audit risk and response (only 8 risks required)**	
	• New client	2
	• Temporary accountant	2
	• FS preparation deadline for bank loan application	2
	• Training costs capitalised	2
	• Goods in transit	2
	• Increase in receivables days	2
	• Redundancy provision	2
	• Directors' bonus disclosure	2
	• Credit note for faulty goods	2
	• Late supplier payment run	2
	Max 8 issues, 2 marks each	**16**
(d)	**Substantive procedures for redundancy costs**	
	1 mark per well-described procedure	
	Restricted to	**5**
Total		**30**

Examiner's comments

This question tested candidates' knowledge of engagement letters, pre-acceptance factors, audit risks and responses and substantive procedures. Overall performance was satisfactory.

Part (a) required candidates to explain the purpose of an audit engagement letter and list four items which should be included in an audit engagement letter. One mark was available for each well explained point regarding the purpose and ½ mark for each item to be included. This is a knowledge area that has been tested in previous sessions. Performance was mixed. Candidates were able to confidently list four items which should be included and so scored the two available marks. In fact, many candidates listed more than four points, the most common correct answers were scope, fees, auditor and management responsibilities. However, few candidates scored well in relation to the purpose of an engagement letter. Many provided vague answers and focused their responses on what an engagement letter is rather than why it is required. Candidates are reminded that they must take care in carefully reading the requirement and only answering the question asked.

Part (b) required an explanation of why five specified pre-acceptance factors should have been considered by the auditor prior to accepting Scarlet Co as a new audit client. One mark was available for each well explained point. Candidates were required to focus their answers on why pre-acceptance factors such as 'management integrity' and 'the outgoing auditor's response' should be considered. Unfortunately, many focused on what the factors were rather than why they were considered. In addition, many of the explanations given were circular in nature. For example, in explaining why 'management integrity' was considered it was common to see answers such as, 'it is important because we need to consider if management have integrity'. This would not have gained any credit because it did not explain why management integrity was important, that for example if management lack integrity there is a greater risk of fraud and intimidation. For the factor of 'independence and objectivity' many candidates simply listed types of ethical threats, rather than explaining that independence needed to be considered so that ethical threats could be assessed and relevant safeguards could be applied where relevant. The factor of 'resources available at the time of the audit' should have focused on whether sufficient audit staff of appropriate technical knowledge and experience were available. However, many answers focused on whether management had staff available to answer auditor's queries.

Part (c) required candidates to identify and describe audit risks and to explain the auditor's response to each in planning the audit of Scarlet Co. Performance was satisfactory. Marks were awarded for identification of audit risks (½ mark each), explanation of audit risks (½ mark each) and an appropriate auditor's responses to each risk (1 mark each). The scenario contained more than eight risks, so it was pleasing that most candidates planned their time carefully and generally only attempted to list the required number of points. Candidates generally identified the risks well. This session it was pleasing to see that many candidates identified from the opening paragraph of the scenario that Scarlet Co was a new client and therefore resulted in an increased detection risk. The main risk which was not identified or misunderstood by candidates related to the payment run made to suppliers on the first day after the year end. This created a window dressing risk in relation to bank and trade payables, but few candidates who identified this risk understood that. Candidates must take the time to carefully read the scenario, noting dates and other relevant information, to ensure that they correctly understand the audit risks arising. As in previous sessions, many candidates did not adequately explain the risk. To explain the risk, candidates need to state the specific area of the financial statements impacted with an assertion (for example cut-off, valuation etc.), or, a reference to over/under/misstated, or, a reference to inherent/control/ detection risk. 'Misstated' was only awarded if it was clear the balance could be either over/understated. As stated in previous examiner's reports, a significant proportion of candidates did not clearly state the specific area of the financial statement impacted. As an example, for the issue relating to the training costs capitalised within the addition of the specialised machine, only noting 'assets could be overstated' was not awarded credit. Candidates must demonstrate adequate understanding of the accounting issues and clearly state the specific area of the financial statements, in this case 'property plant and equipment could be overstated' to be awarded the ½ implication mark. Candidates' performance in relation to auditor's responses continues to be mixed. While an auditor's response does not have to be a detailed procedure, rather an approach the audit team will take to address the identified risk, the responses given were often too weak or not related to the actual audit risk. For example, in response to the risk of the directors' bonus, many candidates focused on auditing a profit figure on which they believed the bonus was based or recalculating the bonus. However, there was no indication in the scenario that the bonus was based on profit or that there was a calculation issue. Instead the response should have focused on the actual risk of separate disclosure as indicated in the scenario and therefore should have considered 'reviewing the disclosure of the bonus for compliance with legislation'.

Additionally, there was an increase in management rather than auditor responses. For example, for the risk of goods in transit, rather than focusing on auditing completeness of inventory and trade payables at the year end, many responses considered what would happen if inventory was damaged in transit or the risk of stockouts due to the three-week delivery time. Future candidates are advised that audit risk is and will continue to be an important element in the syllabus and must be understood. Candidates must ensure that they include adequate question practice as part of their revision on this key topic.

Part (d) required candidates to describe substantive procedures the auditor should perform in relation to the redundancy costs. One mark was available for each well-described procedure. Many candidates failed to provide sufficient detail in their procedures, or they were too brief. For example, many candidates stated 'review board minutes' without specifying that this was being done to confirm whether the redundancy had been announced pre year end. Failing to provide the required detail meant that this test would not have scored any marks. In addition, many irrelevant tests such as 'compare the redundancy provision to prior year' or 'write to the lawyers for confirmation of the provision' demonstrated a lack of understanding of the scenario and gained no marks. Candidates who scored marks focused on recalculation of the provision, confirming the redundancy payment to post-year-end bank statements and agreeing the redundancies to employment records. Candidates are reminded they must take the time to read the question requirements carefully and spend time thinking about what is needed prior to writing their answers.

209 HARLEM *Walk in the footsteps of a top tutor*

Key answer tips

Part (a) asks for specific ratios to be calculated from the information provided. The question specifically states that formulas are not required, therefore, do not waste time typing these out as no marks will be awarded.

Part (b) asks for audit risks and responses. This requirement is examined every sitting. You must make sure the risk relates to either a risk of material misstatement or a detection risk. Read through the scenario to identify information which refers to something that will appear in the financial statements, e.g. intangible assets, property, loans and briefly explain the accounting treatment that should be applied. Think about common mistakes that the client could make either deliberately to manipulate the financial statements or unintentionally. State whether the item in the financial statements is at risk of under or overstatement. The response must be a response of the auditor, not the client and must directly relate to the risk you have given. The response may be a procedure or may be an approach that the auditor will take.

Part (c) covers quality management procedures in respect of supervision and review of the audit team's work. Think about the role of the supervisor and the purpose of the review of working papers.

Part (d) asks for substantive procedures in respect of the valuation of trade receivables. You must give answers which focus on valuation, as marks will not be awarded for procedures which test any of the other assertions.

Part (e) asks for substantive procedures in respect of the disposal of plant and machinery. Again, you must focus on the requirement. Any procedures which relate to plant and equipment in general will not earn marks.

(a) Ratios to assist in planning the audit:

	20X5	**20X4**
Gross profit margin	4,500/23,200 × 100 = **19.4%**	4,600/21,900 × 100 = **21%**
Inventory holding period	2,100/18,700 × 365 = **41 days**	1,600/17,300 × 365 = **34 days**
Gearing	13,000/(10,000 + 13,000) × 100 = **56.5%**	11,000/(9,500 + 11,000) × 100 = **53.7%**
OR	13,000/10,000 × 100 = **130%**	11,000/9,500 × 100 = **116%**
Interest cover	(450 + 290)/290 = **2.6**	(850 + 250)/250 = **4.4**

(b) Audit risk and auditor's response

Audit risk	Auditor's response
Revenue recognition The finance director is planning on reducing the estimated return rate for goods sold on a sale or return basis to wholesale customers from 10% to 5%. IFRS 15 *Revenue from Contracts with Customers* provides that revenue and cost of sales should only be accounted for to the extent that the company foresees that the goods will not be returned. For the goods which may be returned, the company should recognise a refund liability. If, after 60 days, the goods are not returned, then this liability is reversed and revenue is recognised. By reducing the return rate, there is a risk that revenue and cost of sales may be overstated and liabilities understated.	Discuss the basis of the revised assumption of a 5% return rate with the finance director. Review a period of 60 days to quantify the levels of return in the specified period and compare this to the assumed rate of 5%. Discuss any significant variations with the finance director.
Patent The company purchased a patent for $800,000 at the end of the prior year which has a useful life of four years. The carrying amount in the forecast financial statements is $800,000 which is the same as the prior year. In accordance with IAS 38 *Intangible Assets*, this intangible asset should be amortised over its four-year life. It does not appear that management has correctly accounted for the amortisation. Intangible assets and profits are overstated.	Agree the useful life of the patent is four years to supporting documentation. The amortisation charge should be calculated and the appropriate journal adjustment discussed with management, in order to ensure the accuracy of the charge and that the intangible is correctly valued at the year end.
Surplus plant and machinery Surplus plant and machinery was sold during the year, resulting in a loss on disposal of $160,000. Significant profits or losses on disposal are an indication that the depreciation policy of plant and machinery may not be appropriate. Therefore, depreciation may be understated and profit and assets overstated.	Recalculate the loss on disposal calculations and agree all items to supporting documentation. Discuss the depreciation policy for plant and machinery with the finance director to assess its reasonableness. Review for other significant gains or losses on disposal of property, plant and equipment to assess the reasonableness of the company's depreciation policies.

Audit risk	**Auditor's response**
Financial controller fraud Harlem Co's financial controller has allegedly carried out a number of fraudulent transactions at the company. The investigation into the extent of the fraud has only recently commenced. There is a risk that she may have undertaken a significant level of fraudulent transactions leading to an increased control risk which has not yet been identified. These would need to be written off to the statement of profit or loss. If these have not been uncovered by the year end, the financial statements could include errors resulting in the misstatement of profits.	Discuss with the finance director the details of the fraud perpetrated by the financial controller and what procedures have been adopted to date to identify any adjustments which are needed in the financial statements. Additional substantive testing should be conducted over the affected areas of the accounting records. In addition, the team should maintain their professional scepticism and be alert to the risk of further fraud and errors.
Unfair dismissal claim In May 20X5, the financial controller was dismissed and is threatening to sue the company for unfair dismissal. If it is probable that Harlem Co will make payment to the financial controller, a provision for unfair dismissal is required to comply with IAS 37 *Provisions, Contingent Liabilities and Contingent Assets.* If the payment is possible rather than probable, a contingent liability disclosure would be necessary. If Harlem Co has not done this, there is a risk over the completeness of any provisions or contingent liabilities disclosures.	The audit team should discuss with management and request confirmation from the company's lawyers of the existence and likelihood of success of any claim from the former financial controller.
Inventory holding period Harlem Co has had production problems which have affected the quality of a significant batch of tyres. In addition, the inventory holding period has increased from 34 to 41 days. Inventory may be overvalued as its net realisable value (NRV) may be below its cost. If the tyres can be rectified, the rectification costs may mean that cost exceeds net realisable value. If the tyres cannot be rectified, the inventory may need to be written off completely. There is a risk of overstatement of inventory.	Discuss with the finance director whether any write downs will be made to the affected tyres, and what, if any, modifications may be required with regards to the quality. Testing should be undertaken to confirm cost and NRV of the affected products in inventory and that all inventory on a line-by-line basis is valued correctly.

Audit risk	Auditor's response
Receivables valuation A significant customer has been granted a six-month payment break and the receivables collection period has increased from 38 to 51 days. An allowance for credit losses/receivables has historically been maintained, and it is anticipated that it will remain at the prior year level. There is a risk that receivables will be overvalued as some balances may not be recoverable and so will be overstated if adequate allowance for credit losses/ receivables has not been made.	Review and test the controls surrounding how the finance director identifies old or potentially irrecoverable receivables balances and credit control to ensure that they are operating effectively. Discuss with the director the rationale for maintaining the allowance for credit losses/receivables at the same level as the prior year, despite the increase in receivables collection period and the payment break granted to a large customer. Extended post-year-end cash receipts testing and a review of the aged list of individual customer balances to be performed to assess valuation and the need for an increased level of allowance for credit losses/receivables.
Purchase control deficiencies The report to management issued after the prior year audit highlighted significant deficiencies relating to the purchases cycle. If these deficiencies have not been rectified, the controls over purchases and payables may continue to be weak leading to increased control risk and risk of misstatements arising. Cost of sales, expenses and trade payables may not be complete or accurate.	Discuss with management whether the purchases cycle recommendations suggested by Brooklyn & Co were implemented successfully this year. If so, undertake tests of these controls to assess if they are operating efficiently. If the controls are not in place or operating efficiently, adopt a fully substantive approach for confirming the completeness and accuracy of cost of sales and other expenses and trade payables.

Audit risk	**Auditor's response**
Restructure of finance Harlem Co intends to restructure its debt finance after the year end. However, the interest cover has declined from 4.4 to 2.6 and the level of gearing has increased from 53.7% to 56.5%. In order to maximise the chances of securing the debt finance restructure, Harlem Co will need to present financial statements which show the best possible position and performance. The worsening interest cover and gearing ratio increases the risk that the directors may manipulate the financial statements, by overstating profits and assets and understating debt liabilities.	Brooklyn & Co should ensure that there is a suitably experienced audit team. Also, adequate time should be allocated for team members to obtain an understanding of the company and the significant risks of overstatement of profits and assets and understatement of debt, including attendance at an audit team briefing. The team needs to maintain professional scepticism and be alert to the increased risk of manipulation. Significant estimates and judgements should be carefully reviewed in light of the misstatement risk.
Bonus issue Harlem Co has issued shares during the year via a bonus issue. Share capital within equity should increase by the value of the shares and a reserve should decrease accordingly. If the company has not accounted for a bonus issue before, there is a risk that it could have been incorrectly treated with equity being under or overstated. In addition, legal issues may arise if the shares have not been issued in accordance with the company's statutory constitution. Additionally, bonus issues require disclosure in the financial statements and there is a risk that these may be incomplete or inaccurate.	Review the treatment of the bonus issue and agree the increase in shares to the share register and share certificates, and agree that the corresponding reduction in reserves is correct. Review board minutes for authorisation and terms of the bonus issue and review if the transaction has been conducted in line with this approval. Review the statutory constitution documents to confirm the legality of the share issue. Review the adequacy of the bonus issue disclosures in the financial statements.

(c) Supervision and review of the assistants' work

Supervision

During the audit, the supervisor should keep track of the progress of the audit engagement to ensure that the audit timetable is met and should ensure that the audit manager and partner are kept updated of progress.

The competence and capabilities of individual members of the engagement team should be considered, including whether they have sufficient time to carry out their work, whether they understand their instructions and whether the work is being carried out in accordance with the planned approach to the audit.

In addition, part of the supervision process should involve addressing any significant matters arising during the audit, considering their significance and modifying the planned approach appropriately.

The supervisor would also be responsible for identifying matters for consultation or consideration by the audit manager or engagement partner of Harlem Co.

Review

The supervisor would be required to review the work completed by the assistants and consider whether this work has been performed in accordance with professional standards and other regulatory requirements and if the work performed supports the conclusions reached and has been properly documented.

The supervisor should also consider whether all significant matters have been raised for partner attention or for further consideration and where appropriate consultations have taken place, whether appropriate conclusions have been documented.

(d) Valuation of trade receivables

- Discuss with the finance director the rationale for not increasing the allowance for trade receivables and review its overall adequacy.
- Obtain a breakdown of the opening allowance and consider if the receivables provided for in the prior year have been recovered to assess the reasonableness of the prior levels of allowances.
- Review the aged list of individual customer balances to identify any old or slow-moving receivable balances and discuss the status of these balances with the credit controllers to assess whether they are likely to be received.
- Review whether there are any after-date cash receipts for old or slow-moving receivable balances.
- Review customer correspondence with the significant customer and others to identify any balances which are in dispute or are unlikely to be paid.
- Review board minutes to identify whether there are any significant concerns in relation to payments by customers.
- Calculate the potential level of trade receivables which are not recoverable and assess whether this is material or not and discuss with management.

(e) Disposals of plant and machinery

- Obtain a breakdown of disposals, cast the list and review the non-current asset register to confirm that all assets have been removed.
- Select a sample of disposals and agree sale proceeds to supporting documentation such as sundry sales invoices.
- Recalculate the profit/loss on disposal and agree to the trial balance and statement of profit or loss.
- Recalculate the depreciation charge for a sample of disposals to confirm the calculations are correctly applied as per the company policy of a pro rata basis or a full year in the year of acquisition and none in the year of disposal.
- Review the disclosure of the disposals in the draft financial statements and ensure it is in line with IAS 16 *Property, Plant and Equipment*.

Marking guide

		Marks
(a)	**Ratios**	
	• Gross profit margin	1
	• Inventory holding period	1
	• Gearing	1
	• Interest cover	1
		4
(b)	**Audit risks and responses (only 8 required)**	
	• Sale or return assumption	2
	• Intangible asset amortisation	2
	• Significant losses on disposal	2
	• Financial controller dismissal	2
	• Unfair dismissal claim	2
	• Inventory valuation	2
	• Recoverability of receivables	2
	• Purchases cycle control deficiencies	2
	• Intention to restructure finance	2
	• Bonus issue of shares	2
	Max 8 issues, 2 marks each	**16**
(c)	**Supervising and reviewing audit assistants' work**	
	• Monitor the progress of the audit engagement to ensure the audit timetable was met	1
	• Consider the competence and capabilities of team members re sufficient available time, understanding of instructions and if work in accordance with planned approach	1
	• Address any significant matters arising, consider their significance and modifying the approach	1
	• Responsible for identifying matters for consultation/consideration by senior team members	1
	• Work performed in line with professional standards and other requirements	1
	• Work supports conclusions reached and properly documented	1
	• Significant matters raised for partner attention or further consideration	1
	• Appropriate consultations have taken place with conclusions documented	1
	Restricted to	**4**
(d)	**Substantive procedures – Valuation of trade receivables**	
	• Discuss with management adequacy of trade receivables allowance	1
	• Outcome of prior year allowance	1
	• Review aged trade receivables listing to identify old balances	1
	• After-date cash testing	1
	• Review customer correspondence for evidence of disputes	1
	• Recalculate potential irrecoverable balances and assess adequacy of allowance	1
	Restricted to	**3**
(e)	**Substantive procedures – Disposal of plant and machinery**	
	• Obtain breakdown of disposals, cast and agree removal to non-current asset register	1
	• Select sample of disposals and agree sales proceeds to invoice	1
	• Recalculate the profit/loss on disposal and agree to trial balance	1
	• Recalculate depreciation to confirm applied on a pro rata basis	1
	• Review disclosures and confirm in line with accounting standards	1
	Restricted to	**3**
Total		**30**

Examiner's comments

Part (a) for four marks required a calculation of four specified ratios for both the current and prior year. Most candidates were able to generate enough marks to pass this part of the requirement, however few received full marks. Candidates were able to confidently calculate the gross profit margin and inventory holding period. However, candidates struggled in particular to calculate interest cover and some miscalculated the gearing ratio. The calculation of interest cover required candidates to add back finance costs to the profit before tax. Many failed to do this correctly and this may explain the weaker performance on this ratio. Candidates must ensure that they are able to calculate a range of key ratios used in analytical procedures.

Part (b) for 16 marks required candidates to identify and describe eight audit risks and to explain the auditor's response to each in planning the audit of Harlem Co. Performance was satisfactory. Marks were awarded for the identification of an audit risk (½ mark each), explanation of the audit risks (½ mark each) and an appropriate auditor's responses to each risk (1 mark each). The scenario contained more than eight risks so it was pleasing that most candidates planned their time carefully and generally only attempted to list the required number of points. Candidates generally identified the risks well. However, having correctly identified the relevant fact from the scenario a significant number did not understand the associated audit risk. For example, the company's intention to restructure the debt finance post year end gave rise to a manipulation risk in the current year financial statements. Many candidates incorrectly stated that the company had taken out a new loan and therefore the risk of classification needed to be addressed. This was incorrect, as Harlem Co had not taken out any loans in the current year. In addition, the risk arising on the amortisation of the intangible asset was poorly answered by candidates. Many failed to appreciate that the asset was purchased in the prior year, therefore audit work confirming the cost would have been undertaken in the prior year.

For the current year the auditor needed to focus on whether the amortisation had been appropriately charged. Candidates must take the time to carefully read the scenario, noting dates and other relevant information, to ensure that they correctly understand the audit risks arising.

As in previous diets, many candidates did not adequately explain the risk. To explain the risk candidates need to state the specific area of the financial statements impacted with an assertion (for example cut off, valuation etc.), or, a reference to over/under/misstated, or a reference to inherent/ control/ detection risk. A reference to a balance being misstated was only awarded credit if it was clear the balance could be either over/understated. A significant minority of candidates did not clearly state the specific area of the financial statement impacted. For example, for the issue relating to the loss on disposal of surplus plant and machinery, answers which noted 'assets could be overstated' were not awarded credit. Candidates must clearly state the specific area of the financial statements, for example 'property plant and equipment could be overstated' to be awarded the ½ implication mark. Candidates' performance in relation to auditor's responses continues to be mixed. While an auditor's response does not have to be a detailed procedure, rather an approach the audit team will take to address the identified risk, the responses given were often too weak or not related to the actual audit risk. For example, in response to the quality control issue with inventory, the response 'inspect the tyres' was not sufficient to gather evidence over the NRV of these tyres. Candidates needed to explain how they would confirm the valuation, for example by 'discussing with management whether the tyres will be written down'. Future candidates are advised that audit risk is and will continue to be an important element in the syllabus and must be understood. Candidates must ensure that they include adequate question practice as part of their revision on this key topic.

Part (c) on quality management responsibilities, where attempted, was disappointing. A significant proportion of candidates did not even attempt this question. For those who did, general audit objectives or ethical points were given, rather than those for quality management.

Part (d) for three marks required candidates to describe substantive procedures the auditor should perform in relation to the valuation of trade receivables. One mark was available for each well-described procedure. Performance on this requirement was satisfactory. Many candidates were able to provide an appropriate number of well described audit procedures such as after-date cash receipts testing and analytical review procedures. Some candidates suggested procedures which would not address the risk of valuation such as, undertaking a receivables circularisation or agreeing the receivables balance to the financial statements. Procedures unrelated to valuation were not awarded credit.

Part (e) for three marks required candidates to describe substantive procedures the auditor should perform in relation to the disposal of plant and machinery. One mark was available for each well-described procedure. Performance on this requirement was disappointing. Many candidates failed to provide procedures focused on disposals, instead they gave a list of generic property, plant and equipment procedures. This wasted time and often meant that candidates only scored one to two marks at best. Candidates who scored well focused on recalculation of the loss on disposal, confirming the plant and machinery had been removed from the asset register and calculation of depreciation to the point of sale. Candidates are reminded they must take the time to read the question requirements carefully and spend time thinking about what is needed prior to writing their answers rather than listing out generic tests.

210 PEONY *Walk in the footsteps of a top tutor*

Key answer tips

Part (a) asks for a definition and explanation of materiality and performance materiality. This requires knowledge from the text book and the relevant auditing standard. Each constructed response question is likely to have one requirement which is knowledge based and therefore you must take time to learn key definitions and be able to provide an explanation.

Part (b) asks for audit risks and responses. This requirement is examined every sitting. You must make sure the risk relates to either a risk of material misstatement or a detection risk. Read through the scenario to identify information which refers to something that will appear in the financial statements, e.g. intangible assets, property, loans and briefly explain the accounting treatment that should be applied. Think about common mistakes that the client could make either deliberately to manipulate the financial statements or unintentionally. State whether the item in the financial statements is at risk of under or overstatement. The response must be a response of the auditor, not the client and must directly relate to the risk you have given. The response may be a procedure or may be an approach that the auditor will take.

(a) Materiality and performance materiality

Materiality and performance materiality are dealt with under ISA 320 *Materiality in Planning and Performing an Audit*. Auditors need to establish the materiality level for the financial statements as a whole, as well as assess performance materiality levels, which are lower than the overall materiality for the financial statements as a whole.

Materiality

Materiality is defined in ISA 320 as follows: 'Misstatements, including omissions, are considered to be material if they, individually or in the aggregate, could reasonably be expected to influence the economic decisions of users taken on the basis of the financial statements.'

If the financial statements include a material misstatement, then they will not present fairly (give a true and fair view) the position, performance and cash flows of the entity.

A misstatement may be considered material due to its size (quantitative) and/or due to its nature (qualitative) or a combination of both. The quantitative nature of a misstatement refers to its relative size. A misstatement which is material due to its nature refers to an amount which might be low in value but due to its prominence and relevance could influence the user's decision, for example, directors' transactions.

As per ISA 320, materiality is often calculated using benchmarks such as 5% of profit before tax or 1% of total revenue or total assets. These values are useful as a starting point for assessing materiality, however, the assessment of what is material is ultimately a matter of the auditor's professional judgement. It is affected by the auditor's perception of the financial information, the needs of the users of the financial statements and the perceived level of risk; the higher the risk, the lower the level of overall materiality.

In assessing materiality, the auditor must consider that a number of errors each with a low value may, when aggregated, amount to a material misstatement.

Performance materiality

Performance materiality is defined in ISA 320 as follows: 'The amount set by the auditor at less than materiality for the financial statements as a whole to reduce to an appropriately low level the probability that the aggregate of uncorrected and undetected misstatements exceeds materiality for the financial statements as a whole.'

Hence performance materiality is set at a level lower than overall materiality for the financial statements as a whole. It is used for testing individual transactions, account balances and disclosures. The aim of performance materiality is to reduce the risk that the total of all of the errors in balances, transactions and disclosures exceeds overall materiality.

(b) Audit risk and auditor's response

Audit risk	Auditor's response
Reliance on internal audit The external audit team may place reliance on the controls testing work undertaken by the IA department. If reliance is placed on irrelevant or poorly performed testing, then the external audit team may form an incorrect conclusion on the strength of the internal controls at Peony Co. This could result in them performing insufficient levels of substantive testing, thereby increasing detection risk.	The external audit team should meet with IA staff, read their reports and review their files relating to store visits to ascertain the nature of the work undertaken. Before using the work of IA, the audit team will need to evaluate and perform audit procedures on the entirety of the work which they plan to use, in order to determine its adequacy for the purposes of the audit. In addition, the team will need to reperform some of the testing carried out by IA to assess its adequacy.
Misclassification of expenses Forecast ratios from the finance director show that the gross profit margin is expected to increase from 56% to 60% and the operating profit margin is expected to decrease from 21% to 18%. This movement in gross profit margin is significant and inconsistent with the fall in operating profit margin. There is a risk that costs may have been omitted or included in operating expenses rather than cost of sales. Misclassification of expenses would result in understatement of cost of sales and overstatement of operating expenses.	The classification of costs between cost of sales and operating expenses should be reviewed in comparison to the prior year and any inconsistencies investigated.
Inventory valuation Peony Co's inventory valuation policy is selling price less average profit margin, as this is industry practice. Inventory should be valued at the lower of cost and net realisable value (NRV). IAS 2 *Inventories* allows this as a cost calculation method as long as it is a close approximation to cost. If this is not the case, then inventory could be under or overvalued.	Testing should be undertaken to confirm cost and NRV of inventory and that on a line-by-line basis the goods are valued correctly. In addition, valuation testing should focus on comparing the cost of inventory to the selling price less margin for a sample of items to confirm whether this method is actually a close approximation to cost.

Audit risk	Auditor's response
Perpetual inventory system The company utilises a perpetual inventory system at its warehouse rather than a full year-end count. Under such a system, all inventory must be counted at least once a year with adjustments made to the inventory records on a timely basis. Inventory could be under or overstated if the perpetual inventory counts are not all completed, such that some inventory lines are not counted in the year.	The timetable of the perpetual inventory counts should be reviewed and the controls over the counts and adjustments to records should be tested.
Inventory record exceptions During the interim audit, it was noted that there were significant exceptions with the inventory records being higher than the inventory in the warehouse. As the year-end quantities will be based on the records, this is likely to result in overstated inventory.	The level of adjustments made to inventory should be considered to assess their significance. This should be discussed with management as soon as possible as it may not be possible to place reliance on the inventory records at the year end, which could result in the requirement for a full year-end inventory count.
Obsolete PPE A number of assets which had not been fully depreciated were identified as being obsolete. This is an indication that the company's depreciation policy of non-current assets may not be appropriate, as depreciation in the past appears to have been understated. If an asset is obsolete, it should be written off to the statement of profit or loss. Therefore, depreciation may be understated and profit and assets overstated.	Discuss the depreciation policy for non-current assets with the finance director and assess its reasonableness. Enquire of the finance director if the obsolete assets have been written off. If so, review the adjustment for completeness.
Advertising expenditure Peony Co is planning to include a current asset of \$0.7m, which relates to advertising costs incurred and adverts shown on TV before the year end. The costs were incurred and adverts shown in the year ending 20X5 and there is no basis for including them as a current asset at the year end. The costs should be recognised in operating expenses in the current year financial statements.	Discuss with management the rationale for including the advertising as a current asset. Request evidence to support the assessment of probable future cash flows, and review for reasonableness. Review supporting documentation for the advertisements to confirm that all were shown before the 20X5 year end.

Audit risk	**Auditor's response**
If these costs are not expensed, current assets and profits will be overstated.	Request that management remove the current asset and record the amount as an expense in the statement of profit or loss.
Outsourced payroll function During the year, Peony Co outsourced its payroll function to an external service organisation. A detection risk arises as to whether sufficient and appropriate evidence is available at Peony Co to confirm the completeness and accuracy of controls over the payroll cycle and liabilities at the year end.	Discuss with management the extent of records maintained at Peony Co for the period since May 20X5 and any monitoring of controls which has been undertaken by management over payroll. Consideration should be given to contacting the service organisation's auditor to confirm the level of controls in place. A type 1 or type 2 report could be requested.
Data transfer The payroll function was transferred to the service organisation from 1 May 20X5, which is five months prior to the year end. If any errors occurred during the transfer process, these could result in wages and salaries being under/overstated.	Discuss with management the transfer process undertaken and any controls which were put in place to ensure the completeness and accuracy of the data. Where possible, undertake tests of controls to confirm the effectiveness of the transfer controls. In addition, perform substantive testing on the transfer of information from the old to the new system.
Bank loan A $3m loan was obtained in June 20X5. This finance needs to be accounted for correctly, with adequate disclosure made. The loan needs to be allocated between non-current and current liabilities. Failure to classify the loan correctly could result in misclassified liabilities.	Reperform the company's calculations to confirm that the split of the loan note is correct between non-current and current liabilities and that total financing proceeds of $3m were received. In addition, the disclosures for this loan note should be reviewed in detail to ensure compliance with relevant accounting standards.

Audit risk	Auditor's response
Redundancy provision Peony Co is planning to make approximately 60 employees redundant after the year end. The timing of this announcement has not been confirmed; if it is announced to the staff before the year end, then under IAS 37 *Provisions, Contingent Liabilities and Contingent Assets*, a redundancy provision will be required at the year end as a constructive obligation will have been created. Failure to provide or to provide an appropriate amount will result in an understatement of provisions and expenses.	Discuss with management the status of the redundancy announcement; if before the year end, review supporting documentation to confirm the timing. In addition, review the basis of and recalculate the redundancy provision.

Marking guide

		Marks
(a)	**Materiality and performance materiality**	
	• Materiality definition	1
	• Material due to size or nature	1
	• Materiality benchmarks	1
	• Depends on judgement and risk	1
	• Performance materiality definition	1
	• Used for testing individual balances	1
	• Set at lower level than materiality	1
	Restricted to	**4**
(b)	**Audit risks and responses (only 8 required)**	
	• Reliance on internal audit –– increased detection risk	2
	• Unusual movement in margins	2
	• Inventory valuation policy	2
	• Perpetual inventory system	2
	• Obsolete PPE	2
	• Advertising expenditure	2
	• Use of payroll service organisation	2
	• Transfer of data to service organisation	2
	• Bank loan	2
	• Redundancy plan	2
	Max 8 issues, 2 marks each	**16**
Total		**20**

Examiner's comments

Candidates' overall performance on this question was satisfactory.

Part (a) required candidates to define and explain materiality and performance materiality. One mark was available for each well-explained point. This is a knowledge area which has been tested in previous exam sessions. Performance was mixed. A significant number of candidates correctly described performance materiality as 'being lower than materiality' (1 mark) and 'comprised of small aggregated errors' (1 mark). However, it was disappointing that a number of candidates were not familiar with the commonly used benchmarks for quantitative materiality.

Part (b) required candidates to identify and describe eight audit risks and to explain the auditor's response to each in planning the audit of Peony Co. Performance was satisfactory. Marks were awarded for identification of audit risk (½ mark each), explanation of audit risks (½ mark each) and an appropriate auditor's response to each risk (1 mark each). The scenario contained more than eight risks so it was pleasing that most candidates planned their time carefully and generally only attempted to list the required number of points. Candidates identified the risks well. However, a significant minority of candidates noted 'the client had been an audit client for a number of years and hence the auditor would be too familiar with the client'. This was not awarded any credit, as this is a risk to the auditor's independence which should be considered prior to continuing with the engagement. As in previous exam sessions, many candidates did not adequately explain the risk. To explain the risk, candidates need to state the specific area of the financial statements impacted with an assertion (for example, cut-off, valuation etc.), or a reference to over/under/misstated, or a reference to inherent/control/detection risk. Misstated was only awarded credit if it was clear the balance could be either over or understated. A significant minority of candidates stated 'inventory could be misstated due to the inventory records being higher than physical counts'. This was not awarded credit as the balance could clearly only be 'overstated'. A significant minority of candidates did not clearly state the specific area of the financial statement impacted. For the above example stating 'current assets could be overstated' without any reference to inventory was not awarded credit. Candidates must clearly demonstrate that they understand the specific area of the financial statements impacted, to be awarded the ½ implication mark. Candidates' performance in relation to auditor's responses continues to be mixed. While an auditor's response does not have to be a detailed procedure, rather an approach the audit team will take to address the identified risk, the responses given were often too weak. For example, in response to the possible errors in the transfer of data to the service organisation, the response 'check the transfers' was not sufficient, candidates needed to explain how, for example, by 'performing substantive testing on the transfer of information from the old to the new system or performing tests of controls to confirm the effectiveness of the transfer controls'. A significant number of candidates gave management rather than auditor's response. For example, when discussing the redundancy plan a number of candidates noted 'there may be a lack of staff for future expansion'. This was not awarded credit. Future candidates are advised that audit risk is and will continue to be an important element in the syllabus and must be understood. Candidates must ensure that they include adequate question practice as part of their revision on this key topic.

211 DARJEELING *Walk in the footsteps of a top tutor*

Key answer tips

Part (a) asks for an explanation of why analytical procedures are used during three stages of an audit. This is knowledge that you should have learned from the text book. Think about what an analytical procedure is – evaluation of plausible relationships between information. Think about the three stages of an audit – planning, final audit and completion. Then link them together – why is it useful to identify inconsistent relationships when planning, when performing the final audit and when completing the audit.

Part (b) asks for ratios to be calculated from the information provided. Remember that the ratios are to help you identify audit risks. You are not evaluating the financial performance of the company.

Part (c) asks for audit risks and responses. This requirement is examined every sitting. You must make sure the risk relates to either a risk of material misstatement or a detection risk. Read through the scenario to identify information which refers to something that will appear in the financial statements, e.g. revenue, property, inventory and briefly explain the accounting treatment that should be applied. Think about common mistakes that the client could make either deliberately to manipulate the financial statements or unintentionally. State whether the item in the financial statements is at risk of under or overstatement.

The response must be a response of the auditor, not the client and must directly relate to the risk you have given.

Part (d) asks for substantive procedures in respect of the faulty inventory. You must describe procedures that will help you evaluate whether the faulty inventory has been correctly accounted for in the financial statements. Make sure your procedures relate to the faulty inventory as there will be no marks for general audit procedures in relation to inventory.

Part (e) requires substantive procedures in relation to revenue. There should be some marks available here for general revenue procedures. However, there is information in the scenario which should be used to provide procedures specific to Darjeeling Co.

(a) Analytical procedures

Analytical procedures can be used at all stages of an audit, however, ISA 315 (Revised 2019) *Identifying and Assessing the Risks of Material Misstatement* and ISA 520 *Analytical Procedures* identify three particular stages.

During the planning stage, analytical procedures must be used as risk assessment procedures in order to help the auditor to obtain an understanding of the entity and assess the risk of material misstatement.

During the final audit, analytical procedures can be used to obtain sufficient appropriate evidence. Substantive procedures can either be tests of detail or substantive analytical procedures.

At the final review stage, the auditor must design and perform analytical procedures which assist them when forming an overall conclusion as to whether the financial statements are consistent with the auditor's understanding of the entity.

(b) Ratios to assist in planning the audit

	20X5	**20X4**
Gross profit margin	7,410/19,850 = **37.3%**	6,190/16,990 = **36.4%**
Inventory holding period	1,850/12,440 × 365 = **54 days**	1,330/10,800 × 365 = **45 days**
OR		
Inventory turnover	12,440/1,850 = **6.7**	10,800/1,330 = **8.1**
Receivables collection period	2,750/19,850 × 365 = **51 days**	1,780/16,990 × 365 = **38 days**
Payables payment period	1,970/12,440 × 365 = **58 days**	1,190/10,800 × 365 = **40 days**
Current ratio	4,600/(1,970 + 810) = **1.65**	3,670/1,190 = **3.08**
Quick ratio	2,750/(1,970 + 810) = **0.99**	(3,670 – 1,330)/1,190 = **1.97**

(c) Audit risks and auditor's response

Audit risk	**Auditor's response**
R&D During the year, Darjeeling Co has spent \$0.9m on developing new product lines, some of which are in the early stages of development. This expenditure is classed as research and development under IAS 38 *Intangible Assets*. The standard requires research costs to be expensed to profit or loss and only development costs to be capitalised as an intangible asset. The company has included all of this expenditure as an intangible asset. If research costs have been incorrectly classified as development expenditure, there is a risk that intangible assets could be overstated and expenses understated.	Obtain a breakdown of the expenditure and verify that it relates to the development of the new products. Review expenditure documentation to determine whether the costs relate to the research or development stage. Discuss the accounting treatment with the finance director and ensure it is in accordance with IAS 38.

Audit risk	**Auditor's response**
PPE Darjeeling Co purchased and installed a new manufacturing line. The costs include purchase price (\$2.2m), installation costs (\$0.4m) and a five-year servicing and maintenance plan (\$0.5m). As per IAS 16 *Property, Plant and Equipment*, the cost of an asset includes its purchase price and directly attributable costs only. IAS 16 does not allow servicing and maintenance costs to be capitalised as part of the cost of a non-current asset, as they are not directly related to the cost of bringing the asset to its working condition. The servicing costs relate to a five-year period and so should be charged to profit or loss over this time. The upfront payment represents a prepayment for five years; as the services are received, the relevant proportion of the cost should be charged to profit or loss. If the service for 20X5 has been carried out, then \$0.1m (\$0.5m/5) should be charged to profit or loss. Therefore property, plant and equipment (PPE) and profits are overstated and prepayments are understated.	Review the purchase documentation for the new manufacturing line to confirm the exact cost of the servicing and that it does relate to a five-year period. Discuss the accounting treatment with the finance director and the level of any necessary adjustment to ensure treatment is in accordance with IAS 16.
Bank loan The company has borrowed \$4m from the bank via an eight-year loan. This loan needs to be correctly split between current and non-current liabilities in order to ensure correct disclosure. Current and non-current liabilities will be misstated if the split is incorrect.	During the audit, the team would need to confirm that the \$4 million loan finance was received. In addition, the split between current and non-current liabilities and the disclosures for this loan should be reviewed in detail to ensure compliance with relevant accounting standards and local legislation. Details of security should be agreed to the bank confirmation letter.
Finance costs As the level of debt has increased, there should be additional finance costs as the loan has an interest rate of 5%. There is a risk that this has been omitted from the statement of profit or loss leading to understated finance costs and overstated profit.	The finance costs should be recalculated and any increase agreed to the loan documentation for confirmation of the 5% interest rate. Interest payments should be agreed to the bank ledger account and bank statements to confirm the amount was paid and is not therefore a year-end payable.

Audit risk	**Auditor's response**
Planned stock exchange listing Darjeeling Co intends to undertake a stock exchange listing in the next 12 months. In order to maximise the success of the potential listing, Darjeeling Co will need to present financial statements which show the best possible position and performance. The directors therefore have an incentive to manipulate the financial statements, by overstating revenue, profits and assets.	Earl & Co should ensure that there is a suitably experienced audit team. Also, adequate time should be allocated for team members to obtain an understanding of the company and the significant risks of overstatement of revenue, profits and assets, including attendance at an audit team briefing. The team needs to maintain professional scepticism and be alert to the increased risk of manipulation. Significant estimates and judgements should be carefully reviewed in light of the misstatement risk.
Receivables valuation The receivables collection period has increased from 38 to 51 days and management has extended the credit terms given to customers on the condition that sales order quantities were increased. The increase in the receivables collection period could be solely due to these increased credit terms. However, it could also be due to an increased risk over the recoverability of receivables. Receivables may be overvalued and expenses understated.	Review and test the controls surrounding how Darjeeling Co identifies receivables balances which may not be recoverable and procedures around credit control to ensure that they are operating effectively. Extended post-year-end cash receipts testing and a review of the aged list of individual customer balances to be performed to assess valuation. Also consider the adequacy of any allowance for credit losses/ receivables.
Price promise This year the company made a 'price promise' to match the price of its competitors for similar products. Customers are able to claim the difference from the company for one month after the date of purchase of goods. The company should account for the price promise in accordance with IFRS 15 *Revenue from Contracts with Customers.* As the company may be required to provide a refund, the anticipated refund amount should not be initially recognised as revenue but instead as a refund liability until the one-month price promise period has ended.	Discuss with management the basis of the refund liability of $0.25m and obtain supporting documentation to confirm the reasonableness of the assumptions and calculations.

Audit risk	Auditor's response
This is a highly subjective area, with many judgements required with regards to the level of likely refund due. As this is a new liability, the directors may not have correctly accounted for this sum resulting in overstated revenue, under/overstated profits and liabilities.	
Refunds for product recall Darjeeling Co has stopped further sales of one of its paint products and a product recall has been initiated for any goods sold since June. This product recall will result in Darjeeling Co paying refunds to customers. The sales will need to be removed from the 20X5 financial statements and a refund liability recognised. Also, inventory will need to be reinstated, albeit at a possibly written down value. Failing to account for this correctly could result in overstated revenue, understated liabilities and misstated inventory.	Review the list of sales of the paint product made between June and the date of the recall, agree that the sales have been removed from revenue and the inventory included. If the refunds have not been paid before the year end, review the draft financial statements to confirm that it is included within current liabilities.
Inventory valuation – damaged paint The company is holding a number of damaged paint products in inventory and overall the inventory holding period has increased from 45 days to 54 days. Due to the issue with the paint consistency, the quality of these products is questionable and management is investigating whether these products can be rectified. There is a risk that this inventory may be overvalued as its net realisable value may be below cost.	Discuss with the finance director whether any write downs will be made to this product, and what, if any, modifications will be required to rectify the quality of the product. Testing should be undertaken to confirm cost and NRV of the affected paint products held in inventory and that on a line by line basis the goods are valued correctly.
Movement in revenue and margins Revenue has increased by 16.8% in the year; and the gross profit margin has increased slightly from 36.4% to 37.3%. This is a significant increase in revenue. Along with the increase in gross profit margin, may be related to the increased credit period and price promise promotion or could be due to an overstatement of revenue.	During the audit a detailed breakdown of sales will be obtained, discussed with management and tested in order to understand the sales increase. Also increased cut-off testing should be undertaken to verify that revenue is recorded in the right period and is not overstated.

Audit risk	Auditor's response
Going concern uncertainties The payables payment period has increased from 40 to 58 days. The current ratio has decreased from 3.08 to 1.65. The quick ratio has also decreased from 1.97 to 0.99. In addition, the bank balance has moved from \$0.56m to an overdraft of \$0.81m. These are all indicators that the company could be experiencing a reduction in its cash flow which could result in going concern difficulties or uncertainties. These uncertainties may not be adequately disclosed in the financial statements.	Detailed going concern testing to be performed during the audit, including the review of cash flow forecasts and the underlying assumptions. These should be discussed with management to ensure that the going concern basis is reasonable.

(d) Faulty inventory

- Obtain a breakdown of the damaged goods held in inventory and returned from customers and cast to confirm its accuracy.
- From the breakdown, agree the damaged goods quantities manufactured since June to production records; and agree to sales records the quantities sold.
- Agree on a sample basis the returns from customers as per the breakdown back to sales returns documentation to confirm the existence of the returns quantities.
- Discuss with management the current status of their plans for this product line and whether they are able to rectify the damage and then sell the goods on. If so, agree the costs of rectification to supporting documentation.
- If the damaged inventory has been rectified and sold post year end, agree to the sales invoice to assess NRV in line with the new cost of the product.
- Agree the cost of damaged goods to supporting documentation to confirm the raw material cost, labour cost and any overheads attributed to the cost.
- Discuss with management if the goods have been written down; if so, follow through the write down to the inventory valuation to confirm.
- Inspect monthly board meeting minutes from June 20X5 onwards to obtain further information regarding the faulty paint and its possible resale value.

(e) Revenue

- Compare the overall level of revenue against prior years and budget for the year and investigate any significant fluctuations.
- Perform a proof-in-total calculation for revenue, creating an expectation of the average price for the main paint products multiplied by the increased sales volumes for this year. This expectation should be compared to actual revenue and any significant fluctuations should be investigated.
- Obtain a schedule of sales for the year broken down into the main product categories and compare this to the prior year breakdown and for any unusual movements, discuss with management.

- Calculate the final gross profit margin for Darjeeling Co and compare this to the prior year and investigate any significant fluctuations.
- Select a sample of sales invoices for customers and agree the sales prices back to the price list or customer master data information to ensure the accuracy of invoices.
- For a sample of invoices, recalculate invoice totals including discounts and sales tax.
- Select a sample of credit notes raised, trace through to the original invoice and ensure the invoice has been correctly removed from sales.
- Select a sample of customer orders and agree these to the despatch notes and sales invoices through to inclusion in the detailed sales listing and revenue general ledger accounts to ensure completeness of revenue.
- Select a sample of despatch notes both pre and post year end and follow these through to sales invoices in the correct accounting period to ensure that cut-off has been correctly applied.
- For sales made under the price promise, compare the level of claims made to date with the refund liability recognised and assess whether it is reasonable.
- For a sample of sales invoices issued between June and the product recall, trace to subsequent credit notes to confirm that the sale has been removed from revenue.

Marking guide		
		Marks
(a)	**Analytical procedures**	
	• Must be used at planning as risk assessment tool	1
	• Can be used to gather evidence during fieldwork	1
	• Must be used at completion to confirm overall conclusion	1
		3
(b)	**Ratios**	
	• Gross profit margin	1
	• Inventory holding period	1
	• Receivables collection period	1
	• Payables payment period	1
	• Current ratio	1
	• Quick ratio	1
	Max 3 ratios, ½ for each calculation	**3**
(c)	**Audit risks and responses (only 8 risks required)**	
	• Treatment of research and development costs	2
	• Incorrect capitalisation of PPE costs	2
	• New significant loan finance	2
	• Finance costs	2
	• Risk of manipulation due to potential listing	2
	• Recoverability of receivables	2
	• Accounting for 'price promise'	2
	• Product recall	2
	• Inventory valuation	2
	• Significant increase in revenue and gross profit margin	2
	• Cash flow difficulties	2
	Max 8 issues, 2 marks each	**16**

(d)	**Substantive procedures – faulty inventory**	
	• Obtain schedule of faulty inventory, cast and agree to inventory listing	1
	• Agree quantities affected to manufacturing and sales records	1
	• Agree a sample of returns to relevant documentation	1
	• Discuss issue with management and likelihood of subsequent sale	1
	• Agree any post-year-end sales to invoice and assess NRV	1
	• Agree costs of faulty goods to supporting documentation	1
	• Discuss any write down with management	1
	• Inspect board minutes for evidence of resale or additional costs	1
	Restricted to	**3**
(e)	**Substantive procedures – revenue**	
	• Compare to prior year and investigate differences	1
	• Perform a proof-in-total and investigate differences	1
	• Obtain a schedule of revenue by product line and compare to prior year and investigate differences	1
	• Calculate final gross profit margin and investigate differences	1
	• Agree a sample of orders to GDN, invoice and GL	1
	• Perform cut-off testing using GDNs from before and after year end	1
	• For sales made under the price promise, compare level of claims to refund liability	1
	• For a sample of June invoices in relation to the faulty goods, trace to subsequent credit notes	1
	Restricted to	**5**
Total		**30**

Examiner's comments

This question was based on Darjeeling Co, which develops and manufactures specialist paint products. This question tested candidates' knowledge of analytical procedures, ratios, audit risks and responses and substantive procedures for inventory and revenue. Overall candidates' performance was satisfactory.

Part (a) required candidates to explain why analytical procedures are used during the three stages of an audit. One mark was awarded for each well explained point. It was pleasing to see that many candidates were able to clearly explain WHY analytical review procedures were used at three distinct stages in the audit process. However, a number of candidates spent time detailing what analytical procedures were and gave examples, rather than why they were used. This is a knowledge area, which has been tested in previous diets. Candidates are again reminded to read the question requirement carefully and to ensure that they are only answering the question set.

Part (b) required candidates to calculate ratios for the current and prior year. Candidates performed well, with many scoring full marks. However, a significant minority of candidates provided more than the three required ratios. Additionally, some candidates simply stated the ratio formula. However, marks were only awarded (½ mark) for each year's calculation. Therefore, no credit was available for workings or stating of ratio formulae. Some candidates simply provided the formula or working but not the final calculation.

Part (c) required candidates to identify and describe eight audit risks and to explain the auditor's response to each in planning the audit of Darjeeling Co. Performance on this question was satisfactory. Marks were awarded for identification of an audit risk (½ mark each), explanation of the audit risk (½ mark each) and an appropriate auditor's response to each risk (1 mark each). The scenario contained more than eight risks so it was pleasing that most candidates planned their time carefully and generally only attempted to list the required number of points. As in previous diets, although candidates identified the risks, many candidates did not adequately explain the risk. To explain the risk, candidates need to state the area of the financial statements impacted with an assertion (for example cut-off/valuation etc.), or a reference to over/under/misstated, or a reference to inherent/control/detection risk. For example, candidates often correctly identified that the company had made a price promise to customers and therefore recognised a refund liability, this was awarded ½ mark for identification, however, no further credit was awarded for explanations relating to the business implications of false claims. To be awarded the ½ explanation mark candidates need to clearly state the audit implication, for example, that 'profit and the liability may be misstated'. Candidates should ensure that when identifying audit risks they use the scenario fully and rather than listing generic risks they use the detail provided. For example, service and maintenance costs had been included within the cost of a new manufacturing line capitalised into property, plant and equipment. The audit risk therefore related to the incorrect capitalisation of the service and maintenance costs and answers should have focused on this specific issue. However, a significant number of candidates provided generic risks and responses relating to the treatment of assets vs expenses. Candidate performance in relation to auditor's responses continues to be mixed. While an auditor's response does not have to be a detailed audit procedure, rather an approach the audit team will take to address the identified risk, the responses given were often too weak such as 'discuss with management'. This is not a sufficient response to deal with any identified audit risk and candidates need to be able to use their knowledge of audit procedures to provide a valid response which would adequately address the risk identified.

Future candidates must take note that audit risk is and will continue to be an important element of the syllabus and must be understood. Candidates must also ensure that they include adequate question practice as part of their revision of this key topic.

Part (d) required candidates to describe substantive procedures the auditor should perform in relation to faulty products held within year-end inventory. One mark was awarded for each well described procedure. Performance on this requirement was disappointing. Many candidates failed to provide three procedures, and those listed often focused on the wrong areas. Unfortunately, many answers focused on standard inventory count procedures rather than focusing on the key issue of valuation. It can only be assumed that candidates saw the words 'inventory' and 'at the year end' in the requirement and launched into year-end inventory count procedures without further thought. Again, candidates must take the time to read the question requirements carefully and spend time thinking about what is needed prior to writing their answers. Where valuation was considered many answers were vague such as 'recalculate net realisable value' without any detail of how this should be performed. Some procedures such as 'discuss with management' were provided but without any detail as to what exactly should be discussed. As addressed in previous examiner's reports, candidates must strive to understand substantive procedures. Learning a generic list of tests will not translate to exam success, as they must be applied to the question requirement.

Part (e) required candidates to describe substantive procedures the auditor should perform in relation to revenue. One mark was awarded for each well described procedure. Performance on this requirement was satisfactory. The most common procedures provided by candidates were analytical review procedures, cut-off tests and tests of detail tracing to goods received notes, invoices and the ledger. Many provided a sufficient number of procedures to pass this requirement. However, some substantive procedures were often vague, for example, 'review transactions to ensure cut-off is appropriate'. Other examples of procedures which were not adequately described such as 'compare revenue to the prior year' (awarded ½ mark), for the full 1 mark, candidates needed to also state 'and investigate any significant differences'. Also cut-off procedures were sometimes recommended to be undertaken using sales invoices rather than goods received notes, which would only have scored ½ mark.

212 BLACKBERRY *Walk in the footsteps of a top tutor*

Key answer tips

Part (a) asks for the auditor's responsibility in relation to prevention and detection of fraud and error. A good answer needs to refer to the requirements of the relevant auditing standard, ISA 240. If you can't remember the main points of the ISA, take a common sense approach and think about a logical answer to score at least some marks.

Part (b) asks for audit risks and responses. This requirement is examined every sitting. You must make sure the risk relates to either a risk of material misstatement or a detection risk.

Read through the scenario to identify information which refers to something that will appear in the financial statements, e.g. revenue, property, inventory and briefly explain the accounting treatment that should be applied. Think about common mistakes that the client could make either deliberately to manipulate the financial statements or unintentionally. State whether the item in the financial statements is at risk of under or overstatement. The response must be a response of the auditor, not the client and must directly relate to the risk you have given.

Part (c) asks for substantive procedures over completeness of trade payables. The scenario contains information relating to a risk with trade payables, therefore, try to suggest at least one procedure to address this risk to demonstrate application skills. Pay attention to the requirement to only consider the assertion of completeness. No marks will be awarded for procedures which address the other assertions.

Part (d) asks for a description of the quality management deficiencies in the additional paragraph of scenario provided. This is a relatively new syllabus area but should be quite straightforward if you apply your auditing knowledge.

(a) Fraud responsibility

Loganberry & Co must conduct an audit in accordance with ISA 240 *The Auditor's Responsibilities Relating to Fraud in an Audit of Financial Statements* and is responsible for obtaining reasonable assurance that the financial statements taken as a whole are free from material misstatement, whether caused by fraud or error.

In order to fulfil this responsibility, Loganberry & Co is required to identify and assess the risks of material misstatement of the financial statements due to fraud.

They need to obtain sufficient appropriate audit evidence regarding the assessed risks of material misstatement due to fraud through designing and implementing appropriate responses. In addition, Loganberry & Co must respond appropriately to fraud or suspected fraud identified during the audit.

When obtaining reasonable assurance, Loganberry & Co is responsible for maintaining professional scepticism throughout the audit, considering the potential for management override of controls and recognising the fact that audit procedures which are effective in detecting error may not be effective in detecting fraud.

To ensure that the whole engagement team is aware of the risks and responsibilities for fraud and error, ISA 240 requires that a discussion is held within the team. For members not present at the meeting, Blackberry Co's audit engagement partner should determine which matters should be communicated to them.

Loganberry & Co must report any actual or suspected fraud to appropriate parties.

(b) Audit risks and auditor's responses

Audit risk	Auditor's response
Inventory valuation Blackberry Co values its inventory at the lower of cost and net realisable value. Cost includes both production and general overheads. IAS 2 *Inventories* requires that costs included in valuing goods and services should only be those incurred in bringing inventory to its present location and condition. Although production overheads meet these criteria, general overheads do not. If these are included in inventory cost, then this will result in over-valued inventory.	Discuss with management the nature of the overheads included in inventory valuation. If general overheads are included, request management remove them from the valuation to be included in the draft financial statements. Review supporting documentation to verify those overheads deemed to be of a production nature are valid.
Inventory count after year end The company is planning to undertake the full year-end inventory counts after the year end and then adjust for movements from the year end. If the adjustments are not completed accurately, then the year-end inventory could be under or overstated.	The auditor should attend the inventory count held after the year end and note details of goods received and despatched post year end, in order to agree to the reconciliation. During the final audit, the year-end inventory adjustments schedule should be reviewed in detail and agreed to supporting documentation obtained during the inventory count for all adjusting items.
Patent A patent has been purchased for $1.1m and this grants Blackberry Co the exclusive right for three years to customise its portable music players to gain a competitive advantage in the industry. Management has expensed the full	The audit team will need to agree the purchase price to supporting documentation and confirm the useful life is three years as per the contract. Discuss with management the reason for fully expensing the $1.1m paid, and request they correct the treatment.

Audit risk	**Auditor's response**
amount paid to the current year statement of profit or loss. In accordance with IAS 38 *Intangible Assets*, this should have been included as an intangible asset and amortised over its three-year life. As the sum has been fully expensed and not treated in accordance with IAS 38, intangible assets and profits are understated.	The correcting journal should be reviewed and the amortisation charge recalculated in order to ensure the accuracy of the charge and that the intangible is correctly valued.
Share issue During the year Blackberry Co has raised new finance through issuing $1.2m of shares at a premium. This needs to be accounted for correctly, with adequate disclosure made and the equity finance needs to be allocated correctly between share capital and share premium. If this is not done, then the accounts may be misstated due to a lack of disclosure or share capital and share premium may be misstated.	The audit team should confirm that proceeds of $1.2m were received and that the split of share capital and share premium is correct and appropriately recorded. In addition, the disclosures for this finance should be reviewed in detail to ensure compliance with relevant accounting standards and local legislation.
Fraud In May 20X5, it was discovered that a significant teeming and lading fraud had been carried out by four members of the receivables ledger department. There is a risk that the full impact of the fraud has not been quantified and any additional fraudulent transactions would need to be written off in the statement of profit or loss. If these have not been uncovered, the financial statements could be misstated. In addition, individual receivable balances may be under/overstated as customer receipts have been misallocated to other receivable balances.	Discuss with the finance director what procedures have been adopted to fully identify and quantify the impact of the teeming and lading fraud. In addition, discuss with the finance director, what controls have been put in place to identify any similar frauds. Review the receivables listing to identify any unusual postings to individual receivable balances as this could be further evidence of fraudulent transactions. In addition, the team should maintain their professional scepticism and be alert to the risk of further fraud and errors.

Audit risk	**Auditor's response**
Outsourced receivables ledger processing During the year Blackberry Co outsourced its receivables ledger processing to an external service organisation. A detection risk arises as to whether sufficient and appropriate evidence is available at Blackberry Co to confirm the completeness and accuracy of controls over the sales and receivables cycle and balances at the year end.	Discuss with management the extent of records maintained at Blackberry Co for the period since the receivables ledger was outsourced and any monitoring of controls undertaken by management over sales and receivables. Consideration should be given to contacting the service organisation's auditor to confirm the level of controls in place.
Data transfer The receivables ledger processing has been transferred to the service organisation during the year. If any errors occurred during the transfer process, these could result in sales and receivables being under/overstated.	Discuss with management the transfer process undertaken and any controls put in place to ensure the completeness and accuracy of the data. Where possible, undertake tests of controls to confirm the effectiveness of the transfer controls. In addition, perform substantive testing on the transfer of information from the old to the new system.
Unfair dismissal claim The financial accountant of Blackberry Co was dismissed and is threatening to sue the company for unfair dismissal. If it is probable that Blackberry Co will make a payment to the financial accountant, a provision for unfair dismissal is required. If the payment is possible rather than probable, a contingent liability disclosure would be necessary. If Blackberry Co has not done this, there is a risk over the completeness of any provisions or contingent liabilities.	The audit team should request confirmation from the company's lawyers of the existence and likelihood of success of any claim from the former financial accountant.

Audit risk	**Auditor's response**
Supplier statement reconciliations No supplier statement or trade payables account reconciliations will be performed until the financial accountant is replaced which means no reconciliation will be performed at the year end. This a direct control which is being overridden and as such there is an increased risk of errors within trade payables and the year-end payables balance may be under or overstated.	The audit team should increase their testing on trade payables at the year end, including performing supplier statement reconciliations, with a particular focus on completeness of trade payables. Request management prepare a year-end trade payables account reconciliation. The audit team should undertake a detailed review of this reconciliation with a focus on any unusual reconciling items.
Contingent asset A current asset of $360,000 has been included within the financial statements. It represents an anticipated pay out from liquidators handling the bankruptcy of a customer who owed Blackberry Co $0.9m which has been written off during the year. The company has not received a formal notification from the liquidators confirming the payment and this would therefore represent a possible contingent asset. To comply with IAS 37 *Provisions, Contingent Liabilities and Contingent Assets*, this should not be recognised until the receipt is virtually certain. With no firm response to date, the inclusion of this sum overstates profit and current assets.	Discuss with management whether any notification of payment has been received from the liquidators and review the related correspondence. If virtually certain, the treatment adopted is correct. If payment has been received, agree to post-year-end bank ledger account. If receipt is not virtually certain, management should be requested to remove it from profit and receivables. If the receipt is probable, the auditor should request management include a contingent asset disclosure note.

(c) Substantive procedures over completeness of trade payables

- Obtain the trade payables leger, recalculate to confirm arithmetical accuracy and agree to the financial statements.
- Perform supplier statement reconciliations for suppliers where statements are available. Discuss any discrepancies with management.
- Perform a supplier circularisation for significant suppliers where no supplier statement is available and agree the balance per the circularisation to the individual supplier balance.
- Agree a sample of pre-year-end GRNs to purchase invoices and into the list of individual supplier balances.
- Calculate the trade payables payment period, compare with credit terms/prior year and discuss significant differences with management.

(d) Quality management deficiencies

Quality management deficiency	**Recommendation**
Audit senior has been instructed to take on the roles of audit senior and audit manager. Taking on both roles without additional time will mean there is insufficient time to fulfil the responsibilities of each role to the level of quality required. In addition, the audit senior is unlikely to be sufficiently experienced to take on the role of audit manager without any additional supervision. This increases the risk that the work is not performed in accordance with ISAs and ISQM.	An experienced audit manager should be assigned to the audit. If this is not possible in the current timeframe, the audit engagement partner should speak with management of Blackberry Co to arrange an extension to the deadline to accommodate another audit manager to be assigned when resources allow.
The work of the audit senior/manager is not expected to be reviewed until the day before the audit clearance meeting. If additional work is required as a result of the review, there will not be sufficient time for this to be performed. This will mean sufficient and appropriate evidence is not obtained to be able to draw reasonable conclusions to support the auditor's report.	The work must be reviewed on a timely basis to enable any review points to be actioned properly.
The audit engagement partner has instructed the audit senior to reduce sample sizes and procedures. The sample sizes and procedures included in the audit plan have been chosen in response to the risk assessment and planning performed. This will mean sufficient and appropriate evidence is not obtained to be able to draw reasonable conclusions to support the auditor's report.	Changes to the audit plan should only be made where it is appropriate to do so, e.g. if the risk level is reassessed, not because of convenience or lack of time. The planned procedures must be performed and either additional staff assigned to the audit, or an extension to the deadline agreed with the client.

Marking guide

		Marks
(a)	**Fraud responsibilities**	
	• ISA 240 responsibilities	2
	• Respond appropriately	2
		4
(b)	**Audit risks and responses (only 8 risks required)**	
	• Inventory valuation	2
	• Inventory count after year-end date	2
	• Accounting treatment of patent	2
	• Share issue	2
	• Receivables ledger fraud	2
	• Use of service organisation	2
	• Transfer of data to service organisation	2
	• Claim for unfair dismissal	2
	• Supplier statement and trade payables account reconciliations not performed	2
	• Contingent asset	2
	Max 8 issues, 2 marks each	**16**
(c)	**Substantive procedures for payroll expense**	
	• Obtain the trade payables leger, cast, and agree to the financial statements	1
	• Perform supplier statement reconciliations	1
	• Perform a supplier circularisation for significant suppliers where no supplier statement is available	1
	• Agree a sample of pre-year-end GRNs to purchase invoices and the list of individual supplier balances	1
	• Calculate the trade payables payment period, compare with credit terms/prior year and discuss significant differences with management	1
	Maximum	**4**
(d)	**Quality management deficiencies**	
	• Audit senior taking on audit manager role – too much work/lack of experience	2
	• Audit senior's work to be reviewed the day before the audit clearance meeting – too late if additional work required	2
	• Reduction in sample sizes and procedures – sufficient and appropriate evidence will not be obtained	2
		6
Total		**30**

Examiner's comments

This question was based on Blackberry Co, a manufacturer of portable music players. This question tested the areas of fraud and error, and audit risks and responses. Candidates' performance was mixed.

Part (a) required candidates to describe the auditor's responsibilities in relation to the prevention and detection of fraud and error. One mark was awarded for each well described point. Some candidates performed very well on this requirement and clearly had an excellent understanding of the requirements of ISA 240 *The Auditor's Responsibilities Relating to Fraud in an Audit of Financial Statements*, however, a number of candidates described management's responsibilities rather than auditor's responsibilities and therefore did not answer the requirement of the question. In addition, although many candidates understood that the auditors are not responsible for preventing fraud, some candidates were not clear that the auditor is also not responsible for detecting all errors due to fraud/error. A number of candidates described substantive procedures to detect fraud/error, and again these were not awarded credit as the question asked for 'the responsibilities' of the auditors. This is a knowledge area, which has been tested in previous diets. Candidates are again reminded to read the question requirement carefully and to ensure that they are only answering the question set.

Part (b) required candidates to describe eight audit risks and to explain the auditor's response to each in planning the audit of Blackberry Co. Performance on this question was mixed. Marks were awarded for identification of each audit risk (½ mark each), explanation of each risk (½ mark each) and an appropriate auditor's response to each risk (1 mark each). The scenario contained more than eight risks so it was pleasing that most candidates planned their time carefully and generally only attempted to list the required number of points. As in previous diets, although candidates identified the risks, many of them did not adequately explain the risk.

To explain the audit risk, candidates need to state the area of the financial statements impacted with an assertion (for example, cut-off/valuation, etc.), or a reference to over/under/misstated, or a reference to inherent/control/detection risk.

For example, candidates often correctly identified the financial accountant suing for unfair dismissal, this was awarded ½ mark for identification, however no further credit was awarded for the explanation that 'costs may not be included'. To be awarded the ½ explanation mark candidates need to clearly state the implication, for example, that 'provisions may be understated', or 'provisions may not be complete'. Candidate performance in relation to auditor's responses continues to be mixed. While an auditor's response does not have to be a detailed audit procedure, rather an approach the audit team will take to address the identified risk, the responses given were often too weak such as 'discuss with management'. This is not a sufficient response to deal with any identified audit risk and candidates need to be able to use their knowledge of audit procedures to provide a valid response which would adequately address the risk identified. Future candidates must take note audit risk is and will continue to be an important element of the syllabus and must be understood. Candidates must also ensure that they include adequate question practice as part of their revision of this key topic.

213 PRANCER CONSTRUCTION *Walk in the footsteps of a top tutor*

Key answer tips

Part (a) asks for the preconditions of an audit. This is knowledge you either know or don't know. If you don't know it move on and try to compensate by scoring well on other requirements.

Part (b) asks for areas to be included in the audit strategy for Prancer Construction. This requires you to identify the main areas of an audit strategy and apply that knowledge to the specific details of the client in the scenario. Easy marks can be earned here for referring to obtaining an understanding of the internal controls, calculating preliminary materiality and selecting the audit team. These are all things that are done at the planning stage and would be included in the audit strategy.

Part (c) asks for audit risks and responses. This requirement is examined every sitting. You must make sure the risk relates to either a risk of material misstatement or a detection risk. The response must be a response of the auditor, not the client.

(a) Preconditions for the audit

ISA 210 *Agreeing the Terms of Audit Engagements* states that auditors should only accept a new audit engagement when it has been confirmed that the preconditions for an audit are present.

To assess whether the preconditions for an audit are present, Cupid & Co should have determined whether the financial reporting framework to be applied in the preparation of Prancer Construction Co's financial statements is acceptable.

In considering this, the auditor should have assessed the nature of the entity, the nature and purpose of the financial statements and whether law or regulation prescribes the applicable reporting framework.

In addition, the firm should have obtained the agreement of Prancer Construction Co's management that it acknowledges and understands its responsibility for the following:

– Preparation of the financial statements in accordance with the applicable financial reporting framework, including where relevant, their fair presentation.

– For such internal control as management determines is necessary to enable the preparation of financial statements which are free from material misstatement, whether due to fraud or error.

– To provide Cupid & Co with access to all relevant information for the preparation of the financial statements, any additional information which the auditor may request from management and unrestricted access to personnel within Prancer Construction Co from whom the auditor determines it necessary to obtain audit evidence.

(b) Areas to be included in the audit strategy document

The audit strategy sets out the scope, timing and direction of the audit and helps the development of the audit plan. ISA 300 *Planning an Audit of Financial Statements* and the conforming amendments of ISA 220 (Revised) set out areas which should be considered and documented as part of the audit strategy document and are as follows:

Main characteristics of the engagement

The audit strategy should consider the main characteristics of the engagement, which define its scope. For Prancer Construction Co, the following are examples of things which should be included:

- Whether the financial information to be audited has been prepared in accordance with the relevant financial reporting framework.
- Whether automated tools and audit techniques will be used and the effect of IT on audit procedures.
- The availability of key personnel at Prancer Construction Co.

Reporting objectives, timing and nature of communication

It should ascertain the reporting objectives of the engagement to plan the timing of the audit and the nature of the communications required, such as:

- The audit timetable for reporting including the timing of interim and final stages.
- Organisation of meetings with Prancer Construction Co's management to discuss any audit issues arising.
- Any discussions with management regarding the reports to be issued.
- The timings of the audit team meetings and review of work performed.

Significant factors affecting the audit

The strategy should consider the factors which, in the auditor's professional judgement, are significant in directing Prancer Construction Co's audit team's efforts, such as:

- The determination of materiality for the audit.
- The need to maintain a questioning mind and to exercise professional scepticism in gathering and evaluating audit evidence.

Preliminary engagement activities and knowledge from previous engagements

It should consider the results of preliminary audit planning activities and, where applicable, whether knowledge gained on other engagements for Prancer Construction Co is relevant, such as:

- Results of any tests over the effectiveness of internal controls.
- Evidence of management's commitment to the design, implementation and maintenance of sound internal controls.
- Volume of transactions, which may determine whether it is more efficient for the audit team to rely on internal controls.
- Significant business developments affecting Prancer Construction Co, such as the improvement in building practices and construction quality.

Nature, timing and extent of resources

The audit strategy should ascertain the nature, timing and extent of resources necessary to perform the audit, such as:

– The human, technological and intellectual resources assigned.

– Assignment of audit work to the team members including the assignment of appropriately experienced team members to areas where there may be higher risks of material misstatement.

– Setting the audit budget including appropriate time set aside for areas where there may be higher risks of material misstatement.

(c) Audit risks and auditor's responses

Audit risk	**Auditor's response**
New audit client Prancer Construction Co is a new client for Cupid & Co. As the team is not familiar with the accounting policies, transactions and balances of the company, there will be an increased detection risk on the audit.	Cupid & Co should ensure it has a suitably experienced team. In addition, adequate time should be allocated for team members to obtain an understanding of the company and the risks of material misstatement including a detailed team briefing to cover the key areas of risk.
Work-in-progress (WIP) Prancer Construction Co is likely to have a material level of WIP at the year end, being construction WIP as well as ongoing maintenance services, as Prancer Construction Co has annual contracts for many of the buildings constructed. The level of WIP will need to be assessed at the year end. Assessing the percentage completion for partially constructed buildings is likely to be quite subjective, and the team should consider if they have the required expertise to undertake this. If the percentage completion is not correctly calculated, the inventory valuation may be under or overstated.	The auditor should discuss with management the process they will undertake to assess the percentage completion for WIP at the year end. This process should be reviewed by the auditor while attending the year-end inventory counts. In addition, consideration should be given as to whether an independent expert is required to value the WIP or if a management expert has been used. If the work of an expert is to be used, then the audit team will need to assess the competence, capabilities and objectivity of the expert.

Audit risk	**Auditor's response**
Increased inventory The latest management accounts contain \$2.1 million of completed properties; this balance was \$1.4 million in September 20X4. IAS 2 *Inventories* requires that inventory should be stated at the lower of cost and NRV. The increase in inventory may be due to an increased level of pre-year-end orders. Alternatively, it may be that Prancer Construction Co is struggling to sell completed properties. This may indicate that they are overvalued.	Detailed cost and net realisable value (NRV) testing to be performed at the year end and the aged inventory report to be reviewed to assess whether inventory requires to be written down.
Attendance at inventory counts At the year end there will be inventory counts undertaken at all 11 of the building sites in progress. It is unlikely that the auditor will be able to attend all of these inventory counts, increasing detection risk, and therefore they need to ensure that they obtain sufficient evidence over the inventory counting controls, and completeness and existence of inventory for any sites not visited.	The auditor should assess for which of the building sites they will attend the counts. This will be those with the most material inventory or which according to management have the most significant risk of misstatement. For those not visited, the auditor will need to review the level of exceptions noted during the count and discuss with management any issues, which arose during the count.
Warranty provision Prancer Construction Co offers its customers a building warranty of five years, which covers any construction defects. A warranty provision will be required under IAS 37 *Provisions, Contingent Liabilities and Contingent Assets*. Calculating warranty provisions requires judgement as it is an uncertain amount. The finance director anticipates this provision will be lower than last year as the company has improved its building practices and the quality of its finished properties. However, there is a risk that this provision could be understated, especially in light of the overdraft covenant relating to a minimum level of net assets and is being used as a mechanism to manipulate profit and asset levels.	Discuss with management the basis of the provision calculation, and compare this to the level of post-year-end claims, if any, made by customers. In particular, discuss the rationale behind reducing the level of provision this year. Compare the prior year provision with the actual level of claims in the year, to assess the reasonableness of the judgements made by management.

Audit risk	**Auditor's response**
Non-refundable deposit Customers who wish to purchase a property are required to place an order and a 5% non-refundable deposit prior to the completion of the building. These deposits should not be recognised as revenue in the statement of profit or loss until the performance obligations as per the contracts have been satisfied. This is likely to be when the building is finished and the sale process is complete. Instead, the deposits should be recognised as a contract liability within current liabilities. Management may have incorrectly recognised the deposits as revenue, resulting in overstated revenue and understated liabilities.	Discuss with management the treatment of deposits received in advance, to ensure it is appropriate. During the final audit, undertake increased testing over the cut-off of revenue and completeness of contract liabilities.
Overvaluation of receivables An allowance for credit losses/receivables has historically been maintained, but it is anticipated that this will be reduced. Some balances may not be recoverable if adequate allowance for credit losses/ receivables is not made. There is a risk that receivables will be overvalued. In addition, reducing the allowance for credit losses/receivables will increase asset values and would improve the covenant compliance, which increases the manipulation risk further.	Review and test the controls surrounding how the finance director identifies old or potentially irrecoverable receivables balances and credit control to ensure that they are operating effectively. Discuss with the director the rationale for reducing the allowance for credit losses/ receivables. Extended post-year-end cash receipts testing and a review of the aged list of individual customer balances to be performed to assess valuation and the need for an increased allowance for credit losses/ receivables.
Overdraft covenants Prancer Construction Co has a material overdraft which has minimum profit and net assets covenants attached to it. If these covenants were to be breached, the overdraft balance would become instantly repayable. If the company does not have sufficient cash to meet this repayment, then there could be going concern implications.	Review the covenant calculations prepared by the company at the year end and identify whether any defaults have occurred; if so, determine the effect on the company. The team should maintain their professional scepticism and be alert to the risk that profit and/or net assets have been overstated to

Audit risk	Auditor's response
In addition, there is a risk of manipulation of profit and net assets to ensure that covenants are met.	ensure compliance with the covenants.
Trade payables Preliminary analytical review of the management accounts shows a payables payment period of 56 for June 20X5, compared to 87 days for September 20X4. It is anticipated that the year-end payables payment period will be even lower. The forecast profit is higher than last year, indicating an increase in trade, also the company's cash position has continued to deteriorate and therefore, it is unusual for payables payment period to have decreased. There is an increased risk of errors within trade payables and the year-end payables may be understated.	The audit team should increase their testing on trade payables at the year end, with a particular focus on completeness of payables. A payables circularisation or review of supplier statement reconciliations should be undertaken.

Marking guide

		Marks
(a)	**Preconditions for the audit**	
	• Determination of acceptable framework	1
	• Agreement of management responsibilities	1
	• Preparation of financial statements	1
	• Internal control	1
	• Access to information	1
	Restricted to	**3**
(b)	**Audit strategy document**	
	• Main characteristics of the audit	1
	• Reporting objectives	1
	• Significant factors affecting the audit	1
	• Preliminary engagement activities	1
	• Nature, timing and extent of resources	1
	Restricted to	**3**
(c)	**Audit risks and responses (only 7 risks required)**	
	• New client, increased detection risk	2
	• Work-in-progress	2
	• Increased inventory	2
	• Warranty provision	2
	• Attendance at inventory counts	2
	• Revenue overstated	2
	• Receivables allowance and valuation	2
	• Overdraft covenants	2
	• Trade payables	2
	Max 7 issues, 2 marks each	**14**
Total		**20**

Examiner's comments

This question was based on a property construction company, Prancer Construction Co. This question tested the areas of preconditions, the audit strategy document and audit risks and responses.

Part (a) required the steps the firm should take to confirm whether the preconditions for the audit were in place. Where it was answered, candidates performed unsatisfactorily on this question, which is disappointing as candidates did not perform well the last time this area was tested. It was clear from candidate answers that those who had studied preconditions were able to score all three marks and those who had not studied it failed to score any marks. Those candidates who did not score well tended to focus on ethical threats or pre-acceptance procedures such as gaining professional clearance from the previous auditors, checking the audit firm had adequate resources and competence to undertake the audit. This is a knowledge area and has been tested in previous diets. Candidates must practise past exam questions and ensure they study the breadth of the syllabus.

Part (b) required an identification of three main areas, other than audit risks, to be included within Prancer Construction Co's audit strategy document and an example for each area. This question, where attempted, was poorly answered by most candidates. Most candidates did not answer both parts of the requirement, failing to identify the areas of an audit strategy. This is a knowledge area and demonstrated a gap in candidates' technical knowledge. Where candidates did score marks this was for providing examples, the most common answers given were around materiality, timetable and audit team. Those candidates who did not score well either did not attempt the question or focused on audit risks, despite the question requirement clearly stating "other than audit risks" and then explained inherent, control and detection risks.

Part (c) required an identification and description of seven audit risks from the scenario and the auditor's response for each. Performance on this question was mixed. Marks were awarded for identification of audit risk (½ mark each), explanation of audit risk by referring to the assertion and account balance impacted (½ mark each) and an appropriate auditor's response to each risk. (1 mark each). The scenario contained more than seven risks so it was pleasing that most candidates planned their time carefully and generally only attempted to list the required number of points. As in previous diets, a significant number of candidates tended to only identify facts from the scenario such as "inventory has increased significantly on the prior year"; this would only have scored a maximum of ½ mark. This point did not explain the impact on the financial statements or why this was an audit risk and therefore cannot be awarded the ½ mark for explanation.

To adequately explain audit risk, candidates need to state the area of the accounts impacted with either an assertion (e.g. cut off, valuation etc.), a reference to under/over/misstated, or a reference to inherent, control or detection risk. In addition, many candidates incorrectly explained the audit risk. For example, they correctly identified that the auditor was not able to attend all the year-end inventory counts, this would have gained ½ mark but incorrectly stated that this would then lead to inventory being misstated. The issue is that if the auditor does not attend all counts this results in an increased detection risk. Also, weaker candidates argued that the decrease in trade payable days led to a going concern risk, this was not the case, as with trade payables decreasing there was a completeness of payables risk. Many candidates incorrectly assumed the fact the company had a material overdraft was an audit risk and so focused ongoing concern procedures, rather than recognising that the risk actually related to the covenants attached to the overdraft and the possible manipulation of profit or assets in order to meet these.

Candidate performance in relation to auditor's responses continues to be mixed. While an auditor's response does not have to be a detailed audit procedure, rather an approach the audit team will take to address the identified risk, the responses given were often too weak such as 'discuss with management'. This is not a sufficient response to deal with any identified audit risk and candidates need to be able to use their knowledge of audit procedures to provide a valid response which would adequately address the risk identified. A minority of candidates continue to give business advice, such as recommending management charge for the free five-year warranty provided or implementing improved credit control procedures to address the receivables valuation risk. In addition, some responses were impractical, for example suggesting that the audit firm recruit more staff in order to attend all inventory counts. Future candidates must take note audit risk is and will continue to be an important element of the syllabus and must be understood, and candidates must ensure that they include adequate question practice as part of their revision of this key topic.

214 HURLING *Walk in the footsteps of a top tutor*

Key answer tips

Part (a) is a frequently examined requirement asking for definitions of audit risk and the components of audit risk. Take time to learn definitions of common auditing terms such as these.

Part (b) asks for audit risks and responses. This requirement is examined every sitting. You must make sure the risk relates to either a risk of material misstatement or a detection risk. The response must be a response of the auditor, not the client.

Part (c) asks for ethical threats and safeguards from the scenario. To earn a full mark for each threat you must explain how the auditor's objectivity could be impaired i.e. how their behaviour could be affected by the situation which would result in them being biased towards the client.

(a) Audit risk and the components of audit risk

Audit risk is the risk that the auditor expresses an inappropriate audit opinion when the financial statements are materially misstated. Audit risk is a function of two main components, being the risk of material misstatement and detection risk. Risk of material misstatement is made up of a further two components, inherent risk and control risk.

Inherent risk is the susceptibility of an assertion about a class of transaction, account balance or disclosure to a misstatement which could be material, either individually or when aggregated with other misstatements, before consideration of any related controls.

Control risk is the risk that a misstatement which could occur in an assertion about a class of transaction, account balance or disclosure and which could be material, either individually or when aggregated with other misstatements, will not be prevented, or detected and corrected, on a timely basis by the entity's controls.

Detection risk is the risk that the procedures performed by the auditor to reduce audit risk to an acceptably low level will not detect a misstatement which exists and which could be material, either individually or when aggregated with other misstatements. Detection risk is affected by sampling and non-sampling risk.

(b) Audit risks and auditor's responses

Audit risk	**Auditor's response**
Upgrade of website	
Hurling Co upgraded its website during the year at a cost of $1.1m. The costs incurred should be correctly allocated between expenses recognised in the statement of profit or loss and asset expenditure which should be capitalised. Intangible assets and expenses will be misstated if expenditure has been treated incorrectly.	Review a breakdown of the costs and agree to invoices to assess the nature of the expenditure. If asset expenditure, agree to inclusion within the asset register. If expenses, agree to the statement of profit or loss.
In addition, as the website has been upgraded, there is a possibility that the new processes and systems may not record data reliably and accurately. This may lead to a risk over completeness and accuracy of data in the underlying accounting records.	The audit team should document the revised system and undertake tests over the completeness and accuracy of data recorded from the website to the accounting records.
Warehouse acquisition Hurling Co has entered into a transaction to purchase a new warehouse for $3.2m and it is anticipated that the legal process will be completed by the year end. Only assets which physically exist at the year end should be included in property, plant and equipment. If the transaction has not been completed by the year end, there is a risk that assets are overstated if the company incorrectly includes the warehouse at the year end.	Discuss with management as to whether the warehouse purchase was completed by the year end. If so, inspect legal documents of ownership, such as title deeds ensuring these are dated prior to 1 October 20X5 and are in the company name.

Audit risk	**Auditor's response**
Irredeemable preference shares Significant finance has been obtained in the year, as the company has issued $5m of irredeemable preference shares. This finance needs to be accounted for correctly, with adequate disclosure made. As the preference shares are irredeemable, they should be classified as equity rather than non-current liabilities. Failing to correctly classify the shares could result in understated equity and overstated non-current liabilities.	Review share issue documentation to confirm that the preference shares are irredeemable. Confirm that they have been correctly classified as equity within the accounting records and that total financing proceeds of $5m were received. In addition, the disclosures for this share issue should be reviewed in detail to ensure compliance with relevant accounting standards.
Appropriateness of asset lives The finance director has extended the useful lives of fixtures and fittings from three to four years, resulting in the depreciation charge reducing. Under IAS 16 *Property, Plant and Equipment*, useful lives are to be reviewed annually, and if asset lives have genuinely increased, then this change is reasonable. However, there is a risk that this reduction has occurred in order to boost profits. If this is the case, then fixtures and fittings are overvalued and profit overstated.	Discuss with the directors the rationale for any extensions of asset lives and reduction of depreciation rates. Also, the four-year life should be compared to how often these assets are replaced, to assess the useful life of assets.
Receivables valuation A customer of Hurling Co has been encountering difficulties paying their outstanding balance of $1.2m and Hurling Co has agreed to a revised credit period. If the customer is experiencing difficulties, there is an increased risk that the receivable is not recoverable and hence is overvalued.	Review the revised credit terms and identify if any after-date cash receipts for this customer have been made. Discuss with the finance director whether there is an intention to make an allowance for this receivable. If not, review whether any existing allowance for uncollectable accounts is sufficient to cover the amount of this receivable.

Audit risk	Auditor's response
Sales-related bonus scheme A sales-related bonus scheme has been introduced in the year for sales staff, with a significant number of new customer accounts on favourable credit terms being opened pre year end. This has resulted in a 5% increase in revenue. Sales staff seeking to maximise their current year bonus may result in new accounts being opened from poor credit risks leading to irrecoverable receivables. In addition, there is a risk of sales cut-off errors as new customers could place orders within the two-month introductory period and subsequently return these goods post year end.	Increased after-date cash receipts testing to be undertaken for new customer account receivables. Increased sales cut-off testing will be performed along with a review of any post-year-end returns as they may indicate cut-off errors.
Product recall **Inventory valuation** Hurling Co has halted further sales of its new product Luge and a product recall has been initiated for any goods sold in the last four months. If there are issues with the quality of the Luge product, inventory may be overvalued as its NRV may be below its cost.	Discuss with the finance director whether any write downs will be made to this product, and what, if any, modifications may be required with regards the quality. Testing should be undertaken to confirm cost and NRV of the Luge products in inventory and that on a line-by-line basis the goods are valued correctly.
Provision for refunds Additionally, products of Luge sold within the last four months are being recalled, this will result in Hurling Co paying customer refunds. The sale will need to be removed and a refund liability should be recognised along with the reinstatement of inventory, although the NRV of this inventory could be of a minimal value. Failing to account for this correctly could result in overstated revenue and understated liabilities and inventory.	Review the list of sales made of product Luge prior to the recall, agree that the sale has been removed from revenue and the inventory included. If the refund has not been paid pre year end, agree it is included within current liabilities.

Audit risk	**Auditor's response**
Legal action Petanque Co, a customer of Hurling Co, has announced that it intends to commence legal action for a loss of information and profits as a result of the Luge product sold to them. If it is probable that the company will make payment to the customer, a legal provision is required. If the payment is possible rather than probable, a contingent liability disclosure would be necessary. If Hurling Co has not done this, there is a risk over the completeness of any provisions or the necessary disclosure of contingent liabilities.	Caving & Co should write to the company's lawyers to enquire of the existence and likelihood of success of any claim from Petanque Co. The results of this should be used to assess the level of provision or disclosure included in the financial statements.
Audit timetable – detection risk The finance director has requested that the audit completed one week earlier than normal so that results can be reported earlier. A reduction in the audit timetable will increase detection risk and place additional pressure on the team in obtaining sufficient and appropriate evidence. In addition, the finance team of Hurling Co will have less time to prepare the financial information leading to an increased risk of errors arising in the financial statements.	The timetable should be confirmed with the finance director. If it is to be reduced, then consideration should be given to performing an interim audit to reduce the pressure on the final audit. The team needs to maintain professional scepticism and be alert to the increased risk of errors occurring.
Proposed dividend The company is intending to propose a final dividend once the financial statements are finalised. This amount should not be provided for in the 20X5 financial statements as the obligation only arises once the dividend is announced, which is post year end. In line with IAS 10 *Events After the Reporting Date* the dividend should only be disclosed. If the dividend is included, this will result in an overstatement of liabilities and understatement of equity.	Discuss the issue with management and confirm that the dividend will not be included within liabilities in the 20X5 financial statements. The financial statements need to be reviewed to ensure that adequate disclosure of the proposed dividend is included.

(c) Ethical threats and appropriate safeguards

Ethical threat	**Appropriate safeguard**
The finance director is keen to report Hurling Co's financial results earlier than normal and has asked if the audit can be completed in a shorter time frame. This may create an intimidation threat on the team as they may feel under pressure to cut corners and not raise issues in order to satisfy the deadlines and this could compromise the objectivity of the audit team and quality of audit performed.	The engagement partner should discuss the timing of the audit with the finance director to understand if the audit can commence earlier, so as to ensure adequate time for the team to gather evidence. If this is not possible, the partner should politely inform the finance director that the team will undertake the audit in accordance with all relevant ISAs and quality management standards. Therefore, the audit is unlikely to be completed earlier. If any residual concerns remain or the intimidation threat continues, then Caving & Co may need to consider resigning from the engagement.
A non-executive director (NED) of Hurling Co has just resigned and the directors have asked whether the partners of Caving & Co can assist them in recruiting to fill this vacancy. This represents a self-interest threat as the audit firm cannot undertake the recruitment of members of the board of Hurling Co, especially a NED who will have a key role in overseeing the audit process and audit firm.	Caving & Co is able to assist Hurling Co in that it can undertake roles such as reviewing a shortlist of candidates and reviewing qualifications and suitability. However, the firm must ensure that it is not seen to undertake management decisions and so must not seek out candidates for the position or make the final decision on who is appointed.
The engagement quality reviewer (EQR) assigned to Hurling Co was until last year the audit engagement partner. This represents a familiarity threat as the partner will have been associated with Hurling Co for a long period of time and so may not retain professional scepticism and objectivity.	As Hurling Co is a listed company, then the previous audit engagement partner should not be involved in the audit for at least a period of five years. An alternative EQR should be appointed instead.

Ethical threat	**Appropriate safeguard**
Caving & Co provides taxation services, the audit engagement and possibly services related to the recruitment of the NED. There is a potential self-interest or intimidation threat as the total fees could represent a significant proportion of Caving & Co's income and the firm could become overly reliant on Hurling Co. This could result in the firm being less challenging or objective due to fear of losing such a significant client.	Caving & Co should assess whether audit, recruitment and taxation fees would represent more than 15% of gross practice income for two consecutive years. If the recurring fees are likely to exceed 15% of annual practice income this year, additional consideration should be given as to whether the recruitment and taxation services should be undertaken by the firm. In addition, if the fees do exceed 15%, then this should be disclosed to those charged with governance at Hurling Co. If the firm retains all work, it should arrange for a pre-issuance (before the audit opinion is issued) or post-issuance (after the opinion has been issued) review to be undertaken by an external accountant or by a regulatory body.
The finance director has suggested that the audit fee is based on the profit before tax of Hurling Co which constitutes a contingent fee. Contingent fees give rise to a self-interest threat and are prohibited under ACCA's *Code of Ethics and Conduct*. If the audit fee is based on profit, the team may be inclined to ignore audit adjustments which could lead to a reduction in profit.	Caving & Co will not be able to accept contingent fees and should communicate to those charged with governance at Hurling Co that the external audit fee needs to be based on the time spent and levels of skill and experience of the required audit team members.
At today's date, 20% of last year's audit fee is still outstanding and was due for payment three months ago. A self-interest threat can arise if the fees remain outstanding, as Caving & Co may feel pressure to agree to certain accounting adjustments in order to have the previous year and this year's audit fee paid. In addition, outstanding fees could be perceived as a loan to a client which is strictly prohibited.	Caving & Co should discuss the reasons why the final 20% of last year's fee has not been paid with those charged with governance and request the fees are paid. The auditor's report for this year must not be issued until the fees from last year have been paid.

Marking guide		
		Marks
(a)	**Define audit risk and its components**	
	• Audit risk	2
	• Inherent risk	1
	• Control risk	1
	• Detection risk	1
		4
(b)	**Audit risks and responses (only 8 risks required)**	
	• Upgrade of website: Capitalisation of website costs OR Completeness and accuracy of data due to new website	2
	• Warehouse acquisition	2
	• Classification of preference shares	2
	• Appropriateness of asset useful lives	2
	• Irrecoverable receivable	2
	• Sales staff bonus scheme	2
	• Product recall: Inventory valuation OR provision for refunds	2
	• Legal action	2
	• Audit timetable, increased detection risk	2
	• Accounting for proposed dividend	2
	Max 8 issues, 2 marks each	**16**
(c)	**Ethical threats and appropriate safeguards** (only 5 threats required)	
	• Intimidation threat – audit timetable	2
	• Self-interest threat – recruitment	2
	• Familiarity threat – EQR	2
	• Self-interest/intimidation threat – fees	2
	• Self-interest threat – contingent fee	2
	• Self-interest threat – outstanding fees	2
	Max 5 issues, 2 marks each	**10**
Total		**30**

Examiner's comments

This question was based on a listed company, Hurling Co, a manufacturer of computer components. This question tested the areas of audit risks and responses, and ethical threats and safeguards.

Part (a) required candidates to define audit risk and the components of audit risk. This question was generally well answered with the majority of candidates demonstrating a reasonably good knowledge of the area tested. Up to 1 mark was awarded for each definition of audit risk and its components. Most candidates correctly identified the three components of audit risk, however, some candidates did not describe the components correctly. For example, inherent risk was often described only as 'the risk due to the nature of the business', rather than 'the susceptibility of an account balance or class of transaction to misstatement before related controls'. In key knowledge areas such as this, candidates must ensure that they are technically accurate in order to score full marks.

Part (b) required identification and description of eight audit risks from the scenario and the auditor's response to each. Performance on this question was mixed. Marks were awarded for identification of audit risk (½ marks each), explanation of audit risk (½ marks each) and an appropriate auditor's response to each risk (1 mark each). The scenario contained more than eight risks so it was pleasing that most candidates planned their time carefully and generally only attempted to list the required number of issues. Some candidates however included ethical issues from part (c) of the question in their answer to part (b). For example, incorrectly stating that the outstanding prior year audit fee was an audit risk rather than recognising that this is an ethical issue which can threaten auditor independence but does not influence the risk of material misstatement in the financial statements. A number of candidates did not clearly identify and explain certain audit risks from the scenario. For example, some candidates incorrectly noted the issue of a 'new warehouse' could result in 'incorrect allocation of assets and expenses'. However, the issue was that the acquisition of the new warehouse may not have been completed by the year end so there is a risk of existence/rights and obligations not transferred. A large number of candidates are still not explaining how each issue could impact on audit risk and therefore were not awarded the ½ mark for explanation. To adequately explain audit risk, candidates need to state the area of the accounts impacted with either an assertion (e.g. cut off, valuation etc.), a reference to under/over/misstated, or a reference to inherent, control or detection risk. For example, many candidates correctly identified the legal action raised by the customer as an issue (½ mark) but then incorrectly stated the explanation of the risk as this could lead to a loss of customer goodwill/reputational damage for the company. This is an explanation of the risk from the company's perspective and does not explain how the financial statements are impacted. To gain the second ½ mark candidates need to refer to either that liabilities may be understated if a provision is needed but not included or that the financial statements may be misstated as contingent liability disclosure is required.

Candidate performance in relation to auditor's responses continues to be mixed. While an auditor's response does not have to be a detailed audit procedure, rather an approach the audit team will take to address the identified risk, the responses given were often too weak such as 'discuss with management'. This is not a sufficient response to deal with any identified audit risk and candidates need to be able to use their knowledge of audit procedures to provide a valid response which would adequately address the risk identified. A minority of candidates discussed business risks and therefore concentrated their responses on what management should do rather than the auditor. For example, advising management not to issue irredeemable preference shares and instead to consider alternative forms of finance.

This is not a valid response as it does not address the audit risk identified and it is not within the remit of the auditor to provide this type of guidance.

An assessment of audit risk, is a fundamental factor in planning and assessing the risks of an audit of an entity, and this remains a highly examinable area and candidates must ensure that they include adequate question practice as part of their revision of this key topic.

Part (c) required an identification and explanation of five ethical threats faced by the auditor and how these threats should be reduced. Performance in this question was satisfactory. Marks were awarded for identification of the issue and type of threat (½ marks each), explanation of the threat (½ marks each) and a safeguard to reduce this threat (1 mark each). Most candidates were able to identify relevant issues from the scenario, however some candidates did not provide the correct category of threat. For example, some candidates incorrectly categorised the contingent audit fee and the outstanding prior year audit fees as intimidation threats rather than self-interest threats. Candidates are reminded that they must be comfortable with the categories of threats and how they arise in line with ACCA's Code of Ethics and Conduct. Some candidates identified threats where there was not an issue. A frequent misunderstanding being that the tax work resulted in a self-review threat. This was not correct as the tax work undertaken related to tax returns so would not have had an effect on the tax balance in the audited financial statements. Candidates often did not explain the issues correctly, or in sufficient detail. For example, explaining the threat of self-interest resulting from contingent audit fees, as simply that the auditor will not be independent is not sufficient. Candidates needed to comment on the possibility of the auditor ignoring audit adjustments which reduce profits in order to maintain the fee level in order to obtain the explanation ½ mark. Some candidates thought an issue had to be identified for each of the categories of ethical threats of self-review, self-interest etc. This resulted in them trying to identify a situation from the scenario to fit each of the types of threats. This is not the correct approach to take as it is unlikely that the scenario will be based around one of each of the five ethical threats. The second part of the question required safeguards to reduce the risks to an acceptable level. A safeguard should be an action not just a statement of the rules. For example, to simply state that contingent audit fees should never be accepted is a statement rather than an action and therefore cannot constitute a safeguard. To obtain the 1 mark for a safeguard, candidates should have recommended that the firm decline this fee structure and to explain to the client that the audit fee is based on time and risk. Some responses were too brief or impractical. For example, for the threat of outstanding prior year fees, the response given by some candidates was that the auditor should resign. Resignation is an option for auditors, but it is the last resort and was not appropriate for this threat. To obtain the 1 mark for a safeguard, candidates should have recommended that either a revised payment schedule be arranged with the client and or that further work on this year's audit should be delayed until the outstanding audit fee is paid.

215 CENTIPEDE *Walk in the footsteps of a top tutor*

Key answer tips

In part (a), the matters to consider before accepting the audit should include the matters that might prevent the auditor from being able to accept the engagement such as ethical issues which cannot be safeguarded or other risks mentioned in the scenario.

Part (b) asks for ratios to be calculated from the information provided. Remember that the ratios are to help you identify audit risks. You are not evaluating the financial performance of the company.

Part (c) Audit risk and response is examined every sitting. You must make sure the risk relates to either a risk of material misstatement or a detection risk. Risks can be identified from the ratios you have calculated or from the scenario information. The response must be a response of the auditor, not the client.

Part (d) requires knowledge from the text book on how to manage conflicts of interest.

(a) Matters to be considered prior to accepting the audit of Centipede Co

ISA 220 (Revised) *Quality Management for an Audit of Financial Statements* provides guidance to Ant & Co on the steps it should have taken in accepting the new audit client, Centipede Co. It sets out a number of processes which the auditor should perform prior to accepting a new engagement.

Ant & Co should have considered any issues which might arise which could threaten compliance with ACCA's Code of Ethics and Conduct or any local legislation, such as the level of fees from Centipede Co, to ensure it is not unduly reliant on these fees, as well as considering whether any conflicts of interest arise with existing clients. If issues arise, then their significance must be considered.

In addition, the firm should have considered whether it was competent to perform the work and whether it has appropriate resources available, as well as any specialist skills or knowledge required for the audit of Centipede Co.

Ant & Co should have considered what it already knows about the directors of Centipede Co. The reputation and integrity of the directors should have been considered. If necessary, the firm should have obtained references.

Additionally, Ant & Co should have considered the level of risk attached to the audit of Centipede Co and whether this was acceptable to the firm. As part of this, it should have considered whether the expected audit fee was adequate in relation to the risk of auditing Centipede Co.

Ant & Co should have communicated with the outgoing auditor of Centipede Co to assess if there were any ethical or professional reasons why the appointment should not have been accepted. Permission should have been obtained from Centipede Co's management to contact the previous auditor. If this was not given, the engagement should have been refused. Once received, the response from the previous auditor should have been carefully reviewed for any issues which could affect acceptance.

(b) Ratios to assist the audit supervisor in planning the audit

	20X5	**20X4**
Gross profit margin	9,390/25,230 = **37.2%**	7,165/21,180 = **33.8%**
Inventory holding period	2,360/15,840 × 365 = **54 days**	1,800/14,015 × 365 = **47 days**
Payables payment period	3,500/15,840 × 365 = **81 days**	2,800/14,015 × 365 = **73 days**
Current ratio	3,950/4,080 = **0.97**	3,530/2,800 = **1.26**

(c) Audit risks and auditor's responses

Audit risk	**Auditor's response**
New audit client Centipede Co is a new client for Ant & Co and is a listed company. As the team is not familiar with the accounting policies, transactions and balances of the company, there will be an increased detection risk on the audit.	Ant & Co should ensure a suitably experienced team is assigned. Also, adequate time should be allocated for team members to obtain an understanding of the company and the risks of material misstatement, including attendance at an audit team briefing.
Perpetual inventory system The company utilises a perpetual inventory system at its warehouse rather than a full year-end count. Under such a system, all inventory must be counted at least once a year with adjustments made to the inventory records on a timely basis. Inventory could be under or overstated if the perpetual inventory counts are not complete.	The completeness of the perpetual inventory counts should be reviewed and the controls over the counts and adjustments to records should be tested.

Audit risk	**Auditor's response**
Inventory record exceptions During the interim audit, it was noted that there were significant exceptions with the inventory records being higher than the inventory in the warehouse. As the year-end quantities will be based on the records, this is likely to result in overstated inventory.	The level of adjustments made to inventory should be considered to assess their significance. This should be discussed with management as soon as possible as it may not be possible to place reliance on the inventory records at the year end, which could result in the requirement for a full year-end inventory count.
Inventory valuation During the interim audit, it was noted that there were some lines of inventory which according to the records were at least 90 days old. In addition, the inventory holding period has increased from 47 to 54 days. It would appear that there may be an increase in slow-moving inventory. The valuation of inventory as per IAS 2 *Inventories* should be at the lower of cost and net realisable value. There is a risk that obsolete inventory has not been appropriately written down and inventory is overvalued.	The aged inventory report should be reviewed and discussed with management to assess if certain lines of products are slow moving. Detailed cost and net realisable value testing to be performed to assess whether an allowance or write down of inventory is required.
Branch records Centipede Co maintains accounting records at four additional sites which were not visited during the interim audit, and the records from these sites are incorporated monthly into the general ledger. Ant & Co need to ensure that it has obtained sufficient appropriate audit evidence over all the accounting records of the company, not just for those at head office. There is a detection risk if the team does not visit or undertake testing of the records at these sites. Further, if the interface does not occur appropriately, there is a risk that accounting records are incomplete.	Discuss with management the significance and materiality of the records maintained at the four sites. The team should visit some of these sites during the final audit to undertake testing of the records held there. In addition, automated tools and techniques could be utilised by the team to sample test the monthly interface of data from each site to head office to identify any errors.

Audit risk	Auditor's response
Disposal of building During 20X5 a building was disposed of with a loss on disposal of $825,000. Significant profits or losses on disposal are an indication that the depreciation policy for land and buildings may not be appropriate. Therefore, depreciation may be understated and profit and assets overstated. In addition, there is a risk that the disposal has not been removed appropriately from the accounting records.	Recalculate the loss on disposal and agree to supporting documentation. Discuss the depreciation policy for buildings with the finance director to assess its reasonableness. Review the level of losses on disposal generated from other asset sales to ascertain if this is a more widespread issue. Agree that the asset has been removed from the non-current asset register.
Legal action A customer of Centipede Co has commenced legal action against Centipede Co for a loss of profits claim. If it is probable that the company will make payment to the customer, a legal provision is required. If the payment is possible rather than probable, a contingent liability disclosure would be necessary. If Centipede Co has not done this, there is a risk over the completeness of any provisions and the necessary disclosure of contingent liabilities.	Ant & Co should write to the company's lawyers to enquire of the existence and likelihood of success of any claim from the wholesale customer. The results of this should be used to assess the level of provision or disclosure included in the financial statements
Directors' remuneration disclosure The directors have not disclosed the individual names and payments for each of the directors' remuneration. This is in line with IFRS Standards but disclosure of this is required by local legislation. In cases where the local legislation is more comprehensive than IFRS Standards, it is likely the company must comply with the local legislation. The directors' remuneration disclosure will not be complete and accurate if the names and individual payments are not disclosed in accordance with the relevant local legislation and hence the financial statements will be misstated as a result of the non-compliance.	Discuss this matter with management and review the requirements of the local legislation to determine if the disclosure in the financial statements is appropriate.

Audit risk	**Auditor's response**
Revenue growth Revenue has grown by 19% in the year; however, cost of sales has only increased by 13%. This is a significant increase in revenue and along with the increase in gross margin from 33.8% to 37.2% may be due to an overstatement of revenue.	During the audit, a detailed breakdown of sales will be obtained, discussed with management and tested in order to understand the sales increase. Also increased cut-off testing should be undertaken to verify that revenue is recorded in the right period and is not overstated.
Operating expenses Operating expenses have increased by 51% compared with an increase in cost of sales of only 13% and revenue of 19%. The increase in operating expenses is significant and unusual and there is a risk that operating expenses have been overstated possibly due to misclassification of costs between operating expenses and cost of sales.	The classification of costs between cost of sales and operating expenses will be compared with the prior year to ensure consistency. Also increased cut-off testing should be performed at the year end to ensure that costs are complete.
Going concern The overall liquidity of the company is in decline with the current and quick ratios decreasing from 1.26 to 0.97 and 0.62 to 0.39 respectively. In addition, the cash balances have decreased significantly over the year, and the company now has an overdraft of $580,000 at the end of the year. Further, the trade payables payment period has increased from 73 to 81 days, implying the company is struggling to meet its liabilities as they fall due. All of these changes in key ratios could signal going concern difficulties.	Detailed going concern testing to be performed during the audit as there may be a doubt over going concern and the basis of accounting should be discussed with management to ensure that the going concern basis is reasonable.

(d) Safeguards to deal with conflict of interest

- Both Centipede Co and its rival competitor should be notified that Ant & Co would be acting as auditors for each company and, if necessary, consent obtained.
- Advise one or both clients to seek additional independent advice.
- Use separate engagement teams, with different engagement partners and team members. Once an employee has worked on one audit, such as Centipede Co, then they should be prevented from being on the audit of the competitor for a period of time.
- Implement procedures to prevent access to information, for example, strict physical separation of both teams, confidential and secure data filing.

- Communicate clear guidelines for members of each engagement team on issues of security and confidentiality. These guidelines could be included within the audit engagement letters.
- Use confidentiality agreements signed by employees and partners of the firm.
- A senior individual in Ant & Co not involved in either audit should regularly monitor the application of the above safeguards.

Marking guide		
		Marks
(a)	**Matters to be considered prior to accepting the audit of Centipede Co**	
	• Compliance with ACCA's Code of Ethics and Conduct	1
	• Competent	1
	• Reputation and integrity of directors	1
	• Level of risk of Centipede Co audit	1
	• Fee adequate to compensate for risk	1
	• Write to outgoing auditor after obtaining permission to contact	1
	• Previous auditor permission to respond	1
	• Review response for any issues	1
	Restricted to	**5**
(b)	**Ratio calculations (½ mark for each year)**	
	• Gross profit margin	1
	• Inventory holding period/Inventory turnover	1
	• Payables payment period	1
	• Current ratio	1
	Max 4 ratios	**4**
(c)	**Audit risks and responses (only 8 risks required)**	
	• New client, increased detection risk	2
	• Perpetual inventory count adjustments	2
	• Valuation of inventory	2
	• Branch records	2
	• Disposal of building	2
	• Legal case	2
	• Directors remuneration disclosure	2
	• Revenue growth	2
	• Misclassification between cost of sales and operating expenses	2
	• Going concern	2
	Max 8 issues, 2 marks each	**16**
(d)	**Safeguards to deal with conflict of interest**	
	• Notify Centipede Co and its competitor	1
	• Advise seek independent advice	1
	• Separate engagement teams	1
	• Procedures prevent access to information	1
	• Clear guidelines on security and confidentiality	1
	• Confidentiality agreements	1
	• Monitoring of safeguards	1
	Restricted to	**5**
Total		**30**

Examiner's comments

Part (a) required candidates to discuss matters to consider before accepting an audit. Candidates who scored well discussed the competence/resources available of the audit firm, the contact with previous auditors, ethical considerations and the preconditions of an audit. Some candidates focused on one area in too much detail, for example, only describing the various ethical considerations that could arise. Some candidates incorrectly focussed on the removal of the prior year auditor. Few candidates discussed money laundering or risk considerations.

Part (b) tested candidates' ability to calculate ratios which would assist in the planning of an audit. This question was generally well answered. Some candidates however only wrote the ratio formula and did not actually calculate the ratio. The current and quick ratios were also sometimes confused. Some candidates incorrectly calculated inventory days using revenue rather than cost of sales.

Part (c) required candidates to identify and explain the risks from a scenario and give an auditor's response to address the risks. As noted in previous Examiner's Reports a fundamental factor in planning and assessing the risks of an audit of an entity is an assessment of audit risk, and this remains a highly examinable area. Audit risk questions typically require a number of audit risks to be identified (½ marks each), explained (½ marks each) and an auditor's response to each risk (1 mark each). Performance in the audit risk question in December 2016 was mixed. The scenario contained a significant number of issues, and most candidates were able to identify the required number of issues. A significant number of candidates did not explain how each issue could impact on the audit risk and therefore were not awarded the second ½ mark. To explain audit risk candidates need to state the area of the accounts impacted with an assertion (e.g. cut-off, valuation etc.), or, a reference to under/over/misstated, or, a reference to inherent, control or detection risk. Misstated was only awarded if it was clear that the balance could be either over or understated. For example, when explaining the risk of inventory days increasing (½ marks for the issue), credit was only awarded for the audit risk of inventory being overstated (½ marks for the explanation). Auditor's responses were mixed. While an auditor's response does not have to be a detailed audit procedure, rather an approach the audit team will take to address the identified risk, the responses given were sometimes either too weak e.g. 'discuss with management' or, did not address the issue due to a failure to understand the risk. In comparison to recent exam sessions, it was pleasing that fewer candidates discussed business risks in December 2016. However, a minority of candidates continued to concentrate their responses on what management should do rather than the auditor. For example, in relation to inventory, an inappropriate response was to 'put in a FIFO system for inventory'.

Part (d) covered safeguards an audit firm should implement to ensure that a conflict of interest is properly managed. Candidates who scored well discussed a range of safeguards such as the audit team configuration, procedures to prevent access to information, notifying the client to obtain consent, and, obtaining confidentiality agreements. However, some candidates concentrated too much on just one area. For example, listing as different points, separate teams, restriction on reassignment of audit team members, and, different engagement partners – when all three are examples of team configuration. Some candidates focused on ethical issues, such as ensuring the auditor has no shares in the client, which was not relevant for this question. Candidates need to be clear when describing the safeguards, for example candidates often mentioned that confidentiality agreements were required but often were unclear who the agreement should be with, occasionally incorrectly noting that the agreement should be with the client.

216 AQUAMARINE *Walk in the footsteps of a top tutor*

Key answer tips

Requirements (a) and (b) cover frequently examined areas of the syllabus. Knowledge questions such as part (a) can be examined in section B, and you must take time to learn key definitions and requirements of the auditing standards.

In part (b) make sure you describe audit risks and not business risks. Make sure the response is the response of the auditor and not the client.

Part (c) is trickier. This highlights the importance of revising all areas of the syllabus as any area can be tested. If you can't answer the requirement don't waste time, move onto a different question.

(a) Audit risk and its components

Audit risk is the risk that the auditor expresses an inappropriate audit opinion when the financial statements are materially misstated.

Audit risk is a function of two main components, being the risk of material misstatement and detection risk.

Risk of material misstatement is made up of a further two components, inherent risk and control risk.

Inherent risk is the susceptibility of an assertion about a class of transaction, account balance or disclosure to a misstatement which could be material, either individually or when aggregated with other misstatements, before consideration of any related controls.

Control risk is the risk that a misstatement which could occur in an assertion about a class of transaction, account balance or disclosure and which could be material, either individually or when aggregated with other misstatements, will not be prevented, or detected and corrected, on a timely basis by the entity's controls.

Detection risk is the risk that the procedures performed by the auditor to reduce audit risk to an acceptably low level will not detect a misstatement which exists and which could be material, either individually or when aggregated with other misstatements. Detection risk is affected by sampling and non-sampling risk.

(b) Audit risks and auditors' responses

Audit risks	**Auditors' responses**
Work-in-progress (WIP) Aquamarine Co undertakes continuous production and the WIP balance at the year end is likely to be material. As production will not cease, the exact cut-off of the WIP will need to be assessed. If the cut-off is not correctly calculated, the inventory valuation may be under or overstated.	The auditor should discuss with management the process they will undertake to assess the cut-off point for WIP at the year end. This process should be reviewed by the auditor while attending the year-end inventory count. In addition, consideration should be given as to whether an independent expert is required to value the WIP. If so, this will need to be arranged with consent from management and in time for the year-end count.
PPE Aquamarine Co has ordered $720,000 of plant and machinery, two-thirds of which may not have been received by the year end. Only assets which physically exist at the year end should be included in property, plant and equipment. If items not yet delivered have been capitalised, PPE will be overstated. Consideration will also need to be given to depreciation and when this should commence. If depreciation is not appropriately charged when the asset is available for use, this may result in assets and profit being over or understated.	Discuss with management as to whether the remaining plant and machinery ordered have arrived; if so, physically verify a sample of these assets to ensure existence and ensure only appropriate assets are recorded in the non-current asset register at the year end. Determine if the asset received is in use at the year end by physical observation and if so, if depreciation has commenced at an appropriate point.
Patent A patent has been purchased for $1.3 million and is recognised at cost in the financial statements. The patent exclusive rights for the next five years. In accordance with IAS 38 *Intangible Assets*, this should be amortised over its five-year life. Management has not correctly accounted for the patent as no amortisation has been charged. Intangible assets and profits are overstated.	The audit team will need to agree the purchase price to supporting documentation and to confirm the useful life is five years. The amortisation charge should be calculated and management informed that an adjustment is required in order to ensure that the intangible asset is appropriately valued at the year end.

Audit risks	**Auditors' responses**
Bank loan The company has borrowed $1.2 million from the bank via a five-year loan. This loan needs to be correctly split between current and non-current liabilities. There is a risk of incorrect disclosure if the loan is not correctly split between current and non-current liabilities.	During the audit, the team would need to confirm that the $1.2 million loan finance was received. In addition, the split between current and non-current liabilities and the disclosures for this loan should be reviewed in detail to ensure compliance with relevant accounting standards. Details of security should be agreed to the bank confirmation letter.
Finance costs As the level of debt has increased, there should be additional finance costs. There is a risk that this has been omitted from the statement of profit or loss. Finance costs may be understated and profit overstated.	The finance costs should be recalculated and any increase agreed to the loan documentation for confirmation of interest rates. Interest payments should be agreed to the bank ledger account and bank statements to confirm the amount was paid and is not therefore a year-end payable.
Outsourced payroll function During the year Aquamarine Co outsourced its payroll processing to an external service organisation. The audit team will need to verify controls at the third party.	Discuss with management the extent of records maintained at Aquamarine Co and any monitoring of controls undertaken by management over the payroll charge.
A detection risk arises as to whether sufficient and appropriate evidence is available at Aquamarine Co to confirm the completeness and accuracy of controls over payroll. If not, another auditor may be required to undertake testing at the service organisation.	Consideration should be given to contacting the service organisation's auditor to confirm the level of controls in place.
Data transfer The payroll processing transferred to Coral Payrolls Co in January 20X5. Errors may have occurred during the transfer process. There is a risk that the payroll charge and related employment tax liabilities are under/overstated.	Discuss with management the transfer process undertaken and any controls put in place to ensure the completeness and accuracy of the data. Where possible, undertake tests of controls to confirm the effectiveness of the transfer controls. In addition, perform substantive testing on the transfer of information from the old to the new system.

Audit risks	**Auditors' responses**
Revaluation of land and buildings The land and buildings are to be revalued at the year end. It is likely that the revaluation surplus/deficit will be material. The revaluation needs to be carried out and recorded in accordance with IAS 16 *Property, Plant and Equipment*. Non-current assets may be incorrectly valued.	Discuss with management the process adopted for undertaking the valuation, including whether the whole class of assets was revalued and if the valuation was undertaken by an expert. This process should be reviewed for compliance with IAS 16.
Valuation of receivables Receivables at the end of May 20X5 are considerably higher than the prior year. The receivables may not be recoverable and allowance for credit losses may not have been made. There is a risk that receivables may be overvalued.	Discuss with management the reasons for the increase in receivables and management's process for identifying potential irrecoverable debt. Test controls surrounding management's credit control processes. Extended post-year-end cash receipts testing and a review of the aged list of individual customer balances to be performed to assess valuation. Also consider the adequacy of any allowance for credit losses/ receivables.
Redundancy provision Aquamarine Co is planning to make approximately 65 employees redundant after the year end. The timing of this announcement has not been confirmed; if it is announced to the staff before the year end, then under IAS 37 *Provisions, Contingent Liabilities and Contingent Assets* a redundancy provision will be required at the year end. Failure to provide will result in an understatement of provisions and expenses.	Discuss with management the status of the redundancy announcement; if before the year end, review supporting documentation to confirm the timing. In addition, review the basis of and recalculate the redundancy provision.

(c) Payroll service organisations

Additional factors Amethyst & Co should consider in relation to Aquamarine Co's use of the service organisation, Coral Payrolls Co include:

- The audit team should gain an understanding of the services being provided by Coral Payrolls Co, including the materiality of payroll and the basis of the outsourcing contract.
- They will need to assess the design and implementation of internal controls over Aquamarine Co's payroll at Cora Payrolls Co.

- The team may wish to visit Coral Payrolls Co and undertake tests of controls to confirm the operating effectiveness of the controls.
- If this is not possible, Amethyst & Co should contact Coral Payrolls Co's auditors to request either a type 1 (report on description and design of controls) or type 2 report (on description, design and operating effectiveness of controls).
- Amethyst & Co is responsible for obtaining sufficient and appropriate evidence, therefore no reference may be made in the auditor's report regarding the use of information from Coral Payrolls Co's auditors.

Marking guide

		Marks
(a)	**Audit risk and its components**	
	• Audit risk	2
	• Inherent risk	1
	• Control risk	1
	• Detection risk	1
		5
(b)	**Audit risks and responses (only 6 risks required)**	
	• Work-in-progress	2
	• Existence of plant and machinery ordered	2
	• Valuation of intangible asset	2
	• New loan finance obtained	2
	• Completeness of finance costs	2
	• Use of service organisation	2
	• Transfer of data to service organisation	2
	• Valuation of land and buildings	2
	• Overvaluation of receivables	2
	• Redundancy provision	2
	Max 6 issues, 2 marks each	**12**
(c)	**Payroll service organisations**	
	• Gain an understanding of the services being provided	1
	• Assess the design and implementation of internal controls over Aquamarine Co's payroll at Coral	1
	• Visit Coral and undertake tests of controls	1
	• Contact Coral's auditors to request either a type 1 or type 2 report	1
	• No reference in auditor's report of use of information from Coral's auditors	1
	Restricted to	**3**
Total		**20**

Examiner's comments

Performance in the audit risk question, as in many previous exams continues to be mixed. The scenario contained more issues than were required to be discussed. A significant minority identified more issues than necessary, often combining risks into one point. This approach sometimes resulted in a lack of detail in the risk and also led to unfocused auditor responses. In addition, a large number of candidates often did not explain how each issue could result in an audit risk or impact on the financial statements and therefore were not awarded the explanation ½ mark. To explain audit risk candidates need to state the area of the financial statements impacted with an assertion (e.g. cut-off, valuation etc.), or, a reference to under/over/misstated, or, a reference to inherent, control or detection risk. Misstated was only awarded if it was clear that the balance could be either over or understated. In addition, many candidates misunderstood the implication of payroll being outsourced, failing to understand that there was an increased detection risk with regards to access to outsourced records and the risk of data being incorrectly transferred to the service organisation.

The provision of relevant auditor responses continues to be a poorly attempted area and candidates are once again reminded to ensure that this area of the syllabus is adequately studied and practised. While an auditor's response does not have to be a detailed audit procedure, rather an approach the audit team will take to address the identified risk, the responses given were sometimes either too weak e.g. "discuss with management" or, did not address the issue due to a failure to understand the risk (e.g. in response to a possible understated provision, an incorrect response was to "undertake going concern testing'). In comparison to recent exam sessions, it was disappointing that a significant minority of candidates discussed business risks and therefore concentrated their responses on what management should do rather than the auditor (e.g. in relation to the plant and machinery ordered pre year end, an inappropriate response was that the auditor should contact the supplier to ensure the delivery was on time). Further it was pleasing to note that many candidates presented their answers well using a two-column approach with audit risk in one column and the related response in the other column.

In addition, there was a knowledge-based question which required a definition of audit risk and its components. This question was generally well answered with candidates demonstrating reasonable knowledge of the area tested. Some candidates failed to maximise their marks as their explanation of inherent risk was incomplete. In key knowledge areas such as this, candidates must be technically correct in order to score full marks.

217 VENUS *Walk in the footsteps of a top tutor*

Key answer tips

Requirements (a) and (b) cover knowledge of engagement letters. For part (a) think of sensible reasons why a contract with a client may need to be amended. Part (b) has been examined many times before and students should be able to score reasonably well on this.

In part (c) you are asked for sources of information, i.e. where the auditor can obtain information to help plan the audit. Make sure you include an explanation of how the information will be used to score the full mark.

Part (d) asks for audit risks which are examined at every sitting. Audit risks need to relate to either a risk of material misstatement or a detection risk. For risk of material misstatement, identify a balance in the scenario that is at risk of misstatement and explain why you believe it could be misstated. This is usually because the client has failed to apply the relevant accounting standards correctly. The accounting standards examinable for ACCA Financial Accounting are examinable for this exam.

Detection risks are the risks the auditor does not detect material misstatements in the financial statements e.g. when it is a new audit client or if there is a tight reporting deadline.

For the response, make sure it relates to the risk, not the balance in general. Try and be as specific as possible, simply saying more testing is required will not be sufficient. State the nature of the tests that should be performed.

(a) Engagement letters

Engagement letters for recurring/existing clients should be revised if any of the following factors are present:

- Any indication that the entity misunderstands the objective and scope of the audit, as this misunderstanding would need to be clarified.
- Any revised or special terms of the audit engagement, as these would require inclusion in the engagement letter.
- A recent change of senior management or significant change in ownership. The letter is signed by a director on behalf of those charged with governance. If there have been significant changes in management they need to be made aware of what the audit engagement letter includes.
- A significant change in nature or size of the entity's business. The approach taken by the auditor may need to change to reflect the change in the entity and this should be clarified in the engagement letter.
- A change in legal or regulatory requirements. The engagement letter is a contract; hence if legal or regulatory changes occur, then the contract could be out of date.

- A change in the financial reporting framework adopted in the preparation of the financial statements. The engagement letter clarifies the role of auditors and those charged with governance, it identifies the reporting framework of the financial statements and if this changes, then the letter requires updating.
- A change in other reporting requirements. Other reporting requirements may be stipulated in the engagement letter; hence if these change, the letter should be updated.

(b) Matters to be included in an audit engagement letter

- The objective and scope of the audit
- The responsibilities of the auditor
- The responsibilities of management
- Identification of the financial reporting framework for the preparation of the financial statements
- Expected form and content of any reports to be issued
- Elaboration of the scope of the audit with reference to legislation
- The form of any other communication of results of the audit engagement
- The fact that some material misstatements may not be detected
- Arrangements regarding the planning and performance of the audit, including the composition of the audit team
- The expectation that management will provide written representations
- The basis on which fees are computed and any billing arrangements
- A request for management to acknowledge receipt of the audit engagement letter and to agree to the terms of the engagement
- Arrangements concerning the involvement of internal auditors and other staff of the entity
- Any obligations to provide audit working papers to other parties
- Any restriction on the auditor's liability
- Arrangements to make available draft financial statements and any other information
- Arrangements to inform the auditor of facts which might affect the financial statements, of which management may become aware during the period from the date of the auditor's report to the date the financial statements are issued.

(c) Understanding an entity

Prior year financial statements

Provides information in relation to the size of a company as well as the key accounting policies, disclosure notes and whether the audit opinion was modified or not.

Discussions with the previous auditors/access to their files

Provides information on key issues identified during the prior year audit as well as the audit approach adopted.

Prior year report to management

If this can be obtained from the previous auditors or from management, it can provide information on the internal control deficiencies noted last year. If these have not been rectified by management, then they could arise in the current year audit as well and may impact the audit approach.

Accounting systems notes/procedural manuals

Provides information on how each of the key accounting systems operates and this will be used to identify areas of potential control risk and help determine the audit approach.

Discussions with management

Provides information in relation to the business, any important issues which have arisen or changes to accounting policies from the prior year.

Review of board minutes

Provides an overview of key issues which have arisen during the year and how those charged with governance have addressed them.

Current year budgets and management accounts

Provides relevant financial information for the year to date. It will help the auditor during the planning stage for preliminary analytical review and risk identification.

Company website

Recent press releases from the company may provide background on the business during the year as this will help in identifying the key audit risks.

Financial statements of competitors

This will provide information about the company's competitors, in relation to their financial results and their accounting policies. This will be important in assessing the performance in the year and also when undertaking the going concern review.

(d) Audit risk and auditor's responses

Audit risk	**Auditor's response**
Appropriateness of asset lives The directors have reviewed the asset lives and depreciation rates of plant and machinery, resulting in the depreciation charge reducing. Under IAS 16 *Property, Plant and Equipment*, asset lives should be reviewed annually, and if the asset lives have increased as a result of this review such that the depreciation decreases, then this change may be reasonable. This reduction may have occurred in order to achieve profit targets, due to the introduction of the bonus system.	Discuss with the directors the rationale for any extensions of asset lives and reduction of depreciation rates. The revised useful life of a sample of assets should be compared to how often these assets are replaced, as this provides evidence of the useful life of assets.

Audit risk	**Auditor's response**
There is a risk that plant and machinery is overvalued and profit overstated if this is the case.	
Inventory count Due to staff availability, the company is planning to undertake a full year-end inventory count days before the year end and then adjust for movements to the year end. The adjustments may not be made accurately or completely. There is a risk that inventory could be under or overstated.	During the final audit the year-end inventory adjustments schedule should be reviewed in detail and supporting documentation obtained for all adjusting items. The audit team should increase the extent of inventory cut-off testing at the year end.
Fire damaged inventory In June, a fire damaged inventory such that it has been written down from \$0.9 million to \$0.2 million which is its scrap value. This write down should have been charged to profit or loss. If the goods remain unsold after the year end, the scrap value may be overstated. There is a risk of inventory being overvalued.	Discuss with management the basis of the \$0.2 million scrap value attributed. Review whether any of the goods were sold pre or post year end and at what value; this should assess whether the attributed scrap value is reasonable. If none have been sold, discuss with management the possibility of further write downs.
Contingent asset An insurance claim for \$0.7 million has been submitted and the proceeds included within profit or loss. The company has not received a reply from the insurance company and this would therefore represent a possible contingent asset. To comply with IAS 37 *Provisions, Contingent Liabilities and Contingent Assets*, this should not be recognised until the receipt is virtually certain. With no response to date, the inclusion of this sum overstates profit and receivables.	Discuss with management whether any response has been received from the insurance company and review the related correspondence. If virtually certain, the treatment adopted is correct. If not, management should be requested to remove it from profit and receivables. If the receipt is probable, the auditor should request management include a contingent asset disclosure note.

Audit risk	Auditor's response
Unreconciled differences The bank reconciliations for May and June both contain unreconciled amounts, and the finance director believes the overall differences to be immaterial. Errors in bank reconciliations could represent large errors which net off to a small amount. If the differences are not fully reconciled, it could result in bank balances being under or overstated. Unreconciled amounts in the bank could have arisen due to fraud.	Discuss this issue with the finance director and request that the September reconciliation is fully reconciled. The reconciling items should be tested in detail and agreed to supporting documentation. Throughout the audit, the team should be alert to the risk of fraud and maintain professional scepticism.
Directors' bonus scheme A directors' bonus scheme was introduced which is based on achieving a target profit before tax. There is a risk the directors might feel under pressure to manipulate the results through the judgements taken or through the use of provisions. There is a risk of material misstatement of the financial statements in general to increase the bonus payment.	Throughout the audit, the team will need to be alert to this risk and maintain professional scepticism. Detailed review and testing on judgemental decisions, including treatment of provisions, and compare treatment against prior years. Any journal adjustments affecting profit should be tested in detail. In addition, a written representation should be obtained from management confirming the basis of any significant judgements.
Reporting timetable – detection risk The finance director has requested that the audit commence earlier than normal so that results can be reported earlier. The audit may be rushed in order to complete by the deadline. There will also be a shorter subsequent events period to obtain evidence. A reduction in the audit timetable will increase detection risk and place additional pressure on the team in obtaining sufficient and appropriate evidence.	The timetable should be confirmed with the finance director. If it is to be reduced, then consideration should be given to performing an interim audit to reduce the pressure on the final audit.

Marking guide

	Marks
(a) Changes to engagement letter	
• Entity misunderstands the objective and scope of the audit	1
• Revised or special terms of the audit	1
• Recent change of senior management/change in ownership	1
• Change in nature or size of the entity's business	1
• Change in legal or regulatory requirements	1
• Change in the financial reporting framework	1
• Change in other reporting requirements	1
Restricted to	**2**
(b) Engagement letter contents	
• Objective/scope	½
• Responsibilities of auditor	½
• Responsibilities of management	½
• Identification of framework for financial statements	½
• Form/content reports	½
• Elaboration of scope	½
• Form of communications	½
• Some misstatements may be missed	½
• Arrangement for audit	½
• Written representations required	½
• Basis of fees/billing	½
• Management acknowledge letter	½
• Internal auditor arrangements	½
• Obligations to provide working papers to others	½
• Restriction on auditor's liability	½
• Arrangements to make draft financial statements available	½
• Arrangements to inform auditors of subsequent events	½
Restricted to	**2**
(c) Understanding an entity	
• Prior year financial statements	1
• Previous auditor/access to their files	1
• Prior year report to management	1
• Accounting systems notes	1
• Discussions with management	1
• Review of board minutes	1
• Current year budgets and management accounts	1
• Company website	1
• Financial statements of competitors	1
Restricted to	**4**
(d) Audit risks and responses (only 6 risks required)	
• Depreciation rates and asset lives	2
• Adjustments for movements in inventory to the year-end date	2
• Write down of inventory	2
• Contingent asset	2
• Unreconciled differences on bank reconciliations	2
• Manipulation of profit due to directors' bonus	2
• Reporting timetable shortened	2
Max 6 issues, 2 marks each	**12**
Total	**20**

Examiner's comments

Candidates were presented with a question at this sitting based on a manufacturing company and asked to assess audit risk and responses. As noted in previous Examiner's reports; a fundamental factor in planning and assessing the risks of an audit of an entity is an assessment of audit risk, and this remains a highly examinable area. Audit risk questions typically require a number of audit risks to be identified (½ marks each), explained (½ marks each) and an auditor's response to each risk (1 mark each). Performance was mixed. It was encouraging that candidates generally identified the issues correctly from the scenario. However, candidates sometimes did not explain how each issue could impact on the audit risk and therefore were not awarded the full mark. To explain the audit risk candidates need to state for each issue if this could result in a balance being over stated, under stated, misstated, misclassified, a going concern problem or refer to a relevant assertion. In addition, many candidates misunderstood the implication of the inventory being counted before the year end and thought the problem was the lack of staff for the count as opposed to the roll forward adjustments which would be necessary. The provision of relevant auditor's responses continues to be a poorly attempted area and candidates are once again reminded to ensure that this area of the syllabus is adequately studied and practised. While an auditor's response does not have to be a detailed audit procedure, rather it should set out an approach the audit team will take to address the identified risk, the responses given were sometimes either too weak (e.g. in response to the directors' bonus being based on profits a weak response was to 'audit the profit or loss account') or, did not address the issue (e.g. in response to the un-reconciled differences on the bank reconciliation, a weak response was to 'obtain a bank confirmation') It was pleasing to note that few candidates discussed business risks. A minority of candidates however did propose, in relation to the director's bonus being based on profits, the inappropriate response that the auditor should inform management not to base bonuses on profit levels in the future.

218 SYCAMORE *Walk in the footsteps of a top tutor*

Key answer tips

Requirements (a) (c) and (d) require repetition of information from the text book – responsibilities of the auditor in respect of fraud and error, quality management and the difference between an audit and a review engagement.

In part (b) audit risks need to relate to either a risk of material misstatement or a detection risk. For risk of material misstatement, identify a balance in the scenario that is at risk of misstatement and explain why you believe it could be misstated. This is usually because the client has failed to apply the relevant accounting standard correctly. The accounting standards examinable for ACCA Financial Accounting are examinable for this exam.

Detection risks are the risks the auditor does not detect material misstatements in the financial statements e.g. when it is a new audit client or if there is a tight reporting deadline.

For the response, make sure it relates to the risk, not the balance in general. Try and be as specific as possible, simply saying more testing is required will not be sufficient. State the nature of the tests that should be performed.

(a) Fraud responsibility

Maple & Co must conduct an audit in accordance with ISA 240 *The Auditor's Responsibilities Relating to Fraud in an Audit of Financial Statements* and are responsible for obtaining reasonable assurance that the financial statements taken as a whole are free from material misstatement, whether caused by fraud or error.

In order to fulfil this responsibility, Maple & Co is required to identify and assess the risks of material misstatement of the financial statements due to fraud.

They need to obtain sufficient appropriate audit evidence regarding the assessed risks of material misstatement due to fraud, through designing and implementing appropriate responses. In addition, Maple & Co must respond appropriately to fraud or suspected fraud identified during the audit.

When obtaining reasonable assurance, Maple & Co is responsible for maintaining professional scepticism throughout the audit, considering the potential for management override of controls and recognising the fact that audit procedures which are effective in detecting error may not be effective in detecting fraud.

To ensure that the whole engagement team is aware of the risks and responsibilities for fraud and error, ISAs require that a discussion is held within the team. For members not present at the meeting, Sycamore's audit engagement partner should determine which matters are to be communicated to them.

If fraud is detected, the auditor must report this to management and those charged with governance.

(b) Audit risks and auditors' responses

Audit risks	Auditor's responses
Profit on disposal of PPE Surplus plant and equipment was sold during the year, resulting in a profit on disposal of $210,000. Significant profits or losses on disposal are an indication that the depreciation policy of plant and equipment may not be appropriate. Depreciation may be overstated as a result. In addition, as there is a minimum profit loan covenant, there is a risk that this profit on disposal may not have been correctly calculated, resulting in overstated profits.	Discuss the depreciation policy for plant and equipment with the finance director to assess its reasonableness. Recalculate the profit and loss on disposal calculations and agree all items to supporting documentation.
Finance director fraud Sycamore Co's previous finance director left in December after it was discovered that fraud had been committed with regards to expenses claimed. There is a risk that the finance director may have undertaken other fraudulent transactions; these would need to be written off in the statement of profit or loss. If these have not been uncovered, the financial statements could include errors.	Discuss with the new finance director what procedures have been adopted to identify any further frauds by the previous finance director. In addition, the team should maintain their professional scepticism and be alert to the risk of further fraud and errors.

Audit risks	Auditor's responses
Competence of finance director The new finance director was appointed in January 20X5 and was previously a financial controller of a bank. Sycamore Co is a pharmaceutical company which is very different to a bank. There is a risk that the new finance director is not sufficiently competent to prepare the financial statements. The financial statements could contain errors.	During the audit, careful attention should be applied to any changes in accounting policies and in particular any key judgemental decisions made by the finance director.
Development costs During the year, Sycamore Co has spent $1.8 million on developing new products; these are at different stages and the total amount has been capitalised as an intangible asset. In order to be capitalised it must meet all of the criteria under IAS 38 *Intangible Assets*. There is a risk that some projects may not reach final development stage and hence should be expensed rather than capitalised. Intangible assets and profit could be overstated.	A breakdown of the development expenditure should be reviewed and tested in detail to ensure that only projects which meet the capitalisation criteria are included as an intangible asset, with the balance being expensed.
New bank loan Sycamore Co has borrowed $2.0 million from the bank via a ten-year loan. There is a risk that the loan is not split between current and non-current liabilities correctly resulting in incorrect disclosure. In addition, the loan should result in additional finance costs. There is a risk that this has been omitted from the statement of profit or loss, leading to understated finance costs and overstated profit.	During the audit, the team would need to confirm that the $2.0 million loan finance was received. In addition, the split between current and non-current liabilities and the disclosures for this loan should be reviewed in detail to ensure compliance with relevant accounting standards. The finance costs should be recalculated and any increase agreed to the loan documentation for confirmation of interest rates and bank ledger account and bank statements to confirm the amount was paid and is not therefore a year-end payable.

Audit risks	**Auditor's responses**
Overdraft covenants The new loan has a minimum profit target covenant. If this is breached, the loan would be instantly repayable. There is a risk of manipulation of profit to ensure the covenant is met. There is a risk the liability is incorrectly allocated as a non-current liability rather than a current liability if the covenant is breached. If the company does not have sufficient cash to meet this repayment, then there could be going concern implications with a risk of inadequate disclosure of going concern issues.	The team should maintain their professional scepticism and be alert to the risk that profit has been overstated to ensure compliance with the covenants. Review the covenant calculations prepared by the company at the year end and identify whether any defaults have occurred. Review the disclosure of the loan as a current liability. Review cash flow forecasts and enquire of management how they will deal with any need to make the loan repayment.
Sales returns There have been a significant number of sales returns made subsequent to the year end. As these relate to pre-year-end sales, they should be removed from revenue in the draft financial statements and the inventory reinstated. If the sales returns have not been correctly recorded, then revenue will be overstated and inventory understated.	Review a sample of the post-year-end sales returns and confirm if they relate to pre-year-end sales, that the revenue has been reversed and the inventory included in the year-end ledgers. In addition, the reason for the increased level of returns should be discussed with management. This will help to assess if there are underlying issues with the net realisable value of inventory.
Outsourced payroll function During the year, Sycamore outsourced its payroll function to an external service organisation. A detection risk arises as to whether sufficient and appropriate evidence is available at Sycamore to confirm the completeness and accuracy of controls over the payroll cycle and liabilities at the year end.	Discuss with management the extent of records maintained at Sycamore for the period since the payroll function was outsourced, and any monitoring of controls which has been undertaken by management over payroll. Consideration should be given to contacting the service organisation's auditor to confirm the level of controls in place. A type 1 or type 2 report could be requested.

Audit risks	Auditor's responses
Data transfer The payroll function was transferred to the service organisation from January 20X5, which is several months prior to the year end. If any errors occurred during the transfer process, these could result in wages and salaries being under/overstated.	Discuss with management the transfer process undertaken and any controls which were put in place to ensure the completeness and accuracy of the data. Where possible, undertake tests of controls to confirm the effectiveness of the transfer controls. In addition, perform substantive testing on the transfer of information from the old to the new system.
Inventory count movements During Sycamore Co's year-end inventory count there were movements of goods in and out. If these goods in transit were not carefully controlled, then goods could have been omitted or counted twice. This would result in inventory being under or overstated.	During the final audit, the goods received notes and goods despatch notes received during the inventory count should be reviewed and followed through into the inventory count records as correctly included or not.

(c) Quality management

Briefing/direction of the team

The audit team should be informed of their responsibilities, the objectives of their work, the nature of the client's business and any other relevant information to enable them to perform their work efficiently and effectively. This will enable them to identify material misstatements and know which areas require greater attention. The audit team should also be informed of their responsibility to contribute to the quality of the audit and that threats to quality should not result in failure to perform planned procedures.

Supervision – tracking the progress of the audit

The audit supervisor should keep track of the progress of the audit in order to ensure the work is being completed on time or whether action needs to be taken such as bringing in additional staff to help complete the work or whether to agree an extended deadline with the client.

Supervision – addressing significant matters

The audit supervisor will also ensure that significant matters are being dealt with promptly. If issues are resolved as soon as they are identified the audit is more likely to be completed within the agreed timeframe.

Supervision – considering competence of team

The audit supervisor will consider the competence of the audit team and will provide additional coaching if required. Where necessary, work may need to be reassigned to a more experienced team member. The supervisor should be available for the team members to refer to in case of any queries.

Consultation

Consultation will be required where the team does not have the necessary expertise. The audit supervisor should identify any areas where consultation with an expert is required and make arrangements for such consultation whether this is referring the matter to another person within the audit firm or using an external expert.

Review of work

Each team member's work should be reviewed by someone more senior. This is to ensure the work has been to the required standard. The reviewer may identify additional work that needs to be performed before a conclusion can be drawn reducing the risk that material misstatements go undetected.

EQR

An engagement quality review will be necessary for listed clients and other high-risk clients, for example to provide an additional safeguard for clients where independence issues have been identified.

The engagement quality reviewer should be someone independent of the audit team who has no prior knowledge of the client and is able to assess the judgemental areas of the audit with an objective mind. The EQR will review the proposed audit opinion and assess whether there is sufficient appropriate evidence to support that opinion before it is issued.

Documentation

Audit work must be documented to provide evidence that the work was performed in accordance with professional standards and provides a basis for the audit opinion issued. Documentation should enable an experienced auditor to understand the nature, timing and extent of the procedures performed, the results of those procedures and any significant judgements formed. If the auditor's report is called into question at a later date, the audit documentation should be able to prove that the auditor had performed the audit to the required level of quality. Documentation therefore provides protection in the event of a negligence claim.

(d) **(i)** **Review engagements**

Review engagements are often undertaken as an alternative to an audit, and involve a practitioner reviewing financial data, such as six-monthly figures. This would involve the practitioner undertaking procedures to state whether anything has come to their attention which causes the practitioner to believe that the financial data is not in accordance with the financial reporting framework.

A review engagement differs to an external audit in that the procedures undertaken are not nearly as comprehensive as those in an audit, with procedures such as analytical review and enquiry used extensively. In addition, the practitioner does not need to comply with ISAs as these only relate to external audits.

(ii) Levels of assurance

The level of assurance provided by audit and review engagements is as follows:

External audit

This provides comfort that the financial statements present fairly in all material respects (or are true and fair) and are free of material misstatements.

A high but not absolute level of assurance is provided. This is known as reasonable assurance.

Review engagements

The practitioner gathers sufficient evidence to be satisfied that the subject matter is plausible.

In this case negative assurance is given whereby the practitioner confirms that nothing has come to their attention which indicates that the subject matter contains material misstatements.

Marking guide

		Marks
(a)	**Fraud responsibility**	
	• Reasonable assurance FS free from material misstatement, whether caused by fraud or error	1
	• Identify and assess the risks of material misstatement due to fraud	1
	• Obtain sufficient appropriate audit evidence	1
	• Respond appropriately to fraud identified during the audit	1
	• Maintain professional scepticism throughout the audit	1
	• Discussion within the engagement team	1
	• Report fraud to management and those charged with governance	1
	Restricted to	**5**
(b)	**Audit risks and responses (only 8 risks required)**	
	• Profit on disposal	
	• Fraud of previous finance director	2
	• Competence of new finance director	2
	• Treatment of capitalised development expenditure	2
	• New bank loan	2
	• Loan covenants	2
	• Post-year-end sales returns	2
	• Use of payroll service organisation	2
	• Transfer of data to service organisation	2
	• Goods in and out during the inventory count	2
		2
	Max 8 issues, 2 marks each	**16**
(c)	**Quality management**	
	• Briefing/direction of the team	1
	• Supervision – tracking the progress of the audit	1
	• Supervision – addressing significant matters	1
	• Supervision – considering competence of team	1
	• Consultation	1
	• Review of work	1
	• EQR	1
	• Documentation	1
	Restricted to	**5**

(d)	(i)	**Purpose of review engagements and difference from an audit**	
		• Description of review engagements	1
		• Difference to external audit	1
			2
	(ii)	**Level of assurance provided by audit and reviews**	
		• Level of assurance of external audit	1
		• Level of assurance of review engagements	1
			2
Total			**30**

Examiner's comments

Part (a) required an explanation of auditor's responsibilities in relation to the prevention and detection of fraud and error. This question was answered unsatisfactorily and candidates need to be better prepared to tackle questions on core auditor responsibilities. The question required candidates to discuss the auditor's responsibilities in this area; it did not require an explanation of directors' responsibilities. Unfortunately, many candidates wasted time providing this and there were no marks available for this. In addition, some answers strayed into providing procedures for detecting fraud and error rather than just addressing responsibilities. Candidates are again reminded to read the question carefully and to ensure that they are answering the question that has been set. The majority of candidates were able to gain marks for reporting fraud to management or those charged with governance, for the auditors' general responsibility to detect material misstatements caused by fraud or error or that the auditors are not responsible for preventing fraud or error.

Part (b) required an identification and description of audit risks from the scenario and the relevant auditor's response for each. Performance on this question was mixed and performance in relation to this core area of the syllabus remains overall disappointing. Candidates who scored well in this question went on to describe how the point identified from the scenario was an audit risk by referring to the assertion and the account balance impacted. As in previous diets, a significant number of candidates tended to only identify facts from the scenario such as 'the previous finance director had been claiming fraudulent expenses from the company' but failed to describe how this results in an audit risk, thus limiting the marks that can be scored to ½ marks. To gain the full 1 mark candidates needed to refer to the risk of other fraudulent expenses being claimed resulting in an impact on profit, as the financial statement impact must be referred to. Only by connecting the fact from the scenario to the relevant assertion and area of the financial statements will the candidate have adequately explained the audit risk. Unfortunately many candidates yet again focused on business risks rather than audit risks, and explained the risk in terms of the impact on Sycamore rather than the financial statements risk and hence how it affects the auditor. As in previous sittings, many candidates performed poorly with regards to the auditor's responses. Many candidates gave business advice, such as undertaking quality control procedures over inventory to prevent the increased level of sales returns. In addition a significant proportion of candidates failed to appreciate that the inventory count had already occurred, hence auditor responses focused on procedures to adopt at the count were not relevant in the circumstances. Audit responses need to be practical and should relate to the approach (i.e. what testing) the auditor will adopt to assess whether the balance is materially misstated or not. Once again this was due to a failure to read the scenario carefully. Candidates should read the questions carefully and plan an appropriate response. Future candidates must take note audit risk is and will continue to be an important element of the syllabus and must be understood, and they would benefit from practising audit risk questions.

Part (d) (i) required an explanation of the purpose of review engagements and how they differed to an external audit and (d) (ii) tested the levels of assurance for audits and review engagements. Overall this question was answered unsatisfactorily. Few candidates were able to explain the purpose of a review engagement and many candidates failed to score any marks for (d) (i). Where the question was attempted many candidates repeated points that were then given in (d) (ii). Candidates performed better in (d) (ii) and many produced clear and concise answers which addressed the levels of assurance for each specified type of engagements. A minority of candidates however just referred to positive and negative assurance without linking them back to the two types of engagements.

219 RECORDER COMMUNICATIONS *Walk in the footsteps of a top tutor*

Key answer tips

Part (a) is a straightforward knowledge question. Notice that the question asks for the benefits of planning. Answers which just state what activities are performed at the planning stage will not score marks. As planning is the most important stage of the process, students should be aware of the reasons why it is important to plan the audit.

In part (b) audit risks need to relate to either a risk of material misstatement or a detection risk. For risk of material misstatement, identify a balance in the scenario that is at risk of misstatement and explain why you believe it could be misstated. This is usually because the client has failed to apply the relevant accounting standard correctly. Detection risks are the risks the auditor does not detect material misstatements in the financial statements e.g. when it is a new audit client or if there is a tight reporting deadline. For the response, make sure it relates to the risk, not the balance in general. Try and be as specific as possible, simply saying more testing is required will not be sufficient. State the nature of the tests that should be performed.

Parts (c) and (d) require procedures over two very specific areas. Make sure you give specific answers that address the requirement.

Part (e) asks for the auditor's responsibilities to consider laws and regulations during the audit. This requires knowledge of the relevant auditing standard, ISA 250 *Consideration of Laws and Regulations in an Audit of Financial Statements.*

(a) Benefits of audit planning

- It helps the auditor to devote appropriate attention to important areas of the audit.
- It helps the auditor to identify and resolve potential problems on a timely basis.
- It helps the auditor to properly organise and manage the audit engagement so that it is performed in an effective and efficient manner.
- It assists in the selection of engagement team members with appropriate levels of capabilities and competence to respond to anticipated risks and the proper assignment of work to them.

- It facilitates the direction and supervision of engagement team members and the review of their work.
- It assists, where applicable, in the coordination of work done by experts.

(b) Audit risks and responses

Audit risk	Auditor's response
New audit client Recorder Communications Co (Recorder) is a new client for Piano & Co. As the team is not so familiar with the accounting policies, transactions and balances of Recorder, there will be an increased detection risk on the audit.	Piano & Co should ensure a suitably experienced team is assigned. Also, adequate time should be allocated for team members to obtain an understanding of the company and the risks of material misstatement.
Purchases cut-off Recorder purchases goods from South Asia and the goods are in transit for two weeks. Therefore, at the year end only goods which have been received into the warehouse should be included in the inventory balance and a respective payables balance recognised. At the year end there is a risk that the cut-off of inventory, purchases and payables may not be accurate.	The audit team should undertake detailed cut-off testing of goods in transit from the suppliers in South Asia to ensure that the cut-off is complete and accurate.
Perpetual inventory counts The company undertakes continuous (perpetual) inventory counts at its central warehouse. Under such a system all inventory must be counted at least once a year with adjustments made to the inventory records. Inventory could be under or overstated if the continuous (perpetual) inventory counts are not complete and the inventory records accurately updated for adjustments.	The completeness of the continuous (perpetual) inventory counts should be reviewed. In addition, the level of adjustments made to inventory should be considered to assess whether reliance on the inventory records at the year end will be acceptable.
Inventory valuation A number of older models of mobile phones are included within inventory which will be sold at a significantly discount. Inventory will be overstated if these have not been written down to the lower of cost and net realisable value.	Review the aged inventory listing to identify items which need to be discounted and compare with the inventory allowance made, if any. Perform detailed NRV and cost testing to ensure the old items are valued appropriately.

Audit risk	Auditor's response
Sales-related bonus A sales-related bonus scheme has been introduced in the year. This may lead to sales cut-off errors with employees aiming to maximise their current year bonus, or fictitious sales being created meaning some of the customers signed up for contracts may not actually exist. Revenue and receivables could be overstated as a result.	Increased sales cut-off testing will be performed along with a review of any post-year-end cancellations of contracts as they may indicate cut-off errors. External confirmation of receivables to confirm that customers exist and represent valid amounts due.
Receivables valuation Receivables are considerably higher than the prior year and there are concerns about the creditworthiness of some customers. There is a risk that some receivables may be overvalued if they are not recoverable and adequate allowance for credit losses is not made.	Extended post-year-end cash receipts testing and a review of the aged list of individual customer balances to be performed to assess valuation. Also consider the adequacy of any allowance for credit losses/ receivables.
Revaluation of property Recorder has a policy of revaluing its land and buildings and these valuations have been updated during the year. Property, plant and equipment could be under or overvalued if the recent valuation has not been carried out in accordance with IAS 16 *Property, Plant and Equipment* and adequate disclosures may not have been made in the financial statements.	Discuss with management the process adopted for undertaking the valuation, including whether the whole class of assets was revalued and if the valuation was undertaken by an expert. This process should be reviewed for compliance with IAS 16. Review the disclosures of the revaluation in the financial statements for compliance with IAS 16.
Directors' bonus remuneration The directors have each been paid a significant bonus and separate disclosure of this in the financial statements is required by local legislation. The directors' remuneration disclosure will not be complete and accurate if the bonus paid is not disclosed in accordance with the relevant local legislation.	Discuss this matter with management and review the disclosure in the financial statements to ensure compliance with local legislation.

(c) Audit procedures for continuous (perpetual) inventory counts

- Attend at least one of the continuous (perpetual) inventory counts to review whether the controls over the inventory count are adequate.
- Confirm that all of the inventory lines have been counted or are due to be counted at least once a year by reviewing the schedules of counts undertaken/due to be undertaken.
- Review the adjustments made to the inventory records on a monthly basis to gain an understanding of the level of differences arising on a month by month basis.
- Discuss with management how they will ensure that year-end inventory will not be under or overstated. If significant differences consistently arise, this could indicate that the inventory records are not adequately maintained.
- Consider attending the inventory count at the year end to undertake test counts of inventory from records to floor and from floor to records in order to confirm the existence and completeness of inventory.

(d) Substantive procedures for directors' bonus and remuneration

- Obtain a schedule of the directors' remuneration including the bonus paid and cast the addition of the schedule to confirm arithmetical accuracy.
- Agree the individual bonus payments to the payroll records.
- Inspect the bank ledger account and bank statements to confirm the amount of each bonus paid.
- Review the board minutes to confirm whether any additional bonus payments relating to this year have been agreed.
- Obtain a written representation from management confirming the completeness of directors' remuneration including the bonus.
- Review any disclosures made of the bonus and assess whether these are in compliance with local legislation.

(e) Auditor responsibilities in relation to laws and regulations

- The auditor must perform audit procedures to help identify non-compliance with laws and regulations that may have a material impact on the financial statements.
- The auditor must obtain sufficient, appropriate evidence regarding compliance with laws and regulations that have a direct effect on the financial statements e.g. the requirement to separately disclose directors' bonuses.
- The auditor must perform audit procedures to help identify non-compliance with other laws and regulations that may have a material impact on the financial statements.
- Where the auditor becomes aware of non-compliance with laws and regulations they must obtain an understanding of the act and circumstances in which it occurred and evaluate the effect on the financial statements.
- The auditor must report non-compliance to management and those charged with governance.

- If the non-compliance has a material effect on the financial statements, the auditor must modify the audit opinion with a qualified or adverse opinion.
- The auditor must consider whether they have any legal or ethical responsibility to report non-compliance to third parties.

Marking guide

		Marks
(a)	**Importance of planning**	
	• Important areas of the audit	1
	• Identify potential problems	1
	• Effective and efficient audit	1
	• Selection of engagement team members and assignment of work	1
	• Direction, supervision and review	1
	• Coordination of work	1
	Maximum	**5**
(b)	**Audit risks and responses (only 7 risks required)**	
	• New client leading to increased detection risk	2
	• Cut-off of goods in transit	2
	• Continuous (perpetual) inventory counts	2
	• Inventory valuation	2
	• Sales related bonus – overstatement of revenue and receivables	2
	• Receivables – overvaluation	2
	• Valuation of land and buildings	2
	• Directors' bonus remuneration	2
	Max 7 issues, 2 marks each	**14**
(c)	**Perpetual inventory count procedures**	
	• Attend one of the continuous (perpetual) inventory counts to review whether the controls are adequate	1
	• Review the schedule of counts to confirm completeness of all inventory lines	1
	• Review the adjustments made to the inventory records	1
	• If significant differences, discuss with management how they will ensure that year-end inventory will not be under or overstated	1
	• Attend the inventory count at the year end to undertake test counts to confirm the completeness and existence of inventory	1
	Maximum	**3**
(d)	**Substantive procedures**	
	• Cast schedule of directors' remuneration including the bonus paid	1
	• Agree the individual bonus payments to the payroll records	1
	• Agree bonus paid to the bank ledger account and bank statements	1
	• Review the board minutes to confirm any additional bonus payments	1
	• Obtain written representation from management	1
	• Review disclosures to assess compliance with local legislation	1
	Maximum	**4**

(e)	**Auditor responsibilities in relation to laws and regulations**	
	• Identify non-compliance that has a material effect on the financial statements	1
	• Obtain sufficient, appropriate evidence regarding compliance with laws and regulations that have a direct effect on the financial statements	1
	• Perform audit procedures to help identify non-compliance with other laws and regulations	1
	• Understand the act and circumstances in which the non-compliance occurred and evaluate the effect on the financial statements	1
	• Report non-compliance to management and those charged with governance	1
	• If the non-compliance is material, modify the audit opinion	1
	• Consider whether there is any legal or ethical responsibility to report non-compliance to third parties	1
	Maximum	**4**
Total		**30**

Examiner's comments

Part (a) required candidates to explain the importance of audit planning. Candidates' performance was satisfactory on this question. Many candidates were able to confidently identify that planning resulted in sufficient attention being devoted to important areas/audit risks, selection of an appropriate audit team, an efficient and effective audit and resolution of issues in a timely manner. Where candidates did not score enough marks to pass, this tended to be because they focused on the contents of an audit strategy and plan, which was not the specific focus of the question. Often candidates identified the procedures which would be considered prior to planning, such as confirming the independence of auditors or used to obtain an understanding of the entity resulting in some candidates focusing on what was done at the planning stage rather than explaining the importance of planning.

Part (b) required identification and description of audit risks from the scenario and the auditor's response for each. Performance on this question was mixed. The scenario contained significantly more than the number of risks required and so candidates were able to easily identify enough risks, and strong answers went on to describe how the point identified from the scenario was an audit risk by referring to the assertion and the account balance impacted. As in previous diets, some candidates tended to only identify facts from the scenario such as 'Recorder purchases goods from a supplier in South Asia and the goods are in transit for two weeks' but failed to describe how this could impact audit risk; this would only have scored ½ marks. To gain 1 mark the point needed to be developed to also explain that this could result in issues over the completeness of inventory. More so than in previous diets, candidates disappointingly provided business risks rather than audit risks with answers such as stock outs due to the two-week transit period and possible damage to inventory during transit. As a result, these candidates then provided responses related to how management should address these business risks rather than how the auditor should respond. This meant that out of a potential 2 marks per risk, candidates would only score ½ marks for the identification of the issue from the scenario. Some candidates also identified irrelevant risks such as Recorder undertaking continuous inventory counts. While an audit risk was present around inventory in relation to the effectiveness of the perpetual inventory system, very few candidates explained the risk in this manner instead focusing on the lack of a full year-end count. This demonstrated a lack of understanding of continuous inventory counts. Additionally, many candidates performed poorly with regards to the auditor's responses. Many candidates gave business advice, such as changing the salesmen's bonus structure or provided vague responses such as perform detailed substantive testing or maintain professional scepticism. Responses which start with 'ensure that......' are unlikely to score marks as they usually fail to explain exactly how the auditor will address the audit risk. Audit responses need to be practical and should relate to the approach (i.e. what testing) the auditor will adopt to assess whether the balance is materially misstated or not. Most candidates presented their answers well, adopting a two-column approach with audit risk in one column and the related response next to it. This helps candidates to ensure that for every risk identified there is a related response and candidates are encouraged to continue to use this approach where appropriate.

Part (c) required procedures the auditor should perform in order to place reliance on the continuous counts for inventory. Candidates' performance was disappointing. Many candidates provided lengthy answers on procedures to be carried out when attending a year-end inventory count or procedures to verify valuation or completeness/existence of inventory, suggesting that a significant proportion of candidates do not understand continuous inventory counts, the risks associated with this and therefore the areas the auditor needs to focus on. A small proportion of candidates correctly identified that it was important to confirm if all inventory items were counted at least once a year and also to assess the level of adjustments made during these counts. Inventory is a key element of the financial statements and candidates need to be able to provide relevant procedures for both full year-end counts as well as continuous counting.

Part (d) required substantive procedures for confirming the directors' bonus payment made during the year. Candidates' performance was disappointing. Unfortunately, many candidates focused on the authorisation of the bonus; this is not a substantive procedure and would not have scored any marks. A significant minority thought that the directors' bonus was based on sales which was not the case. The scenario stated that salesmen's bonuses were based on sales, hence candidates either confused these two items or failed to read the scenario properly. They then looked to recalculate the bonus based on sales levels which was not appropriate in the circumstances. A number of vague procedures were suggested such as obtaining written representations or reading board minutes without explaining what for. Analytical procedures were suggested; however, they were unlikely to be valid procedures as bonuses by their nature tend to vary each year.

INTERNAL CONTROLS

220 SILVER CO *Walk in the footsteps of a top tutor*

Key answer tips

Part (a) This is a knowledge-based requirement to describe four matters the auditor should consider in determining whether a deficiency in internal controls is weak. Elements of audit theory, not related to the question scenario, are frequently examined, so ensure that you understand the theory as well as the practical aspects of auditing. Ensure also that you provide sufficient description/narrative to enable the examiner to award marks.

Part (b) This is a big requirement, so ensure that you work methodically though the question scenario to identify deficiencies in the inventory count arrangements. Having identified a deficiency, explain why it is a deficiency and then state a control recommendation to deal with the deficiency. Here, a tabular presentation of your answer helps to provide structure and focus.

(a) Significant deficiencies

ISA 265 *Communicating Deficiencies in Internal Control to Those Charged with Governance and Management* details the matters the external auditor should consider in determining whether a deficiency in internal controls is significant including:

- The likelihood of the deficiencies leading to material misstatements in the financial statements in the future.
- The susceptibility to loss or fraud of the related asset or liability.
- The subjectivity and complexity of determining estimated amounts.
- The financial statement amounts exposed to the deficiencies.
- The volume of activity which has occurred or could occur in the account balance or class of transactions exposed to the deficiency or deficiencies.
- The importance of the controls to the financial reporting process.
- The cause and frequency of the exceptions detected as a result of the deficiencies in the controls.
- The interaction of the deficiency with other deficiencies in internal control.

(b) Deficiencies and recommendations

Control deficiency	Control recommendation
Movements of goods in and out of the company's factory and warehouse are being made on the day of the inventory count. While production cannot stop, there is a risk that the inventory count will be incorrect if there are movements of goods during the count which are not adequately controlled. Goods could be included in the count when they should not be, resulting in double counting or omitted from the count when they should be included.	Any raw materials likely to be needed on 30 September 20X5 should be estimated and set aside and included within the work in progress valuation. The company should try to minimise planned dispatches for the day of the count. Goods to be dispatched to customers should be set aside so that they can be excluded from inventory. Raw materials received from suppliers and finished goods received from the factory should be delivered to a different part of the warehouse and counted separately for inclusion as part of raw materials or finished goods at the end of the count.
The count is to be undertaken by 20 teams from the warehouse and will be overseen by the warehouse supervisor. While warehouse staff will be familiar with the inventory of the company, this represents a lack of segregation of duties as they are not independent and hence could deliberately conceal fraud and/or error.	There should be a different department involved in the inventory count to ensure adequate segregation of roles. For example, the teams could be comprised of one counter from the warehouse and one from finance. In addition, the count should not be overseen by the warehouse supervisor. Instead, a responsible official such as the financial controller should oversee the count.
The inventory sheets detail the quantities held at the date of the count. If quantities are contained on the inventory sheets, counters may not undertake a full physical count of the inventory on hand, instead relying on the pre-populated numbers. This could result in over or understated inventory quantities.	The inventory count sheets should not contain details of quantities but should instead only include product codes. This should ensure that counters physically count the inventory and record the actual quantities on hand on the inventory count sheets.
There are 20 teams comprising of two individuals and there is no clear or defined division of responsibilities within the team. As a consequence, both members of the team could be counting, instead of one counting and one recording. There is a risk that errors or omissions may go unnoticed.	The roles of the team members should be defined in the count instructions and split so that one individual is responsible for counting and one for recording the results. In addition, for each team, test counts should be carried out by the count supervisor to ensure that each team is counting effectively.

Control deficiency	**Control recommendation**
When an area has been counted, it is marked off on the warehouse map in the office rather than marking the warehouse bays as counted. There is a risk that if the map is not updated properly, a warehouse bay could be omitted or double-counted resulting in incorrect inventory quantities being recorded.	All warehouse bays which have been counted should be physically marked as such so that it is not missed or double-counted. All warehouse bays should be inspected at the end of the count to ensure that all areas/items have been marked to ensure the completeness of the count.
Inventory is only being counted by one counting team. When the inventory count is then compared to the book quantities, it will be difficult to ascertain whether differences are due to counting errors or are genuine adjustments, resulting in errors in the final inventory valuation.	Once the first count has been completed, a second count should be undertaken by a team who did not perform the first count. Any differences on the first count should be notified to the count supervisor and a third count undertaken if necessary. Sample checks should be carried out by the count supervisor to ensure that items are being counted properly.
There is a large quantity of spare parts which are not being counted on the grounds that they are unusable. All items in the warehouse should be counted irrespective of whether they are old, damaged or obsolete as otherwise there is a risk that inventory is understated. Furthermore, if these items are not counted and included on the inventory sheets, there is a risk that items could be misappropriated.	This area of the warehouse should be included on the count sheets and warehouse map and included in the count to ensure that all items are counted. If the items are potentially obsolete, this should be flagged on the inventory count sheets to allow consideration of their subsequent valuation by the finance team following the count.
Completed inventory sheets are passed to the warehouse assistant for an immediate update to the inventory records. There does not appear to be any investigation into differences between physical inventory and the inventory records prior to the adjustment being made. Significant variations could be an indication of fraud or inaccuracies in the recording of inventory which could result in under or overstated inventory.	All differences should be investigated to establish whether the inventory records are incorrect, or the count has been inaccurate. Once the investigation is completed, only then should the inventory records be amended.

Control deficiency	**Control recommendation**
The warehouse supervisor is going to undertake the valuation of work in progress at the year end which has previously been carried out by an expert. The warehouse supervisor is familiar with the company's products, but may not have the necessary expertise to determine the stage of completion of different products, resulting in mistakes and inventory being over or understated.	A specialist should continue to be used to value the work in progress at the year end and the basis for the valuation should be agreed with the specialist to ensure it is appropriate. If the company no longer wishes to use a specialist this year, the warehouse supervisor could perform the valuation and have the specialist check the valuation.
The company has 30 sofas in its warehouse which belong to a third party and they are to be stored alongside similar products to Silver Co. If these sofas are not segregated from Silver Co's own inventory, they may be counted and included in the inventory valuation resulting in overstated inventory.	The sofas belonging to the third party should be separated from the inventory of Silver Co and clearly marked to avoid them being included in the count and the final inventory valuation.

ACCA marking guide

		Marks
(a)	Significant deficiencies	
	1 mark per well-described point	
	Restricted to	4
(b)	Deficiencies and recommendations	
	Movement of goods	2
	Count teams	2
	Sheets include quantity	2
	Division of responsibilities	2
	Counted areas	2
	One team	2
	Spare parts excluded	2
	No investigation of differences	2
	WIP valuation	2
	Third party sofas	2
	Other	2
	Maximum 8 issues, 2 marks each	16
Total		**20**

Examiner's comments

Requirement (a)

This is a knowledge requirement and has been tested in previous exam sessions. Some knowledge requirements, such as this one, have an opening statement, sometimes referenced to an ISA, and this is useful for setting the scene and providing clarification on the aim of the question requirement. Question requirements such as this demonstrate the importance of having a detailed understanding of the ISAs, and in this case ISA 265 *Communicating Deficiencies in Internal Control to Those Charged with Governance and Management*.

It is important that candidates understand exactly what the question is asking, especially for knowledge questions, where they should be aiming to score full marks. It is also important that candidates note that they do not need to use the scenario to answer this requirement.

For this session candidates were required to describe matters in determining whether a deficiency is significant for 4 marks. As the requirement verb was 'describe', candidates need to ensure that they include sufficient detail in their answers. Simply providing a few words such as 'materiality of deficiency' is not enough for a description. Candidates therefore need to consider whether they have written enough.

Commonly awarded points included complexity of deficiencies and frequency of deficiencies. However, these points would only gain ½ mark as they are too brief. To gain the additional ½ mark, candidates need to consider the complexity when determining estimates and the frequency of exceptions identified as a result of the deficiencies.

It is also important that candidates pay attention to any elements of the requirement which are highlighted. In this session the word FOUR was in capitals. This was specifically done to focus candidates' answers, so that they would know to provide four well described answers. Additionally, there was a note under the requirement which stressed that the scenario did not need to be referred to in answering this requirement. Notes and capitalisation of words in requirements are there to guide candidates and to help, candidates should be careful not to ignore them.

It is imperative that future candidates ensure that they devote adequate time to learning the knowledge areas of the syllabus as well as practising knowledge questions.

Requirement (b)

Marks are awarded for identification of deficiencies (½ mark each), explanation of the implication of the deficiency to the company (½ mark each) and an appropriate control recommendation to address each deficiency (1 mark each).

The first step in tackling a deficiencies question is to read through the scenario in full, this gives an understanding of what the potential answer points are as some deficiencies are easier to explain than others. Having looked at the whole scenario, candidates should reread it, drafting their answer as they go along. Do not be daunted by the length of the scenario, be methodical and keep re-reading the requirement to stay focused.

In identifying deficiencies, it is important to record what the actual deficiency from the scenario is. Candidates can pick the fact from the scenario but fail to spot what the actual deficiency is. For example, in this session some candidates stated that 'the company manufactures goods 24 hours a day, seven days a week'. This is not a deficiency. When copying and pasting facts from the scenario, care must be taken to identify a relevant deficiency. It was pleasing to see that candidates did not identify as many irrelevant deficiencies as has been seen in other sessions.

The least commonly provided deficiency related to inventory records being updated without investigation of any count differences. To gain the ID marks for the warehouse supervisor valuing the work in progress (WIP) deficiency, it was important to note that the issue related WIP. Some candidates simply stated the warehouse supervisor has suggested undertaking this valuation this year, without linking this to WIP. No credit was given for this.

Having identified deficiencies, candidates are required to explain the implication to the business to be awarded credit. For example, a valid explanation for the deficiency 'the count is overseen by the warehouse supervisor' (identification ½ mark awarded), would have been 'the warehouse supervisor is not independent and so may conceal errors or potential fraud.' Answers which just stated 'the supervisor is not independent' would not have gained credit as it does not explain how a lack of independence will impact the business.

The explanation needs to be specific to each deficiency, as it is not sufficient to state 'this will result in fraud/error' as all deficiencies can lead to increased fraud and error. A clear understanding of how the deficiency will result in fraud and error is needed. Also, it was apparent that some deficiencies were misunderstood by candidates. For the deficiency 'inventory records are updated without investigation of count difference' candidates incorrectly explained that the warehouse assistant who updated the records was too junior to undertake this role and therefore recommended that someone more senior do this. No credit was given for this explanation or the recommendation as the seniority of the individual updating the records was not what the deficiency related to.

The next part of the requirement is for candidates to describe control recommendations. To gain the 1 mark available it is imperative that the descriptions of the recommendations are detailed enough. Additionally, recommendations must be actions rather than just objectives, recommendations which are phrased as 'ensure that....' are unlikely to gain much credit.

Candidates need to take care to ensure that recommendations are well described, clearly address the specific control deficiency identified and are practical suggestions. For the deficiency relating to movements of goods in/out of the warehouse during the count, many candidates incorrectly recommended that the company should stop all movements of goods during the count, despite the scenario clearly stating that movements would need to continue for operational reasons. Candidates must read the scenario carefully when making recommendations.

It is important that recommendations are as complete as possible. For the deficiency of 'no clear division of responsibilities within the team', the recommendation of 'responsibilities should be allocated within the team' would not gain any credit, as they have not said HOW these responsibilities should be allocated. The recommendation needs to state that 'one team member should count and the other record the quantities' to gain the available 1 mark.

221 PETRA *Walk in the footsteps of a top tutor*

Key answer tips

Part (a) requires control objectives of a sales system. A control objective focuses the reason for a control procedure being required, i.e. a risk that needs to be mitigated. One way to generate ideas is to think about the assertions that need to be confirmed e.g. transactions should be completely recorded, recorded in the correct accounting period, recorded accurately. However, this needs to be broken down into the stages of a transaction such as order, dispatch, invoicing, recording.

Part (b) asks for direct controls and tests of controls relating to the scenario. A direct control is one which will reduce the risk of material misstatement. Make sure the controls are direct as companies will have many controls in place but not all of them will be direct.

Part (c) the looks at the opposite side of controls and asks for deficiencies and recommendations. Here you need to explain the deficiencies and why the company should want to overcome them, therefore they should be explained as risks to the business that could have negative consequences such as reduced cash flow/profit/revenue. The recommendation should focus on what the company can do to overcome the deficiency. Try and be as specific as possible. Sometimes control recommendations need more than one part to be complete so you will need to give both parts in order to score the mark.

Part (d) requires substantive procedures over purchases and other expenses. Substantive procedures are procedures designed to detect misstatements in a balance as opposed to tests of controls. Think about how you can obtain evidence over the accuracy, occurrence, completeness, cut-off and classification of the transactions. Make sure the procedures you give explain how the evidence will be obtained and the objective of the procedure. Also remember that substantive procedures include analytical procedures as well as tests of detail, so simple comparisons between current year and prior year will score marks.

Part (e) looks at a different syllabus area of corporate governance. The requirement asks for corporate governance deficiencies and recommendations so it is a similar question to part (c) but focusing on how the company is directed and controlled by those charged with governance. This requires knowledge and understanding of the corporate governance code. Make sure you explain how the company does not comply with the code and why this is a potential issue. When giving a recommendation, make sure you are as detailed as possible.

(a) Control objectives of a sales system

- To ensure that orders are only accepted if goods are available to be processed for customers.
- To ensure that all orders are recorded completely and accurately.
- To ensure that goods are not supplied to customers who are poor credit risks.
- To ensure that goods are dispatched for all orders on a timely basis.
- To ensure that only genuine sales supported by a valid order are recognised in revenue.

- To ensure that the correct quantity of goods is dispatched and they are of an adequate quality.
- To ensure that all goods dispatched are correctly invoiced at authorised prices.
- To ensure that all invoices raised are recorded as revenue in the correct accounting period.
- To ensure that sales discounts are only provided up to an agreed limit.
- To ensure that all sales and related receivables are recorded at an appropriate amount in the correct accounts.
- To ensure that cash received is allocated against the correct customer and invoices to prevent disputes.
- To ensure that overdue receivables are followed up on a timely basis.
- To ensure that irrecoverable receivables are identified and written off appropriately.

(b) Direct controls and tests of controls

Direct control	**Test of control**
Supervision clock card Factory staff are issued with clock cards which they are required to swipe to enter and exit the factory and this process is supervised by security staff. This ensures that genuine employees are only paid for the work actually done and reduces the risk of employees being paid but not completing their required hours. In addition, due to the supervision it is unlikely that one employee could fraudulently clock-in on behalf of other employees	Observe the use of clock cards by employees when entering and exiting the factory and confirm that security staff are supervising the process.
Gross to net checks The payroll supervisor selects a sample of payslips, recalculates the gross to net pay calculations and compares their results to the output from the payroll system and investigates any discrepancies. This reduces the risk that the automated system generates errors during the payroll processing. Any errors would be identified on a timely basis to prevent wages being over or underpaid.	Review the weekly payslips sampled by the payroll supervisor for evidence of a signature to confirm that the review of calculations has been undertaken. For a sample of weekly payrolls, reperform the gross to net pay calculation and compare to the payroll system. Discuss any discrepancies with the payroll supervisor. Enquire of the payroll supervisor whether any discrepancies have been noted during the year between the gross to net pay calculations and the figures generated by the payroll system and how these were resolved.

Direct control	**Test of control**
Revised rates Revised pay rates for factory staff are input by a clerk into the payroll system. Each entry is checked by a senior clerk for input errors prior to processing and their review is evidenced via signature of the listing. This reduces the risk of input errors resulting in over/underpayment of wages and salaries to employees.	Obtain the payroll listing for the factory staff used for the pay rate increase and review for evidence of signature by the senior clerk who checks for input errors.
Segregation of duties The pay packets are prepared by two staff members using system generated payslips with one staff member preparing and one checking the pay packets. This is evidenced by each staff member signing the weekly listing. This ensures there is segregation of duties and reduces the likelihood of errors or staff members fraudulently increasing the pay packets for friends and family member without being identified.	Observe the preparation of the pay packets, ensuring that one member prepares the wages using the system generated payslips and that the second member checks pay packets for accuracy. For a sample of weeks throughout the year, inspect the weekly payroll listing for evidence of signature by two members of staff involved in the preparation of the pay packets.

(c) Control deficiencies and recommendations

Control deficiency	**Control recommendation**
Credit limits A credit check is performed on all new customers, after which a credit limit is set by the finance director, and these limits remain unchanged unless the customer requests an increase. If credit limits are not reviewed regularly, they could be out of date, resulting in limits being too high and therefore sales being made to poor credit risks or, alternatively, too low and therefore Petra Co losing potential revenue.	Credit limits should continue to be set by the finance director, however, these limits should be reviewed on a regular basis and amended as appropriate by a responsible official.

Control deficiency	**Control recommendation**
No copy of sales order kept by sales department Customer orders are recorded on a pre-printed three-part form. No copy of the order form is sent to the sales department of Petra Co and hence they would not be able to monitor if orders are being fulfilled on a timely basis. If orders are not fulfilled on a timely basis, this would reduce customer goodwill.	The sales order form should be amended to become four-part, with the fourth copy being sent to the sales department. Upon dispatch, the goods dispatch note should be matched to the order. A regular review of unmatched orders should be undertaken by the sales department to identify any unfulfilled orders.
Discounts not reviewed Sales staff have discretion to grant sales discounts to customers of up to 8% but discounts granted are not reviewed. This could result in unauthorised discounts in excess of 8% being allowed and a loss of revenue as they may award unrealistic discounts simply to meet sales targets.	All discounts to be granted to customers should be authorised in advance by a responsible official, such as the sales director. If this is not practical, then the supervisor of the sales staff should undertake this role. A copy of the authorisation should be sent to the sales department and the customer's master file data amended for discounts allowed by a responsible official. The master file data system should be amended to prohibit discounts in excess of 8% being entered. On a regular basis, the sales director should undertake a review of discount levels granted on sales orders and ensure they are in line with authorised levels.
Master data access Access to the master file data for suppliers is available to all those in the purchasing department who are able to make changes. As all members of the purchasing department can make changes to data and therefore add new suppliers to the payables ledger system, this increases the risk of fraud and payments being made to fictitious suppliers.	Amendments to master file data should be restricted so that only authorised members of the department are able to make changes. In addition, a log of changes to master file data, including details of which staff member made the change, should be produced and reviewed by a responsible official on a regular basis and signed as evidence of their review.

Control deficiency	**Control recommendation**
No GRN to finance GRNs and orders are matched and filed in the warehouse and the finance department does not receive a copy. Therefore, on receipt of purchase invoices, they are not being agreed to the relevant GRNs and orders prior to input into the payables ledger. This could result in invoices being paid for goods which were not received or ordered.	A copy of the GRN should be provided on a timely basis to the finance department. On receipt, all purchase invoices should be matched to the related GRN and purchase order and this should be undertaken prior to the invoice being logged in the payables ledger.
Document count controls A payables ledger clerk only utilises document count controls when inputting invoices into the payables ledger. Document count controls can confirm the completeness of input. However, they do not verify the accuracy or validity of input. If the invoices are not input correctly, suppliers may not be paid on time or may be paid incorrect amounts. This could lead to a loss of supplier goodwill or suppliers withdrawing credit facilities.	The payables ledger clerk should instead input the invoices in batches and apply information processing controls, such as control totals, rather than just completeness checks to ensure both completeness and accuracy over the input of purchase invoices. In addition, sequence checks should be built into the system to ensure completeness of input.

(d) Substantive procedures for purchases and other expenses

- Calculate the operating profit and gross profit margin and compare to the prior year and to budget and investigate any significant differences.
- Review monthly purchases and other expenses to identify any significant fluctuations and discuss with management.
- Review the annual purchases and other expenses on a line-by-line basis, compare to the prior year and investigate any significant differences.
- Recalculate the accuracy of a sample of purchase invoice totals and related taxes and confirm that the expense has been correctly included in the general ledger.
- Recalculate the year-end prepayments and accruals to ensure the accuracy of the expense charge included in the profit or loss.
- Select a sample of post-year-end expense invoices and ensure that any expenses relating to the current year have been accrued.
- Select a sample of expense payments from the bank ledger/cash book and trace to the relevant expense account in the general ledger to ensure the expense has been included and classified correctly.

- Select a sample of goods received notes (GRNs) from throughout the year. Agree them to purchase invoices and the detailed purchase listing to ensure the completeness of purchases.
- Select a sample of GRNs immediately before and after the year end. Agree to the detailed purchase listing to ensure the expense is recorded in the correct accounting period.

(e) Corporate governance deficiencies and recommendations

Deficiency	**Recommendation**
Marketing director as Chair It is proposed that the current marketing director be appointed as the Chair of the company when the current Chair retires. As a former executive director, this director has been previously recently employed by the company and so will not be independent on appointment as advised by corporate governance principles. A lack of independence may result in the Chair not bringing the necessary level of independence and objective judgement to the role.	The Chair of Petra Co should be independent on appointment and hence the marketing director should not be appointed as Chair, as they have been an employee within the last five years and therefore not considered independent. An individual who is fully independent of Petra Co should be appointed to the role of Chair when the current Chair retires.
Frequency of director re-election Annually at the company's general meeting, two directors are subject to re-election. The shareholders should review on a regular basis that the composition of the board of directors is appropriate, and they do this by regular re-election of all directors.	All directors should be subject to annual re-election by the shareholders. At the current year's general meeting, it should be proposed that all directors should be subject to re-election.
NEDs no financial experience All members of the audit committee were previously involved in sales or purchasing related roles. At least one member of the audit committee should have recent and relevant financial experience. None of the non-executive directors (NEDs) appears to have held a financial role and so it is unlikely they possess the required financial experience to be able to understand the financial statements.	The company should consider recruiting a new independent NED who has the required recent and relevant financial experience. This process may be undertaken as part of the re-election process for directors.

Deficiency	**Recommendation**
Annual bonus NEDs The NEDs' remuneration is in the form of an annual bonus. However, remuneration paid to NEDs should reflect the time and responsibilities attached to the role, as the inclusion of performance related elements, especially those tied to short-term performance targets, can affect the independence of NEDs.	The remuneration of the NEDs should be revised so they are paid an annual fee for their services, which is unrelated to how Petra Co performs, and should reflect the time commitment and responsibilities attached to the role. The board as a whole should determine an appropriate level of remuneration for the NEDs.

ACCA marking guide

		Marks
(a)	**Control objectives of a sales system**	
	1 mark per well-explained point	
	Restricted to	**4**
(b)	**Direct controls and tests of controls**	
	• Supervision clock card	2
	• Gross to net checks	2
	• Revised rates	2
	• Segregation of duties	2
	Max 3 issues, 2 marks each	**6**
(c)	**Control deficiencies and recommendations**	
	• Credit limits	2
	• No copy of sales order in sales department	2
	• Discounts not reviewed	2
	• Master data access	2
	• No GRN to finance	2
	• Document count controls	2
	Max 5 issues, 2 marks each	**10**
(d)	**Substantive procedures over purchases and other expenses**	
	1 mark per well-described procedure	
	Restricted to	**4**
(e)	**Corporate governance deficiencies and recommendations**	
	• Marketing director as Chair	2
	• Frequency of director re-election	2
	• NEDs no financial experience	2
	• Annual bonus NEDs	2
	Max 3 issues, 2 marks each	**6**
Total		**30**

Examiner's comments

Requirement (a). This is a knowledge requirement and has been tested in previous exam sessions. Candidates were required to list four control objectives for Petra Co's sales system. As the requirement verb was 'list', candidates did not need to write as much detail as would be required for a 'describe' requirement. Providing four bullet points of the control objectives would be sufficiently detailed. It is also important that candidates noted that they did not need to use the scenario to answer this requirement. Therefore, candidates only needed to use their knowledge of a standard sales cycle to tackle this requirement. It would be good exam technique to answer part (a) of Petra Co prior to reading the detailed scenario. This would avoid the risk of candidates confusing their answer with deficiencies from the sales system of Petra Co.

Candidates who used their knowledge of sales systems and understood that the requirement was for control objectives were able to generate enough points. Commonly awarded points included 'ensure that orders are only accepted if goods are available for dispatch,' 'ensure that orders are recorded completely and accurately,' ensure that goods are not supplied to poor credit risks' and 'ensure that goods are dispatched on a timely basis.'

Unfortunately, in this session it was more common to see answers which provided controls rather than objectives or listed tests of controls. Many candidates ignored the note advising that the scenario did not need to be referred to. These candidates provided controls from within the scenario, such as 'Petra Co carried out credit checks for all new customers.' Unfortunately, this is not a control objective and so to gain credit the objective should be 'to ensure that goods are not supplied to poor credit risks.' This objective is then put into practice using the control of carrying out credit checks for new customers. Where controls, rather than objectives, were provided, no marks were awarded.

Additionally, some candidates ignored the requirement to provide objectives specifically for the sales system and gave objectives for the payroll or purchasing system. Candidates must ensure that they carefully read the question requirements, paying particular attention to key words and must not disregards notes which refer to not needing to use the scenario. This is done to help candidates to produce relevant, tailored answers in a timely basis.

Requirement (b). Marks were awarded for identification of direct controls (½ mark each), explanation of the implication of the direct control to the company (½ mark each) and an appropriate test of control for each control (1 mark each). In common with risks questions, the scenario will typically contain more than the number of direct controls required, so it is important that candidates plan their time carefully and only attempt to list the required number of points. With this type of requirement, good exam technique is absolutely critical.

As stated in previous examiner's reports, candidates should be prepared to answer questions which cover direct controls and tests of controls, control deficiencies and recommendations or a combination of both. Petra Co examines both direct controls and deficiencies and focuses on different parts of the internal control system. Questions may also be set where direct controls and deficiencies are tested but in relation to a single part of a company's internal control system.

It is important that having read the question requirement, candidates take the time to ensure they fully understand what the requirement involves. This session there were a number of candidates who listed deficiencies rather than controls or provided controls relating to the sales and purchases systems. These would not gain any credit as they are not answering the question asked.

In order to be a direct control, candidates need to consider whether the control as described has been appropriately designed and is being operated in such a way that it would in fact prevent or detect a material misstatement. Therefore, when identifying direct controls, it is important that the control described is complete. For example, the fact that 'staff each have a unique clock card which they use to enter/exit the factory' is not in itself a direct control. Additional checks would need to be undertaken to ensure that the clock cards are being used correctly. To be effective as a direct control, the process of employees using their clock cards would need to be supervised by security staff who would ensure, for example, that staff are not clocking in/out other employees.

Some candidates are under the misconception that each sentence in the scenario contains a direct control or deficiency. This is not the case. The scenario will include information which describes the way in which the system operates but not all of this information will indicate a direct control or deficiency. Candidates who then break down each line into a different point end up wasting time and not gaining credit. In this session, some candidates split a direct control into two points. As only three controls were required, this resulted in very few marks being gained. For example, the payroll system automatically calculating gross and net pay and the payroll supervisor reperforming a sample of these calculations are not separate controls as any automatically generated calculations would need to be checked for system errors by an appropriate person.

Having identified direct controls, candidates then need to explain each control. In considering this it is important to think about what the aim of the control is, what potential misstatement is being prevented or detected. The explanation needs to be specific to each control. It is not sufficient to state 'this will prevent fraud and error' as all controls aim to prevent or detect fraud and error in some way. A clear understanding of specifically how the control will prevent fraud and error is needed. For example, in this session the scenario contained a control whereby revised pay rates are checked when input into the payroll system. An appropriate explanation would be that the aim of this control is to ensure that this reduces the risk of input errors. It is important to include the reference to input errors as this is the key focus of the control and is needed for the ½ mark. Simply stating that this reduces the risk of fraud and errors will not gain credit.

The last part of the requirement is for candidates to describe tests of controls for each direct control identified. To gain the 1 mark available, it is imperative that the descriptions of the tests are detailed enough. A test which starts with 'check' is unlikely to provide sufficient detail as to how exactly the auditor will test the control, detail must be given on specifically what is being done to achieve a check, the word itself is not enough. Also, the control must be fully tested. For 'the control over the supervision of clock cards', simply recommending 'observe the clock in/out process' would only gain ½ mark as the test needs to 'confirm that this process is supervised' to gain 1 mark.

In addition, it must be remembered that tests of controls are procedures carried out by the auditor, therefore candidates need to ensure that they focus on what the auditor should do rather than provide recommendations for management.

In considering how to test the control, a useful starting point is to consider if there are any documents which can be inspected as this is likely to provide strong evidence that the control is operating. However, when describing the test, it is important to clearly state what document is being inspected and also for what purpose. In this session, the scenario contained a direct control where pay packets are prepared by one employee and recounted by a second member of staff, and both employees sign the weekly payroll listing on completion of the task. In testing this control an appropriate response would be that the 'weekly payroll listings are inspected' and in this case that it is 'for evidence of signature by the two employees who prepared and checked the pay packets.'

In addition, tests such as 'observe' should be used rarely as they do not generally score as well as inspection or some enquiry type procedures. Where more reliable evidence sources are available, these should be used to test the controls. In addition, candidates should ensure that they do not confuse tests of control with substantive procedures. For the control over the preparation of pay packets, some candidates suggested 'agree the contents of pay packets to the payroll listing to confirm they are correct' however, this is a substantive procedure rather than a test of control and so would not have gained any credit.

Requirement (c). Marks are awarded for identification of deficiencies (½ mark each), explanation of the implication of the deficiency to the company (½ mark each) and an appropriate control recommendation to address each deficiency (1 mark each).

The first step in tackling a deficiencies question is to read through the scenario relating to the sales and purchases systems in full, this gives an understanding of what the potential answer points are as some deficiencies are easier to explain than others. Having looked at the whole scenario then candidates should re-read it, drafting their answer as they go along. Do not be daunted by the length of the scenario, be methodical and keep re-reading the requirement to stay focused. In a multi-cycle question such as Petra Co there is likely to be a good cross section of points across each of the two systems presented and only five deficiencies are required.

In identifying deficiencies, it is important to record what the actual deficiency from the scenario is. Candidates can pick the fact from the scenario but fail to spot what the actual deficiency is. Candidates must also be careful not to identify irrelevant deficiencies. In this session irrelevant points identified included new customers being set up by an accounting clerk in the receivables ledger master file; sales orders not being sequentially numbered; no segregation of duties within the warehouse department; and credit limits being set by the finance director rather than sales director.

The least commonly provided deficiencies related to 'GRNs not being received by the finance department as they are filed in the warehouse' and 'payables clerk only using document count controls when logging invoices into the payables ledger.' To gain the ID marks for the document count controls deficiency it was important to note that the issue was that ONLY document count controls were used, as on their own they only confirm completeness of input and not accuracy or validity.

Having identified deficiencies, candidates are required to explain the implication to the business to be awarded credit. For example, a valid explanation for the deficiency 'the sales department not receiving a copy of the sales orders' (identification ½ mark awarded), would have been 'this will result in the sales department finding it difficult to monitor unfulfilled orders resulting in a loss of revenue and customer goodwill.' Answers which just stated 'cannot monitor for unfulfilled orders' would not have gained credit as it does not explain how it will impact the business.

The explanation needs to be specific to each deficiency, as just as with direct controls it is not sufficient to state 'this will result in fraud/error' as all deficiencies can lead to increased fraud and error. A clear understanding of how the deficiency will result in 'fraud and error' is needed. In particular for the deficiency of 'all members of the purchasing department have access to master file data' the explanation needs to focus on how this could lead to an increased risk of fictitious suppliers being added rather than a generic comment relating to 'an increased risk of fraud and error'.

The next part of the requirement is for candidates to describe control recommendations. To gain the 1 mark available it's imperative that the descriptions of the recommendations are detailed enough. Additionally, recommendations must be actions rather than just objectives, recommendations which are phrased as 'ensure that....' are unlikely to gain much credit.

Candidates need to take care to ensure that recommendations are well described, clearly address the specific control deficiency identified and are practical suggestions. It is important that where a document should be reviewed then it needs to be clear who should review this and when. For the 'credit limits not being reviewed after being set' deficiency, the recommendation of 'limits should be regularly reviewed' would only gain ½ marks as it needs to state that this review should be 'undertaken by the finance or sales director'.

Requirement (d). For substantive procedures requirements, one mark is available for each well-described procedure, therefore candidates should aim to produce four tests for this requirement. Candidates should plan their time accordingly.

When describing substantive procedures, one of the key things to consider is the level of detail provided. Many candidates fail to score well in this type of requirement because their procedures are vague or too brief. Tests must be sufficiently detailed noting clearly which source document should be used and what for. Candidates must ensure that they can distinguish between a substantive procedure and a test of control. Many candidates lose marks in this type of requirement by mixing up these procedures. Where substantive procedures are required for an account balance subject to an accounting standard then considering the rules of the standard can help in generating targeted substantive procedures.

Candidates who focused on 'casting the purchase listing and agreeing to financial statements', 'recalculating purchase invoices,' 'analytical review of total/monthly purchases to prior year/budget,' and 'cut off testing' were able to gain credit. However, to be awarded the full 1 mark per analytical review procedure, it is important that having compared purchases to prior year or budget that any significant fluctuations are investigated/discussed with management. Without reviewing the fluctuations only ½ marks are awarded. Also, when undertaking cut-off testing its important to use GRNs as the source document rather than purchase invoices.

Incorrect answers focused on auditing trade payables rather than purchases. Unfortunately, many candidates listed multiple payables tests rather than purchases procedures. Other incorrect procedures included 'obtaining written representations' when purchases and other expenses is not a judgemental account balance and so written representations would not be necessary.

Requirement (e). For corporate governance questions, candidates are generally asked to identify and explain a set number of corporate governance deficiencies from a given scenario and give a relevant recommendation to ensure compliance with corporate governance principles. Candidates are awarded ½ mark for identifying the deficiency and ½ mark for explaining the implication of the deficiency. Candidates are awarded 1 mark for each well explained recommendation.

In order to be awarded the identify ½ marks, candidates are required to identify the deficiency from the scenario and it was pleasing to see that most candidates were able to confidently undertake this. However, there were a number of incorrect points identified as deficiencies such as the non-executive directors (NEDs) are all member of the audit committee and so lack independence; the directors' salary is set by the remuneration committee; and the chair cannot be proposed by the nomination committee as this should be undertaken by a shareholder vote/board of directors. These incorrect points demonstrate a lack of technical knowledge around corporate governance deficiencies.

Having identified the deficiency, the next step is to clearly explain the implication of the deficiency. Candidates often fail to do this and miss out on the ½ marks available. The explanation needs to be clear how this results in a corporate governance issue. For example, just stating that 'this is poor corporate governance' would not be awarded credit. For the deficiency of directors not being subject to regular re-election, many candidates struggled to explain why this would be an issue. To gain the ½ mark available they needed to explain that shareholders need to regularly review whether the board composition is appropriate.

Additionally, for the deficiency of the NEDs all having been involved in sales and purchasing roles, many candidates incorrectly thought that these NEDs had been employed at Petra Co within sales and purchasing. Therefore, their explanation focused on how these NEDs were not independent of the company. However, the scenario was clear in that they had these roles before they joined Petra Co. The explanation should have focused on how none of the NEDs had financial experience and so would not be sufficiently experienced to review the financial statements in their role within the audit committee.

The final step is to then suggest a recommendation to ensure compliance with corporate governance principles and it is important that this is phrased as an action; often candidates provide objectives rather than actions. For example, for the deficiency relating to NEDs only having sales and purchasing experience, a recommendation of 'NEDs need financial experience' will not be awarded credit. In order to gain the one mark available, the recommendation must give a clear action, for example 'a new NED with financial experience should be appointed.'

Additionally, some candidates did not explain an appropriate recommendation for the deficiency of 'non-executive's remuneration is based on profit growth'. A recommendation of 'remuneration should be based on long-term growth or based on share options' would not be awarded credit. In order to gain the one mark available, the recommendation should be 'non-executive's remuneration should be based on their time commitment, responsibilities or on a fixed annual fee.'

222 DALEY *Walk in the footsteps of a top tutor*

Key answer tips

Part (a) requires knowledge of the five components of internal control. Most constructed response questions will include a knowledge requirement such as this which requires key elements of the auditing standards to be memorised. If you don't know it, move on to the next part rather than waste valuable time. You can always come back to it later if you have time.

Part (b) asks for control deficiencies, recommendations and tests of controls. Deficiencies are where the controls are not working effectively and therefore provide opportunity for fraud and error. You must fully explain the deficiency in terms of the effect on the company. If management are to take action, they must be concerned about the potential consequences of the deficiency. When providing recommendations for improvement, be as specific as possible. For the test of control, describe how the auditor would obtain evidence that the client has implemented the control suggested.

Part (c) asks for substantive procedures over the bank balances. Substantive procedures are procedures designed to detect misstatements in a balance as opposed to tests of controls. Think about how you can obtain evidence over the existence, valuation, completeness, rights and classification of the bank balances. Make sure the procedures you give explain how the evidence will be obtained and the objective of the procedure.

In part (d) you are asked for deficiencies and recommendations but this time in respect of the company's corporate governance practices. This requires knowledge and understanding of the corporate governance code. Make sure you explain how the company does not comply with the code and why this is a potential issue. When giving a recommendation, make sure you are as detailed as possible.

(a) Components of a system of internal control

Component of internal control	**Description**
Control environment	The control environment includes the governance and management functions and the attitudes, awareness and actions of those charged with governance and management concerning the entity's system of internal control and its importance in the entity. The control environment sets the tone of an organisation, influencing the control consciousness of its people and provides the overall foundation for the operation of other components. The control environment encompasses many elements, such as how management's responsibilities are carried out (such as creating and maintaining the entity's culture and demonstrating management's commitment to integrity and ethical values); how those charged with governance demonstrate independence from management and exercise oversight of the entity's system of internal control; how the entity assigns authority and responsibility in pursuit of its objectives; how the entity attracts, develops and retains competent individuals in alignment with its objectives; and how the entity holds individuals accountable for their responsibilities in pursuit of the entity's system of internal control.
Entity's risk assessment process	The entity's risk assessment process is an iterative process for identifying and analysing risks to achieve the entity's objectives and forms the basis for determining the risks to be managed. For financial reporting purposes, the entity's risk assessment process includes how management identifies business risks relevant to the preparation of financial statements in accordance with the entity's applicable financial reporting framework. It estimates their significance, assesses the likelihood of their occurrence, and decides upon actions to respond to and manage them and the results thereof.
Entity's process to monitor the system of internal control	Monitoring of controls is a continual process to assess the effectiveness of internal control performance over time. It involves assessing the effectiveness of controls and taking necessary remedial actions on a timely basis. Management accomplishes the monitoring of controls through ongoing activities, separate evaluations, or a combination of the two. Ongoing monitoring activities are often built into the normal recurring activities of an entity and include regular management and supervisory activities.

Component of internal control	Description
Information system and communication	The information system relevant to the preparation of the financial statements consists of the activities, policies and records designed and established to initiate, record, process, and report entity transactions (as well as events and conditions) and to maintain accountability for the related assets, liabilities, and equity. Communication which involves providing an understanding of individual roles and responsibilities may be through policy and accounting and financial reporting manuals. It may be made electronically, orally or through management actions.
Control activities	Control activities include controls which are designed to ensure proper application of policies in all the components of the entity's system of internal control and include both direct and indirect controls. Control activities include information processing controls and general IT controls and may be manual or automated in nature. They have various objectives and are applied at various organisational and functional levels. They may include authorisation and approvals, reconciliations, verifications, physical or logical controls and/or segregation of duties.

(b) Deficiencies, controls and test of controls

Control deficiency	Control recommendation	Test of control
No checks of data At the end of each week, the key card system transfers the hours worked to the payroll system. As the system is automated, no checks are performed. As there are no checks performed on the transfer of hours worked from the key card system to the payroll system, errors and overpayments could be made resulting in a loss of employee goodwill.	The transfer of hours worked from the key card system to the payroll should be checked by a senior official in the payroll department and this check should be evidenced by way of signature.	Review a sample of weeks transferred from the key card system to the payroll system for evidence that they have been checked by a senior official prior to the payroll being finalised.

Control deficiency	**Control recommendation**	**Test of control**
Edit report not reviewed		
The payroll clerk reperforms payroll calculations and amends the payroll data if there are any errors. The edit report of the amendments is not reviewed. The payroll clerk could make errors when making the amendments or could fraudulently revise payroll data to inflate the pay of friends or family. This could result in incorrect payments being made to employees and incorrect deductions being made resulting in loss of employee goodwill and misstated payroll expenses.	The edit report should be reviewed on a weekly basis by a senior official from the payroll department before the payroll is finalised and any payments made. Any unusual amendments should be investigated. This review should be evidenced (likely by way of signature) and the results of any investigations should be recorded.	For a sample of weekly edit reports, confirm that these have been signed as reviewed by a senior official from the payroll department. For a sample of amendments, agree to record of investigation and confirm appropriate action taken.
PPE physical verification		
The internal audit (IA) department undertakes physical verification of assets each year. As in the prior years, IA will only complete the comparison at one factory and one warehouse in the year to 30 September 20X5. Daley Co has ten factories, ten warehouses and a head office. Therefore, on this basis, it will take over ten years to physically verify all 21 sites. If the non-current asset register is not physically verified on a regular basis, there is an increased risk of assets being misappropriated as there is no check that the assets still exist in their correct location. In addition, obsolete assets may not be identified on a timely basis.	The board should set a policy to ensure comparisons must be carried out more frequently (for example, every two years). IA should review its programme of visits to assess if additional resources could be devoted to ensure that all 21 sites are visited in a shorter period. This would ensure that physical verification of all assets could be completed more regularly. During visits, any assets which cannot be located should be investigated fully to identify where they could be. If they cannot be located, then they should be written off.	Review the board minutes for evidence of new policy set by the board regarding frequency of IA visits. Review IA programme to assess whether visits are in line with new policy. Review records from physical verification visits by IA to ensure comparisons have been performed and any unidentified and obsolete assets have been written off following approval by the board or a responsible official.

Control deficiency	Control recommendation	Test of control
Change to asset policy		
During the year, the company's accounting policy was changed by the financial controller so that items of a capital (asset) nature are only capitalised if they exceed $20,000. While it can be normal practice for a threshold to be set for capitalisation, this represents a significant change to an accounting policy which does not appear to have been discussed or approved at board level. This threshold is too high, as over time this will result in a significant amount of costs which should be capitalised being written off to the statement of profit or loss and understated property, plant and equipment.	Significant changes to an accounting policy should be discussed and approved at board level. A record of any decisions should be included in the board minutes. The capitalisation limit should be reduced to a more appropriate limit, such as $1,000, so that assets and profitability are more accurately reported.	Review board minutes for evidence that changes to accounting policies have been discussed and approved. Discuss with the finance director the capitalisation limit and for a sample of capital items over $1,000, agree that they have been correctly capitalised in the statement of financial position.
Finance director review		
The finance director authorises the monthly supplier payments listing, but only views the total amount of payments to be made. Without looking at the detail of the payments list, as well as supporting documentation, there is a risk that suppliers could be being paid an incorrect amount, or that sums are being paid to fictitious suppliers.	The finance director should review the whole payments list prior to authorising. As part of this, the finance director should agree the amounts to be paid to supporting documentation, as well as reviewing the supplier names to identify any duplicates or any unfamiliar names. This should be evidenced by signing the supplier payments listing.	A sample of payment listings should be reviewed to verify that the finance director has agreed the amounts payable to supporting documentation prior to the bank transfer being made.
No petty cash receipts		
There is no requirement for receipts for sundry purchases paid for out of petty cash to be returned to the finance department.	A petty cash book should be maintained so that the amount borrowed, date and employee name is recorded together with details of the sundry purchase made.	A sample of petty cash transactions from the record book should be reviewed to ensure all cash issued has been accounted for and

Control deficiency	Control recommendation	Test of control
This could result in sundry purchases being made which are for non-business-related items or the cash could be being misappropriated.	In addition to returning excess cash back to the finance department, employees should also be required to promptly return a receipt for sundry purchases. The petty cash book should then be updated to record the excess cash and the receipt. A member of the finance department should reconcile the petty cash on a weekly basis and if any receipts are missing, they should be investigated further with the employees who made the petty cash purchases during that week. The reconciliations should be reviewed by a responsible official who should evidence their review.	receipts provided for expenses. A sample of reconciliations should also be reviewed to ensure these are approved.
Bank reconciliations The company maintains four bank accounts but only the main current account is reconciled on a monthly basis, with the other three bank accounts being reconciled quarterly. If all bank accounts are not reconciled on a monthly basis, errors or fraud may not be spotted on a timely basis.	All bank accounts should be reconciled each month and any reconciling items on the bank reconciliation statements should be investigated and corrected, where necessary. The reconciliations should be reviewed by a responsible official who should evidence their review.	Review a sample of bank reconciliation statements for all bank accounts to ensure they are being completed and reviewed on monthly basis.

(c) Substantive procedures over the bank balances

- Obtain a bank confirmation letter from Daley Co's bank for all of its bank accounts.
- Agree all accounts listed on the bank confirmation letter to Daley Co's bank reconciliations and trial balance to ensure completeness of bank balances.
- Obtain the year-end bank reconciliations and cast to ensure mathematical accuracy.

- Agree the balance per cash book/bank ledger account on the year-end bank reconciliation statements to the cash book/trial balance/financial statements.
- Agree the balance per the bank reconciliations to the year-end bank confirmation letter and bank statements.
- Trace all outstanding lodgements/deposits to the pre-year-end cash book/bank ledger account, post-year-end bank statement and also to the paying-in book pre year end.
- Trace all unpresented cheques through to the pre-year-end cash book/bank ledger account and post-year-end bank statements. For any unusual amounts or delays, obtain explanations from management.
- Examine any old unpresented cheques to assess if they need to be written back as they are no longer valid.
- Examine the bank confirmation letter for details of any security provided by the company or any legal right of set-off as this may require disclosure.
- Review the cash book/bank ledger account and bank statements for any unusual items or large transfers around the year end as this may be evidence of window dressing.

(d) Corporate governance deficiencies and recommendations

Deficiency	**Recommendation**
During the year, the Chair resigned and Fred Johnson, who is currently the chief executive, took over the role. If Fred Johnson is both the Chair and chief executive, Fred will have unfettered power of decision making and will effectively be responsible for running the company and the board.	Fred Johnson should resign as the Chair and only carry out the role of chief executive. An independent non-executive should be appointed to fill the Chair's role.
The Chair recently wrote to all shareholders to inform them that any questions or comments they may have could only be raised at the company's annual general meeting (AGM). Restricting shareholders to only raising concerns at the AGM will not ensure regular effective engagement with the owners of the company. This could result in the board making decisions which are not in line with the wishes of major shareholders.	The Chair of Daley Co should take steps to encourage regular effective engagement with major shareholders in addition to the AGM. This could be in the form of regular meetings and would aim to seek shareholders' views on the company's governance and performance against strategy.

Deficiency	**Recommendation**
Non-executive directors' remuneration is based on pre-tax profit targets agreed by the board at the start of the year. Non-executive directors' remuneration should not be based on pre-determined profit targets as their pay should not be based on how the company performs as this would reduce their independence.	Daley Co should pay the non-executive directors an annual fee for their services to the company and this fee should be unrelated to the company's financial performance, but rather based on time committed and responsibilities of the role.
The company currently does not have an audit committee as the board views the internal control environment as very effective. The lack of an audit committee means there is no oversight in the company to enable the directors to discharge their responsibilities for accountability appropriately and there will not be a means of the company maintaining its independent relationship with the external auditors.	The company should consider establishing an audit committee as quickly as possible. The audit committee should be comprised of at least three non-executive directors and one of these non-executive directors should have recent and relevant financial expertise. The committee as a whole should have appropriate competence in the industry.

ACCA marking guide		
		Marks
(a)	**Components of a system of internal control**	
	• Control environment	1
	• Entity's risk assessment process	1
	• Entity's process to monitor the system of internal control	1
	• Information system and communication	1
	• Control activities	1
	Restricted to	**5**
(b)	**Internal control deficiencies controls and tests of controls (only 5 required)**	
	• No checks of data	3
	• Edit report not reviewed	3
	• PPE physical verification	3
	• Change to asset capitalisation policy	3
	• Finance director only reviews payment total	3
	• No receipts for petty cash	3
	• Quarterly bank reconciliations	3
	Max 5 issues, 3 marks each	**15**
(c)	**Substantive procedures over the bank balances**	
	1 mark per well-described procedure	
	Restricted to	**4**

(d)	**Corporate governance deficiencies and recommendations**	
	• CEO is also Chair	2
	• Shareholder engagement	2
	• Remuneration of non-executive directors	2
	• No audit committee	2
	Restricted to	**6**
Total		**30**

Examiner's comments

Part (a). This is a knowledge requirement which has been tested in previous exam sessions. Knowledge requirements such as this often have an opening statement, sometimes referenced to an ISA, which is useful for setting the scene and providing clarification on the aim of the question requirement. It is especially important that candidates understand exactly what the question is asking, especially for knowledge questions, where candidates should be aiming to score full marks. For this session, candidates were required to describe the components of an entity's system of internal control. As the requirement verb was 'describe' candidates needed to ensure that they wrote enough detail in their answers. Simply providing a few words such as 'identification of risk' is not sufficient as a description. Therefore, when reviewing their answers, candidates need to consider whether they have written enough. Candidates were provided the five components from ISA 315 (Revised 2019) *Identifying and Assessing the Risks of Material Misstatement* in a table, with one mark available for each description. However, a significant proportion of candidates did not gain credit as their answers were circular. For example, 'the risk assessment process relates to managements method for assessing risk' is simply a repetition of the words for the risk assessment process component, and therefore would not gain any credit. Commonly awarded points included 'management's attitude or awareness,' 'process to assess effectiveness of internal control' and 'process for identifying risk.' However, these points would each only gain ½ marks as they are too brief or only part of the description. The component most candidates struggled with was information system and communication. Many candidates incorrectly assumed that this related to an information technology (IT) system rather than relating to records to process transactions, assets and liabilities to maintain accountability. It is imperative that future candidates ensure that they devote adequate time to learning the knowledge areas of the syllabus as well as practising this style of knowledge question.

Part (b). Marks are awarded for identification of deficiencies (½ mark each), explanation of the implication of the deficiency to Daley Co (½ mark each), an appropriate control recommendation to address each deficiency (1 mark each) and an appropriate test of control for each control (1 mark each). The scenario will typically contain more than the number of deficiencies required, so it is important that candidates plan their time carefully and only attempt to list the required number of points. With this type of requirement good exam technique is absolutely crucial. The first step in tackling a control deficiencies question is to read through the scenario in full. This gives an understanding of what the potential answer points are as some deficiencies are easier to explain than others. Having read the whole scenario then candidates should re-read it, drafting their answer as they go along. Do not be daunted by the length of the scenario; be methodical and keep re-reading the requirement to stay focused. In a multi-cycle question such as Daley Co there is likely to be a good cross section of points across each of the three cycles presented and only five deficiencies are required. In identifying deficiencies, it is important to record what the actual deficiency from the scenario is. Candidates can pick the fact from the scenario but fail to spot what the actual deficiency is. Candidates must also be careful not to identify irrelevant deficiencies. In this diet it was pleasing to see that most candidates were able to appropriately identify relevant deficiencies. The least commonly provided deficiencies related to the physical verification of sites not being completed regularly enough and the bank accounts only being reconciled quarterly. The deficiency relating to the bank reconciliations was quite straightforward and candidates who identified this point often scored well, therefore it is surprising that so few candidates provided this point. It is possible that, as it was detailed at the end of the scenario, some candidates simply did not read the whole scenario before they began to write their answer. This demonstrates weak exam technique. With each deficiency being worth three marks, it is important to pick the five most straightforward points to maximise marks. Having identified deficiencies, candidates are required to explain the implication to the business to be awarded credit. For example, a valid explanation for the deficiency 'accounting policy changed resulting in capital items under $20,000 being expensed rather than capitalised' (identification ½ mark awarded), would have been 'this limit is too high and could result in capital expenditure incorrectly written off to profit and loss resulting in understated property, plant and equipment.' Answers which just stated 'that this is not in line with IAS 16 *Property, Plant and Equipment*' would not have gained credit as it does not explain why this is not in accordance with the standard, or how it will impact the business. The explanation needs to be specific to each deficiency. It is not sufficient to state 'this will result in fraud/error' as all deficiencies lead to increased chance of fraud and/or error. A clear understanding of how the deficiency will result in 'fraud and error' is needed. In particular, for the deficiency of 'FD only reviews the bank payments list totals,' the explanation needs to focus on how this could lead to an increased risk of payments to fictitious suppliers rather than a generic comment relating to 'an increased risk of fraud and error.' The next part of the requirement is for candidates to describe control recommendations. To gain the 1 mark available, it's imperative that the descriptions of the controls are detailed enough. Additionally, recommendations must be actions rather than just objectives. Recommendations which are phrased as 'ensure that….' are unlikely to gain much credit, as the recommendations must be clear and actionable. Candidates must take care to ensure that their recommendations are well described, clearly address the specific control deficiency identified and are practical suggestions. Many candidates often just repeat the converse of the deficiency, though to obtain the recommendation mark more detail is needed. For the 'edit report of amendments not being reviewed' deficiency, the recommendation of 'the payroll manager should review the edit reports' would only gain ½ marks as its needs to state that this review should be evidenced, and any unusual amendments investigated. Additionally, for this same deficiency some candidates recommended that only the payroll manager should make amendments to the payroll. This would not have gained credit as the deficiency relates to an edit report not being reviewed rather than the seniority of the person amending the payroll. The last part of the requirement is for candidates to describe a test of controls for each control recommended. To gain the 1 mark available it is important that the descriptions of the tests are detailed enough. A test which starts with 'check' is unlikely to provide sufficient detail as to how exactly the auditor will test the control. In addition, it must be remembered that tests of controls are procedures carried out by the auditor. Therefore, candidates must ensure that they focus on what the auditor should do rather than provide recommendations for management. In considering how to test the control, a useful starting point is to consider if there are any documents which can be inspected as this is likely to provide strong evidence the control is operating. However, when describing the test it is important to clearly state which document is being inspected and also for what purpose. In this session the scenario contained a deficiency where only the totals on the bank payments list were reviewed. In testing the control recommendation of 'the FD should review the payments list for unfamiliar items and evidence this review by signature,' an appropriate response would be that the 'bank payments lists are inspected' and in this case that it is 'for evidence of review by the FD.' In addition, tests such as 'observe' do not score as well as inspection or some enquiry type procedures. Where more reliable evidence sources are available they should be used to test the controls. In this session, 'observation' was not credited for any of the deficiency recommendations as in each case more reliable evidence could be generated through enquiry or inspection. Candidates should ensure that they do not confuse tests of control with substantive procedures.

Part (c). For substantive procedures requirements, one mark is available for each well-described procedure, therefore candidates should aim to produce four tests for this requirement. Candidates should plan their time accordingly. Also, candidates should note that it is not necessary to write out the question requirement at the beginning of their answer. This does not gain any credit and wastes candidates' time. When describing substantive procedures one of the key things to consider is the level of detail provided. Many candidates fail to score well in this type of requirement because their procedures are vague or too brief. Tests must be sufficiently detailed, noting clearly which source document should be used and for what purpose. Candidates must ensure that they can distinguish between a substantive procedure and a test of control. Many candidates lose marks in this type of requirement by mixing up these procedures. Where substantive procedures are required for an account balance subject to an accounting standard then considering the rules of the standard can help in generating targeted substantive procedures. It is important when auditing bank balances to consider in detail the elements of the bank reconciliation as this is the main focus of the auditor's testing. Utilising knowledge from Financial Accounting, about how the bank statement is reconciled to the year-end balance as per the cash book/bank ledger account, should provide candidates with sufficient points to audit. When auditing the reconciliation candidates must be clear as to which time period the various source documents relate to. For example, in testing outstanding lodgements, to be a valid reconciling item on the reconciliation, the audit test should be to 'agree to the pre-year-end cash book/bank ledger account and the post-year-end bank statements.' Where candidates were not specific as to whether the bank statements were pre or post year end then full credit could not be awarded. Candidates who focused on 'obtaining a bank letter and agreeing the balance per the bank to the reconciliation,' 'agreeing the cash book/bank ledger account balance at the year end to the trial balance and financial statements,' 'reviewing the year-end bank statements for unusual items or window dressing,' and 'reviewing disclosure' as well as testing outstanding lodgements and payments were able to gain credit. Incorrect answers focused on auditing opening balances or the petty cash balance despite the requirement only being for bank balances. In many substantive procedure questions, analytical procedures can be an important source of evidence, but for one off types of expenditure and bank balances then analytical review is unlikely to be useful.

Part (d). For corporate governance questions, candidates are generally asked to identify and explain a set number of corporate governance deficiencies from a given scenario and give a relevant recommendation to ensure compliance with corporate governance principles. Candidates are awarded ½ marks for identifying the deficiency and ½ marks for explaining the implication of the deficiency. Candidates are awarded 1 mark for each well-explained recommendation. In order to be awarded the identification ½ marks, candidates are required to identify the deficiency from the scenario and it was pleasing to see that most candidates were able to confidently undertake this. The next step is to clearly explain the implication of the deficiency. Candidates often fail to do this and miss out on the ½ marks available. The explanation needs to be clear about how this results in a corporate governance issue. For example, just stating that 'this is poor corporate governance' would not be awarded credit. For the deficiency of Chair and CEO being the same individual, many candidates struggled to explain why this would be an issue. To gain the ½ marks available they needed to explain that there could be an abuse of power by one individual as both are key roles. Even where candidates attempted an explanation, these were often weak as they did not explain adequately why the deficiency causes poor corporate governance. The final step is to then suggest a recommendation to ensure compliance with corporate governance principles. It is important that this is phrased as an action; often candidates provide objectives rather than actions. For example, for the deficiency relating to non-executive's remuneration being based on pre-tax profits, a recommendation of 'remuneration should not be based on short-term profits' will not be awarded credit. In order to gain the one mark available, the recommendation must give a clear action, for example 'non-executive's remuneration should be based on their time commitment, responsibilities or on a fixed annual fee.'

223 WHITTAKER *Walk in the footsteps of a top tutor*

Key answer tips

Part (a) asks for matters when determining whether a control deficiency is significant. Think about which type of deficiencies a client might be more concerned about and therefore more likely to want to do something about because the consequences could be significant, as compared with deficiencies where the consequences might not be so detrimental for the company. All section B questions are likely to include a knowledge requirement. Often, these questions require knowledge of an auditing standard and therefore they can be difficult to answer unless you have revised the specific audit guidance, therefore, plan some of your revision time to go over these areas.

Part (b) asks for direct controls and tests of controls. Direct controls reduce the risk of material misstatement. Look for evidence of segregation of duties, authorisation, reconciliations, etc. The control must be complete to be effective, e.g. sequential numbering of invoices must be accompanied with a regular sequence check to ensure the sequence is complete in order for the control to be effective. A bank reconciliation must be reviewed by a responsible official to ensure it has been performed properly. For the full mark, explain what the control aims to achieve, for example, the risk that the control is designed to mitigate.

When describing a test of control, you need to say how the auditor will obtain evidence that the control is working effectively. This may come from inspecting a document for evidence of authorisation or reperforming a control such as a reconciliation to ensure the client staff have performed the control effectively.

Part (c) asks for control deficiencies and recommendations in respect of the internal control system. This is examined frequently and with plenty of past exams to practise, this type of question should be straightforward. Fully explain the deficiency in terms of the effect on the company. If management are to take action, they must be concerned about the potential consequences of the deficiency. When providing recommendations for improvement, be as specific as possible.

(a) Determining deficiencies in internal control

ISA 265 *Communicating Deficiencies in Internal Control to Those Charged With Governance and Management* details matters the external auditor should consider when determining whether a deficiency in internal control is significant, including:

- The likelihood of the deficiency (or deficiencies) resulting in material misstatements in the financial statements in the future.
- The susceptibility to loss or fraud of the related asset or liability.
- The subjectivity and complexity of determining estimated amounts.
- The amounts exposed to the deficiencies.
- The volume of activity which has occurred or could occur in the account balance or class of transaction exposed to the deficiency or deficiencies.
- The importance of the identified deficient controls to the financial reporting process.
- The cause and frequency of the exceptions identified as a result of the deficiencies in the controls.
- The interaction of the deficiency with other deficiencies in internal control.

(b) Direct controls and test of controls

Direct control	**Test of control**
New system tested The new sales system was fully tested prior to its implementation and the new and old systems are being run in parallel until the year end with internal audit (IA) performing checks on the output and following up on any discrepancies. This reduces the risk that data is lost or data is not processed correctly if there are issues associated with the operation of the new system. This reduces the risk of processing errors and misstatements in the accounting records.	The audit team should review the procedures and documentation relating to the testing which has been undertaken and agree that the tests undertaken are appropriate and that any errors were fully investigated and resolved. The audit team should review IA's testing schedule to understand what checks are being undertaken and when they are expected to be complete. For IA checks which have been completed, the audit team should obtain and review documentation which details the test performed and any follow up actions to confirm the tests are appropriate and to understand how errors or inconsistencies have been communicated and resolved. For a new transaction being entered into the system, the audit team should observe the transaction being recorded in the old and new system and agree that the information is processed and output is generated consistently between the two systems.

Direct control	**Test of control**
Credit check New customers undergo a full credit check and a credit limit is set using an automated system. The credit limit is approved by the sales director who evidences that review. Requiring a credit check reduces the risk of lost revenue and uncollectable trade receivables as only creditworthy customers are able to place orders. The automated process should ensure that no bias is included in accepting creditworthy customers or setting the credit limit which helps ensure the credit limit set is appropriate and that receivables are recoverable.	The audit team should select a sample of new customer accounts opened in the period and confirm, by reference to information on the system, that a credit check has been performed. They should also agree there is evidence of approval, such as a signature or electronic sign-off, by the sales director before the credit limit is set. For a sample of new customers, the audit team should obtain a copy of the first order placed by the customer and agree that the date of the first order was after the credit check was completed.
Aged receivables review The receivables ledger clerk performs a monthly review of the aged receivables listing and identifies those aged more than 30 days which are followed up with the relevant customers by the credit control department. The regular review of the aged receivables listing and subsequent action by credit control should ensure that debts are collected on a timely basis which reduces the risk of irrecoverable debts. It should also ensure that balances are appropriately identified as irrecoverable and accounted for accordingly.	The audit team should obtain a copy of the aged receivables report downloaded and confirm there is evidence of review, such as a signature or electronic sign-off, by the receivables ledger clerk. The audit team should enquire as to which receivables balances are passed to credit control and should confirm this is appropriate based on Whittaker Co's credit control policies. The audit team should review a sample of follow-up documentation from credit control to confirm action taken.

Direct control	Test of control
Account reconciliations The accounts clerk performs a monthly trade receivables account reconciliation and resolves errors on a timely basis. The reconciliation is reviewed and approved by the financial controller. Regular reconciliation of the list of individual customer balances and the trade receivables account helps to ensure that the receivables balance presented in the financial statements is accurate. Timely identification and correction of errors ensures that recording issues are resolved and the accounting records are accurate. Review by the financial controller helps to ensure the accuracy of the reconciliation.	The audit team should review the file of trade receivables account reconciliations and confirm that these are being performed on a monthly basis. For a sample of reconciliations with reconciling items trace to supporting documentation to confirm that errors have been corrected. The team should also review the reconciliations for a signature or electronic sign-off as evidence of approval and review by the financial controller.

(c) Control deficiencies and recommendations

Control deficiency	Control recommendation
No joiner forms When additional staff are required at short notice, joiners' forms are not completed. Instead, they are added to payroll following email notification from the production supervisor. The production supervisor may not include all the relevant details on the email to payroll. This could result in the temporary employees not receiving the correct pay or not being paid on time, resulting in a loss of employee goodwill. The addition of employees to the payroll without authorisation from HR also increases the risk of fictitious individuals being added.	A joiner form should be completed for all new employees, whether temporary or permanent. The authorised joiner form should then be sent to payroll on the day the employee commences employment. Payroll should then sign the form as being actioned. Payroll should not set up new employees without an authorised joiner form.

Control deficiency	Control recommendation
Overtime reviewed quarterly Staff are paid overtime on a monthly basis but the overtime worked reports are only reviewed every quarter after the overtime has been paid. Reviewing overtime worked reports quarterly after employees have been paid is too infrequent. This could result in employees being paid for hours not worked, hence increasing costs or not being paid enough overtime which could result in loss of employee goodwill.	The production supervisor should review and authorise overtime worked reports before they are passed to the payroll department for processing. This will ensure the correct levels of overtime are paid to the correct employees. The payroll department should be instructed not to process any overtime worked reports which have not been reviewed and authorised.
Calculations not checked The wages and deductions calculations are automatically performed by the payroll system but no checks are carried out to confirm the calculations are accurate. There is a risk that any system errors which occur during the payroll processing would not be identified. This could result in wages being over or under calculated, leading to an additional payroll cost or loss of employee goodwill. In addition, statutory deductions may be over or underpaid, giving rise to compliance issues.	For a sample of employees, a senior member of the payroll team should recalculate the gross to net pay workings and compare their results to the output from the payroll system. Any discrepancies should be investigated. These calculations should be signed as approved before payments are made.
Bonus The HR manager decides on bonuses based on employee performance and has confirmed the bonuses to the payroll department. There are no approved parameters for the bonus level so it is purely based on the discretion of one individual who could pay bonuses inappropriately, leading to extra costs or loss of employee goodwill.	The bonus payments should be determined in line with specified and documented criteria and approved by the board. The HR director or other responsible official should provide payroll with a list detailing approved bonuses per employee. Payroll should be informed only to action payment of a bonus or any other change on receipt of written authorisation approved by the board.

Control deficiency	Control recommendation
Input errors The bonuses were input into the system and a number of employees subsequently notified the payroll department of errors in their pay. It appears that bonuses were input without any additional review. This increases the risk of errors arising within payroll. In addition, it appears that the bonus issues have only been investigated for the employees who have complained that their bonus is inaccurate. It is more likely that complaints will arise from an employee who is underpaid and therefore there is a risk that other employees have been overpaid which increases the payroll cost.	The bonuses should be reviewed to agree they are in line with documentation provided by HR. The bonuses should be input by one clerk and checked by a second payroll clerk for any errors. Any changes to the payroll should trigger an exception report which a senior member of the payroll department should authorise.
Internet banking The internet banking log in details are saved in a central location which is accessible to all payables ledger staff. There is a risk that staff are fraudulently setting up payees or making withdrawals from the bank, resulting in an increased risk of loss due to misappropriation of funds.	The internet banking log in details should not be documented and should be known to only select staff with appropriate authority. Any changes to payees should be documented on a change report which is extracted from the internet banking system and reviewed by the finance director on a regular basis to confirm changes are expected.
Reconciling items The reconciling items on the bank reconciliation are only investigated by the financial controller if the sum of reconciling items is significant. The bank reconciliations could contain significant errors, but a low overall number of reconciling items, as there could be compensating errors which cancel each other out. If reconciling items are not reviewed, then this reduces the effectiveness of the bank reconciliations and also results in a lack of assurance that bank reconciliations are being carried out properly.	The reconciling items should be reviewed by the financial controller on a weekly basis, even if they are not significant, and they should evidence their review by way of signature on the bank reconciliation

ACCA marking guide

		Marks
(a)	**Determining deficiencies in internal control**	
	• The likelihood of the deficiency (or deficiencies) resulting in material misstatements	1
	• The susceptibility to loss or fraud	1
	• The subjectivity and complexity of determining estimated amounts	1
	• The amounts exposed to the deficiencies	1
	• The volume of activity which has occurred or could occur in the associated account balance or class of transaction	1
	• The importance to the financial reporting process	1
	• The cause and frequency of the exceptions identified	1
	• The interaction of the deficiency with other deficiencies	1
	Restricted to	**4**
(b)	**Direct controls and tests of controls** (only 3 required)	
	• New system tested	2
	• Credit check	2
	• Aged receivables review	2
	• Account reconciliations	2
	Max 3 issues, 2 marks each	**6**
(c)	**Control deficiencies and recommendations** (only 5 required)	
	• No joiner forms	2
	• Overtime reviewed quarterly	2
	• Calculations not checked	2
	• Bonus	2
	• Input errors	2
	• Internet banking	2
	• Reconciling items	2
	Max 5 issues, 2 marks each	**10**
Total		**20**

Examiner's comments

Requirement (a). This is a knowledge requirement which has been tested in previous exam sessions. For knowledge requirements such as this, it is important that candidates understand exactly what the question is asking, especially where candidates should be aiming to score full marks. For this session candidates were required to describe matters in determining whether a deficiency is significant for 4 marks. As the requirement verb was 'describe' candidates need to ensure that they include sufficient detail in their answers. Simply providing a few words such as 'materiality of deficiency' is not enough for a description. Candidates therefore need to consider whether they have written enough. Commonly awarded points included 'complexity of deficiencies' and 'frequency of deficiencies.' However, these points would only gain ½ marks as they are too brief. To gain the additional ½ marks, candidates need to consider 'the complexity when determining estimates' and 'the frequency of exceptions identified as a result of the deficiencies'. It is also important that candidates pay attention to any elements of the requirement which are highlighted. In this session the word FOUR was in capitals. This was specifically done to focus candidates' answers, so that they would know to provide four well described answers. Additionally, there was a note under the requirement which stressed that the scenario did not need to be referred to in answering this requirement. Unfortunately, during this session some candidates ignored this note and provided control deficiencies from the scenario which were required for part (c). Notes and capitalisation of words in requirements are there to guide candidates and to help, candidates should be careful not to ignore them. It is imperative that future candidates ensure that they devote adequate time to learning the knowledge areas of the syllabus as well as practicing this style of knowledge question.

Requirement (b). Marks are awarded for identification of direct controls (½ mark each), explanation of the implication of the direct control to the company (½ mark each) and an appropriate test of control for each control (1 mark each). In common with risks questions, the scenario will typically contain more than the number of direct controls required, so it is important that candidates plan their time carefully and only attempt to list the required number of points. With this type of requirement good exam technique is absolutely critical. As stated in previous Examiner's reports, candidates should be prepared to answer questions which cover direct controls and tests of controls, control deficiencies and recommendations or a combination of both. Whittaker Co examines both direct controls and deficiencies and focuses on different parts of the internal control system. Questions may also be set where direct controls and deficiencies are tested but in relation to a single part of a company's system. In order to be a direct control, candidates need to consider whether the control as described has been appropriately designed and is being operated in such a way that it would in fact prevent or detect a material misstatement. Therefore, when identifying direct controls, it is important that the control described is complete. For example, the fact that the monthly reconciliations are performed, that in itself is not a direct control. Additional checks would need to be undertaken to ensure that the process has been undertaken fully. To be effective as a direct control, the reconciliations would need to be reviewed by a responsible official who would ensure that any errors have been resolved. Some candidates are under the misconception that each sentence in the scenario contains a direct control. This is not the case. The scenario will include information which describes the way in which the system operates but not all of this information will indicate a direct control. Candidates who then break down each line into a different point end up wasting time and not gaining credit. In this session some candidates split a direct control into two points. As only three controls were required, this resulted in very few marks being gained. For example, the automatic credit check and review of credit limits by the sales director are not separate controls as any system generated credit limit would need to be reviewed for reasonableness by a responsible official. Having identified direct controls, candidates then need to explain each control. In considering this it is important to think about what the aim of the control is, what potential misstatement is being prevented or detected. The explanation needs to be specific to each control. It is not sufficient to state 'this will prevent fraud and error' as all controls aim to prevent or detect fraud and error in some way. A clear understanding of specifically how the control will prevent fraud and error is needed. For example, in this session the scenario contained a control whereby a new sales system was implemented and internal audit fully tested the system by comparing output from the old and new systems. An appropriate explanation would be that the aim of this control is to ensure that this reduces the risk of loss of/ incomplete data when transferring to the new system. The last part of the requirement is for candidates to describe tests of controls for each direct control identified. To gain the 1 mark available it is imperative that the descriptions of the tests are detailed enough. A test which starts with 'check' is unlikely to provide sufficient detail as to how exactly the auditor will test the control, detail must be giving on specifically what is being done to achieve a check, the word itself is not enough. In addition, it must be remembered that tests of controls are procedures carried out by the auditor, therefore candidates need to ensure that they focus on what the auditor should do rather than provide recommendations for management. In considering how to test the control, a useful starting point is to consider if there are any documents which can be inspected as this is likely to provide strong evidence that the control is operating. However, when describing the test, it is important to clearly state what document is being inspected and also for what purpose. In this session, the scenario contained a direct control where the aged receivables report was reviewed and passed to credit control for the chasing of overdue debts. In testing this control an appropriate response would be that the 'aged receivables reports are inspected' and in this case that it is 'for evidence of review by credit control'. In addition, in describing tests of controls, it is important that key elements of the control are tested. This session the scenario contained a direct control over automatic credit checks and review of limits by the sales director. Some candidates recommended that in order to test this 'a dummy customer should be entered into the system to see if a credit limit is generated'. This is not a valid test in this situation as the system would not be able to generate a credit limit as there would not be any real world data on which to assess the creditworthiness of the customer. In addition, tests such as 'observe' do not score as well as inspection or some enquiry type procedures. Where more reliable evidence sources are available, these should be used to test the controls. In this session, 'observation' was not credited for any of the direct controls as in each case more reliable evidence could be generated through enquiry or inspection. In addition, candidates should ensure that they do not confuse tests of control with substantive procedures. For the control over the review of aged receivables reports, some candidates suggested 'review after-date cash receipts' however, this is a substantive procedure rather than a test of control and so would not have gained any credit. Direct controls and tests of controls are a key requirement in internal control questions and future candidates must ensure they practice these types of questions in advance of their exam.

Requirement (c). Marks are awarded for identification of deficiencies (½ mark each), explanation of the implication of the deficiency to the company (½ mark each) and an appropriate control recommendation to address each deficiency (1 mark each). The scenario will typically contain more than the number of deficiencies required and it remains important that candidates plan their time carefully and only attempt to list the required number of points. Continuing to apply good exam technique and time management skills is critical. The first step in tackling a deficiencies question is to read through the whole scenario in full, this gives an understanding of what the potential answer points are as some deficiencies are easier to explain than others. Having looked at the whole scenario then candidates should re-read it, drafting their answer as they go along. Do not be daunted by the length of the scenario, be methodical and keep re-reading the requirement to stay focused. In a multi cycle question such as Whittaker Co there is likely to be a good cross section of points across each of the two cycles presented. In identifying deficiencies, it is important to record what the actual deficiency from the scenario is. Candidates can pick the fact from the scenario but fail to spot what the actual deficiency is. For example, candidates identified from the scenario 'the overtime reports are reviewed on a quarterly basis'. However, the actual issue was that the reports are being reviewed after the overtime has been paid. This was required for the ½ mark available for identification of the deficiency as simply stating part of what was in the scenario did not sufficiently detail the deficiency. Candidates must also be careful not to identify irrelevant deficiencies. For example, in the scenario it stated that the accounts clerk undertakes bank reconciliations on a weekly basis. This is not a deficiency, as it's sufficiently regular for bank reconciliations to be undertaken weekly. Therefore, any answers which criticised this method and recommended daily bank reconciliations did not gain credit. Other incorrect answers focused on the production supervisor being too junior to review the overtime and the financial controller not reviewing the bank reconciliations as this should be undertaken by the finance director. Candidates often incorrectly identify deficiencies relating to accounts/finance clerks being too junior to undertake any elements of internal controls systems. This demonstrates a lack of understanding of internal control systems and candidates should take time to develop their knowledge by practising past exam questions. Having identified deficiencies, candidates are required to explain the implication to the business to be awarded credit. For example, a valid explanation for the deficiency 'staff added to the payroll without joining forms being completed' (identification ½ mark awarded), would have been 'this could result in fictitious employees being added to the payroll'. Answers which just stated 'the production supervisor may recruit staff without relevant experience' would not have gained credit as it is unlikely that the supervisor would not know what skills are required to undertake the role. The key implication to the company is that if appropriate checks are not completed then the payroll system could be fraudulently circumvented. The explanation needs to be specific to each deficiency, as it is not sufficient to state 'this will result in fraud/error' as all deficiencies can lead to increased fraud and error. A clear understanding of how the deficiency will result in 'fraud and error' is needed. In particular for the deficiency of 'automatic wage calculations are not checked' the explanation needed to focus on how system errors may not be identified on a timely basis rather than a generic comment relating to 'an increased risk of fraud and error'. The last part of the requirement is for candidates to describe control recommendations. To gain the 1 mark available it's imperative that the descriptions of the controls are detailed enough. Additionally, recommendations must be actions rather than just objectives, recommendations which are phrased as 'ensure that....' are unlikely to gain much credit. Candidates must be sure to describe 'how' something is to be ensured. Candidates need to take care to ensure that recommendations are well described, clearly address the specific control deficiency identified and are practical suggestions. Many candidates often just repeat the converse of the deficiency, and to obtain the recommendation mark more detail is needed. For the lack of joiner forms deficiency, the recommendation of 'joiner forms should be completed for all new staff member' would only gain ½ marks as candidates need to state who should complete these forms, for example human resources. Additionally, for the wages calculations not being checked deficiency, simply recommending that 'a responsible official should recalculate a sample of calculations' was not sufficient as these calculations need to be checked against the payroll system to fully identify whether any system errors have arisen.

224 POMERANIAN *Walk in the footsteps of a top tutor*

Key answer tips

Part (a) requires knowledge of limitations of internal control components. These limitations are the reasons why the auditor cannot rely 100% on the control system of the client and must always perform substantive procedures over material balances.

Part (b) asks for control deficiencies and recommendations. Deficiencies are where the controls are not working effectively and therefore provide opportunity for fraud and error. Fully explain the deficiency in terms of the effect on the company. If management are to take action, they must be concerned about the potential consequences of the deficiency. When providing recommendations for improvement, be as specific as possible. For the test of control, describe how the auditor would obtain evidence that the client has implemented the control suggested.

(a) Limitations of controls

Human error in the design of or application of an internal control

An entity may have an adequate internal control process over a particular area of the financial statements. However, human error in applying that control gives rise to an inherent limitation, for example a staff member may review a bank reconciliation but not identify an error.

There may also be a flaw in the design of internal control whereby there is an error in the design of, or change to, an internal control which means it does not operate as intended.

Circumvention of internal control

No system of internal control will be completely effective at preventing and detecting fraud and error. Employees may manipulate deficiencies in an entity's internal control for personal gain or to conceal fraudulent activity. This is more likely to be possible where there is collusion between employees.

Management override of internal control

Management is in a position of power to override an entity's internal control regardless of the strength of the system of internal control. Such management override could be to conceal information or for personal financial gain.

Use of judgement on the nature and extent of controls

Management is responsible for implementing controls which are designed to prevent, detect and correct material misstatements and safeguard the company's assets. Professional judgement will be needed to determine the type and extent of internal controls needed within the company and certain controls may be absent or ineffective. In particular, systems may be designed to deal with routine transactions and may therefore be inadequate in respect of non-routine transactions.

(b) Control deficiencies and recommendations

Control deficiency	Control recommendation
Credit limits not reviewed Credit limits set by the sales director are only changed when a customer requests an increase. If credit limits are not reviewed regularly they could be out of date, resulting in limits being too high and therefore sales being made to poor credit risks or, alternatively, too low and therefore Pomeranian Co losing potential revenue.	Credit limits should continue to be set by the sales director, however these limits should be reviewed and amended as appropriate on a regular basis by a responsible official for example the finance director or sales director.
GDNs sent weekly to finance Goods despatch notes (GDNs) are sent to the finance department on a weekly basis. If the finance department does not promptly receive GDNs, this could result in goods being despatched but being invoiced late. This could result in revenue cut-off issues and understated receivables.	The copies of the GDNs should be sent to the finance department on a more frequent basis, such as daily. The finance department should undertake a sequence check of the GDNs to ensure none are missing for processing.
No credit controller The company's credit controller is currently on maternity leave for six months and no one has taken over the credit controller's duties. Therefore, during this period no one has been responsible for monitoring and chasing ageing receivables. This could result in an increased risk of irrecoverable receivables and lead to customers not paying their outstanding balances on time, or at all, leading to reduced cash flows.	During the period of the maternity leave an alternative member of the finance department should be trained in the credit control role (or a temporary credit controller recruited) and assigned responsibility for reviewing the aged receivables listing and following up on any overdue customers.

Control deficiency	**Control recommendation**
Reconciliations only reviewed if differences The monthly trade receivables account reconciliation is only reviewed by the financial controller if there are any unreconciled differences. The reconciliation could reconcile but still contain significant errors as there could be compensating errors which cancel each other out or it may have been incorrectly prepared or manipulated and this would not be identified. If the reconciliation is not reviewed, then this significantly reduces its effectiveness.	The reconciliations should be reviewed by the financial controller on a monthly basis, even if there are no exceptions, and the review should be evidenced by way of signature on the reconciliation.
Authorisation limits too high Asset expenditure items below \$0.5m are authorised by the relevant head of department. \$0.5m is a significant sum and although department heads undertake the authorisation process, there is still considerable scope for non-business use or surplus assets being purchased leading to reduced profits and cash flow for Pomeranian Co.	The authorisation level for department heads should be significantly reduced to a more appropriate level, such as \$25,000. Any sums in excess of this should be approved by the board. If this proves too onerous, an asset expenditure committee of senior employees should be established for authorisation of assets. This committee should report to the board.
PPE verification work not as scheduled The internal audit department (IA) undertakes physical verification of assets each year. It is supposed to verify all assets over a three-year cycle, however in the current year IA will only complete the relevant procedures at one factory and one warehouse. The company has five factories and warehouses and a head office. Therefore, on this basis it will take over five years to physically verify all 11 sites. If the non-current asset register is not physically verified on a regular basis, there is an increased risk of assets being misappropriated or obsolete assets still being included in the register, as there is no check that the assets still exist in good working order.	IA should review its programme of visits to assess if additional resources could be devoted to ensure that all 11 sites are visited in line with the policy of three years. This would ensure that physical verification of all assets could be completed more regularly. During visits any assets which cannot be located should be investigated fully to identify where they could be. If they cannot be located then they should be written off.

Control deficiency	Control recommendation
Warehouse manager supervising counts The warehouse manager at each of the company's five sites is responsible for supervising the monthly perpetual inventory counts and ensuring that the counting teams are following their instructions. The warehouse managers may wish to hide inefficiencies and inventory discrepancies so that their departments are not criticised. This could result in inventory count records being inaccurate as well as an increase in inventory frauds.	The inventory counts should be supervised by an independent person, such as a member of Pomeranian Co's IA department.
Standard costs out of date The company costs its inventory using standard costs, which are not being kept up to date. If the standard costs were last reviewed two years ago there is the risk that the costs are misstated as changes in raw materials and wages costs may not have been adjusted for. This could result in inventory and profits being misstated. In addition, for year-end reporting, IAS 2 Inventories only allows standard costs to be used for valuation purposes, if they are a close approximation to actual costs, which is unlikely if the standard costs remain unchanged for a long period of time. Therefore, the inventory cost may not be in line with IAS 2.	A review of all standard costs currently in use should be undertaken by a senior manager in the production department. Actual costs for materials, labour and overheads should be ascertained and compared to the proposed standard costs to ensure they are a close approximation. The revised standard costs should be reviewed by the production director who should evidence this review. At least annually, a review of the standard costs should be undertaken by the production director to ensure they are up to date.
Exception report not reviewed Access to the master file data for suppliers is available to all those in the purchasing department and the monthly exception report of changes to master file data is not reviewed. All members of the purchasing department could amend data and, potentially, add new suppliers to the payables system, and as the exception report is not reviewed it is unlikely that this would be identified. This leads to an increased risk of fraud as clerks could add fictitious suppliers and then place fraudulent orders without detection.	The monthly exception report of changes to master file data should be reviewed by a responsible official, who should evidence this review. Any unauthorised or unexpected changes should be investigated and appropriate action taken. The ability to make amendments to master file data should be restricted to those required and authorised to make changes to this data.

Control deficiency	**Control recommendation**
Purchase invoices not agreed to GRNs Purchase invoices are not agreed to the relevant goods received notes (GRNs) prior to authorisation and input. This could result in invoices being paid for goods which were not received, resulting in increased costs.	All purchase invoices should be matched to both the purchase order and the related GRN. The details should be agreed prior to the invoice being authorised and logged in the payables system.

ACCA marking guide

		Marks
(a)	**Limitations of controls**	
	• Human error	1
	• Circumvention/collusion	1
	• Management override	1
	• Use of judgement on nature and extent of controls	1
	Restricted to	**4**
(b)	**Control deficiencies and recommendations (only 8 required)**	
	• Credit limits not reviewed	2
	• GDNs sent weekly to finance department	2
	• No credit controller	2
	• Reconciliations only reviewed if differences	2
	• Authorisation limits too high	2
	• PPE verification work not as scheduled	2
	• Warehouse manager supervising inventory counts	2
	• Standard costs out of date	2
	• Exception report not checked	2
	• Purchase invoices not agreed to GRNs	2
	Max 8 issues, 2 marks each	**16**
Total		**20**

Examiner's comments

Requirement (a). As with all knowledge requirements, it is important that candidates understand exactly what the question is asking for, especially where candidates should be aiming to score full marks. For this session, candidates were required to describe limitations of internal control for 4 marks. As the requirement verb was 'describe' candidates need to ensure that they write enough detail in their answers. Simply providing a few words such as 'human error' is not enough for a description. Candidates therefore need to consider whether they have developed the point sufficiently.

When attempting this requirement, it is important to identify the limitation and then provide some form of description of how this is a limitation. ½ mark was credited for the identification of the limitation and ½ mark for the description of it. For example, ½ mark would have been awarded for 'management override of control' and ½ mark for going on to say 'management using their position to ignore the controls in place for their own personal benefit'.

It is also important that candidates pay attention to any elements of the requirement which are highlighted. In this session the word 'limitations' was in capitals. This was specifically done to focus candidates' answers, so that they would not provide answers which related to other aspects of internal control. Additionally, there was a note under the requirement which stressed that the scenario did not need to be referred to in answering this requirement. Unfortunately, in this session many candidates ignored the word 'limitations' and the note and incorrectly focused on types of controls such as authorisation, components of internal control or provided control deficiencies from the scenario. Notes and key words highlighted in requirements are there to guide candidates and to help, do not ignore them.

It is imperative that future candidates ensure that they devote adequate time to learning the knowledge areas of the syllabus as well as practicing this style of knowledge question.

Requirement (b). Marks are awarded for identification of deficiencies (½ mark each), explanation of the implication of the deficiency to the company (½ mark each) and an appropriate control recommendation to address each deficiency (1 mark each).

The scenario will typically contain more than the number of deficiencies required and it remains important that candidates plan their time carefully and only attempt to list the required number of points. Continuing to apply good exam technique and time management skills is critical.

The first step in tackling a deficiencies question such as Pomeranian Co is to read through the whole scenario in full. This gives an understanding of what the potential answer points are as some deficiencies are easier to explain than others. Candidates may find it helpful to use the highlight function at this stage to mark the key points in the scenario which indicate a deficiency. Having looked at the whole scenario then candidates should re-read it, select the points they are to address in their response and then draft their answer as they go along. Do not be daunted by the length of the scenario, be methodical and keep re-reading the requirement to stay focused. In a multi-cycle question such as Pomeranian Co there is likely to be a good cross section of points across each of the cycles presented.

In identifying deficiencies, it is important to record what the actual deficiency from the scenario is. Candidates appear to be able to pick the relevant fact from the scenario but often fail to describe it in terms of a deficiency. For example, candidates identified from the scenario 'the finance clerk matches the invoices to the relevant purchase order and then passes the documents to the finance director for authorisation prior to input.' This is the relevant information from the scenario however, the actual deficiency which should have been derived from this information was that the invoices are only agreed to orders and not to goods received notes before being authorised for payment. A reference to the lack of checking to the goods received note would be required for the ½ mark available for identification of the deficiency.

Candidates must also be careful not to identify irrelevant deficiencies. For example, in the scenario it stated that the company maintains a perpetual inventory system. This in itself is not a deficiency, as it is a perfectly acceptable method for recording inventory as long as the process is well-managed and records are regularly updated and checked. Therefore, responses which identified this method as a deficiency and recommended a full year-end inventory count did not gain credit. Other answers incorrectly stated that the company should not value inventory using standard costs, that asset verifications should be undertaken over one year (which would not be practical) and that clerks were too junior to complete any tasks irrespective of the level of supervision or review by senior staff.

Having identified deficiencies, candidates are required to explain the implication to the business to be awarded credit. For example, a valid explanation for the deficiency 'only assets from two of the eleven sites will have been physically verified by the year end' (identification ½ mark awarded), would have been 'this could result in obsolete assets not being identified in the asset register in a timely manner.' The explanation of the deficiency must be sufficiently detailed and specific to the deficiency identified. Continuing with the example of the physical verification of assets deficiency, answers which just stated 'assets may be misstated' would not have gained credit as it does not fully explain **how** assets may be misstated.

Many candidates explain deficiencies by stating that 'this will result in fraud/error'. This explanation is not sufficiently detailed as all deficiencies can lead to increased fraud and error. A clear understanding of how the deficiency will result in fraud and error is needed. In Pomeranian Co this applied particularly to the deficiency of 'trade receivables account reconciliation is only reviewed where there are unreconciled differences.' The explanation needed to focus on how the receivables balance could contain errors rather than a generic comment relating to 'an increased risk of fraud and error.'

The last part of the requirement is for candidates to describe control recommendations. To gain the 1 mark available it is imperative that the descriptions of the controls are detailed enough. Details to consider would include what needs to be done, who it needs to be carried out by and how often does this need to take place. Additionally, recommendations must be actions rather than just objectives. Recommendations which are phrased as 'ensure that....' are unlikely to gain much credit as they set out what needs to be achieved rather than the process or procedure that needs to be put in place.

Candidates need to take care to ensure that recommendations are well described, clearly address the specific control deficiency identified and are practical suggestions. Many candidates often just repeat the converse of the deficiency, and to obtain the recommendation mark more detail is needed. For the credit limits deficiency, the recommendation of 'the credit limits should be regularly reviewed' would only gain ½ mark. To achieve a full mark the recommendation would need to state who should undertake this review, for example the sales or finance director. Additionally, for the deficiency relating to the warehouse managers supervising their own counts, simply recommending that 'a suitable person should supervise the count' was not sufficient. To gain full credit the recommendation would need to specify who this person should be. In this case, an appropriate suggestion would be a member of the internal audit department.

225 CASTLE COURIER *Walk in the footsteps of a top tutor*

Key answer tips

Part (a) is a straightforward knowledge requirement on documentation of systems. This is examined frequently so learn the methods and the advantages and disadvantages of each.

Part (b) asks for direct controls and tests of controls. Direct controls reduce the risk of material misstatement. Look for evidence of segregation of duties, authorisation, reconciliations, etc.

The control must be complete to be effective, e.g. sequential numbering of invoices must be accompanied with a regular sequence check to ensure the sequence is complete in order for the control to be effective. A bank reconciliation must be reviewed by a responsible official to ensure it has been performed properly. For the full mark, explain what the control aims to achieve, for example, the risk that the control is designed to mitigate. When describing a test of control, you need to say how the auditor will obtain evidence that the control is working effectively. This may come from inspecting a document for evidence of authorisation or reperforming a control such as a reconciliation to ensure the client staff have performed the control effectively.

Part (c) asks for control deficiencies and recommendations. Deficiencies are where the controls are not working effectively and therefore provide opportunity for fraud and error. Fully explain the deficiency in terms of the effect on the company. If management are to take action, they must be concerned about the potential consequences of the deficiency. When providing recommendations for improvement, be as specific as possible. For the test of control, describe how the auditor would obtain evidence that the client has implemented the control suggested.

Part (d) requires substantive procedures on the payroll expense. Substantive procedures are used to test the payroll figure which appears in the financial statements. The assertions relevant to transactions and events such as completeness, accuracy, occurrence and cut-off should be tested. This can be achieved with analytical procedures as well as tests of detail.

(a) Documenting systems

	Description	**Disadvantage**
Narrative notes	Narrative notes consist of a written description of the system. They detail what occurs in the system at each stage including related controls which operate at each stage.	They may prove to be time-consuming and cumbersome if the internal control system is complex. It may make it more difficult to identify if any internal controls are missing in narrative notes.

	Description	Disadvantage
Internal control questionnaires	Internal control questionnaires contain a list of questions for each major transaction cycle. They use questions designed to assess whether internal controls exist.	Internal controls may be overstated if the client is aware that the auditor is looking for a particular answer. Unusual controls may not be included on a standard questionnaire and hence may not be identified.

(b) Direct controls and tests of control

Direct control	Test of control
Sequence checks All staff members are issued with a sequentially numbered key card. Sequence checks and checks on the data recorded are carried out by the human resources (HR) supervisor. This ensures that payroll records are complete, that employees are paid for hours worked and that all hours are recorded.	For a sample of key cards and data recorded in the clocking-in system, carry out a sequence check to identify if there are any gaps in the sequence. Review details of checks carried out by the HR supervisor to identify any gaps in the sequence and check they have evidenced their review by way of signature.
HR review of clocking in process The clocking-in process is monitored by a camera on entry to the distribution centre and video footage is reviewed by HR every week. This will prevent staff members fraudulently clocking-in for other employees and hence employees will only be paid for actual hours worked ensuring occurrence of payroll.	For a sample of weeks, review the log of the recordings to identify who reviewed that week's footage to ensure it has been reviewed by a member of the HR department. Review the log for any gaps in the review process and discuss these findings with HR.
Payroll calculations reperformed The payroll clerk confirms the transfer of hours and calculations has been done accurately by recalculating, for a sample of employees, their gross to net pay. This check is also reviewed by the payroll supervisor who evidences their review. This reduces the risk that errors occur in the automated transfer and calculations during the payroll processing. Any errors would be identified on a timely basis to prevent salaries being over or under paid.	For a sample of months, review the calculations of gross to net pay for evidence that the calculations have been performed. Confirm the signature of the payroll supervisor as evidence that they have reviewed the report. For any anomalies, enquire of the reasons and what action was taken to resolve the issue. For a sample of months, reperform the gross to net pay calculations and compare to the payroll system and the calculations prepared by the payroll clerk. Discuss any discrepancies with the payroll supervisor.

Direct control	Test of control
Password updated monthly The payroll system is password-protected and the payroll manager changes the password on a monthly basis using a random password generator. This reduces the risk of fraud by preventing unauthorised changes being made to the standing data and unauthorised access to sensitive payroll information.	Attempt to login to the payroll system using a password which should be out of date. Confirm that the system has rejected access.
Account reconciliations performed Each month, the finance director carries out a payroll account reconciliation and investigates any differences. This will ensure the payroll expense and employment tax liability is accurate and is not misstated in the year-end financial statements.	For a sample of months, review the payroll account reconciliations and make enquiries of the finance director of any errors, how they arose and what action was taken to ensure they do not arise in the future. Reperform a sample of account reconciliations and compare results with those prepared by the finance director. Discuss any discrepancies with the finance director.
Tax liability calculation reviewed The amount due to the tax authority is calculated by the payroll supervisor who then passes it to the financial controller for review. This ensures that the amount paid to the tax authority is correct. It also creates segregation of duties between the payroll supervisor calculating the liability and the financial controller reviewing the calculation which reduces the risk of error.	Review a sample of calculations of the monthly employment tax liability for evidence of review by the financial controller confirming the calculation is correct and that payment can be made.

(c) Control deficiencies and recommendations

Control deficiency	Control recommendation
Holiday requests not authorised Department managers are required to approve all employees' holiday forms, however, this does not always occur. This could result in employees taking unauthorised leave which could lead to operational difficulties if there are shortages of staff at critical periods.	Employees should receive written confirmation when their holiday has been approved and should be informed that they will not be able to take holiday without this notification. Any payments for unused holiday should be authorised by department managers prior to payment.

Control deficiency	**Control recommendation**
In addition, payments for untaken holiday may be made in error as holiday records may be incorrect.	
Lack of segregation of duties The financial controller prepares the bank transfers for the payroll and also authorises these to be paid. This lack of segregation of duties increases the risk of fraud/error as the financial controller could pay themselves or certain employees more than they are due without this being detected.	Once the bank transfer has been prepared by the financial controller, it should be passed to the finance director to be reviewed and authorised for payment. The review and authorisation should be evidenced by the finance director.
Edit report not checked The payroll clerk amends the payroll and an edit report of changes is produced but this report is not reviewed. As the edit report is not checked, errors made by the payroll clerk when updating the system will not be identified promptly. This may result in new employees not being paid at all, errors being made in payments to new employees or leavers being paid after they have left the company. This would lead to loss of employee goodwill and errors in accounting records for wages and salaries. It could also result in an increased risk of fraud as fictitious employees could be added by the payroll clerk.	The payroll supervisor or a member of the finance team should review all edit reports and agree changes made to the details on the joiner/leavers forms. Any discrepancies should be investigated promptly and the payroll system updated for any errors or omissions. The payroll supervisor should evidence their review on the edit report with their signature.
Temporary staff not processed by HR The HR department is responsible for processing joiners and leavers, but due to staff illness, the operations manager has processed temporary new drivers and notified payroll. The operations manager may not carry out all the required procedures for processing temporary new drivers as the manager may not be using appropriate documentation. This could result in temporary employees not being set up in the payroll records correctly, resulting in the late payment of wages, incorrect statutory deductions being calculated and incomplete payroll records.	All staff appointments, including temporary staff, should only be processed by the HR department to ensure that correct procedures are followed. If it is not possible for the HR department to carry out all of the detailed processing due to staff shortages, a member of the HR team should review the leaver/joiner form and authorise it before it is sent to the payroll department. The payroll department should be notified not to accept any new joiner information unless approved by a member of HR.

Control deficiency	Control recommendation
Only overtime > 5 hours authorised Only overtime in excess of five hours per week needs authorisation by the operations manager. This means that employees could claim to have worked up to five hours overtime without authorisation resulting in payments being made to employees for hours not worked and additional payroll costs.	All overtime, including that below five hours, should be authorised by a responsible official before being processed in the payroll. This authorisation should be evidenced by way of signature.
Cash wages collected without ID Where cash wages are paid, the driver is only required to provide their name to collect their pay packet. Payment of wages without proof of identity or signature increases the risk that wages could be paid to incorrect employees either in error or due to fraud resulting in a loss of cash.	All drivers collecting cash pay packets should provide a form of identification to the finance staff member before the pay packet is handed to them. The driver should also be required to sign for their pay packet.
No approved bonus parameters The operations manager decides on the bonus to be paid to delivery drivers each quarter and there are no approved parameters for the bonus levels. Without approved parameters, the operations manager may award excessive bonuses or pay additional sums to friends and family members resulting in additional payroll costs.	Approved bonus parameters should be established by the board. All bonuses should be determined by a senior official, such as the sales director, in line with these parameters, who should communicate the bonus in writing to the payroll department.
Driver's breaks not monitored Delivery drivers must take breaks throughout the day which are not monitored. Drivers could take longer breaks than those authorised resulting in payments being made to employees for time not worked. Conversely, if drivers do not take the required breaks, they may be in breach of law and regulations which require drivers to take regular breaks, hence the company is at risk of fines.	The company should monitor the activity of the delivery drivers through electronic means, for example, by using tracking devices attached to their vehicles to ensure that the prescribed breaks are taken by the employees. Data should be downloaded and reviewed by a responsible official on a regular basis.

(d) Substantive procedures on payroll expense

- Cast a sample of payroll records to confirm completeness and accuracy and agree the total wages and salaries expense per the payroll system to the trial balance.
- Recalculate the gross and net pay figures for a sample of employees and agree to the payroll records.
- For a sample of wage payments, agree the total net pay per the payroll records to the bank transfer listing and to the bank ledger account.
- Perform a proof-in-total of wages and salaries, incorporating joiners and leavers and the pay increase/bonuses. Compare this to the actual wages and salaries expense in the financial statements and investigate any significant differences.
- Compare the total payroll figure this year to the prior year, identify any significant differences and discuss with management.
- Review monthly payroll charges, compare this to the prior year and budgets and discuss any significant differences with management.
- Calculate overtime costs as a percentage of total wages. Compare this to the prior year and discuss any significant differences with management.
- Agree a sample of individual wages and salaries per the payroll to personnel records and records of hours worked per the clocking-in system.
- Reperform the calculation of statutory deductions and agree to supporting documentation to confirm whether correct deductions for this year have been made in the payroll.
- Select a sample of joiners and leavers, agree their start/leaving date to supporting documentation, recalculate their first/last salary to ensure it is accurate.
- Recalculate holiday pay for a sample of employees and agree to holiday records and daily rate applied.
- Select a sample of employees from HR records and agree salaries per HR records to the payroll records to confirm the accuracy of the payroll expense.
- Agree the payroll account reconciliation to accounting records and investigate any differences.

ACCA marking guide		
		Marks
(a)	**Methods of documenting internal controls**	
	• Narrative notes	2
	• Internal control questionnaires	2
	Restricted to	**4**
(b)	**Direct controls and tests of control (only 4 required)**	
	• Sequence checks on key cards/data	2
	• HR review of clocking in process	2
	• Payroll calculations reperformed	2
	• Password updated monthly	2
	• Account reconciliations performed	2
	• Tax liability calculation reviewed	2
	Max 4 issues, 2 marks each	**8**

(c)	**Control deficiencies and recommendations (only 6 required)**	
	• Holiday requests not authorised	2
	• FC prepares and authorises bank transfer	2
	• Edit report not checked	2
	• Temporary staff not processed by HR	2
	• Only overtime above five hours authorised	2
	• Cash wages collected without identification	2
	• No approved bonus parameters	2
	• Driver's breaks not monitored	2
	Max 6 issues, 2 marks each	**12**
(d)	**Substantive procedures for payroll expense** 1 mark per well-described procedure	
	Restricted to	**6**
Total		**30**

Examiner's comments

Part (a). This is a relatively straightforward knowledge requirement which has been tested in previous exam sessions. For knowledge requirements such as this it is important that candidates understand exactly what the question is asking, especially where candidates should be aiming to score full marks. For this session two methods for documenting systems were provided in a table; narrative notes and questionnaires. The first part of the requirement was a description of the method and 1 mark was available for each method. Where the requirement verb is 'describe' as was the case in this instance, candidates need to ensure that they include enough detail in their answers.

When describing a given method it is important to think about the words used; for example stating that 'internal control questionnaires are questionnaires' does not give any additional detail on what the method actually is as it just repeats the words given in the question. An appropriate response would have been 'a list of questions used to assess if the controls exist'.

Similarly, in this session some candidates only gained ½ mark for the description of the narrative notes as they simply stated that they 'were written'. To gain a full mark a response would need to provide further explanation, for example 'they provide detail of what happens at each stage in the system'.

Having described the method, the next part of the requirement is to provide an explanation of a disadvantage. It is important to read the requirement carefully and highlight key parts, in this case that only disadvantages are required. This session some candidates incorrectly provided advantages as well as disadvantages or provided advantages instead of disadvantages. The requirement asked for 'a' disadvantage and so only one per method is needed and if well explained would gain 1 mark. As with the description of the method it is important to provide sufficient detail in answers. Stating 'time consuming' or 'cumbersome' without any further development is not a sufficiently detailed response to gain 1 mark.

Part (b). Marks are awarded for identification of direct controls (½ mark each), explanation of the control (½ mark each) and an appropriate test of control for each control (1 mark each). In common with risks questions the scenario will typically contain more than the number of direct controls required, so it is important that candidates plan their time carefully and only attempt to list the required number of points. With this type of requirement good exam technique is absolutely critical. As stated in previous Examiner's reports candidates should be prepared to answer questions which cover direct controls and tests of controls, control deficiencies and recommendations or a combination of both. Castle Courier Co examines both direct controls and deficiencies and focuses solely on the payroll system. Questions may also be set where direct controls and deficiencies are tested but in relation to different parts of a company's system, for example direct controls in the sales system and deficiencies in the purchases system.

The first step in tackling a single system direct controls and deficiencies question, such as Castle Courier Co, is to read through the whole scenario in full. This gives an understanding of what the potential answer points are for both direct controls and deficiencies. It is critical in a question like this that candidates can distinguish between direct controls and deficiencies. Candidates must take care not to identify a direct control where in fact there is a deficiency. If the scenario includes a description of a control which is not operating effectively then this is a deficiency and NOT a direct control. For example, in Castle Courier Co the scenario states that 'an edit report is generated which records the changes made to the payroll system, but this report is not reviewed.' In this case the fact that 'an edit report of changes to the system is generated', is not a direct control. This control is not operating correctly as the report is not reviewed. This should instead be identified as a deficiency.

When undertaking the first read through of the scenario it would be good exam technique to use the highlight function, using one colour for direct controls and a different colour for deficiencies. This would provide a visual aid for quickly spotting both controls and deficiencies. Having looked at the whole scenario and highlighted relevant points candidates should pick their strongest points based on the number set out in the requirement (in this case four), re-read them from the scenario, drafting their answer as they go along. Do not be daunted by the length of the scenario, be methodical and keep re-reading the requirement to stay focused.

In order to be a direct control, candidates need to consider whether the control as described has been appropriately designed and is being operated in such a way that it would in fact prevent or detect a material misstatement. Therefore, when identifying direct controls, it is important that the control described is complete. For example, the fact that the payroll system automatically calculates gross and net pay is not in itself a direct control. Additional checks would need to be undertaken to ensure that the system is correctly calculating the wages and any deductions. Similarly, some candidates simply focused on the employee key cards being sequentially numbered. To be effective as a direct control sequence checks would need to be carried out to identify any gaps to ensure completeness of the records. The sequential numbering is an important element of the system as it allows the sequence checking to take place, but in itself is not a control.

Some candidates are under the misconception that each sentence in the scenario contains a direct control. This is not the case. The scenario will include information which describes the way in which the system operates but not all of this information will indicate a direct control. Candidates who then break down each line into a different point end up wasting time and not gaining credit. In this session some candidates split one direct control into two or three points. As only four controls were required this resulted in very few marks being gained.

Having identified direct controls, candidates then need to explain each control. In considering this it is important to think about what the aim of the control is, what potential misstatement is being prevented or detected. The explanation needs to be specific to each control. It is not sufficient to state 'this will prevent fraud and error' as all controls aim to prevent or detect fraud and error in some way. A clear understanding of specifically how the control will prevent fraud and error is needed. For example, in this session the scenario contained a control whereby HR review video footage of the clocking-in process. An appropriate explanation would be that the aim of this control is to ensure that staff members cannot clock-in other employees, resulting in staff only being paid for actual hours worked.

The last part of the requirement is for candidates to describe tests of controls for each direct control identified. To gain the 1 mark available it is imperative that the descriptions of the tests are detailed enough. A test which starts with 'check' is unlikely to provide sufficient detail as to how exactly the auditor will test the control. In addition, it must be remembered that tests of controls are procedures carried out by the auditor, therefore candidates need to ensure that they focus on what the auditor should do rather than provide recommendations for management.

In considering how to test the control, a useful starting point is to consider if there are any documents which can be inspected as this is likely to provide strong evidence the control is operating. However, when describing the test it is important to clearly state what document is being inspected and also for what purpose. In this session the scenario contained a key control where the payroll tax liability is calculated by the payroll supervisor and reviewed by the financial controller. In testing this control an appropriate response would be that the 'monthly tax liability calculations are being inspected' and in this case that it is 'for evidence of review by the financial controller'.

In addition, in describing tests of controls, it is important that key elements of the control are tested. This session the scenario contained a direct control over passwords being changed monthly. Some candidates recommended that in order to test this 'a fictitious password should be used to attempt to enter the system, which should then be rejected'. This is not a valid test in this situation. A fictitious password would of course not access the system but this would not confirm that passwords are changed on a monthly basis. An appropriate way to test that the passwords are changed each month is to use one of the expired passwords to attempt to access the system. In addition, tests such as 'observe' do not score as well as inspection or some enquiry type procedures.

Part (c). Marks are awarded for identification of deficiencies (½ mark each), explanation of the implication of the deficiency to the company (½ mark each) and an appropriate control recommendation to address each deficiency (1 mark each). In common with direct controls requirements the scenario will typically contain more than the number of deficiencies required and it remains important that candidates plan their time carefully and only attempt to list the specified number of points. Continuing to apply good exam technique and time management skills is critical. Having completed the direct controls requirement candidates should complete their second read through of the scenario, transferring the highlighted deficiencies into their answer. In this session some candidates had already addressed a number of deficiencies incorrectly as direct controls in part (b) and therefore failed to identify them in their response for part (c) of the question requirement and so were not able to gain credit. Additionally, a significant proportion of candidates identified deficiencies where in fact a control was operating. For example, a common incorrect answer was 'the payroll clerk recalculates gross to net pay' with candidates believing that the payroll clerk was too junior to undertake these checks. This was not a deficiency but instead part of a direct control including the subsequent review of this process by a supervisor.

In identifying deficiencies, it is important to record what the actual deficiency from the scenario is. Candidates appear able to pick the relevant fact from the scenario but often fail to describe it in terms of a deficiency. For example, in Castle Courier Co, candidates identified from the scenario 'overtime over five hours is authorised' but the actual issue was that overtime under five hours is not authorised. This was required for the ½ mark available for identification of the deficiency. Candidates must also be careful not to identify irrelevant deficiencies. For example, in the scenario it stated that some temporary drivers were paid in cash. This in itself is not a deficiency. How a company chooses to pay its wages and salaries is a business decision, the auditor would only be focused on whether the payment method is well controlled. Other incorrect answers focused on monthly processes and reconciliations not being frequent enough and clerks being too junior to undertake any tasks.

Having identified deficiencies candidates are required to explain the implication to the business to be awarded credit. For example, a valid explanation for the deficiency 'holiday request forms are not always authorised' (identification ½ mark awarded), would have been 'this could result in employees taking unauthorised leave which could lead to staff shortages and operational difficulties.' In common with direct control requirements, the explanation needs to be specific to each deficiency, as it is not sufficient to state 'this will result in fraud/error' as all deficiencies can lead to increased fraud and error. A clear understanding of how the deficiency will result in 'fraud and error' is needed.

The last part of the requirement is for candidates to describe control recommendations. To gain the 1 mark available it is imperative that the descriptions of the controls are detailed enough. Details to consider would include what needs to be done, who it need to be done by and how often does this need to take place. Additionally, recommendations must be actions rather than just objectives. Recommendations which are phrased as 'ensure that….' are unlikely to gain much credit. For the holiday forms deficiency, the recommendation of 'ensure that holiday request forms are authorised' is an objective and does not explain how this should be undertaken. Candidates need to take care to ensure that recommendations are well described, clearly address the specific control deficiency identified and are practical suggestions. Many candidates often just repeat the converse of the deficiency, and to obtain the recommendation mark more detail is needed.

Part (d). For substantive procedures requirements, one mark is available for each well-described procedure, therefore candidates should aim to produce six tests for this requirement. Candidates should plan their time accordingly. Also, candidates should note that it is not necessary to write out the question requirement at the beginning of their answer, it does not gain any credit and is a waste of time.

When describing substantive procedures one of the key things to consider is the level of detail provided. Many candidates fail to score well in this type of requirement because their procedures are vague or too brief. Tests must be sufficiently detailed noting clearly which source document should be used. For example, in this session many candidates included, 'agree to bank ledger account and bank statements' without specifying that this was being done to agree the net pay or statutory deductions. Also 'recalculate gross to net pay for a sample of employees' would only gain ½ mark as it needs to be agreed back to the underlying payroll records to ensure payroll is accurate.

Candidates must ensure that they can distinguish between a substantive procedure and a test of control. Many candidates lose marks in this type of requirement by mixing up these procedures. For example, in this session some candidates provided tests of controls such as 'reviewing that the drivers' bonuses have been authorised.' The purpose of this procedures is to ensure that the controls over the bonus allocations are operating effectively, therefore this is not a substantive procedure.

Analytical procedures are an important source of evidence when auditing payroll and there are a number of examples which would be relevant in this case for example, comparison of monthly payroll with the prior year and investigation of any significant differences. Candidates who included analytical procedures in their answers were able to gain credit.

In this session many candidates included irrelevant tests such as 'obtaining written representations', 'reviewing disclosure' or focused on authorisation of overtime and bonuses. This demonstrates a lack of understanding of the scenario and the purpose of substantive procedures.

Take the time to read the question requirements carefully and spend time thinking about what is needed prior to producing an answer.

226 SWIFT *Walk in the footsteps of a top tutor*

Key answer tips

Part (a) is a straightforward knowledge requirement. This has been examined many times before so students should be able to answer this part of the question well.

Part (b) asks for direct controls and tests of controls. Direct controls reduce the risk of material misstatement. Look for evidence of segregation of duties, authorisation, reconciliations, etc. The control must be complete to be effective, e.g. sequential numbering of invoices must be accompanied with a regular sequence check to ensure the sequence is complete in order for the control to be effective. A bank reconciliation must be reviewed by a responsible official to ensure it has been performed properly. For the full mark, explain what the control aims to achieve, for example, the risk that the control is designed to mitigate. When describing a test of control, you need to say how the auditor will obtain evidence that the control is working effectively. This may come from inspecting a document for evidence of authorisation or reperforming a control such as a reconciliation to ensure the client staff have performed the control effectively.

(a) Documenting systems

	Description	**Advantage**
Narrative notes	Narrative notes consist of a written description of the system. They detail what occurs in the system at each stage and include details of any controls which operate at each stage.	They are simple to record; after discussion with staff members, these discussions are easily written up as notes. They can facilitate understanding by all members of the audit team, especially more junior members who might find alternative methods too complex.
Flowcharts	Flowcharts are a diagrammatic illustration of the internal control system. Lines usually demonstrate the sequence of events and standard symbols are used to signify controls or documents.	With flowcharts it is easy to view the system in its entirety as it is all presented together in one diagram. Due to the use of standard symbols for controls, it can be effective in identifying missing controls.

	Description	Advantage
Questionnaires	Internal control questionnaires (ICQs) or internal control evaluation questionnaires (ICEQs) contain a list of questions for each major transaction cycle. ICQs are used to assess whether controls exist whereas ICEQs assess the effectiveness of the controls in place.	Questionnaires are quick to prepare, which means they are a timely method for recording the system. If drafted thoroughly they ensure that all controls present within the system are considered and recorded, hence missing controls or deficiencies are clearly highlighted by the audit team.

(b) Direct controls and tests of control

Direct control	Test of control
Segregation of duties Swift Co has a separate human resources (HR) department, which is responsible for setting up all new employees. Having a segregation of roles between HR and payroll departments reduces the risk of fictitious employees being set up and also being paid (occurrence of payroll costs) which would result in overstatement of payroll costs.	Review the job descriptions of payroll and HR to confirm the split of responsibilities with regards to setting up new joiners. Discuss with members of the payroll department the process for setting up new joiners and agree new joiners to documentation initiated by HR.
Unique employee number All new employees are assigned a unique employee number by HR. The payroll system is unable to process new joiners without the inclusion of the unique employee number. As payroll staff are unable to set up new joiners without the employee number from the joiner form it reduces the risk of fictitious employees being set up by payroll (occurrence of payroll costs).	Attempt to add a new joiner to the payroll system without a unique employee number, the system should reject this addition.
Review of exception report On a monthly basis an exception report of changes to payroll standing data is produced and reviewed by the payroll manager. This ensures that any unauthorised amendments to standing data are identified and investigated on a timely basis so that the data used when the payroll is run is valid and accurate.	Select a sample of monthly exception reports and review for evidence of review and follow up of any unexpected changes by the payroll manager.

Direct control	Test of control
Recalculation of gross to net pay The payroll supervisor selects a sample of payslips and recalculates the gross to net pay calculations, compares the results to the output from the payroll system and investigates any discrepancies. This reduces the risk that the automated system generates errors during the payroll processing. Any errors would be identified on a timely basis to prevent wages being over or under paid.	Review the monthly payslips sampled by the payroll supervisor for their signature for evidence the review of calculations has been undertaken. For a sample of monthly payrolls reperform the gross to net pay calculation and compare to the payroll system, discuss any discrepancies with the payroll supervisor.
Authorisation of purchase orders Purchase orders up to $5,000 are authorised by the purchasing manager and above $5,000 by the purchasing director. This ensures that goods are only purchased which are required by Swift Co and relate to genuine business expenses (occurrence of purchases).	Select a sample of purchase orders and review for evidence of authorisation in accordance with authorisation limits. Agree this to the appropriate signature on the approved signatories list.
Goods received checked The warehouse department agrees the receipt of goods from suppliers to a copy of the purchase order and confirms the quantity and quality of the goods received and signs the goods received notes (GRNs) to evidence the checks. This ensures that Swift Co is not recording liabilities and subsequently paying for the receipt of inferior quality goods or for goods it did not order.	During the interim audit observe the warehouse department when receiving goods to understand the level of checks being undertaken. Review a sample of GRNs held in the warehouse department for signature, as evidence of checks being undertaken on receipt of goods.
Control totals on purchase invoices Purchase invoices are logged into the detailed list of purchases in batches, utilising control totals. Utilising control totals ensures both completeness and accuracy over the input of purchase invoices. If the invoices are not all input completely and accurately payables may be misstated.	Select a sample of control total sheets and review for evidence of control totals being utilised and the clerk's signature.

Direct control	**Test of control**
Supplier statement reconciliations Supplier statement reconciliations are undertaken on a monthly basis and these are reviewed by the financial controller. This ensures that any errors in the recording of purchases and payables are identified and corrected in a timely manner and therefore that payables are complete and accurate.	Review the file of reconciliations to ensure that they are being performed on a regular basis and that they have been reviewed by a responsible official. Reperform a sample of the reconciliations to ensure that they have been carried out appropriately and discrepancies investigated.
Authorisation of bank transfer list The finance director authorises the bank transfer payment list for suppliers after agreeing the amounts to be paid to supporting documentation and reviewing for any duplicate payments. This reduces the risk that suppliers could be being paid an incorrect amount, or that sums are being paid to fictitious suppliers which will cause misstatement of payables.	Review the payments list for evidence of review by the finance director. Enquire of accounts staff what supporting documentation the finance director requests when undertaking this review.

ACCA marking guide

		Marks
(a)	**Methods of documenting internal controls**	
	Narrative notes	2
	Flowcharts	2
	Questionnaires	2
		6
(b)	**Direct controls and test of controls** (only 7 required)	
	Segregation of duties between HR and payroll	2
	Unique employee number to process joiners	2
	Review of exception report	2
	Recalculation of gross to net pay	2
	Authorisation of purchase orders	2
	Goods agreed to purchase order/quality/quantity	2
	Control totals used for invoice input	2
	Supplier statement reconciliations	2
	Authorisation of bank transfer list	2
	Max 7 issues, 2 marks each	**14**
Total		**20**

Examiner's comments

Part (a) is a relatively straightforward knowledge requirement which has been tested in previous exam sessions. Knowledge requirements such as this often have an opening statement, sometimes referenced to an ISA, and this is useful for setting the scene and providing clarification on the aim of the question requirement. It is especially important that candidates understand exactly what the question is asking, especially for knowledge questions, where candidates should be aiming to score full marks. In Swift Co, three methods for documenting systems were provided in a table; narrative notes, flowcharts and questionnaires. The first part of the requirement was a description of the method and 1 mark was available for each method. As the requirement verb was 'describe' candidates need to ensure that they write enough detail in their answers, simply stating 'list of questions' for questionnaires is not enough for a description. Candidates therefore need to consider whether they have provided sufficient detail. When describing a given method it is important to think about the words used; for example, 'narrative notes are notes' does not give any detail on what the method actually is as it is essentially just repeating the same words given in the question and therefore will not gain any credit. An appropriate response for narrative notes would have been 'a written description of what occurs in the system at each stage'. In this session some candidates misunderstood what flowcharts were confusing a graphic illustration with a graph. Having described the method, the next part of the requirement is to provide an explanation of an advantage. It is important to read the requirement carefully and highlight key parts, in this case that only advantages are required. This session some candidates incorrectly provided disadvantages. The requirement asked for 'an' advantage and so only one per method is needed and if well explained would gain 1 mark. Again, it is important to provide sufficient detail in answers. Also, it is important to think about those advantages specific to each method. Providing the same advantages for all three methods is unlikely to gain sufficient credit, as each method and its advantages are different. It is imperative that future candidates ensure that they devote adequate time to learning the knowledge areas of the syllabus as well as practising this style of knowledge question.

In part (b) marks are awarded for identification of key controls (½ mark each), explanation of the key control (½ mark each) and an appropriate test of control for each control (1 mark each). In common with risks questions the scenario will typically contain more than the number of key controls required, so it is important that candidates plan their time carefully and only attempt to list the required number of points. With this type of requirement good exam technique is absolutely critical. Candidates should be prepared to answer questions which cover key controls and tests of control, control deficiencies and recommendations or a combination of both. The exam technique required is similar, however it is vitally important that candidates identify exactly what they are being required to do. This session many candidates did not provide key controls and instead identified controls from the scenario and attempted to turn them into deficiencies along with recommendations, this would have gained no credit. For example, some candidates identified correctly from the scenario that exception reports were produced and reviewed by the payroll manager, but then went on to state in their answer that this was a deficiency as someone else should review the exceptions for better segregation of duties. The first step in tackling a key controls question is to read through the whole scenario in full, this gives an understanding of what the potential answer points are as some key controls are easier to explain than others. Having looked at the whole scenario, candidates should then re-read it, drafting their answer as they go along.

Do not be daunted by the length of the scenario, be methodical and keep re-reading the requirement to stay focused. A key control is a control which has been appropriately designed to prevent or detect material misstatement. As such when identifying key controls, it is important that the control described is complete. When attempting questions of this type and identifying key controls, candidates should ask themselves 'why would the auditor want to place reliance on this particular control' and 'what is it about the control which would prevent or detect a material misstatement'. Assessing the information in the scenario in this way will allow candidates to ensure that they are identifying all aspects of the control. For example, Swift Co's system contained a control relating to monthly supplier statement reconciliations being performed and reviewed by the financial controller. Candidates who simply focused on the preparation of the reconciliations did not gain the identification ½ mark, as the complete control includes the review of the reconciliations to ensure that all differences have been resolved. It is the identification and resolution of these differences which ensures that liabilities are complete and accurate. Similarly, employees having a unique identification number on its own is not a key control. Instead the focus needs to include how the unique number ensures that only genuine employees are paid wages. When identifying key controls, candidates must also think about the relevance of the issue identified to the auditor. This session many irrelevant points were identified from the scenario which were not key controls. Employees being paid by bank transfer is not a key control, conversely if wages are paid in cash this is not in itself a deficiency. How a company chooses to pay its wages and salaries is a business decision, the auditor would only be focused on the key controls surrounding the payment method. Other incorrect answers included goods received notes being sent to the finance department – this is a crucial part of the process but is not in itself a control.

Having identified key controls, candidates then need to explain the control. In considering this it is important to think about what the aim of the control is, what potential misstatement is being prevented or detected. The explanation needs to be specific to each control. It is not sufficient to state 'this will prevent fraud and error' as all controls aim to prevent or detect fraud and/or error in some way. A clear understanding of specifically how the control will 'prevent fraud and error' is needed. For example, in this session the scenario contained a control whereby the finance director reviewed the payments list to supporting documentation prior to authorising. The aim of this control is to ensure that invalid, duplicate or fictitious payments are identified. Note how this explanation describes the specific type of fraud or error that the control prevents. The last part of the requirement is for candidates to describe tests of control for each key control identified. To gain the 1 mark available it is imperative that the descriptions of the tests are detailed enough. A test which starts with 'check' is unlikely to provide sufficient detail as to how exactly the auditor will test the control. In addition, it must be remembered that tests of controls are procedures carried out by the auditor, therefore candidates need to ensure that they focus on what the auditor should do rather than provide recommendations for management. A useful starting point when considering how to test a control is to consider if there are any documents which can be inspected for evidence that the control is operating. However, when describing the test, it is important to clearly state what document is being inspected and also for what purpose. In this session the scenario contained a key control of authorisation of purchase orders. In testing this control it is necessary to state that the 'purchase orders are being inspected' and in this case that it is 'for evidence of review by the relevant authoriser'. In addition, in describing tests of controls, tests such as 'observe' do not score as well as inspection, enquiry or reperformance procedures. For some controls it is perfectly acceptable for observation to be used as an audit procedure, such as 'observing the warehouse team when undertaking detailed checks on receipt of goods.' However, 'observing the finance director agreeing the payments list to supporting documentation' will not gain credit as instead 'the payments list should be reviewed for evidence of the director's review' as this provides stronger audit evidence. In Swift Co, 'observation' is only an appropriate response in relation to the warehouse department checks on goods received, as for all other controls it would have been possible to perform stronger tests of controls to gather more conclusive evidence on whether the control is operating effectively.

227 SNOWDON *Walk in the footsteps of a top tutor*

Key answer tips

Part (a) asks for matters when determining whether a control deficiency is significant. Think about which type of deficiencies a client might be more concerned about and therefore more likely to want to do something about because the consequences could be significant, as compared with deficiencies where the consequences might not be so detrimental for the company. All section B questions are likely to include a knowledge requirement. Often, these questions require knowledge of an auditing standard and therefore they can be difficult to answer unless you have revised the specific audit guidance, therefore, plan some of your revision time to go over these areas.

Part (b) asks for direct controls and tests of controls. Direct controls reduce the risk of material misstatement. Look for evidence of segregation of duties, authorisation, reconciliations, etc. The control must be complete to be effective, e.g. sequential numbering of invoices must be accompanied with a regular sequence check to ensure the sequence is complete in order for the control to be effective. A bank reconciliation must be reviewed by a responsible official to ensure it has been performed properly. For the full mark, explain what the control aims to achieve, for example, the risk that the control is designed to mitigate.

When describing a test of control, you need to say how the auditor will obtain evidence that the control is working effectively. This may come from inspecting a document for evidence of authorisation or reperforming a control such as a reconciliation to ensure the client staff have performed the control effectively.

Part (c) asks for control deficiencies and recommendations in respect of the internal control system. This is examined frequently and with plenty of past exams to practise, this type of question should be straightforward. Fully explain the deficiency in terms of the effect on the company. If management are to take action, they must be concerned about the potential consequences of the deficiency. When providing recommendations for improvement, be as specific as possible.

(a) Significant deficiencies

Examples of matters the external auditor may consider in determining whether a deficiency in internal controls is significant include:

- The likelihood of the deficiencies leading to material misstatements in the financial statements in the future.
- The susceptibility to loss or fraud of the related asset or liability.
- The subjectivity and complexity of determining estimated amounts.
- The financial statement amounts exposed to the deficiencies.
- The volume of activity that has occurred or could occur in the account balance or class of transactions exposed to the deficiency or deficiencies.
- The importance of the controls to the financial reporting process.

- The cause and frequency of the exceptions detected as a result of the deficiencies in the controls.
- The interaction of the deficiency with other deficiencies in internal control.

(b) Direct controls and tests of control

Direct control	Test of control
Asset classification checks Asset expenditure purchase orders are classified by the finance department between assets and expenses using guidelines established by the finance director, this is noted on the purchase order. The finance director also sample checks the classification is correctly applied. The use of finance department guidelines and sample checks by the finance director should reduce the risk of an incorrect assessment and of understated/overstated profits, assets and incorrect depreciation charges.	Select a sample of asset expenditure purchase orders and review evidence of the classification being noted. For a sample of orders compare the classification noted with the finance director's guidelines to assess whether the classification was correctly undertaken. Review purchase orders for evidence of the finance director's sample checks for example, by signature.
Segregation of duties Snowdon Co has a separate human resources (HR) department, which is responsible for setting up all new employees. Having a segregation of roles between HR and payroll departments reduces the risk of fictitious employees being set up and also being paid which would result in overstatement of payroll costs.	Review the job descriptions of payroll and HR to confirm the split of responsibilities with regards to setting up new joiners. Discuss with members of the payroll department the process for setting up new joiners and agree new joiners to documentation initiated by HR.
Pre-printed new joiner forms Pre-printed forms are completed by HR for new employees, and includes assignment of a unique employee number, and once verified a copy is sent to the payroll department. The payroll system is unable to process new joiners without the inclusion of the employee's unique number. As payroll is unable to set up new joiners without the forms and employee number, it reduces the risk of fictitious employees being set up by payroll which would result in overstatement of payroll costs.	Select a sample of new employees added to the payroll during the year, review the joiner forms for evidence of completion and the allocation of a unique employee number which was received by payroll prior to being added to the system. Select a sample of edit reports for changes to payroll during the year; agree a sample of new employees added to payroll to the joiner's forms. Attempt to add a new joiner to the payroll system without a unique employee number, the system should reject this addition.

Direct control	Test of control
Bank reconciliations The cashier reconciles the bank statements to the bank ledger account monthly and this reconciliation is reviewed and investigated by the financial controller, who evidences that review by way of signature on the bank reconciliation. The bank reconciliation is a key control which reduces the risk of fraud. Monthly review and investigation ensure that fraud and errors are identified on a timely basis, reducing the risk of misstatement of the bank and cash balance.	Review the file of bank reconciliations to confirm that there is one for each month. Inspect a sample of monthly bank reconciliations for evidence of investigation and review by the financial controller. For a sample of months reperform the bank reconciliation and where differences have occurred discuss and investigate these with the financial controller.

(c) Control deficiencies and recommendations

Control deficiency	Control recommendation
IA staff shortages Snowdon Co has experienced significant staff shortages within its internal audit (IA) department, and the department is currently under- resourced. This has resulted in a reduction in their programme of work for the year. Maintaining an IA department is an important control as it enables senior management to test whether controls are operating effectively within the company. If the team has staff shortages, this reduces the effectiveness of this monitoring control.	Senior management should consider recruiting additional employees to join the IA department or outsourcing the IA function. In the interim, employees from other departments, such as finance, could be seconded to IA to assist them with audits. It must be ensured that these reviews do not cover controls operating in the department in which the employees normally work.
Asset budgets exceeded Some departments have already significantly exceeded their annual asset expenditure budgets. It appears that purchase orders for assets are being placed without being agreed back to annual budgets, resulting in overspends. The increased expenditure may be due to increased levels of services being provided, or it could be due to a lack of control over the asset expenditure process, resulting in increased costs and reduced profits.	The company's monthly management accounts should include an analysis of asset expenditure against budget and prior year per department. Each department head should include narrative which explains the significant variances to date. Purchase orders for assets should be compared to the annual department budgets as part of the authorization process. Any spend in excess of the budget should be referred for authorisation to the finance director.

Control deficiency	**Control recommendation**
Physical verification of assets The IA department undertakes physical verification of assets each year for the four largest centres as well as five of the other centres, randomly selected. The company has 45 centres as well as a head office and warehouse, hence if each year the four largest sites are visited this can result in the other sites only being visited every eight years. If the non-current asset register is not physically verified on a regular basis, there is an increased risk of assets being misappropriated as there is no check that the assets still exist in their correct location. In addition, obsolete assets will not be identified on a timely basis.	IA should review its programme of visits to assess if additional resources could be devoted to ensuring that all sites are visited over a shorter period, for example, five years. This would ensure that physical verification of all assets could be completed more regularly. For sites visited any assets which cannot be located should be investigated fully. If it cannot be located, then it should be written off. Each centre should submit a list of assets with serial numbers to IA, who should compare these to the non-current asset register. Those sites with significant variations should be prioritised for a site visit by IA.
Amendment of standing data All members of the payroll department can amend employees' standing data in the payroll system as they have access to the password. As all members of payroll can amend standing data this may result in errors or unauthorised changes being made, leading to incorrect payment of wages and increased risk of fraud.	The password to amend standing data should be changed and only communicated to senior members of the payroll department. If all members of payroll need the ability to amend standing data, the system should be changed to require authorisation of all changes by a senior member of payroll. Edit reports should be generated for all standing data changes with clear reference to who made the change and who authorised it. These edit reports should be regularly reviewed by a responsible official and they should evidence this review with a signature.
Lack of segregation of duties The senior payroll manager reviews the bank transfer listing prior to authorising the payments and if any discrepancies are noted, always makes the adjustment in the payroll records for any changes required. Discrepancies may arise due to the payroll records or the bank transfer listing being incorrect. Assuming the discrepancies are always in the payroll records may result in incorrect amendments being made to payroll or incorrect amounts paid to employees.	The senior payroll manager should not be able to process changes to the payroll system as well as authorise payments. Discrepancies should be thoroughly investigated, and adjustments made in the relevant record as required. The authorisation of the bank transfer listing should be undertaken by an individual outside the payroll department, such as the finance director.

Control deficiency	Control recommendation
In addition, there is a lack of segregation of duties as it is the payroll team which processes the amounts and the senior payroll manager who authorises payments. The senior manager could fraudulently increase or incorrectly amend the amounts to be paid to certain employees, process this payment as well as amend the records.	
Credit limits not reviewed After passing a credit check a credit limit is set for all new customers by the sales director, but these credit limits are not reviewed after this unless a review is requested by the customer. If credit limits are not reviewed regularly, they could be out of date, resulting in limits being too high and sales being made to poor credit risks or too low and Snowdon Co losing potential revenue.	Credit limits should continue to be set by the sales director; however, these limits should be reviewed and amended as appropriate on a regular basis by a responsible official.
Invoices only chased after 90 days Client services managers are given responsibility to chase customers directly for payment once an invoice is outstanding for 90 days. This is considerably in excess of the company's credit terms of 30 days which will lead to poor cash flow. Further, client services managers are more likely to focus on customer relationships and generating further revenues rather than chasing payments. This could result in an increase in irrecoverable balances and reduced profit and cash flows.	A credit controller should be appointed, and it should be their role, rather than the client services managers, to chase any outstanding sales invoices which are more than 30 days old.

ACCA marking guide

		Marks
(a)	**Significant deficiencies**	
	• Likelihood of leading to material misstatement	1
	• Susceptibility to loss or fraud	1
	• Subjectivity and complexity of amounts	1
	• Amount exposed to deficiency	1
	• Volume of activity	1
	• Importance to financial reporting process	1
	• Cause and frequency of exceptions	1
	• Interaction with other deficiencies	1
	Restricted to	**4**

(b)	**Direct controls and tests of control (only 3 required)**	
	• Asset expenditure classification	2
	• HR department/payroll department	2
	• Processing new joiners	2
	• Bank reconciliations	2
	Max 3 issues, 2 marks each	**6**
(c)	**Control deficiencies and recommendations (only 5 required)**	
	• IA staff shortages	2
	• Asset expenditure budgets exceeded	2
	• Physical verification of assets	2
	• Amendment of standing data	2
	• Changes made in payroll records	2
	• Credit limits not reviewed	2
	• Invoices only chased after 90 days	2
	Max 5 issues, 2 marks each	**10**
Total		**20**

Examiner's comments

This question tested candidates' knowledge of significant deficiencies, key controls and tests of control and control deficiencies and recommendations.

Part (a) required candidates to describe matters the auditor may consider in determining if a deficiency was significant. Many candidates did not attempt this part of the question and where it was answered, many provided irrelevant points. A significant number of candidates provided answers around the components of internal control, such as control environment and monitoring of controls. Others focused on what a 'good' or 'bad' internal control was. A significant minority listed deficiencies from the scenario, which was required for part (c) of the question. For those candidates who provided valid answers, most tended to pick up ½ mark per point rather than one mark, due to a lack of detail. Correct answers tended to focus on matters related to 'an increased risk of fraud' or 'material misstatements'. Candidates are reminded once again that questions in this syllabus area usually contain a knowledge-based requirement. These are straightforward marks, provided candidates spend the necessary time learning the knowledge and practicing past questions.

Part (b) required candidates to identify and explain from the scenario three key controls and tests of control to assess if the key controls were operating effectively in the internal control system of Snowdon Co. The scenario was multicycle and covered the non-current asset, payroll, sales and bank cycles. Key control questions such as this typically require key controls to be identified (½ mark each), explained (½ mark each) which must cover the implication of the key control for the company and a relevant test of control to test if the control is operating effectively (1 mark). Candidates struggled to identify correct key controls from the scenario. There were more controls than were required to be discussed. However, in many instances, candidates confused deficiencies with key controls. For example, a commonly provided incorrect point was 'credit limits are set for new customers by the sales director'. In this instance this was not a key control as the lack of subsequent review meant that the control was not operating effectively. Instead the correct conclusion would be that the lack of review was a control deficiency. For a key control to gain credit, it must be complete. It must be appropriately designed and, if operating effectively, would prevent or detect a material misstatement. If the credit limits referred to above had been regularly reviewed, then this would have been a valid key control. Other examples of key controls incorrectly identified included 'having an internal audit (IA) department'. As this was understaffed it was not operating effectively as a control and therefore should have been recognised as a deficiency. Another identified by many candidates was 'the payroll manager reviews the list of bank payments', however as the scenario went on to say that if discrepancies arose the manager always changed the payroll without first investigating the differences this gave rise to a deficiency rather than a key control. Similarly, 'each training centre having an asset budget', was not an effective control as the scenario stated that these budgets were being exceeded. Again, the lack of control over asset expenditure should have been identified as a control deficiency. Valid key controls identified were bank reconciliations being reviewed, and the need for the unique employee number to process new joiners in the payroll system. The identification of a key control would have scored ½ mark. In order to gain the other ½ mark candidates needed to clearly explain the implication of the control and many appeared to struggle with this. For example, having a separate HR and payroll department carrying out the tasks described means that there is a reduced risk of fictitious employees being set up. Candidates must clearly explain what the control is aiming to prevent to be awarded the ½ explanation mark. Candidates' answers for the tests of control were adequate and where one mark per test was not awarded this tended to be due to a lack of detail. Candidates must ensure that they are as prepared for a question on key controls as they are for deficiencies as they are both highly examinable. Future candidates need to ensure that they have undertaken adequate question practice of all examinable control systems.

Part (c) required candidates to identify and explain from the scenario five deficiencies and to provide a control recommendation to address each of these deficiencies. Performance was satisfactory. Internal control deficiency questions such as this typically require internal control deficiencies to be identified (½ mark each), explained (½ mark each) which must cover the implication of the deficiency to the company and a relevant recommendation to address the deficiency (1 mark). The scenario in the exam contained more issues than were required to be discussed. It was pleasing that the majority of students were able to identify five deficiencies. However, a significant proportion of candidates had already addressed a number of deficiencies incorrectly as key controls in part (b) and therefore failed to identify them for part (c) of the question requirement and so did not gain credit. Additionally, some candidates identified key controls as deficiencies. For example, a common incorrect answer was 'bank reconciliations are undertaken by the cashier and reviewed by the financial controller' with candidates believing that the financial controller should undertake the reconciliations rather than the cashier. This was not a deficiency but rather a key control. The cashier undertaking the reconciliation process is perfectly acceptable, and together with the review by the financial controller constitutes a key control. A number of points did score well, however. These included the deficiencies relating to access to standing data, physical inspection of assets and lack of regular review of credit limits. Some candidates were able to identify the deficiencies but clearly did not understand them as they were unable to explain the implication of these deficiencies. Candidates are required to explain the implication to the business to be awarded credit. For example, a valid explanation for the deficiency 'sales invoices only chased after 90 days' (identification ½ mark awarded), would have been 'this could increase the risk of irrecoverable receivables/result in poor cash flow management'. Candidates were able to provide recommendations to address the deficiencies identified however the recommendations were often not described in enough detail or were phrased as objectives. For the IA department deficiency, the recommendation of 'ensure enough staff' is an objective and did not explain how this should be undertaken to address the staff shortages in the IA department.

228 AMBERJACK *Walk in the footsteps of a top tutor*

Key answer tips

Part (a) requires knowledge of limitations of internal control components. These limitations are the reasons why the auditor cannot rely 100% on the control system of the client and must always perform substantive procedures over material balances.

Part (b) asks for control deficiencies and recommendations in respect of a cash system. This is examined frequently and with plenty of past papers to practise, this type of question should be straightforward. Fully explain the deficiency in terms of the effect on the company. If management are to take action, they must be concerned about the potential consequences of the deficiency. When providing recommendations for improvement, be as specific as possible.

A covering letter is also required. Marks will be awarded for a letter format, appropriate greeting, disclaimer and sign off.

(a) Limitations of internal control components

- Human error – mistakes made by those responsible for performing controls.
- Ineffective controls – controls which do not work as intended.
- Collusion of staff – staff work together (collude) to bypass the control of segregation of duties.
- The abuse of power by those with ultimate controlling responsibility (management override) – management may falsify accounting records or post unauthorised journals to present a different result in the financial statements.
- Use of management judgement on the nature and extent of controls it chooses to implement.

(b) Report to management

Board of directors
Amberjack Co
21 Under the Sea
Shorelife City
Shark Country

1 July 20X5

Dear Directors,

Audit of Amberjack Co for the year ended 30 April 20X5

Please find enclosed the report to management on deficiencies in internal controls identified during the audit for the year ended 30 April 20X5. The appendix to this report considers deficiencies in the sales and despatch system and recommendations to address those deficiencies.

Please note that this report only addresses the deficiencies identified during the audit and if further testing had been performed, then more deficiencies may have been reported.

This report is solely for the use of management and if you have any further questions, then please do not hesitate to contact us.

Yours faithfully

An audit firm

Appendix

Control deficiency	Control recommendation
Customer credit limits Customer credit limits are set by receivables ledger clerks. Receivables ledger clerks are not sufficiently senior and so may set limits too high, leading to irrecoverable debts, or too low, leading to a loss of sales.	Credit limits should be set by a senior member of the receivables ledger department and not by receivables ledger clerks. These limits should be regularly reviewed by a responsible official.
Customer master data not reviewed Receivables ledger clerks record new customer details and credit limits in the customer master data file and these changes are not reviewed. There is a risk that customers could be set up incorrectly resulting in a loss of customer goodwill and sales revenue. In addition, the receivables ledger clerks are not senior enough to be given access to making changes to master file data as this could increase the risk of fraud.	Receivables ledger clerks should not be able to access the master data file to add new customers or make amendments. Any such additions/ amendments to master file data should be restricted so that only supervisors and above can make changes. An exception report of changes made should be generated and reviewed by a responsible official.
Credit controller not replaced Amberjack Co's credit controller is currently on secondment for six months to the internal audit department and has not been replaced. During this period, it does not appear that anyone else has been responsible for monitoring ageing receivables. This could result in an increased risk of irrecoverable debts and lead to customers not paying their outstanding balances on time, or at all, leading to reduced cash flows.	During the period of the secondment, an alternative member of the finance department should be trained in the credit control role and assigned responsibility for reviewing the aged receivables listing and following up on any overdue customers.

Control deficiency	**Control recommendation**
GDNs not sequentially numbered Goods despatch notes (GDN) are given the same number as the order number to which they relate. The sales invoices are only raised on receipt of a GDN, and without separate sequential numbers, it is difficult for Amberjack Co to identify if any GDNs are missing as they are not likely to be raised in the same sequence as the sales orders. If GDNs are missing and the company fails to raise invoices in a timely manner, this could lead to a loss of revenue.	GDNs should all be sequentially numbered using a sequence which is different to the order number. On a regular basis, a sequence check of GDNs should be undertaken to identify any missing despatch notes.
Insufficient copies of GDN Once orders are processed, copies of GDNs are sent to the finance department, customer and remain in the warehouse. However, the sales order department of Amberjack Co does not receive a copy of the GDN. If the sales order department does not receive a copy of the completed GDNs, it is not able to monitor if orders are being fulfilled on a timely basis. This could result in a loss of revenue and customer goodwill.	The GDN should be amended to be at least four-part. One copy should be sent to the sales order department. Once the copy of the GDN has been received by the order department, it should be matched to the order. A regular review of unmatched orders should be undertaken by the sales order department to identify any unfulfilled orders.
Sales invoice processing Additional staff has been drafted in to help the sales clerks produce the sales invoices. As the extra staff will not be as experienced as the sales clerks, there is an increased risk of mistakes being made in the sales invoices. This could result in customers being under or overcharged leading to misstated revenue or dissatisfied customers.	Only the sales clerks should be able to raise sales invoices. As Amberjack Co is expanding, consideration should be given to recruiting and training more permanent sales clerks who can produce sales invoices. If this is not currently possible, temporary staff should be adequately trained and additional input checks on invoices should be introduced.

Control deficiency	Control recommendation
Manual recording of discounts Discounts given to customers who purchased goods during the 10% off weekend are manually entered onto the sales invoices by sales clerks. This could result in unauthorised sales discounts being given as there does not seem to be any authorisation required. In addition, a clerk could forget to manually enter the discount or enter an incorrect level of discount for a customer, leading to the sales invoice being overstated and a loss of customer goodwill. Unauthorised discounts in excess of 10% would result in a loss of revenue, either due to error or fraud.	During the period of any special offers, such as the 10% off weekend, the authorised sales prices file should be updated by a responsible official. These changes should be reviewed for any input errors, this review should be evidenced. The invoicing system should confirm that orders were placed during the discount weekend. Hence the sales invoices for these periods should automatically contain the reduced prices. The invoicing system should be amended to prevent sales clerks from being able to manually enter sales discounts onto invoices.
Customer statements not generated Customer statements are no longer being generated and sent to customers. If statements are not sent regularly, this increases the likelihood of errors and any disputed invoices not being quickly identified and resolved by Amberjack Co. This could lead to cash flow issues.	Amberjack Co should produce monthly customer statements for all customers and send them out promptly.
Trade receivables account only reconciled annually The trade receivables account is only reconciled at the end of April in order to verify the year-end balance. If the receivables account is only reconciled annually, there is a risk that errors will not be spotted promptly. Receivables may be misstated.	The trade receivables account should be reconciled on a monthly basis to identify any errors which should be investigated and corrected. The reconciliations should be reviewed by a responsible official and they should evidence their review by way of signature.

Marking guide			
			Marks
(a)	**Limitations of internal control components**		
	• Human error		1
	• Ineffective controls		1
	• Collusion of staff		1
	• Abuse of power/management override		1
	• Use of management judgement		1
		Restricted to	**4**

(b)	**Control deficiencies and recommendations (only 7 required)**	
	• Customer credit limits	2
	• Customer master data not reviewed	2
	• Credit controller not replaced	2
	• Goods despatch notes (GDNs) not sequentially numbered	2
	• Insufficient copies of GDN	2
	• Sales invoice processing	2
	• Manual recording of discounts	2
	• Customer statements no longer raised	2
	• Trade receivables account only reconciled annually	2
	Max 7 issues, 2 marks each and 2 marks for covering letter	**16**
Total		**20**

Examiner's comments

Part (b) required candidates to provide a report to management which identified and explained from the scenario seven deficiencies and controls to address each of these deficiencies. Candidates were also required to provide a covering letter. Performance was satisfactory. Internal control deficiency questions such as this typically require internal control deficiencies to be identified (½ mark each), explained (½ mark each) which must cover the implication of the deficiency to the company and a relevant recommendation to address the deficiency (1 mark). The scenario in the exam contained more issues than were required to be discussed. The majority of candidates were able to identify the required number of deficiencies. However, a significant minority of candidates identified irrelevant or incorrect deficiencies. For example, many candidates were concerned about sales prices only being updated every six months or that sales invoices were prepared using quantities from goods despatch notes. These are not deficiencies and therefore were not awarded any credit. Some candidates did not clearly understand/explain the implication of the deficiency. Candidates are required to explain the implication to the business to be awarded credit. For example, a candidate who correctly identified the deficiency 'discounts are manually entered onto sales invoices' (identification ½ mark awarded), would not have received credit for the explanation 'discounts could be unauthorised'. Candidates must clearly explain the implication to the business, for example that 'this could result in a loss of revenue or loss of customer goodwill', to be awarded the ½ explanation mark. Candidates were able to provide recommendations to address the deficiencies identified however often the recommendations were not described in enough detail. For example, the recommendation that 'credit limits should be set by senior members of the sales department, rather than the clerks' was only awarded ½ mark. Candidates needed to also recommend that 'these limits should be regularly reviewed' to be awarded the full 1 mark. It was disappointing that few candidates provided a covering letter, and of these, few letters contained suitable disclaimer statements. An example disclaimer stating that 'this report only addressed deficiencies identified during the audit and if further testing had been undertaken more deficiencies may have been reported' was required. Internal control questions remain a highly examinable area and future candidates need to ensure that they have undertaken adequate question practice of all examinable control systems.

229 FREESIA *Walk in the footsteps of a top tutor*

Key answer tips

Part (a) requires knowledge from the text book. Use subheadings to make it easy for the marker to see that you have answered both advantages and disadvantages of each type of method.

Part (b) requires the control deficiencies within the sales, purchases and payroll systems to be identified. Use the specific information in scenario rather than giving generic deficiencies. There are always more deficiencies than you need so choose the ones you can write well about. Suggest controls the client can implement to address the control deficiency. Be specific about which member of client staff should be responsible for the control and how frequently they should perform the control. Tests of controls are the audit procedures the auditor will perform to obtain evidence to prove the control suggested is in place and working effectively. Be specific about how they would do this.

Part (c) asks for substantive procedures. A substantive procedure is used to detect material misstatement in the figure. Tests of controls will not score marks. Think about procedures that can be performed to confirm accuracy of the accrual, completeness of the accrual, etc.

Part (d) requires corporate governance deficiencies within the scenario to be explained and a recommendation provided for each. Knowledge of the Corporate Governance Code is required here. Work through on a line by line basis and consider whether the information suggests that the company is compliant with the requirements of the corporate governance best practice.

(a) Documenting systems

	Description	**Advantage**
Narrative notes	Narrative notes consist of a written description of the system. They detail what occurs in the system at each stage and include any controls which operate at each stage.	They are simple to record; after discussion with staff members, these discussions are easily written up as notes. They can facilitate understanding by all members of the audit team, especially more junior members who might find alternative methods too complex.

	Description	**Advantage**
Questionnaires	Internal control questionnaires (ICQs) or internal control evaluation questionnaires (ICEQs) contain a list of questions for each major transaction cycle. ICQs are used to assess whether controls exist whereas ICEQs assess the effectiveness of the controls in place.	Questionnaires are quick to prepare, which means they are a timely method for recording the system. They ensure that all controls present within the system are considered and recorded, hence missing controls or deficiencies are clearly highlighted to the audit team.

(b) Deficiencies, controls and test of controls

Control deficiency	**Control recommendation**	**Test of control**
Credit limits Customer credit limits are set by sales ledger clerks. Sales ledger clerks are not sufficiently senior. Limits may be set which are too high, leading to irrecoverable debts, or too low, leading to a loss of sales.	Credit limits should be set by a senior member of the sales department and not by sales ledger clerks. These limits should be regularly reviewed by a responsible official.	For a sample of new customers accepted in the year, review the authorisation of the credit limit, and ensure that this was performed by a responsible official. Enquire of sales ledger clerks as to who can set credit limits.
Orders numbers Customer orders are given a number based on the sales person's own identification number. These numbers are not sequential. Without sequential numbers, it is difficult for Freesia Co to identify missing orders and to monitor if all orders are being despatched in a timely manner. If orders are not despatched in a timely manner, this could lead to a loss of customer goodwill.	Sales orders should be sequentially numbered. On a regular basis, a sequence check of orders should be undertaken to identify any missing orders.	Reperform the control by undertaking a sequence check of sales orders. Discuss any gaps in the sequence with sales ordering staff.

Control deficiency	Control recommendation	Test of control
Segregation of duties Lily Shah, a finance clerk, is responsible for several elements of the cash receipts system due to posting the bank transfer receipts from the bank statements to the bank ledger account, updating the list of individual customers and performing the bank reconciliations. There is a lack of segregation of duties. Errors will not be identified on a timely basis. There is also an increased risk of fraud.	The key roles of posting bank receipts, updating the list of individual customers and performing bank reconciliations should be split between different individuals. If this is not practical, then as a minimum, the bank reconciliations should be undertaken by another member of the finance team.	Review the file of completed bank reconciliations to identify who prepared them. Review the log of IDs of individuals who have posted bank receipts and updated the list of individual customers to assess whether these are different individuals. Discuss with the financial controller which members of staff undertake the roles of processing of bank receipts and updating of the bank ledger account and list of individual customers.
Insufficient copies of GRN GRNs are only sent to the finance department. Failing to send a copy to the purchase ordering department means that it is not possible to monitor the level of unfulfilled orders. This could result in a significant level of unfulfilled orders leading to stock-outs and a consequent loss of sales. In addition, if the GRN is lost, then it will not be possible for the finance department to match the invoice to proof of goods being received. This could result in a delay to the invoice being paid and a loss of supplier goodwill.	The GRN should be created in three parts with one copy of the GRN being sent to the ordering department. The second copy should be held at the warehouse and the third sent to the finance department. A purchase ordering clerk should agree their copy of the GRN to the purchase order and change the order status to complete. On a regular basis, a review should be undertaken for all unfulfilled orders and these should be followed up with the relevant supplier.	Review the file of copy GRNs held by the purchase ordering department and review for evidence that these are matched to orders and flagged as complete. Review the file of unfulfilled purchase orders for any overdue items and discuss their status with an ordering clerk.

Control deficiency	Control recommendation	Test of control
Controls over inputting of invoices Camilla Brown, the purchase ledger clerk, only utilises document count controls when inputting invoices into the purchases system. Document count controls can confirm the completeness of input. However, they do not verify the accuracy or validity of input. If the invoices are not input correctly, suppliers may not be paid on time, or paid incorrect amounts leading to an overpayment or loss of supplier goodwill who may withdraw credit facilities.	The purchase ledger clerk should instead input the invoices in batches and apply information processing controls, such as control totals, rather than just completeness checks to ensure both completeness and accuracy over the input of purchase invoices. In addition, sequence checks should be built into the system to ensure completeness of input.	The audit team should utilise test data procedures to assess whether data can be entered without the use of batch control totals and also whether sequence checks are built into the system. Observe the inputting of purchase invoices and identify what information processing controls are utilised by the clerk.
Out of date standard costs The company values its inventory using standard costs, which are not being kept up-to-date. If the standard costs were reviewed 18 months ago, there is the risk that the costs are misstated as changes in raw materials and wages inflation may not have been adjusted for. This could result in inventory being under or overvalued and profits being misstated. For year-end reporting, IAS 2 *Inventories* only allows standard costs to be used for valuation purposes if they are a close approximation to actual costs, which is unlikely if the standard costs remain unchanged for a long period of time. Therefore, the valuation may not be in line with IAS 2.	A review of all standard costs currently in use should be undertaken by a senior manager in the production department. Actual costs for materials, labour and overheads should be ascertained and compared to the proposed standard costs to ensure they are a close approximation. The revised standard costs should be reviewed by the production director who should evidence this review. At least annually, a review of the standard costs should be undertaken to ensure they are up-to-date.	Obtain a copy of the standard costs used for inventory valuation, assess when the review was last undertaken and inspect for evidence of review by the production director.

Control deficiency	Control recommendation	Test of control
Overtime not authorised Overtime is not authorised prior to being paid. The information per employee is collated and submitted to payroll by a production clerk, but not authorised. The production director is only informed about overtime levels via quarterly reports. These reports are reviewed sometime after the payments have been made which could result in unauthorised overtime or amounts being paid incorrectly and Freesia Co's payroll cost increasing.	All overtime should be authorised by a responsible official prior to the payment being processed by the payroll department. This authorisation should be evidenced in writing.	Review the overtime report for evidence of authorisation and note the date this occurred to ensure that this was undertaken prior to the payment of the overtime.
Bank transfer authorisation The finance director compares the total of the list of bank transfers with the total to be paid per the payroll records. There could be employees omitted or fictitious employees added to the payment listing so that, although the total payments list agrees to payroll totals, there could be fraudulent or erroneous payments being made.	The finance director, when authorising the payments, should on a sample basis perform checks from the human resource department's staff records to payment list and vice versa to confirm that payments are complete and only made to bona fide employees. The finance director should sign the payments list as evidence that these checks have been undertaken.	Obtain a sample of payments lists and review for signature by the finance director as evidence that the control is operating correctly.

(c) **Accrual for employment tax payable**

- Compare the accrual for employment tax payable to the prior year, investigate any significant differences.
- Agree the year-end employment tax payable accrual to the payroll records to confirm accuracy.
- Reperform the calculation of the accrual for a sample of employees to confirm the accuracy.

- Undertake a proof-in-total test for the employment tax accrual by multiplying the payroll cost for June 20X5 with the appropriate tax rate. Compare this expectation to the actual accrual and investigate any significant differences.
- Agree the subsequent payment to the post-year-end bank ledger account and bank statements to confirm completeness.
- Review any correspondence with tax authorities to assess whether there are any additional outstanding payments due. If so, confirm they are included in the year-end accrual.
- Review any disclosures made of the employment tax accrual and assess whether these are in compliance with accounting standards and legislation.

(d) Corporate governance deficiencies and recommendations

Deficiency	**Recommendation**
The finance director is a member of the audit committee. The audit committee should be made up entirely of independent NEDs. The role of the committee is to maintain objectivity with regards to financial reporting; this is difficult if the finance director is a member of the committee as the finance director will be responsible for the preparation of the financial statements.	The audit committee must comprise independent NEDs only, therefore the finance director should resign from the committee.
The remuneration for directors is set by the finance director. However, no director should be involved in setting their own remuneration as this may result in excessive levels of pay being set.	There should be a fair and transparent policy in place for setting remuneration levels. The NEDs should form a remuneration committee to decide on the remuneration of the executives. The board as a whole should decide on the pay of the NEDs.
Executive remuneration includes a significant annual profit related bonus. Remuneration should motivate the directors to focus on the long-term growth of the business, however, annual targets can encourage short-term strategies rather than maximising shareholder wealth.	The remuneration of executives should be restructured to include a significant proportion based on long-term company performance. For example, executives could be granted share options with a minimum vesting and holding period of five years, as this would encourage focus on the longer-term position.

Deficiency	Recommendation
The chair has sole responsibility for liaising with the shareholders and answering any of their questions. This is a role which the board as a whole should undertake.	All members of the board should be involved in ensuring that satisfactory dialogue takes place with shareholders, for example, all should attend meetings with shareholders such as the annual general meeting. The board should state in the annual report the steps taken to ensure that the members of the board, and in particular the non-executive directors, develop an understanding of the views of major shareholders about the company.

ACCA marking guide

		Marks
(a)	**Methods of documenting internal control systems**	
	• Narrative notes	2
	• Questionnaires	2
	Restricted to	**4**
(b)	**Control deficiencies, recommendations, tests of controls (only 6 required)**	
	• Credit limits	3
	• No sequential numbering of orders	3
	• Segregation of duties – cash receipts	3
	• Insufficient copies of GRN	3
	• Controls over inputting of invoices	3
	• Out-of-date standard costs	3
	• Overtime not authorised	3
	• Authorisation of bank transfer	3
	Max 6 issues, 3 marks each	**18**
(c)	**Substantive procedures – accrual for employment tax**	
	• Compare to prior year and investigate differences	1
	• Agree accrual to year-end payroll records	1
	• Recalculate accrual and consider reasonableness	1
	• Perform proof-in-total and investigate variances	1
	• Confirm post-year-end payment	1
	• Review correspondence with tax authorities for any additional liabilities	1
	• Review disclosure and confirm in line with accounting standards	1
	Restricted to	**4**
	Corporate governance deficiencies and recommendations (2 issues required)	
	• Composition of audit committee	2
	• Finance director sets remuneration	2
	• Executive directors' remuneration	2
	• Only the chair liaises with shareholders	2
	Max 2 issues, 2 marks each	**4**
Total		**30**

Examiner's comments

Part (a) required candidates to describe documenting internal control systems using narrative notes and questionnaires and explain an advantage of using each method. Performance in this knowledge-based question was satisfactory. There were some good responses, however, a number of candidates were unable to describe each method in enough detail to sufficiently differentiate the two methods of documentation. A number of candidates also discussed the disadvantages of each method, which was not a requirement of the question. In addition, a number of responses described types of questionnaires in too much detail given the marks available. Candidates are reminded to read the question requirement carefully to ensure that they are only answering the question set and to consider the marks available when writing their answers.

Part (b) required candidates to identify and explain from the scenario six deficiencies, recommend a control to address each of these deficiencies, and describe a test of control the external auditors should perform. Performance was satisfactory. Internal control deficiency questions such as this typically require internal control deficiencies to be identified (½ mark each), explained (½ mark each) which must cover the implication of the deficiency to the company, a relevant recommendation to address the deficiency (1 mark), and a test of control the external auditors should perform to assess of the control is operating effectively (1 mark). The scenario in the exam contained more issues than were required to be discussed. It was pleasing that the majority of candidates were able to identify six deficiencies. Very few candidates, however, identified the lack of controls over the accuracy of purchase invoice entry, or the lack of sufficient copies of goods received notes. A minority of candidates identified irrelevant or unrealistic deficiencies. For example, a significant number of candidates were concerned about the range of work performed by the warehouse staff although this was not flagged as an issue in the scenario. Some candidates did not clearly understand/explain the implication of the deficiency. Candidates are required to explain the implication to the business to be awarded credit. For example, a candidate who correctly identified the deficiency 'credit limits are set by the sales ledger clerks' (identification ½ mark awarded), no credit was awarded for the explanation 'the sales ledger clerk is not senior enough'. Candidates must clearly explain the implication to the business that 'this could result in irrecoverable debts if limits set are too high or loss of sales if limits are too low' to be awarded the ½ explanation mark. Candidates were able to provide recommendations to address the deficiencies identified, however, often the recommendations were not described in enough detail. For example, the recommendation that 'sales orders should be sequentially numbered' was awarded only ½ mark, candidates needed to also recommend that 'there should be regular sequence checks' to be awarded the full one mark. Candidates were also able to describe tests of controls the external auditor should perform, however, often they were not described in enough detail. For example, the test of control of 'reviewing the authorised overtime report' was awarded only ½ mark, candidates needed to recommend the auditor also 'notes the date of review to ensure the report is authorised prior to payment' to be awarded the full one mark. It was pleasing that many candidates followed the instructions to set their answer out in three columns, being control deficiency, control recommendation and test of control. Internal control questions remain a highly examinable area and future candidates need to ensure that they have undertaken adequate question practice of all examinable control systems.

Part (c) required candidates to describe substantive procedures the auditor should perform in relation to a year-end accrual for employment tax payable. One mark was available for each well-described procedure. Performance on this requirement was disappointing. Many candidates failed to provide four procedures, and those listed often focused on payroll expenses and deductions rather than the relevant year-end accrual. Candidates must take the time to read the question requirements carefully and spend time thinking about what is needed prior to writing their answers.

Part (d) required candidates to describe two corporate governance deficiencies faced by Freesia Co and provide a recommendation to address each to ensure compliance with corporate governance principles. One mark was available per well-explained deficiency and one mark per recommendation. Performance was mixed. Candidates generally identified two deficiencies, however, often did not adequately explain why each was a deficiency. For example, a significant number of candidates correctly identified that 'the finance director decides on the directors' remuneration' (½ mark), however, only stronger candidates explained 'this could result in setting excessive pay' (½ mark). Weaker candidates simply explained this deficiency as being 'against corporate governance rules' and were not awarded the second ½ mark. Recommendations were mixed. A significant number of candidates did not state a clear action as a recommendation. No mark was awarded for giving a statement rather than an action. For example, 'the finance director should not set the remuneration' was not awarded credit. Candidates needed to recommend 'a remuneration committee of non-executive directors should be established to set executives' pay' for one mark.

230 CAMOMILE *Walk in the footsteps of a top tutor*

Key answer tips

Part (a) requires an explanation of the importance of the external auditor communicating with those charged with governance, and asks for two matters which would be communicated. This requires knowledge of ISA 260. Most questions in the constructed response section of the exam will start with a knowledge requirement such as this so make sure you learn the key requirements of the auditing standards as well as being able to tackle the scenario based, application requirements which follow.

Part (b) asks for control deficiencies and recommendations in respect of a cash system. This is examined frequently and with plenty of past papers to practise, this type of question should be straightforward. Fully explain the deficiency in terms of the effect on the company. If management are to take action, they must be concerned about the potential consequences of the deficiency. When providing recommendations for improvement, be as specific as possible.

(a) (i) Importance of communicating with those charged with governance

In accordance with ISA 260 *Communication with Those Charged with Governance*, it is important for the auditors to report to those charged with governance as it helps in the following ways:

- It assists the auditor and those charged with governance in understanding matters related to the audit, and in developing a constructive working relationship. This relationship is developed while maintaining the auditor's independence and objectivity.
- It helps the auditor in obtaining, from those charged with governance, information relevant to the audit. For example, those charged with governance may assist the auditor in understanding the entity and its environment, in identifying appropriate sources of audit evidence and in providing information about specific transactions or events.

- It helps those charged with governance in fulfilling their responsibility to oversee the financial reporting process, thereby reducing the risks of material misstatement of the financial statements.
- It promotes effective two-way communication between the auditor and those charged with governance.

(ii) Matters to be communicated to those charged with governance

- The auditor's responsibilities with regards to providing an opinion on the financial statements and that they have carried out their work in accordance with International Standards on Auditing.
- The auditor should explain the planned approach to the audit as well as the audit timetable.
- Any key audit risks identified during the planning stage should be communicated.
- In addition, any significant difficulties encountered during the audit should be communicated.
- Also significant matters arising during the audit, as well as significant accounting adjustments.
- During the audit, any significant deficiencies in the internal control system identified should be communicated in writing or verbally.
- How the external auditor and internal auditor may work together and any planned use of the work of the internal audit function.
- Those charged with governance should be notified of any written representations required by the auditor.
- Other matters arising from the audit which are significant to the oversight of the financial reporting process.
- If any suspected frauds are identified during the audit, these must be communicated.
- If the auditors are intending to make any modifications to the audit opinion, these should be communicated to those charged with governance.
- For listed entities, a confirmation that the auditors have complied with ethical standards and appropriate safeguards have been put in place for any ethical threats identified.

(b) Control deficiencies and recommendations

Control deficiency	Control recommendation
Petty cash differences Each restaurant maintains a petty cash float of $400, and at any point in time the receipts and funds present should equal the float. It has been noted by the internal audit (IA) department that on occasions there are differences due to the fact that no log is maintained of petty cash requests. This could be as a result of sundry items being purchased without the relevant receipt or voucher being returned. There is also a possibility that the cash is being misappropriated by staff members, or being spent on non-business-related items.	A petty cash log should be maintained so the purchase of sundry items is recorded in the log along with the sum borrowed, date and employee. On purchase of the items, the relevant employee should return the relevant receipt or voucher and any funds not spent. The log should be updated to confirm return of funds and receipts. On a weekly basis, the restaurant manager should reconcile the petty cash and if any receipts are missing, these should be followed up with the relevant employee. If it is cash which is missing, then this should be investigated further with the employees who made petty cash purchases during that period.
Access to tills To speed up the cash payment by customers, for each venue the tills have the same log on code and these codes are changed fortnightly. In the event of cash discrepancies arising in the tills, it would be difficult to ascertain which employees may be responsible as there is no way of tracking who used which till. This could lead to cash being easily misappropriated.	Each employee should be provided with a unique log on code and this is required to be entered when using the tills. In order to facilitate the investigation of till differences, employees should be allocated to a specific till point for their shift. Any discrepancies which arise should initially be double checked to ensure they are not arithmetical errors. If still present, the relevant employees who had access to the till can be identified and further investigations can be undertaken.
Tills reconciled in total The reconciliations of the tills to the daily sales readings are performed in total for all five tills at each venue rather than for each till. This means that when exceptions arise, it will be difficult to identify which till caused the difference. Therefore, employees may require further till training or may have undertaken fraudulent transactions.	The reconciliations should be undertaken on an individual till by till basis rather than in aggregate and any discrepancies noted should be investigated immediately.

Control deficiency	Control recommendation
Lack of segregation of duties The cashing up of tills along with the recording of any cash discrepancies is undertaken by just one individual, the restaurant manager. There is a fraud risk as the manager could remove some of the cash and then simply record that there was an exception on the daily sales list. In addition, as there is no segregation of duties, the restaurant manager could, fraudulently or by error, record the total sales as per each till incorrectly leading to incorrect identification of discrepancies.	The cashing up process should be undertaken by two individuals together, ideally an assistant manager and the restaurant manager. One should count the cash and the other record it. Any exceptions to the till reading should be double checked to confirm that they are not simply arithmetical errors. If still present, the relevant employees who had access to the till can be identified and further investigations can be undertaken.
Risk of incomplete sales sheets Daily sales sheets are scanned and emailed to head office on a weekly basis. There is a possibility that some sales sheets could be misplaced by the restaurant manager. This will result in incomplete sales and cash receipts data being recorded into the accounting system.	Daily sales sheets for each venue should be sequentially numbered and remitted to head office on a daily basis. At head office, a sequence check should be undertaken on a regular basis to identify any missing sheets and any gaps should be investigated further. Once received, the cashier should post the sales and cash data for all six venues on a daily basis. Once processed, they should then be signed as posted by the cashier and filed away securely.
Security of cash Cash is stored in a safe at each venue and the restaurant manager stores the safe key in a drawer of their desk when not in use. Although cash is banked on a daily basis, there could still be a significant sum of cash onsite each day. There is a risk of significant cash losses due to theft if access to the safe key is not carefully controlled.	The current key lock safe should be replaced with a safe with a digital code. Only authorised personnel should have the code which should be updated on a regular basis.

Control deficiency	Control recommendation
Cashier duties The cashier is responsible for several elements of the cash receipts system. The cashier receives the daily sales sheets from restaurants, agrees that cash has cleared into the bank statements, updates the bank ledger account and undertakes the bank reconciliations. There is a lack of segregation of duties and errors will not be identified on a timely basis.	These key roles should be split between different members of the finance team, with ideally the bank reconciliations being undertaken by another member of the team.
Credit card statements not reconciled The cashier is not checking that payments made by credit card have resulted in cash being received by Camomile Co. The credit card statements are not reviewed or reconciled, they are just filed away. There is a risk that receipts of cash by credit card may have been omitted and this would not be identified on a timely basis as the bank is only reconciled every two months. This may result in difficulties in resolving any discrepancies with the credit card company.	The cashier should reconcile the credit card vouchers per restaurant to the monthly statement received from the card company. The daily amounts per the statement should be agreed to the bank statement to ensure that all funds have been received. This reconciliation should be reviewed by a responsible official, such as the financial controller, who should evidence by signature that the review has been undertaken.
Infrequent bank reconciliations The bank reconciliations are only carried out every two months. The bank reconciliation is a direct control which reduces the risk of fraud and identifies errors. If not performed regularly, it will not be effective at identifying fraud and errors on a timely basis.	The bank reconciliations should be performed on a monthly basis rather than every two months. The financial controller should continue to review each reconciliation and evidence that review by way of signature on the bank reconciliation.

Detail of payment list not reviewed The finance director only views the total amount of payments to be made rather than the amounts to be paid to each supplier. Without looking at the detail of the payments list, as well as supporting documentation, there is a risk that suppliers could be being paid an incorrect amount, or that sums are being paid to fictitious suppliers. This will cause loss for the company.	The finance director should review the whole payments list prior to authorising. As part of this, the finance director should agree the amounts to be paid to supporting documentation, as well as reviewing the supplier names to identify any duplicates or any unfamiliar names. The finance director should evidence that review by signing the bank transfer list.

Marking guide

			Marks
(a)	**(i)**	**Importance of communicating with TCWG**	
		• Assists understanding of matters related to the audit	1
		• Obtains information relevant to the audit	1
		• Assists TCWG discharge their responsibilities	1
		• Promotes effective two-way communication	1
		Restricted to	**2**
	(ii)	**Matters to communicate to TCWG** 1 mark for any relevant and well-described example	**2**
(b)		**Control deficiencies and recommendations (only 8 issues required)**	
		• Petty cash differences	2
		• Access to tills	2
		• Tills reconciled in total	2
		• Lack of SOD – reconciling cash	2
		• Risk of incomplete daily sales sheets	2
		• Security of cash – access to safes	2
		• Lack of SOD – cashier	2
		• Credit card statements are not reconciled	2
		• Frequency of bank reconciliations	2
		• Payment list not adequately reviewed	2
		Max 8 issues, 2 marks each	**16**
Total			**20**

Examiner's comments

Part (a) required candidates to explain why it is important to report to those charged with governance and to then provide two examples of matters which may be communicated. Candidates' performance was disappointing. The majority of candidates were unable to explain why auditors communicate, and instead simply provided examples of matters to report for part (a)(i); these were then repeated for part (a)(ii). Candidates tended to gain the two available example marks for reporting suspected frauds and significant deficiencies or matters. This is a knowledge area, which has been tested in previous diets. Candidates must practise past exam questions, ensure they study the breadth of the syllabus and ensure their responses are relevant to the requirement.

Part (b) required candidates to identify and explain from the scenario eight deficiencies in respect of the cash receipts and payments system and provide a recommendation to address each of these deficiencies. Performance was disappointing.

Internal control deficiency questions such as this typically require internal control deficiencies to be identified (½ mark each), explained (½ mark each) which must cover the implication of the deficiency to the company and a relevant recommendation to address the deficiency (1 mark). The scenario in the exam contained more issues than were required to be discussed, however, unlike previous diets, it was noted that a significant minority of candidates did not identify the required eight points. This is possibly because they were less prepared for a scenario based on the cash receipts and payments system, having only focused on sales, purchases or payroll systems. Internal controls questions remain a highly examinable area and future candidates need to ensure that they have undertaken adequate question practice of all examinable control systems.

The deficiencies most candidates were able to identify were the frequency of the bank reconciliation process, access to the safe, the restaurant manager solely cashing up tills and all tills having the same log on code. However, a significant minority of candidates identified irrelevant or unrealistic deficiencies. Some candidates identified that the company's internal audit was too small or that a centralised purchasing department should be implemented. However, the requirement was to focus on the cash system and these points were unrelated to the control system being examined, hence were not awarded any credit. Incorrect answers such as 'employees are not supervised when they enter cash receipts from customers into the tills' were not credited as they were not deficiencies and demonstrated a lack of understanding of a cash system.

In addition, some candidates did not clearly understand/ explain the implication of the deficiency. Candidates are required to explain the implication to the business to be awarded credit. For example, a candidate who correctly identified the deficiency 'cash tills are only cashed up by one individual' (identification ½ mark awarded), no credit was awarded for the explanation 'this could lead to an increased risk of fraud'. Candidates must clearly explain the implication to the business of any system errors not being identified, such as 'the restaurant manager may steal the cash and conceal the error or fraud as no one else is present during the cashing up process ' to be awarded the ½ explanation mark. In addition, some candidates correctly identified the deficiency 'bank reconciliations are only performed every two months' but failed to provide any implication at all, thereby restricting marks awarded. Candidates were able to provide some good recommendations to address the deficiencies identified. However, some of the recommendations were not described in enough detail or were auditor responses rather than control recommendations for management

231 RASPBERRY *Walk in the footsteps of a top tutor*

Key answer tips

Part (a) asks for direct controls and tests of controls. Direct controls reduce the risk of material misstatement. Look for evidence of segregation of duties, authorisation, reconciliations, etc. The control must be complete to be effective, e.g. sequential numbering of invoices must be accompanied with a regular sequence check to ensure the sequence is complete in order for the control to be effective. A bank reconciliation must be reviewed by a responsible official to ensure it has been performed properly. For the full mark, explain the risk that the control is designed to mitigate. When describing a test of control, you need to say how the auditor will obtain evidence that the control is working effectively. This may come from inspecting a document for evidence of authorisation or observing client staff perform their work to see whether the do what they are supposed to.

Part (b) asks for control deficiencies and recommendations. This is examined frequently and with plenty of past papers to practise, this type of question should be easy and students should be able to earn most of the marks available. Fully explain the deficiency in terms of the effect on the company. If management are to take action, they must be concerned about the potential consequences of the deficiency. When providing recommendations for improvement, be as specific as possible. For the test of control, describe how the auditor would obtain evidence that the client has implemented the control suggested.

Part (c) is a knowledge requirement asking for the differences between the role of internal audit and external audit. Knowledge requirements such as this are likely to feature in most constructed response questions so allocate some revision time to learning this type of content.

Part (d) asks for assignments that the internal audit department could perform. Think about the purpose of the IAD to help generate ideas. The internal audit department perform checks on the company to make sure it is running as efficiently and effectively as possible. This includes making sure the company minimises the risk of fraud and error, complies with laws and regulations, etc.

(a) Direct controls and tests of controls

Direct control	**Test of control**
Segregation of duties Raspberry Co has a separate human resources (HR) department which is responsible for setting up all new employees. Having a segregation of roles between human resources and payroll departments reduces the risk of fictitious employees being set up and paid. This ensures occurrence of payroll costs which will lead to overstatement.	Review the job descriptions of payroll and HR to confirm the split of responsibilities with regards to setting up new joiners. Discuss with members of the payroll department the process for setting up new joiners and for confirmation that the process is initiated by HR.

Direct control	Test of control
Pre-printed new joiner forms Pre-printed forms are completed by HR for all new employees, and includes assignment of a unique employee number, and once verified, a copy is sent to the payroll department. Payroll is unable to set up new joiners without information from these forms. The use of pre-printed forms ensures that all relevant information, such as tax IDs, is obtained about employees prior to set up. This minimises the risk of incorrect wage and tax payments and the associated misstatement of payroll costs. In addition, as payroll is unable to set up new joiners without the forms and employee number, it reduces the risk of fictitious employees being set up by payroll thereby ensuring occurrence of payroll costs in respect of new joiners.	Select a sample of new employees added to the payroll during the year, review the joiner forms for evidence of completion of all parts and that the information was verified as accurate and was received by payroll prior to being added to the system. Select a sample of edit reports for changes to payroll during the year; agree a sample of new employees added to payroll to the joiners' forms.
Data processing checks The quarterly production bonus is input by a clerk into the payroll system, each entry is checked by a senior clerk for input errors prior to processing, and they evidence their review via signature. This reduces the risk of input errors resulting in misstatement of payroll costs and over/underpayment of the bonus to employees.	If attending Raspberry Co at the time of bonus processing, observe the clerk inputting and senior clerk checking the bonus payments into the payroll system. In addition, obtain listings of quarterly bonus payments and review for evidence of signature by the senior clerk who checks for input errors.
Clock card process monitored Production employees are issued with clock cards and are required to swipe their cards at the beginning and end of their shift, this process is supervised by security staff 24 hours a day. This ensures that genuine employees are only paid for the work actually done, and reduces the risk of employees being paid but not completing their eight-hour shift. In addition, due to the supervision it is unlikely that one employee could swipe in others. This ensures occurrence of payroll costs and reduces the risk of overstatement.	Observe the use of clock cards by employees when entering the power station. Confirm the security team is supervising the process and following up on discrepancies through discussions with the security staff.

Direct control	**Test of control**
Automatic transfer of data The clock card information identifies the employee number and links into the hours worked report produced by the payroll system. As the hours worked are automatically transferred into the payroll system, this reduces the risk of input errors in entering hours to be paid in calculating payroll, ensuring accuracy of payroll costs.	Utilise test data procedures to input dummy clock card information, verify this has been updated into the payroll system.
Exception reports On a quarterly basis, exception reports of changes to payroll standing data are produced and reviewed by the payroll director. This ensures that any unauthorised amendments to standing data are identified and resolved on a timely basis. This reduces the risk of over or understatement of payroll costs.	Select a sample of quarterly exception reports and review for evidence of review and follow up of any unexpected changes by the payroll director.
Security process over cash For production employees paid in cash, cash is received weekly from the bank by a security company. It is likely the sum of money required to pay over 175 employees would be considerable. It is important that cash is adequately safeguarded to reduce the risk of misappropriation and misstatement of cash balances.	Enquire of payroll clerks how cash is delivered to Raspberry Co for weekly pay packets. Review a sample of invoices from the security company to Raspberry Co for delivery of cash.
Segregation of duties The pay packets are prepared by two members of staff with one preparing and one checking the pay packets and this is evidenced by each staff member signing the weekly listing. This ensures there is segregation of duties which prevents fraud and errors not being identified which could result in misstatement of payroll costs.	Observe the preparation of the pay packets ensuring that two members of staff are involved and that pay packets are checked for accuracy. For a sample of weeks throughout the year, inspect the weekly payroll listing for evidence of signature by the two members of staff involved in the preparation of the pay packets.

(b) Control deficiencies and recommendations

Control deficiency	**Control recommendation**
Production bonus set by supervisor Production supervisors determine the amount of the discretionary bonus to be paid to employees. Production supervisors could pay extra bonuses to friends or family members. This will result in additional payroll costs.	The bonus should be determined by a responsible official, such as the production director and should be formulated based on a written policy. If significant in value, the bonus should be formally agreed by the board of directors. The bonus should be communicated in writing to the payroll department.
No calculation checks The wages calculations are generated by the payroll system and there are no checks performed. Therefore, if system errors occur during the payroll processing, this would not be identified. This could result in wages being over or under calculated, leading to an additional payroll cost or loss of employee goodwill.	A senior member of the payroll team should recalculate the gross to net pay workings for a sample of employees and compare their results to the output from the payroll system. These calculations should be signed as approved before payments are made.
No monitoring of student loan deductions Student loan deduction forms are completed by relevant employees and payments are made directly to the third party until the employee notifies HR that the loan has been repaid in full. As the payments continue until the employee notifies HR, and employees are unlikely to be closely monitoring payments. There is the risk that overpayments may be made, which then need to be reclaimed, leading to employee dissatisfaction. In the case of underpayments, Raspberry Co has an obligation to remit funds on time and to reconcile to annual loan statements. If the company does not make payments in full and on time, this could result in non-compliance by both the company and employee, which could result in fines or penalties.	The payroll department should maintain a schedule, by employee, of payments made to third parties, such as the central government as well as the cumulative balance owing. On a regular basis, at least annually, this statement should be reconciled to the loan statement received from the government and sent to the employee for agreement. In accordance with the schedule, payments which are due to cease shortly should be confirmed in writing with the third party, prior to stopping.

Control deficiency	**Control recommendation**
Holiday requests not always authorised Holiday request forms are required to be completed and authorised by relevant line managers, however, this does not always occur. This could result in employees taking unauthorised leave, resulting in production difficulties if an insufficient number of employees are present to operate the power plant. In addition, employees taking unauthorised leave could result in an overpayment of wages.	Employees should be informed that they will not be able to take holiday without completion of a holiday request form, with authorisation from the line manager. Payroll clerks should not process holiday payments without agreement to the authorised holiday form.
Lack of segregation of duties The senior payroll manager reviews the bank transfer listing prior to authorising the payments and also amends the payroll records for any changes required. There is a lack of segregation of duties as it is the payroll team which processes the amounts and the senior payroll manager who authorises payments. The senior manager could fraudulently increase the amounts to be paid to certain employees, process this payment as well as amend the records.	The senior payroll manager should not be able to process changes to the payroll system as well as authorise payments. The authorisation of the bank transfer listing should be undertaken by an individual outside the payroll department, such as the finance director.
Distribution of pay packets The pay packets are delivered to the production supervisors, who distribute them to employees at the end of their shift. The supervisor is not sufficiently independent to pay wages out. They could adjust pay packets to increase those of close friends whilst reducing others. In addition, although the production supervisors know their team members, payment of wages without proof of identity increases the risk that wages could be paid to incorrect employees.	All pay packets should be distributed by the payroll department, directly to employees, upon sight of the employee's clock card and photographic identification as this confirms proof of identity. The payroll department should undertake a reconciliation of pay packets issued to production supervisors, wages distributed with employee signatures to confirm receipt and pay packets returned to payroll due to staff absences. Any differences should be investigated immediately. As employees work eight-hour shifts over 24 hours, consideration should be given to operating a shift system for the payroll department on wages pay out day.

Control deficiency	Control recommendation
	This will ensure that there are sufficient payroll employees to perform the wages pay out for each shift of employees, with the same level of controls in place.
Variances not analysed Monthly management accounts do not analyse the variances between actual and budgeted wages and salaries. This is because there are no overtime costs. However, wages and salaries are a significant expense and management needs to understand why variances may have arisen. These could occur due to extra employees being recruited which were not budgeted for, or an increase in wage pay out rates. The board would need to monitor the wages and salaries costs as if they are too high, then this would impact the profitability of the company.	The monthly management accounts should be amended to include an analysis of wages and salaries compared to the budgeted costs. These should be broken down to each relevant department and could also include an analysis of headcount numbers compared to budget.

(c) Role of internal and external audit

	External audit	Internal audit
Objective	Express an opinion on the truth and fairness of the financial statements in a written report	Improve the company's operations by reviewing the efficiency and effectiveness of internal controls
Reporting	Reports to shareholders	Reports to management or those charged with governance
Availability of report	Publicly available	Not publicly available. Usually only seen by management or those charged with governance
Scope of work	Verifying the truth and fairness of the financial statements	Wide in scope and dependent on management's requirements
Appointment and removal	By the shareholders of the company	By the audit committee or board of directors
Relationship with company	Must be independent of the company	May be employees (which limits independence) or an outsourced function (which enhances independence)

(d) Assignments for internal audit department (IAD)

Value for money review – The IAD could be asked to assess whether Raspberry Co is obtaining value for money in areas such as asset expenditure.

Review of financial/operational controls – The IAD could undertake reviews of controls at head office and the power station and make recommendations to management over such areas as the purchasing process as well as the payroll cycle.

Monitoring asset levels – The IAD could undertake physical verification of property, plant and equipment (PPE) at the production site and head office and compare the assets seen to the PPE register. There is likely to be a significant level of PPE and the asset register must be kept up to date to ensure continuous production. If significant negative differences occur, this may be due to theft or fraud.

Regulatory compliance – Raspberry Co produces electricity and operates a power station, hence it will be subject to a large number of laws and regulations such as health and safety and environmental legislation. The IAD could help to monitor compliance with these regulations.

IT system reviews – Raspberry Co is likely to have a relatively complex computer system linking production data to head office. The IAD could be asked to perform a review over the computer environment and controls.

Cash controls – Raspberry Co's internal auditors could undertake controls testing over cash payments. 70% of employees are paid in cash rather than bank transfer, therefore on a weekly basis cash held is likely to be significant, therefore the cash controls in payroll should be tested to reduce the level of errors.

Fraud investigations – The IAD can be asked to investigate any specific cases of suspected fraud as well as review the controls in place to prevent/detect fraud.

Marking guide

		Marks
(a)	**Direct controls and tests of control (only 5 controls required)**	
	• Separate HR department	2
	• Pre-printed joiners' forms	2
	• Data processing checks on bonus information	2
	• Use of clock cards and process supervised	2
	• Direct transfer between clock card and payroll systems	2
	• Exception reports for changes to payroll data	2
	• Security process over cash	2
	• SOD over pay packets	2
	Max 5 direct controls, 2 marks each	**10**
(b)	**Control deficiencies and recommendations (only 5 issues required)**	
	• Production bonus set by supervisor	2
	• No independent checks on wage calculations	2
	• No monitoring of student loan payments	2
	• Holiday requests not always authorised	2
	• Lack of SOD in payroll department	2
	• Pay packets not delivered by independent staff/no evidence of distribution	2
	• Monthly management accounts not analysed	2
	Max 5 issues, 2 marks each	**10**

(c)	**Role of internal and external audit**		
	• Objective		1
	• Reporting		1
	• Availability of report		1
	• Scope of work		1
	• Appointment and removal		1
	• Relationship with company		1
		Restricted to	**5**
(d)	**Internal audit assignments**		
	• Value for money		1
	• Financial/operational review		1
	• Monitoring assets		1
	• Regulatory compliance		1
	• IT systems		1
	• Cash controls		1
	• Fraud investigation		1
		Restricted to	**5**
Total			**30**

Examiner's comments

Part (a) required candidates to identify and explain from the scenario direct controls in respect of the payroll system described which the auditor may seek to place reliance on, and describe a test of control the auditor should perform to assess if each of the controls is operating effectively. Candidates' performance on this requirement was disappointing. Questions such as this typically require the direct control to be identified (½ mark each), explained as to why it is a direct control (½ mark each) and a test of control provided (1 mark). The scenario in the exam contained more direct controls than were required to be discussed and it was disappointing that many candidates did not identify the required number of controls noted in the question. Candidates are encouraged to familiarise themselves with the requirements of ISA 330 *The Auditor's Responses to Assessed Risks* which states that tests of controls should only be performed on controls which are suitably designed to prevent, or detect and correct, a material misstatement, to help them consider what constitutes a direct control. Although a number of candidates identified, for ½ mark each, the direct controls of separate human resources and payroll departments, supervision of the clocking-in process, and segregation of duties in the preparation of the pay packets, many candidates did not clearly explain the control and so were not awarded the second ½ mark. To explain why the control is direct, candidates must explain how the control will prevent or detect and correct a misstatement. For example, to explain the fact that the company operates a separate human resources and payroll department as a direct control, candidates must state 'it would reduce the risk of fictitious employees being set up' to be awarded the ½ mark, explanations such as 'this is good segregation of duties' was not a sufficient explanation to be awarded credit. A significant number of candidates incorrectly included control deficiencies in part (a). For example, identifying that 'the senior payroll manager agrees BACs payments to the payroll' was not awarded credit as a direct control as there was a lack of segregation of duties, as if errors were noted, the senior payroll manager also amended the records, which would have prevented the auditor from placing reliance on this control. This point should actually be included as a deficiency in part (b). In common with previous diets, candidates continue to find tests of control challenging. Many candidates confused substantive procedures for tests of control and tests were often vague or incomplete. For example, 'look at the bonus listing' without saying why, i.e. 'for evidence of review', or 'observe the clocking in process' without reference to the overview of the process by the security staff. Tests of control are very commonly tested and future candidates need to ensure that they have undertaken adequate question practice.

Part (b) required candidates to identify and explain from the scenario deficiencies in respect of the payroll system and provide a recommendation to address each of these deficiencies. Many candidates performed well in this requirement. Internal control deficiency questions such as this typically require internal control deficiencies to be identified (½ mark each), explained (½ mark each) which must cover the implication of the deficiency to the company and a relevant recommendation to address the deficiency (1 mark). The scenario in the exam contained more issues than were required to be discussed and it was pleasing that many candidates identified the required number of issues noted in the question. However, some candidates did not clearly understand/explain the implication of the deficiency. Candidates are required to explain the implication to the business to be awarded credit. For example, a candidate who correctly identified the deficiency 'wage calculations generated by the system are not checked' (identification ½ mark awarded), no credit was awarded for the explanation 'this could lead to errors'. Candidates must clearly explain the implication to the business of any system errors not being identified such as 'wages may be over/under calculated' or 'wages may be overpaid' or 'loss of employee goodwill', to be awarded the ½ explanation mark. Many candidates were able to provide good recommendations to address the deficiencies identified. However, some of the recommendations were not described in enough detail, for example, in relation to management accounts not analysing budget versus actual for wages and salaries, a recommendation 'management accounts should be amended to include an analysis of wages and salaries' was awarded ½ mark, for the full 1 mark candidates needed to go on to say 'and this should be compared to budget' or 'should include a commentary'. It was pleasing that many candidates followed the instructions to set their answer out in two columns being control deficiency and control recommendation. Internal controls questions remain a highly examinable area and future candidates need to ensure that they have undertaken adequate question practice.

Part (d) required candidates to describe assignments the internal audit department of Raspberry Co would carry out. Up to 1 mark was awarded for each well-described point. Performance was mixed. Some candidates only listed the assignments rather than describing them and therefore were awarded ½ mark for each. Candidates are again reminded to pay attention to the verb used in the requirement to ensure they are providing sufficiently detailed answers. Common misunderstandings by a number of candidates were 'the internal auditor prepares the financial statements' and 'internal auditors implement the controls'. Some candidates described the differences between internal and external audit, which was not the purpose of the requirement. Further, some candidates included many examples of financial/operational controls which the internal audit department could test, however, this only demonstrated one type of assignment so was awarded only 1 mark overall. In addition, some candidates described assignments, which would not be relevant to an electric power station client, for example 'internal auditors undertaking mystery shopping'. This is principally a knowledge area, which has been tested in previous diets. Candidates must practise past exam questions, ensure they study the breadth of the syllabus and ensure their responses are relevant to the scenario.

232 COMET PUBLISHING *Walk in the footsteps of a top tutor*

Key answer tips

Part (a) asks for steps to confirm systems documentation. Again, this is straight from the text book knowledge and students should commit this knowledge to memory.

Part (b) asks for control deficiencies, recommendations and tests of controls. This is examined frequently and with plenty of past papers to practise, this type of question should be easy and students should be able to earn most of the marks available. Fully explain the deficiency in terms of the effect on the company. If management are to take action, they must be concerned about the potential consequences of the deficiency. When providing recommendations for improvement, be as specific as possible. For the test of control, describe how the auditor would obtain evidence that the client has implemented the control suggested.

Part (c) asks for substantive procedures over purchases and expenses. A substantive procedure tests the number in the financial statements. You must give substantive procedures and not tests of controls for this requirement. Don't make the mistake of testing payables. The question asks for purchases. Purchases are the transactions that took place throughout the year. Payables are only the invoices unpaid at the year end. They are not the same figures. Focus on testing GRNs, purchase invoices and the detailed purchase listing. Analytical procedures can also be used as substantive procedures.

Part (d) is a regularly seen requirement asking for safeguards to address a conflict of interest. This is rote learned knowledge from the text book and all students should be able to score most, if not all, of the marks available.

(a) Steps to confirm prior year flowcharts and system notes

- Obtain the system notes from last year's audit and ensure that the documentation on the purchases and payables system covers all expected stages and is complete.
- Review the audit file for indications of weaknesses in the system and note these for investigation this year.
- Review the prior year report to management to identify any recommendations which were made over controls in this area as this may highlight potential changes which have been made in the current year.
- Obtain system documentation from the client, potentially in the form of a procedure manual. Review this to identify any changes made in the last 12 months.
- Interview client staff to ascertain whether systems and controls have changed including the stores and warehouse to ensure that the flowcharts and notes produced last year is correct.
- Perform walk-through tests by tracing a sample of transactions through the purchases and payables system to ensure that the flowcharts and systems notes contained on the audit file are accurate.
- During the walk-through tests, confirm the systems notes and flowcharts accurately reflect the control procedures which are in place and can be used to identify controls for testing.

(b) Control deficiencies, control recommendations and tests of control

Control deficiency	Control recommendation	Test of control
No inter-branch transfers It is not possible for a store to order goods from other local stores for customers. Instead, customers are told to contact the other stores or use the company website. Customers are less likely to contact individual stores themselves and this could result in the company losing valuable sales. In addition, some goods which are slow moving in one store may be out of stock at another; if goods could be transferred between stores, then overall sales may be maximised.	An inter-branch transfer system should be established between stores, with inter-branch inventory forms being completed for store transfers. This should help stores whose inventory levels are low but are awaiting deliveries from the suppliers.	During the interim audit, arrange to visit a number of the stores, discuss with the store manager the process for ordering of inventory items, in particular whether it is possible to order from other branches. At each store, inspect a sample of completed inter-branch inventory forms for confirmation the control is operating.
Authorisation of orders Purchase orders below $1,000 are not authorised and are processed solely by the purchase order clerk who is also responsible for processing invoices. This could result in non-business-related purchases and there is an increased fraud risk as the clerk could place orders for personal goods up to the value of $1,000, which is significant.	All purchase orders should be authorised by a responsible official. Authorised signatories should be established with varying levels of purchase order authorisation.	Select a sample of purchase orders and review for evidence of authorisation, agree this to the appropriate signature on the approved signatories list.

Control deficiency	**Control recommendation**	**Test of control**
GRNs not processed regularly Goods received notes (GRNs) are sent to the accounts department every two weeks. This could result in delays in suppliers being paid as the purchase invoices could not be agreed to a GRN and also recorded liabilities being understated. Additionally, any prompt payment discounts offered by suppliers may be missed due to delayed payments.	A copy of the GRNs should be sent to the accounts department on a more regular basis, such as daily. The accounts department should undertake a sequence check of the GRNs to ensure none are missing for processing.	Enquire of the accounts clerk as to the frequency of when GRNs are received to assess if they are being sent promptly. Undertake a sequence check of GRNs held by the accounts department and discuss any missing items with the accounts clerk.
Insufficient parts to GRN GRNs are only sent to the accounts department. Failing to send a copy to the ordering department could result in a significant level of unfulfilled orders leading to a loss of sales and stock-outs.	The GRN should be created in three parts and a copy of the GRN should be sent to the purchase order clerk, Oli Dancer, who should agree this to the order and change the order status to complete. On a regular basis Oli should then review for all unfulfilled orders and chase these with the relevant supplier.	Review the file of copy GRNs held by the purchase ordering clerk, Oli Dancer, and review for evidence that these are matched to orders and flagged as complete. Review the file of unfulfilled purchase orders for any overdue items and discuss their status with Oli Dancer.
Lack of segregation of duties The purchase ordering clerk, Oli Dancer, has responsibility for ordering goods below $1,000 and for processing all purchase invoices for payment. There is a lack of segregation of duties and this increases the risk of fraud and non-business-related purchases being made.	The roles of purchase ordering and processing of the related supplier invoices should be allocated to separate members of staff.	Observe which member of staff undertakes the processing of purchase invoices and confirm this is not the purchase ordering clerk, Oli Dancer. Inspect a copy of the company's organisation chart to identify if these tasks have now been allocated to different roles.

Control deficiency	Control recommendation	Test of control
Detail of payments list not reviewed The finance director authorises the bank transfer payment list for suppliers; however, but only views the total amount of payments to be made. Without looking at the detail of the payments list, as well as supporting documentation, there is a risk that suppliers could be being paid an incorrect amount, or that sums are being paid to fictitious suppliers.	The finance director should review the whole payments list prior to authorising. As part of this, the finance director should agree the amounts to be paid to supporting documentation, as well as reviewing the supplier names to identify any duplicates or any unfamiliar names. The finance director should evidence that review by signing the bank transfer list.	Review the payments list for evidence of review by the finance director. Enquire of accounts staff what supporting documentation the finance director requests when undertaking this review.
Supplier statement reconciliations Supplier statement reconciliations are no longer performed. This may result in errors in the recording of purchases and payables not being identified in a timely manner.	Supplier statement reconciliations should be performed on a monthly basis for all suppliers and these should be reviewed by a responsible official.	Review the file of reconciliations to ensure that they are being performed on a regular basis and that they have been reviewed by a responsible official. Reperform a sample of the reconciliations to ensure that they have been carried out appropriately.

(c) Substantive procedures in relation to purchases and other expenses

- Calculate the operating profit and gross profit margins and compare them to last year and budget and investigate any significant differences.
- Review monthly purchases and other expenses to identify any significant fluctuations and discuss with management.
- Discuss with management whether there have been any changes in the key suppliers used and compare this to the detailed purchase listing to assess completeness and accuracy of purchases.
- Recalculate the accuracy of a sample of purchase invoice totals and related taxes and ensure expense has been included in the correct general ledger code.
- Recalculate the prepayments and accruals charged at the year end to ensure the accuracy of the expense charge included in the statement of profit or loss.
- Select a sample of post-year-end expense invoices and ensure that any expenses relating to the current year have been included.

- Select a sample of payments from the bank ledger account and trace to expense account to ensure the expense has been included and classified correctly.
- Select a sample of goods received notes (GRNs) from throughout the year; agree them to purchase invoices and the detailed purchase listing to ensure the completeness of purchases.
- Select a sample of GRNs just before and after the year end; agree to the detailed purchase listing to ensure the expense is recorded in the correct accounting period.

(d) Safeguards to deal with conflict of interest

- Both Comet Publishing Co and its rival competitor, Edmond Co, should be notified that Halley & Co would be acting as auditors for each company and, if necessary, consent should be obtained from each.
- Advising one or both clients to seek additional independent advice.
- The use of separate engagement teams, with different engagement partners and team members; once an employee has worked on one audit, such as Comet Publishing Co, then they would be prevented from being on the audit of the competitor for a period of time.
- Procedures to prevent access to information, for example, strict physical separation of both teams, confidential and secure data filing.
- Clear guidelines for members of each engagement team on issues of security and confidentiality. These guidelines could be included within the audit engagement letters.
- Potentially the use of confidentiality agreements signed by employees and partners of the firm.
- Regular monitoring of the application of the above safeguards by a senior individual in Halley & Co not involved in either audit.

Marking guide		
		Marks
(a)	**Steps to confirm prior year flowcharts**	
	• Review PY notes and confirm all stages covered	1
	• Review PY file for weaknesses not actioned	1
	• Review PY report to management	1
	• Review client system documentation for changes	1
	• Interview client staff to confirm client processes	1
	• Walk-through tests to confirm notes	1
	• Walk-through tests to confirm procedures	1
	Restricted to	**5**
(b)	**Control deficiencies, recommendations and tests of control**	
	• No inter-branch transfers	3
	• Not all purchase orders are authorised	3
	• GRNs not processed regularly	3
	• GRNs not sent to purchasing department	3
	• Segregation of duties in relation to purchases	3
	• Authorisation of bank payments	3
	• Supplier statement reconciliations not performed	3
	Max 5 issues, 3 marks each	**15**

(c)	**Substantive tests in relation to purchases and other expenses**	
	• Calculate operating and gross profit margin and compare to PY	1
	• Review monthly purchases and investigate unexpected difference	1
	• Discuss changes in key suppliers and compare to detailed purchase listing	1
	• Recalculate a sample of purchase invoices	1
	• Recalculate prepayments and accruals	1
	• Review post-year-end invoices for pre-year-end liabilities	1
	• Sample of bank ledger account payments to appropriate expense account	1
	• GRNs to purchase invoice to detailed purchase listing	1
	• Cut-off testing using GRNs	1
	Restricted to	**5**
(d)	**Safeguards to deal with conflict of interest**	
	• Notify both parties and obtain consent	1
	• Advise client to seek independent advice	1
	• Separate engagement teams	1
	• Prevent access to information	1
	• Clear guidelines on security and confidentiality provided to client	1
	• Confidentiality agreements	1
	• Monitor safeguards	1
	Max	**5**
Total		**30**

Examiner's comments

This question was based on Comet Publishing Co, a book retailer with ten stores. This question tested candidates' knowledge of systems documentation, control deficiencies, control recommendations and tests of control, substantive procedures for purchases and other expenses as well as conflicts of interests.

Part (a) required candidates to explain the steps the auditor should take to confirm the accuracy of the flowcharts and systems notes held in the prior year audit file for the purchases and payables cycle. Performance on this question, when answered, was very disappointing. Only a minority of candidates understood what flowcharts and system notes were and therefore recommended procedures such as discussions with management on changes to the system; observing the operation of the system or walkthrough tests and updating the systems documentation to reflect any changes. These candidates scored well in this question. Unfortunately, the majority of candidates did not seem to understand what flowcharts and system notes were or simply saw that the question contained the words 'purchases and payables' and hence provided a long list of substantive procedures or compliance tests for auditing purchases and trade payables. This was not what was required and candidates are again reminded that it is imperative that they address the requirement set. In addition, a significant minority of candidates demonstrated a fundamental lack of understanding in relation to what a flowchart is or its purpose with suggestions of 'agreeing prior year flowcharts to those of the current year and investigating significant differences', or 'agreeing flowcharts to financial statements' and 'agree flowcharts to purchase invoices'. Internal control is a key part of the syllabus and candidates must be prepared for both knowledge and application questions in this area. There are few knowledge areas in syllabus area C, hence candidates should have learnt these areas and practised past exam questions.

Part (b) required candidates to identify and explain from the scenario five deficiencies in respect of the purchases and payables cycle, provide a recommendation to address each of these deficiencies and a test of control to assess if each control, if implemented, is operating effectively. Candidates' performance was mixed. It was pleasing that many candidates followed the instructions to set their answer out in three columns being deficiency, recommendation and test of control. Internal control questions such as this typically require internal control deficiencies to be identified (½ mark each), explained (½ mark each) which must cover the implication of the deficiency to the company, a relevant recommendation to address the deficiency (1 mark) and a test of control (1 mark).

Internal controls questions remain a highly examinable area. The scenario in the exam contained more issues than were required to be discussed and it was therefore disappointing that some candidates did not identify the required number of issues noted in the question. In addition, it was unfortunate that a number of candidates identified facts from the scenario which were not deficiencies, and the related control recommendation and test of control would not have been relevant and therefore did not gain credit. Irrelevant points included 'the store manager raises the requisitions personally/with no authorisation' this failed to understand that at this point it is just a request (still internal to the company) and not at order stage which is where the authorisation is needed. Also, some candidates flagged that the 'warehouse team received goods from suppliers' and that this was somehow problematic as it should be a manager who received goods from suppliers. Candidates were also concerned about overstocking of books and that there was a significant risk of obsolescence or damage which was unlikely in the circumstances. In addition, some candidates did not clearly understand/explain the implication of the deficiency. For example, there was concern that the finance director reviewing the payments list resulted in a lack of segregation of duties, rather than a lack of detailed information being given to approve payments, which could result in invalid or fictitious payments. Many candidates were able to provide good recommendations to address the deficiencies. However, some of the recommendations were either poorly described, did not clearly address the specific control deficiency identified or were impractical suggestions. For example, in relation to the lack of supplier statement reconciliations, some recommended that the company simply hire more staff rather than recommending that the company undertake monthly reconciliations and that these should be reviewed by a responsible official. The final part of the requirement was for tests of controls. In common with previous diets, candidates did not perform well. Many candidates confused substantive procedures for tests of control and too often tests were vague or incomplete. For example, "review for supplier statement reconciliations" which is not clear about exactly what the reconciliations are being reviewed for. Also "observation" is often suggested as a test of control, while it is a valid audit procedure, it is not always the most appropriate one when testing controls and is rarely sufficient on its own. Tests of control are very commonly tested and future candidates need to ensure that they have undertaken adequate question practice.

Part (c) required candidates to describe substantive procedures the auditor should perform to obtain sufficient and appropriate audit evidence in relation to purchases and other expenses. Performance on this requirement was very disappointing. One mark was awarded for each well-described procedure. The most common procedures provided by candidates included analytical review against prior year or budget, detailed tests agreeing to invoices and goods received notes (GRN) or cut-off tests. However, a significant number of candidates provided procedures which were relevant to trade payables rather than purchases and expenses; these would not have gained credit as they did not answer the question asked. For example, many candidates described audit procedures such as trade payable circularisations. Candidates are reminded to read the question requirement carefully and to ensure that they are answering the question set. Following on from part (b), candidates also gave tests of control, such as 'review for authorisation of purchase orders' rather than substantive procedures. Further, many candidates provided vague and incomplete tests. For example, 'agree purchases to GRNs and invoices' would only be awarded ½ mark as this is an incomplete test of detail as it does not follow the transaction into the books of prime entry. Further cut-off tests were incorrectly described using purchase invoices rather than GRNs, these would have only been awarded ½ mark. Candidates are again reminded to think about the aim of the procedure when they are describing substantive tests.

Part (d) required candidates to explain safeguards the auditor should implement in order to address a potential conflict of interest created by the audit firm which also audited the main competitor of Comet Publishing Co. This question was well answered with the majority of candidates demonstrating a good knowledge of the ethical area tested. Many candidates correctly identified safeguards such as informing both companies, separate engagement teams and keeping information confidential. A number of candidates also included the need for confidentiality agreements. Less commonly suggested safeguards included the need to seek independent advice, and monitoring of safeguards. Also, where independent advice was suggested this was in the context of asking for legal advice, which was not relevant. In addition, many candidates suggested monitoring of the audit work undertaken by each team rather than the application and monitoring of the ethical safeguards. Some candidates repeated safeguards in slightly different ways, such as having separate audit teams and suggesting separate engagement partners. These are not two points and hence would have only gained one mark in total rather than two. Also, some made several suggestions on how information could be kept confidential: separate offices, password protection, storing audit files in different locations. Ultimately these are all examples of the same point and so only received credit once.

233 EQUESTRIAN *Walk in the footsteps of a top tutor*

Key answer tips

Part (a) is a straightforward knowledge requirement asking for the control activities as given in ISA 315 (Revised 2019) and examples of each. This should not cause any problems. If in doubt, give examples of controls in your own workplace.

Part (b) asks for direct controls and tests of controls. Direct controls reduce the risk of material misstatement. Look for evidence of segregation of duties, authorisation, reconciliations, etc. The control must be complete to be effective, e.g. sequential numbering of invoices must be accompanied with a regular sequence check to ensure the sequence is complete in order for the control to be effective. A bank reconciliation must be reviewed by a responsible official to ensure it has been performed properly. When describing a test of control, make sure you focus on obtaining evidence that the control is working effectively.

Part (c) asks for control deficiencies and recommendations. You must fully explain the deficiency in terms of the effect on the company. If management are to take action, they must be concerned about the potential consequences of the deficiency. When providing recommendations for improvement, be as specific as possible.

Part (d) Advantages and disadvantages of outsourcing the internal audit function is a straightforward knowledge requirement. Aim for an equal number of advantages and disadvantages. Use subheadings to make it clear in your answer clear which are the advantages and which are the disadvantages.

(a) Control activities

Segregation of duties

Assignment of roles or responsibilities to ensure the tasks of authorising and recording transactions and maintaining custody of assets are carried out by different people, thereby reducing the risk of fraud and error in the normal course of their duties. For example, the payables ledger clerk recording invoices in the list of individual suppliers, and the finance director authorising the payment of those purchase invoices.

Verifications

Controls which compare two or more items with each other or compare an item with a policy. Verifications include information processing controls such as the use of batch control totals when entering transactions into the system.

Authorisation

Approval of transactions by a suitably responsible official or higher level of management to ensure transactions are valid and genuine. For example, authorisation by a responsible official of all purchase orders.

Physical or logical controls

Restricting access to physical assets as well as computer programs and data files, thereby reducing the risk of theft of assets or data. For example, cash being stored in a safe which only a limited number of employees are able to access.

Reconciliations

Reconciliations compare two or more data elements to confirm completeness or accuracy of the data. For example, the bank ledger account being reconciled to the bank statements on a regular basis to identify any discrepancies which can then be resolved on a timely basis.

(b) Direct controls and tests of controls

Direct control	Test of control
System changes monitored by IA Changes to the accounting systems are monitored by the internal audit department, as evidenced by the change to the receivable system. This reduces the risk of errors, loss of data and incorrect processing of information which could result in misstatement of receivables.	Inspect the internal audit department's documentation of the changeover of the receivables system and the checks made to ensure that the checks have been performed and that they were completed appropriately. For a sample of receivables, agree the data in the old system to the data in the new system at several points in time during the year.

Direct control	Test of control
Credit checks and credit limits set and reviewed regularly All new customers are required to undergo a full credit check and credit limits are set with appropriate authorisation by the sales director. Credit limits are reviewed on a regular basis and an authorised form is required to make any changes to the limit. This means sales are only made to customers that are likely to pay in full and on time, reducing the risk of irrecoverable debts and overstatement of receivables.	Inspect a sample of customer files to ensure a credit check has been obtained and review the date it was performed to ensure it is up to date. Inspect the customer's account within the system to ensure credit limits have been put in place and inspect the email authorisation by the sales director to confirm the correct limit has been entered into the system. Inspect evidence of the credit limit review performed by the sales managers during the year. For a sample of customers whose credit limit has changed in the year, obtain the credit limit review form and inspect for evidence of authorisation by the sales director.
Use of approved price list Sales invoices are prepared using the company price list. The price list is updated quarterly, meaning up to date prices are used when the invoices are raised, reducing the risk of errors when raising invoices and ensuring accuracy of revenue.	Inspect the price list for approval by the directors and review the last modified date to ensure it has been reviewed in the last three months. Agree the prices in the system to the approved price list. Obtain a copy of the current price list and, for a sample of invoices, agree that the correct prices have been used. Enquire of management who has authority to amend standing data such as prices in the system to ensure only persons of suitable authority have access. Try to input a change to the prices in the system using a used ID of a clerk to ensure that they system does not allow access to this standing data.
Authorisation of sales discounts Discounts must be requested by a sales manager and authorised by the sales director. This reduces the risk of fraud which will result in misstatement of revenue.	With Equestrian Co's permission, attempt to process an invoice with a sales discount that has not been authorised by the sales director. The system should reject the invoice. Inspect a sample of sales orders with discounts given for evidence of the sales director's signature authorising the discount and confirm the discount given is within the approved range of 2% – 10%.

Direct control	Test of control
Segregation of duties Payments are made by the cashier's office and recorded by the purchase ledger team. This segregation of duties prevents fraud and error as one person is not responsible for the physical cash and updating the ledger which would enable someone to conceal the fraud. This reduces the risk of misstatement of payables and cash balances.	Observe the process of payments from the cashier's office to ensure segregation of duties is in place. Inspect the accounts team organisational chart to ensure appropriate segregation of duties between the cashier's office and purchase ledger team.
Invoices marked as paid Invoices are stamped as 'paid' and filed separately from invoices not yet paid. This prevents invoices from being paid twice which would result in unnecessary cash outflow and understatement of payables.	Inspect the file of paid invoices and ensure they are kept separate from invoices not yet paid. Inspect them for evidence they have been stamped as 'Paid'.

(c) Control deficiencies and recommendations

Control deficiency	Control recommendation
Physical verification of assets Physical verification of assets within the non-current asset register has not been undertaken for some time. A current programme has started but is only 15% complete, due to staff shortages. If non-current assets are not physically verified on a regular basis, there is an increased risk of assets being misappropriated or misplaced as there is no check that the assets still exist in their correct location.	Additional resources should be devoted to completing the physical verification of all assets within the register. If any assets cannot be located, they should be written off. Following this full review, on a monthly basis a sample of assets at the sites should be agreed back to the register to confirm existence.
Staff shortages in the IA department Equestrian Co has experienced significant staff shortages within its internal audit (IA) department. Maintaining an IA department is an important control as it enables senior management to test whether controls are operating effectively within the company. If the team has staff shortages or lack of experience, this reduces the effectiveness of this monitoring control.	Senior management should consider recruiting additional employees to join the IA department. If this is not possible, consideration should be given to outsourcing the internal audit function. In the interim, employees from other departments, such as finance, could be seconded to IA to assist them with the internal audits, provided these reviews do not cover controls operating in the department where the employees normally work.

Control deficiency	**Control recommendation**
Lack of segregation of duties During the year, the human resources (HR) department has been busy, therefore the payroll department has set up new joiners to the company. This is a lack of segregation of duties, as employees are able to set up new joiners in the payroll system and process their pay, this leads to an increased risk of fictitious/ duplicate employees being set up.	The HR director should review the workloads of the department as a matter of urgency to assess whether other tasks can be re-prioritised as payroll should cease to set up new joiners. This role must immediately revert back to HR to undertake. Additionally, a review should be undertaken of all new joiners set up by payroll with agreement to employee files to confirm that all new employees are bona fide.
Lack of approval for wage increase The wage rate has been increased by the HR director and notified to the payroll supervisor by email. As payroll can be a significant expense for a business, any decision to increase this should be made by the board as a whole and not just by the HR director. In addition, the notification of the payroll increase was via email and the payroll supervisor was able to make changes to the payroll standing data without further authorisation. This increases the risk of fraud or errors arising within payroll.	All increases of pay should be proposed by the HR department and then formally agreed by the board of directors. Upon agreement of the pay rise, a written notification of the board decision should be sent to the payroll supervisor who enters the revised pay rate into the system. This change should trigger an exception report for the payroll director, and the new rate should not go live until the director has signed off the changes.
Access to high value inventory High value inventory is stored in a secure location across all nine warehouses and access is via a four-digit code, which is common to all sites. A considerable number of people will be aware of the codes and could access inventory at any of the nine sites. This significantly increases the risk of fraud through theft and misstatement of inventory.	The access codes for all of the sites should be changed. Each site should have a unique code, known to a small number of senior warehouse employees. These codes should be changed on a regular basis.

Control deficiency	Control recommendation
Incomplete perpetual counts Monthly perpetual inventory counts are supposed to be undertaken at each of the nine warehouses, but some of these are outstanding. In order to rely on inventory records for decision making and the year-end financial statements, all lines of inventory must be counted at least once a year, with high value or high turnover items counted more regularly. If the counts are outstanding, some goods may not be counted, and the inventory records may be incorrect.	The programme of perpetual inventory counts should be reviewed for omissions. Any lines which have been missed out should be included in the remaining counts. At the year end, if any lines are identified as having not been counted, the company should organise an additional count to ensure that all items are confirmed to inventory records.
Bank reconciliations not always reviewed The bank reconciliations are only reviewed by the financial controller if the sum of reconciling items is significant, therefore some reconciliations are not being reviewed. The financial controller relies solely on the accounts clerk's notification that the bank reconciliations require review. The bank reconciliations could contain significant errors, but a low overall number of reconciling items, as there could be compensating errors which cancel each other out. Bank reconciliations are a direct control which reduces the risk of fraud. If they are not reviewed, then this reduces its effectiveness and also results in a lack of assurance that bank reconciliations are being carried out at all or on a timely basis.	The bank reconciliations should be reviewed by the financial controller on a monthly basis, even if there are no reconciling items. The financial controller should evidence their review by way of signature on the bank reconciliation.
Invoices not paid on time Invoices are authorised by the finance director, but payment is only made 75 days after receipt of the invoice. There is the risk that Equestrian Co is missing out on early settlement discounts. Also, failing to pay in accordance with the supplier's payment terms can lead to a loss of supplier goodwill as well as the risk that suppliers may refuse to supply goods to the company.	The policy of making payment after 75 days should be reviewed. Consideration should be given to earlier payment if the settlement discounts are sufficient. If not, invoices should be paid in accordance with the supplier's payment terms.

(d) Outsourcing internal audit

Advantages

Staffing

Equestrian Co wishes to expand its internal audit department in terms of size and specialist skills. If it outsources, there will be no need to spend money on recruiting further staff as the service provider will provide the staff members.

Immediate solution

As the current internal audit department is small, outsourcing can provide the number of staff needed straight away. If Equestrian Co was to recruit, it would take more time to obtain the additional people required.

Skills and experience

A service provider is likely to have a large pool of staff available to provide the internal audit service to Equestrian Co and is likely to have staff with specialist skills already available.

Cost control

Outsourcing can be an efficient means to control the costs of internal audit as any associated costs such as training will be eliminated as the service provider will train its own employees. In addition, the costs for the internal audit service will be agreed in advance. This will ensure that Equestrian Co can budget accordingly.

Flexibility

If the internal audit department is outsourced, Equestrian Co will have total flexibility in its internal audit service. Staff can be requested from the service provider to suit the company's workload and requirements. This will ensure that, when required, extra staff are readily available for as long or short a period as needed.

Disadvantages

Existing internal audit department

Equestrian Co has an existing internal audit department. If the staff cannot be redeployed elsewhere in the company, then they may need to be made redundant and this could be costly for Equestrian Co. Staff may oppose the outsourcing if it results in redundancies.

Increased costs

As well as the cost of potential redundancies, the internal audit fee charged by the service provider may increase over time, proving to be very expensive.

Knowledge of company

The service provider will allocate available staff members to work on the internal audit assignment. This may mean that each visit the staff members are different and hence they may not fully understand the systems of Equestrian Co. This will decrease the quality of the services provided and increase the time spent by Equestrian Co's employees in explaining the system to the internal auditors.

Loss of in-house skills

If the current internal audit team is not deployed elsewhere in the company, valuable internal audit knowledge and experience may be lost. If Equestrian Co then decided at a future date to bring the service back in-house, this might prove to be too difficult.

Confidentiality

Knowledge of company systems and confidential data will be available to the service provider. Although the engagement letter would include confidentiality clauses, this may not stop breaches of confidentiality.

Control

Once outsourced, Equestrian Co will need to discuss areas of work and timings well in advance with the service provider which means losing some control over the activities of its internal audit department.

ACCA marking guide		
		Marks
(a)	**Control activities**	
	• Segregation of duties	1
	• Verification	1
	• Authorisation	1
	• Physical or logical controls	1
	• Reconciliations	1
	Restricted to	**4**
(b)	**Direct controls and tests of control**	
	• System changes overseen by internal audit	2
	• Credit checks performed, credit limits set and reviewed	2
	• Invoices raised using approved price list	2
	• Discounts authorised	2
	• Segregation of duties for payment of invoices	2
	• Paid invoices marked and recorded separately	2
	Max 5 direct controls, 2 marks each	**10**
(c)	**Control deficiencies and recommendations**	
	• Assets not physically verified	2
	• Internal audit staff shortages	2
	• Payroll setting up new staff	2
	• Lack of approval for wage increase	2
	• Inappropriate access to high value inventory	2
	• Perpetual inventory counts not complete	2
	• Bank reconciliations not always reviewed	2
	• Invoices not paid in line with supplier's terms	2
	Max 5 issues, 2 marks each	**10**
(d)	**Outsourcing internal audit**	
	Advantages	
	• Staffing – no need to recruit	1
	• Immediate solution	1
	• Skills and experience increased	1
	• Cost control	1
	• Flexibility of service	1
	Disadvantages	
	• Potential redundancies for existing internal audit staff	1
	• Increased costs as fees may increase over time	1
	• Knowledge of company and systems reduced	1
	• Loss of in-house skills	1
	• Confidentiality issues	1
	• Control of department reduced	1
	Restricted to	**6**
Total		**30**

Examiner's comments

Part (a) was a knowledge-based requirement asking candidates to describe four different types of control activities and for each type to provide an example control a company could implement. Performance was very disappointing. Many candidates did not attempt this requirement. The first ½ mark was awarded for each type of control activity described and the second ½ mark for a relevant control example. Few candidates described the five control activities. Segregation of duties and physical or logical controls were the two most common control activities identified. However, most candidates who did identify these two activities only named and did not describe them so were not awarded the first ½ mark. If a candidate identified a control activity correctly they generally gave a relevant example for the second ½ mark.

Part (c) required candidates to identify and explain from the scenario the deficiencies in Equestrian Co's internal controls and provide a recommendation to address each of these deficiencies. Candidates' performance was mixed. Internal control questions typically require internal control deficiencies to be identified (½ marks each), explained (½ marks each), and a relevant recommendation to address the control (1 mark). Internal controls questions remain a highly examinable area. The scenario in the exam contained more issues than were required to be discussed and it was therefore disappointing that some candidates did not identify the required number of issues noted in the question. In addition, some candidates put more than one deficiency as one point in their answer. For example, some candidates identified 'physical verification of assets had not been completed for some time' due to 'internal audit shortages' and ½ mark was awarded for identifying each of these issues (i.e. 1 mark in total). However, when issues are combined in this manner they are often not individually well explained and neither is a separate recommendation noted for each. In addition, some candidates did not clearly explain the implication of the deficiency. For example, if PPE is not regularly physically verified some candidates stated that an incorrect carrying amount of PPE could arise. This is not fully explaining the implication of the deficiency, i.e. that there may be a possible misappropriation of assets or assets included in the register which cannot be verified. Most candidates were able to provide good recommendations to address the deficiencies. However, some of the recommendations were either poorly described, did not clearly address the specific control deficiency identified or were impractical suggestions. For example, recommending that monthly counts are carried out to address the deficiency that perpetual inventory counts are outstanding for some sites does not remedy the deficiency as monthly counts should already be performed, the issue is that the company is not adhering to their own policy. In addition, many candidates recommended that the company undertake a full year-end count, despite being told in the scenario that this was not an option.

Part (d) required advantages and disadvantages of outsourcing the internal audit department. Candidates performed well on this question. Many candidates were able to identify a good range of points and the mark allocation was adhered to. Many answers were well structured with sub headings for advantages and disadvantages which facilitated the marking of this question. Those candidates who did not score well tended to provide very little detail in their answers, such as for advantages simply stated 'lower costs' or 'more flexibility' these are far too brief to score the 1 mark available per point. The requirement asked candidates to 'explain' their points and this does not provide adequate explanation. Candidates must pay attention to the requirement verb and provide the required level of detail.

234 CATERPILLAR *Walk in the footsteps of a top tutor*

Key answer tips

Part (a) is a straightforward knowledge requirement. This has been examined many times before so students should be able to answer this part of the question well.

Part (b) asks for direct controls and tests of controls. Direct controls reduce the risk of material misstatement. Look for evidence of segregation of duties, authorisation, reconciliations, etc. The control must be complete to be effective, e.g. sequential numbering of invoices must be accompanied with a regular sequence check to ensure the sequence is complete in order for the control to be effective. A bank reconciliation must be reviewed by a responsible official to ensure it has been performed properly. To test the control, you need to describe how the auditor would obtain evidence that the control works effectively. Be careful not to suggest performing the control as the auditor requires evidence that the client has implemented the control within their business.

Part (c) is a controls deficiency question which appears in every exam. You must fully explain the deficiency in terms of the effect on the company. If management are to take action, they must be concerned about the potential consequences of the deficiency. When providing recommendations for improvement, be as specific as possible.

(a) Control objectives – cash receipts system

- To ensure that all valid cash receipts are received and banked promptly.
- To ensure all cash receipts are recorded in the bank ledger account.
- To ensure that all receipts are recorded at the correct amounts in the bank ledger account.
- To ensure that cash receipts are correctly posted to the general ledger.
- To ensure that cash receipts are recorded in the correct accounting period.
- To ensure that cash is safeguarded to prevent theft.

(b) Direct controls and tests of control

Direct control	**Test of control**
Daily till reconciliations At the end of each day, the tills are closed down with daily readings of sales taken. These are reconciled to the total of the cash in the tills and the credit card payment slips and any discrepancies are noted. Daily cashing up procedures should ensure that the cash is controlled and reduces the risk of fraud through theft as employees are aware that the assistant manager will be looking for cash discrepancies. This reduces the risk of misstatement within the cash balance.	For a sample of stores visited, the auditor should review the file of daily reconciliations to ascertain if end of day till reconciliations have taken place on a daily basis. For reconciliations with discrepancies, discuss with the store manager what actions were taken and how these differences were resolved.
Cash collected by security company Cash received from customers is taken to the bank daily via collection by a security company. This ensures that cash is safeguarded and that the risk of theft when transferring to the bank is minimised. This reduces the risk of misstatement within the cash balance.	During the store visits, enquire of staff how the cash is transferred to the bank. A sample of invoices from the collection company should be reviewed and confirmed that charges are made for daily collections. In addition, during these visits observe the cash collection process carried out by the security company.
Data transfer to head office The daily sales readings from the tills along with the cash and credit card data are transferred to head office through a daily interface into the sales and cash receipts records. This should ensure that sales and cash records are updated on a prompt basis and are complete and accurate.	During the interim audit at head office, compare the daily sales readings from individual stores, including some visited by the audit team, to the sales and cash receipt records within the general ledger. Review the date on which the sales and cash receipt records were updated to ensure this occurred promptly. Any discrepancies should be discussed with the clerk responsible for overseeing this process.
Checks on amounts banked On a daily basis the clerk agrees that the cash banked and the credit card receipts from the credit card company have been credited to the bank statements in full. This should ensure the completeness of cash receipts, as they are transferred in from two sources, being the security company and the credit card operator.	Discuss with the clerk responsible for reconciling the cash and credit card receipts, the process undertaken. Review the daily reconciliations the clerk has completed to confirm the process has been undertaken as described.

(c) Cash system deficiencies and controls

Control deficiency	Control recommendation
Incomplete IA checks The IA department only undertakes cash control visits to the 20 largest stores as this is where most issues are expected to arise. However, Caterpillar Co has 45 stores in total which means over half of the stores are not being checked. This increases the likelihood of control errors, as these stores may not comply with company procedures. As it is a cash business heightens the chance of frauds through theft occurring.	Caterpillar's IA department should have a rolling programme of visits to all 45 stores. This programme can have a bias to large and high-risk stores, but it should ensure that all stores are visited on a cyclical basis.
No individual log on codes for tills All store employees are able to use each till and none have an individual log on code when using the tills. Allowing all employees access to the till points increases the risk of fraud and error arising. Also, in the event of cash discrepancies arising in the tills, it would be difficult to ascertain which employees may be responsible as there is no way of tracking who used which till.	Only employees for whom criminal record/credit checks have been undertaken should be able to use the tills to take customer payments. Each employee should have a designated till and a log on code, which is required for each payment transaction.
Employees can serve friends/family Where employees' friends or family members purchase clothes in store, the employee is able to serve them at the till point. There is a significant fraud risk as employees could fail to put the goods through the till, but retain the cash paid by the friend/family members. Additionally, they could give the goods away for free or undercharge for goods sold, thereby granting unauthorised discounts.	Caterpillar Co should instigate a policy whereby employees are unable to serve friends or family members at the till points. They should be required to request that a manager or supervisor put these goods through the till. In addition, CCTV cameras could be placed in the shops, near to the till points to record the daily till transactions. This would act as a deterrent to employees as well as provide evidence in the case of fraudulent transactions occurring. Also, Caterpillar Co should carry out regular inventory counts to identify if goods in the stores are below the levels in the inventory records, as this could identify goods being given away for free.

Control deficiency	**Control recommendation**
Junior sales clerk sent to bank If a store needs change, a junior sales clerk is sent to the bank by a till operator to change it into smaller denominations. There is a risk of the cash being misplaced or stolen on the way to the bank or collusion between the junior clerk and till operator as no record appears to be kept of the money removed from the till in these instances and no confirmation of how much cash is returned is carried out.	Caterpillar's head office should stipulate a float amount per till and how the note denominations should be comprised. When assigning the cash float in the morning, the store manager should ensure that this policy is adhered to. If during the day, further smaller denomination notes are required, the store manager should authorise a member of staff to obtain cash from the bank and should fully record movements in and out of the till.
Lack of segregation of duties One clerk is responsible for several elements of the cash receipts system. The clerk oversees the daily interface from stores, agrees that cash has cleared into the bank statements and undertakes the bank reconciliations. There is a lack of segregation of duties and errors will not be identified on a timely basis as well as increasing the risk of fraud.	These key roles should be split between a few individuals, with ideally the bank reconciliations being undertaken by another member of the finance team.
Bank reconciliations not always reviewed The bank reconciliations are only reviewed by the financial controller if there are any unreconciled amounts. The bank reconciliation could reconcile but still contain significant errors as there could be compensating errors which cancel each other out. In addition, for a cash-based business, the bank reconciliation is a direct control which reduces the risk of fraud. If it is not reviewed, then this reduces its effectiveness.	The bank reconciliations should be reviewed by the financial controller on a monthly basis, even if there are no exceptions, there should evidence of this review by way of signature on the bank reconciliation.

Marking guide

		Marks
(a)	**Control objectives – cash receipts system**	
	• All valid cash receipts are received & banked promptly	1
	• All cash receipts are recorded in the bank ledger account	1
	• All receipts are recorded at the correct amounts in the bank ledger account	1
	• Cash receipts are correctly posted to the general ledger	1
	• Cash receipts are recorded in the correct accounting period	1
	• Cash is safeguarded to prevent theft	1
	Restricted to	**4**

(b)	**Direct controls and tests of control**	
	• Daily sales readings taken from tills and reconciled to cash and credit card payment slips, exceptions noted	2
	• Cash collected daily and taken to the bank by security company	2
	• Daily interface to head office for sales, cash and credit card data into sales and cash receipts books	2
	• Daily agreement of cash banked by security company and cash received from credit card company into bank statements	2
	Max 3 direct controls, 2 marks each	**6**
(c)	**Control deficiencies and recommendations**	
	• Internal audit only visits 20 largest stores rather than all 45	2
	• All employees able to use tills and no individual log on codes	2
	• Employees can serve friends and family members at the till points	2
	• Junior sales clerks given cash and sent to the bank	2
	• Lack of segregation of duties in head office	2
	• Bank reconciliations not always reviewed by the financial controller	2
	Max 5 issues, 2 marks each	**10**
Total		**20**

Examiner's comments

Part (a) required candidates to state control objectives of a cash receipts system. Candidates' performance was disappointing. A significant number of candidates identified control procedures rather than control objectives. In addition, many candidates did not link objectives specifically to the cash receipts system.

Part (b) required candidates to identify (½ marks each), explain (½ marks each) the direct controls from the scenario and describe a test of control that the auditor could perform (1 mark each). Performance was mixed in this question. Candidates often correctly identified direct controls from the scenario but few explained why it was a direct control. The tests of controls were of a mixed standard. Some of the tests were poorly described and many described substantive rather than control tests. Candidates are advised that to test a control they need to ensure the client has carried out the control.

Part (c) required candidates to identify (½ marks each), explain (½ marks each) the internal control deficiencies from the scenario and describe a test of control for each deficiency that the auditor could perform (1 mark each). Internal control remains a highly examinable area. It was pleasing to note that candidates generally performed well in this question. Candidates were able to identify the internal control deficiencies from the scenario, however many candidates did not clearly explain the implication of the deficiency. In order to gain the ½ explanation mark for the deficiency, candidates must fully explain the impact on the business. Often the explanation of the deficiency was too vague. For example, the implication of there being no individual logons being described as 'could lead to fraud' was not awarded any credit. Candidates needed to explain the implication for the business that 'they would not be able to determine who was in charge of the till if a discrepancy arose'. It was pleasing to note that most candidates were able to identify the required number of issues. Most candidates were able to provide good recommendations to address the deficiencies. However, some of the recommendations were either poorly described, did not clearly address the specific control deficiency identified, were impractical suggestions or were incomplete. For example, for the deficiency 'all employees can access all tills', a common recommendation was 'to have each employee accessing their own till' which would be impractical with only three or four cash tills per store on average. Candidates are reminded that they should tailor their recommendation to the circumstances presented in the scenario.

235 BRONZE *Walk in the footsteps of a top tutor*

Key answer tips

Part (a) is a knowledge question. Take a logical, common sense approach to try and come up with two or three points. Think about how controls impact the financial statements and how this impacts the auditor's work. If you don't know the answer, don't waste time thinking about it, move on to the next part of the question and come back to it later when you have answered the other questions.

Part (b) requires the control deficiencies within the payroll cycle to be identified. Use the specific information in scenario rather than giving deficiencies that could be present in any payroll system. There are always more deficiencies than you need so choose the ones you can write well about. Suggest controls the client can implement to address the control deficiency. Be specific about which member of client staff should be responsible for the control and how frequently they should perform the control.

Tests of controls are the audit procedures the auditor will perform to obtain evidence to prove the control suggested is in place and working effectively. Be specific about how they would do this.

In part (c) you are asked for analytical procedures to confirm payroll. An analytical procedure requires the auditor to form an expectation of the payroll figure to compare with the client's actual figure to assess whether it looks reasonable. Comparisons with prior year, comparison with budget and performing a proof-in-total would be typical analytical procedures for payroll.

Part (d) requires text book knowledge of analytical procedures and their suitability.

Part (e) covers a small syllabus area. An internal audit function may perform work useful to the external auditor, and depending on the level of assessed competence and objectivity of the internal auditors, the external auditor may be able to place reliance on their work instead of performing those procedures. Before placing reliance, the external auditor will need to assess the internal auditor's work to ensure it is appropriate for audit purposes.

(a) Need to obtain an understanding of components of internal control

- One component of audit risk is control risk. To assess control risk the auditor must understand the components of internal control such as the control environment, control activities, etc.
- If the client's system of internal control is weak, there is a greater risk of material misstatement within the financial statements as the control system will not have prevented, or detected and corrected the misstatements occurring.
- If the controls are not effective the auditor cannot rely on the controls as a source of audit evidence and therefore a more substantive approach must be taken to obtaining sufficient and appropriate audit evidence.
- If the control system is effective, reliance can be placed on the controls and less substantive evidence will be required.

(b) Payroll system deficiencies and control recommendations

Control deficiency	Control recommendation	Test of control
Clock in/out process not supervised Employees swipe their cards at the beginning and end of the eight-hour shift. This process is not supervised. This could result in a number of employees being swiped in as present when they are not. This will result in a substantially increased payroll cost for Bronze Co.	The clocking in and out process should be supervised by a responsible official to prevent one individual clocking in multiple employees. A supervisor should undertake a random check of employees by reviewing who has logged in with a swipe card and confirming visually that the employee is present.	Observe the clocking in and out process to ensure it is supervised by a responsible official. Enquire of the supervisor whether they perform a random check of employees.
Employee breaks not monitored Employees are entitled to a 30-minute paid break and do not need to clock out to access the dining area. Employees could be taking excessive breaks. This will result in a decrease in productivity and increased payroll costs.	Employees should be allocated set break times and there should be a supervisor present to ensure that employees only take the breaks they are entitled to.	Review the rota for break-times to ensure break times are formally communicated to staff. Observe the dining area during break times to ensure a supervisor is present.
Temporary staff appointed by factory supervisors Although there is a human resources department, appointments of temporary staff are made by factory production supervisors. The supervisor could appoint unsuitable employees and may not carry out all the required procedures for new joiners. This could result in these temporary employees not receiving the correct pay and relevant statutory deductions causing dissatisfaction of employees.	All appointment of staff, whether temporary or permanent, should only be made by the human resources department.	Inspect the HR procedures manual to ensure that appointments of staff are the responsibility of the HR department. For a sample of employees employed by Bronze Co, inspect the employee's file to ensure the appropriate checks were carried out by the HR department prior to employment.

Control deficiency	Control recommendation	Test of control
Overtime authorised after payment made Overtime reports which detail the amount of overtime worked are sent out quarterly by the payroll department to production supervisors for review. These reports are reviewed after the payments have been made. This could result in unauthorised overtime or amounts being paid incorrectly and Bronze Co's payroll cost increasing.	All overtime should be authorised by a responsible official prior to the payment being processed by the payroll department. This authorisation should be evidenced in writing.	Inspect the overtime reports for evidence of a responsible official's signature authorising the overtime prior to the payment being processed.
Production supervisors determine bonuses Production supervisors determine the amount of the discretionary bonus to be paid to employees. Production supervisors are not senior enough to determine bonuses. They could pay extra bonuses to friends or family members causing increased cost for Bronze Co.	The bonus should be determined by a more senior individual, such as the production director, and this should be communicated in writing to the payroll department.	Inspect the communication of bonuses to the payroll department and ensure it is sent by a senior official.
No input checks on bonuses The bonus is input by a clerk into the payroll system. There is no indication that this input process is reviewed. This could result in input errors or the clerk could fraudulently change the amounts. This could lead to incorrect bonus payments being made and increased payroll costs for Bronze Co.	Once the clerk has input the bonus amounts, all entries should be double checked against the written confirmation from the production director by another member of the team to identify any amounts entered incorrectly.	Observe the payroll clerk inputting the bonus amounts and subsequent check against the written confirmation from the production director by a different member of the team.

Control deficiency	Control recommendation	Test of control
Lack of segregation of duties The payroll manager reviews the bank transfer listing prior to authorising the payments and also amends the payroll records for any changes required. There is a lack of segregation of duties as it is the payroll team which processes the amounts and the payroll manager who authorises payments. The manager could fraudulently increase the amounts to be paid to certain employees, process this payment as well as amend the records causing loss for the company.	The payroll manager should not be able to process changes to the payroll system as well as authorise payments. The authorisation of the bank transfer listing should be undertaken by an individual outside the payroll department, such as the finance director.	Inspect the payroll bank transfer listing for the authorisation signature. Ensure the signature is of a person outside of the payroll department and of suitable authority such as the finance director.
No identity checks on cash payments A payroll clerk distributes cash pay packets to employees without requesting proof of identity. Even if most employees are known to the clerk, there is a risk that without identity checks wages could be paid to incorrect employees. This could result in increased payroll costs or dissatisfied employees if incorrect amounts are received.	The payroll clerks should be informed that all cash wages can only be paid upon sight of the employee's clock card and photographic identification as this confirms proof of identity.	Observe the process of wage collection to ensure that employees can only collect their wages on production of their clock card and photographic ID.

(c) Substantive analytical procedures to confirm payroll expense

- Compare the total payroll expense to the prior year or budget and investigate any significant differences.
- Review monthly payroll charges, compare this to the prior year and budgets and discuss with management any significant variances.
- Compare overtime pay as a percentage of factory normal hours pay to investigate whether it is at a similar level to the prior year and within an acceptable range. Investigate any significant differences.

- Perform a proof-in-total of total wages and salaries, incorporating joiners and leavers and any pay increase. Compare this to the actual wages and salaries in the financial statements and investigate any significant differences.
- Calculate statutory deductions as a percentage of gross pay and compare to the prior year to assess the reasonableness of the statutory deductions. Investigate any significant variances.

(d) Suitability of analytical procedures

- Nature of the balance or class of transactions. Analytical procedures are more suitable to large volume transactions that are predictable over time such as payroll, sales and expenses.
- Reliability of the information being analysed. If the information being analysed is unreliable, the results of the analytical procedures will be unreliable. Reliability of the information will be affected by source, nature and effectiveness of internal controls.
- Relevance to the assertion being tested. Analytical procedures would usually not be used to test the existence assertion of a tangible asset such as inventory or property, plant and equipment as physical inspection of the asset would provide more reliable evidence.
- Precision of expectation. The auditor should consider whether a sufficiently precise expectation can be developed to be able to identify a material misstatement. If not, there is limited use in using analytical procedures.
- Amount of difference between expected amounts and recorded amounts that is acceptable. This will depend on the level of materiality and the desired level of assurance required by the auditor.

(e) Impact on interim and final audit

Interim audit

Scarlet & Co could look to rely on any internal control documentation produced by internal audit (IA) to assess whether the control environment has changed during the year.

If the IA department has performed testing during the year on internal control systems, such as the payroll, sales and purchase systems, then Scarlet & Co could review and possibly place reliance on this work. This may result in the workload reducing and possibly a decrease in the external audit fee.

During the interim audit, Scarlet & Co would need to perform a risk assessment to assist in the planning process. It is possible that the IA department may have conducted a risk assessment and so Scarlet & Co could use this as part of its initial planning process.

Scarlet & Co would need to consider the risk of fraud and error and non-compliance with law and regulations resulting in misstatements in the financial statements. This is also an area for IA to consider, hence there is scope for Scarlet & Co to review the work and testing performed by IA to assist in this risk assessment.

Final audit

It is possible that the IA department may assist with year-end inventory counting and controls and so Scarlet & Co can place some reliance on the work performed by them. Scarlet & Co will still need to attend the count and perform its own reduced testing.

Marking guide

		Marks
(a)	**Need to obtain an understanding of components of internal control**	
	• To assess control risk	1
	• If system of internal control is weak, there is a greater risk of material misstatement within the financial statements	1
	• If the controls are not effective, a more substantive approach must be taken	1
	• If the control system is effective, reliance can be placed on the controls and less substantive evidence will be required	1
	Maximum	**3**
(b)	**Control deficiencies, control recommendations and tests of control**	
	• Clock in/out process unsupervised	3
	• Employee breaks not monitored	3
	• Temporary staff are not appointed by human resources department	3
	• Overtime report reviewed after payment	3
	• Authorisation of discretionary bonus	3
	• No input checks over entry of bonus into payroll	3
	• Payroll manager reviews the bank transfer listing prior to payment and can change payroll records	3
	• No identity checks prior to cash wages pay out	3
	Max 5 issues, 3 marks each	**15**
(c)	**Substantive analytical procedures**	
	• Compare total payroll expense to the prior year or budget and investigate any significant differences	1
	• Review monthly payroll charges, compare to the prior year, budgets, discuss with management	1
	• Compare overtime pay as a percentage of factory normal hours against prior year, investigate any significant differences	1
	• Perform a proof-in-total of total wages and salaries, compare to actual, and investigate any significant differences	1
	• Calculate statutory deductions as a percentage of gross pay and compare to the prior year to assess the reasonableness	1
	Maximum	**4**
(d)	**Suitability of analytical procedures**	
	• Nature of the balance or class of transactions	1
	• Reliability of the information being analysed	1
	• Relevance to the assertion being tested	1
	• Precision of expectation	1
	• Amount of difference between expected amounts and recorded amounts that is acceptable	1
	Maximum	**4**
(e)	**Work performed at interim audit**	
	• Systems documentation	1
	• Testing of systems such as payroll, sales, purchases	1
	• Risk assessment	1
	• Fraud and error, non-compliance with law and regulations	1
	Work performed at final audit	
	• Inventory count procedures	1
	Maximum	**4**
Total		**30**

Examiner's comments

Internal control questions typically require internal controls deficiencies to be identified (½ marks each), explained (½ marks each) and, often, to give a relevant recommendation to address the deficiency (1 mark each). Candidates continue to perform well on internal control questions. Candidates were able to confidently identify internal controls deficiencies from the scenario, however some candidates did not clearly explain the deficiency in terms of how it affects the business. The scenario in the exam will always contain more issues than required to be discussed and it was therefore encouraging that candidates generally applied effective exam technique and focused on providing well explained answers which identified the required number of issues as noted in the question. A minority of candidates, rather than evaluating internal controls just formed a point of view as to how well the company was controlling its operations, and, also included more 'social' factors such as 'the motivational effect of having/not having a bonus system in force in a company' which was not required and does not answer the question. Recommendations to address control deficiencies were on the whole well explained. Most candidates were able to provide good recommendations to address the deficiencies. However occasionally some of the recommendations did not clearly address the specific control deficiency identified and candidates are again reminded to ensure that their recommendation is specifically tailored to the requirements of the scenario.

Part (d) required candidates to explain the impact on the external auditor's work at the interim and final audits if the client was to establish an internal audit department. Performance on this question was unsatisfactory. Where the question was attempted, many candidates failed to score more than 1 mark. What was required was an explanation of tasks that internal audit might perform that the external auditor might then look to rely on in either the interim or final audit. For example, they could utilise systems documentation produced by internal audit during the interim audit. Or they could rely on year-end inventory counts undertaken by internal audit as part of their inventory testing at the final audit. Where candidates achieved 1 mark this was usually for a general comment about relying on the work of internal audit and so reducing substantive procedures.

Mistakes made by candidates were:

- Focusing on the role of internal audit in general.
- Giving lengthy answers on factors to consider when placing reliance on internal audit.
- Providing details of what an external auditor does at the interim and final audit stages.

236 TROMBONE *Walk in the footsteps of a top tutor*

Key answer tips

Part (a) requires repetition of knowledge from the text book of the components of an internal control system. Make sure you explain the components. You do not need to give the full text book definition but make sure some of the key elements are included in your answer.

Part (b) requires the control deficiencies within the payroll cycle to be identified. Use the specific information in scenario rather than giving deficiencies that could be present in any payroll system. There are always more deficiencies than you need so choose the ones you can write well about. Suggest controls the client can implement to address the control deficiency. Be specific about which member of client staff should be responsible for the control and how frequently they should perform the control. Tests of controls are the audit procedures the auditor will perform to obtain evidence to prove the control suggested is in place and working effectively. Be specific about how they would do this.

Parts (c) and (d) ask for substantive procedures. A substantive procedure is used to detect material misstatement in the figure. Tests of controls will not score marks.

(a) Internal control components

ISA 315 (Revised 2019) *Identifying and Assessing the Risks of Material Misstatement* considers the components of an entity's internal control. It identifies the following components:

Control environment

The control environment refers to the set of controls, processes and structures that address:

- how management's oversight responsibilities are carried out
- the independence of and oversight over the entity's system of internal control by those charged with governance
- the entity's assignment of authority and responsibility
- how the entity attracts, develops and retains competent individuals, and
- how the entity holds individuals accountable for their responsibilities in the pursuit of the objectives of the system of internal control.

Entity's risk assessment process

The entity's risk assessment process covers how the entity identifies business risks relevant to financial reporting objectives, assesses the significance of those risks including the likelihood of occurrence, and how the entity addresses those risks.

The entity's process to monitor the system of internal control

This is the client's ongoing process of evaluating the effectiveness of controls over time and taking necessary remedial action in respect of control deficiencies. If the entity has an internal audit function, it will assist with monitoring process.

The information system and communication

The information system and communication consists of all of the activities and policies relevant to the preparation of the financial statements. It includes the procedures within both computerised and manual systems to initiate, record, process, and report entity transactions. It also looks at how the entity communicates significant matters that support the preparation of the financial statements and related reporting responsibilities in the information system.

Control activities relevant to the audit

Control activities are designed to ensure proper application of policies in all the other components of the entity's system of internal control. These include segregation of duties, verifications, reconciliations, physical or logical controls and authorisations.

(b) Payroll system deficiencies, controls and test of controls

Control deficiency	Control recommendation	Test of control
Payroll calculations not checked The wages calculations are generated by the payroll system and there are no checks performed. Therefore, if system errors occur during the payroll processing, this would not be identified. This could result in wages being over or under calculated, leading to an additional payroll cost or loss of employee goodwill.	A senior member of the payroll team should recalculate the gross to net pay workings for a sample of employees and compare their results to the output from the payroll system. These calculations should be signed as approved before payments are made.	Review a sample of the gross to net pay calculations for evidence that they are undertaken and signed as approved.
Changes to standing data Annual wages increases are updated in the payroll system standing data by clerks. Payroll clerks are not senior enough to be making changes to standing data as they could make mistakes. This could lead to incorrect payment of wages causing dissatisfied employees. In addition, if they can access standing data, they could make unauthorised changes.	Payroll clerks should not have access to standing data changes within the system. The annual wages increase should be performed by a senior member of the payroll department and this should be checked by another responsible official for errors.	Ask a clerk to attempt to make a change to payroll standing data; the system should reject this attempt. Review the log of standing data amendments to identify whether the wage rate increases were changed by a senior member of payroll.

Control deficiency	Control recommendation	Test of control
Authorisation of overtime Overtime worked by employees is not all authorised by the relevant department head, as only overtime in excess of 30% of standard hours requires authorisation. This increases the risk that employees will claim for overtime even though they did not work these additional hours. This will result in additional payroll costs for Trombone Co.	All overtime hours worked should be authorised by the relevant department head. This should be evidenced by signature on the employees' weekly overtime sheets.	Review a sample of employee weekly overtime sheets for evidence of signature by relevant department head.
No checks on time off taken Time taken off as payment for overtime worked should be agreed by payroll clerks to the overtime worked report; however, this has not always occurred. Employees could be taking unauthorised leave if they take time off but have not worked the required overtime. This will cause loss for the company.	Payroll clerks should be reminded of the procedures to be undertaken when processing the overtime sheets. They should sign as evidence on the overtime sheets that they have agreed any time taken off to the relevant overtime report.	Select a sample of overtime sheets with time taken off and confirm that there is evidence of a check by the payroll clerk to the overtime worked report.
Review of overtime The overtime worked report is emailed to the department heads and they report by exception if there are any errors. If department heads are busy or do not receive the email and do not report to payroll on time, it will be assumed that the overtime report is correct even though there may be errors.	All department heads should report to the payroll department on whether or not the overtime report is correct. The payroll department should follow up on any non-replies and not make payments until agreed by the department head.	For a sample of overtime reports emailed to department heads confirm that a response has been received from each head by reviewing all responses.

Control deficiency	**Control recommendation**	**Test of control**
This could result in the payroll department making incorrect overtime payments which could cause additional cost for the company or a loss of employee goodwill.		
Department head cover for authorisation Department heads are meant to arrange for annual leave cover so that overtime sheets are authorised on a timely basis; however, this has not always happened. If overtime sheets are authorised late, overtime payments will be delayed. This will cause employee dissatisfaction.	Department heads should be reminded of the procedures with regards to annual leave and arrangement of suitable cover. During annual leave periods, payroll clerks should monitor that overtime sheets are being submitted by department heads on a timely basis and follow up any late sheets.	Discuss with payroll clerks the process they follow for obtaining authorisation of overtime sheets, in particular during periods of annual leave. Compare this to the process which they should adopt to identify any control exceptions.
Detail of payments list not checked The finance director reviews the total list of bank transfers with the total to be paid per the payroll records. There could be employees omitted along with fictitious employees added to the payment listing, so that the total payments list still agrees to the payroll totals even though it is incorrect. This could mean fraudulent payments are able to be made causing loss for the company.	The finance director when authorising the payments should on a sample basis perform checks from payroll records to payment list and vice versa to confirm that payments are complete and only made to *bona fide* employees. The finance director should sign the payments list as evidence that these checks have been undertaken.	Obtain a sample of payments list and review for signature by the finance director as evidence that the control is operating correctly.

(c) Substantive procedures in relation to completeness and accuracy of payroll

- Agree the total wages and salaries expense per the payroll system to the trial balance, investigate any differences.
- Cast a sample of payroll records to confirm completeness and accuracy of the payroll expense.
- For a sample of employees, recalculate the gross and net pay and agree to the payroll records to confirm accuracy.

- Recalculate the statutory deductions to confirm whether correct deductions for this year have been made in the payroll.
- Compare the total payroll expense to the prior year and investigate any significant differences.
- Review monthly payroll charges, compare this to the prior year and budgets and discuss with management for any significant variances.
- Perform a proof-in-total of total wages and salaries, incorporating joiners and leavers and the annual pay increase. Compare this to the actual wages and salaries in the financial statements and investigate any significant differences.
- Select a sample of joiners and leavers, agree their start/leaving date to supporting documentation, recalculate that their first/last pay packet was accurately calculated and recorded.
- Agree the total net pay per the payroll records to the bank transfer listing of payments and to the bank ledger account.
- Agree the individual wages and salaries per the payroll to the personnel records for a sample.
- Select a sample of weekly overtime sheets and trace to overtime payment in payroll records to confirm completeness of overtime paid.

(d) Substantive procedures in relation to income tax payable accrual

Procedures the auditor should adopt in respect of auditing this accrual include:

- Agree the year-end income tax payable accrual to the payroll records to confirm accuracy.
- Recalculate the accrual to confirm accuracy.
- Agree the subsequent payment to the post-year-end bank ledger account and bank statements to confirm completeness.
- Review any correspondence with tax authorities to assess whether there are any additional outstanding payments due; if so, agree they are included in the year-end accrual.
- Review any disclosures made of the income tax accrual and assess whether these are in compliance with accounting standards and legislation.

Marking guide

		Marks
(a)	**Components of internal control**	
	• Control environment – oversight responsibilities of management and those charged with governance (up to 2 marks)	2
	• Entity's risk assessment – process for identifying business risk	1
	• The entity's process to monitor the system of internal control – to assess effectiveness of internal controls	1
	• Information system and communication – procedures to record an entity's transactions, assets and liabilities	1
	• Control activities – segregation of duties, authorisation, etc.	1
	Note to markers: Please award credit for reasonable explanations of internal control components.	
	Restricted to	**5**

(b)	**Control deficiencies, recommendations and tests of control**	
	• Payroll calculations not checked	3
	• Payroll clerks update standing data for wages increases	3
	• Authorisation of overtime sheets only undertaken if overtime exceeds 30% of standard hours	3
	• Time off as payment for overtime not checked to overtime worked report	3
	• Review of overtime worked reports by department heads	3
	• Authorisation of overtime sheets when department heads on annual leave	3
	• Finance director only reviews totals of payroll records and payments list	3
	Max 5 issues, 3 marks each	**15**
(c)	**Substantive procedures in relation to completeness and accuracy of payroll**	
	• Agree wages and salaries per payroll to trial balance	1
	• Cast payroll records	1
	• Recalculate gross and net pay	1
	• Recalculate statutory deductions	1
	• Compare total payroll to prior year	1
	• Review monthly payroll to prior year and budget	1
	• Proof-in-total of payroll and agree to the financial statements	1
	• Verify joiners/leavers and recalculate first/last pay	1
	• Agree wages and salaries paid per payroll to bank transfer list and bank ledger account	1
	• Agree the individual wages and salaries as per the payroll to the personnel records	1
	• Agree sample of weekly overtime sheets to overtime payment in payroll records	1
	Restricted to	**6**
(d)	**Substantive procedures in relation to accrual for tax payable**	
	• Agree to the payroll records to confirm the accuracy of the accrual	1
	• Recalculate the accrual	1
	• Agree the subsequent payment to the post-year-end bank ledger account and bank statements	1
	• Review any correspondence with tax authorities to assess whether there are any additional outstanding payments due, if so, agree they are included in the year-end accrual	1
	• Review disclosures and assess whether these are adequate and in compliance	1
	Restricted to	**4**
Total		**30**

Examiner's comments

Part (a) asked candidates to identify and briefly explain the components of an entity's internal control. Candidates' performance was mixed on this question with many not even attempting it. There were some candidates who had clearly revised this area and were able to confidently identify the five components and explain what they related to. Some candidates were confused by 'information systems' and incorrectly related this solely to a computer environment. Many candidates were only able to identify the components and either did not provide an explanation or it was incorrect. Also, a significant minority of candidates explained the components from the perspective of what this meant for the audit firm rather than the company. In addition, a significant minority of candidates did not understand the question requirement, or did not have sufficient technical knowledge of this area and so instead of providing components, such as, control environment and control activities, focused on providing a list of internal controls such as authorisation or segregation of duties controls.

Part (b) required candidates to identify and explain deficiencies in the payroll system, recommend controls to address these deficiencies, and a test of control for each of these recommendations that could be used to assess if it was operating effectively if implemented. The first two parts of this questions were answered satisfactorily by candidates, however the tests of controls proved challenging for many. Candidates were able to comfortably identify deficiencies from the scenario, although a minority of candidates identified deficiencies which were generic to payroll systems rather than specific to the question, such as references to 'clock cards', which were not a component of the system under review. Also, some candidates identified points which were not valid deficiencies, such as employees being able to complete their own overtime sheets, being allowed a choice between days off or payment of overtime and overtime sheets being entered by payroll clerks. Although sufficient deficiencies were identified by many candidates, they did not always adequately explain what the deficiency meant to Trombone. For example, candidates identified the deficiency that 'the overtime worked reports are not always checked,' however some failed to explain the implication of this in that it could lead to employees taking days off when they had not worked the overtime hours required. The requirement to provide controls was answered satisfactorily. Most candidates were able to provide good recommendations to address the deficiencies; however, in some instances these recommendations were too brief. Candidates have a tendency to state control objectives rather than valid procedures which can be implemented by the client. In addition, some recommendations failed to address the deficiency identified, for example where department heads failed to assign a deputy to authorise overtime whilst on annual leave, many candidates simply recommended that this control already existing control be put in place, rather than addressing how the control should be amended to ensure it was followed at all times. The requirement for tests of controls was answered unsatisfactorily. Many candidates are still confusing substantive procedures and test of controls. A significant number of candidates suggested substantive procedures such as 'recalculating gross and net pay calculations', rather than a test of control which might be to 'review evidence of the recalculation of payroll'. Candidates need to review their understanding of these different types of audit procedures and ensure that they appreciate that substantive tests focus on the number within the financial statements whereas test of controls are verifying if client procedures are operating. In many instances candidates focused on reperforming the control rather than testing it had operated. Observation of a control was commonly suggested by candidates, however in many cases this is not an effective way of testing that a control has operated throughout the year.

Part (c) required substantive procedures to confirm the completeness and accuracy of the payroll expense. On the whole candidates performed well in this area. A good proportion of candidates were able to suggest practical payroll procedures such as analytical review of prior year and current year charges or undertaking a proof-in-total calculation. Other common answers included recalculation of a sample of payroll calculations or statutory deductions.

Common mistakes made by candidates were:

- Giving objectives rather than procedures 'ensure that the gross and net pay calculations are correct', this is not a detailed substantive procedure and so would not score any marks.

- Lack of detail in tests such as 'check that the payroll calculations are correct', this would not score any marks as it does not explain what should be checked or how this testing would be carried out.
- Providing tests of controls rather than substantive procedures, such as focusing on authorisation of payroll.

The requirement verb was to 'describe' therefore sufficient detail was required to score the 1 mark available per test. Candidates are reminded yet again that substantive procedures are a core topic area and they must be able to produce relevant detailed procedures and to apply their knowledge to different areas of the financial statements.

Part (d) required substantive procedures in respect of the year-end accrual for tax payable on employment income. Where answered, performance on this requirement was disappointing. Candidates were provided with a short scenario to explain how the employment taxes were remitted to the taxation authorities and that at the year end there would be an accrual for any outstanding amount. The scenario was provided so that candidates could apply their knowledge of accruals to the specific circumstances; however, from the answers provided it seems that some did not take notice of detail provided. Many answers demonstrated that candidates did not know what a tax accrual was and hence suggested procedures focused on 'discussions with management' or 'obtaining written representations'. This accrual was not judgemental and so the above procedures would not have scored many marks. Those candidates that scored well suggested answers such as 'recalculation of the accrual,' 'comparison with prior year or months' and 'verifying the subsequent payment after the year end'.

237 LILY WINDOW GLASS *Walk in the footsteps of a top tutor*

Tutor's top tips

Part (a) Controls deficiencies and recommendations questions are usually quite straight-forward, however, you must explain the deficiencies and controls in sufficient detail to score marks. If you are too brief you will only score ½ marks.

Part (b) Audit procedures performed during the inventory count will include a mixture of tests of controls and substantive procedures. Make sure you give procedures that will be done during the count, which is usually conducted at the year-end date, and not procedures that will be performed during the final audit.

Parts (c) and (d) Automated tools and techniques include audit software, test data and data analytics. Data analytics is an emerging technology in the auditing profession. Look out for examiner articles on the use of data analytics.

(a) Inventory count arrangements

Control deficiency	Control recommendation
Warehouse manager supervises the count The warehouse manager is planning to supervise the inventory count. The warehouse manager is familiar with the inventory, but has overall responsibility for the inventory and so is not independent. The warehouse manager may want to hide inefficiencies and any issues that arise to avoid criticism of the department.	An alternative supervisor who is not normally involved with the inventory, such as an internal audit manager, should supervise the inventory count. The warehouse manager and warehouse team should not be involved in the count at all.
No division of responsibilities There are ten teams of counters, each team having two members of staff. However, there is no clear division of responsibilities within the team. Therefore, both members of staff could count together rather than checking each other's count. Errors in the count may not be identified.	Each team should be informed that both members are required to count their assigned inventory separately. Therefore, one counts and the second member checks that the inventory has been counted correctly.
IA teams performing counts The internal audit teams are undertaking inventory counts. Internal audit should review the controls and perform sample test counts to confirm the count is being performed accurately and effectively. Issues with the count may not be identified resulting in an ineffective count.	The internal audit counters should sample check the counting undertaken by the ten teams to provide an extra control over the completeness and accuracy of the count.
Counted areas not flagged Once areas are counted, the teams are not flagging the aisles as completed. Some areas of the warehouse could be double counted or missed out. This will increase the risk of the inventory quantities being either under or overstated.	All aisles should be flagged as completed, once the inventory has been counted. In addition, internal audit or the count supervisor should check at the end of the count that all 20 aisles have been flagged as completed.

Control deficiency	Control recommendation
Additional sheets not sequentially numbered Inventory not listed on the sheets is to be entered onto separate sheets, which are not sequentially numbered. The supervisor will be unable to ensure the completeness of all inventory sheets. This could result in understatement of inventory.	Each team should be given a blank sheet for entering any inventory count which is not on their sheets. This blank sheet should be sequentially numbered, any unused sheets should be returned at the end of the count, and the supervisor should check the sequence of all sheets at the end of the count.
Inventory sheets not signed There is no indication that the completed count sheets are signed by the counting team. If any issues arise with the counting in an aisle, it will be difficult to follow up as the identity of the counting team will not be known.	All inventory sheets should be signed by the relevant team upon completion of an aisle. When the sheets are returned, the supervisor should check that they have been signed.
Damaged goods not separated Damaged goods are not being stored in a central area, and instead the counter is just noting on the inventory sheets the level of damage. It will be difficult for the finance team to decide on an appropriate level of write down if they are not able to see the damaged goods. The inventory value for the damaged items may not be appropriate. In addition, if these goods are left in the aisles, they could be inadvertently sold to customers or moved to another aisle.	Damaged goods should be clearly flagged by the counting teams and at the end of the count appropriate machinery should be used to move all damaged windows to a central location. This will avoid the risk of selling these goods. A senior member of the finance team should then inspect these goods to assess the level of any write down or allowance.
Inventory movements during the count Lily Window Glass Co undertakes continuous production and so there will be movements of goods during the count. Goods may be missed or double counted due to movements in the warehouse. Inventory records could be under or overstated as a result.	It is not practical to stop all inventory movements as the production needs to continue. However, any raw materials required for 31 December should be estimated and put to one side. These will not be included as raw materials and instead will be work-in-progress. The goods which are manufactured on 31 December should be stored to one side, and at the end of the count should be counted once and included within finished goods.

Control deficiency	Control recommendation
	Any goods received from suppliers should be stored in one location and counted once at the end and included as part of raw materials. Goods to be despatched to customers should be kept to a minimum for the day of the count.
Competence of warehouse manager to assess WIP The warehouse manager is to assess the level of work-in-progress and raw materials. In the past, a specialist has undertaken this role. It is unlikely that the warehouse manager has the experience to assess the level of work-in-progress as this is something that the factory manager would be more familiar with. In addition, the warehouse manager will also estimate the quantity of raw materials. A mistake could be made when assessing the quantities. Inventory could be materially misstated.	A specialist should be utilised to assess both work-in-progress and the quantities of raw materials.
Third-party inventory included in count Inventory owned by third parties is also being counted by the teams with adjustments being made by the finance team to split these goods out later. There does not appear to be a method for counters to identify which items are third-party inventory. There is a risk that these goods may not be correctly removed from the inventory count sheets, resulting in inventory being overstated.	All inventories belonging to third parties should be moved to one location. This area should be clearly marked and excluded from the counting process.

(b) Procedures during the inventory count

- Observe the counting teams of Lily Window Glass to confirm whether the inventory count instructions are being followed correctly.
- Select a sample and perform test counts from inventory sheets to warehouse aisle and from warehouse aisle to inventory sheets.
- Confirm the procedures for identifying and segregating damaged goods are operating correctly.
- Select a sample of damaged items as noted on the inventory sheets and inspect these windows to confirm whether the level of damage is correctly noted.

- Observe the procedures for movements of inventory during the count, to confirm that no raw materials or finished goods have been omitted or counted twice.
- Obtain a photocopy of the completed sequentially numbered inventory sheets for follow up testing on the final audit.
- Identify and make a note of the last goods received notes (GRNs) and goods despatch notes (GDNs) for 31 December in order to perform cut-off procedures.
- Observe the procedures carried out by the warehouse manager in assessing the level of work-in-progress and consider the reasonableness of any assumptions used.
- Discuss with the warehouse manager how estimation of the raw materials quantities is performed. To the extent that it is possible, reperform the procedures adopted by the warehouse manager.
- Identify and record any inventory held for third parties (if any) and confirm that it is excluded from the count.

(c) Audit procedures using automated tools and techniques

- The audit team can use audit software to calculate the inventory holding period for the year-to-date to compare against the prior year to identify whether inventory is turning over more slowly, as this may be an indication that it is overvalued.
- Audit software can be utilised to produce an aged inventory analysis to identify any slow-moving goods, which may require write down or an allowance.
- Cast the inventory listing to confirm the completeness and accuracy of inventory.
- Audit software can be used to select a representative sample of items for testing to confirm net realisable value and/or cost.
- Audit software can be utilised to recalculate cost and net realisable value for a sample of inventory.
- Verify cut-off by testing whether the dates of the last GRNs and GDNs recorded relate to pre year end; and that any with a date of 1 August 20X5 onwards have been excluded from the inventory records.
- Use audit software to confirm whether any inventory adjustments noted during the count have been correctly updated into final inventory records.

(d) Advantages

- Enables the audit team to test a large volume of inventory data accurately and quickly.
- If audit software is utilised on the audit of Lily, then as long as the company does not change its inventory system, it can be cost effective after setup.
- Test data can test program controls within the inventory system as well as general IT controls, such as passwords.
- Allows the team to obtain information directly from the system and test the actual inventory system and records rather than printouts from the system which could be incorrect.
- Potentially reduces the level of human error in testing and hence provide a better quality of audit evidence.

- Results from the use of automated techniques can be compared with traditional audit testing; if these two sources agree, then overall audit confidence will increase.
- The use of automated tools and techniques frees up audit team members to focus on judgemental and high-risk areas, rather than number crunching.
- Enables the auditor to perform audit procedures throughout the year rather than just at the year end.

Disadvantages

- The cost in the first year will be high as there will be significant set up costs, it will also be a time-consuming process which increases costs.
- As this is the first time that automated tools and techniques will be used on Lily's audit, then the team may require training.
- If Lily's inventory system is likely to change in the foreseeable future, then costly revisions may be required.
- The inventory system may not be compatible with the audit firm's technology, in which case bespoke software may be required which will increase the audit costs.
- If testing is performed over the live inventory system, then there is a risk that the data could be corrupted or lost.
- If testing is performed using copy files rather than live data, then there is the risk that these files are not genuine copies of the actual files.
- There must be adequate systems documentation available. If this is not the case for Lily, then it will be more difficult to devise appropriate automated procedures due to a lack of understanding of the inventory system.
- The data obtained may not be complete which will limit the assurance that can be obtained.
- The inventory balance is still influenced by subjective estimates and management judgement, e.g. work-in-progress and allowance for slow-moving inventory. Therefore, audit staff with appropriate experience and scepticism will still be required to audit these areas.

Marking guide

		Marks
(a)	**Control deficiencies and recommendations**	
	• Warehouse manager supervising the count	2
	• No division of responsibilities within each counting team	2
	• Internal audit teams should be checking controls and performing sample counts	2
	• No flagging of aisles once counting complete	2
	• Additional inventory listed on sheets which are not sequentially numbered	2
	• Inventory sheets not signed by counters	2
	• Damaged goods not moved to central location	2
	• Movements of inventory during the count	2
	• Warehouse manager not qualified or experienced to assess the level of work-in-progress and raw materials	2
	• Third-party inventory included in the count	2
	Max 7 issues, 2 marks each	**14**

(b)	**Audit procedures during the inventory count**	
	• Observe the counters to confirm if inventory count instructions are being followed	1
	• Perform test counts inventory to sheets and sheets to inventory	1
	• Confirm procedures for damaged goods are operating correctly	1
	• Inspect damaged goods to confirm whether the level of damage is correctly noted	1
	• Observe procedures for movements of inventory during the count	1
	• Obtain a photocopy of the completed inventory sheets	1
	• Identify and make a note of the last goods received notes and goods despatch notes	1
	• Observe the procedures carried out by warehouse manager in assessing the level of work-in-progress	1
	• Discuss with the warehouse manager how the raw material quantities were estimated	1
	• Identify inventory held for third parties and ensure excluded from count	1
	Restricted to	**6**
(c)	**Substantive procedures**	
	• Calculate the inventory holding period	1
	• Produce an aged inventory analysis to identify any slow-moving goods	1
	• Cast the inventory listing	1
	• Select a sample of items for testing to confirm net realisable value (NRV) and/or cost	1
	• Recalculate cost and NRV for sample of inventory	1
	• Confirm cut-off	1
	• Confirm whether inventory adjustments noted during the count have been updated to inventory records.	1
	Restricted to	**4**
(d)	**Advantages**	
	• Test a large volume of inventory data accurately and quickly	1
	• Cost effective after setup	1
	• Test data can test program controls as well as general IT controls	1
	• Test the actual inventory system and records rather than printouts from the system	1
	• Potentially reduces the level of human error in testing	1
	• Results can be compared with traditional audit testing	1
	• Free up audit team members to focus on judgemental and high risk areas	1
	Disadvantages	
	• Costs in the first year will be high	1
	• Team may require training	1
	• Changes in the inventory system may require costly revisions	1
	• The inventory system may not be compatible with the audit firm's software	1
	• If testing the live system, there is a risk the data could be corrupted or lost	1
	• If using copy files rather than live data, there is the risk that these files are not genuine copies	1
	• Adequate systems documentation must be available	1
	• Data may not be complete	1
	• Still requires audit staff with appropriate experience and scepticism to audit inventory	1
	Restricted to	**6**
Total		**30**

Examiner's comments

Part (a) required candidates to identify and explain, for the inventory count arrangements of Lily, deficiencies and suggest a recommendation for each deficiency. Most candidates performed very well on this part of the question. They were able to confidently identify deficiencies from the scenario. However, some candidates did not address the question requirement fully as they did not 'identify and explain'. Candidates identified, but did not go on to explain why this was a deficiency. For example, 'additional inventory sheets are not numbered' would receive ½ mark, however to obtain the other ½ mark they needed to explain how this could cause problems during the inventory count such as 'the additional sheets could be lost resulting in understated inventory quantities'. The requirement to provide controls was also well answered. Most candidates were able to provide practical recommendations to address the deficiencies. The main exception to this was with regards to the issue of continued movements of goods during the count. The scenario stated that Lily undertakes continuous production; therefore, to suggest 'that production is halted for the inventory count' demonstrated a failure to read and understand the scenario. The scenario is designed to help candidates and so they should not ignore elements of it. Some candidates incorrectly identified deficiencies from the scenario, demonstrating a fundamental lack of understanding of the purpose of an inventory count. For example, a significant minority believed that inventory sheets should contain inventory quantities when in fact this is incorrect, as this would encourage markers to just agree the stated quantities rather than counting properly.

In addition, candidates felt that counters should not use ink on the count sheets as pencil would be easier for adjustments, again this is incorrect, as if the counts are in pencil then the quantities could be erroneously amended after the count. Also, candidates felt that there should be more warehouse staff involved in the count, despite the self-review risk. Many candidates set their answer out in two columns being deficiency and recommendation. However, those who explained all of the deficiencies and then separately provided all of the recommendations tended to repeat themselves and possibly wasted some time. In addition, it was not uncommon to see candidates provide many more answers than required.

Part (b) required procedures the auditor should undertake during the inventory count of Lily. Performance was unsatisfactory on this part of the question. The requirement stated in capitals that procedures DURING the count were required; however, a significant proportion of candidates ignored this word completely and provided procedures both before and after the count. Many answers actually stated 'before the count...', candidates must read the question requirements properly. Those candidates who had read the question properly often struggled to provide an adequate number of well-described points. The common answers given were 'to observe the inventory counters' although candidates did not make it clear what they were observing for; or 'undertake test counts' but with no explanation of the direction of the test and whether it was for completeness or existence. Some candidates provided all possible inventory tests, in particular focusing on NRV testing. This demonstrated that candidates had learnt a standard list of inventory tests and rather than applying these to the question set just proceeded to list them all. This approach wastes time and tends not to score well as of the answers provided very few tended to be relevant.

Part (c) required a description of four audit procedures that could be carried out for inventory using automated tools and techniques (ATTs). Performance on this question was unsatisfactory. Candidates needed to apply their knowledge of ATTs to inventory procedures, many failed to do this. Again, lots of candidates did not read the question properly and so despite the requirement to apply their answer to inventory, they proceeded to refer to tests on receivables and payables. Also, many candidates appear not to actually understand what ATTs are, who uses them and how they work. Therefore, many answers focused on the company using ATTs rather than the auditor, many procedures given were not related to ATTs for example 'discuss inventory valuation with the directors' or 'agree goods received notes to purchase invoices'. Those candidates who scored well tended to mainly focus on analytical review procedures for inventory that could be undertaken as part of audit software tests.

Part (d) required an explanation of the advantages and disadvantages of using ATTs. This question was on the whole answered well. Candidates were able to identify an adequate number of points to score well on this part of the question. The main advantages given related to saving time; reducing costs; improving the accuracy of testing and the ability to test larger samples. A minority of candidates failed to explain their advantages; answers such as 'saves time' were commonly provided, this is not an explanation and so would not have scored well. The main disadvantages given related to increased costs; training requirements and the corruption of client data. It was apparent that candidates had learnt a standard list of points for ATTs.

238 PEAR INTERNATIONAL *Walk in the footsteps of a top tutor*

Key answer tips

Part (a) asks for direct controls and tests of controls. Direct controls reduce the risk of material misstatement. Look for evidence of segregation of duties, authorisation, physical controls etc. For the full mark, explain the risk that the control is designed to mitigate. When describing a test of control, you need to say how the auditor will obtain evidence that the control is working effectively. This may come from inspecting a document for evidence of authorisation or observing a client staff perform their work to see whether they do what they are supposed to.

Part (b) Controls deficiencies and recommendations questions are usually quite straightforward, however, you must explain the deficiencies and controls in sufficient detail to score marks. Fully explain the deficiency in terms of the effect on the company. If you are too brief you will only score ½ marks. When providing recommendations for improvement, be as specific as possible.

Part (c) requires substantive procedures in respect of additions and disposals of plant and equipment. A substantive procedure is used to detect material misstatement in the financial statements. Think of how you would obtain evidence that the client has correctly included the additions and removed the disposals.

Part (d) asks for factors to be considered when deciding on whether an internal audit function is necessary. This is a straightforward knowledge question. If you can't remember the information from the text book, think about the type of companies that typically have an internal audit function – large and often listed companies. Then consider why they have them, for example to give comfort to the directors that the controls established are sufficient and appropriate.

(a) Direct controls and tests of controls

Direct control	Test of control
Validation checks The website has controls to check the validity of the data entered by the customer. This reduces the risk of orders being processed incorrectly, goods not being delivered to the correct location and card payments not being received. This ensures accuracy of sales.	Input a sales order into the website with various incorrect details to check that the system would reject the order.
Credit checks and credit limits Credit checks are performed for retail customers prior to being accepted with a credit limit being set by a sales manager This reduces the risk of irrecoverable debts, which can cause loss to the company and will result in overstatement of receivables if not written off.	Inspect a sample of customer files to ensure a credit check has been obtained and an appropriate credit limit set by the sales manager.
Invoices raised from GDN Sales invoices are raised from the GDN. This ensures the invoice relates to the actual quantity and type of goods despatched rather than the order which may be different. This reduces the risk of customers being invoiced incorrectly for goods not received which will result in misstatement of sales revenue.	For a sample of invoices agree the quantity and type of goods to the GDN. Inspect the GDN for evidence of being matched to invoices to ensure the control has been performed.
Regular customer statements and follow up of overdue debts Customer statements are sent on a regular basis, which reminds customers of the invoices they need to pay and also means they can check if there are any errors in the invoices. Alongside the follow up of overdue debts the risk of irrecoverable debts is reduced, which would cause loss to the company and could result in overstatement of receivables if not written off.	For a sample of customers, inspect copies of the monthly statements to confirm that they are actually sent out, and review evidence of follow up of overdue debts such as notes of phone calls or emails sent to customers.

Direct control	**Test of control**
Inventory levels checked Inventory levels are checked on a regular basis prior to the purchase of raw materials. This ensures only necessary goods and services are procured, reducing the risk of loss to the company. This reduces the risk of inappropriate levels of stock being maintained which could result in obsolescence and overstatement of inventory if not valued appropriately at the lower of cost and net realisable value.	Observe the weekly stock check process being performed by the factory supervisors in a number of factory locations. Inspect a sample of requisitions for evidence of inventory levels being checked first, such as a signature.
Requisitions authorised Requisitions are authorised by the factory managers before being sent to the procurement department. This ensures only necessary goods and services are procured, reducing the risk of loss to the company. This reduces the risk of inappropriate levels of stock being maintained which could result in obsolescence and overstatement of inventory if not valued appropriately at the lower of cost and net realisable value.	Inspect a sample of requisitions for evidence of authorisation, such as a signature.
Approved supplier list Pear has an approved supplier list which gives assurance about the quality of goods and reliability of the suppliers. Poor quality supplies will affect the product sold to the customers, leading to customer complaints and possible returns which could result in inappropriate inventory valuation.	For a sample of purchase orders placed, agree the supplier name to the approved supplier list. Observe a member of the procurement team attempting to place an order with an unapproved supplier. The system should not allow it to proceed.

(b) Control deficiencies and recommendations

Control deficiency	**Control recommendation**
Website and inventory system not integrated Currently the website is not integrated into inventory system. This can result in Pear accepting customer orders when the goods are not available. This can cause them to lose sales and customer goodwill.	The website should be updated to include an interface into the inventory system; this should check inventory levels and only process orders if adequate inventory is held. If inventory is out of stock, this should appear on the website with an approximate waiting time.
Customer signatures not obtained For goods despatched by local couriers, customer signatures are not always obtained. Customers may falsely claim that they have not received their goods. Pear would not be able to prove that the goods had in fact been delivered and may result in goods being sent out twice. This could cause loss for the company.	Pear should remind all local couriers that customer signatures must be obtained as proof of delivery and payment will not be made for any despatches with missing signatures.
Unfulfilled sales orders There have been a number of situations where sales orders have not been fulfilled in a timely manner. This can lead to a loss of customer goodwill and if it persists will damage the reputation of Pear as a reliable supplier.	Once goods are despatched they should be matched to sales orders and flagged as fulfilled. The system should automatically flag any outstanding sales orders past a predetermined period, such as five days. This report should be reviewed by a responsible official.
Sales discounts set by sales team Sales discounts are set by Pear's sales team. In order to boost their sales, members of the sales team may set the discounts too high. This will lead to a loss of revenue and profit for the company.	All members of the sales team should only be given authority to grant sales discounts up to a set limit. Any sales discounts above these limits should be authorised by sales area managers or the sales director. Regular review of sales discount levels should be undertaken by the sales director, and this review should be evidenced.

Control deficiency	**Control recommendation**
Supplier statement reconciliations Supplier statement reconciliations are no longer performed. Errors in the recording of purchases and payables may not be identified in a timely manner. This could result in late or incorrect payments to suppliers and a loss of supplier goodwill.	Supplier statement reconciliations should be performed on a monthly basis for all suppliers and these should be reviewed by a responsible official.
Changes to master file Changes to supplier details in the master file can be undertaken by payables ledger clerks. Key supplier data may be accidently amended or fictitious suppliers being set up. This increases the risk of fraud and loss for the company.	Only payables ledger supervisors should have the authority to make changes to master file data. This should be controlled via passwords. Regular review of any changes to master file data by a responsible official and this review should be evidenced.
Authorisation of purchase requisitions Purchase requisitions are authorised by production supervisors. Production supervisors are not sufficiently independent or senior to authorise asset expenditure. This could lead to unnecessary cost for the company if asset expenditure is not needed by the company or if the best price is not obtained.	Asset expenditure authorisation levels to be established. Production supervisors should only be able to authorise low value items, any high value items should be authorised by the board.

(c) Substantive procedures

Additions of property and equipment

- Obtain a breakdown of additions, cast the list and agree to the non-current asset register to confirm completeness of plant & equipment (P&E).
- Select a sample of additions from the breakdown and agree the cost to supplier invoice to confirm valuation.
- Verify rights and obligations by agreeing the addition of plant and equipment to a supplier invoice in the name of Pear International Co.
- Review nature of the items included on the list of additions to confirm that they relate to assets rather than repairs and maintenance.
- For a sample of additions recorded in on the breakdown, physically verify them on the factory floor to confirm existence.

Disposals

- Obtain a breakdown of disposals, cast the list and agree all assets have been removed from the non-current asset register to confirm existence.
- Select a sample of disposals from the breakdown and agree the sale proceeds to supporting documentation such as sundry sales invoices.
- Recalculate the profit/loss on disposal and agree to the income statement.

(d) Need for internal audit

- **Scale, diversity and complexity of activities** – the more complex and diverse the activities of the company, the greater the need for internal checks which can be performed by an internal audit function.
- **Number of employees** – if the company employs a large number of people, the risk of fraud and error increases. An internal audit function may be beneficial as it will act as a deterrent for fraud and may detect frauds through the work performed.
- **Cost/benefit considerations** – if the cost of running an internal audit function outweighs the benefits obtained, the directors may decide there is no need for one.
- **Level of assurance required by management** – senior management may want to have assurance that the controls of the company are adequate and receive advice on risk and control to help them fulfil their responsibilities.
- **Corporate governance** – the desire to be seen to be adopting best practice voluntarily to increase confidence of shareholders and other stakeholders.

Tutorial note

Having an internal audit department is generally considered to be 'best practice,' rather than being required by law. This allows flexibility in the way internal audit is established to suit the needs of a business. In small, or owner managed businesses there is unlikely to be a need for internal audit because the owners are able to exercise more direct control over operations, and are accountable to fewer stakeholders.

ACCA marking guide

		Marks
(a)	**Direct controls and tests of control**	
	• Website validity checks	2
	• Credit checks and credit limits set	2
	• Invoices generated from GDN	2
	• Regular customer statements and follow up of overdue debts	2
	• Inventory levels checked regularly and prior to ordering	2
	• Purchase requisitions authorised	2
	• Approved supplier list	2
	Max 5 direct controls, 2 marks each	**10**
(b)	**Control deficiencies and recommendations**	
	• Website not integrated into inventory system	2
	• Customer signatures	2
	• Unfulfilled sales orders	2
	• Sales discounts	2
	• Supplier statement reconciliations	2
	• Payables master file data	2
	• Authorisation of asset expenditure	2
	Max 5 issues, 2 marks each	**10**

(c)	**Substantive procedures**	
	Additions	
	• Cast list of additions and agree to non-current asset register	1
	• Agree cost to recent supplier invoice	1
	• Agree name of company on the purchase invoice	1
	• Review nature of additions to confirm asset expenditure	1
	• Physically verify additions to confirm existence	1
	Disposals	
	• Cast list of disposals and agree removed from non-current asset register	1
	• Agree sale proceeds to sundry sales invoices	1
	• Recalculate the profit/loss on disposal	1
	Max	**6**
(d)	**Need for internal audit factors**	
	• Scale and diversity of business activities	1
	• Number of employees	1
	• Cost versus benefit	1
	• Level of assurance required by senior management	1
	• Corporate governance	1
	Max	**4**
Total		**30**

Examiner's comments

Part (a) required candidates to identify direct controls and recommend tests of controls to assess if the internal controls of Pear were operating effectively. The requirement to provide tests of control was not answered well. Many candidates simply repeated their controls and added 'to check that' or 'to make sure'. These are not tests of control. Also, many candidates suggested that the control be tested through observation. For example, 'observe the process for authorisation of sales discounts'. This is a weak test as it is likely that if the auditor is present that the control will operate effectively; instead a better test would be 'to review sales invoices for evidence of authorisation of discounts by sales manager.'

Part (b) required candidates to identify and explain deficiencies and suggest a control for each deficiency. Most candidates performed well on this part of the question. They were able to confidently identify deficiencies from the scenario. However, many candidates did not address the question requirement fully as they did not 'identify and explain'. Candidates identified, but did not go on to explain why this was a deficiency. For example 'couriers do not always record customer signatures as proof of delivery' would receive ½ mark, however to obtain the other ½ mark they needed to explain how this could cause problems for the company such as customers could dispute receipt of goods and Pear would need to resend them. The requirement to provide controls was generally well answered. Some candidates gave objectives rather than controls for example 'Pear should ensure that all sales are forwarded to the despatch department' without explaining what the control should be to ensure that this happened. In addition, some candidates provided controls which were just too vague to attain the 1 mark available per control.

The requirement was for five deficiencies; it was not uncommon to see candidates provide many more than five. Often in one paragraph they would combine two or three points such as authorisation of credit limits and of sales discounts. When points were combined, some candidates did not fully provide controls and tests of controls for each of the given points, therefore failing to maximise their marks.

Part (c) required substantive procedures the auditor should perform on year-end property, plant and equipment (PPE) additions and disposals. Performance was mixed on this part of the question. Candidates who scored well often did so by providing a number of tests for each area, each test was average and so scored ½ mark each and so they managed to attain full marks in this way. However, some candidates provided detailed procedures and so achieved the 1 mark available per test. This is better utilisation of time. The requirement verb was to 'describe' therefore sufficient detail was required to score 1 mark per test. Candidates are reminded that substantive procedures are a core topic area and they must be able to produce relevant detailed procedures. Many tests given were just too brief. Answers such as 'check accounting records to ensure correct treatment of disposals' are far too vague as it does not explain how we gain comfort that disposals have been recorded correctly.

In addition, answers such as 'ensure that additions are correctly included' are objectives rather than substantive procedures. Other common mistakes made by candidates were:

- Providing general PPE tests such as for depreciation, rather than just focusing on additions and disposals.
- Giving unrealistic tests such as 'to physically verify on the factory floor that an asset has been disposed of' if it's been disposed of then how can it be physically verified!
- Focusing too much on whether the asset has been disposed of for the best possible price; this is a concern of management and not of the auditor.

SUBSTANTIVE PROCEDURES, COMPLETION AND REPORTING

239 LATTE CO *Walk in the footsteps of a top tutor*

Key answer tips

Part (a).

(a) Substantive procedures for existence and valuation of trade receivables

- Obtain a breakdown of the list of customer balances and agree it to the trade receivables balance in the trial balance and financial statements.
- Calculate the average receivables collection period for 20X5, compare it to the receivables collection period for 20X4 and investigate any significant differences.
- Review the aged receivables to identify any slow moving or old balances. Discuss the status of these balances with the credit controller and/or finance director to assess the likelihood of payment.
- Review board minutes to identify whether there are any significant concerns in relation to payments by customers.
- Review the after-date cash receipts and follow through to pre year-end receivable balances.

- Discuss with the finance director the basis for the decrease in allowance for receivables given the $1.1m increase in the receivables balance and agree any change in assumptions to supporting documentation.
- Obtain a breakdown of the allowance for receivables calculation, recalculate and agree the amount of the allowance is accurate.
- Inspect a sample of post year-end sales returns/credit notes to assess whether an additional allowance against receivables is required.
- Select a sample of goods despatched notes (GDN) before and just after the year end and follow through to receivables to ensure they are recorded in the correct accounting period.
- For any slow moving/aged balances, review customer correspondence to assess whether there are any invoices in dispute or unlikely to be paid and discuss with management.
- Select a sample of year-end receivables balances and agree back to valid supporting documentation of sales invoices, GDN and sales order to ensure existence.

(b) Substantive procedures re provision for legal claim

- Obtain and review a copy of the claim made and any correspondence with the former employee to understand the basis for and the amount claimed.
- Review correspondence with Latte Co's lawyers, or with the client's permission contact the lawyers, to establish the likelihood of success of the claim and the expected amount payable to ascertain whether a provision or disclosure as a contingent liability is required.
- Inspect relevant board minutes/discuss with the finance director to ascertain whether payment is probable and the basis for the provision.
- Review the post year-end bank ledger account and bank statements to identify whether any payment has been made in respect of the claim and compare the actual payment to provision created to assess whether the amount provided is reasonable.
- Obtain a written representation from management to confirm the completeness of the provision.
- Review the financial statements for disclosure of the provision for legal claims to ensure compliance with IAS 37 *Provisions, Contingent Liabilities and Contingent Assets*.

(c) Substantive procedures re bank loan –

- Obtain a copy of the loan documentation to confirm the amount borrowed, the repayment terms and the interest rate applicable.
- Request a bank confirmation letter from the bank to confirm the outstanding balance and any security provided and agree the details to the loan balance within the trial balance at the year end/financial statements.
- In respect of the receipt of the loan and payments made to the bank, agree the amounts to the original loan documentation and to the bank ledger account and bank statements.

- Review correspondence with the bank to identify whether any late payment penalties have been levied in respect of the late payment and agree these are included as a finance cost in the period.
- Confirm that repayments have been correctly allocated into their capital and interest elements and accounted for accordingly.
- Recalculate the amount included as a finance cost in the year by reference to the interest rate and amounts outstanding during the year.
- Review the loan agreement for details of covenants and recalculate to identify if any breaches have occurred. Discuss the impact of any breaches with the finance director.
- Review the disclosure of non-current liabilities in the draft financial statements, including any security provided and confirm that it is in accordance with accounting standards and local legislation. Additionally, confirm that the split of current and non-current loans in the financial statements is correct.

(d) Auditor's report

(i) Factors to consider

As Latte Co is listed, a key audit matters (KAM) section will be required in the auditor's report in accordance with ISA 701 Communicating Key Audit Matters in the Independent Auditor's Report. The audit engagement partner would have considered whether the matter was communicated to those charged with governance as KAM are selected from matters communicated with those charged with governance. The audit engagement partner would have also considered the level of risk in relation to the valuation of the provision and, as determining the size of the liability is an accounting estimate, the level of judgement involved. The audit engagement partner will have also considered whether, in their professional judgement, the matters regarding the valuation of the provision were of most significance in the audit of Latte Co's financial statements for the year ended 31 March 20X5.

(ii) Contents of KAM

The KAM section of the auditor's report should include a reference to the audit risk in relation to the valuation of the provision and the level of judgement required in making this assessment. It should detail why this issue was considered to be an area of significance in the audit and therefore determined to be a KAM. It must also explain how the matter was addressed in the audit and the auditor should provide a brief overview of the audit procedures adopted as well as detailing that a review was undertaken of any related disclosures.

ACCA marking guide		
		Marks
(a)	Substantive procedures for existence and valuation of trade receivables 1 mark per well-described procedure Restricted to	6
(b)	Substantive procedures re provision for legal claim 1 mark per well-described procedure Restricted to	4
(c)	Substantive procedures re bank loan 1 mark per well-described procedure Restricted to	5
(d)	Auditor's report 1 mark per well-explained point Restricted to	5
Total		**20**

Examiner's comments

General comments

This 20-mark question is based on Macchiato & Co, an audit firm due to commence the audit of Latte Co, a listed company which supplies catering equipment. This question tests candidates' knowledge of substantive procedures and auditor's reports.

Requirements (a) and (c) examine substantive procedures for trade receivables, a legal claim and a bank loan. Requirement (a) is for 6 marks, (b) for 4 marks and (c) for 5 marks and time allocation should be based on 1.8 minutes per mark. Therefore, the available time should be split as follows; 11 minutes for requirement (a), 7 minutes for (b) and 9 minutes for (c).

One mark is available for each well-explained procedure therefore candidates should aim to produce 6 tests for requirement (a), 4 for (b) and 5 for (c). Candidates must strive to understand substantive procedures and apply good exam technique. This includes tailoring procedures to the specific requirements of the question. Too often candidates have rote learnt a set of standard tests and these are then produced for each requirement without consideration of their relevance to the scenario provided. This approach tends to generate few marks. Audit procedures must be sufficiently detailed noting clearly which source document should be used. For example, tests such as 'review disclosures' would only score ½ mark. To score a full mark the procedure should go on to say, 'in accordance with accounting standards/relevant legislation'.

Part (a) – 6 marks

For substantive procedures requirements, one mark is available for each well described procedure, therefore candidates should aim to produce six tests for this requirement. Candidates should plan their time accordingly. The question was tailored to two assertions, existence and valuation, and these were capitalised in the requirement to aid candidates. Any procedures not related to these assertions, such as 'review disclosures' will not gain credit.

When describing substantive procedures, one of the key things to consider is the level of detail provided. Many candidates fail to score well in this type of requirement because their procedures are vague or too brief. Tests must be sufficiently detailed, noting clearly which source document should be used and for what purpose.

For example, in this session some candidates included, 'review after-date cash receipts' and would have only gained ½ mark. To gain the 1 mark available, this test would need to be expanded to 'follow these receipts through to the pre year end receivables balance'. 'Reviewing customer correspondence for disputed balances' would only have gained ½ mark, as this needs to be 'discussed with management with regards to whether an allowance may be required' to gain 1 mark.

Candidates must ensure that they can distinguish between a substantive procedure and a test of control. Many candidates lose marks in this type of requirement by mixing up these procedures. Where substantive procedures are required for an account balance subject to an accounting standard then considering the rules of the standard can help in generating targeted substantive procedures.

In many substantive procedure questions analytical procedures can be an important source of evidence, but for one-off types of expenditure, analytical review is unlikely to be useful. For trade receivables, valid analytical procedures such as comparing the trade receivables to the prior year with significant differences being discussed with management would gain the full one mark. Candidates who compare the balance to the prior year to identify any significant differences only gained ½ mark as the process of comparing current to prior year only identifies the differences. To gain the other ½ mark these significant differences need to be investigated or discussed further with management.

Candidates who focused on casting the receivables listing and agreeing to financial statements, reviewing after-date cash receipts, reviewing the aged receivables reports for slow-moving balances and discussing with management the need for an allowance, reviewing customer correspondence for balances in dispute and undertaking analytical review procedures were able to gain credit.

Some candidates had not read the scenario carefully as it clearly stated that a trade receivables confirmation (circularisation) would not be performed, therefore no credit was awarded for this procedure. Additionally, some candidates went further and listed the steps which should be followed when undertaking a confirmation.

When generating substantive procedures for trade receivables or trade payables, it is imperative that the focus of the tests is on the statement of financial position balance rather than on revenue or purchases. In this session some candidates incorrectly provided revenue procedures such as recalculate the total on the sales invoices and agree goods dispatched notes to the sales invoice and listing of sales invoices. These did not gain credit. Take the time to read the question requirements carefully and spend time thinking about what is needed prior to producing an answer.

Part (b) – 4 marks

Good exam technique is important for a requirement like this. While some knowledge of accounting for legal claims would have been helpful, the key here is to think logically. It is possible to produce a good answer by thinking through the issues which are relevant for any provision.

For example, whether it should be recognised and if so, at what amount. Procedures can then be designed to address these issues using the information from the scenario to add detail.

Straightforward procedures which gained credit in this session included reviewing employee correspondence, contact the lawyers to establish the likely outcome of the claim, reviewing board minutes to ascertain the probable amount and likelihood of payment, reviewing the post-year-end cash book/bank ledger for payments made and agreeing this to the provision,' obtaining written representations on management's view of the outcome of the claim, and reviewing the disclosures for compliance with IAS 37/accounting standards.

Careful thought should be given to the nature of the legal claim and the context of the scenario. This claim related to an employee claiming for an injury sustained at work, therefore, as it related to an individual employee injury it is unlikely that further claims from other employees exist. Hence, any procedures which considered the issue of other or future claims would not gain any credit.

Additionally, some candidates did not consider the one-off nature of this claim and therefore suggested comparing the provision for the current year to the prior year. This is unlikely to provide useful evidence as it is unlikely the company had a similar claim in the prior year.

Also, this was a single claim and therefore no credit was awarded for recalculating the provision or casting the list of legal claim provisions. Candidates must carefully read the information in the question and tailor their answers accordingly.

Part (c) – 5 marks

The scenario for this part of the question was quite brief. Key points included that a new three-year loan had been taken out to finance the purchase of new equipment, the loan attracts interest at 5%, quarterly repayments are due, and the March repayment was paid late after the year end. Candidates should consider how this information could be used to tailor the procedures, the impact they would have on the financial statements and then the evidence which would be available.

When generating procedures for bank loans, it's important to note that it is the year-end balance which is audited but this will be made up of $1m initially received, plus interest at 5% less any capital repaid. In this case, the question states that the quarterly instalment of $105,000 includes interest. By considering each of these issues, appropriate substantive procedures can be derived. For example, the initial loan proceeds can be agreed to the cash book/bank ledger and bank statement, and the split of the loan repayment between capital and interest can be recalculated. The loan can also be agreed to a loan agreement which would contain such details as the repayment period and interest to be charged. The scenario also states that it is a three-year loan which means that part of the loan will be a current liability and part will be a non-current liability. As part of the review of the disclosure of the loan, the auditor will need to recalculate the split between current and non-current liabilities to confirm it is correct. The model answer shows other relevant procedures.

Using the information in the scenario carefully will ensure that answers are focussed on the right issues and avoids inappropriate procedures being included. A number of candidates incorrectly assumed that the March repayment being paid 15 days late meant there was a going concern issue and so listed several going concern procedures.

No credit was awarded for this as the payment was simply late, therefore no going concern issues arose and candidates should instead have focused on late payment penalties. Some candidates focused on auditing the new equipment, which was purchased by the company. No credit was awarded for this as the requirement was clearly for the bank loan.

Other common inappropriate tests included discussing with management why they were obtaining new loans, bank reconciliation procedures, comparing the loans to the prior year, or obtaining a written representation, even this was not a judgemental audit area. Others included a procedure reviewing board minutes for authorisation of the loans. This is a test of control and not a substantive procedure.

Part (d) – 5 marks

Although audit reports feature regularly in the AA exam, there are several ways in which they can be tested, and candidates must be prepared for any type of question on audit reports. For this session, 5 marks were awarded for the factors to be considered and for the contents of the KAM section.

The starting point with this type of requirement is to consider what knowledge a candidate has with regards to ISA 701 *Communicating Key Audit Matters in the Independent Auditor's Report*. Knowledge of this standard will help in considering what influences the decision as to whether an issue is a KAM or not. Although the scenario related to the legal claim, knowledge marks could be easily obtained without reference to the scenario.

Candidates should focus on three to four points that the engagement partner would consider such as the level of risk relating to this issue, whether it would be reported to those charged with governance, the significance of the matter and the level of judgement required in forming a conclusion on the truth and fairness of this issue.

The next step would be to move onto the content of the KAM section of the audit report. Here candidates should consider reporting WHAT the issue is – that there was a risk over the valuation of the legal claim provision. WHY the issue is considered a KAM – due to the fact it was high risk with significant auditor judgement required. HOW the issue was addressed during the audit – with details of audit procedures adopted along with a review of the disclosures. One point for each of these would have been sufficient to maximise the available marks. The model answer shows the key points which should be included for each of these.

It was pleasing to see that some candidates had revised the area of KAM for this session. These candidates were generally able to consider factors in determining if the issue was a KAM but still struggled with the contents.

Some candidates incorrectly assumed they needed to attempt to draft the KAM paragraph rather than just describing its content. Other common incorrect answers attempted to answer this question as if it related to a modified audit opinion. It is important to revise all audit report options and not to simply assume that the focus of the question will contain a modified opinion. Auditor's reports are a core area of the syllabus and knowledge of the ISAs in this area is imperative.

240 HERON *Walk in the footsteps of a top tutor*

Key answer tips

Procedures must focus on the specific aspects of the scenario/requirement rather than being general procedures over the balance. This means that for this question the focus must be on PPE additions, not existing assets, in part (a) and the provision for legal claim, not any issues relating to inventory or going concern, in part (c).

Procedures are always worth a maximum of 1 mark for a well-explained procedure so give enough procedures for the mark allocation. Make sure you give substantive procedures and not tests of control. A substantive procedure is one which will detect material misstatement at the assertion level.

Part (d) focuses on subsequent events and whether the event described is an adjusting or non-adjusting event. You must explain your conclusion. In addition, procedures must be described to form a conclusion on any required amendment. These procedures must be procedures that would be performed at the completion stage to form a conclusion rather than procedures which would have been performed during the main part of audit testing.

(a) Substantive procedures for additions to plant and equipment

- Obtain the detailed breakdown of the costs incurred for the new manufacturing line, cast the breakdown and confirm that it is included in the non-current assets register in order to confirm completeness of the addition.
- Confirm the purchase price of $2·7m and delivery and installation costs of $0·3m to supplier invoices and that the invoices are in the name of Heron Co in order to confirm valuation and rights and obligations.
- Discuss the treatment of the refundable purchases tax of $0·5m with the finance director as this should be excluded from cost. Agree to inclusion in the tax control account.
- Request that management expenses the $0·1m training costs and to profit or loss as they are not eligible for capitalisation. Confirm to a journal entry that the adjustment has been made.
- Review the breakdown of the costs of $0·2m incurred when testing the new line. Discuss with management and agree to supporting documentation to confirm the nature of these costs to ensure they are eligible for capitalisation.
- Select a sample from the non-current assets register and physically verify the new manufacturing line on the factory floor to confirm existence.
- Discuss with management the basis of the eight-year useful life and how it was derived and agree to supporting documentation such as the replacement policy.
- Recalculate the depreciation charge to confirm that the calculations have been appropriately time apportioned and that depreciation only commenced from December 20X4 when the asset was brought into use.

(b) Substantive procedures for provision for bank balances

- Obtain a bank confirmation letter from Heron Co's bankers for all four of its accounts.
- Agree all balances listed on the bank confirmation letter to the company's bank reconciliations or the trial balance/general ledger in order to ensure completeness of bank balances.
- For the current account, obtain Heron Co's bank reconciliation and cast it to check the additions in order to ensure arithmetical accuracy.
- Agree the balance per the bank reconciliation to an original year-end bank statement and to the bank confirmation letter.
- Agree the reconciliation's balance per the bank ledger/cash book to the year-end bank ledger/cash book.
- Trace all the outstanding lodgements to the pre-year-end bank ledger/cash book, post-year-end bank statement and also to the paying-in book pre year end.
- Trace all unpresented cheques through to a pre-year-end bank ledger/cash book and post-year-end bank statement. For any unusual amounts or significant delays, obtain explanations from management.
- Examine any old unpresented cheques to assess whether they need to be written back.
- Review the bank ledger/cash book and bank statements for any unusual items or large transfers around the year end, as this could be evidence of window dressing.
- Examine the bank confirmation letter for details of any security provided by Heron Co, with regards to the bank overdraft or any legal right of set-off as these may require disclosure.
- For the savings accounts, review any reconciling items on the year-end bank reconciliations and agree to supporting documentation.
- Review the financial statements to ensure that the disclosure of bank balances is complete and accurate, and that the overdraft is within current liabilities and the savings accounts within current assets.

(c) Substantive procedures re provision for legal claim

- Discuss with management the facts of the case to determine the nature of the claim and why only $0·6m provided.
- Review correspondence with Heron Co's lawyers or, with the client's permission, obtain confirmation from the client's lawyer about the likely outcome and possibility of payment.
- Inspect correspondence received from the customer regarding the claim in order to assess whether a provision should be recognised and, if so, whether the amount of the provision is reasonable.
- Inspect the post year-end bank ledger/cash book and bank statements to identify whether any payments have been made and compare any actual payments to the amounts provided in the financial statements.

- Inspect relevant board minutes and discuss with the finance director to ascertain whether payment is probable and the basis for the provision.
- Review the expense accounts in the statement of profit or loss for inclusion of legal costs and agree to correspondence from the legal advisers.
- Obtain a written representation from management that they believe the provision is valued appropriately and is complete.
- Review the financial statement disclosures relating to the provision to ensure they are in compliance with IAS 37 *Provisions, Contingent Liabilities and Contingent Assets*.

(d) Subsequent event

(i) The information regarding Sparrow Co's cash flow difficulties was received on 14 July 20X5, after the year end, but provides further evidence of the recoverability of the receivable balance at the year end. If Sparrow Co is experiencing cash flow difficulties just a few months after the year end, it is highly unlikely that the $692,000 was recoverable as at 31 May 20X5 and hence this is an adjusting event in accordance with IAS 10 *Events after the Reporting Period*.

The receivables balance is overstated and consideration should be given to adjusting this balance, if material, either through the use of an allowance for receivables or by writing off the balance relating to Sparrow Co depending on the assessment of the recoverability of the balance.

The total amount outstanding at the year end was $692,000 and is material as it represents 7.8% (0·692m/8·9m) of profit before tax and 1.1% (0·692m/65·4m) of total assets.

The directors should amend the 20X5 financial statements by making an allowance or by writing off the receivable balance relating to Sparrow Co, depending on their assessment.

(ii) The following audit procedures should be applied to form a conclusion as to the adjustment:

- The correspondence with the customer should be reviewed to assess whether there is any likelihood of payment.
- Discuss with management and review board minutes to obtain an understanding as to why they feel an adjustment is not required.
- Review the post-year-end bank ledger/cash book and bank statements to see if any payments have been received from the customer.

ACCA marking guide		
		Marks
(a)	**Substantive procedures for plant and equipment**	
	• Obtain detailed breakdown of costs, cast and agree to non-current asset register - completeness	1
	• Confirm purchase price to supplier invoices – valuation and rights and obligations	1
	• Discuss the treatment of refundable purchase tax with the finance director	1
	• Request that management expenses the training costs and confirm the adjustment to a journal entry	1
	• Review the breakdown of costs incurred for testing the new line and discuss with management to ensure they are eligible for capitalisation	1
	• Physically verify the new manufacturing line for existence	1
	• Assess the reasonableness of the eight-year useful life	1
	• Recalculate the depreciation charge to confirm appropriate time apportionment	1
	Restricted to	**5**
(b)	**Substantive procedures for bank balances**	
	• Obtain bank confirmation letter for all accounts	1
	• Agree all balances on the confirmation letter to the bank reconciliations or trial balance/general ledger	1
	• For the current account, obtain Heron Co's bank reconciliation and cast it to ensure arithmetical accuracy.	1
	• Agree the balance per the bank reconciliation to an original year-end bank statement and to the bank confirmation letter	1
	• Agree the reconciliation's balance per the bank ledger/cash book to the year-end bank ledger/cash book.	1
	• Trace outstanding lodgements to the pre-year-end bank ledger/cash book, post-year-end bank statement and paying-in book pre year end	1
	• Trace unpresented cheques to a pre-year-end bank ledger/cash book and post-year-end bank statement. For any unusual amounts or significant delays, obtain explanations from management	1
	• Examine any old unpresented cheques to assess whether they need to be written back	1
	• Review the bank ledger/cash book and bank statements for any unusual items or large transfers around the year end	1
	• Examine the bank confirmation letter for details of any security provided by Heron Co	1
	• For the savings accounts, review any reconciling items on the year-end bank reconciliations	1
	• Review the financial statements to ensure that the disclosure of bank balances is complete and accurate	1
	Restricted to	**5**

(c)	**Substantive procedures for legal claim**	
	• Discuss the facts with management	1
	• Review correspondence with Heron Co's lawyers	1
	• Inspect correspondence with the customer	1
	• Inspect the post-year-end bank ledger/cash book and bank statements to identify whether any payments have been made	1
	• Inspect relevant board minutes and discuss with the finance director to ascertain whether payment is probable	1
	• Review the expense accounts for inclusion of legal costs	1
	• Obtain a written representation from management that they believe the provision is valued appropriately and is complete	1
	• Review the financial statement disclosures relating to the provision to ensure they are in compliance with IAS 37	1
	Restricted to	**5**
(d)	**Subsequent event**	
	(i) Discussion of issue	
	– Provides further evidence of the recoverability of the receivable balance at the year end – adjusting event	1
	– Receivable balance overstated and adjustment required	1
	– Materiality calculation and conclusion	1
	– Financial statements should be amended by making an allowance or writing off the receivable balance	1
	(ii) Procedures	
	– Review customer correspondence	1
	– Discuss with management/review board minutes	1
	– Review post-year-end receipts from the customer	1
	Restricted to	**5**
Total		**20**

Examiner's comments

General comments

One mark is available for each well-explained procedure. Candidates must strive to understand substantive procedures and apply good exam technique. This includes tailoring procedures to the specific requirements of the question. Additionally, tests must be sufficiently detailed noting clearly which source document should be used. For example, tests such as 'review disclosures' would only score ½ mark. To score a full mark the procedure should go on to say, 'in accordance with accounting standards/relevant legislation'. Also recommending 'obtain a written representation' without explaining what for, will not generate any marks.

Requirement (a)

The scenario for this requirement detailed that the company had incurred capital expenditure on the purchase of a new manufacturing line. The scenario contained detail of the various costs incurred including the purchase price, delivering and installation, refundable purchase tax, training and quality control costs. A key point in the scenario was that all of the costs had been capitalised within non-current assets.

It is important to consider what issue the scenario contains, and this is then compared to the question requirement. In some cases, question requirements can sometimes focus on a specific assertion such as valuation or completeness or on a particular element of an account balance, such as just additions, and where this is the case, care must be taken to ensure that any substantive procedures listed only relate to this assertion or account element.

Spending time understanding the issue and carefully reading the question requirement ensures that any procedures listed are tailored and more likely to score marks. As the requirement was only for additions, then general property, plant and equipment procedures would not gain credit.

The scenario contained significant detail of the various costs capitalised as part of the new manufacturing line. Candidates should have considered whether each cost element is allowable expenditure under IAS 16 *Property, Plant and Equipment*. At least one substantive procedure should then have been generated to test each cost element. For example, the refundable purchase tax should be excluded from the asset cost and therefore should be agreed to the tax account. There were five cost elements included within the cost capitalised and if candidates had listed one well explained substantive procedure per cost element, they would have been awarded five marks.

Procedures such as 'casting the additions and agree to the non-current asset register', 'agreeing additions to invoices to ensure in company name and correct value capitalised', 'physically inspecting the addition', 'recalculation of depreciation for correct time period,' 'discussing the basis of the useful life' and 'reviewing the disclosure for compliance with relevant accounting standards' would all gain credit.

In this session some candidates included procedures such as 'obtain written representations,' 'reviewing the minutes for authorisation of the additions' or 'comparison against the prior year for the additions.' Requesting written representation should be restricted to areas where the auditor is relying on management's judgement or there is little independent evidence available. This is not the case with additions. In addition, some of these procedures would not gain credit as they were tests of control rather than substantive or they do not help to gather sufficient evidence relating to additions. Tests must be tailored to fit with the requirement and scenario.

Requirement (b)

The scenario for this part of the question was quite brief, key points included that there were three savings accounts, and the main current account was overdrawn. Candidates should consider how this information could be used to tailor the procedures. It is important to note that just because the current account is overdrawn, this does not change the main focus of the substantive procedures. The bank reconciliation for this account should be audited in detail, regardless of whether it is a current asset or liability. Candidates often incorrectly focus on going concern procedures, simply because there is an overdraft and no credit at all would be awarded for these procedures as they are not relevant when auditing the year end bank balance.

It is important when auditing bank balances to consider in detail the elements of the bank reconciliation as this is the main focus of the auditor's testing. Utilising knowledge from Financial Accounting and how the bank statement is reconciled to the year-end balance as per the cash book, should provide candidates with sufficient points to audit. When auditing the reconciliation, candidates must be clear as to what time period the various source documents relate to. For example, in testing outstanding lodgements, to be a valid reconciling item on the reconciliation, the audit test should be to 'agree to the pre-year-end bank ledger/cash book and the post-year-end bank statements.' Where candidates were not specific as to whether the bank statements were pre or post year end then full credit was not awarded.

Procedures such as 'casting the bank reconciliation,' 'obtaining a bank confirmation letter,' 'reviewing the disclosures,' and 'agreeing unpresented cheques and outstanding lodgements to the pre-year-end bank ledger/cash book and post-year-end bank statement' would all gain credit. However, some of these procedures would only gain ½ marks, for example 'obtain a bank letter' on its own would only have scored ½ marks. To obtain 1 mark, the test needed to agree to the balance per the bank on the reconciliation.

Candidates struggled to generate a sufficient number of relevant detailed procedures. A significant number of procedures did not make it clear whether the source they were agreeing to/from, such as the bank statement, was pre or post year end. Also, some tests were very vague, 'agree the bank reconciliation to the bank statement' would not gain any credit as it is not clear which line in the reconciliation is being audited and whether the bank statement is at the year end or post year end. Also, many candidates simply recommended 'reperform the bank reconciliation' and that was their sole focus on the bank reconciliation. These candidates then went on to recommend 'analytical review against the prior year or budget', 'recalculating bank interest', 'reviewing the signatures for authorising payment' and 'obtaining written representations'. None of these procedures gained credit.

Requirement (c)

Good exam technique is important for a requirement like this. While some knowledge of accounting for legal claims would have been helpful, the key here is to think logically. It is possible to produce a good answer by thinking through the issues which are relevant for any provision, for example whether it should be recognised and if so, at what amount. Procedures can then be designed to address these issues using the information from the scenario to add detail.

Straightforward procedures which gained credit in this session included 'reviewing customer correspondence', 'contact the lawyers to establish the likely outcome of the claim,' 'reviewing board minutes to ascertain the probable amount and likelihood of payment,' 'obtaining written representations on managements view of the outcome of the claim' and 'reviewing the disclosures for compliance with IAS 37/accounting standards.'

Careful thought should be given to the nature of the legal claim and the context of the scenario. This claim related to a customised dye and no inventory of this dye was held at the year end. As the product was customised, this means it was produced solely for the customer, Parrot Co. Therefore, there cannot be any further claims from other customers relating to this dye. Hence any procedures which considered the issue of other or future claims would not gain any credit. Also, the requirement is solely in relation to the legal claim provision and the company does not hold any inventory at the year end. However, this session candidates did focus procedures on confirming the valuation of inventory of the customised dye. These procedures would not gain any credit.

Additionally, some candidates did not consider the one-off nature of this claim and therefore suggested 'comparing the provision for the current year to the prior year', which is unlikely to provide useful evidence as it is unlikely the company had a similar claim in the prior year. Candidates must carefully read the information in the question and tailor their answers accordingly.

Requirement (d)

This requirement focused on subsequent events and marks are awarded for an explanation of whether the financial statements require amendment (3 marks) and audit procedures to conclude on whether an amendment is needed (2 marks).

The starting point with this type of requirement is to consider the accounting from IAS 10 *Events After the Reporting Period* and to decide whether the event in the scenario is adjusting or non-adjusting. The scenario contained information relating to a customer, Sparrow Co, which had a significant year-end receivables balance and had just informed Heron Co that they were unable to make any payments for the foreseeable future. Using relevant accounting knowledge, candidates should then explain the key points that determine whether the financial statements require amendment.

Credit would be gained for the following, 'provides evidence over recoverability at the year end' and 'is an adjusting subsequent event.' In order to assess whether the financial statements require amendment, the materiality of the receivables balance should be calculated. Having concluded that the balance owing was material and an adjusting event then candidates need to actually answer the requirement and state that the financial statements do need amendment. Furthermore, it should be clear exactly how the financial statements would be amended, in this case through an allowance or a write down of the balance.

In this session some candidates incorrectly assumed that the requirement of the financial statements needing amendment somehow related to an audit report and whether this would be modified or not. This was not an audit report question. Any procedures relating to audit reports did not gain any credit.

Having considered part (i) of this requirement, candidates then need to describe two detailed audit procedures to assess whether the receivable balance at the year end should be amended. Straightforward procedures such as 'reviewing customer correspondence from Sparrow Co to assess the likelihood of payment,' 'reviewing the post-year-end period for any payments made by Sparrow Co' and 'discussing with the directors why they believe payment will be made and so have not adjusted the financial statements' would all gain credit. Only two procedures were needed and it is important that they related to Sparrow Co and the issue of whether they had or were likely to make payment. Generic receivables procedures, relating to all trade receivables, would not gain any credit.

It is important that candidates adequately prepare themselves for questions from any part of syllabus area E and not just assume that there will be a question on audit reports.

241 PACIFIC *Walk in the footsteps of a top tutor*

Key answer tips

Part (a) asks for procedures over completeness of trade payables and accruals. Your procedures must address the risk that some of these liabilities have been omitted from the financial statements. To test the assertion of completeness, your procedures must start from outside of the accounting records.

Part (b) asks for procedures in respect of a provision for a legal claim. Remember that a provision is an estimate, therefore management may deliberately understate the provision as the amount is uncertain. Professional scepticism needs to be exercised when auditing this type of balance.

Part (c) asks for substantive analytical procedures over revenue. In the requirement, the word analytical is emphasised to highlight that the procedures should be analytical rather than tests of detail. Analytical procedures include comparisons, trends and ratios. The most meaningful evidence comes from analysing disaggregated data such as analysing revenue by product line or by store.

In respect of (a), (b), and (c), procedures are worth one mark if they contain sufficient detail.

For (a) and (b), the procedures can be a mixture of tests of detail and analytical procedures.

Part (d) asks for the impact on the auditor's report if the issue remains unresolved. This is a very common requirement and should be straightforward to answer if you have prepared for the exam by practising past exams. Start by giving a brief description of the issue i.e. how the financial statements are affected. Next, assess the materiality of the misstatement. If the misstatement is material, consider whether it is pervasive. This will lead you to the appropriate type of opinion. Finish off by stating how other sections of the report will be affected e.g. the basis for opinion.

(a) Substantive procedures for trade payables and accruals

- Calculate the payables payment period for Pacific Co, compare to prior years and investigate any significant differences, in particular any decrease this year due to the inclusion of the payment run on 1 June.
- Compare the total trade payables, or significant supplier balances, and good received not invoiced (GRNI) accrual against the prior year and investigate any significant differences.
- Compare the list of accruals this year to the prior year to identify any missing items or unusual fluctuations and discuss with management.
- Discuss with management the process they have undertaken to quantify the misstatement of trade payables due to the payment run and consider the materiality of the error in isolation as well as with other misstatements found.
- Review the journal entry processed to correct the misstatement of trade payables due to the payment run to ensure all errors have been included.

- Select a sample of purchase invoices received around the year end. Ascertain, through reviewing goods received notes (GRNs), if the goods were received pre or post year end. If post year end, then confirm that they have been excluded from the ledger.
- Review after-date payments; if they relate to the current year, then follow through to the list of individual supplier balances or GRNI accrual to ensure they are recorded in the correct period.
- Reperform a sample of supplier statement reconciliations and agree these to the list of individual supplier balances. Investigate any reconciling items.
- Select a sample of trade payables balances and perform a trade payables' circularisation. Follow up any non-responses and any reconciling items between the balance confirmed and the trade payables' balance.
- Select a sample of GRNs before the year end and after the year end and follow through to inclusion of the liability in the correct period's payables balance to ensure correct cut-off.

(b) Substantive procedures for provision for legal claims

- Enquire with the directors or inspect relevant supporting documentation to confirm if a present obligation exists at the year end.
- Discuss with directors how the mislabelling of ingredients is alleged to have occurred and whether it is likely that any other customers have been affected.
- Discuss the claim with management and review the internal investigation report in order to gain an insight into the circumstances which led to the mislabelling.
- Inspect board minutes to ascertain whether payment is probable.
- Inspect post-year-end bank statements to identify whether any payments have been made in respect of the claim.
- Review correspondence with Pacific Co's lawyers or with the client's permission, contact the lawyers and obtain confirmation regarding the claim to assess whether a provision should be recognised and whether the amount of the provision is material.
- Review correspondence or discuss with lawyers the likelihood and amount of other potential future claims.
- If evidence indicates that it is only possible that the claim will be successful, inspect the financial statement for contingent liability disclosures to ensure compliance with IAS 37 *Provisions, Contingent Liabilities and Contingent Assets.*
- Obtain a written representation from management confirming their view that they have an obligation at the year end in respect of the claim and that it is appropriate to include a provision.

(c) Substantive analytical procedures for revenue

- Compare the overall level of revenue against prior years and discuss the reasons for the 9·4% increase with management and agree to supporting documentation.
- Compare the overall level of revenue against the budget for the year and investigate any significant fluctuations.
- Obtain a schedule of sales for the year disaggregated into the eight main product lines and compare this to the prior year breakdown and budget to understand what impact the new products have had on revenue. For any unusual movements, discuss with management.

- Obtain a schedule of sales for the year analysed for the existing 13 stores. Compare this to the prior year and discuss any unusual movements/significant fluctuations with management.
- Perform a proof-in-total calculation for revenue. The prior year revenue for the eight main product lines should be taken and an adjustment should be made for sales from the new product lines and for the new store for approximately nine months. This expectation should be compared to actual revenue and whether this equates to 9·4% growth over the prior year. Any significant fluctuations should be investigated.
- Calculate the gross profit margin for Pacific Co and compare this to the prior year and investigate any significant fluctuations.

(d) Auditor's report

The financial statements contain a provision for legal claims of $0.5m, however, audit work has identified that the provision should be $0.8m. Hence the provision is understated and profits overstated by $0.3m. The argument that the provision is a reasonable estimate is not valid.

The error of $0.3m represents 7.3% of profit before tax (0.3m/4.1m) and hence is a material matter.

If the finance director refuses to increase the provision, the audit opinion will be modified due to a material misstatement. As provisions are understated and the error is material but not pervasive, a qualified opinion would be necessary.

A basis for qualified opinion paragraph would be needed subsequent to the opinion paragraph and would explain the material misstatement in relation to the understated provision for the legal claims and the effect on the financial statements. The opinion paragraph would be qualified 'except for'.

ACCA marking guide		
		Marks
(a)	**Substantive procedures for trade payables and accruals**	
	• Calculate the payables payment period	1
	• Compare trade payables and GRNI accrual to prior year	1
	• Compare accruals listing to prior year	1
	• Discuss with management how they have quantified the misstatement of trade payables due to the payment run	1
	• Review correcting journal	1
	• Test purchase invoices received around the year end	1
	• Review after-date payments	1
	• Reperform supplier statement reconciliations	1
	• Perform a trade payables circularisation	1
	• Test GRNs around the year end	1
	Restricted to	5
(b)	**Substantive procedures for provision for legal claims**	
	• Ascertain if a present obligation exists through discussion or inspection of documentation	1
	• Discuss with directors how the mislabelling occurred	1
	• Obtain an insight into the issue by reviewing the investigation report or discussing with management	1
	• Inspect board minutes for probability of the claim	1
	• Inspect post-year-end bank statements	1
	• Review correspondence with Pacific Co's lawyers re amount of the claim	1
	• Review correspondence with Pacific Co's lawyers re probability of potential future claims	1
	• Review financial statement disclosures for compliance with IAS 37	1
	• Obtain written representation from management	1
	Restricted to	6

(c)	**Substantive analytical procedures for revenue**	
	• Compare total revenue with prior year	1
	• Compare total revenue with budget	1
	• Obtain schedule of disaggregated sales by product line and compare to prior year breakdown and budget	1
	• Obtain schedule of sales by store and compare to prior year	1
	• Perform a proof-in-total calculation for revenue	1
	• Calculate gross profit margin and compare to prior year	1
	Restricted to	**4**
(d)	**Auditor's report**	
	• Discussion of issue	1
	• Materiality calculation	1
	• Type of modification	2
	• Impact on report	1
	Restricted to	**5**
Total		**20**

Examiner's comments

Part (a). The scenario for this requirement detailed that Pacific Co had kept the payables ledger open in error for one day after the year end, and as a result a significant payment run for suppliers had been made on 1 June 20X5 and recorded in the year-end payables ledger. The finance director had corrected the error via a journal. It is important to consider what issue the scenario contains, and then compare this to the question requirement. As in this case, question requirements can sometimes focus on a specific assertion such as valuation or completeness and where this is the case, care must be taken to ensure that any substantive procedures listed only relate to this assertion.

Spending time understanding the issue and carefully reading the question requirement ensures that any procedures listed are tailored and more likely to score marks. As the requirement was only for completeness, procedures needed to focus on this specific assertion, as any procedures not related to completeness would not gain credit. Procedures such as 'casting the payables listing and agreeing to the trial balance and financial statements,' 'reviewing after date cash payments and agreeing to the payables ledger for the relevant period,' 'reperforming supplier statement reconciliations,' 'undertaking a payables circularisation' and analytical review would all gain credit.

In this session some candidates included procedures such as 'review whether the disclosure is in accordance with accounting standards' or 'obtain written representations.' These procedures would not gain credit as they do not help to gather sufficient evidence as to the completeness of trade payables and accruals. Requesting written representation should be restricted to areas where the auditor is relying on management's judgement or there is little independent evidence available. This is not the case with completeness of payables and tests must be tailored to fit with the requirement and scenario.

When generating substantive procedures, it is important to ensure the tests have sufficient detail and are clear. For example, 'perform a trade payables circularisation' would only be awarded ½ marks. For the full mark candidates had to also say 'and investigate any reconciling items between the balance confirmed and trade payables balance.'

Part (b). Good exam technique is important for a requirement like this. While some knowledge of accounting for legal claims would have been helpful the key here is to think logically. It is possible to produce a good answer by thinking through the issues which are relevant for any provision, for example whether it should be recognised and if so, at what amount. Procedures can then be designed to address these issues using the information from the scenario to add detail.

Straightforward procedures which gained credit in this session included 'reviewing customer correspondence,' 'contact the lawyers to establish the likely outcome of the claims,' 'reviewing the post year-end cashbook for payments made and agreeing this to the provision,' 'obtaining written representations on managements view of the outcome of the claims' and 'reviewing the disclosures for compliance with IAS 37/accounting standards.'

Careful thought should be given to the nature of the legal claims and the context of the scenario. It was clear from the scenario that a number of claims had been received from customers by the year end, each alleging an allergic reaction, therefore it was possible that further claims relating to products sold pre year end could arise subsequent to the year end. Therefore, substantive procedures are needed to confirm the amounts claimed by the year end, as well as considering whether this provision is complete as further claims could arise. This session, many candidates did not consider this issue of future of claims.

Additionally, some candidates did not consider the 'one-off' nature of this claim and therefore suggested 'comparing the provision for the current year to the prior year.' This is unlikely to provide useful audit evidence as it is unlikely the company had a similar claim in the prior year. Candidates must carefully read the information in the question and tailor their answers accordingly.

Part (c). It is important to carefully consider any element of the requirement which is capitalised when tackling substantive procedure questions. Here 'substantive analytical' is capitalised, therefore only analytical review procedures, and not tests of detail, will gain credit. To gain full credit, four well explained analytical procedures are required.

The next step is to review the scenario to consider whether there is any information which will help to tailor the procedures. In the case of Pacific Co the scenario details that there has been an increase in revenue over the prior year, that management information is available across the eight key product lines as well as per store, and that there have been some new product lines launched as well as a new store opening. Using this information should help candidates to produce procedures such as 'compare revenue by each of the eight main products lines and compare this to the prior year or budget' and 'compare monthly revenue for the original 13 stores to the prior year.' Additionally, a detailed proof in total procedure which incorporates the changes in product lines and store numbers would also gain credit.

In addition to the above scenario specific points, 'comparing total or monthly revenue to the prior year and budget' as well a review of gross margins would all be awarded credit. To be awarded the full 1 mark per analytical review procedure it is important that having compared revenue to prior year or budget then any significant fluctuations are investigated/discussed with management. Without reviewing the fluctuations only ½ marks are awarded.

Unfortunately, many candidates this diet struggled to generate more than two analytical review procedures and then instead listed tests of detail, such as 'casting the detailed sales list' or 'agreeing to sales invoices and good despatch notes.' No credit was awarded as this was not the question requirement.

Part (d). Although audit reports feature regularly in the AA exam, there are several ways in which they can be tested, and candidates must be prepared for any type of question on audit reports. In this diet, the issue which needed to be considered related to the provision for legal claims being understated by $0.3m, as it should be $0.8m rather than the $0.5m provided in the financial statements. Auditor's report questions have shown a gradual improvement in recent diets and performance for this question was satisfactory.

Marks are awarded for a discussion of the issue (1 mark), assessment of the materiality of the issue (1 mark), a description of the type of modification (2 marks) and the resultant impact on the auditor's report (1 mark).

It was pleasing to see that more candidates attempted to discuss the issue. In order to be awarded the mark for discussing the issue, candidates needed to not just re-write the fact from the question. Candidates needed to explain that the provision should be \$0.8m rather than the \$0.5m currently provided (½ marks), and that without adjustment provisions would be understated and profit overstated (½ marks).

Unfortunately, some candidates did not correctly calculate materiality as they used the full provision amount of \$0.8m rather than the under provision of \$0.3m. If materiality had been correctly calculated, then ½ marks would have been awarded, with a further ½ marks for the assessment that this was material.

Candidates satisfactorily described the type of modification and the impact on the auditor's report. When considering the type of modification candidates are reminded that no credit is awarded for 'qualified report' or 'the audit report is modified' as it is the opinion rather than the report which has been modified. Some candidates continue to list all possible options in a scatter gun approach as seen in previous diets, which simply wastes their time.

Auditor's reports are a core area of the syllabus and knowledge of the ISAs in this area is imperative.

242 SPINACH *Walk in the footsteps of a top tutor*

Key answer tips

Part (a) requires audit procedures over revenue. The procedures can be a mixture of tests of detail and analytical procedures. Think about the documentation that exists to support the sales transactions. If doing analytical procedures, think about how you can assess the reasonableness of the figure through comparisons, trends and ratios.

Part (b) requires procedures before and during the inventory count. For procedures before the count, think about how you would need to prepare to attend the count. What information would be useful to look at in advance. For procedures performed during the count, remember that the auditor will perform a mixture of tests of controls and substantive procedures. Testing the assertion of existence is the one of the main reasons for attending the count, but the auditor will also obtain evidence over cut-off, completeness and valuation.

Part (c) requires procedures in relation to the issue of share capital. The issue of share capital raises finance for the company so think about the double entry that is used to account for a share issue. In this case, the shares were issued at a premium, therefore, procedures will need to be performed to ensure the premium is calculated correctly and classified correctly.

Part (d) requires knowledge of key audit matters: how the auditor determines the key audit matters to include in the report and the content of the matter to be included in the report. You either know this or you don't. Knowledge requirements such as this test your detailed knowledge of the auditing standards. It is important to spend some of your revision time learning the main requirements of the auditing standards as most constructed response questions will contain a knowledge requirement.

(a) Revenue

- Cast a breakdown of revenue and agree to the general ledger, trial balance and draft financial statements.
- Compare the overall level of revenue against prior year/budget and investigate any significant fluctuations.
- Obtain a breakdown of sales analysed by month and compare this to the prior year/month. Investigate any significant fluctuations.
- Obtain a schedule of sales for the year disaggregated into the main product categories/by type of customer by month and compare this to the prior year breakdown. Discuss any unusual movements with management.
- Perform a proof in total calculation for revenue by taking the prior year revenue and increasing it for the three new product lines launched in February 20X5 and the price rise in line with inflation from September 20X4 and other known factors. This expectation should be compared to actual revenue and any significant fluctuations should be investigated.
- Calculate the gross profit margin for Spinach Co for the year, compare this to the prior year and investigate any significant fluctuations.
- Select a sample of sales invoices for wholesale customers and agree the sales prices back to the price list or customer master data information, noting whether the price was pre or post the price increase, to confirm the accuracy of invoices.
- For a sample of invoices, recalculate invoice totals including any discounts and sales tax.
- Select a sample of credit notes raised, trace through to the original invoice and ensure the invoice has been correctly removed from sales.
- Select a sample of despatch notes and agree these to sales invoices through to inclusion in the detailed sales listing and revenue accounts in the general ledger to confirm completeness of revenue.
- Select a sample of despatch notes both pre and post year end and follow these through to sales invoices in the correct accounting period to ensure that cut-off has been correctly applied.
- Select a sample of website sales made in the final week prior to the year end and where goods were despatched post year end, confirm that the sale proceeds received are recorded as deferred income (contract liability) rather than as revenue.

(b) Inventory count procedures

Before the count

- Review the prior year audit files to identify whether there were any particular warehouses where significant inventory issues arose last year.
- Discuss with management whether any of the warehouses this year are new, whether any significant changes have occurred this year with regards to inventory items or if any warehouses have experienced significant control issues.
- Decide which of the six warehouses the audit team members will attend, basing this on materiality and risk of each site.

- Obtain a copy of the proposed inventory count instructions, review them to identify any control deficiencies and, if any are noted, discuss them with management prior to the counts.
- Discuss with management whether third-party inventory is stored in any of the other warehouses and what the procedures are for ensuring that third-party inventory is omitted from the counts.

During the count

- Observe the counting teams of Spinach Co to confirm whether the inventory count instructions are being followed correctly.
- Select samples of inventory and perform test counts from inventory sheets to physical inventory and from physical inventory to inventory sheets.
- Observe the counts in order to confirm that the procedures for identifying and segregating damaged goods are operating correctly and inspect inventory for evidence of any damaged or slow-moving items.
- Observe the procedures for movements of inventory during the counts, in order to confirm that all movements have ceased.
- Discuss with the internal audit supervisors how any raw materials quantities have been estimated. Where possible, reperform the procedures adopted by the supervisors.
- Obtain a copy of the completed sequentially numbered inventory sheets for follow up testing at the final audit.
- Obtain copies of the last goods received notes (GRNs) and goods despatch notes (GDNs) for 31 July and request copies of GRNs and GDNs raised on 1 August in order to perform cut-off procedures as at the year end.
- Observe the procedures carried out by Spinach Co's staff in identifying third-party inventories are operating correctly and review the completed inventory count sheets to confirm no third-party inventory is included.

(c) Substantive procedures for issue of share capital

- Review board minutes to confirm the number of additional shares issued in May 20X5 and the issue price.
- Agree the issue of shares is permitted from a review of any statutory constitution agreements in place.
- Review legal documentation, correspondence or share issue prospectus to confirm the details of the share issue.
- Agree the issue of new shares to the share register.
- Inspect the bank ledger account and bank statements for evidence of the amount of cash received from the share issue.
- Where the sum received is less than $4.3m, confirm the difference is treated as share capital called up but not paid in the financial statements.
- Recalculate the split of proceeds between the nominal value of shares and premium on issue and agree correctly recorded within share capital and share premium account (other components of equity).
- Review the disclosure of the share issue in the draft financial statements and ensure it is in line with relevant accounting standards and local legislation.

(d) Auditor's report

(i) Factors to consider

As Spinach Co is listed, a key audit matters (KAM) section will be required in the auditor's report. The audit partner would have considered whether the matter was communicated to those charged with governance as KAM are selected from matters communicated to those charged with governance. The audit partner would have also considered the level of risk in relation to the valuation of inventory and, as determining the net realisable value is an accounting estimate, the level of judgement involved. The audit partner would have also considered whether, in their professional judgement, the matters regarding the valuation of inventory were of most significance in the audit of Spinach Co's financial statements for the year ended 31 July 20X5.

(ii) Contents of KAM

The KAM section of the auditor's report should include a reference to the audit risk in relation to the valuation of inventory and the level of judgement required in making this assessment. It should detail why this issue was considered to be an area of significance in the audit and therefore determined to be a KAM. It should also explain how the matter was addressed in the audit and the auditor should provide a brief overview of the audit procedures adopted as well as detailing that a review was undertaken of any related disclosures.

ACCA marking guide

		Marks
(a)	**Substantive procedures for revenue**	
	• Cast a breakdown of revenue and agree to the general ledger, trial balance and draft financial statements	1
	• Compare the overall level of revenue against prior year/budget and investigate any significant fluctuations	1
	• Obtain a breakdown of sales analysed by month and compare this to the prior year/month. Investigate any significant fluctuations	1
	• Compare sales for the year disaggregated into the main product categories/by type of customer by month and to the prior year	1
	• Perform a proof in total calculation for revenue	1
	• Calculate the gross profit margin for the year and compare to the prior year	1
	• For a sample of sales invoices for wholesale customers, agree the sales prices back to the price list or customer master data	1
	• For a sample of invoices, recalculate invoice totals including any discounts and sales tax	1
	• Trace a sample of credit notes through to the original invoice and ensure the invoice has been correctly removed from sales	1
	• Select a sample of despatch notes, agree to sales invoices and into the detailed sales listing and revenue accounts to confirm completeness	1
	• Select a sample of despatch notes and sales invoices pre and post year end to ensure appropriate cut-off	1
	• For a sample of website sales made in the final week prior to the year end and where goods were despatched post year end, confirm the sale proceeds are recorded as deferred income (contract liability)	1
	Restricted to	5

(b)	**Inventory count procedures**	
	Before the count	1
	• Review the prior year audit files to identify issues	1
	• Discuss with management whether any of the warehouses this year are new, whether any significant changes have occurred or if any warehouses have experienced significant control issues	1
	• Decide which warehouses to attend based on materiality and risk	1
	• Obtain and review a copy of the proposed inventory count instructions for control deficiencies	1
	• Discuss with management whether third-party inventory is stored	1
	During the count	1
	• Observe the counting teams to confirm whether the inventory count instructions are being followed correctly	1
	• Select samples of inventory and perform two-way test counts	1
	• Observe the counts to confirm that the procedures for identifying and segregating damaged goods are operating correctly and inspect inventory for evidence of any damaged or slow-moving items	1
	• Observe to confirm that all movements have ceased	1
	• Discuss with the internal audit supervisors how any raw materials quantities have been estimated	1
	• Obtain a copy of the completed sequentially numbered inventory sheets	1
	• Obtain copies of the last goods received notes (GRNs) and goods despatch notes (GDNs) for 31 July and request copies of GRNs and GDNs raised on 1 August in order to perform cut-off procedures	1
	• Observe the procedures for identifying third-party inventories and confirm no third-party inventory is included in the count sheets	1
	Restricted to	**6**
(c)	**Substantive procedures for share capital**	
	• Review board minutes to confirm the number of additional shares issued and the issue price	1
	• Agree the issue of shares is permitted from a review of any statutory constitution agreements in place	1
	• Review legal documentation, correspondence or share issue prospectus to confirm the details of the share issue	1
	• Agree the issue of new shares to the share register	1
	• Inspect the bank ledger account and bank statements for evidence of the amount of cash received from the share issue	1
	• Confirm any unpaid amounts are treated as share capital called up but not paid in the financial statements	1
	• Recalculate the split of proceeds between the nominal value of shares and premium on issue and agree to the financial statements	1
	• Review the disclosure of the share issue in the draft financial statements for compliance with relevant accounting standards and local legislation	1
	Restricted to	**4**
(d)	**Factors/content for key audit matters**	
	• Matters communicated to those charged with governance	1
	• Assessment of risk	1
	• Areas of judgement	1
	• Effect on audit	1
	• Description of issue	1
	• Why determined KAM	1
	• How addressed in audit	1
	Restricted to	**5**
Total		**20**

Examiner's comments

Requirement (a). The scenario for this requirement detailed information about how Spinach Co generates sales to its individual customers via its website, and to wholesale customers through the sales ordering department, with the latter sales on credit. Candidates should then consider why this information has been provided and its relevance. The scenario also details that website sales are paid in full at the point of order and therefore the only receivables would be wholesale customers. The scenario also states that goods are typically despatched seven days after the date of order. Individual website customers are therefore paying in advance of the despatch of goods and at the year end there would be deferred income for any customers who had paid but not had their order despatched by 31 July. Candidates should then have considered substantive procedures to confirm that the cut off of revenue and deferred income is complete and accurate. Additionally, the scenario contained information about inflationary sales price increases and new product lines launched in February 20X5. Candidates should spend time understanding this information and then applying it to generate tailored procedures. Analytical procedures are very useful when auditing revenue and can be used to generate several valid tests. Comparisons can be made between total or monthly revenue and the prior year or budget; a breakdown of key product lines or customers can be compared to the prior year as well as a review of the gross margin for the current and prior year. In all cases however, any significant fluctuations must be investigated, not just identified, and discussed with management. Another useful analytical review procedure is a proof in total where the prior year is adjusted for any known fluctuations in the year such as the new product lines, and then compared to the actual revenue in the year with significant fluctuations investigated. Carefully reading the scenario and question requirement ensures that any procedures listed are tailored and more likely to score marks. Procedures such as casting a breakdown of sales, varied analytical procedures, recalculating sales invoice totals, agreeing sales prices to the authorised price lists and cut-off procedures would all gain credit. Where the question requirement is for revenue then no credit will be awarded for any receivables procedures. In this session it was common to see candidates stray into receivables tests such as 'reviewing after-date cash receipts' and 'considering whether an allowance for receivables was necessary'. Also, where detailed tests were provided, rather than testing to or from the sales listing, incorrect answers focused on the receivables listing when agreeing to sales invoices and goods despatch notes (GDNs). This was not valid and so would not have gained the available 1 mark. Additionally, when listing these types of detailed tests, the key point when the sale should be recognised is when the goods have been despatched and so tests should begin or end with the GDN rather than the sales order. In this session some candidates focused on whether the inflationary price increases had been appropriately applied and whether this was a reasonable benchmark for increasing prices. This is not a concern of the auditor, but rather for management and so would not have gained credit. Care must also be taken not to produce tests of controls such as 'reviewing the board minutes for evidence of the authorisation of the inflationary price increases', as these are not substantive procedures and would not gain any credit. Many candidates suggested 'reviewing disclosure of revenue' however this would not have gained any credit as revenue, along with most profit or loss account balances, does not require disclosure notes. When generating substantive procedures, it is important to ensure the tests have sufficient detail and are clear. For example, 'perform a cut off test' without describing what the actual test is and what documents should be used will not gain any marks. It is important to stress that the source document is GDNs before and after the year end and that these need to be agreed to sales invoices to ensure they have been included in the correct accounting period. If sales invoices had been used as the source document rather than GDNs then only ½ marks would have been awarded.

Requirement (b). In common with part (a) it is important to carefully consider the requirement and review the scenario to understand what issue is being addressed. In this case the scenario indicated that a full year-end inventory count would be undertaken across the company's six warehouses. In addition, the scenario stressed that there would be no significant work in progress (WIP), that third-party inventory is stored at the company's largest warehouse and that there would be no movements of goods in or out of the warehouses during the count. The requirement strictly focused on procedures both before and during the count and although not required, it would be useful to split the procedures into before and then during the count as this helps to ensure a good cross section of points are covered. Unfortunately, many candidates did not carefully read the requirement and therefore listed procedures which would be undertaken after the count on the final audit e.g. 'reviewing aged inventory records for slowing-moving goods' or 'casting inventory records back to the trial balance', these procedures would not gain any credit as they were not addressing the question requirement. Procedures before the count which will gain credit are those which relate to understanding the risks associated with the various warehouses, as the scenario stated that not all six warehouses would be attended by the auditor. Therefore, reviewing the prior year audit files and discussions with management concerning control issues across the sites would gain credit. In addition, inventory count instructions would need to be reviewed in detail to identify whether any control deficiencies may arise, as these would need to be discussed in advance of the count. Candidates who simply stated 'obtain inventory count instructions' would not have gained credit as simply obtaining them is not undertaking an audit procedure, they need to be reviewed. Moving onto during the count it is important to consider the role the auditor is undertaking, which is to test whether the controls over the count are functioning correctly, to obtain information for the final audit such as a copy of the completed inventory count sheets, and for the auditor to undertake detailed testing to confirm the completeness and existence of the inventory records. In testing the controls, a key procedure would be to 'observe the counters to ensure the inventory count instructions are being followed correctly'. Having gained credit for this procedure some candidates then laboured this point by listing various elements of the instructions which should be confirmed e.g. 'observe the counters are flagging inventory once counted'. These candidates listed several procedures surrounding the count process which should be confirmed or observed which did not gain any further marks. In addition, many candidates incorrectly provided statements of what controls should be in place within the count, e.g. 'inventory should be counted in teams of two' would not gain credit as this is not an audit procedure. In this session many candidates did not utilise the scenario correctly. For example, it was stated that WIP was not significant, therefore the auditor would not have focused on auditing this balance, hence no credit was awarded for any WIP procedures. Also, the scenario stated that there was third-party inventory stored in one warehouse and so candidates should have focused on confirming controls over the segregation of these goods from the count. However, many candidates instead focused on Spinach Co holding its goods in other third-party warehouses, which was not alluded to in the scenario at all. It is crucial that candidates read the scenario carefully and do not just focus on individual words.

Requirement (c). The scenario for this requirement was short and simply detailed that shares were issued at a premium in May 20X5. The rationale for the share issue was to purchase a factory, however this is irrelevant for the question requirement, which focused on the share issue itself. Focusing on whether the factory was purchased or auditing this purchase in any way would not gain credit as it is not answering the question asked. In considering where to start, it is useful to consider the accounting for the share issue as this then provides areas to audit. The share issue would have generated cash proceeds and as the issue was at a premium the share capital and share premium accounts would have been credited. Therefore, procedures which 'inspected the bank ledger account or bank statements for evidence of the share issue proceeds of $4.3m' would have gained credit. Also, the shares would need to be recorded within share capital at nominal value, therefore 'agreeing the issue of the shares to the share register'. The premium would need to be recorded in the share premium account, hence 'recalculating the split of the proceeds and agreeing to the share capital and share premium accounts' are all procedures would each have gained 1 mark each. Other straightforward procedures which gained credit included 'reviewing the disclosure of the share issue in the financial statements', 'agreeing the share issue details to relevant documentation such as share issue prospectus' and 'reviewing board minutes to confirm the number of shares issued and the issue price'. Common incorrect procedures included 'analytical review of the share capital to the prior year' which is pointless as we know the balance has changed over the year. 'Reviewing the board minutes to confirm the issue of shares was authorised' is a test of control and so does not gain credit. 'Obtaining a written representation over the share issue' would also not be relevant as requesting written representation should be restricted to areas where the auditor is relying on management's judgement or there is little independent evidence available. This is not the case with an issue of share capital.

Requirement (d). Although audit reports feature regularly in the AA exam, there are several ways in which they can be tested, and candidates must be prepared for any type of question on audit reports. For this session 5 marks were awarded for the factors to be considered and for the contents of the KAM section. The starting point with this type of requirement is to consider what knowledge a candidate has with regards to ISA 701 *Communicating Key Audit Matters in the Independent Auditor's Report*. Knowledge of this standard will help in considering what influences the decision as to whether an issue is a KAM or not. Although the scenario related to the valuation of inventory, knowledge marks could be easily obtained without reference to the scenario. Candidates should focus on three to four points that the engagement partner would consider. Such as the level of risk relating to this issue, whether it would be reported to those charged with governance, the significance of the matter and the level of judgement required in forming a conclusion on the truth and fairness of this issue. The next step would be to move onto the content of the KAM section of the audit report. Here candidates should consider reporting WHAT the issue is – that there was a risk over the valuation of inventory. WHY the issue is considered a KAM – due to the fact it was high risk with significant auditor judgement required. HOW the issue was addressed during the audit – with details of audit procedures adopted along with a review of the disclosures. One point for each of these three would have been sufficient to maximise the available marks. The model answer shows the key points which should be included for each of these three. This session it was pleasing to see that some candidates had revised the area of KAM. These candidates were generally able to consider factors in determining if the issue was a KAM but struggled with the contents. Some candidates incorrectly assumed they needed to attempt to draft the KAM paragraph rather than just describing its content. Other common incorrect answers attempted to answer this question as if it related to a modified audit opinion. It is important to revise all audit report options and not to simply assume that the focus of the question will contain a modified opinion. Auditor's reports are a core area of the syllabus and knowledge of the ISAs in this area is imperative.

243 DANUBE *Walk in the footsteps of a top tutor*

Key answer tips

Part (a) requires audit procedures over land and buildings. The land and buildings have been revalued during the year therefore procedures must focus on this aspect and whether the relevant accounting standard has been followed with regard to revaluations.

Part (b) requires the additional audit procedures necessary when exceptions arise from a receivables circularisation. The auditor still needs to obtain evidence in respect of these balances so think about alternative procedures that can be performed.

Part (c) requires procedures over the provision and the receivable arising from the sale of defective goods. This requires application of the requirements of IAS 37 in relation to provisions and contingent assets. Procedures must focus on whether the requirements of the standard have been met.

Part (d) requires knowledge of key audit matters: how the auditor determines the key audit matters to include in the report and the content of the matter to be included in the report.

(a) Land and buildings

- Obtain a schedule of all land and buildings, cast and agree to the trial balance and financial statements.
- Consider the competence and capability of the valuer, by assessing through enquiry their qualification, membership of a professional body and experience in valuing these types of assets.
- Review the assumptions and method adopted by the valuer in undertaking the revaluation to confirm the reasonableness and compliance with principles of IAS 16.
- Agree the schedule of revalued land and buildings to the valuation statement provided by the valuer and to the non-current asset register.
- Agree all land and buildings on the non-current asset register to the valuation report to ensure completeness of the land and buildings valued to ensure all assets in the same category have been revalued in line with IAS 16.
- Recalculate the total revaluation adjustment and agree correctly recorded in the revaluation surplus.
- Recalculate the depreciation charge for the year and confirm that for assets revalued at July 20X4, the depreciation was based on cost before the revaluation and based on the valuation after on a pro rata basis.
- For a sample of land and buildings from the non-current asset register, physically verify to confirm existence.
- For a sample of land and buildings trace back to the non-current asset register and general ledger to confirm completeness.
- Review the financial statements disclosures relating to land and buildings to ensure they comply with IAS 16.

(b) Exceptions in the trade receivables circularisation

Nile Co

- For the non-response from Nile Co, with the client's permission, the team should arrange to send a follow-up confirmation request.
- If Nile Co does not respond to the follow up, then with the client's permission, the auditor should telephone the customer and ask whether they are able to respond in writing to the confirmation request.
- If there is still no response, then the auditor should undertake alternative procedures to confirm the balance owing from Nile Co. These would include detailed testing of the balance by a review of after-date cash receipts and agreeing to sales invoices and goods despatch notes (GDN).

Congo Co

- For the response from Congo Co the auditor should investigate the difference of $14,132, and identify whether this relates to timing differences or whether there are possible errors in the records of Danube Co.
- If the difference is due to timing, such as cash in transit, details of the difference should be agreed to post-year-end cash receipts in the bank ledger account.
- If the difference relates to goods in transit, then details should be agreed to a pre-year-end GDN.
- The list of individual customer balances should be reviewed to identify any possible mispostings as this could be a reason for the difference with Congo Co.

(c) Provision and receivable arising from the sale of defective goods

- Review the correspondence with Kalama Kids Co and establish the details of the claim to assess whether a present obligation as a result of a past event has occurred.
- Review correspondence with Thames Co, the supplier of the hoverboards, to assess whether they accept liability for the defect.
- Review correspondence with Danube Co's legal advisers or, with the client's permission, contact the legal advisers to obtain their view as to the probability of either the legal claim from the customer and the request for reimbursement from the supplier being successful as well as any likely amounts to be paid or received.
- Discuss with management/enquire of the legal adviser as to whether any other customers of Danube Co have experienced problems with sales of hoverboards and therefore the likelihood of any potential future claims.
- Review board minutes to establish whether the directors believe that either claim will be successful or not.
- Review the post-year-end bank ledger account to assess whether any payments have been made to the customer or cash received from the supplier and compare with the amounts recognised in the financial statements.
- Discuss with management why they have included a receivable for the claim against the supplier as this is possibly a contingent asset and should only be recognised as an asset if the receipt of cash is virtually certain. Consider the reasonableness of the proposed treatment.

- Obtain a written representation confirming management's view that the lawsuit by Kalama Kids Co is likely to be successful and the claim against Thames Co is virtually certain and hence a provision and a receivable are required to be included.
- Review the adequacy of the disclosures of the lawsuit and supplier claim in the draft financial statements to ensure they are in accordance with IAS 37.

(d) (i) Factors to consider

As Danube Co is listed, a Key Audit Matters (KAM) section will be required in the auditor's report. The audit partner would have considered whether the matter was communicated to those charged with governance as KAM are selected from matters communicated with those charged with governance. The audit partner would also have considered whether the issue relating to the claims was an area of higher assessed risk of material misstatement or a significant risk and as it is an accounting estimate the level of judgement involved. The audit partner will have also considered whether, in their professional judgement, the matters regarding the claim and counter-claim were of most significance in the audit of Danube Co's financial statements for the year ended 31 March 20X5 therefore requiring significant auditor attention.

(ii) Contents of KAM section

The KAM section of the auditor's report should provide a description of the issue. It should detail why this issue was considered to be an area of most significance in the audit and therefore determined to be a KAM. It would include a reference to the audit risk of completeness of the provision and recognition of the receivable and the level of judgement required in making this assessment. It should also explain how the matter was addressed in the audit and the auditor should provide a brief overview of the audit procedures adopted as well as making a reference to any related disclosures.

ACCA marking guide

		Marks
(a)	**Substantive procedures for land and buildings**	
	1 mark per well-described procedure	
	Restricted to	**6**
(b)	**Procedures in relation to the trade receivables circularisation exceptions**	
	Nile Co	2
	Congo Co	2
	Restricted to	**4**
(c)	**Substantive procedures for provision and receivable arising from the sale of defective goods**	
	1 mark per well-described procedure	
	Restricted to	**5**
(d)	**Key audit matters**	
	Matter communicated to those charged with governance	1
	Assessment of risk	1
	Areas of judgement	1
	Effect on audit	1
	Description of issue	1
	Why determined KAM	1
	How addressed in audit	1
	Restricted to	**5**
Total		**20**

Examiner's comments

1 mark is available for each well-explained procedure. Candidates must strive to understand substantive procedures and apply good exam technique. This includes tailoring procedures to the specific requirements of the question. Additionally, tests must be sufficiently detailed noting clearly which source document should be used. For example, tests such as 'review disclosures' would only score ½ mark. To score a full mark the procedure should go on to say 'in accordance with accounting standards/relevant legislation.' Also, recommending 'obtain a written representation' without explaining what for will not generate any marks.

Requirement (a). The scenario for this requirement detailed that the company had changed its accounting policy for land and buildings from the cost model to the revaluation model and that a revaluation of all land and buildings had taken place during the year. As is the case for Danube Co, it is important to consider what issue the scenario focuses on when looking at the question requirement. Here, the revaluation is an important factor. In other cases, the focus is provided in the requirement. For example, the question requirements can ask for procedures which relate to specific assertions such as valuation or completeness. Where this is the case, care must be taken to ensure that any substantive procedures listed only relate to this assertion.

Spending time understanding the issue and carefully reading the question requirement ensures that any procedures listed are tailored and more likely to score marks. As the requirement was for land and buildings then the procedures need to focus on this specific category of property, plant and equipment (PPE) rather than focusing on all types of PPE.

Procedures such as agreeing the revaluation to a valuation report and considering the independence and experience of the valuer would gain credit. However, also note that more straightforward procedures such as casting the schedule of land and buildings, recalculating depreciation and physically verifying the land and buildings would also have been relevant.

Care must also be taken when requesting written representations. These should be restricted to areas where the auditor is relying on management's judgement or there is little independent evidence available.

When generating substantive procedures, it is important to ensure the tests have sufficient detail and are clear. For example, 'recalculate the depreciation' would be awarded ½ mark. For the full mark candidates should make some reference to the basis of the calculation. An appropriate response would be to add 'and confirm depreciation is based on the correct valuation/pro rata'.

Requirement (b). In common with part (a) it is important to carefully consider the requirement and review the scenario to understand what issue is being addressed. In this case the scenario indicated that a receivables circularisation had been undertaken and two customer accounts, Nile Co and Congo Co, had exceptions. Nile Co had not responded and Congo Co had confirmed a balance lower than the balance contained within Danube Co's receivables listing.

The substantive procedures which will gain credit are those which are targeted on resolving the exceptions. In tackling this requirement, it is important to note that there are four marks available for two exceptions, therefore each exception relates to two marks and two detailed procedures per exception would be required to maximise marks. Information regarding the mark split was provided in a note to the requirement.

In approaching this question candidates should consider what circumstances could have given rise to each exception and suggest procedures to address this. In the case of Nile Co, as no response has been received then the logical first step would be to 'send a follow up confirmation request with the client's permission.' If no response is received, then candidates should consider what alternative procedures could be adopted, such as 'review after-date cash receipts to confirm the year-end receivable,' to gain the other available mark.

For Congo Co the issue relates to a difference of $14,132. Candidates need to consider why the customer would have a lower sum owing than Danube Co has recorded. The two most logical reasons would be due to cash in transit at the year end from Congo Co to Danube Co or due to goods in transit from Danube Co to Congo Co. One audit procedure to test each of these reasons would result in two marks. In generating tests for in transit items it is important to list exactly what records will be reviewed and whether these are before or after the year end. Failing to be specific would result in full marks not being awarded. Candidates need to be clear that for cash in transit, the post-year-end bank ledger account would be reviewed and for goods in transit, the pre-year-end goods despatch notes would be tested.

Requirement (c). Good exam technique is important for a requirement like this. The scenario for this requirement detailed that Danube Co had sold some hoverboards to a customer and it was alleged that these were faulty and the customer was therefore suing Danube Co. However, Danube Co was counter claiming against its supplier that had supplied the hoverboards. Therefore, a provision for the claim from the customer and a receivable for the counter claim on the supplier were recognised in the draft financial statements. It is important to consider how the issue in the scenario links to the question requirement. In this case the requirement clearly relates only to the provision and receivable and so candidates should only provide substantive procedures for these two balances.

A significant minority of candidates also provided tests relating to the defective inventory of hoverboards. However, the scenario clearly stated there were no hoverboards in inventory at the year end and the question requirement only related to the provision and receivable. Candidates must carefully read the information in the question and tailor their answers accordingly.

While some knowledge of accounting for legal claims would have been helpful the key here is to think logically. It is possible to produce a good answer by thinking through the issues which are relevant for any provision, for example whether it should be recognised and if so, at what amount. Procedures can then be designed to address these issues using the information from the scenario to add detail.

Procedures which gained credit in this session included 'reviewing customer/supplier correspondence', 'reviewing the post-year-end bank ledger account for payments made/received and agreeing this to the financial statements' and 'obtaining written representations on management's view of the outcome of each of the claims.' The most common incorrect procedure, other than those relating to inventory, was 'to recalculate the provision.' For a single claim/counter claim this would not be appropriate as there is nothing to calculate.

Requirement (d). Although auditors' reports feature regularly in the AA exam, there are several ways in which they can be examined, and candidates must be prepared for a range of question types on auditor's reports. For this session the requirement for 5 marks tested the factors to be considered when determining KAM and the contents of the KAM section.

The starting point with this type of requirement is to consider what knowledge a candidate has with regards to ISA 701 *Communicating Key Audit Matters in the Independent Auditor's Report*. Knowledge of this standard will help in considering what influences the decision as to whether an issue is a KAM or not. Although the scenario related to the provision and receivable from the sale of defective goods, many of the marks available could be obtained for stating basic points derived from the ISA. Candidates should be reminded of the importance of being familiar with all of the ISAs relevant to section E of the syllabus.

Based on the marks available, candidates should focus on two to three points that the engagement partner would consider. These would include the level of risk relating to this issue, whether it would be reported to those charged with governance and the level of judgement involved.

The next step would be to move onto the content of the KAM section of the auditor's report. Here candidates should consider reporting WHAT the issue is, WHY the issue is considered a KAM and HOW the issue was addressed during the audit. One point for each of these three would have been sufficient to maximise the available marks for this part.

This session it was clear that many candidates had not revised the area of KAM and as a result were unable to tackle this question requirement. Common incorrect answers attempted to answer this question as if it related to a modified audit opinion. It is important to revise all aspects of auditors' reports included in the syllabus and candidates should not simply assume that the focus of the question will be a modified opinion.

244 PURRFECT CO *Walk in the footsteps of a top tutor*

Key answer tips

Part (a) requires audit procedures over inventory valuation. There will be no marks awarded for procedures which focus on other assertions such as existence. Focus on the valuation rules as given in the relevant accounting standard.

Part (b) requires audit procedures in relation to a specific receivable balance. Design procedures which provide evidence that the customer is likely to pay the outstanding balance.

Part (c) requires audit procedures over legal claims. The claim must be accounted for in accordance with the relevant accounting standard therefore procedures should focus on obtaining evidence to confirm that this is the case.

Part (d) asks for the audit reporting implications if the issue is unresolved. First you should discuss what the issue is i.e. what the client has done wrong. Calculate whether the adjustment required is material. If the issue is not material it won't impact the auditor's report. If it is material consider whether it is material and pervasive as this will impact the type of opinion that should be given. Remember to include the key wording of the opinion you are suggesting as well as any other impact on the auditor's report.

(a) Inventory of Vego Dog

- Obtain and cast the inventory listing of Vego Dog products and agree the total cost of $2.4m to inventory records.
- Agree the quantity of Vego Dog products shown as held at the year end to the year-end inventory count records.
- Request a breakdown of the cost calculation of each unit of this product and discuss with management how the standard cost was derived.
- Recalculate the cost calculations to confirm that the quantity multiplied by the standard cost is $2.4m.
- For a sample of finished goods items, obtain standard cost cards and agree:
  - raw material costs to recent purchase invoices
  - labour costs to time sheets or wage records

  - overheads allocated to invoices and that they are of a production nature.

- Compare sales prices over time to establish if the price has been reduced because of falling demand to determine whether an allowance is required.

- Compare actual sales units per month to budgeted sales per month from before and after the year end to establish how much lower actual sales are than expected and discuss with management.

- Select a sample of items included in inventory of Vego Dog and review post-year-end sales invoices to ascertain if net realisable value (NRV) is above cost or if an adjustment is required.

(b) Receivable due from Ellah Co

- Review correspondence with Ellah Co to establish if there was a discussion about payment difficulties and whether Ellah Co intends to fully settle the outstanding amount.

- Review the age of the outstanding debt with Ellah Co and discuss the circumstances with the credit controller to establish if it has exceeded the agreed credit terms and consider if an allowance is required.

- Review post-year-end receipts from Ellah Co to establish how much of the debt was recovered by the audit completion date and to assess how much of the year-end balance remains outstanding.

- Inspect board minutes to identify whether there are any significant concerns in relation to payments by Ellah Co.

- Discuss with management of Purrfect Co why no allowance has been made in respect of this debt and assess the justification.

(c) Contamination – legal claims

- Review customer correspondence to establish the details of the claims and the amounts being claimed.

- Review correspondence with Purrfect Co's lawyers or, with the client's permission, contact the lawyers to establish the likely outcome of the customer claims made to date.

- Discuss with the lawyers the likelihood and amount of potential future claims.

- Inspect board minutes to establish details of the circumstances of the contamination and to ascertain management's view as to the likelihood that the existing claims will be successful and the extent of possible future claims.

- Compare levels of returns and claims to date against sales volumes of the product to assess the potential level of future claims.

- Review post-year-end payments for damage settlements and compare with any amounts provided at the year end to assess the reasonableness of the provision.

- Obtain written representations from management that there have been no other contamination incidents and no other product liability claims of which management are aware and for which provision may be required.

- Review the draft financial statements to establish that the legal claims have been appropriately provided for or disclosed in accordance with IAS 37 *Provisions, Contingent Liabilities and Contingent Assets*.

(d) Issue and impact on auditor's report

According to IAS 37, the possibility of additional claims should be disclosed as a contingent liability as it is possible but not probable and quantifiable.

As the claims may be significant, this issue represents a matter which is fundamental to users' understanding of the financial statements. The impact on the auditor's report depends on whether this matter is deemed to be adequately disclosed in the financial statements.

Adequate disclosure

If Purrfect Co adequately discloses the issue, then an unmodified audit opinion should be given but the auditor's report should include an emphasis of matter paragraph. This would draw attention to the disclosure in the financial statements by cross-referencing the user to the note in the financial statements which discloses the possible claims, emphasising that the audit opinion is unmodified.

Inadequate disclosure

If there is no disclosure in the financial statements or the disclosure is considered to be inadequate, then this indicates that the financial statements are materially misstated. As this lack of adequate disclosure is likely to be material but not pervasive, then a qualified opinion will be given. A basis for qualified opinion paragraph will be added to the auditor's report discussing the matter and the opinion paragraph will be modified to state that 'except for' the failure to adequately disclose the matter, the financial statements give a true and fair view.

ACCA marking guide

			Marks
(a)	**Substantive procedures for inventory of Vego Dog**		
	1 mark per well-described procedure		
		Restricted to	**6**
(b)	**Substantive procedures for receivable due from Ellah Co**		
	1 mark per well-described procedure		
		Restricted to	**4**
(c)	**Substantive procedures for contamination – legal claims**		
	1 mark per well-described procedure		
		Restricted to	**5**
(d)	**Issue and impact on auditor's report**		
	Discussion of issue		1
	Adequate disclosure		2
	Inadequate disclosure		2
			5
Total			**20**

Examiner's comments

Parts (a) – (c) examine substantive procedures for inventory valuation, receivables and legal claims. 1 mark is available for each well-explained procedure therefore candidates should aim to produce six tests for requirement (a), four for (b) and five for (c). Candidates must think carefully about applying good exam technique. This includes tailoring procedures to the specific requirements of the question. Additionally, tests must be sufficiently detailed noting clearly which source document should be used. For example, tests such as 'review disclosures' would only score ½ mark. To score a full mark the procedure should go on to say, 'in accordance with accounting standards/relevant legislation'. Also recommending that the auditor should 'obtain a written representation' without explaining what for, will not generate any marks.

Part (a). The scenario for this requirement detailed that a new product line had been launched in the year, but sales were lower than expected and there is a material amount of finished goods in inventory at the year end. One of the key words in requirement (a) is 'valuation' and combined with the scenario it is clear that the substantive procedures must focus on whether the inventory of this specific product line is overvalued at the year end. Also, it is important to have noted that the inventory was all finished goods. Therefore, any tests relating to work in progress (WIP) would not be relevant. Spending time understanding the issue and carefully reading the question requirement ensures that any procedures listed are tailored and therefore more likely to score marks. As the requirement asks for procedures relating to valuation specifically then the procedures need to focus on confirming the cost of the inventory, confirming the net realisable value (NRV) and considering whether any write down or allowance is required. Additionally, any other procedures which might flag that this new product line is overvalued would also gain credit. It is also important to appreciate that the requirement only relates to the Vego Dog product line, therefore any general inventory wide procedures are not relevant. This clearly highlights the need to tailor tests to the specifics of the scenario and requirement rather than producing lists of rote-learned procedures. In this session however, many candidates included procedures which did not address the specifics of the scenario or the requirement. Many included procedures relating to WIP such as 'recalculate WIP based on stage of completion,' 'discuss the basis of the WIP with management', or procedures which would have been carried out at the inventory count. Similarly, 'review the disclosure of this inventory in the financial statements' would not have gained credit as it does not provide evidence relating to valuation. When generating the substantive procedures for valuation a logical approach would be to firstly consider how to verify cost and then how to assess the NRV. Well-described procedures relating to the standard cost include; 'agreeing the material costs to recent purchase invoices,' 'agreeing labour costs to payroll or wage records' and 'reviewing the nature of the overheads allocated to ensure they are production related'. To establish NRV 'reviewing a sample of post-year-end invoices for this product line to assess if the NRV is above cost' would be a suitable response. When considering NRV it is important to ensure that the tests provided are focused and detailed, as procedures such as 'confirm inventory is valued at lower of cost and NRV' will not gain credit as there are no details as to how this confirmation will occur or how the evidence is obtained. Candidates must ensure that they can distinguish between a substantive procedure and a test of control. Many candidates lose marks in this type of requirement by mixing up these procedures. For example, in this session some candidates provided tests of controls which would be undertaken when attending the inventory count, rather than providing substantive procedures for valuation.

Part (b). In common with part (a) it is important to carefully consider the requirement. Although substantive procedures for receivables are required, this question only relates to one receivable balance which is owing from a customer, Ellah Co. A review of the scenario reinforces that Ellah Co is struggling and is therefore less likely to be able to pay the sum of $2.6m owing. The substantive procedures which will gain credit are those which are targeted on confirming whether Ellah Co is likely to, or has, paid any of the sum owing. Therefore, any general receivable procedures which relate to all receivables would not gain credit. For example, 'calculate receivable collection period and compare to the prior year and investigate any significant differences,' and 'reviewing the disclosure in the financial statements' are procedures relevant for receivables as a whole as opposed to addressing the issues relating to Ellah Co. Procedures which can confirm whether Ellah Co has paid any of the sums owing, such as after-date cash receipts testing and comparison to the sum now owing would gain credit, as well as reviewing correspondence with Ellah Co, evidence obtained through discussions with management or reviewing of board minutes. However, the level of detail included is important, as 'discuss with management' with little detail of what is being discussed would have gained no credit. To gain the 1 mark available it needs to be clear what is being discussed and that this is relevant to the receivable due from Ellah Co.

Part (c). Good exam technique is important for a requirement like this. While some knowledge of accounting for legal claims would have been helpful the key here is to think logically. It is possible to produce a good answer by thinking through the issues which are relevant for any provision, for example whether it should be recognised and if so, at what amount.

Procedures can then be designed to address these issues using the information from the scenario to add detail. For example, the information provides a sum of $1.9m for claims to date. Agreement of these to relevant supporting claims/documentation would form the basis of an appropriate test. Other procedures which gained credit in this session included casting the provision, reviewing customer correspondence, contacting the lawyers to establish the likely outcome of the claims reviewing the disclosures for compliance with IAS 37/accounting standards and agreeing the provision to the financial statements. Careful thought should be given to the nature of the legal claims and the context of the scenario. It is clear from the scenario that the amount of $1.9m only relates to claims received by the year end, however due to the nature of the circumstances it is possible that further claims relating to goods sold pre year end would arise. Therefore, appropriate substantive procedures would include those which provide evidence as to whether the provision is complete. Additionally, some candidates did not consider the 'one-off' nature of this claim and therefore suggested 'comparing the provision for the current year to the prior year'. This is unlikely to provide useful evidence as it is unlikely the company had a similar claim in the prior year. Candidates must carefully read the information in the question and tailor their answers accordingly.

Part (d). There are several ways in which auditors' reports can be examined, and candidates must be prepared for a range of question types on this area of the syllabus. For this requirement marks are awarded for a discussion of the issue (1 mark), and the impact on the auditor's report of adequate disclosure (2 marks) and inadequate disclosure (2 marks).

The starting point with this type of requirement is to identify the issue. This should be relatively straightforward as the details will be provided in the additional information. In this case the issue presented relates to whether the contingent liability for future contamination legal claims has been adequately disclosed in the financial statements. Many candidates still do not attempt this part and therefore cannot be awarded the 1 mark available for this. In order to be awarded the mark for discussing the issue however, candidates should not just re-write the fact from the question but need to explain what the impact is. In this case this would include an explanation that the contingent liability should be disclosed as it is a possible obligation (½ mark) and that the effect on the auditor's report depends on the adequacy of the disclosure (½ mark).

In this requirement there is no need to consider materiality as no financial data has been provided in the scenario and the information states that the engagement partner has confirmed that the contingent liability requires disclosure, therefore the accounting treatment has been agreed.

The question then requires candidates to consider the impact on the auditor's report of adequate and inadequate disclosure. Therefore, answers should be clearly split into two parts. In this session candidates that structured their answers in this way generated more relevant answers and ensured that they considered both aspects of the requirement. Those who did not clearly address the two outcomes separately often failed to consider the impact of adequate disclosure or produced answers where it was not clear which aspect of the requirement was being answered. If the contingent liability has been adequately disclosed, then the key point is that the auditor's report would contain an unmodified opinion as the financial statements are true and fair. However, candidates should also consider whether any additional information would be required in the auditor's report. If this issue is fundamental to users understanding, then an emphasis of matter paragraph which is cross referenced to the notes in the financial statements would be necessary.

If the opinion is to be modified, the type of modified opinion which is appropriate should be identified (i.e. qualified opinion, adverse opinion, disclaimer of opinion) and whether this is due to a material misstatement or due to an inability to obtain sufficient and appropriate audit evidence.

In respect of Purrfect Co if the disclosure is inadequate then there is a material misstatement which is likely to be material not pervasive and therefore a qualified opinion is appropriate. It should also be remembered that a modified opinion will affect the basis for opinion paragraph. For example, it will include an explanation of why the opinion is modified. The sample answer shows the key points which should be included.

Auditors' reports are a core area of the syllabus. Knowledge of the ISAs in this area is imperative and candidates must ensure that they are familiar with, and use the terminology as set out in the ISAs.

245 SAGITTARII & CO *Walk in the footsteps of a top tutor*

Key answer tips

Part (a) requires audit procedures over income. Use the scenario to identify the types of income received and devise procedures to obtain evidence for each type. Remember that substantive procedures include analytical procedures as well as tests of detail.

Part (b) requires audit procedures in relation to a restructuring provision. The provision must be accounted for in accordance with the relevant financial reporting standard therefore procedures should focus on obtaining evidence that this is the case.

Part (c) requires audit procedures over the bank loan. Think about the different supporting documentation that should be available for the initial loan and the loan liability at the year end.

Part (d) asks for the audit reporting implications if the issue is unresolved. First you should discuss what the issue is i.e. what the client has done wrong. Calculate whether the adjustment required is material. If the issue is not material it won't impact the auditor's report. If it is material consider whether it is material and pervasive as this will impact the type of opinion that should be given. Remember to include the key wording of the opinion you are suggesting as well as any other impact on the auditor's report.

(a) Substantive procedures for Vega Vista Co's income

- Obtain a schedule of all Vega Vista C o's income and cast to confirm completeness and accuracy of the balance and agree to the trial balance.
- Compare the individual categories of income of festival ticket sales, sundry sales and donations against prior years and investigate any significant differences.
- For the annual festival, construct a proof-in-total calculation of the number of tickets sold, approximately 15,000, multiplied by the ticket price of $35. Compare this to the income recorded and discuss any significant differences with management.
- For tickets sold on the day of the festival reconcile from ticket stubs the number of tickets sold multiplied by $35 and agree these sales to cash banked in the bank statement.
- Discuss with management their procedures for ensuring advance ticket sales for the September 20X5 festival are excluded from income and instead recognised as deferred income in the statement of financial position.
- Select a sample of advance ticket sales made online, agree that the transaction has been excluded from current year income and follow through to inclusion in deferred income.
- Agree journal entry to transfer prior year deferred income relating to the 20X4 festival to current year income to the ledger and agree figures to prior year financial statements.

- For sundry sales, obtain a breakdown of the income received per stall and agree to supporting documentation provided by each stall holder. Recalculate the fixed percentage received is as per the agreement/contract made with Vega Vista Co.
- Compare sundry sales per stall holder to prior year sales data and investigate any significant differences.
- For monthly donations, trace a sample of donations from sign up documentation to the bank statements, bank ledger account and income listing to ensure that they are recorded completely and accurately.
- For a sample of new donors in the year, agree the monthly sum and start date from their completed forms and trace to the monthly donations received account and agree to the bank ledger account and bank statements.

(b) Substantive procedures for Canopus Co's restructuring provision

- Cast the breakdown of the restructuring provision to ensure it is correctly calculated and agree the total to the trial balance.
- Review the board minutes where the decision to restructure the production process was taken and confirm the decision was made in March 20X5.
- Review the announcement to shareholders and employees in late March, to confirm that this was announced before the year end.
- Obtain a breakdown of the restructuring provision and confirm that only direct expenditure relating to the restructuring is included.
- Review the expenditure to confirm that there are no retraining costs of existing staff included.
- For the costs included within the provision, including acquisitions of plant and machinery, agree to supporting documentation, such as purchase invoices, to confirm validity and value of items included.
- Review post-year-end payments/invoices relating to the expenditure and compare the actual costs incurred to the amounts provided to assess whether the amount of the provision is reasonable.
- Obtain a written representation confirming management discussions in relation to the announcement of the restructuring and to confirm the completeness of the provision.
- Review the adequacy of the disclosures of the restructuring provision in the financial statements and assess whether these are in accordance with IAS 37 *Provisions, Contingent Liabilities and Contingent Assets.*

(c) Substantive procedures for Canopus Co's bank loans

- Obtain a schedule of opening and closing loans detailing any changes during the year. Cast the schedule to confirm its accuracy and agree the closing balances to the trial balance and draft financial statements.
- For the new loan taken out in the year, review the loan agreement to confirm the amount borrowed, the repayment terms and the interest rate applicable.
- For the new loan taken out in the year, agree the loan proceeds of $4.8 million per the loan agreement to the bank ledger account and bank statements.
- For loans repaid, agree the final settlement amount per bank correspondence to payments out during the year in the bank ledger account and bank statements.
- Agree the quarterly repayment of the new loan of $150,000 paid on 31 March 20X5 to the bank ledger account and bank statement.

- Recalculate the split of the loan repayment made on 31 March 20X5 between interest and principal, recalculate interest and agree to inclusion in statement of profit or loss, and outstanding loan balance reduced by principal amount repaid.
- Review the bank correspondence and loan agreements for confirmation of any early settlement charges incurred on the loans repaid. Agree that these were charged to the statement of profit or loss as a finance charge.
- Obtain direct confirmation at the year end from the loan provider of the outstanding balances and any security provided. Agree confirmed amounts to the loans schedule.
- Review all loan agreements for details of covenants and recalculate all covenants to identify any potential or actual breaches.
- Review the disclosure of non-current liabilities in the draft financial statements, including any security provided and assess whether these are in accordance with accounting standards and local legislation. Additionally, confirm that the split of current and non-current loans in the financial statements is correct.

(d) Impact on auditor's report

The restructuring provision of $2.1 million includes $270,000 of costs which do not meet the criteria for inclusion as per IAS 37 *Provisions, Contingent Liabilities and Contingent Assets*. Hence by including this amount the provision and expenses for this year are overstated and profits understated.

The error is material as it represents 2.3% of total equity and liabilities/ total assets (0.27m/11.6m) and hence the finance director should adjust the financial statements by removing this cost from the provision and instead expensing it to profit or loss as it is incurred. The argument that the provision is judgemental and has been deemed reasonable by the board is not valid. IAS 37 has strict criteria for what can and cannot be included within a restructuring provision. For example, training costs for existing staff must be specifically excluded.

If the finance director refuses to amend this error the audit opinion will be modified due to a material misstatement. As management has not complied with IAS 37 and the error is material but not pervasive, a qualified opinion would be appropriate.

A basis for qualified opinion paragraph would be included after the opinion paragraph and would explain the material misstatement in relation to the incorrect treatment of the restructuring provision and the effect on the financial statements. The opinion paragraph would be qualified 'except for'.

ACCA marking guide			
			Marks
(a)	**Substantive procedures for income** 1 mark per well-described procedure		
		Restricted to	5
(b)	**Substantive procedures for restructuring provision** 1 mark per well-described procedure		
		Restricted to	5
(c)	**Substantive procedures for bank loans** 1 mark per well-described procedure		
		Restricted to	5

(d)	**Issue and impact on auditor's report**	
	Discussion of issue	1
	Materiality calculation and assessment	1
	Type of modification required	2
	Impact on auditor's report	1
		5
Total		**20**

Examiner's comments

Parts (a) – (c) examine substantive procedures for income, restructuring provisions and bank loans. Each requirement is for 5 marks so time allocation should be evenly split. One mark is available for each well-explained procedure therefore candidates should aim to produce five tests for each requirement. Candidates must strive to understand substantive procedures and apply good exam technique. This includes tailoring procedures to the specific requirements of the question. Additionally, tests must be sufficiently detailed noting clearly which source document should be used. For example, tests such as 'review disclosures' would only score ½ mark. To score a full mark the procedure should go on to say, 'in accordance with accounting standards/relevant legislation'. Also recommending 'obtain a written representation' without explaining what for, will not generate any marks.

Part (a). The key point to note for this requirement is the nature of the entity and the balance being audited as this will have an impact on the type of procedures which will be performed. This question requires substantive procedures in relation to income for a not for profit charity. The charity's main sources of income are donations and ticket sales for charity events therefore testing sales invoices and goods despatch notes which may be valid in other circumstances, would not be relevant. This clearly highlights the need to tailor tests to the specifics of the scenario rather than producing lists of rote-learned procedures. In this session however, many candidates included procedures such as; 'agreeing to sales invoices and goods despatch notes (GDN)' and 'cut-off procedures of GDNs around the year end'. These procedures would not have gained credit as they were not relevant for the charity described in the scenario. Analytical procedures are an important source of evidence when auditing revenue and there are a number of examples which would be relevant in this case for example, comparison of different categories of income with the prior year and investigation of any significant differences. Note should be taken of the details provided in the scenario. In this question, information is given about the sale price of tickets for the festival and the approximate number of people expected to attend. This information can be used to describe a detailed proof in total procedure.

Careful thought should be given as to why information has been included in the question and how it can be used to make procedures as specific as possible. The scenario also suggests that completeness and cut-off of income are key risks. Again, this information is there to help, trying to encourage candidates to think about these assertions and focus their procedures accordingly. The treatment of the advance ticket sales by Vega Vista Co would be a key consideration for the auditor to confirm that the income has been recorded in the relevant accounting period. Candidates must ensure that they can distinguish between a substantive procedure and a test of control. Many candidates lose marks in this type of requirement by mixing up these procedures. For example, in this session some candidates provided test of controls such as 'observing the cash collection at the festival.' The purpose of the observation is to ensure that the controls over the cash collection are operating effectively, therefore this is not a substantive procedure.

246 ENCORE *Walk in the footsteps of a top tutor*

Key answer tips

Part (a) requires audit procedures over additions and disposals of vehicles only. There will be no marks awarded for procedures which focus on vehicles in general.

Part (b) requires audit procedures in relation to valuation of receivables. There will be no marks awarded for procedures which focus on other assertions such as existence. Valuation is affected by recoverability of debts and whether customers are able, and likely, to pay.

Part (c) requires audit procedures over a breach of regulations. The relevant auditing standard requires the auditor to obtain evidence as to the potential effect on the financial statements therefore procedures should focus on potential penalties that could be imposed and whether they have been appropriately recognised.

Part (d) asks for the audit reporting implications if the issue is unresolved. First you should discuss what the issue is i.e. what the client has done wrong. Calculate whether the adjustment required is material. If the issue is not material it won't impact the auditor's report. If it is material consider whether it is material and pervasive as this will impact the type of opinion that should be given. Remember to include the key wording of the opinion you are suggesting as well as any other impact on the auditor's report.

(a) Vehicles additions and disposals

- Cast the schedule of additions to vehicles, cast it and agree the total to the disclosure note for property, plant and equipment. Agree the cost of the vehicles given in part-exchange to the disclosure note to confirm that they have been removed from cost carried forward.
- For a sample of new vehicles on the schedule of additions agree the cost to the purchase invoice, ensuring that the recorded cost includes the cash amount paid plus the trade-in allowance for the old vehicle. Confirm that the invoice is made out to Encore Co.
- Physically inspect a sample of additions, confirming that the registration number of the vehicle agrees to that on the non-current asset register.
- Review the non-current asset register to confirm that the 20 old vehicles were removed and that the 20 new vehicles were included.
- Recalculate the loss on disposal of \$1.1 m (\$1.8 – (\$4.6m – \$3.9m) and agree to the trial balance and statement of profit or loss.
- Agree the cash payment of \$3.9m to the bank ledger account and bank statement.
- Recalculate the depreciation expense, confirming that the depreciation expense was based on the old vehicles until 1 February and on the cost of the new vehicles after that date.
- Recalculate accumulated depreciation on the vehicles disposed of and confirm that this has been removed from accumulated depreciation carried forward.

- In light of the loss on disposal, review depreciation rates on existing vehicles to establish if the carrying amount of other vehicles may be overstated.
- Discuss with management Encore Co's history of vehicle replacement to establish if vehicles are being used for the entire period of their estimated useful life.
- Discuss with management why trade-in allowances were so much lower than the carrying amounts of the vehicles to provide further evidence as to whether depreciation policies are reasonable.
- Review the notes to the financial statements to ensure that disclosure of the additions and disposals is in accordance with IAS 16 *Property, Plant and Equipment*.

(b) Valuation of trade receivables

- Review the aged receivables listing to identify old or slow-moving balances. Discuss the status of these balances with the credit controller to assess whether the customers are likely to pay or if an allowance for credit losses/receivables is required.
- Review whether there are any after-date cash receipts for old/slow-moving receivable balances.
- Review correspondence with customers in order to identify any balances which are in dispute or unlikely to be paid and discuss with management whether any allowance is required.
- Review board minutes to identify whether there are any significant concerns in relation to outstanding receivables balances and assess whether the allowance is reasonable.
- Obtain a breakdown of the allowance for trade receivables. Recalculate it and compare it to any potentially irrecoverable balances to assess if the allowance is adequate.
- Review the payment history for evidence of slow paying by any customers who were granted credit in the period when there was no credit controller and who may not, therefore, have been properly scrutinised.
- Discuss with the finance director the rationale for maintaining the allowance at the same level in light of the increase in the receivables collection period and the absence of a credit controller.
- Inspect post-year-end sales returns/credit notes and consider whether an additional allowance against receivables is required.

(c) Potential breach of regulations

- Review correspondence with the transport authority to establish details of the complaint and the number of times the breach has allegedly occurred.
- Enquire of the directors why they are unwilling to provide or make disclosure, whether they accept that any breaches took place but believe that the effect is immaterial or whether they dispute their occurrence.
- Review Encore Co's policies and procedures to record driving hours and rest periods and compare to the regulations to determine the likelihood that breaches have occurred and how frequently.

- Review correspondence with the transport authority to establish if there have been discussions about other instances of potential non-compliance.
- Review correspondence with Encore Co's legal advisers or, with the client's permission, contact the lawyers to establish their assessment of the likelihood of the breach being proven and any fines that would be payable.
- Review the board minutes to ascertain management's view as to the likelihood of payment to the transport authority.
- Obtain a written representation to the effect that the directors are not aware of any other breaches of laws or regulations that would require a provision or disclosure in the financial statements.
- Inspect the post-year-end bank ledger account and bank statements to identify whether any fines have been paid.

(d) Auditor's report

The breaches in regulations and the initial investigation into the breaches occurred before the year end. The announcement by the authorities that they are taking legal action provides further evidence regarding these conditions which existed at the yearend date therefore IAS 10 *Events after the Reporting Period* would classify this as an adjusting subsequent event.

As it seems probable that the fine will be payable, a provision must be included rather than merely the disclosure. Failure to make such a provision will cause profits to be overstated and provisions to be understated.

The potential fine of $850,000 (17 × $50,000) is 16% ($850k/$5.3m) of profit before tax and 2.1% ($850k/$40.1 m) of total assets. It is therefore material.

If the directors refuse to make a provision, then Velo & Co should issue a modified opinion on the grounds that there is a material misstatement of profit and liabilities.

As this is material but not pervasive a qualified opinion would be appropriate.

A basis for qualified opinion paragraph would be included after the opinion paragraph.

This would explain the material misstatement in relation to the non-recognition of the provision and the effect on the financial statements.

The opinion paragraph would be qualified 'except for'.

ACCA marking guide			
			Marks
(a)	**Substantive procedures for vehicle additions and disposals** 1 mark per well-described procedure		
		Restricted to	6
(b)	**Substantive procedures for valuation of trade receivables** 1 mark per well-described procedure		
		Restricted to	5
(c)	**Substantive procedures for breach of regulations** 1 mark per well-described procedure		
		Restricted to	4
(d)	**Issue and impact on auditor's report**		
	• Discussion of issue		1
	• Materiality calculation and assessment		1
	• Type of modification required		2
	• Impact on auditor's report		1
			5
Total			20

Examiner's comments

Overall performance was mixed.

Part (a) required the candidate to describe substantive procedures for Encore Co's vehicle additions and disposals. Performance on this requirement was satisfactory. One mark was awarded for each well-described audit procedure. Those candidates who had practiced past questions scored well, noting procedures such as 'agreeing additions to invoices to ensure in company name and correct value capitalised', 'physically inspecting the addition', and 'recalculation of depreciation for correct time period'. Weaker candidates either did not provide sufficient detail in their tests or were vague such as, 'review relevant documents to ensure the accuracy of the amount capitalised' however this did not detail what documents should be reviewed. In addition, some provided test of controls such as 'reviewing board minutes for evidence of authorisation of the additions. The scenario contained a part exchange and some candidates were confused by this. However, if candidates had focused on standard additions and disposals tests then they would have comfortably passed this requirement. Candidates are reminded that substantive procedures are an important part of the syllabus and it is imperative they are able to provide relevant procedures for all areas of the financial statements listed in the syllabus.

Part (b) required the candidate to describe substantive procedures in relation to the valuation of Encore Co's trade receivables. Performance on this requirement was mixed. One mark was awarded for each well-described audit procedure. While the question required procedures for valuation, a significant number of candidates listed generic procedures for trade receivables such as reviewing disclosure. Others included procedures which focused on auditing revenue rather than trade receivables such as agreeing back to sales orders and invoices. These procedures were not awarded any credit as they were not focused on valuation of trade receivables. Candidates must carefully read the requirement of the question and tailor their answers accordingly.

The most common procedures which gained credit included 'after-date cash receipts', 'review of aged receivables balances' and 'recalculation of the allowance'. Analytical review of 'comparing receivables to the prior year and investigating significant differences' would have gained 1 mark. No credit was awarded for 'calculating receivables collection period' as this information was already provided in the scenario. Additionally, some of the procedures provided lacked detail, for example 'review correspondence with customers' with little detail of what the correspondence is being reviewed for would have gained no credit. To gain the one mark available it needed to be clear that 'the correspondence was reviewed to identify any balances in dispute, and these should be discussed with management'. As addressed in previous examiner's reports candidates must strive to understand substantive procedures. Learning a generic list of tests will not translate to exam success, as they must be applied to the question requirements.

Part (c) required the candidate to describe substantive procedures in relation to the potential breach in traffic regulations by Encore Co. One mark was awarded for each well-described audit procedure. Many candidate answers were incomplete. For a requirement of four marks, four well-described substantive procedures are required. However, many answers contained only a few procedures, some of which were either inappropriate, vague or lacking sufficient detail. Common inappropriate tests included 'contacting the transport authority' rather than reviewing correspondence with the authority and 'comparing the fine to the prior year' which would not have been appropriate as the breach of regulation was not an event which occurred annually. Those candidates who gained credit focused on reviewing bank statements for post-year-end payment of the fine, enquiries with the lawyer and discussions with management relating to the likelihood of payment.

Part (d) required a discussion of an issue and the impact on the auditor's report if the issue remained unresolved. The issue presented related to a post-year-end notification of transport regulation having been breached, and therefore a provision was required. Auditor's report questions have shown a gradual improvement in recent sessions but the performance for this question was mixed. Marks are awarded for a discussion of the issue (1 mark), assessment of the materiality of the issue (1 mark), a description of the type of modification (up to 2 marks) and the resultant impact on the auditor's report (1 mark). Many candidates did not discuss the issue. In order to be awarded the mark for discussing the issue candidates should not just re-write the fact from the question. Candidates needed to explain that the announcement of legal action by the authority post year end was an adjusting subsequent event (½ mark), and that without adjustment provisions would be understated and profit overstated (½ mark). In addition, unfortunately many candidates did not correctly calculate materiality. The scenario was clear that the impact of one breach was $50,000 and there were 17 breaches. Hence the error was $850,000 and not $50,000. If the error and then materiality had been correctly calculated, then ½ mark would have been awarded with a further ½ mark for the assessment that this was material. Candidates satisfactorily described the type of modification and the impact on the auditor's report. When considering the type of modification candidates are reminded that they must state whether the audit opinion is modified or not, and if modified, the type of modification required. In addition, a minority of candidates included reference to Emphasis of Matter paragraphs as part of their answers, this was incorrect and would not have gained credit. It was pleasing to note that many answers only provided one option for the auditor's report, rather than providing all possible options in a scatter gun approach as seen in previous sessions.

247 SPADEFISH *Walk in the footsteps of a top tutor*

Key answer tips

Part (a) requires audit procedures to investigate exceptions arising from a receivables circularisation. Where differences are found, these must be investigated to understand the reasons for the differences. This may be due to errors, which will need to be corrected, or due to timing differences, which will need to be confirmed.

Part (b) requires audit procedures in relation to the allowance for credit losses/receivables. The client must make an allowance for expected credit losses. Your procedures should focus on whether the provision is likely to be adequate to cover the credit losses which may occur in the future. Remember that the client is likely to want to make as little allowance as possible as the greater the allowance, the lower the level or reported profits and assets.

Part (c) requires an explanation of the going concern indicators of a client. Your explanation needs to describe the impact to the company of the indicator identified.

Part (d) requires procedures to assess whether the company is a going concern. Some procedures can be general procedures that must always be performed in relation to going concern, such as obtaining a written representation or reviewing and assessing the cash flow forecast. However, you should always try to include some procedures specific to the scenario information.

(a) Exceptions in the receivables circularisation

The following steps should be undertaken in regard to the exceptions arising in the positive receivables circularisation:

Albacore Co

- For the non-response from Albacore Co, with the client's permission, the team should arrange to send a follow-up circularisation.
- If Albacore Co does not respond to the follow up, then with the client's permission, the auditor should telephone the customer and ask whether they are able to respond in writing to the circularisation request.
- If there is still no response, then the auditor should undertake alternative procedures to confirm the balance owing from Albacore Co. Such as detailed testing of the balance by agreeing to sales invoices and goods despatch notes (GDN).

Flounder Co

- For the response from Flounder Co, with a difference of $5,850 the auditor should identify any disputed amounts, and identify whether these relate to timing differences or whether there are possible errors in the records of Triggerfish.
- If the difference is due to timing, such as cash in transit, this should be agreed to post-year-end cash receipts in the bank ledger account.
- If the difference relates to goods in transit, then this should be agreed to a pre-year-end GDN.

Menhaden Co

- The reason for the credit balance with Menhaden should be discussed with the credit controller or finance department to understand how a credit balance has arisen.
- Review the list of individual suppliers to identify if Menhaden is a supplier as well as a customer; if so, a purchase invoice may have been posted in error to the receivables rather than payables.
- If the difference is due to credit notes, this should be agreed to pre-year-end credit notes issued around the year-end date.
- The list of individual customer balances should be reviewed to identify any possible mispostings as this could be a reason for the difference with Menhaden Co.

(b) Allowance for credit losses/trade receivables

- Discuss with the finance director the rationale for not providing against any receivables and consider the reasonableness of the allowance.
- Obtain a breakdown of the opening allowance of $125,000 and consider if the receivables provided for in the prior year have been fully recovered as a result of the additional credit control procedures or if they have now been fully written off.
- Inspect the aged list of individual customer balances to identify any old or slow-moving receivable balances and discuss the status of these balances with the credit controllers to assess whether they are likely to be received.
- Review whether there are any after-date cash receipts for identified old or slow-moving receivable balances.
- Review customer correspondence to identify any balances which are in dispute or are unlikely to be paid and confirm if these have been considered when determining the allowance.
- Inspect board minutes to identify whether there are any significant concerns in relation to payments by customers and assess if these have been considered when determining the allowance.
- Recalculate the potential level of trade receivables which are not recoverable and compare to allowance and discuss differences with management.

(c) Going concern indicators

Marlin Co has paid some of its suppliers considerably later than usual and only after many reminders; hence some of them have withdrawn credit terms meaning the company must pay cash on delivery. This suggests that the company is struggling to meet its liabilities as they fall due. This will also put significant additional pressure on the company's cash flow, because the company will have to pay for goods on delivery but is likely to have to wait for cash from its receivables due to credit terms.

Marlin Co's main supplier who provides over 60% of the company's specialist equipment has just stopped trading. If the equipment is highly specialised, there is a risk that Marlin Co may not be able to obtain these products from other suppliers which would impact on the company's ability to trade. More likely, there are other suppliers available but they may be more expensive or may not offer favourable credit terms which will increase the outflows of Marlin Co and worsen the cash flow position.

Marlin Co's overdraft has grown significantly during the year and is due for renewal within the next month. If the bank does not renew the overdraft and the company is unable to obtain alternative finance, then it may not be able to continue to meet its liabilities as they fall due, especially if suppliers continue to demand cash on delivery, and the company may not be able to continue to trade.

In order to conserve cash, Marlin Co has decided not to pay a final dividend for the year ended 30 April 20X5. This may result in shareholders losing faith in the company and they may attempt to sell their shares; in addition, they are highly unlikely to invest further equity, and Marlin Co may need to raise finance to repay its overdraft.

(d) Going concern procedures

- Obtain the company's cash flow forecast and review the cash in and outflows. Assess the assumptions for reasonableness and discuss the findings with management to understand if the company will have sufficient cash flows.
- Perform a sensitivity analysis on the cash flows to understand the margin of safety the company has in terms of its net cash in/outflow.
- Evaluate management's plans for future actions, including their contingency plans in relation to ongoing financing and plans for generating revenue, and consider the feasibility of these plans.
- Review the company's post-year-end sales and order book to assess if the levels of trade are likely to increase and if the revenue figures in the cash flow forecast are reasonable.
- Review any agreements with the bank to determine whether any covenants have been breached, especially in relation to the overdraft.
- Review any bank correspondence to assess the likelihood of the bank renewing the overdraft facility.
- Review post-year-end correspondence with suppliers to identify if any have threatened legal action or any others have refused to supply goods.
- Inspect any contracts or correspondence with suppliers to confirm supply of the company's specialist equipment. If no new supplier has been confirmed, discuss with management their plans to ensure the company can continue to meet customer demand.
- Enquire of the lawyers of Marlin Co as to the existence of any litigation.
- Perform audit tests in relation to subsequent events to identify any items which might indicate or mitigate the risk of going concern not being appropriate.
- Review the post-year-end board minutes to identify any other issues which might indicate further financial difficulties for the company.
- Review post-year-end management accounts to assess if in line with cash flow forecast.
- Consider whether any additional disclosures as required by IAS 1 Presentation of Financial Statements in relation to material uncertainties over going concern should be made in the financial statements.
- Consider whether the going concern basis is appropriate for the preparation of the financial statements.
- Obtain a written representation confirming the directors' view that Marlin Co is a going concern.

Marking guide

		Marks
(a)	**Audit procedures – trade receivables circularisation**	
	• Albacore Co	3
	• Flounder Co	3
	• Menhaden Co	3
	Restricted to	**8**
(b)	**Substantive procedures – allowance for trade receivables**	
	• Discuss the rationale and reasonableness with the finance director	1
	• Obtain breakdown of opening allowance and confirm recovered	1
	• Inspect the aged receivables listing and discuss old or slow-moving balances	1
	• Perform after-date cash testing on identified old and slow-moving balances	1
	• Review customer correspondence for evidence of disputed balances	1
	• Inspect board minutes for balances which may not be recovered	1
	• Recalculate potential level of irrecoverable balance and compare to allowance and discuss differences	1
	Restricted to	**4**
(c)	**Going concern indicators**	
	• Withdrawal of credit – impact explained	1
	• Loss of main supplier – impact explained	1
	• Overdraft facility due for renewal – impact explained	1
	• No final dividend – impact explained	1
	Restricted to	**3**
(d)	**Going concern procedures**	
	• Obtain cash flow forecast and assess assumptions	1
	• Perform sensitivity analysis on cash flow forecast	1
	• Evaluate management's plans for future actions	1
	• Review post-year-end order book to assess levels of trade	1
	• Review agreements with the bank to determine whether any covenants breached	1
	• Review bank correspondence for evidence of renewal	1
	• Review correspondence with suppliers for dispute/legal action	1
	• Inspect contracts with supplier to confirm supply	1
	• Obtain confirmation from company lawyers about any legal action	1
	• Review post-year-end board minutes for any indications of financial difficulties	1
	• Review management accounts to assess if in line with cash flow	1
	• Review financial statement disclosure	1
	• Consider if going concern basis is appropriate	1
	• Obtain a written representation	1
	Restricted to	**5**
Total		**20**

Examiner's comments

Overall performance was disappointing.

Part (a) for eight marks required candidates to describe procedures the auditor should perform to resolve exceptions noted during a receivables circularisation for Triggerfish Co. Performance on this requirement was very disappointing. One mark was awarded for each well-described audit procedure. Candidates were provided with three customer balances as per Triggerfish's receivables listing and the response from the receivables circularisation. It was disappointing to see that a significant minority of candidates did not even attempt this requirement or simply provided one very brief procedure for each of the three exceptions. Of the three customer balances, Albacore Co was best attempted by candidates. Well prepared candidates gained marks for procedures such as after-date cash receipts testing as an alternative procedure, chasing the customer to request a response or sending a follow up circularisation request. The second balance in respect of Flounder Co related to a potential overstatement or timing difference. The third balance in respect of Menhaden Co was a credit balance in the receivables listing but a debit balance in the circularisation response. Candidates seemed to really struggle with these exceptions and other than suggesting 'discuss the reason for the difference with management' they could not provide many other relevant procedures. Candidates incorrectly focused on 'agreeing to sales invoices and goods despatch notes' or trying to understand how the credit balance in Menhaden Co may have occurred, without providing any procedures. For the balance with Flounder Co, candidates needed to focus their tests on items which could have been in transit at the year end to have caused the difference. Procedures around cash in transit or goods in transit were required. For the balance with Menhaden Co, procedures should have focused on credit notes or identifying mispostings. A significant minority of candidates produced very repetitive responses, providing audit procedures for Albacore Co and then simply copying these tests for each of the other two exceptions. Candidates should note that duplicating tests will not result in credit being awarded more than once. Candidates are reminded that substantive procedures are an important part of the syllabus and it is imperative they are able to attempt different types of question requirements.

Part (b) for four marks required candidates to describe substantive procedures the auditor should perform to obtain sufficient and appropriate evidence in relation to Triggerfish Co's allowance for receivables. Performance on this requirement was also very disappointing. One mark was awarded for each well-described audit procedure. It was disappointing that despite the question requiring procedures for the allowance for receivables, a significant number of candidates listed generic procedures for trade receivables such as receivables circularisation, cut off testing and reviewing disclosure. The majority of these procedures were not awarded any credit as they were not focused on the allowance. Candidates must carefully read the requirement of the question and tailor their answers accordingly.

Where candidates did attempt to audit the allowance, many of the procedures were not relevant. For example, undertaking analytical review of the allowance when the scenario stated it had been significantly reduced in the year, and reviewing board minutes for authorisation of the allowance were not awarded credit as they were not valid. As addressed in previous examiner's reports candidates must strive to understand substantive procedures. Learning a generic list of tests will not translate to exam success, as they must be applied to the question requirements.

Part (c) for four marks required the candidate to identify and explain indicators that Marlin Co was not a going concern. Questions such as this typically require indicators to be identified (½ mark each) and explained (½ mark each). Performance was satisfactory. The scenario contained more issues than were required to be discussed.

The majority of students were able to identify three going concern indicators as required. A number of candidates incorrectly identified that 'suppliers being paid later than usual' was a going concern indicator. Many companies choose to pay suppliers late in order to maximise working capital, and on its own this would not be enough to raise concerns over going concern. Instead credit was awarded for 'suppliers having withdrawn credit or requiring cash on delivery.' The explanation of the indicators caused difficulties for some candidates, with generic answers being given such as 'this will cause cash flow problems for the company'. In order to be awarded the second ½ mark, candidates needed to explain how the indicator could cause cash flow issues for Marlin Co. Those candidates who did not score well provided going concern indicators which were not in the scenario such as 'sale of significant assets', these had clearly been learnt as a generic list of indicators of going concern.

Part (d) for five marks required candidates to describe audit procedures to assess whether Marlin Co was a going concern. Performance was satisfactory on this requirement. One mark was awarded for each well-described substantive procedure. Those candidates who had practiced past questions scored well, noting procedures such as reviewing the cash flow forecast, discussions with management regarding future plans, reviewing board minutes and obtaining a written representation. Those candidates who did not score well provided procedures which lacked sufficient detail, for example, 'discuss with management' without explaining what was to be discussed. Vague procedures such as this are not awarded any credit. In addition, some candidates provided irrelevant procedures such as undertaking ratio analysis or reviewing bank statements. These procedures would not provide evidence as to whether the company was a going concern or not and so were not awarded any credit.

248 HYACINTH *Walk in the footsteps of a top tutor*

Key answer tips

This question focuses mainly on substantive procedures. A substantive procedure is used to test the figures in the financial statements with the aim of identifying material misstatements. One approach to generating audit procedures is to think about the assertions which need to be tested and design a procedure which does that. Another approach that can be used is to think about the audit techniques of inspection, enquiry, etc. and design procedures using those techniques. Whilst you may be able to use generic procedures learned from the text book, be careful to make sure the procedures you give address any specific issues mentioned in the scenario. For a balance such as research and development costs, think about how you can confirm whether the criteria from the relevant accounting standard have been met.

Part (d) requires discussion of a subsequent event. First of all discuss whether the event is an adjusting or non-adjusting event. You will need to assess whether the impact of the event is material. Next, suggest procedures that will provide sufficient appropriate evidence as to the level of adjustment if it is an adjusting event or the information that will need to be disclosed if it is a material non-adjusting event.

(a) Inventory valuation

- Obtain the breakdown of WIP and agree a sample of WIP assessed during the inventory count to the WIP schedule, agreeing the percentage completion to that recorded at the inventory count.
- For a sample of inventory items (finished goods and WIP), obtain the relevant cost sheets and agree raw material costs to recent purchase invoices, labour costs to time sheets or payroll records and confirm overheads allocated are of a production related nature.
- Examine post-year-end credit notes to determine whether there have been returns which could signify that a write down is required.
- Select a sample of year-end finished goods and compare cost with post-year-end sales invoices to ascertain if net realisable value (NRV) is above cost or if an adjustment is required.
- Discuss the basis of WIP valuation with management and assess its reasonableness.
- Select a sample of items included in WIP at the year end and ascertain the final unit cost price by verifying costs to be incurred to completion to relevant supporting documentation. Compare to the unit sales price included in sales invoices post-year-end to assess NRV.
- Review aged inventory reports and identify any slow-moving goods, discuss with management why these items have not been written down or if an allowance is required.
- For the defective batch of product Crocus, review board minutes and discuss with management their plans for selling these goods, and why they believe these goods have a NRV of $90,000.
- If any Crocus products have been sold post year end, review the sales invoice to assess NRV.
- Agree the cost of $450,000 for product Crocus to supporting documentation to confirm the raw material cost, labour cost and any overheads attributed to the cost.
- Confirm if the final adjustment for the damaged product is $360,000 ($450,000 – $90,000) and discuss with management if this adjustment has been made. If so, follow through the write down to confirm.

(b) Research and development

- Obtain and cast a schedule of intangible assets, agree the closing balances to the general ledger, trial balance and draft financial statements.
- Discuss with the finance director the rationale for the four-year useful life and consider its reasonableness.
- Recalculate the amortisation charge for a sample of intangible assets which have commenced production and confirm that it is in line with the amortisation policy of straight line over four years and that amortisation only commenced from the point of production.
- For the three new computing software projects, discuss with management the details of each project along with the stage of development and whether it has been capitalised or expensed.

- For those expensed as research, agree the costs incurred to invoices and supporting documentation and to inclusion in profit or loss.
- For those capitalised as development, agree costs incurred to invoices.
- Confirm technically feasible and intention to complete the project by discussion with development managers or review of feasibility reports.
- Review market research reports to confirm Hyacinth Co has the ability to sell the product once complete and probable future economic benefits will arise.
- Review the costs, projected revenue and cash flow budgets for the each of the three projects to confirm Hyacinth Co has adequate resources to complete the development stage and that probable future economic benefits exist. Agree the budgets to supporting documentation.
- Review the disclosures for intangible assets in the draft financial statements to verify that they are in accordance with IAS 38 *Intangible Assets.*

(c) Sales tax liability

- Agree the year-end sales tax liability in the trial balance to the tax return/ reconciliation submitted to the tax authority and cast the return/reconciliation.
- Agree the quarterly sales tax charged equates to 15% of the last quarter's sales as per the detailed sales day listing.
- Recalculate the sales tax incurred as per the reconciliation is equal to 15% of the final quarter's purchases and expenses as per the detailed purchase listing.
- Recalculate the amount payable to the tax authority as being sales tax charged less sales tax incurred.
- Compare the year-end sales tax liability to the prior year balance or budget and investigate any significant differences.
- Agree the subsequent payment to the post-year-end bank ledger account and bank statements to confirm completeness and that it has been paid in line with the terms of the tax authority.
- Review any current and post-year-end correspondence with the tax authority to assess whether there are any additional outstanding payments due. If so, confirm they are included in the year-end liability.
- Review any disclosures made of the sales tax liability to ensure that it is shown as a current liability and assess whether disclosures are in compliance with accounting standards and legislation.

(d) Subsequent event

A flood has occurred at the off-site warehouse and property, plant and equipment and inventory valued at $0.7 million have been damaged and now have no scrap value. The directors do not believe they are likely to be able to claim on the company's insurance for the damaged assets. This event occurred after the reporting period and is not an event which provides evidence of a condition at the year end and so this is a non-adjusting event.

The damaged assets of $0.7 million are material as they represent 10.9% ($0.7m/$6.4m) of profit before tax and 3.0% ($0.7m/$23.2m) of total assets. As a material non-adjusting event, the assets do not need to be written down to zero in this financial year.

However, the directors should consider including a disclosure note detailing the flood and the value of assets impacted.

The following audit procedures should be applied to form a conclusion on any amendment:

- Obtain a schedule showing the damaged property, plant and equipment and agree the net book value to the non-current asset register to confirm the total value of affected assets.
- Obtain a schedule of the water damaged inventory, visit the off-site warehouse and physically inspect the impacted inventory. Confirm the quantity of goods present in the warehouse to the schedule; agree the original cost to pre-year-end production costs.
- Review the condition of other PPE and inventory to confirm all damaged assets identified.
- Review the damaged property, plant and equipment and inventory and discuss with management the basis for the zero scrap value assessment.
- Discuss with management why they do not believe that they are able to claim on their insurance; if a claim were to be made, then only uninsured losses would require disclosure, and this may be an immaterial amount.
- Discuss with management whether they will disclose the effect of the flood, as a non-adjusting event, in the year-end financial statements.

Marking guide

		Marks
(a)	**Substantive procedures – valuation of inventory**	
	• Agree percentage completion recorded at inventory count to final inventory records	1
	• Confirm costs to invoice/timesheets	1
	• Inspect post-year-end sales invoices for finished goods to assess NRV	1
	• Discuss basis of WIP valuation with management	1
	• Inspect WIP valuation with sales prices less costs to complete	1
	• Review aged inventory reports and discuss allowance	1
	• Discuss with management basis of valuation for Crocus products	1
	• Inspect post-year-end sales value of Crocus products	1
	• Confirm adjustment regarding Crocus products	1
	Restricted to	**6**
(b)	**Substantive procedures – R&D expenditure**	
	• Obtain schedule, cast and agree to trial balance	1
	• Review reasonableness of useful lives	1
	• Recalculate amortisation and confirm in line with policy	1
	• Discuss with management treatment of costs for new products	1
	• Agree research costs expensed	1
	• For capitalised costs, confirm IAS 38 criteria met	1
	• Inspect budgets to confirm adequate resources to complete	1
	• Review disclosure and confirm in line with accounting standards	1
	Restricted to	**4**

(c)	**Substantive procedures – accrual for sales tax liability**	
	• Obtain schedule/return, cast and agree to trial balance	1
	• Recalculate sales tax in relation to sales and agree to return	1
	• Recalculate sales tax in relation to purchases and agree to return	1
	• Recalculate overall amount due to tax authority	1
	• Compare liability to prior year end, investigate differences	1
	• Confirm payment to post-year-end bank ledger account and bank statements	1
	• Review correspondence with the tax authority for evidence of additional liability	1
	• Review disclosure and confirm in line with IAS 37	1
	Restricted to	**4**
(d)	**Subsequent event**	
	• Discussion of amendment	3
	• Audit procedures	3
		6
Total		**20**

Examiner's comments

This question tested candidates' knowledge of substantive procedures for inventory, research and development, and the year-end sales tax liability. The question also tested candidates' knowledge of the treatment of subsequent events in the financial statements. Overall performance was mixed.

Part (a) for six marks required candidates to describe substantive procedures the auditor should perform to obtain sufficient and appropriate audit evidence in relation to the valuation of Hyacinth Co's inventory. Performance on this requirement was disappointing. One mark was awarded for each well-described audit procedure. The most common procedures provided by candidates were confirming raw material costs to purchase invoices, and comparing post-year-end sales invoices to cost to assess net realisable value. While it was pleasing that a significant number of candidates noted analytical review procedures, these were often not adequately explained for a full one mark. For example, many candidates only noted 'compare year-end inventory days with the prior year' (this was awarded ½ mark), for an additional ½ mark the candidate needed to also state 'and investigate any significant differences'. It was disappointing that despite the requirement stating procedures for the 'valuation' of inventory, a significant number of candidates listed procedures for the existence and completeness of inventory such as 'attending the inventory count'. This was not awarded any credit. Candidates must carefully read the requirement of the question and tailor their answers accordingly. In addition, many candidates did not specifically refer to audit procedures for the Crocus product which had not met customer quality and technical standards. Candidates are advised again to carefully read the scenario and tailor their procedures to address the issues described.

Part (b) for four marks required candidates to describe substantive procedures the auditor should perform to obtain sufficient and appropriate evidence in relation to Hyacinth Co's research and development expenditure. Performance on this requirement was mixed. One mark was awarded for each well-described audit procedure. The most common procedures provided by candidates were to cast the schedule of intangible assets, agree it to the trial balance, and discuss with management if the new projects were capitalised or expensed. In order to score well in this very commonly tested area, candidates needed to explain how a procedure should be performed. For example, 'ensure the four-year amortisation policy is reasonable' would not have gained full credit. The candidate needed to explain how the auditor could achieve this. For one mark the candidate needed to state 'discuss with the finance director the rationale for the four-year useful life and consider its reasonableness'.

While it was pleasing that a significant number of candidates noted the auditor should 'review the disclosures of intangibles in the financial statements' (½ mark), it was disappointing that candidates did not also state 'and verify that they are in line with accounting standards' to be credited a further ½ mark. Candidates are reminded that substantive procedures must be well explained to be awarded a full one mark. It was pleasing that candidates noted (for 1 mark) that 'if capitalised, agree compliance with the criteria in IAS 38 for capitalisation'. However, it was disappointing that few candidates suggested detailed testing to ensure this compliance. For example, very few candidates noted 'review market research reports to confirm the ability to sell the product'. It was disappointing that many candidates listed generic audit procedures, which were not relevant to the scenario. For example, a significant number of candidates noted analytical review procedures with the prior year, which was not appropriate.

As addressed in previous examiner's reports, candidates must strive to understand substantive procedures. Learning a generic list of tests will not translate to exam success, as they must be applied to the question requirements.

Part (c) for four marks required candidates to describe substantive procedures to obtain sufficient and appropriate audit evidence in relation to Hyacinth Co's year-end sales tax liability. Performance was disappointing. One mark was awarded for each well-described audit procedure. The most common procedures provided by candidates were analytical review procedures and after-date cash payment. A significant minority of candidates disappointingly listed procedures for revenue rather than sales tax, and/or listed procedures to audit the sales tax system throughout the year rather than testing the year-end liability. Candidates again are advised to read the question carefully.

Part (d) for six marks required candidates to (i) explain whether the financial statements required amendment in relation to a flood and (ii) describe audit procedures, which should be performed in order to form a conclusion on any required amendment. One mark was available per valid point and the marks were split equally between each part.

Performance for part (i) was reasonable. A significant number of candidates scored well by calculating materiality, concluding the 'matter was material', and stating that 'the financial statements required amendment'. However, it was disappointing that few candidates stated either that 'a disclosure note was necessary' or specifically stated that 'it was a non-adjusting event'.

Performance for part (ii) was disappointing. Despite the scenario stating that 'the company is unlikely to be able to claim on its insurance', a significant number of candidates inappropriately suggested 'writing to the insurance company'. A significant number of candidates also discussed the potential impact on the auditor's report, but this was not a requirement of the question. Candidates are again reminded to read the question requirement carefully.

249 JASMINE *Walk in the footsteps of a top tutor*

Key answer tips

This question focuses mainly on substantive procedures. A substantive procedure is used to test the figures in the financial statements with the aim of identifying material misstatements. One approach to generating audit procedures is to think about the assertions which need to be tested and design a procedure which does that. Another approach that can be used is to think about the audit techniques of inspection, enquiry, etc. and design procedures using those techniques. Whilst you may be able to use generic procedures learned from the text book, be careful to make sure the procedures you give address any specific issues mentioned in the scenario. For example, part (a) asks for substantive procedures over receivables excluding performing a circularisation. Part (b) requires procedures over Jasmine's bank balance which include an overdraft and savings accounts. It also states that the accounts are not reconciled and that the overdraft is due for renewal, therefore procedures will need to be performed in respect of these issues.

Part (c) requires procedures over the going concern status of Jasmine. Here you need to perform procedures that will provide sufficient appropriate evidence that the company can afford to pay its liabilities when they fall due. You will need to obtain evidence to assess the likely cash inflows and outflows for the year ahead.

Part (d) asks for the audit reporting implications if adequate and inadequate disclosures regarding going concern are made. Remember that the audit opinion should only be modified if the financial statements are not prepared in accordance with the financial reporting framework. If the financial statements are prepared properly, the auditor may need to include additional communication to the users regarding matters disclosed by the client if they are fundamental to the user's understanding.

(a) Trade receivables

- Obtain the aged receivables listing and agree to the balance on the trade receivables account and trial balance.
- Review the aged list of customer balances to identify any old or slow-moving balances, discuss the status of these balances with the credit controller to assess whether they are likely to pay.
- Select a representative sample of trade receivables and review for any after-date cash receipts. Ensure that a sample of old/slow-moving receivable balances is also selected.
- Review customer correspondence to identify any balances which are in dispute or unlikely to be paid and discuss with management.
- Review board minutes to identify whether there are any significant concerns in relation to payments by customers.
- Calculate the average receivables collection period and compare this to the prior year and investigate any significant differences.
- Inspect post-year-end sales returns/credit notes and consider whether an additional allowance against receivables is required.

- Obtain a breakdown of the allowance for trade receivables, recalculate and compare to any potentially irrecoverable balances to assess if the allowance is adequate.
- Select a sample of goods despatch notes (GDN) immediately before and after the year end and follow through to the list of individual customer balances to ensure they are recorded in the correct accounting period.
- Select a sample of year-end receivables balances and agree back to valid supporting documentation of sales invoices, GDNs and sales orders to ensure existence.

(b) Bank balances

- Obtain a bank confirmation letter from Jasmine Co's bankers for all of its accounts.
- Agree all accounts listed on the bank confirmation letter to the company's bank reconciliations or the trial balance/general ledger to ensure completeness of bank balances.
- For the current account, obtain Jasmine Co's bank reconciliation and cast to check the additions to ensure arithmetical accuracy.
- Agree the balance per the bank reconciliation to an original year-end bank statement and to the bank confirmation letter.
- Agree the reconciliation's balance per the bank ledger account to the year-end bank ledger account.
- Trace all the outstanding lodgements to the pre-year-end bank ledger account, post-year-end bank statement and also to the pre-year-end paying-in book.
- Trace all unpresented cheques through to a pre-year-end bank ledger account and post-year-end bank statement. For any unusual amounts or significant delays, obtain explanations from management.
- Examine any old unpresented cheques to assess whether they need to be written back as they are no longer valid to be presented.
- Review the bank ledger account and bank statements for any unusual items or large transfers around the year end, as this could be evidence of window dressing.
- Examine the bank confirmation letter for details of any security provided by Jasmine Co, with regards to the bank overdraft or any legal right of set-off as this may require disclosure.
- For the savings bank accounts, review any reconciling items on the year-end bank reconciliations and agree to supporting documentation.
- Review the financial statements to ensure that the disclosure of bank balances is complete and accurate and classified appropriately between current assets and current liabilities.

(c) Going concern procedures

- Obtain the company's cash flow forecast and review the cash inflows and outflows. Assess the assumptions for reasonableness and discuss the findings with management to understand if the company will have sufficient cash.
- Perform a sensitivity analysis on the cash flows to understand the margin of safety the company has in terms of its net cash in/outflow.

- Evaluate management's plans for future actions, including their contingency plans in relation to ongoing financing and plans for generating revenue, and consider the feasibility of these plans.
- Review the company's post-year-end sales and order book to assess if the levels of trade are likely to increase and if the revenue figures in the cash flow forecast are reasonable.
- Review any agreements with the bank to determine whether any covenants have been breached, especially in relation to the overdraft.
- Review any bank correspondence to assess the likelihood of the bank renewing the overdraft facility.
- Review post-year-end correspondence with suppliers to identify if any have threatened legal action or any others have refused to supply goods.
- With the client's permission, enquire of the lawyers of Jasmine Co as to the existence of any litigation and if so, the likely outcome of any litigation.
- Perform audit tests in relation to subsequent events to identify any items which might indicate or mitigate the risk of going concern not being appropriate.
- Review the post-year-end board minutes to identify any other issues which might indicate further financial difficulties for the company.
- Review post-year-end management accounts to assess if in line with cash flow forecast.
- Consider whether any additional disclosures as required by IAS 1 *Presentation of Financial Statements* in relation to material uncertainties over going concern should be made in the financial statements.
- Consider whether the going concern basis is appropriate for the preparation of the financial statements.
- Obtain a written representation confirming the directors' view that Jasmine Co is a going concern.

(d) Auditor's report

As the outcome regarding the negotiations for the overdraft facility renewal will not be known at the time of signing the auditor's report, there is a material uncertainty which may cast significant doubt on the company's ability to continue as a going concern. The impact on the auditor's report depends on whether this uncertainty is deemed to be adequately disclosed in the financial statements.

Disclosure adequate

If the disclosures are adequate, then the auditor's report will need to include a material uncertainty related to going concern section.

The section will state that the audit opinion is not modified, indicate that there is a material uncertainty and will cross reference to the disclosure note made by management.

It would be included after the opinion and basis for opinion paragraph.

Disclosure inadequate

If the disclosures made by management are not adequate, the audit opinion will need to be modified as there is a material misstatement relating to inadequate disclosure.

The failure to adequately disclose is likely to be material but not pervasive due to the ongoing nature of the negotiations and so a qualified opinion will be issued.

The opinion paragraph will state that 'except for' the failure to adequately disclose the uncertainty, the financial statements give a true and fair view.

The report will contain a basis for opinion paragraph, subsequent to the opinion paragraph, explaining that a material uncertainty exists and that the financial statements do not adequately disclose this matter.

Marking guide		
		Marks
(a)	**Substantive procedures – trade receivables**	
	• Obtain aged receivables listing, cast and agree to TB	1
	• Review listing for old balances and discuss with management	1
	• Perform cash after-date testing	1
	• Inspect customer correspondence for evidence of disputed items and discuss with management	1
	• Calculate receivables collection period, compare to PY and investigate differences	1
	• Inspect post-year-end returns and consider need for additional allowance	1
	• Obtain a breakdown of the allowance, recalculate and consider adequacy	1
	• Select sample of GDNs from before and after year end and confirm recorded in correct period	1
	• Select a sample of balances and agree to order, GDN and invoice	1
	Restricted to	**5**
(b)	**Substantive procedures – bank balances**	
	• Bank confirmation letter	1
	• Agree to bank reconciliation and TB	1
	• Cast bank reconciliations	1
	• Testing on bank reconciliations (1 mark per relevant procedure)	4
	• Review bank ledger account and bank statements for window dressing	1
	• Examine bank letter for evidence of security granted	1
	• Review financial statement disclosure	1
	Restricted to	**5**
(c)	**Going concern procedures**	
	• Obtain cash flow forecast and assess assumptions	1
	• Perform sensitivity analysis on cash flow forecast	1
	• Evaluate management's plans for future actions	1
	• Review post-year-end order book to assess levels of trade	1
	• Review agreements with the bank to determine whether any covenants breached	1
	• Review bank correspondence for evidence of renewal	1
	• Review correspondence with suppliers for dispute/legal action	1
	• Obtain confirmation from company lawyers about any legal action	1
	• Review post-year-end board minutes for any indications of financial difficulties	1
	• Review management accounts to assess if in line with cash flow	1
	• Review financial statement disclosure	1
	• Consider if going concern basis is appropriate	1
	• Obtain a written representation	1
	Restricted to	**5**
(d)	**Issue and impact on auditor's report**	
	• Discussion of issue	1
	• Disclosure adequate	2
	• Disclosure inadequate	2
		5
Total		**20**

Examiner's comment

This question tested candidates' knowledge of substantive procedures for trade receivables and bank, going concern procedures and auditor's reports. Overall performance was mixed.

Part (a) for five marks required candidates to describe substantive procedures the auditor should perform to obtain sufficient and appropriate audit evidence in relation to Jasmine's trade receivables. Performance on this requirement was satisfactory. One mark was awarded for each well-described substantive procedure. Those candidates who had practised past questions scored well, noting procedures such as after-date cash receipts testing, analytical review procedures, review of aged receivables reports and discussions with management regarding recoverability and allowances. Although many candidates recommended cut-off testing, candidates once again suggested using invoices rather than goods despatch notes. Those candidates who did not score well provided procedures which lacked sufficient detail. For example, 'discuss receivables with management' without explaining what was to be discussed. Vague procedures such as this are not awarded any credit. In addition, despite the scenario stating that a trade receivables circularisation was not going to be performed, it was disappointing to see that many candidates still recommended procedures relating to the circularisation. Candidates must carefully read the scenario and tailor their procedures accordingly.

Part (b) for five marks required candidates to describe substantive procedures the auditor should perform to obtain sufficient and appropriate audit evidence in relation to the company's bank balances. Performance on this requirement was disappointing. As in part (a), one mark was awarded for each well-described substantive procedure. Disappointingly, the substantive procedures often lacked detail and failed to focus specifically on auditing the bank balances. Candidates seemed to note that the bank balance was an overdraft and so focused ongoing concern procedures. Whether the bank balance is a current asset or liability, the principal focus of the procedures should have been to audit the bank reconciliation in detail, however, very few candidates did this. The most common procedures listed included 'obtain a bank letter' which on its own would only have scored ½ mark. To obtain 1 mark the test needed to agree the account names to the trial balance or to agree the balance given to the bank reconciliation. Vague references to auditing the bank reconciliation were given, such as 'ensure the bank statement balance matches the bank ledger account balance'. In order to score well in this very commonly tested area, candidates needed to focus on each line in the bank reconciliation and provide procedures to confirm that each line represented a valid reconciling item between the bank statement and bank ledger account.

Part (c) for five marks required candidates to describe going concern procedures. Many candidates performed well on this requirement. Again, one mark was available for each well-described procedure. This area has been tested extensively in previous diets and many candidates were able to provide a sufficient number of valid going concern procedures. A minority of procedures were too brief or vague, often not giving the source for the test, or stating 'ensure' without explaining how the test would achieve this. For example, 'obtain written representations' would not have gained any credit.

To obtain the available mark the procedure should be 'obtain a written representation confirming the directors' view that Jasmine Co is a going concern'. In addition, a minority of candidates suggested 'the auditor should call the bank to ask if they will renew the company's bank overdraft'. This is impractical as the bank will not provide such a response to the auditor.

Part (d) for five marks required a discussion of an issue and the impact on the auditor's report of adequate and inadequate disclosure. The issue being brief going concern disclosures made in the financial statements. Auditor's report questions have shown a gradual improvement in recent diets so it is very disappointing that performance for this requirement was poor. Marks were awarded for a discussion of the issue (1 mark), the impact on the auditor's report of adequate disclosure (2 marks) and inadequate disclosure (2 marks). It was disappointing that candidates often do not discuss the issue. In order to be awarded the mark for discussing the issue, candidates should not just re-write the issue from the question. In this case candidates needed to explain that as the outcome of the overdraft renewal would not be known until after the auditor's report was signed, this was a material uncertainty (½ mark) and that the effect on the auditor's report depends on the adequacy of the disclosure (½ mark). The question then required candidates to consider the impact on the auditor's report of adequate and inadequate disclosure. Answers should have addressed each of these outcomes and this was clearly flagged in the requirement. To score well, candidates should have considered whether any additional information would be required in the auditor's report for 'adequate disclosure' and if the opinion would be impacted. Inadequate disclosure resulted in a modification of the opinion and as a result, candidates tended to perform better. Many answers were poorly structured as they did not split out the two possible outcomes and it was at times difficult to see which points related to which outcome, resulting in difficulties in allocating marks. Incorrect answers for adequate disclosure focused on the use of emphasis of matter paragraphs. For inadequate disclosure some candidates suggested an adverse opinion, despite the scenario stating that the engagement partner was satisfied with the use of the going concern basis. In addition, many answers failed to consider whether the audit opinion was modified or not.

250 GOOSEBERRY *Walk in the footsteps of a top tutor*

Key answer tips

Part (a) asks for substantive procedures in relation to research and development. Think about the accounting treatment required by the relevant accounting standard and design procedures to test whether the treatment is appropriate. In the case of R&D there are a number of criteria which must be met in order for the costs to be capitalised. Generate audit procedures around each of these criteria to obtain evidence as to whether the costs should be capitalised or expensed. Don't forget the easy marks such as recalculating the breakdown of costs and agreeing the total to the financial statements.

Part (b) requires substantive procedures depreciation. Depreciation is an estimate and as such is an area of management judgement. Management may use an inappropriate depreciation rate to manipulate the financial statements. Your audit procedures should therefore not just focus on the calculation of depreciation but also whether the rate used by the client is appropriate.

Part (c) requires substantive procedures over director's bonuses. Once again, easy marks can be earned for recalculating the list of bonuses and agreeing to the financial statements. For other procedures think about the supporting documentation that provide evidence as to whether the figures are accurate and complete.

Part (d) asks for the audit reporting implications if the issue is unresolved. First you should discuss what the issue is i.e. what the client has done wrong. Calculate whether the adjustment required is material. If the issue is not material it won't impact the auditor's report. If it is material consider whether it is material and pervasive as this will impact the type of opinion that should be given. Remember to include the key wording of the opinion you are suggesting as well as any other impact on the auditor's report.

(a) Research and development

- Obtain and cast a schedule of intangible assets, detailing opening balances, amounts capitalised in the current year, amortisation and closing balances.
- Agree the closing balances to the general ledger, trial balance and draft financial statements.
- Discuss with the finance director the rationale for the three-year useful life and consider its reasonableness.
- Recalculate the amortisation charge for a sample of intangible assets which have commenced production and confirm it is in line with the amortisation policy of straight line over three years and that amortisation only commenced from the point of production.
- For the nine new projects, discuss with management the details of each project along with the stage of development and whether it has been capitalised or expensed.
- For those expensed as research, agree the costs incurred to invoices and supporting documentation and to inclusion in profit or loss.

- For those capitalised as development, agree costs incurred to invoices and confirm technically feasible by discussion with development managers or review of feasibility reports.
- Review market research reports to confirm Gooseberry Co has the ability to sell the product once complete and probable future economic benefits will arise.
- Review the disclosures for intangible assets in the draft financial statements to verify that they are in accordance with IAS 38 *Intangible Assets*.

(b) Depreciation

- Discuss with management the rationale for the changes to property, plant and equipment (PPE) depreciation rates, useful lives, residual values and depreciation methods and ascertain how these changes were arrived at.
- Confirm the reasonableness of these changes, by comparing the revised depreciation rates, useful lives and methods applied to PPE to industry averages and knowledge of the business.
- Review the asset expenditure budgets for the next few years to assess whether the revised asset lives correspond with the planned period until replacement of the relevant asset categories.
- Review the non-current asset register to assess if the revised depreciation rates have been applied.
- Review and recalculate profits and losses on disposal of assets sold/scrapped in the year, to assess the reasonableness of the revised depreciation rates.
- Select a sample of PPE and recalculate the depreciation charge to ensure that the non-current asset register is correct and ensure that new depreciation rates have been appropriately applied.
- Obtain a breakdown of depreciation by asset categories, compare to prior year; where significant changes have occurred, discuss with management and assess whether this change is reasonable.
- For asset categories where there have been a minimal number of additions and disposals, perform a proof-in-total calculation for the depreciation charged on PPE, discuss with management if significant fluctuations arise.
- Review the disclosure of the depreciation charges and policies in the draft financial statements and ensure it is in line with IAS 16 *Property, Plant and Equipment*.

(c) Directors' bonuses

- Obtain a schedule of the directors' bonus paid in May 20X5 and cast the schedule to ensure accuracy and agree amount disclosed in the financial statements.
- Review the schedule of current liabilities and confirm the bonus accrual is included as a year-end liability.
- Agree the individual bonus payments to the payroll records.
- Recalculate the bonus payments and agree the criteria, including the exclusion of intangible assets, to supporting documentation and the percentage rates to be paid to the directors' service contracts.
- Confirm the amount of each bonus paid post year end by agreeing to the bank ledger account and bank statements.
- Agree the amounts paid per director to board minutes to ensure the sums included in the current year financial statements are fully accrued and disclosed.

- Review the board minutes to identify whether any additional payments relating to this year have been agreed for any directors.
- Obtain a written representation from management confirming the completeness of directors' remuneration including the bonus.
- Review the disclosures made regarding the bonus paid to directors and assess whether these are in compliance with local legislation.

(d) Impact on auditor's report

One of the new health and beauty products Gooseberry Co has developed in the year does not meet the recognition criteria under IAS 38 *Intangible Assets* for capitalisation but has been included within intangible assets.

This is contrary to IAS 38, as if the criteria are not met, then this project is research expenditure and should be expensed to the statement of profit or loss rather than capitalised.

The error is material as it represents 6.9% of profit before tax (0.44m/6.4m) and 1.2% of total assets (0.44m/37.2m).

Management should adjust the financial statements by removing this amount from intangible assets and charging it to the statement of profit or loss instead. IAS 38 requires costs to date to be expensed; if the project meets the recognition criteria in 20X6, then only from that point can any new costs incurred be capitalised. Any costs already expensed cannot be written back to assets.

If management refuses to amend this error, then the auditor's opinion will need to be modified. As management has not complied with IAS 38 and the error is material but not pervasive, then a qualified opinion would be necessary.

A basis for qualified opinion paragraph would be needed after the opinion paragraph and would explain the material misstatement in relation to the incorrect treatment of research and development and the effect on the financial statements. The opinion paragraph would be qualified 'except for'.

Marking guide

		Marks
(a)	**Substantive procedures – Research & development**	
	• Cast and agree closing balance to TB and draft FS	1
	• Discuss amortisation policy with management and assess reasonableness	1
	• Recalculate amortisation charge/commenced in line with production	1
	• Discuss new projects and stage of development	1
	• For research costs agree invoices and to profit or loss	1
	• For development costs agree to invoices and confirm meets criteria	1
	• Review market research to confirm ability to sell	1
	• Review disclosures in line with IAS 38	1
	Restricted to	**5**
(b)	**Substantive procedures – depreciation**	
	• Discuss reasons for change with management	1
	• Compare to industry averages and knowledge of business	1
	• Review asset budgets to assess revised lives appropriate	1
	• Agree new rates to non-current asset register	1
	• Recalculate profit/loss on disposal and consider new rates	1
	• Recalculate depreciation charge for a sample of assets	1
	• Perform a proof-in-total on depreciation charge	1
	• Review disclosure is in line with IAS 16	1
	Restricted to	**5**

(c)	**Substantive procedures – directors' bonuses**	
	• Cast schedule of bonuses and agree to TB	1
	• Confirm bonus accrual as current liability	1
	• Agree bonus payments to payroll records	1
	• Recalculate bonus payments in line with contracts	1
	• Confirm post-year-end payment to bank statement	1
	• Review board minutes for additional sums	1
	• Obtain written representation confirming completeness	1
	• Review disclosures in line with local legislation	1
	Restricted to	**5**
(d)	**Issue and impact on auditor's report**	
	• Discussion of issue	1
	• Calculation of materiality and conclusion	1
	• Type of opinion modification required	2
	• Impact on auditor's report	1
		5
Total		**20**

Examiner's comments

This question was based on Gooseberry Co, a company which develops and manufactures health and beauty products and distributes these to wholesale customers. This question tested candidates' knowledge of substantive procedures for research and development, depreciation and directors' bonuses, and auditor's reports.

Part (a) required candidates to describe substantive procedures the auditor should perform to obtain sufficient and appropriate audit evidence in relation to Gooseberry's research and development expenditure. Performance on this requirement was mixed. One mark was awarded for each well-described substantive procedure. Hence for a five-mark requirement, candidates should have provided at least five substantive procedures. Disappointingly this was not the case, as some answers only contained one or two procedures for each area and these were often not well described, resulting in a maximum of ½ mark each. Candidates are severely limiting the opportunity to score marks and are reminded to ensure that they employ effective exam technique. Many procedures were vague, often not giving the source for the test, or stating 'ensure' without explaining how the test would achieve this. For example, 'recalculate expenditure' rather than clearly stating 'recalculate the amortisation charge and confirm it is in line with the company's policy'. Only a minority of strong candidates demonstrated an understanding of IAS 38 *Intangible Assets* and tailored their answer around these criteria.

Part (b) required the candidates to describe substantive procedures the auditor should perform to obtain sufficient and appropriate audit evidence in relation to depreciation. Performance on this requirement was disappointing. As in part (a), one mark was awarded for each well-described substantive procedure. Disappointingly often the substantive procedures were either not well described, or were not related to depreciation. A significant number of candidates did not clearly answer the specific requirement of the question to describe depreciation substantive procedures. Although many candidates were able to correctly suggest recalculating the depreciation charge, candidates often described more general property, plant and equipment substantive procedures including confirming additions and disposals. In addition, many candidates referred to procedures which were not relevant to the requirement or the scenario, for example, verifying the credentials of the valuer, to audit the revaluation of the property, plant and equipment, suggesting that candidates have rote learned a list of procedures from previous questions. Candidates are advised to read the question scenario and requirements carefully and tailor their answer accordingly. In general, there was clear evidence of a lack of tailoring of knowledge to the specific scenario provided. Candidates have clearly learned that the depreciation charge should be compared to the prior year. However, this substantive procedure is not relevant if there is a change in the useful life of the assets in the year as was detailed in this scenario. As addressed in previous examiner's reports candidates must strive to understand substantive procedures. Learning a generic list of tests will not translate to exam success, as they must be applied to the question requirement.

Part (c) required the candidates to describe substantive procedures the auditor should perform to obtain sufficient and appropriate audit evidence in relation to the directors' bonuses. Performance on this requirement for many candidates was pleasing. As in part (a) and (b), one mark was available for each well-described procedure. Many candidates were able to correctly suggest agreeing the bonus payment to the payroll records/payslips, agreeing the bonus criteria to the directors' service contracts, and agreeing the bonus payment to the post-year-end bank ledger account /bank statement. A number of candidates also correctly described agreeing the amounts paid for each director to the board minutes. Some candidates did not describe the substantive procedures in sufficient depth, for example, no credit was awarded for 'ensure the bonus is paid' as this provides no source or clear indication as to how this would be achieved. Candidates are reminded that substantive procedures are a core topic area and they must be able to produce relevant detailed procedures.

Part (d) for five marks required a discussion of an issue and the impact on the auditor's report if the issue remained unresolved. The issue presented related to $440,000 of development costs which had been incorrectly capitalised by the client. Auditor's report questions have shown a gradual improvement in recent diets so it is disappointing that performance for this question was mixed. Marks are awarded for a discussion of the issue (1 mark), assessment of the materiality of the issue (1 mark), a description of the type of modification (up to 2 marks) and the resultant impact on the auditor's report (1 mark). It was disappointing that candidates often do not discuss the issue. In order to be awarded the mark for discussing the issue candidates should not just re-write the fact from the question. Candidates need to explain the effect of the item being incorrectly recorded, i.e. this overcapitalisation results in assets/liabilities/profit being over/understated. Many candidates described the issue as 'development costs are incorrectly capitalised' which was a restatement of fact and were not awarded credit. To be awarded marks candidates should have noted 'the costs should have been expensed to the statement of profit or loss' (½ mark) and therefore 'profit/assets are overstated' (½ mark). It was pleasing that most candidates correctly calculated materiality (½ mark) and concluded whether this was material (½ mark). Candidates attempted to identify the type of modification and the impact on the report, however, many answers were incomplete, for example, many candidates did not refer to a 'material misstatement' or a 'basis for qualified opinion paragraph'. A number of candidates described the impact on the auditor's report if the issue was resolved and also if the issue remained unresolved. The question clearly asked for the impact if the issue remained unresolved. Once again, candidates are advised to read the question requirements carefully.

251 DASHING *Walk in the footsteps of a top tutor*

Key answer tips

Part (a) asks for the steps to obtain a receivables circularisation. Take a methodical approach and think of each and every step involved in the process.

Part (b) requires substantive procedures over receivables for specific assertions. A substantive procedure tests the balance included in the financial statements. Think carefully about the objective of the procedure you are suggesting to ensure you include it under the appropriate assertion.

Part (c) requires substantive procedures over the redundancy provision. Again, a methodical approach can help. Think of how the balance will have been calculated and design procedures to test the calculation. Think about the accounting treatment required by the relevant accounting standard and design procedures to test whether the treatment is appropriate.

Part (d) asks for the audit reporting implications if the issue is unresolved. First you should discuss what the issue is i.e. what the client has done wrong. Calculate whether the adjustment required is material. If the issue is not material it won't impact the auditor's report. If it is material consider whether it is material and pervasive as this will impact the type of opinion that should be given. Remember to include the key wording of the opinion you are suggesting as well as any other impact on the auditor's report.

(a) Steps in undertaking a positive receivables circularisation for Dashing Co

- Obtain consent from the finance director of Dashing Co in advance of undertaking the circularisation.
- Obtain a list of trade receivables at the year end, cast this and agree it to the total on the trade receivables account.
- Select a sample from the receivables list ensuring that a number of nil, old, credit and large balances are selected.
- Circularisation letters should be prepared on Dashing Co's letterhead paper, requesting a confirmation of the year-end receivables balance, and for replies to be sent directly to the audit team using a pre-paid envelope.

  For requests sent by email, the email wording should be drafted by the auditor and provided to the client to send to the customer with a request that replies are emailed directly to the audit team using the email address provided.
- The finance director of Dashing Co should be requested to sign all the letters prior to them being sent out by a member of the audit team. For emails, the auditor should observe the email being sent by client staff.
- Where no response is received, follow this up with another letter, email or a phone call and where necessary alternative procedures should be performed
- When replies are received, they should be reconciled to Dashing Co's receivables records, any differences such as cash or goods in transit should be investigated further.

(b) Receivables

Accuracy, valuation and allocation

- Review the after-date cash receipts and follow through to pre-year-end receivable balances.
- Inspect the aged receivables report to identify any slow-moving balances and discuss these with the credit control manager to assess whether an allowance or write down is necessary.
- For any old/slow-moving balances review customer correspondence to assess whether there are any invoices in dispute.
- Review board minutes of Dashing Co to assess whether there are any material disputed receivables.

Completeness

- Select a sample of goods despatch notes from before the year end, agree to sales invoices and to inclusion in the year-end list of individual customer balances.
- Agree the total on the list of individual customer balances to the trade receivables account and to the trial balance.
- Obtain the prior year aged receivables listing and for significant balances compare to the current year receivables listing for inclusion and amount due. Discuss with management any missing receivables or significantly lower balances.
- Review the list of individual customer balances for any credit balances and discuss with management whether these should be reclassified as payables.

Rights and obligations

- Review bank confirmations and loan agreements for any evidence that receivables have been assigned as security for amounts owed by Dashing Co.
- Review board minutes for evidence that legal title to receivables has been sold onto a third party such as a factor.
- For a sample of receivables, agree the balance recorded on the list of individual customer balances to the original name of the customer on a sales order or a contract.

Tutorial note: Marks will be awarded for any other relevant receivables tests.

(c) Redundancy provision

- Discuss with the directors of Dashing Co as to whether they have formally announced their intention to close the production site and make their employees redundant, to confirm that a present obligation exists at the year end.
- If announced before the year end, review supporting documentation to verify that the decision has been formally announced.
- Review the board minutes to ascertain whether it is probable that the redundancy payments will be paid.
- Obtain a breakdown of the redundancy calculations by employee and cast it to ensure completeness and agree to trial balance.

- Recalculate the redundancy provision to confirm completeness and agree components of the calculation to supporting documentation such as employee contracts.
- Review the post-year-end bank ledger account to identify whether any redundancy payments have been made, compare actual payments to the amounts provided to assess whether the provision is reasonable.
- Obtain a written representation from management to confirm the completeness of the provision.
- Review the disclosure of the redundancy provision to ensure compliance with IAS 37 *Provisions, Contingent Liabilities and Contingent Assets*.

(d) Impact on auditor's report

The company has included a redundancy provision of $110,000 in the draft financial statements, however, audit fieldwork testing has confirmed that the provision should actually be $305,000. The provision is understated and profit before tax overstated if the finance director does not amend the financial statements.

The provision included is $110,000, it should be $305,000 hence an adjustment of $195,000 is required which represents 7.5% of profit before tax (195/2,600) or 1.1% of total assets (195/18,000) and hence is a material matter.

If management does not adjust the redundancy provision, the audit opinion will need to be modified.

As provisions are understated and profit overstated, there is a material misstatement, which is not pervasive.

Therefore, a qualified opinion would be necessary, stating that the opinion is qualified 'except for'.

A basis for qualified opinion paragraph would also need to be included subsequent to the opinion paragraph. This would explain the material misstatement in relation to the redundancy provision and the effect on the financial statements.

Marking guide

		Marks
(a)	**Steps for a receivables circularisation**	
	• Obtain consent from client	1
	• Agree receivables listing to SL	1
	• Select sample including nil, credit, old and large balances	1
	• Prepare letters on company letterhead or emails sent from a client email address	1
	• Letters sent by auditor/emails sent under supervision of auditor	1
	• Where no response, perform alternative procedures	1
	• For replies received, reconcile and investigate differences	1
	Restricted to	**4**
(b)	**Substantive procedures – receivables s**	
	• Accuracy, valuation and allocation tests	2
	• Completeness tests	2
	• Rights and obligations tests	2
	Restricted to	**6**

(c)	**Substantive procedures – redundancy provision**	
	• Discuss with directors when announcement was made	1
	• If before year end, agree to supporting documentation	1
	• Review board minutes for details of redundancy payments	1
	• Obtain a breakdown of redundancy calculations	1
	• Recalculate the redundancy provision	1
	• Review post-year-end bank ledger account for payments	1
	• Obtain written representation	1
	• Review disclosure in FS	1
	Restricted to	**5**
(d)	**Issue and impact on auditor's report**	
	• Discussion of issue	1
	• Calculation of materiality	1
	• Type of opinion modification required	2
	• Impact on auditor's report	1
		5
Total		**20**

Examiner's comments

This question was based on Dashing Co and tested candidates' knowledge of performing a receivables' circularisation, receivables and redundancy provision substantive procedures and auditor's reports.

Part (a) required the steps the auditor should perform in undertaking a positive receivables circularisation. Performance on this requirement was disappointing. One mark was awarded for each well-described step. This was a knowledge area and a straightforward requirement. Candidates should have been able to easily describe enough steps to pass this part of the question. However, a significant minority of candidates did not seem to understand what a receivables circularisation was and so just produced a list of receivables substantive procedures. Other answers incorrectly focused on the differences between positive and negative circularisations which were not requested. Stronger candidates were able to suggest some of the following steps: selecting a sample of receivable balances, sending a letter out, requesting a response, chasing up non-replies, undertaking alternative procedures in the event of no response and reconciling to records for those replies received.

Part (b) required substantive procedures for receivables relating to three specific assertions: (i) accuracy, valuation and allocation, (ii) completeness and (iii) rights and obligations. Candidates' performance was disappointing. One mark was awarded for each well-described substantive procedure. Hence for a six-mark requirement, candidates should have provided at least six substantive procedures. Disappointingly this was not the case, as some answers only contained one for each area and these were often not well described, resulting in maximum of ½ mark each.

In order to gain the available one mark each substantive procedure needed to be sufficiently detailed, and be clearly linked to the relevant assertion. Most candidates either structured their answers into the three sub category headings of (i), (ii) and (iii) or the tests included a reference to which assertion it addressed. Candidates' performance was most disappointing for (iii) rights and obligations, where often no answer was provided. A significant number of candidates provided example procedures which were not related to receivables, but instead focused on revenue or on a receivables circularisation which were specifically excluded from this question requirement. This can only be due to a failure to read the question requirement properly. In addition, many procedures were vague, often not giving the source for the test, or stating 'check' or 'ensure' without explaining how the test would achieve this. In addition, many tests were incomplete such as agreeing goods despatch notes (GDNs) to sales invoices but not then agreeing the invoices to the year-end receivables list, and these GDNs and invoices should have been close to the year end. Also, many of the procedures were tests of control rather than substantive procedures.

Part (c) required substantive procedures for confirming the redundancy provision. Candidates' performance was mixed. Again, one mark was awarded for each well-described substantive procedure. Many candidates were able to correctly suggest recalculation of the provision, obtaining a written representation confirming the completeness of the provision and agreeing to supporting documentation such as board minutes, employment contracts or payroll records. However, there was clear evidence of a lack of tailoring of knowledge to the specific scenario provided. Candidates have clearly learnt that all provisions should be compared to the prior year and that legal advice is required to confirm the amount of the provision. These are not relevant for a redundancy provision as it is unlikely there was a similar provision last year or that the company's lawyers would estimate the costs of redundancy. As addressed in previous examiner's reports candidates must strive to understand substantive procedures. Learning a generic list of tests will not translate to exam success as they must be applied to the question requirement.

The requirement verb for (a), (b) and (c) was to 'describe' therefore sufficient detail was required to score the 1 mark available per procedure. Also, candidates must provide enough tests to score the marks and should assume 1 mark per valid procedure. Candidates are reminded that substantive procedures are a core topic area and they must be able to produce relevant detailed procedures.

Part (d) required a discussion of the specific issue detailed in the requirement and the impact on the auditor's report if the issue remained unresolved. The issue being that the redundancy provision was understated by $195,000. Performance was satisfactory on this question, with an improvement by candidates on the last time this style of question was tested. Some candidates launched straight into assessing materiality without discussing the issue, which was that the redundancy provision should be $305,000 rather than $110,000 (½ mark). Therefore, the provision was understated (½ mark) and hence missed out on the available 1 mark for this. A further mark was available for the calculation and assessment of materiality. A number of candidates incorrectly used the total provision balance of $305,000 in calculating materiality rather than the under provision of $195,000. However, if they then stated that the balance was material they would have gained ½ mark. Many candidates were able to then correctly identify the type of opinion modification required (2 marks available), and attempt to describe the impact on the auditor's report (1 mark). Candidates answers tended to be more focused this session, rather than adopting a scatter gun approach of all possible auditor's report options.

252 AIRSOFT *Walk in the footsteps of a top tutor*

Key answer tips

Part (a) requires substantive procedures over completeness of payables. Make sure your procedures only focus on this one assertion otherwise you will not score marks. The requirement also specifies substantive procedures, therefore tests of controls will not score marks.

Part (b) asks for audit procedures using audit software. Audit software is used to manipulate data and perform calculations which would be time consuming to perform manually.

Parts (c) and (d) require substantive procedures over bank balances and directors' remuneration. Here you are not limited to a specific assertion so any relevant procedures will score marks.

Part (e) focuses on the key audit matters section of an auditor's report. You should learn the different sections of the auditor's report and their purpose.

(a) Trade payables and accruals

- Compare the total trade payables and list of accruals against prior year and investigate any significant differences.
- Select a sample of post-year-end payments from the bank ledger account; if they relate to the current year, follow through to the list of individual supplier balances or accruals listing to ensure they are recorded in the correct period.
- Obtain supplier statements and reconcile these to the list of individual supplier balances, and investigate any reconciling items.
- Select a sample of payable balances and perform a trade payables' circularisation, follow up any non-replies and any reconciling items between the balance confirmed and the trade payables' balance.
- Review after-date invoices and credit notes to ensure no further items need to be accrued.
- Enquire of management their process for identifying goods received but not invoiced or logged in the list of individual supplier balances and ensure that it is reasonable to ensure completeness of payables.

(b) Audit software procedures

- The audit team can use audit software to calculate the payables payment period for the year-to-date to compare against the prior year to identify whether payables days have changed in line with trading levels and expectations. If the ratio has decreased, this may be an indication that payables are understated.
- Audit software can be used to cast the payables and accruals listings to confirm the completeness and accuracy of trade payables and accruals.
- Audit software can be used to select a representative sample of items for further testing of payables balances.

- Audit software can be utilised to recalculate the accruals for goods received not invoiced at the year end.
- Undertake cut-off testing by assessing whether the dates of the last GRNs recorded relate to pre year end; and that any with a date of 1 May 20X5 onwards were excluded from trade payables.

(c) Bank balances

- Obtain a bank confirmation letter from Airsoft Co's bankers for all of its bank accounts.
- Agree all accounts listed on the bank confirmation letter to Airsoft Co's bank reconciliations and the trial balance to ensure completeness of bank balances.
- For all bank accounts, obtain Airsoft Co's bank account reconciliation and cast to ensure arithmetical accuracy.
- Agree the balance per the bank reconciliation to an original year-end bank statement and to the bank confirmation letter.
- Agree the reconciliations balance per the bank ledger account to the year-end bank ledger account.
- Trace all the outstanding lodgements to the pre-year-end bank ledger account, post-year-end bank statement and also to the pre-year-end paying-in-book.
- Trace all unpresented cheques through to a pre-year-end bank ledger account and post-year-end statement. For any unusual amounts or significant delays, obtain explanations from management.
- Examine any old unpresented cheques to assess if they need to be written back as they are no longer valid to be presented.
- Review the bank ledger account and bank statements for any unusual items or large transfers around the year end, as this could be evidence of window dressing.
- Examine the bank confirmation letter for details of any security provided by Airsoft Co or any legal right of set-off as this may require disclosure.
- Review the financial statements to ensure that the disclosure of bank balances is complete and accurate.

(d) Directors' remuneration

- Obtain a schedule of the directors' remuneration, split by salary and bonus paid in April and cast the schedule to ensure accuracy.
- Agree a sample of the individual monthly salary payments and the bonus payment in April to the payroll records.
- Confirm the amount of each bonus paid by agreeing to the bank ledger account and bank statements.
- Review the board minutes to identify whether any additional payments relating to this year have been agreed for any directors.
- Agree the amounts paid per director to board minutes to ensure the sums included are genuine.
- Obtain a written representation from management confirming the completeness of directors' remuneration including the bonus.
- Review the disclosures made regarding the directors' remuneration and assess whether these are in compliance with local legislation.

(e) Key audit matters

Key audit matters (KAM) are those matters which, in the auditor's professional judgement, were of most significance in the audit of the financial statements of the current period. Key audit matters are selected from matters communicated with those charged with governance.

The purpose of including key audit matters in the auditor's report is to help users in understanding the entity, and to provide a basis for the users to discuss with management and those charged with governance about matters relating to the entity and the financial statements. A key part of the definition is that these are the most significant matters. Identifying the most significant matters involves using the auditor's professional judgement.

ISA 701 *Communicating Key Audit Matters in the Independent Auditor's Report* suggests that in determining key audit matters the auditor should take the following into account:

- Areas of higher assessed risk of material misstatement, or significant risks.
- Significant auditor judgements relating to areas in the financial statements which involved significant management judgement.
- The effect on the audit of significant events or transactions which occurred during the period.

The description of each KAM in the Key Audit Matters section of the auditor's report should include a reference to the related disclosures in the financial statements and covers why the matter was considered to be one of most significance in the audit and therefore determined to be a KAM; and how the matter was addressed in the audit.

Marking guide

		Marks
(a)	**Substantive procedures for completeness of payables and accruals**	
	• Compare to prior year and investigate differences	1
	• Post y/e payments to list of individual suppliers	1
	• Supplier statement reconciliations	1
	• Trade payables circularisation	1
	• Review after-date invoices and credit notes	1
	• Enquiry of management process for identifying accruals	1
	Restricted to	**4**
(b)	**Audit software procedures over trade payables and accruals**	
	• Calculate trade payables payment period	1
	• Cast the payables and accruals schedule	1
	• Select sample for circularisation	1
	• Recalculate accruals	1
	• Cut-off testing on GRNs	1
	Restricted to	**3**

(c)	**Substantive procedures – year-end bank balances**	
	• Bank confirmation letter	1
	• Agree to bank reconciliation and TB	1
	• Cast bank reconciliations	1
	• Testing on bank reconciliations (1 mark per relevant procedure)	1
	• Review bank ledger account and bank statements for window dressing	1
	• Examine bank letter for evidence of security granted	1
	• Review financial statement disclosure	1
	Restricted to	**5**
(d)	**Substantive procedures – directors' remuneration**	
	• Cast schedule of remuneration	1
	• Agree payments to payroll records	1
	• Confirm bonus payments to the bank ledger account	1
	• Review board minutes for additional remuneration	1
	• Obtain written representation confirming completeness	1
	• Review financial statement disclosure	1
	Restricted to	**3**
(e)	**Key audit matters**	
	• Definition of KAM	1
	• Purpose of KAM	1
	• Significant matters and areas of judgement	1
	• Examples of KAM	2
	• KAM disclosure	1
	Restricted to	**5**
Total		**20**

Examiner's comments

Part (a) required candidates to describe substantive procedures the auditor should perform to obtain sufficient and appropriate audit evidence in relation to the completeness of Airsoft Co's trade payables and accruals. Performance on this requirement was disappointing. One mark was awarded for each well-described procedure. A number of candidates provided procedures which were not relevant to trade payables or accruals. For example, many candidates described audit procedures for purchases and inventory. Candidates are reminded to read the question requirement carefully and to ensure that they are answering the question set. Further, many candidates provided incomplete tests. For example, 'obtain supplier statements and agree to the payables list' would only be awarded ½ mark as without reference to reconciliation and the investigation of reconciling items, this test does not offer much assurance to the auditor. Candidates are again reminded to think about the aim of the procedure when they are describing substantive tests. Some candidates described audit procedures that did not focus on the completeness assertion. For example, agreeing amounts on the goods received not invoiced listing to post-year-end invoices, will not ensure that all items which should have been accrued at the year end have been included. Candidates are reminded to think carefully about the direction of their procedure when they are tackling completeness and existence testing, and are reminded that assertions are a key element of this syllabus.

Part (b) required candidates to describe audit software procedures which could be carried out during the audit of Airsoft Co's trade payables and accruals. Candidates' performance was disappointing. Some candidates did not attempt this question. Again, one mark was awarded for each well-described procedure. Although specifically advised not to, some candidate repeated their tests from part (a). For example, many candidates repeated the analytical review procedures in (a) in their answer to part (b). Marks were only awarded once. Often candidates did not make it clear the procedure related specifically to payables. For example, using audit software to cast the ledger, without making it clear which ledger exactly did not score the full mark.

Some candidates described control rather than substantive procedures. For example, run dummy data to ensure the payables system is operating correctly, would not be awarded any credit as this is an example of test data and not audit software.

Part (c) candidates to describe substantive procedures the auditor should perform to obtain sufficient and appropriate evidence in relation to Airsoft Co's year-end bank balance. Candidates' performance in this area was mixed. Again, one mark was awarded for each well-described procedure. Candidates who suggested a detailed audit procedure for each line of a standard bank reconciliation performed well on this question, however, some candidate descriptions of the tests were unclear, for example 'trace outstanding lodgements to pre and post year end'. This is another example of an incomplete test as there is no reference to what source documentation is being used to perform this test. When writing substantive procedures candidates are reminded that their procedure should make clear where the information is being drawn from as well as what it is being agreed to. The scenario noted that Airsoft Co had a bank overdraft of $2.6m. Some candidates therefore described a number of going concern audit procedures. However, this was not relevant as, not only was it not asked for in the question, but the scenario clearly showed the company was profitable, with profit before tax of $16.3m and total assets of $66.8m and there was no indication in the question that funding was an issue. Candidates must ensure that they read the requirement and answer the question as set.

Part (d) required candidates to describe substantive procedures the auditor should perform to confirm the directors' remuneration included in the financial statements at the year end. The director's remuneration included their salary and a discretionary bonus. Candidates' performance was disappointing. As in parts (a) (b) and (c) tests were often incomplete or were control tests. The most common incomplete test was simply 'review the disclosures' without going on to say 'to ensure compliance with local legislation'. The most common control test being 'review payroll listings to ensure monthly pay is authorised' The requirement verb for (a) (b) (c) and (d) was to 'describe' therefore sufficient detail was required to score the 1 mark available per procedure. Also, candidates must provide enough tests to score the marks and should assume 1 mark per valid procedure. Candidates are reminded that substantive procedures are a core topic area and they must be able to produce relevant detailed procedures.

Part (e) required candidates to identify a Key Audit Matter (KAM) and explain how the auditor determines and communicates KAM. This was a knowledge-based requirement based on the relatively new standard, ISA 701 Communicating Key Audit Matters in the Independent Auditor's Report. Candidates' performance was very disappointing with some candidates not attempting this requirement. Candidates often incorrectly described a KAM as an important matter that the auditor would consider at the planning stage of an audit. Candidates are reminded that knowledge of Auditor Reporting and the relevant ISAs is a key area of this syllabus.

253 INSECTS4U *Walk in the footsteps of a top tutor*

Key answer tips

Parts (a) to (c) require substantive procedures over three specific issues. Make sure your procedures address the issue described otherwise you will not score marks. The requirement also specifies substantive procedures, therefore tests of controls will not score marks.

Part (d) asks for the impact on the auditor's report if the issue described remains unresolved. You need to refer to materiality considerations to establish whether or not the opinion needs to be modified. Then consider the type of modification. Finally consider any other impact to the report. If the opinion is to be modified, the basis for opinion section will need to explain the reason for the modification.

(a) Completeness of Insects4U Co income

- Obtain a schedule of all Insects4U Co's income and cast to confirm completeness and accuracy of the balance.
- Compare the individual categories of income against prior year and investigate any significant differences.
- For monthly donations, trace a sample of donations received in the bank statements to the bank ledger account to ensure that they are recorded completely and accurately.
- For a sample of new subscribers in the year, agree from their completed subscription form the monthly sum and start date, trace to the monthly donations received account and agree to the bank ledger account and bank statements.
- For donations received in the post, review correspondence from donors, agree to the donations account and trace sums received to the bank ledger account and bank statements to ensure all completely recorded.
- For the charity events, undertake a proof-in-total calculation of the number of tickets sold multiplied by the ticket price, compare this to the income recorded and discuss any significant differences with management.

(b) Spider Spirals Co trade payables

- Calculate the trade payables payment period for Spider Spirals Co and compare to prior years and investigate any significant difference, in particular any decrease for this year due to the payment run on 3 May.
- Compare the total trade payables and list of accruals against prior year and investigate any significant differences.
- Discuss with management the process they have undertaken to quantify the misstatement of trade payables due to the late payment run and cut-off error of purchase invoices and consider the materiality of the error in isolation as well as with other misstatements found.

- Select a sample of purchase invoices received between the period of 1 and 7 May, ascertain through reviewing goods received notes (GRNs) if the goods were received pre or post year end, if post year end, then confirm that they have been excluded from the ledger or follow through to the correcting journal entry.
- Review after-date payments; if they relate to the current year, then follow through to the list of individual supplier balances or accrual listing to ensure they are recorded in the correct period.
- Obtain supplier statements and reconcile these to the list of individual supplier balances, and investigate any reconciling items.
- Select a sample of payables balances and perform a trade payables' circularisation, follow up any non-replies and any reconciling items between the balance confirmed and the trade payables' balance.
- Select a sample of GRNs before the year end and after the year end and follow through to inclusion in the correct period's payables balance, to ensure correct cut-off.

(c) Spider Spirals Co trade receivables

- Review the aged receivables listing to identify any old or slow-moving receivables balances, discuss the status of these balances with the finance director to assess whether they are likely to pay.
- Review customer correspondence to identify any balances which are in dispute or unlikely to be paid.
- Review whether there are any after-date cash receipts for old/slow-moving receivables balances.
- Review board minutes to identify whether there are any significant concerns in relation to payments by customers.
- Calculate the potential level of receivables which are not recoverable and assess whether this is material or not and discuss with management.
- Recalculate the allowance for credit losses/receivables and compare to the potentially irrecoverable balances to assess if the allowance is adequate.
- Inspect post-year-end sales returns/credit notes and consider whether an additional allowance against receivables is required.

(d) Impact on auditor's report

The company made a payment run of $490,000 for payables on 3 May, which is post-year-end. The trade payables which were outstanding at the year end have been understated as they have been recorded as being paid.

In addition, the bank overdraft is overstated as the payments are recorded as coming out of the year-end bank balance. This is evidence of window dressing, as the company has attempted to record a lower level of payable obligations at the year end.

The finance director's argument that no adjustment is necessary because the balances affected are both current liabilities is irrelevant, as although both balances are liabilities, they should each still be materially correct.

The amount of the payment run is $490,000 which represents 6.0% of total liabilities (490/8,100) and hence is a material matter.

If management refuses to adjust for the post-year-end payment run, the audit opinion will need to be modified. As trade payables are understated and the bank overdraft is overstated and there is a material misstatement which is not pervasive, a qualified opinion would be necessary. The opinion paragraph would be qualified 'except for'.

A basis for qualified opinion paragraph would need to be included subsequent to the opinion paragraph. This would explain the material misstatement in relation to the treatment of the trade payables and bank overdraft and the effect on the financial statements.

Marking guide		
		Marks
(a)	**Substantive procedures – completeness of income**	
	• Cast schedule of all of the company's income	1
	• Compare individual categories of income to prior year	1
	• Trace monthly donations from bank statements to bank ledger account	1
	• Agree subscription forms to donations received account, bank ledger account and bank statements	1
	• Review correspondence from donors, agree to donations account, bank ledger account and bank statements	1
	• Perform proof-in-total of tickets sold multiplied by ticket price	1
	Restricted to	**4**
(b)	**Substantive procedures – Spider Spirals Co trade payables**	
	• Calculate the trade payables payment period	1
	• Compare total trade payables and accruals to prior year	1
	• Discuss with management process to quantify misstatement	1
	• Sample invoices received between 1 to 7 May	1
	• Review after-date payments	1
	• Review supplier statements reconciliations	1
	• Perform a trade payables' circularisation	1
	• Cut-off testing pre and post-year-end GRN	1
	Restricted to	**6**
(c)	**Substantive procedures – Spider Spirals Co trade receivables**	
	• Aged receivables report to identify any slow-moving balances	1
	• Review customer correspondence for disputes	1
	• Review the after-date cash receipts	1
	• Review board minutes	1
	• Discuss level of irrecoverable receivables with management	1
	• Recalculate allowance for credit losses/receivables	1
	• Post-year-end sales returns/credit notes	1
	Restricted to	**5**
(d)	**Effect of uncorrected misstatement and impact on auditor's report**	
	• Discussion of issue	1
	• Calculation of materiality	1
	• Type of opinion modification required	2
	• Impact on auditor's report	1
		5
Total		**20**

Examiner's comments

Part (a) required candidates to describe substantive procedures to assess the completeness of income. In this type of question one mark was awarded for each well-described procedure. As in previous diets, performance in questions requiring substantive tests to be described continues to be disappointing. Most candidates did not understand the implications of testing for completeness and/or the implication of being a not-for-profit organisation. Many candidates therefore just gave standard tests over income such as agreeing goods despatch notes to invoices. Many candidates also placed too much emphasis to the cash at bank suggesting a bank reconciliation should be performed, with no reference to donations or income. Most candidates were unable to tailor their knowledge of general substantive procedures to the specific issues in the question requirements, or provided vague tests such as 'check' or objectives of 'ensure that....' As addressed in previous Examiner's Reports candidates must strive to understand substantive procedures. Learning a generic list of tests will not translate to exam success – procedures must be tailored to the specific requirements of the question.

Part (b) required candidates to describe substantive procedures for trade payables as the ledger was kept open one week longer than normal. One mark was awarded for each well-described procedure. Performance in this question was also disappointing. Candidates often listed general trade payable tests and did not relate to the specific requirement of the question. Although many candidates suggested suitable analytical review tests such as compare with prior year figure, few provided a full procedure by ensuring that 'significant differences should be investigated' and hence only scored ½ marks. Many candidates did attempt to explain a cut-off test however often, incorrectly, described sourcing the sample from invoices rather than goods received notes. Many candidates suggested testing purchase orders to goods received notes and invoices, however, this would not verify the year-end trade payable balance.

Part (c) required candidates to describe substantive procedures for trade receivables as the trade receivable days had increased. Again, one mark was awarded for each well-described procedure. Performance in this question was disappointing. Candidates again generally listed general trade receivable tests and did not relate to the specific requirement of the question. Many candidates incorrectly included substantive tests such as analytical review, receivable circularisation, cut-off testing, reconciling the trade receivables account to list of individual customer balances etc., which are not relevant to the question. Candidates must read the question carefully and apply their knowledge to the scenario provided.

Part (d) required candidates to describe the impact on the auditor's report if the issues remained unresolved. Performance was mixed across this question, however overall performance on auditor's reports showed an improvement over previous diets. Most candidates correctly calculated materiality and correctly suggested the type of modification. However, many candidates repeated the facts from the scenario and/or discussed how to resolve the issue. Few candidates noted that the issue resulted in trade payables being understated and therefore the bank overdraft being overstated. While most candidates correctly stated the impact on the auditor's report would be an 'except for' opinion, few discussed the need to include a 'basis of qualified opinion' paragraph.

254 ELOUNDA *Walk in the footsteps of a top tutor*

Key answer tips

Parts (a) to (c) require substantive procedures over three specific issues. Make sure your procedures address the issue described otherwise you will not score marks. The requirement also specifies substantive procedures, therefore tests of controls will not score marks.

Part (d) asks for procedures to assess whether the company is a going concern. This is a regularly examined topic, therefore students should be able to answer this question well.

(a) Revaluation of property, plant and equipment (PPE)

- Obtain a schedule of all PPE revalued during the year and cast to confirm completeness and accuracy of the revaluation adjustment and agree to trial balance and financial statements.
- Consider the competence and capability of the valuer, Martin Dullman, by assessing through enquiry with reference to qualifications, membership of a professional body and experience in valuing these types of assets.
- Consider whether the valuation undertaken provides sufficiently objective audit evidence. Discuss with management whether Martin Dullman has any financial interest in Elounda Co which along with the family relationship could have had an impact on independence of mind.
- Agree the revalued amounts to the valuation statement provided by the valuer.
- Review the valuation report and consider if all assets in the same category have been revalued in line with IAS 16 *Property, Plant and Equipment*.
- Agree the revalued amounts for these assets are included correctly in the non-current asset register.
- Recalculate the total revaluation adjustment and agree correctly recorded in the revaluation surplus.
- Recalculate the depreciation charge for the year to ensure that for the assets revalued during the year, the depreciation was based on the correct valuation and was for 12 months.
- Review the financial statements disclosures relating to the revaluation to ensure they comply with IAS 16.

(b) Inventory valuation

- Obtain a schedule of all raw materials, finished goods and work in progress (WIP) inventory and cast to confirm completeness and accuracy of the balance and agree to trial balance and financial statements.
- Obtain the breakdown of WIP and agree a sample of WIP assessed during the count to the WIP schedule, agreeing the percentage completion as recorded at the inventory count.

- For a sample of inventory items (finished goods and WIP), obtain the relevant cost sheets and confirm raw material costs to recent purchase invoices, labour costs to time sheets or wage records and overheads allocated are of a production nature.
- For a sample of inventory items, review the calculation for equivalent units and associated equivalent unit cost and recalculate the inventory valuation.
- Select a sample of year-end finished goods and review post-year-end sales invoices to ascertain if net realisable value (NRV) is above cost or if an adjustment is required.
- Select a sample of items included in WIP at the year-end and ascertain the final unit cost price, verifying to relevant supporting documentation, and compare to the unit sales price included in sales invoices post year end to assess NRV.
- Review aged inventory reports and identify any slow-moving goods, discuss with management why these items have not been written down or if an allowance is required.
- For the defective chemical compound E243, discuss with management their plans for disposing of these goods, and why they believe these goods have a NRV of $400,000.
- If any E243 has been sold post year end, agree to the sales invoice to assess NRV.
- Agree the cost of $720,000 for compound E243 to supporting documentation to confirm the raw material cost, labour cost and any overheads attributed to the cost.
- Confirm if the final adjustment for compound E243 is $320,000 (720 – 400) and discuss with management if this adjustment has been made; if so follow through the write down to confirm.
- Review the financial statements disclosures relating to inventory and WIP to ensure they comply with IAS 2 *Inventories*.

(c) Bank loan

- Agree the opening balance of the bank loan to the prior year audit file and financial statements.
- For any loan payments made during the year, agree the cash outflow to the bank ledger account and bank statements.
- Review bank correspondence to identify whether any late payment penalties have been levied and agree these have been charged to profit or loss account as a finance charge.
- Obtain direct confirmation at the year end from the loan provider of the outstanding balance and any security provided. Agree confirmed amounts to the loan schedule and financial statements.
- Review the loan agreement for details of covenants and recalculate to identify any breaches in these.
- Agree closing balance of the loan to the trial balance and draft financial statements and that the disclosure is adequate, including any security provided, that the loan is disclosed as a current liability and disclosure is in accordance with accounting standards and local legislation.

(d) Going concern procedures

- Obtain Elounda's cash flow forecast and review the cash in and out flows. Assess the assumptions for reasonableness and discuss the findings with management to understand if the company will have sufficient cash flows to meet liabilities as they fall due.
- Discuss with management their ability to settle the next instalment due for repayment to the bank and the lump sum payment of $800k in October 20X5 and ensure these have been included in the cash flow forecast.
- Review current agreements with the bank to determine whether any key ratios or covenants have been breached with regards to the bank loan or any overdraft.
- Review the company's post-year-end sales and order book to assess the levels of trade and if the revenue figures in the cash flow forecast are reasonable.
- Review post-year-end correspondence with suppliers to identify whether any restrictions in credit have arisen, and if so, ensure that the cash flow forecast reflects the current credit terms or where necessary an immediate payment for trade payables.
- Enquire of the lawyers of Elounda Co as to the existence of litigation and claims; if any exist, then consider their materiality and impact on the going concern basis.
- Perform audit tests in relation to subsequent events to identify any items which might indicate or mitigate the risk of going concern not being appropriate.
- Review the post-year-end board minutes to identify any other issues which might indicate financial difficulties for the company.
- Review post-year-end management accounts to assess if in line with cash flow forecast and to identify any issues which may be relevant to the going concern assessment.
- Consider whether any additional disclosures as required by IAS 1 *Presentation of Financial Statements* in relation to material uncertainties over going concern should be made in the financial statements.
- Obtain a written representation confirming the directors' view that Elounda Co is a going concern.

Marking guide

		Marks
(a)	**Substantive procedures – revaluation**	
	• Cast schedule of PPE revalued this year and agree to TB/FS	1
	• Consider reasonableness of the valuer's qualifications, membership of professional body and experience	1
	• Discuss with management if the valuer has financial interests in the company which may impact independence	1
	• Agree the revalued amounts to the valuation statement	1
	• Consider if all items in the same class of assets have been revalued	1
	• Agree the revalued amounts included correctly in the non-current asset register	1
	• Recalculate the total revaluation adjustment and agree recorded in the revaluation surplus	1
	• Recalculate the depreciation charge for the year	1
	• Review the financial statements disclosures for compliance with IAS 16	1
	Restricted to	**5**

(b)	**Substantive procedures – inventory valuation**	
	• Cast a schedule of all raw materials, finished goods and work in progress (WIP) inventory and agree to TB/FS	1
	• Obtain breakdown and agree sample of WIP from the count to the WIP schedule, agree percentage completion	1
	• Obtain relevant cost sheets and confirm costs to supporting documentation	1
	• Review the calculation for equivalent units and associated equivalent unit cost and recalculate the inventory valuation	1
	• Review post-year-end sales invoices to ascertain if net realisable value (NRV) is above cost	1
	• Ascertain the final unit cost price of WIP and compare to the sales invoices post year end to assess NRV	1
	• Review aged inventory reports, identify slow-moving goods, discuss with management	1
	• Compound E243, discuss with management plans for disposing of goods, why NRV is $400,000	1
	• If any of defective goods have been sold post year end, agree to the sales invoice to assess NRV	1
	• Agree the cost of $720,000 for compound E243 to supporting documentation	1
	• Confirm the final adjustment for compound E243, discuss with management if adjustment made	1
	• Review financial statements disclosures for compliance with IAS 2	1
	Restricted to	**6**
(c)	**Substantive procedures – bank loan**	
	• Agree the opening balance to the prior year audit file and FS	1
	• For loan payments made, agree to bank ledger account and bank statements	1
	• Review the bank correspondence for late payment penalties, agree to statement of profit or loss	1
	• Obtain direct confirmation of year-end balance from bank, agree to the loan schedule	1
	• Review loan agreement for details of covenants and recalculate to identify any breaches	1
	• Agree closing balance to the TB and draft FS and review the disclosure of the current liability bank loan	1
	Restricted to	**4**
(d)	**Going concern procedures**	
	• Review cash flow forecasts	1
	• Review bank loan agreements, breach of key ratios or covenants	1
	• Review post-year-end sales and order book	1
	• Review correspondence with suppliers	1
	• Enquire of lawyers for any litigation	1
	• Subsequent events	1
	• Board minutes	1
	• Management accounts	1
	• Consider additional disclosures under IAS 1	1
	• Written representation	1
	Restricted to	**5**
Total		**20**

Examiner's comments

This question covered the area of audit evidence and going concern. Performance across this question was disappointing.

Parts (a) to (c) were scenario based and required substantive procedures for three areas; revaluation of property, plant and equipment (PPE), WIP valuation and bank loans. A key requirement of this part of the syllabus is an ability to describe relevant audit procedures for a particular class of transactions or event. As in previous diets overall performance in this key syllabus area was once again disappointing. Most candidates were unable to tailor their knowledge of general substantive procedures to the specific issues in the question requirements, or provided vague tests such as 'check' or objectives of 'ensure that....' As addressed in previous Examiner's Reports candidates must strive to understand substantive procedures. Learning a generic list of tests will not translate to exam success – procedures must be tailored to the specific requirements of the question. On the revaluation question many candidates provided general PPE tests on areas of title or additions/disposals. Additionally, candidates focused on authorisation of asset expenditure or discussing why PPE had been revalued. Answers over auditing the WIP valuation were particularly disappointing. A significant proportion of candidates focused on inventory counts rather than valuation. Candidates must read the question and apply their knowledge to the scenario provided. Substantive procedures provided for the bank loan were stronger, however, again genera bank and cash tests were provided rather than for the bank loans. Additionally, some candidates strayed into auditing going concern rather than the liability associated with the bank loan.

Part (d) on going concern procedures was answered satisfactorily. Many candidates were able to generate a sufficient number of points to provide a strong answer. However, some candidates failed to understand the question was about procedures rather than going concern indicators. Additionally, some procedures lacked detail e.g. 'review board minutes' but the procedure failed to explain what this key source of evidence was being reviewed for.

255 ANDROMEDA *Walk in the footsteps of a top tutor*

Key answer tips

Part (a) is a knowledge question regarding reliability of evidence. This requires text book knowledge. Make sure you provide an explanation.

Part (b) asks for audit procedures before and during an inventory count. Procedures to be performed during the count will need to be planned before the count takes place. Procedures will be affected by the level of risk assessed in relation to inventory.

Part (c) requires procedures in relation to a rights issue. Procedures will be required to determine the amount raised by the rights issue and whether it has been classified and disclosed correctly in the financial statements.

Part (d) requires procedures in relation to research and development expenditure. Procedures should focus on whether the accounting requirements from the relevant accounting standard have been followed.

Part (e) asks for the reporting implications of an unresolved issue. Work through the information in a logical manner to arrive at the appropriate suggestion. Document each step of the process as this is what earns the marks. You cannot earn all of the marks available if you only state the opinion required.

(a) Reliability of audit evidence

- The reliability of audit evidence is increased when it is obtained from independent sources outside the entity.
- The reliability of audit evidence which is generated internally is increased when the related controls imposed by the entity, including those over its preparation and maintenance, are effective.
- Audit evidence obtained directly by the auditor is more reliable than audit evidence obtained indirectly or by inference.
- Audit evidence in documentary form, whether paper, electronic or other medium, is more reliable than evidence obtained orally.
- Audit evidence provided by original documents is more reliable than audit evidence provided by photocopies or facsimiles, the reliability of which may depend on the controls over their preparation and maintenance.

(b) Inventory count procedures

Before the count

- Review the prior year audit files to identify whether there were any particular warehouses where significant inventory issues arose last year.
- Discuss with management whether any of the warehouses this year are new, or have experienced significant control issues.
- Decide which of the 12 warehouses the audit team members will attend, basing this on materiality and risk of each site.

- Obtain a copy of the proposed inventory count instructions, review them to identify any control deficiencies and if any are noted, discuss them with management prior to the counts.

During the count

- Observe the counting teams of Andromeda to confirm whether the inventory count instructions are being followed correctly.
- Select a sample of inventory and perform test counts from inventory sheets to warehouse aisle and from warehouse aisle to inventory sheets.
- Confirm the procedures for identifying and segregating damaged goods are operating correctly, and assess inventory for evidence of any damaged or slow-moving items.
- Observe the procedures for movements of inventory during the count, to confirm that all movements have ceased.
- Obtain a photocopy of the completed sequentially numbered inventory sheets for follow up testing on the final audit.
- Identify and make a note of the last goods received notes and goods despatch notes for 31 July in order to perform cut-off procedures.
- Discuss with the internal audit supervisor how any raw materials quantities have been estimated. Where possible, reperform the procedures adopted by the supervisor.

(c) Rights issue

- Review board minutes to confirm the amount of finance to be raised via rights issue.
- Recalculate the amount raised by multiplying the number of shares issued with the share price of $2.50 to confirm accuracy.
- Inspect bank statements to confirm the amount received from the rights issue.
- Recalculate split of share capital and share premium and agree to the financial statements.
- Review financial statement disclosure to confirm compliance with financial reporting framework.

(d) Research and development

- Obtain and cast a schedule of intangible assets, detailing opening balances, amount capitalised in the current year, amortisation and closing balances.
- Agree the opening balances to the prior year financial statements.
- Agree the closing balances to the general ledger, trial balance and draft financial statements.
- Recalculate the amortisation charge for a sample of intangible assets which have commenced production and confirm it is line with the amortisation policy of straight line over five years.
- For the five new projects, discuss with management the details of each project along with the stage of development and whether it has been capitalised or expensed.

- For those expensed as research, agree the costs incurred to invoices and supporting documentation and to inclusion in profit or loss.
- For those capitalised as development, agree costs incurred to invoices and confirm technically feasible by discussion with development managers or review of feasibility reports.
- Review market research reports to confirm Andromeda has the ability to sell the product once complete and probable future economic benefits will arise.
- Review the disclosures for intangible assets in the draft financial statements are in accordance with IAS 38 *Intangible Assets*.

(e) Auditor's report

One of the projects Andromeda has developed in the year does not meet the recognition criteria under IAS 38 *Intangible Assets* for capitalisation but has been included within intangible assets. This is contrary to IAS 38, as if the criteria are not met, then this project is research expenditure and should be expensed to profit or loss rather than capitalised.

The error is material as it represents 11.8% of profit before tax (0.98m/8.3m).

Management should adjust the financial statements by removing this project from intangible assets and charging it to profit or loss instead. The finance director's argument that the balance is immaterial is not correct.

If management refuses to amend this error, then the audit opinion will need to be modified as management has not complied with IAS 38.

The error is material but not pervasive, therefore the opinion paragraph would be qualified 'except for'.

A basis for qualified opinion paragraph would be needed and would explain the material misstatement in relation to the incorrect treatment of research and development and the effect on the financial statements.

Marking guide

		Marks
(a)	**Reliability of evidence**	
	• Reliability increased when it is obtained from independent sources	1
	• Internally generated evidence more reliable when the controls are effective	1
	• Evidence obtained directly by the auditor is more reliable than evidence obtained indirectly or by inference	1
	• Evidence in documentary form is more reliable than evidence obtained orally	1
	• Evidence provided by original documents is more reliable than evidence provided by copies	1
	Restricted to	**4**
(b)	**Inventory count audit procedures**	
	Before the count	
	• Review the prior year audit files to identify significant inventory issues from last year	1
	• Discuss with management if any new warehouses or any sites have significant control issues	1
	• Decide which of the 12 warehouses to attend	1
	• Review a copy of the proposed inventory count instructions	1

	During the count	
	• Observe the counters to confirm if inventory count instructions are being followed	1
	• Perform 2-way test counts	1
	• Confirm procedures for damaged goods	1
	• Observe procedures for movements of inventory	1
	• Obtain a photocopy of the completed inventory sheets	1
	• Identify and make a note of the last GRNs and GDNs	1
	• Discuss with the internal audit supervisor how the raw materials quantities has been estimated	1
	Restricted to	**5**
(c)	**Rights issue**	
	• Review board minutes to confirm finance to be raised via rights issue	1
	• Recalculate the amount raised to confirm accuracy	1
	• Inspect bank statements to confirm amount received	1
	• Recalculate split of share capital and share premium	1
	• Review financial statement disclosure to confirm compliance with financial reporting framework	1
	Restricted to	**3**
(d)	**Research and development**	
	• Cast the schedule of intangible assets	1
	• Agree the opening balances to the prior year financial statements	1
	• Agree the closing balances to the general ledger, trial balance and draft financial statements	1
	• Recalculate amortisation charged in the year and confirm in line with the policy of straight line over five years	1
	• For new projects, discuss with management the stage of development and if capitalised or expensed	1
	• For those expensed as research, agree costs to invoices, supporting documentation and to inclusion in profit or loss	1
	• Agree development costs to invoice and confirm technically feasible by discussion with development managers	1
	• Review market research reports to confirm Andromeda has the ability to sell the product	1
	• Review the disclosures in the financial statements in accordance with IAS 38	1
	Restricted to	**4**
(e)	**Issue and impact on auditor's report**	
	• Discussion of issue	1
	• Calculation of materiality	1
	• Type of opinion modification required	1
	• Impact on auditor's report	1
		4
Total		**20**

Examiner's comments

Part (a) Candidates were firstly asked to explain factors which influence the reliability of audit evidence. One mark was available for each factor. Candidates were required to either fully explain the factor or compare that factor to another source. This question was generally well answered. A minority of candidates did not fully describe each factor e.g. they noted written evidence was reliable but did not explain why it was reliable, or alternatively, did not make a comparison such as written evidence is stronger than oral evidence. It was pleasing that candidates planned their time carefully and generally only described the required number of factors.

In parts (b) and (d), candidates were further provided with a short scenario based question and were required to describe audit procedures that would be performed before and during an inventory count and audit procedures in relation to research and development costs. As in previous sitting and as noted in previous examiner's reports the provision of audit procedures relevant to particular circumstances was not well attempted by the majority of candidates. Most candidates were able to identify that the count procedures should be obtained before the inventory count, however a significant number did not expand to explain the purpose of obtaining this information or the importance of the auditor reviewing the adequacy of these instructions. Candidates often then listed further details to be obtained e.g. location of count, assembling the audit team, whether to use an expert etc. A number of candidates referred to third-party inventory however this was not mentioned in the scenario and therefore any related procedures were not valid. Only the better candidates suggested looking at prior year audit files or, considered the materiality of the sites and control issues at sites. Most candidates did note that during the count the auditor should observe the counters to ensure the instructions were being followed. However, a significant number of candidates then proceeded to list the count procedures that the company's counting team should follow thereby straying into management responsibilities rather than the procedures relevant to the auditor. Some candidates correctly suggested undertaking test counts, while only a minority suggested obtaining copies of the completed count sheets. Overall it was disappointing that candidates did not seem familiar with the auditor's role at an inventory count. In relation to research and development costs, some candidates correctly suggested that the auditor needed to ensure compliance with the capitalisation criteria in IAS 38 and also suggested recalculating the amortisation charge, but few candidates identified any other relevant procedures. Many candidates did not score any marks for this requirement. Although many candidates suggested a review of invoices, the procedure described was most often testing valuation or rights and obligations rather than to ensure correct classification.

Part (e) Candidates were required to discuss the implication on the auditor's report if an issue surrounding research and development costs remained unresolved. This question was well answered. Most candidates stated the issue, being that the project did not meet the capitalisation criteria, however few candidates explained the impact on the financial statements e.g. assets would be overstated and profit understated. The majority of candidates correctly calculated materiality, however a small number of candidates incorrectly calculated materiality based on the size of the project as a percentage of total research and development spend (i.e. 49%), thereby not considering the materiality of the issue to the financial statements as a whole. Overall it was encouraging to note that reporting questions have shown a continued improvement in recent sittings.

256 HAWTHORN *Walk in the footsteps of a top tutor*

Key answer tips

In part (a) make sure you give assertions relevant to transactions and events. Procedures need to be properly described to earn a full mark. Make it clear what the auditor needs to do and what the procedure will achieve.

The scenario for parts (b) to (d) provides details of very specific issues that have occurred during the year. Your procedures need to focus on these issues rather than the balances in general.

(a) **Occurrence**

The transactions and events that have been recorded have actually occurred and pertain to the entity.

Substantive procedures

Select a sample of sales transactions recorded in the detailed sales listing; agree the details back to a goods despatched note (GDN) and customer order.

Review the monthly breakdown of sales per key product, compare to the prior year and budget and investigate any significant differences.

Completeness

All transactions and events that should have been recorded have been recorded.

Substantive procedures

Select a sample of GDNs raised during the year; agree to the sales invoice and that they are recorded in the detailed sales listing.

Review the total amount of sales, compare to the prior year and budget and investigate any significant differences.

Accuracy

The amounts and other data relating to recorded transactions and events have been recorded appropriately.

Substantive procedures

Select a sample of sales invoices and recalculate that the totals and calculation of sales tax are correct.

For a sample of sales invoices, confirm the sales price stated agrees to the authorised price list.

Cut-off

Transactions and events have been recorded in the correct accounting period.

Substantive procedures

Select a sample of pre and post-year-end GDNs and agree that the sale is recorded in the correct period's detailed sales listing.

Review the post-year-end sales returns and agree if they relate to pre-year-end sales that the revenue has been correctly removed from the detailed sales listing.

Classification

Transactions and events have been recorded in the proper accounts.

Substantive procedures

Agree for a sample of sales invoices that they have been correctly recorded within the revenue general ledger account codes and included within revenue in the financial statements.

Presentation

Transactions and events are appropriately aggregated or disaggregated and clearly described, and related disclosures are relevant and understandable in the context of the applicable financial reporting framework.

Substantive procedures

Obtain a breakdown of revenue by account code and cast to ensure accuracy. Agree the breakdown of revenue disclosed in the financial statements to the revenue account codes within the general ledger.

(b) Supplier statement reconciliations

- Select a representative sample of year-end supplier statements and agree the balance to the list of individual supplier balances of Hawthorn. If the balance agrees, then no further work is required.
- Where differences occur due to invoices in transit, confirm from goods received notes (GRN) whether the receipt of goods was pre year end, if so confirm that this receipt is included in year-end accruals.
- Where differences occur due to cash in transit from Hawthorn to the supplier, confirm from the bank ledger account and bank statements that the cash was sent pre year end.
- Discuss any further adjusting items with the payables ledger supervisor to understand the nature of the reconciling item, and whether it has been correctly accounted for.

(c) Bank reconciliation

- Obtain Hawthorn's bank account reconciliation and cast to check the additions to ensure arithmetical accuracy.
- Agree the balance per the bank reconciliation to an original year-end bank statement and to the bank confirmation letter.
- Agree the reconciliation's balance per the bank ledger account to the year-end bank ledger account.
- Trace all the outstanding lodgements to the pre-year-end bank ledger account, post-year-end bank statement and also to paying-in-book pre year end.
- Trace all unpresented cheques through to a pre-year-end bank ledger account and post-year-end statement. For any unusual amounts or significant delays, obtain explanations from management.
- Examine any old unpresented cheques to assess if they need to be written back as they are no longer valid to be presented.

(d) Receivables

- Review the aged receivable ledger to identify any old or slow-moving receivable balances, discuss the status of these balances with the credit controller to assess whether they are likely to pay.
- Select a significant sample of receivables and review whether there are any after-date cash receipts, ensure that a sample of old/slow-moving receivable balances is also selected.
- Review customer correspondence to identify any balances which are in dispute or unlikely to be paid.
- Review board minutes to identify whether there are any significant concerns in relation to payments by customers.
- Calculate the average receivables collection period and compare this to prior year, investigate any significant differences.
- Inspect post-year-end sales returns/credit notes and consider whether an additional allowance against receivables is required.
- Select a sample of goods despatch notes (GDN) before and just after the year end and follow through to the list of individual customer balances to ensure they are recorded in the correct accounting period.
- Select a sample of year-end receivable balances and agree back to valid supporting documentation of GDN and sales order to ensure existence.

Marking guide

		Marks
(a)	**Assertions and substantive procedures relevant to revenue**	
	• Occurrence	
	• Completeness	2
	• Accuracy	2
	• Cut-off	2
	• Classification	2
	• Presentation	2
	Restricted to	**8**
(b)	**Supplier statement reconciliations**	
	• Select a sample of supplier statements and agree the balance to the list of individual supplier balances	1
	• Invoices in transit, confirm via GRN if receipt of goods was pre year end, if so confirm included in year-end accruals	1
	• Cash in transit, confirm from bank ledger account and bank statements the cash was sent pre year end	1
	• Discuss any further adjusting items with the payables ledger supervisor	1
	Restricted to	**3**
(c)	**Bank reconciliation**	
	• Check additions of bank reconciliation	1
	• Bank balance to statement/bank confirmation	1
	• Bank ledger account balance to bank ledger account	1
	• Outstanding lodgements	1
	• Unpresented cheques review	1
	• Old cheques write back	1
	Restricted to	**4**

(d)	**Receivables**	
	• Aged receivables report to identify any slow-moving balances	1
	• Review the after-date cash receipts	1
	• Review customer correspondence to assess whether there are any invoices in dispute	1
	• Review board minutes	1
	• Calculate the average receivables collection period	1
	• Post-year-end sales returns/credit notes	1
	• Cut-off testing of GDN	1
	• Agree to GDN and sales order to ensure existence	1
	Restricted to	**5**
Total		**20**

Examiner's comments

Part (a) comprised (a) (i) which required four assertions relevant to classes of transactions and events and part (a) (ii) which required an example substantive procedure for each assertion identified which would be relevant to the audit of revenue. This question was unrelated to the scenario and was knowledge based, and candidates' performance was unsatisfactory. Assertions are a key element of the syllabus and so it was very disappointing to see that a significant minority of candidates do not know the assertions relevant to classes of transactions and events. A significant proportion of candidates provided existence and valuation which were irrelevant as these are assertions relevant to account balances. Where candidates did correctly identify the assertions they often failed to explain them adequately or did so with reference to assets and liabilities rather than transactions. Also many explanations were too brief or simply repeated the assertion, such as, 'accuracy ensures the amounts in the financial statements are accurate'. A number of candidates provided example procedures which were not relevant when testing revenue, but instead focused on receivables or purchases. This can only be due to a failure to read the question requirement properly. In addition many procedures were vague or incomplete, such as agreeing goods despatch notes to sales invoices but not then agreeing the invoices to the detailed sales listing. Also many of the procedures were tests of control rather than substantive procedures. The direction of the occurrence and completeness tests were often confused resulting in incorrect procedures. The direction of occurrence tests should generally start at accounting records, whereas completeness procedures should begin at source documents.

The remainder of the question provided candidates with three short scenarios detailing matters that had been brought to attention prior to the audit fieldwork and candidates were expected to produce appropriate substantive procedures relevant to each matter. Part (b) required substantive procedures in relation to auditing supplier statement reconciliations. Part (c) required substantive procedures over the bank reconciliation and finally part (d) required substantive procedures in relation to the existence and valuation of receivables. Performance on this question was unsatisfactory. A significant minority did not attempt all parts of this question. Most candidates were unable to tailor their knowledge of general substantive procedures to the specific issues in the scenario and question requirements. Many candidates spotted the terms payables, bank and receivables and proceeded to list all possible tests for these areas. This is not what was required and this approach scored few or no marks. The scenario was provided so that candidates could apply their knowledge. However it seems that many candidates did not take any notice of the scenario at all. As addressed in previous examiner's reports candidates must strive to understand substantive procedures, learning a generic list of tests will not translate to exam success as they must be responsive to the scenario.

In part (b) candidates needed to focus on testing supplier statement reconciliations rather than trade payables in general. The most common correct answer awarded credit was 'agree the supplier statements to the list of individual supplier balances.' Very few candidates scored more than 1 mark. Incorrect answers focused on calculating trade payables days or undertaking a payables circularisation.

In part (c) many candidates focused on auditing the cash balance rather than the bank reconciliation. Hence answers such as casting the bank ledger account, requesting a bank confirmation letter or counting the petty cash balance were not awarded any credit. Preparation of bank reconciliations is part of the Financial Accounting syllabus and therefore candidates should have considered the items which are included as part of the bank reconciliation and focused on deriving tests to audit each component. In addition to verify if unpresented cheques and outstanding lodgements were valid reconciling items, audit procedures should have focused on inclusion in the pre-year-end bank ledger account and post-year-end bank statements. Very few candidates demonstrated an understanding of this point.

In part (d) stronger candidates were able to generate tests focusing on analytical review against prior year balances, review of aged receivables listing or discussions with management about an allowance for receivables. However, a significant proportion of candidates incorrectly suggested undertaking receivables circularisation, including the detailed steps required, this was despite the scenario clearly stating that the finance director had requested that a circularisation not be carried out. The requirement verb was to 'describe' therefore sufficient detail was required to score the 1 mark available per test. Candidates must provide enough tests as they should assume 1 mark per valid procedure. Candidates are reminded yet again that substantive procedures are a core topic area and they must be able to produce relevant detailed procedures.

257 PINEAPPLE BEACH HOTEL *Walk in the footsteps of a top tutor*

Key answer tips

Part (a) is a knowledge requirement covering working paper contents. This is rote-learned knowledge from the text book.

In part (b) make sure you give substantive analytical procedures only. Procedures need to be properly described to earn a full mark. Analytical procedures include comparison of results, trends, ratios and proof-in-totals. Try to suggest ways the auditor can assess the reasonableness of the revenue figure.

Parts (c) and (d) require substantive procedures over two specific issues. Substantive procedures are used to test the amounts included in the financial statements, therefore focus on how to obtain evidence to support the depreciation charge for the new equipment and the claim for food poisoning. These procedures can include both analytical procedures and tests of detail.

Part (e) is a reporting requirement focused on an inability to obtain sufficient appropriate audit evidence due to the directors refusing to provide a signed written representation letter. Take the usual approach to determining the implications for the auditor's report. Consider whether the issue is material, if so, is it material but not pervasive or material and pervasive and choose the appropriate opinion for that issue.

(a) Working papers

- Name of client – identifies the client being audited.
- Year-end date – identifies the year end to which the audit working papers relate.
- Subject – identifies the area of the financial statements that is being audited, the topic area of the working paper, such as receivables circularisation.
- Working paper reference – provides a clear reference to identify the number of the working paper.
- Preparer – identifies the name of the audit team member who prepared the working paper, so any queries can be directed to the relevant person.
- Date prepared – the date that the audit work was performed by the team member; this helps to identify what was known at the time and what issues may have occurred subsequently.
- Reviewer – the name of the audit team member who reviewed the working paper; this provides evidence that the audit work was reviewed by an appropriate member of the team.
- Date of review – the date the audit work was reviewed by the senior member of the team; this should be prior to the date that the auditor's report was signed.
- Objective of work/test – the aim of the work being performed, could be the related assertion; this provides the context for why the audit procedure is being performed.
- Details of work performed – the audit tests performed along with sufficient detail of items selected for testing.
- Results of work performed – whether any exceptions arose in the audit work and if any further work is required.
- Conclusion – the overall conclusion on the audit work performed, whether the area is true and fair.

(b) Analytical procedures to confirm revenue

- Compare revenue for the current year against revenue for the prior year and budget and investigate any unusual fluctuations through discussion with management.
- Compare revenue by category (accommodation, leisure facilities and restaurants) and compare against the prior year and investigate any unusual fluctuations through discussion with management.
- Analyse revenue by category on a month by month basis to assess whether revenue appears reasonable taking into consideration seasonal fluctuations and any potential bad publicity caused by the food poisoning lawsuit.
- Calculate the gross profit margin by category and compare with prior year. Discuss any unusual fluctuations with management.
- Perform a proof-in-total for revenue from accommodation by multiplying the average occupancy rate by the average room rate and compare with actual revenue for accommodation. Discuss any unusual fluctuations with management.

- Perform a proof-in-total for leisure facility membership revenue by multiplying the average number of members by the annual membership fee and compare with actual revenue for leisure memberships. Discuss any unusual fluctuations with management.
- Calculate the average revenue per membership and compare with the annual membership fee to assess reasonableness. Discuss any unusual fluctuations with management.

(c) Depreciation

- Review the reasonableness of the depreciation rates applied to the new leisure facilities and compare to industry averages.
- Review the asset expenditure budgets for the next few years to assess whether there are any plans to replace any of the new leisure equipment, as this would indicate that the useful life is less than 10 years.
- Review profits and losses on disposal of assets disposed of in the year to assess the reasonableness of the depreciation policies.
- Select a sample of new leisure equipment and recalculate the depreciation charge to ensure arithmetical accuracy of the charge.
- Perform a proof-in-total calculation for the depreciation charged on the new equipment, discuss with management if significant fluctuations arise.
- Review the disclosure of the depreciation charges and policies in the draft financial statements.

(d) Food poisoning claim

- Review the correspondence from the customers claiming food poisoning to assess whether Pineapple has a present obligation as a result of a past event.
- Send an enquiry letter to the lawyers of Pineapple to obtain their view as to the probability of the claim being successful.
- Review board minutes to understand whether the directors believe that the claim will be successful or not.
- Review the post-year-end period to assess whether any payments have been made to any of the claimants.
- Discuss with management as to whether they propose to include a contingent liability disclosure or not, consider the reasonableness of this.
- Review the adequacy of any disclosures made in the financial statements to ensure they are in accordance with IAS 37 *Provisions, Contingent Liabilities and Contingent Assets*.

(e) Implications for the auditor's report

- The lack of a signed written representation letter means the auditor does not have sufficient and appropriate audit evidence to be able to form an opinion on the matters covered by the representation.
- As the written representation letter covers many aspects such as confirming the directors have recorded all transactions, the financial statements have been properly prepared and they have provided the auditor with all information for the audit, the refusal to sign the letter casts doubt over management integrity and is likely to be considered material and pervasive.

- The opinion should be modified with a disclaimer of opinion being issued stating that the auditor does not express an opinion on the financial statements due to an inability to obtain sufficient appropriate evidence.
- The basis for opinion will be changed to a basis for disclaimer of opinion and will explain the issue causing the modified opinion.
- The reference to professional standards which is usually included in the basis for opinion section will be moved to the auditor's responsibility section of the report.
- The statement that the auditor has audited the financial statements will be changed to the auditor was engaged to perform an audit.

Marking guide

		Marks
(a)	**Working paper contents**	
	• Name of client	1
	• Year-end date	1
	• Subject	1
	• Working paper reference	1
	• Preparer	1
	• Date prepared	1
	• Reviewer	1
	• Date of review	1
	• Objective of work/test	1
	• Details of work performed	1
	• Results of work performed	1
	• Conclusion	1
	Restricted to	**4**
(b)	**Analytical procedures to confirm revenue**	
	• Compare revenue to prior year and budget	1
	• Compare revenue by category	1
	• Analyse revenue by month – seasonality	1
	• Calculate gross profit margin	1
	• Perform proof-in-total of accommodation revenue	1
	• Perform proof-in-total of leisure facility membership revenue	1
	• Calculate the average revenue per membership	1
	Restricted to	**4**
(c)	**Depreciation**	
	• Review the reasonableness of the depreciation rates	1
	• Review the asset expenditure budgets	1
	• Review profits and losses on disposal for assets disposed of in year	1
	• Recalculate the depreciation charge for a sample of assets	1
	• Perform a proof-in-total calculation	1
	• Review the disclosure in the draft financial statements	1
	Restricted to	**4**

(d)	**Food poisoning claim**	
	• Review the correspondence from the customers	1
	• Enquire of the lawyers as to the probability of the claim being successful	1
	• Review board minutes	1
	• Review the post-year-end period to assess whether any payments have been made	1
	• Discuss with management as to whether they propose to include a contingent liability disclosure	1
	• Review any disclosures made in the financial statements	1
	Restricted to	**4**
(e)	**Implications for the auditor's report**	
	• Auditor is unable to obtain sufficient, appropriate audit evidence	1
	• Material and pervasive due to the matters included	1
	• Disclaimer of opinion – no opinion expressed	1
	• Basis for disclaimer of opinion explains the issue	1
	• Reference to professional standards moved from basis for opinion to auditor's responsibilities	1
	• Wording changed to say the auditor was engaged to perform the audit	1
	Restricted to	**4**
Total		**20**

Examiner's comments

This question required substantive procedures for depreciation and a contingent liability for a food poisoning case. Performance on this question was unsatisfactory. A significant minority did not even attempt this part of the question. Candidates' answers for depreciation tended to be weaker than for the food poisoning. On the depreciation many candidates did not focus their answer on the issue identified, which related to the depreciation method adopted for the assets acquired in the year. In the scenario the issue was headed up as depreciation and so this should have given candidates a clue that they needed to focus just on depreciation. However, a significant proportion of answers were on general PPE tests often without any reference at all to depreciation. In addition, many felt that generic tests such as 'get an expert's advice' or 'obtain management representation' were appropriate tests; they are not. The food poisoning issue tended to be answered slightly better, however again tests tended to be too brief, 'read board minutes', 'discuss with management' or 'discuss with the lawyer' did not score any marks as they do not explain what is to be discussed or what we are looking for in the board minutes.

In addition, a minority of candidates focused on auditing the kitchen and food hygiene procedures with tests such as 'observing the kitchen process' or 'writing to customers to see if they have had food poisoning.' This is not the focus of the auditor and does not provide evidence with regards to the potential contingent liability.

Substantive procedures are a core topic area and future candidates must focus on being able to generate specific and detailed tests.

ADDITIONAL QUESTIONS

258 SAXOPHONE ENTERPRISES *Walk in the footsteps of a top tutor*

Key answer tips

This question requires corporate governance deficiencies within the scenario to be explained and a recommendation provided for each. Knowledge of the Corporate Governance Code is required here. Work through on a line by line basis and consider whether the information suggests that the company is being properly managed and controlled in the best interests of the shareholders.

Corporate governance deficiencies and recommendations

Deficiency	Recommendation
Bill Bassoon is now the chair after having been the chief executive until last year. The chair must be an independent non-executive director and hence cannot have previously been the chief executive of the same company. The roles of chair and chief executive are both very important and carry significant responsibilities. Too much power resides in the hands of one individual.	Bill Bassoon should return to the role of chief executive as this will fill the current vacancy and an independent non-executive director should be recruited to fill the role of chair. Open advertising and/or an external search consultancy should be used for the appointment of the chair.
The board comprises five executives and only three non-executive directors. There should be an appropriate balance of executives and non-executives, to ensure that the board makes the correct objective decisions, which are in the best interest of the stakeholders of the company. The executives can dominate the board's decision-making.	At least half the board, excluding the chair should be independent NEDs. Hence the board of Saxophone should consider recruiting and appointing two additional independent non-executive directors.

Deficiency	**Recommendation**
Bill Bassoon is considering appointing a close friend as a non-executive director. The friend has experience of running a manufacturing company. If this director is a close friend of Bill Bassoon, then it is possible that independence will be compromised. In addition, other than being a former chief executive, the NED does not have any relevant experience of the insurance industry and so it is questionable what value will be added to Saxophone.	Only independent non-executives with relevant experience and skills should be appointed to the board of Saxophone. Appointments should be based on merit and objective criteria and should promote diversity. The close friend of Bill Bassoon is unlikely to meet these criteria, due to having no experience in the insurance industry, and so should not be appointed. Open advertising and/or an external search consultancy should be used for the appointment of the NEDs.
The remuneration for directors is set by Jessie Oboe, the finance director. However, no director should be involved in setting their own remuneration as this may result in excessive levels of pay being set. Jessie may pay more to directors who are willing to support this agenda in board meetings.	The board should establish formal and transparent procedures for developing the policy for executive directors' remuneration. The remuneration committee should determine the policy for executive director remuneration, as well as set the remuneration for the chair, executive directors and senior management.
All directors' remuneration is in the form of an annual bonus. Pay should motivate the directors to focus on the long-term growth of the business. Annual targets can encourage short-term strategies rather than maximising shareholder wealth.	The remuneration of executives should be restructured to include a significant proportion aimed at long-term, sustainable company performance. Shares awards should be released for sale on a phased basis and be subject to a total vesting and holding period of five years or more.
In addition, non-executive directors' pay should not be based on meeting company targets as their pay should be independent of how the company performs.	NED remuneration should be determined by the board. It should reflect time commitment and responsibilities of the role and should not include share options or other performance related elements.
Saxophone does not currently have an audit committee. Audit committees undertake an important role in that they help the directors to satisfy their responsibility of accountability with regards to maintaining an appropriate relationship with the company's auditor. Without an audit committee there is no oversight of the financial reporting processes of the company.	Saxophone should appoint an audit committee as soon as possible. The committee should comprise at least three independent non-executives, one of whom should have relevant financial experience.

Deficiency	**Recommendation**
A new sales director was appointed nine months ago, but has not yet undergone any board training. All directors should receive induction training when they first join the board so that they are fully aware of their responsibilities. The new sales director may not be fully effective in the role without the relevant training and induction.	The new sales director should immediately receive relevant training from Bill Bassoon to ensure that a full understanding of the role and responsibilities is obtained.
Saxophone is not planning to hold an annual general meeting (AGM) as the number of shareholders are such that it would be too costly and impractical. However, the AGM is an important meeting in that it gives the shareholders an opportunity to raise any concerns, receive an answer and vote on important resolutions. The proposal to send the financial statements and resolutions by email is not appropriate as it does not allow shareholders an opportunity to raise relevant questions.	The company should continue to hold the AGM. Sending information by email in advance of the meeting may be practical and save some costs; however, this should not be seen as a replacement for the AGM.

Marking guide	
	Marks
Corporate governance deficiencies and recommendations	
• Chief executive is now chair	2
• Currently only three of eight directors are non-executive, should be at least half	2
• Chair considering appointing a friend as a non-executive	2
• Finance director decides on the remuneration for the directors	2
• Remuneration for all directors in form of annual bonus	2
• No audit committee at present	2
• No induction training for new sales director	2
• No AGM planned as felt impractical and too costly	2
Max 5 issues, 2 marks each	**10**
Total	**10**

Examiner's comments

Candidates performed well on this question. Most candidates were able to confidently identify deficiencies from the scenario. However many could not explain the deficiency, relying on explanations such as 'this is not good corporate governance'. This was not sufficient to score the extra ½ marks available for each point. Candidates needed to be able to explain how these deficiencies impacted the company. In addition a significant proportion of candidates misread the scenario and thought the chair and chief executive was the same person. This was not correct. Bill Bassoon had been the chief executive and was now the chair. Hence answers focused on these key roles being held by the same person rather than the chair not being independent and failed to score marks as a result. Candidates must read the scenario carefully before they start to write. The recommendations provided were not adequate in many cases and often answers gave corporate governance objectives rather than recommendations, such as, 'the board should be balanced between executive and non-executives'. This is an objective; the recommendation should have been to 'appoint additional non-executive directors to ensure a balanced board'.

259 ORANGE FINANCIALS *Walk in the footsteps of a top tutor*

Key answer tips

Part (a) is a typical ethical threats question focusing on threats to objectivity. Remember to explain the threat properly, don't just state the name of the threat but explain how it could affect the auditor's behaviour when performing the audit. For the safeguard, state the relevant guidance from the ACCA Code of Ethics and Conduct.

Part (b) is a straightforward knowledge question. Make sure you take time to learn key definitions and terms such as the elements of an assurance engagement as they are regularly examined.

(a) Ethical threats and appropriate safeguards

Ethical threat	Appropriate safeguard
Orange Financials Co (Orange) has asked the engagement partner of Currant & Co to attend meetings with potential investors. This represents an advocacy threat. The audit firm may be perceived as promoting investment in Orange and this threatens objectivity.	The engagement partner should politely decline this request from Orange, as it represents too great a threat to independence.

Ethical threat	**Appropriate safeguard**
Due to the stock exchange listing, Orange has requested that Currant & Co produce the financial statements. This represents a self-review threat. The auditor may not detect errors in the financial statements they were responsible for preparing, or, may not wish to admit to errors that are detected.	As Orange is currently not a listed company then Currant & Co are permitted to produce the financial statements and also audit them. However, Orange is seeking a listing, therefore, ideally Currant & Co should not undertake the preparation of the financial statements as this would represent too high a risk. If Currant & Co chooses to produce the financial statements then separate teams should undertake each assignment and the audit team should not be part of the accounts preparation process. The preparation must be routine and mechanical in nature, therefore the audit firm must not be responsible for selecting accounting policies or determining accounting estimates.
The assistant finance director of Orange has joined Currant & Co as a partner and has been proposed as the review partner. This represents a self-review threat. The new review partner will not be independent and may not detect errors, or, may not wish to admit to errors that are detected in the financial statements during the period in post as FD when having responsibility for the financial statements. The new review partner will also lack professional scepticism.	This partner must not be involved in the audit of Orange until a cooling-off period has been served. An alternative review partner should be appointed.
Orange has several potential assurance assignments available and Currant & Co wish to be appointed to these. There is a potential self-interest threat as these assurance fees along with the external audit fee could represent a significant proportion of Currant & Co's fee income. The firm may be reluctant to upset its client for fear of losing the work and associated fees.	The firm should assess whether these assignments, along with the audit fee, would represent more than 15% of gross practice income for two consecutive years. These assurance assignments will only arise if the company obtains its listing and hence will be a public interest company. If the recurring fees are likely to exceed 15% of annual practice income then additional consideration should be given as to whether these assignments should be sought by the firm. Fees will need to be discussed with the audit committee.

Ethical threat	Appropriate safeguard
Orange has implied to Currant & Co that they must complete the audit quickly and with minimal questions/issues if they wish to obtain the assurance assignments. This creates an intimidation threat on the team. They may feel pressure to cut corners and not raise issues, and this could compromise the objectivity of the audit team.	The engagement partner should politely inform the finance director that the team will undertake the audit in accordance with all relevant ISAs and the firm's own quality management procedures. This means that the audit will take as long as is necessary to obtain sufficient, appropriate evidence to form an opinion. If any residual concerns remain or the intimidation threat continues then Currant & Co may need to consider resigning from the engagement.
The finance director has offered the team a free weekend away at a luxury hotel. This represents a self-interest threat. The audit team may feel indebted to the client and reluctant to raise issues identified during the audit.	Acceptance of goods and services, unless clearly trivial and inconsequential in value, is not permitted. As it is unlikely that a weekend at a luxury hotel for the whole team has an insignificant value, then this offer should be politely declined.

(b) Elements of an assurance engagement

- A **three-party relationship** comprising of:
  - The intended user who is the person who requires the assurance report.
  - The responsible party, which is the organisation responsible for preparing the subject matter to be reviewed.
  - The practitioner (i.e. an accountant) who is the professional who will review the subject matter and provide the assurance.
- A suitable **subject matter**. The subject matter is the data which the responsible party has prepared and which requires verification.
- The subject matter is then evaluated or assessed against **suitable criteria** in order for it to be assessed and an opinion provided.
- **Sufficient and appropriate evidence** in order to give the required level of assurance.
- A written assurance report containing the conclusion or opinion which is given by the practitioner to the intended user.

Marking guide

		Marks
(a)	**Ethical threats and appropriate safeguards** (only 5 threats required)	
	• Engagement partner attending listing meeting	2
	• Preparation of financial statements	2
	• Assistant finance director as review partner on audit	2
	• Total fee income	2
	• Pressure to complete audit quickly and with minimal issues	2
	• Weekend away at luxury hotel	2
	• Provision of loan at preferential rates	2
	Max 5 issues, 2 marks each	**10**
(b)	**Elements of an assurance engagement**	
	• 3 party relationship – intended user, responsible party, practitioner	1
	• Subject matter	1
	• Suitable criteria	1
	• Sufficient and appropriate evidence	1
	• Written assurance report	1
		5
Total		**15**

Examiner's comments

This question required an explanation of ethical threats from the scenario and a method for reducing each of these threats. This was very well answered with many candidates scoring full marks. Ethics questions are often answered well by candidates and the scenario provided contained many possible threats. Where candidates did not score well this was usually because they only identified rather than explained the ethical threat. In addition some candidates identified the threat but when explaining them they came up with incorrect examples of the type of threat; such as attending the weekend away at a luxury hotel gave rise to a familiarity threat rather than a self-interest threat. The threat which candidates struggled with the most was the intimidation threat caused by management requesting the audit team ask minimal questions. The response given by many candidates was to decline the assurance engagement which does not address the intimidation threat. Instead candidates needed to stress that this issue needed to be discussed with the finance director and that appropriate audit procedures would be undertaken to ensure the quality of the audit was not compromised. In addition when explaining issues some candidates listed many examples of ethical threats; such as 'the assistant finance director being the review partner gives rise to a familiarity, self-review and self-interest threat.' This scatter gun approach to questions is not recommended as it wastes time.

260 VIOLET & CO *Walk in the footsteps of a top tutor*

Key answer tips

This is a typical completion and reporting question and the requirement gives you an approach to use. Discuss the issue, consider if it is material, recommend further procedures and describe the impact on the auditor's report. When discussing the impact on the auditor's report, remember that the opinion is only one element of the report. Consider whether there is a need for any further impact such as a 'basis for' paragraph if you are suggesting the opinion should be modified.

This question also requires discussion of whether a written representation is required in the circumstances described. Written representations should only be used in limited circumstances as client generated evidence is not as reliable as other forms of evidence. Professional scepticism should be used to determine whether a representation is appropriate. Remember also there are specific ISAs which require written representations to be obtained.

Daisy Co

(i) Daisy Co's sales ledger has been corrupted by a computer virus therefore no detailed testing has been performed on revenue and receivables. The audit team will need to see if they can confirm revenue and receivables in an alternative manner. If they are unable to do this, then two significant balances in the financial statements will not have been confirmed.

Revenue and receivables are both higher than the total profit before tax (PBT) of $2 million. Receivables are 170% of PBT and revenue is nearly eight times the PBT, hence this is a very material issue.

(ii) A written representation does not provide sufficient and appropriate evidence over the completeness and accuracy of sales revenue and receivables.

A written representation should only be used where other sufficient and appropriate evidence cannot be expected to exist such as where is it a matter of management judgement or an intention of management.

Alternative procedures can be performed to obtain evidence over revenue and receivables and the auditor should not rely on a written representation as a substitute for more reliable evidence.

(iii) Procedures to be adopted include:

- Discuss with management whether they have any alternative records which detail revenue and receivables for the year.
- Attempt to perform analytical procedures, such as proof-in-total or monthly comparison to last year, to gain comfort in total for revenue and for receivables.

(iv) The auditors will need to modify the opinion as they are unable to obtain sufficient appropriate evidence in relation to two material and pervasive areas, being receivables and revenue.

The opinion paragraph will be a disclaimer of opinion and will state that the auditor does not express an opinion on the financial statements.

A basis for disclaimer of opinion paragraph will explain the limitation in relation to the lack of evidence over revenue and receivables.

Fuchsia Co

(i) Fuchsia Co is facing going concern problems as it has experienced difficult trading conditions and it has a negative cash outflow. However, the financial statements have been prepared using the going concern basis of accounting, even though it is possible that the company is not a going concern.

The prior year financial statements showed a profit of $1.2 million and the current financial statements show a loss before tax of $4.4 million, the net cash outflow of $3.2 million represents 73% of this loss (3.2/4.4) and hence is a material issue.

(ii) A written representation is appropriate in relation to going concern.

ISA 570 *Going Concern* requires the auditor to obtain a written representation confirming that matters affecting going concern have been disclosed to the auditor. This does not preclude the auditor from performing procedures over going concern but a written representation should be obtained as one of those procedures.

However, the written representation cannot be used as means of avoiding a modified opinion if the directors of Fuchsia Co do not make adequate disclosure of the going concern issues.

(iii) Management are confident that further funding can be obtained, however the team is sceptical and so the following procedures should be adopted:

- Discuss with management whether any finance has now been secured.
- Review the correspondence with the finance provider to confirm the level of funding that is to be provided and this should be compared to the net cash outflow of $3.2 million.
- Review the most recent board minutes to understand whether management's view on Fuchsia Co's going concern has altered.
- Review the cash flow forecasts for the year and assess the reasonableness of the assumptions adopted.

(iv) If management refuses to amend the going concern basis, or at the very least make adequate going concern disclosures, the audit opinion will need to be modified.

As the going concern basis is probably incorrect the misstatement is material and pervasive.

The opinion paragraph will be an adverse opinion and will state that the financial statements do not give a true and fair view.

A basis for adverse opinion paragraph will explain the inappropriate use of the going concern basis of accounting.

Marking guide	Marks
Daisy Designs Co	
• Discussion of issue	1
• Calculation of materiality	1
• Written representation	2
• Procedures at completion stage	2
• Type of audit opinion modification required	1
• Impact on auditor's report	1
Fuchsia Co	
• Discussion of issue	1
• Calculation of materiality	1
• Written representation	2
• Procedures at completion stage	2
• Type of audit opinion modification required	1
• Impact on auditor's report	1
Max 6 marks per issue	**12**
Total	**12**

Examiner's comments

This question required a discussion of two issues; an assessment of the materiality of each; procedures to resolve each issue and the impact on the auditor's report if each issue remained unresolved. Performance was mixed on this question. There were a significant minority of candidates who did not devote sufficient time and effort to this question bearing in mind the number of marks available. The requirement to discuss the two issues of Daisy Co's corrupted sales ledger and Fuchsia Co's going concern problem was on whole, answered well by most candidates. In addition, many candidates correctly identified that each issue was clearly material. A significant minority seemed to believe the corruption of the sales ledger was an adjusting event and so incorrectly proceeded to focus on subsequent events. With regards to procedures to undertake at the completion stage, candidates seemed to struggle with Daisy. Given that the sales ledger had been corrupted procedures such as 'agree goods despatch notes to sales invoices to the sales ledger' or 'reconcile the sales ledger to the general ledger' were unlikely to be possible. Most candidates correctly identified relevant analytical procedures and a receivables circularisation. Candidates performed better on auditing the going concern of Fuchsia Co, however some candidates wasted time by providing a long list of going concern tests when only one or two were needed. Performance on the impact on the auditor's report if each issue remained unresolved was unsatisfactory. Candidates still continue to recommend an emphasis of matter paragraph for all reporting questions, this is not the case and it was not relevant for either issue. Candidates need to understand what an emphasis of matter paragraph is and why it is used. A significant number of candidates were unable to identify the correct modification, suggesting that Daisy Co's should be qualified or adverse, as opposed to disclaimer of opinion. Also, some answers contradicted themselves with answers of 'the issue is not material therefore qualify the opinion'. Additionally, many candidates ignored the question requirement to only consider the impact if the issue was unresolved. Lots of answers started with 'if resolved the auditor's report .....' this was not required. In relation to the impact on the auditor's report, many candidates were unable to describe how the opinion paragraph would change and so failed to maximise their marks. Once again future candidates are reminded that the auditor's report is the only output of a statutory audit and hence is considered very important for this exam.

Section 5

SPECIMEN EXAM QUESTIONS

Audit and Assurance (AA) - Specimen Exam

Section A

This section of the exam contains **three OT cases**.

Each OT case contains a scenario which relates to **five OT questions**.

Each question is worth **2 marks** and is compulsory.

This exam section is worth **30 marks** in total.

Select **Next** to continue.

Audit and Assurance (AA) - Specimen Exam

Explain Answer Calculator Scratch Pad

You are an audit manager at Buffon & Co, responsible for the audit of Maldini Co and you have become aware of the following information:

Audit engagement partner
The audit engagement partner for Maldini Co, a listed company, has been in place for approximately eight years and her son has just been offered a role with Maldini Co as a sales manager. This role would entitle him to shares in Maldini Co as part of his remuneration package.

Internal audit function
Maldini Co's board of directors are considering establishing an internal audit function, and the finance director has asked your firm about the differences in the role of internal audit and external audit. If the internal audit function is established, the board has suggested that they may wish to outsource this to Buffon & Co.

Auditor characteristics
Following management's request for information regarding the different roles of internal and external auditors, the audit assistant has collated a list of key characteristics:

(1) Appointed by audit committee
(2) Reports are publicly available to shareholders
(3) Review effectiveness of internal controls to improve operations
(4) Express an opinion on the truth and fairness of the financial statements

Fees
The finance director has suggested to the board that if Buffon & Co are appointed as internal as well as external auditors, then fees should be renegotiated with at least 20% of all internal and external audit fees being based on the profit after tax of the company, as this will align the interests of Buffon & Co and Maldini Co. This fee income would be significant to Buffon & Co.

Q1

Your audit assistant has highlighted a number of potential threats to independence in respect of the audit of Maldini Co.

Identify which of the following represent valid threats to independence, matching each threat to the appropriate category.

Facts	Category of threat
Length of time the audit engagement partner has been in position	Self-interest
Maldini Co's request for advice regarding internal audit	Self-interest
Potential holding of shares by audit partner's son	Familiarity
Possible provision of internal audit services	Self-review
Basis of fee	

Q2

In relation to the audit engagement partner holding the role for eight years, and her son's offer of employment with Maldini Co:

Which of the following safeguards should be implemented in order to comply with ACCA's Code of Ethics and Conduct?

- The audit partner should be removed from the audit team
- An engagement quality control reviewer should be appointed
- A third party such as a professional body should be consulted on key audit judgments
- Buffon & Co should resign from the audit

Q3

In line with ACCA's Code of Ethics and Conduct, which TWO of the following factors must be considered before the internal audit engagement should be accepted?

- Whether the external audit team have the expertise to carry out the internal audit work
- If the assignments will relate to the internal controls over financial reporting
- If management will accept responsibility for implementing appropriate recommendations
- The probable timescale for the outsourcing of the internal audit function

Q4

Match each of the characteristics identified by the audit assistant to the appropriate type of auditor.

Characteristic	Type of auditor
1	Internal auditor
2	Internal auditor
3	External auditor
4	External auditor

Q5

If the internal and external audit assignments are accepted, which of the following statements is TRUE regarding the proposed basis for the fee?

- As long as the total fee received from Maldini Co is less than 15% of the firm's total fee income then no safeguards are needed
- The client should be informed that only the internal audit fee can be based on profit after tax
- The fees should be based on Maldini Co's profit before tax
- No safeguards can be applied and this basis for fee determination should be rejected

Audit and Assurance (AA) - Specimen Exam

Explain Answer **Calculator** **Scratch Pad**

It is 1 July 20X5. Balotelli Co operates a number of hotels providing accommodation, leisure facilities and restaurants. You are an audit supervisor of Mario & Co, conducting the audit of Balotelli Co for the year ended 31 December 20X4. The following information has been brought to your attention.

Non-current assets
Balotelli Co incurred significant capital expenditure during the year updating the leisure facilities at several of the company's hotels. Depreciation is charged on all assets monthly on a straight-line basis (SL) and it is company policy to charge a full month's depreciation in the month of acquisition and none in the month of disposal.The audit team has obtained the following extract of the non-current assets register detailing some of the new leisure equipment acquired during the year:

Date	Description	Cost ($)	Depreciation policy	Charge for the year ($)	Carrying amount ($)
01/05/X4	15 treadmills	18,000	36 months SL	4,000	14,000
15/05/X4	20 exercise bikes	17,000	3 years SL	5,667	11,333
17/08/X4	15 rowing machines	9,750	36 months SL	2,167	7,583
19/08/X4	10 cross trainers	11,000	36 months SL	1,528	9,472
		55,750		**13,362**	**42,388**

In order to verify the depreciation charge for the year the audit team has been asked to recalculate a sample of the depreciation charges. The audit team has also been asked to carry out detailed testing on the valuation of non-current assets.

Food poisoning - litigation
Balotelli Co's directors received correspondence in November 20X4 from a group of customers who have alleged that they suffered severe food poisoning from food eaten at the hotel and are claiming substantial damages. Management have stated that based on discussions with their lawyers the claim is unlikely to be successful.

Trade receivables circularisation

The audit team has obtained the following results from the receivables circularisation:

Customer	Balance per sales ledger ($)	Balance per customer confirmation ($)	Comment
Willow Co	42,500	42,500	
Cedar Co	35,000	25,000	Invoice raised 28 December 20X4
Maple Co	60,000	45,000	Payment made 30 December 20X4
Laurel Co	55,000	55,000	A balance of $20,000 is currently being disputed by Laurel Co

Q6

Which of the following correctly calculates the depreciation expense for the new assets for the year ended 31 December 20X4 and explains the resultant impact on non-current assets?

- Depreciation should be $10,660, assets are understated
- Depreciation should be $18,583, assets are understated
- Depreciation should be $9,111, assets are overstated
- Depreciation should be $12,549, assets are overstated

Q7

Which FOUR of the following audit procedures are appropriate to test the VALUATION assertion for non-current assets?

- ☐ Review board minutes for evidence of disposals during the year and verify that these are appropriately reflected in the non-current asset register
- ☐ Agree a sample of additions included in the non-current assets register to purchase invoice and cash book
- ☐ Review the repairs and maintenance expense account for evidence of items of a capital nature
- ☐ Recalculate the depreciation charge for a sample of assets ensuring that it is being applied consistently and in accordance with IAS 16 Property, Plant and Equipment
- ☐ Review physical condition of non-current assets for any signs of damage
- ☐ Ensure disposals are properly accounted for and recalculate gain/loss on disposal

Q8

Which of the following audit procedures would provide the auditor with the MOST reliable audit evidence regarding the likely outcome of the litigation?

- ○ Request a written representation from management supporting their assertion that the claim will not be successful
- ○ Send a confirmation request to the lawyers of Balotelli Co to obtain their view as to the probability of the claim being successful
- ○ Review the correspondence from the customers claiming food poisoning to assess whether Balotelli Co has a present obligation as a result of a past event
- ○ Review board minutes to understand why the directors believe that the claim will not be successful

Q9

Which TWO of the following are benefits of carrying out a trade receivables circularisation?

- ☐ It provides evidence from an independent external source
- ☐ It provides sufficient appropriate evidence over all balance assertions
- ☐ It improves audit efficiency as all customers are required to respond
- ☐ It improves the reliability of audit evidence as the process is under the control of the auditor

Q10

The audit team has been asked to assess whether any additional work is required on receivables.

Based on the results of the circularisation, match each customer to the appropriate audit procedure.

Customer	Audit procedure
Willow Co	Agreed to post year end cash book and bank statement
Cedar Co	Discuss with management and consider whether amount should be included in allowance for receivables
Maple Co	No further audit procedures required
Laurel Co	Agree to pre year end invoice

Audit and Assurance (AA) - Specimen Exam

Explain Answer | Calculator | Scratch Pad

It is 1 July 20X5. Cannavaro.com is a website design company whose year end was 31 December 20X4. The audit is almost complete and the financial statements are due to be signed shortly. Profit before tax for the year is $3.8m and revenue is $11.2m.

Form and content of auditor's report

The company has only required an audit for the last two years and the board of directors has asked your firm to provide more detail in relation to the form and content of the auditor's report. In particular they have queried why the following elements are included:

(1) Date of report

(2) Addressee

(3) Auditor's responsibilities

(4) Opinion paragraph

Balance due from Pirlo Co

During the audit it has come to light that a key customer, Pirlo Co, with a receivables balance at the year end of $285,000, has just notified Cannavaro.com that they are experiencing cash flow difficulties, meaning they are unable to make any payments for the foreseeable future. The finance directors of Cannavaro.com has notified the auditor that he will write this balance off as an irrecoverable debt in the financial statements for the year ended 31 December 20X5.

Audit work

The audit partner has asked you to perform the following work in respect of the receivables balance due from Pirlo Co:

(1) Make an initial assessment of the materiality of the issue and consider the overall impact on the financial statements.

(2) Perform additional procedures in order to conclude on whether the financial statements require adjustment.

Q11

Match the following elements of the unmodified auditor's report queried by the directors of Cannavaro.com, to the correct explanation for its inclusion.

Element of auditor's report	Reason for inclusion
1	Explains the financial statements are presented fairly
2	Demonstrates the point at which sufficient appropriate evidence has been obtained
3	Clarifies who may rely on the opinion included in the report
4	Explains the role and remit of the audit

Q12

The audit assistant assigned to the audit of Cannavaro.com wants a better understanding of the impact that subsequent events have on the audit and has made the following statements.

Identify, by clicking on the relevant box in the table below, whether each of the following statements is true or false.

All material subsequent events require the numbers in the financial statements to be adjusted	TRUE	FALSE
A non-adjusting event is a subsequent event for which NO amendments to the current year financial statements are required	TRUE	FALSE
The auditor's responsibilities for subsequent events which occur prior to the auditor's report being signed are different from their responsibilities after the auditor's report has been issued	TRUE	FALSE
The auditor should request a written representation confirming that all relevant subsequent events have been disclosed	TRUE	FALSE

Q13

In response to the partner's request, which of the following options correctly summarises the effect of the outstanding balance with Pirlo Co?

Option	Material	Impact on financial statements
A	No	Revenue is overstated
B	No	Gross profit is understated
C	Yes	Profit is overstated
D	Yes	Going concern basis is in doubt

- Option A
- Option B
- Option C
- Option D

Q14

Which TWO of the following audit procedures should be performed to form a conclusion as to whether the financial statements require adjustment?

- Discuss with management the reasons for not amending the financial statements
- Review the cash book post year end for receipts from Pirlo Co
- Send a request to Pirlo Co to confirm the outstanding balance
- Agree the outstanding balance to invoices and sales orders

Q15

The finance director has asked you to outline the appropriate audit opinions which will be provided depending on whether the company decides to amend or not amend the 20X4 financial statements for the issue identified regarding the recoverability of the balance with Pirlo Co.

Complete the following sentences by dragging and dropping the appropriate audit opinions.

If the 20X4 financial statements are not amended, our opinion will be [ ]

If the appropriate adjustment is made to the financial statements, our opinion will be [ ]

Audit opinions	
adverse	disclaimer
unmodified with emphasis of matter paragraph	qualified 'except for'
unmodified	

Audit and Assurance (AA) - Specimen Exam

Flag for Review

Section B

This section of the exam contains **three constructed response questions**.

Each question contains a scenario which relates to one or more requirement(s) which may be split over multiple question screens.

Each question is worth **20 or 30 marks** and is compulsory.

This exam section is worth **70 marks** in total.

Important:

In your live exam you must:

(1) Enter your answer for each question in the response area provided for that question. Any answers entered into a response area provided for a different question will not be marked.

(2) Show all notes/workings that you want the marker to see within the response area provided for the question. Remember, any notes/workings made on the Scratch Pad or on your workings paper will not be marked.

Select **Next** to continue.

Previous Navigator Next

Audit and Assurance (AA) - Specimen Exam

Explain Answer   Æ Symbol   Calculator   Scratch Pad

This scenario relates to five requirements.

Milla Co manufactures fizzy drinks such as cola and lemonade as well as other soft drinks and its year end is 30 September 20X5. It is 1 July 20X5. You are an audit manager of Totti & Co and are currently planning the audit of Milla Co. You attended the planning meeting with the audit engagement partner and finance director last week and the minutes from the meeting are shown below. You are reviewing these as part of the process of preparing the audit strategy document.

Minutes of planning meeting for Milla Co

Milla Co's trading results have been strong this year and the company is forecasting revenue of $85m, which is an increase from the previous year. The company has invested significantly in the cola and fizzy drinks production process at the factory. This resulted in expenditure of $5m on updating, repairing and replacing a significant amount of the machinery used in the production process.

As the level of production has increased, the company has expanded the number of warehouses it uses to store inventory. It now utilises 15 warehouses; some are owned by Milla Co and some are rented from third parties. There will be inventory counts taking place at all 15 of these sites at the year end.

A new accounting general ledger has been introduced at the beginning of the year, with the old and new systems being run in parallel for a period of two months. In addition, Milla Co has incurred expenditure of $4.5m on developing a new brand of fizzy soft drinks. The company started this process in July 20X4 and is close to launching their new product into the market place.

As a result of the increase in revenue, Milla Co has recently recruited a new credit controller to chase outstanding receivables. The finance director thinks it is not necessary to continue to maintain an allowance for receivables and so has released the opening allowance of $1.5m.

The finance director stated that there was a problem in April in the mixing of raw materials within the production process which resulted in a large batch of cola products tasting different. A number of these products were sold; however, due to complaints by customers about the flavour, no further sales of these goods have been made. No adjustment has been made to the valuation of the damaged inventory, which will still be held at cost of $1m at the year end.

As in previous years, the management of Milla Co is due to be paid a significant annual bonus based on the value of year-end total assets.

Q16

(a) Explain audit risk and the components of audit risk.

(5 marks)

(b) Using the minutes provided, describe SEVEN audit risks, and explain the auditor's response to each risk, in planning the audit of Milla Co.

(14 marks)

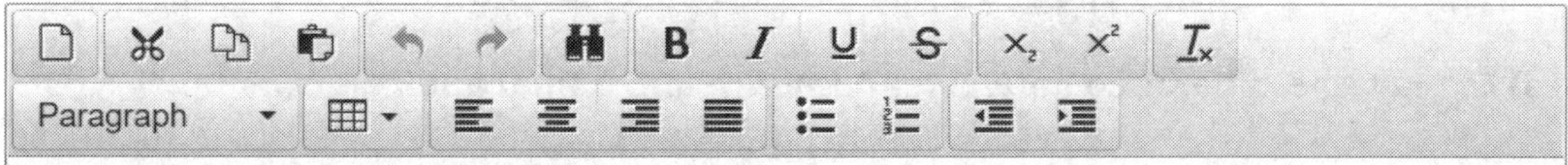

Audit risk	Auditor's response

(c) Identify the main areas, other than audit risks, which should be included within the audit strategy document for Milla Co, and for each area provide an example relevant to the audit.

(4 marks)

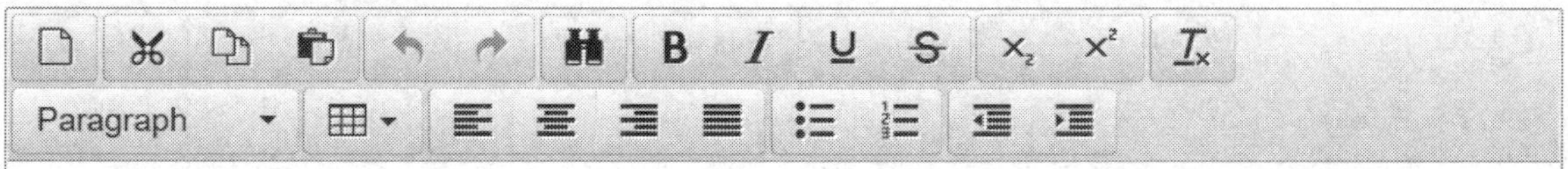

The finance director has requested that the deadline for the 20X6 audit be shortened by a month and has asked the audit engagement partner to consider if this will be possible. The partner has suggested that in order to meet this new tighter deadline the firm may carry out both an interim and final audit for the audit of Milla Co to 30 September 20X6.

(d) Explain the difference between an interim and a final audit.

(3 marks)

(e) Explain the procedures which are likely to be performed during an interim audit of Milla Co and the impact which it would have on the final audit.

(4 marks)

(30 marks)

Audit and Assurance (AA) - Specimen Exam

Explain Answer Æ **Symbol** **Calculator** **Scratch Pad**

This scenario relates to four requirements.

It is 1 July 20X5. Baggio Co is a manufacturer of electrical equipment. It has factories across the country and its customer base includes retailers as well as individuals, to whom direct sales are made through their website. The company's year end is 30 September 20X5. You are an audit supervisor of Suarez & Co and are currently reviewing documentation of Baggio Co's internal control in preparation for the interim audit.

Baggio Co's website allows individuals to order goods directly, and full payment is taken in advance. Currently the website is not integrated into the inventory system and inventory levels are not checked at the time when orders are placed. Inventory is valued at the lower of cost and net realisable value.

Goods are dispatched via local couriers; however, they do not always record customer signatures as proof that the customer has received the goods. Over the past 12 months there have been customer complaints about the delay between sales orders and receipt of goods. Baggio Co has investigated these and found that, in each case, the sales order had been entered into the sales system correctly but was not forwarded to the dispatch department for fulfilling.

Baggio Co's retail customers undergo credit checks prior to being accepted and credit limits are set accordingly by sales ledger clerks. These customers place their orders through one of the sales team, who decides on sales discount levels.

Raw materials used in the manufacturing process are purchased from a wide range of suppliers. As a result of staff changes in the purchase ledger department, supplier statement reconciliations are no longer performed. Additionally, changes to supplier details in the purchase ledger master file can be undertaken by purchase ledger clerks as well as supervisors.

In the past six months, Baggio Co has changed part of its manufacturing process and as a result some new equipment has been purchased. However, there are considerable levels of plant and equipment which are now surplus to requirement. Purchase requisitions for all new equipment have been authorised by production supervisors and little has been done to reduce the surplus of old equipment.

Q17

(a) In respect of the internal control of Baggio Co:

(i) Identify and explain SIX deficiencies;
(ii) Recommend a control to address each of these deficiencies; and
(iii) Describe a test of control Suarez & Co would perform to assess whether each of these controls, if implemented, is operating effectively.

Note: The total marks will be split equally between each part.

(18 marks)

Control deficiency	Control recommendation	Test of control

(b) Describe substantive procedures the auditor should perform at the year end to confirm plant and equipment additions.

(2 marks)

(20 marks)

Audit and Assurance (AA) - Specimen Exam

Explain Answer Æ Symbol Calculator Scratch Pad

This scenario relates to four requirements.

It is 1 July 20X5. Vieri Co manufactures a range of motor cars. You are an audit supervisor of Rossi & Co and are currently preparing the audit programmes for the audit of Vieri Co for the year ended 31 March 20X5. You have had a meeting with your audit manager and he has notified you of the following issues identified during the audit risk assessment process:

Land and buildings

Vieri Co has a policy of revaluing land and buildings, this is undertaken on a rolling basis over a five-year period. During the year Vieri Co requested an external independent valuer to revalue a number of properties, including a warehouse purchased in October 20X4. Depreciation is charged on a pro rata basis.

Work in progress

Vieri Co undertakes continuous production of cars, 24 hours a day, seven days a week. An inventory count is to be undertaken at the year end and Rossi & Co will attend. You are responsible for the audit of work in progress (WIP) and will be part of the team attending the count as well as the final audit. WIP constitutes the partly assembled cars at the year end and this balance is likely to be material. Vieri Co values WIP according to percentage of completion, and standard costs are then applied to these percentages.

Q18

(a) Explain the factors Rossi & Co should consider when placing reliance on the work of the independent valuer.

(5 marks)

(b) Describe the substantive procedures the auditor should perform to obtain sufficient and appropriate audit evidence in relation to the revaluation of land and buildings and the recently purchased warehouse.

(6 marks)

(c) Describe the substantive procedures the auditor should perform to obtain sufficient and appropriate audit evidence in relation to the valuation of work in progress.

(4 marks)

During the audit, the team has identified an error in the valuation of work in progress, as a number of the assumptions contain out of date information. The directors of Vieri Co have indicated that they do not wish to amend the financial statements.

(d) Explain the steps Rossi & Co should now take and the impact on the auditor's report in relation to the directors' refusal to amend the financial statements.

(5 marks)

(20 marks)

Section 6

ANSWERS TO SPECIMEN EXAM QUESTIONS

SECTION A

1

Fact 1 - Partner has been in role for 8 years which contravenes the code and represents a **familiarity** threat.

Fact 2 - Providing information on internal audit does not give rise to a threat to independence.

Fact 3 - Partner's son holding shares represents a **self-interest** threat as a close family member of the partner holds a financial interest.

Fact 4 - Providing internal audit services raises a **self-review** threat as it is likely that the audit team will be looking to place reliance on the control system reviewed by IA.

Fact 5 - This represents fees on a contingent basis and raises a **self-interest** threat as the audit firm's fee will rise if the company's profit after tax increases.

2

If the engagement partner's son accepts the role and obtains shares in the company it would constitute a self-interest threat BUT as the partner has already exceeded the seven year relationship rule, in line with ACCA's Code of Ethics and Conduct, the partner should be rotated off the audit irrespective of the decision made by her son.

As Maldini Co is a listed company an engagement quality control reviewer should already be in place in line with ISA 220.

Consulting a third party on key audt judgments would be a potential safeguard in respect of overdependence on fees but would not be adequate in the circumstances described.

It is unlikely that the firm needs to resign from the audit (due to the stated circumstances) as the threat to objectivity can be mitigated.

3

Statement 1 is inappropriate as the external and internal audit team should be separate and therefore consideration of the skills of the external team is not appropriate in the circumstances.

Statement 4 does not apply in that the timescale of the work is not relevant to consider the threats to objectivity

Statement 2 and 3 are valid considerations -as per ACCA's Code of Ethics and Conduct providing internal audit services can result in the audit firm assuming a management responsibility. To mitigate for this it is appropriate for the firm to assess whether management will take responsibility for implementing recommendations. Further for a listed company the Code prohibits the provision of internal audit services that reviews a significant proportion of the internal controls over financial reporting as these may be relied upon by the external audit team and the self review threat is too great.

4

Internal audit are appointed by the audit committee (external audit by the shareholders) and it is the role of internal audit to review the effectiveness and efficiency of internal controls to improve operations. External audit looks at the operating effectiveness of internal controls on which they may rely for audit evidence. A by-product may be to comment on any deficiencies they have found.

Therefore characteristics 1 and 3 relate to internal audit

The external auditor's report is publicly available to the shareholders of the company (internal audit reports are addressed to management) and the external auditor provides an opinion on the truth and fairness of the financial statements.

Therefore characteristics 2 and 4 relate to external audit.

5

The proposal in relation to the fees is a contingent fee basis which is expressly prohibited by ACCA's Code of Ethics and Conduct and therefore the only viable option here is to reject the fee basis

6

Depreciation should be calculated as:

Treadmills/exercise bikes = (18,000 + 17,000)/36 x 8 months = 7,778
Rowing machines/cross trainers = (9,750 + 11,000)/36 x 5 months = 2,882

Therefore total depreciation is **$10,660** and assets are currently **understated** as too much depreciation has currently been charged.

7

Reviewing board minutes for disposals and verifying that they have been removed from the asset register is a test for existence

Review the expense accounts for items of a capital nature is a test for completeness

All other tests are relevant for valuation

8

While all procedures would be valid in the circumstances only the written confirmation from the company's lawyers would allow the auditor to obtain an expert, third party confirmation on the likelihood of the case being successful. This would provide the auditor with the most reliable evidence in the circumstances

9

As per ISA 505 External Confirmations, the evidence obtained from a trade receivables circularisation should be reliable as it is from an external source and the risk of management bias and influence is restricted due to the process being under the control of the auditor.

Customers are not obliged to answer and often circularisations have a very low response rate. A circularisation will not provide evidence over the valuation assertion for receivables

10

Willow Co - external confirmation has confirmed the balance and no further work on existence is required.

Cedar Co - Represents an invoice in transit and therefore should be confirmed to a pre year end invoice to verify that it is a legitimate timing difference.

Maple Co - Represents a payment in transit and should be agreed to post year end payment to confirm that it is a legitimate timing difference

Laurel Co- Customer is disputing the balance and therefore the need for an allowance against the balance should be assessed.

11

Addressee - sets out who the report is addressed to - usually the shareholders - and is there to clarify who can place reliance on the audit opinion.

Auditor's responsbilities - this paragraph sets out that the auditor is required to express an opinion on the financial statements and seeks to explain the difference between the role of the auditor and those charged with governance. Thus this paragraph sets out the role and remit of the auditor.

Opinion paragraph - this paragraph sets out the auditors conclusion on the financial statements. In an unmodified report this takes the form of the auditor confirming that the financial statements present a true and fair view or are presented fairly.

Date of report - The auditor's report shall be dated no earlier than the date on which the auditor has obtained sufficient appropriate audit evidence on which to base the auditor's opinion on the financial statements. The date of the audit report is important in the case of subsequent events which impact the financial statements.

12

Statement 1 is false as not all subsequent events will require an adjustment to the numbers within the financial statements. IAS 10 Events after the Reporting Period makes a distinction between an adjusting and non-adjusting event. Only material adjusting events would require an amendment to the figures within the financial statements.

Statement 2 is false as while a non-adjusting event would not require a change to the numbers it may require a disclosure to be made. If this is material, non-disclosure could still result in a modification to the auditor's report.

Statement 3 is true as the auditor is required to carry out procedures up to the date of the auditor's report to gain sufficient appropriate evidence that all relevant subsequent events have been identified and dealt with appropriately. After the auditor's report is issued the auditor does not need to actively look for subsequent events.

Statement 4 is true as per ISA 560 Subsequent Events, the auditor is required to obtain written confirmation from management or those charged with governance that all subsequent events have been identified and dealt with in accordance with the appropriate reporting framework.

13

The outstanding balance with Pirlo Co is likely to be irrecoverable as the customer is experiencing financial difficulties The balance is material at 7.5% of PBT and 2.5% of revenue and therefore would need adjusted as without an adjustment the financial statements would be materially misstated as profit and assets are overstated by $285k.

Therefore Option C is correct

14

After date cash testing is the best way for the auditor to assess if the balance is recoverable wholly or in part and therefore the cashbook should be reviewed for any receipts that will change the assessment of the debt after the year end.

The issue should also be discussed with management to understand their reasons for not wanting to amend the financial statements as this may be due to a change in circumstances.

Writing to the customer/agreeing to invoices, while valid procedures during the audit to verify the existence of an outstanding balance, would not allow the auditor to assess the recoverability of the balance which is the key issue in determining whether an adjsutment is required.

15

The debt with Pirlo Co should be written off or included in the allowance for trade receivables. As the balance is material to the financial statements at 7.5% of PBT and 2.5% of revenue.This represents a material misstatement which is material but not pervasive

As such, if no adjustment is made the auditor will be required to provide a qualified 'except for' opinion.

If the required change is made no material misstatement exists and therefore the auditor will be able to issue an unmodified opinion.

SECTION B

16 Milla Cola Co

Milla Cola Co

Audit risk and its components

Audit risk is the risk that the auditor expresses an inappropriate audit opinion when the financial statements are materially misstated. Audit risk is a function of two main components being the risks of material misstatement and detection risk. Risk of material misstatement is made up of two components, inherent risk and control risk.

Inherent risk is the susceptibility of an assertion about a class of transaction, account balance or disclosure to a misstatement that could be material, either individually or when aggregated with other misstatements, before consideration of any related controls.

Control risk is the risk that a misstatement which could occur in an assertion about a class of transaction, account balance or disclosure and which could be material, either individually or when aggregated with other misstatements, will not be prevented, or detected and corrected, on a timely basis by the entity's internal control.

Detection risk is the risk that the procedures performed by the auditor to reduce audit risk to an acceptably low level will not detect a misstatement which exists and which could be material, either individually or when aggregated with other misstatements. Detection risk is affected by sampling and non-sampling risk.

AA Specimen Exam - Section B **Milla Co**		
	Marks available	**Marks awarded**
Requirement – component of audit risk		
Explanation of audit risk	2	
Explanation of components of audit risk: Inherent, control and detection risk	3	
Total marks	5	

Milla Co

Audit risks and responses

Audit risk	Auditor's response
Milla Co has incurred $5m on updating, repairing and replacing a significant amount of the production process machinery. If this expenditure is of a capital nature, it should be capitalised as part of property, plant and equipment (PPE) in line with IAS 16 *Property, Plant and Equipment*. However, if it relates more to repairs, then it should be expensed to the statement of profit or loss If the expenditure is not correctly classified, profit and PPE could be under or overstated.	The auditor should review a breakdown of these costs to ascertain the split of capital and revenue expenditure, and further testing should be undertaken to ensure that the classification in the financial statements is correct.
At the year end there will be inventory counts undertaken in all 15 warehouses. It is unlikely that the auditor will be able to attend all 15 inventory counts and therefore they need to ensure that they obtain sufficient appropriate audit evidence over the inventory counting controls, and completeness and existence of inventory for any warehouses not visited.	The auditor should assess which of the inventory sites they will attend the counts for. This will be any with material inventory or which have a history of significant errors. For those not visited, the auditor will need to review the level of exceptions noted during the count and discuss with management any issues which arose during the count.
Inventory is stored within 15 warehouses; some are owned by Milla Co and some rented from third parties. Only warehouses owned by Milla Co should be included within PPE. There is a risk of overstatement of PPE and understatement of rental expenses if Milla Co has capitalised all 15 warehouses.	The auditor should review supporting documentation for all warehouses included within PPE to confirm ownership by Milla Co and to ensure non-current assets are not overstated.
A new accounting general ledger system has been introduced at the beginning of the year and the old system was run in parallel for two months. There is a risk of opening balances being misstated and loss of data if they have not been transferred from the old system correctly. In addition, the new accounting general ledger system will require documenting and the controls over this will need to be tested.	The auditor should undertake detailed testing to confirm that all opening balances have been correctly recorded in the new accounting general ledger system. They should document and test the new system. They should review any management reports run comparing the old and new system during the parallel run to identify any issues with the processing of accounting information.
Milla Co has incurred expenditure of $4·5 million on developing a new brand of fizzy drink. This expenditure is research and development under IAS 38 *Intangible Assets*. The standard requires research costs to be expensed and development costs to be capitalised as an intangible asset. If Milla Co has incorrectly classified research costs as development expenditure, there is a risk the intangible asset could be overstated and expenses understated.	Obtain a breakdown of the expenditure and undertake testing to determine whether the costs relate to the research or development stage. Discuss the accounting treatment with the finance director and ensure it is in accordance with IAS 38.

The finance director of Milla Co has decided to release the opening provision of $1·5 million for allowance for receivables as he feels it is unnecessary. There is a risk that receivables will be overvalued, as despite having a credit controller, some balances will be irrecoverable and so will be overstated if not provided against. In addition, due to the damaged inventory there is an increased risk of customers refusing to make payments in full.	Extended post year-end cash receipts testing and a review of the aged receivables ledger to be performed to assess valuation and the need for an allowance for receivables. Discuss with the director the rationale for releasing the $1.5m opening allowance for receivables.
A large batch of cola products has been damaged in the production process and will be in inventory at the year end. No adjustment has been made by management. The valuation of inventory as per IAS 2 *Inventories* should be at the lower of cost and net realisable value. Hence it is likely that this inventory is overvalued.	Detailed cost and net realisable value testing to be performed to assess how much the inventory requires writing down by.
Due to the damaged cola products, a number of customers have complained. It is likely that for any of the damaged goods sold, Milla Co will need to refund these customers. Revenue is possibly overstated if the sales returns are not completely and accurately recorded.	Review the breakdown of sales of damaged goods, and ensure that they have been accurately removed from revenue.
The management of Milla Co receives a significant annual bonus based on the value of year-end total assets. There is a risk that management might feel under pressure to overstate the value of assets through the judgements taken or through the use of releasing provisions.	Throughout the audit the team will need to be alert to this risk. They will need to maintain professional scepticism and carefully review judgemental decisions and compare treatment against prior years.

AA Specimen Exam - Section B **Milla Co**		
	Marks available	**Marks awarded**
Requirement – Audit risks and responses (only 7 risks required)		
$5 million expenditure on production process	2	
Inventory counts at 15 warehouses at year end	2	
Treatment of owned v third party warehouses	2	
New general ledger system introduced at the beginning of the year	2	
Release of opening provision for allowance for receivables	2	
Research and development expenditure	2	
Damaged inventory	2	
Sales returns	2	
Management bonus based on asset values	2	
Max 7 issues, 2 marks each	**14**	

Milla Cola Co

Audit strategy document

The audit strategy sets out the scope, timing and direction of the audit and helps the development of the audit plan. It should consider the following main areas:

It should identify the main characteristics of the engagement which define its scope. For Milla it should consider the following:

- Whether the financial information to be audited has been prepared in accordance with IFRS.
- To what extent audit evidence obtained in previous audits for Milla will be utilised.
- Whether computer-assisted audit techniques will be used and the effect of IT on audit procedures.
- The availability of key personnel at Milla.

It should ascertain the reporting objectives of the engagement to plan the timing of the audit and the nature of the communications required, such as:

- The audit timetable for reporting and whether there will be an interim as well as final audit.
- Organisation of meetings with Milla's management to discuss any audit issues arising.
- Location of the 15 inventory counts.
- Any discussions with management regarding the reports to be issued.
- The timings of the audit team meetings and review of work performed.
- If there are any expected communications with third parties.

The strategy should consider the factors that, in the auditor's professional judgement, are significant in directing Milla's audit team's efforts, such as:

- The determination of materiality for the audit.
- The need to maintain a questioning mind and to exercise professional scepticism in gathering and evaluating audit evidence.

It should consider the results of preliminary audit planning activities and, where applicable, whether knowledge gained on other engagements for Milla is relevant, such as:

- Results of previous audits and the results of any tests over the effectiveness of internal controls.
- Evidence of management's commitment to the design, implementation and maintenance of sound internal control.
- Volume of transactions, which may determine whether it is more efficient for the audit team to rely on internal control.
- Significant business developments affecting Milla, such as the change in the accounting system and the significant expenditure on an overhaul of the factory.

The audit strategy should ascertain the nature, timing and extent of resources necessary to perform the audit, such as:

- The selection of the audit team with experience of this type of industry.
- Assignment of audit work to the team members.
- Setting the audit budget.

Tutorial note: *The answer is longer than required for four marks but represents a teaching aid*

AA Specimen Exam - Section B **Milla Co**		
	Marks available	**Marks awarded**
Requirement – Audit strategy document		
Main characteristics of the audit	1	
Reporting objectives of the audit and nature of communications required	1	
Factors that are significant in directing the audit team's efforts	1	
Results of preliminary engagement activities and whether knowledge gained on other engagements is relevant	1	
Nature, timing and extent of resources necessary to perform the audit	1	
Restricted to	**4**	

Milla Co

(d) Differences between an interim and a final audit

Interim audit

The interim audit is that part of the audit which takes place before the year end. The auditor uses the interim audit to carry out procedures which would be difficult to perform at the year end because of time pressure. There is no requirement to undertake an interim audit; factors to consider when deciding upon whether to have one include the size and complexity of the company along with the effectiveness of internal controls.

Final audit

The final audit will take place after the year end and concludes with the auditor forming and expressing an opinion on the financial statements for the whole year subject to audit. It is important to note that the final opinion takes account of conclusions formed at both the interim and final audit.

(e) Procedures which could be undertaken during the interim audit include:

- Review and updating of the documentation of accounting systems at Milla Co
- Discussions with management on the recent growth and any other changes within the business which have occurred during the year to date at Milla Co to update the auditor's understanding of the company.
- Assessment of risks which will impact the final audit of Milla Co.
- Undertake tests of controls on Milla Co's key transaction cycles of sales, purchases and inventory, and credit control.
- Perform substantive procedures on profit and loss transactions for the year to date and any other completed material transactions.

Impact of interim audit on final

If an interim audit is undertaken at Milla Co then it will have an impact on the final audit and the extent of work undertaken after the year end. Firstly, as some testing has already been undertaken there will be less work to be performed at the final audit, which may result in a shorter audit and audited financial statements possibly being available earlier. The outcome of the controls testing undertaken during the interim audit will impact the level of substantive testing to be undertaken. If the controls tested have proven to be operating effectively then the auditor may be able to reduce the level of detailed substantive testing required as they will be able to place reliance on the controls. In addition if substantive procedures were undertaken at the interim audit then only the period from the interim audit to the year end will require to be tested.

AA Specimen Exam - Section B **Milla Co**		
	Marks available	**Marks awarded**
Requirement (d) – Difference between interim and final audit		
Interim audit	2	
Final audit	2	
Restricted to	**3**	
Requirement (e) – Procedures/impact of interim audit on final audit		
Example procedures	3	
Impact on final audit	3	
Restricted to	**4**	

17 Baggio International Co

Baggio Co's internal control assessment

Deficiency	Control recommendations	Test of Control
Currently the website is not integrated into inventory system. This can result in Baggio Co accepting customer orders when they do not have the goods in inventory. This can cause them to lose sales and customer goodwill	The website should be updated to include an interface into the inventory system; this should check inventory levels and only process orders if adequate inventory is held. If inventory is out of stock, this should appear on the website with an approximate waiting time.	Test data could be used to attempt to process orders via the website for items which are not currently held in inventory. The orders should be flagged as being out of stock and indicate an approximate waiting time.
For goods despatched by local couriers, customer signatures are not always obtained. This can lead to customers falsely claiming that they have not received their goods. Baggio Co would not be able to prove that they had in fact despatched the goods and may result in goods being despatched twice.	Baggio Co should remind all local couriers that customer signatures must be obtained as proof of delivery and payment will not be made for any despatches with missing signatures.	Select a sample of despatches by couriers and ask Baggio Co for proof of delivery by viewing customer signatures.
There have been a number of situations where the sales orders have not been fulfilled in a timely manner. This can lead to a loss of customer goodwill and if it persists will damage the reputation of Baggio Co as a reliable supplier.	Once goods are despatched they should be matched to sales orders and flagged as fulfilled. The system should automatically flag any outstanding sales orders past a predetermined period, such as five days. This report should be reviewed by a responsible official.	Review the report of outstanding sales orders. If significant, discuss with a responsible official to understand why there is still a significant time period between sales order and despatch date. Select a sample of sales orders and compare the date of order to the goods despatch date to ascertain whether this is within the acceptable predetermined period.
Customer credit limits are set by sales ledger clerks. Sales ledger clerks are not sufficiently senior and so may set limits too high, leading to irrecoverable debts, or too low, leading to a loss of revenue.	Credit limits should be set by a senior member of the sales ledger department and not by sales ledger clerks. These limits should be regularly reviewed by a responsible official.	For a sample of new customers accepted in the year, review the authorisation of the credit limit, and ensure that this was performed by a responsible official. Enquire of sales ledger clerks as to who can set credit limits.
Sales discounts are set by Baggio Co's sales team. In order to boost their sales, members of the sales team may set the discounts too high, leading to a loss of revenue.	All members of the sales team should be given authority to grant sales discounts up to a set limit. Any sales discounts above these limits should be authorised by sales area managers or the sales director. Regular review of sales	Discuss with members of the sales team the process for setting sales discounts. Review the sales discount report for evidence of review by the sales director.

	discount levels should be undertaken by the sales director, and this review should be evidenced.	
Supplier statement reconciliations are no longer performed. This may result in errors in the recording of purchases and payables not being identified in a timely manner.	Supplier statement reconciliations should be performed on a monthly basis for all suppliers and these should be reviewed by a responsible official.	Review the file of reconciliations to ensure that they are being performed on a regular basis and that they have been reviewed by a responsible official.
Changes to supplier details in the purchase ledger master file can be undertaken by purchase ledger clerks. This could lead to key supplier data being accidently amended or fictitious suppliers being set up, which can increase the risk of fraud.	Only purchase ledger supervisors should have the authority to make changes to master file data. This should be controlled via passwords. Regular review of any changes to master file data by a responsible official and this review should be evidenced.	Request a purchase ledger clerk to attempt to access the master file and to make an amendment, the system should not allow this. Review a report of master data changes and review the authority of those making amendments.
Baggio Co has considerable levels of surplus plant and equipment. Surplus unused plant is at risk of theft. In addition, if the surplus plant is not disposed of then the company could lose sundry income.	Regular review of the plant and equipment on the factory floor by senior factory personnel to identify any old or surplus equipment. As part of the capital expenditure process there should be a requirement to confirm the treatment of the equipment being replaced.	Observe the review process by senior factory personnel, identifying the treatment of any old equipment. Review processed capital expenditure forms to ascertain if the treatment of replaced equipment is stated.
Purchase requisitions are authorised by production supervisors. Production supervisors are not sufficiently independent or senior to authorise capital expenditure.	Capital expenditure authorisation levels to be established. Production supervisors should only be able to authorise low value items, any high value items should be authorised by the board.	Review a sample of authorised capital expenditure forms and identify if the correct signatory has authorised them.

AA Specimen Paper - Section B **Baggio Co**		
	Marks available	**Marks awarded**
Requirement – Control weaknesses, recommendations and tests of controls (only 6 issues required)		
Website not integrated into inventory system	3	
Customer signatures	3	
Unfulfilled sales orders	3	
Customer credit limits	3	
Sales discounts	3	
Supplier statement reconciliations	3	
Purchase ledger master file	3	
Surplus plant and equipment	3	
Authorisation of capital expenditure	3	
6 issues required, 3 marks each	**18**	

Baggio Co

Substantive procedures - additions

- Obtain a breakdown of additions, cast the list and agree to the non-current asset register to confirm completeness of plant and equipment (P&E).
- Select a sample of additions and agree cost to supplier invoice to confirm valuation.
- Verify rights and obligations by agreeing the addition of plant and equipment to a supplier invoice in the name of Baggio Co.
- Review the list of additions and confirm that they relate to capital expenditure items rather than repairs and maintenance.
- Review board minutes to ensure that significant capital expenditure purchases have been authorised by the board.
- For a sample of additions recorded in P&E, physically verify them on the factory floor to confirm existence.

AA Specimen Exam - Section B **Baggio Co**		
	Marks available	**Marks awarded**
Requirement – Substantive procedures for PPE		
Cast list of additions and agree to non-current asset register	1	
Vouch cost to recent supplier invoice	1	
Agree addition to a supplier invoice in the name of Baggio Co to confirm rights and obligations	1	
Review additions and confirm capital expenditure items rather than repairs and maintenance	1	
Review board minutes to ensure authorised by the board	1	
Physically verify them on the factory floor to confirm existence	1	
Other		
Restricted to	**2**	

18 Vieri Motor Cars Co

Vieri Co

Reliance on the work of an independent valuer

ISA 500 *Audit Evidence* requires auditors to evaluate the competence, capabilities including expertise and objectivity of a management expert. This would include consideration of the qualifications of the valuer and assessment of whether they were members of any professional body or industry association.

The expert's independence should be ascertained, with potential threats such as undue reliance on Vieri Co or a self-interest threat such as share ownership considered.

In addition, Rossi & Co should meet with the expert and discuss with them their relevant expertise, in particular whether they have valued similar land and buildings to those of Vieri Co in the past. Rossi & Co should also consider whether the valuer understands the accounting requirements of IAS 16 *Property, Plant and Equipment* in relation to valuations.

The valuation should then be evaluated. The assumptions used should be carefully reviewed and compared to previous revaluations at Vieri Co. These assumptions should be discussed with both management and the valuer to understand the basis of any valuations.

AA Specimen Exam - Section B **Vieri Co**		
	Marks available	**Marks awarded**
Requirement – Reliance on independent valuer		
ISA 500 requires consideration of competence and capabilities of expert	1	
Consider if member of professional body or industry association	1	
Assess independence	1	
Assess whether relevant expertise of type of properties as Vieri Co	1	
Evaluate assumptions	1	
Total marks	**5**	

Vieri Co

Substantive procedures for revaluation of land and buildings

- Obtain a schedule of land and buildings revalued this year and cast to confirm completeness and accuracy of the revaluation adjustment.
- On a sample basis agree the revalued amounts to the valuation statement provided by the valuer.
- Agree the revalued amounts for these assets are included correctly in the non-current assets register.
- Recalculate the total revaluation adjustment and agree correctly recorded in the revaluation surplus.
- Agree the initial cost for the warehouse addition to supporting documentation such as invoices to confirm cost.
- Confirm through a review of the title deeds that the warehouse is owned by Vieri Co.
- Recalculate the depreciation charge for the year to ensure that for assets revalued during the year, the depreciation was based on the correct valuation and for the warehouse addition that the charge was for six months only.
- Review the financial statements disclosures of the revaluation to ensure they comply with IAS 16 *Property, Plant and Equipment*.

AA Specimen Exam - Section B **Vieri Co**		
	Marks available	**Marks awarded**
Requirement – Substantive procedures for revaluation of land and buildings.		
Cast schedule of land and buildings revalued this year	1	
Agree the revalued amounts to the valuation statement provided by the valuer	1	
Agree the revalued amounts included correctly in the non-current assets register	1	
Recalculate the total revaluation adjustment and agree recorded in the revaluation surplus	1	
Agree the initial cost for the warehouse to invoices to confirm cost	1	
Confirm through title deeds that the warehouse is owned by Vieri Co	1	
Recalculate the depreciation charge for the year	1	
Review the financial statements disclosures for compliance with IAS 16 *Property, Plant and Equipment*	1	
Other		
Restricted to	**6**	

Vieri Co

Substantive procedures for valuation of work in progress (WIP)

- Prior to attending the inventory count, discuss with management how the percentage completions are attributed to the WIP, for example, is this based on motor cars passing certain points in the production process.
- During the count, observe the procedures carried out by Vieri Co staff in assessing the level of WIP and consider the reasonableness of the assumptions used.
- Agree for a sample that the percentage completions assessed during the count are in accordance with Vieri Co's policies communicated prior to the count.
- Discuss with management the basis of the standard costs applied to the percentage completion of WIP, and how often these are reviewed and updated.
- Review the level of variances between standard and actual costs and discuss with management how these are treated.
- Obtain a breakdown of the standard costs and agree a sample of these costs to actual invoices or payroll records to assess their reasonableness.
- Cast the schedule of total WIP and agree to the trial balance and financial statements.
- Agree sample of WIP assessed during the count to the WIP schedule, agree percentage completion is correct and recalculate the inventory valuation.

AA Specimen Exam - Section B **Vieri Co**		
	Marks available	**Marks awarded**
Requirement – Substantive procedures for work in progress (WIP)		
Discuss with management how the percentage completions are attributed to WIP	1	
Observe the procedures carried out in the count in assessing the level of WIP; consider reasonableness of the assumptions used	1	
During the count, agree a sample of percentage completions are in accordance with Vieri Co's policies	1	
Discuss with management the basis of the standard costs	1	
Review the level of variances between standard and actual costs	1	
Obtain a breakdown of the standard costs and agree a sample of these costs to actual invoices	1	
Cast the schedule of total WIP and agree to the trial balance and financial statements	1	
Agree sample of WIP assessed during the count to the WIP schedule, agree percentage completion is correct and recalculate the inventory valuation	1	
Other		
Restricted to	**4**	

Vieri Co

Impact of misstatement on auditor's report

Discuss with the management of Vieri Co why they are refusing to make the amendment to WIP. Assess the materiality of the error; if immaterial, it should be added to the schedule of uncorrected misstatements. The auditor should then assess whether this error results in the total of uncorrected misstatements becoming material; if so, this should be discussed with management; if not, there would be no impact on the auditor's report.

If the error is material and management refuses to amend the financial statements, then the auditor's opinion will need to be modified. It is unlikely that any error would be pervasive as although WIP in total is material, it would not have a pervasive effect on the financial statements as a whole. As management has not complied with IAS 2 *Inventories* and if the error is material but not pervasive, then a qualified opinion would be necessary. The opinion paragraph would be qualified 'except for'.

A basis for qualified opinion paragraph would need to be included after the opinion paragraph. This would explain the material misstatement in relation to the valuation of WIP and the effect on the financial statements.

AA Specimen Exam - Section B **Vieri Co**		
	Marks available	**Marks awarded**
Requirement – Impact on auditor's report		
Discuss with management reasons for non-amendment	1	
Assess materiality	1	
Immaterial – schedule of uncorrected adjustments	1	
Material not pervasive – qualified opinion	1	
Opinion paragraph – qualified 'except for'	1	
Basis for qualified opinion paragraph	1	
Restricted to	**5**	